RAPID EYE

"Intelligent journalism and committed writing...RAPID EYE tells you what is really happening. It tells a wider story of a cultural struggle that is crucial to the demands of the 90s; the struggle between life and death."

THE OBSERVER

"Not your average coffee-table book. Covering the esoteric arts and alternative ways of thinking, RAPID EYE is well presented, intelligently argued and easily digestible...Excellent. If it doesn't get closed down it should go a long way in bringing about a reassessment of a sub-culture that, at best, has been looked on as slightly suspect, and at worst, loudly condemned in the usual media. A cut above the rest."

MELODY MAKER

"Book find of the year. RAPID EYE is great!"

SHORT NEWS, NEW YORK

"A journal of note. Full of wild and weird stuff. Great articles. My Producer tells me that I'm only supposed to show you RAPID EYE if I show profound disapproval. Nice."

ANTHONY H. WILSON, 'OTHER SIDE OF MIDNIGHT' GRANADA TV

"Classic stuff – mad people with sane reasons...If you fancy dipping your toes into the horror, insanity and diversity that exists all around us, take a look at the strange collage of ideas and visions in RAPID EYE."

DARK SIDE MAGAZINE

"RAPID EYE is a microscope through which we can see the fractured, fractal nature of the virus we call popular culture, wherin all things are intrinsically bound together. Comprehensive...incisive...incredible. To do justice to this eye opening volume is impossible; suffice to say it's guaranteed to blow your mind. Utterly essential."

OUTLOOK MAGAZINE

"Absolutely jam-packed with interesting stuff. Recommended."

SOUNDS

"Some of the best pop writing to be found...excellent articles."

THE FACE

"'Heavy writing, heady reading' they say. Very good and engrossing, I say. Full of informative stuff – the interview with Genesis P-Orridge surely being the definitive encounter ...Wonderful...strangely constructed...RAPID EYE must be read."

THE INTERNATIONAL TIMES

"The essential counter-culture journal...audibly clear...fragmentary, disturbing. Examining and affirming an increasingly disparate culture of resistance. Recommended."

THE PINK PAPER

"Heavyweight periodical devoted to documenting apocalypse culture. Great pieces ...recommended reading."

i-D MAGAZINE

"Reading RAPID EYE, every experience, every individual, every society changes its meaning. They all relate to one another in an infinite web, in a way you would never imagine possible...Gradually you start to make connections even between the most fantastically different ideas in the book. Ideas which are different in every conceivable respect – apart from one. Articles range from the inspiring to the disturbing. RAPID EYE alternately titillates, repels and confuses. This is a pernicious book. Genius."

NUIT ISIS MAGAZINE

"Visionary...An intelligent and imaginative journal of what they'd call 'de-control', RAPID EYE is beautifully presented and its contents are a veritable treasure-trove of mind activating information. Penetrating...comprehensive...most illuminating. Can a price be put on inspiration?"

N.M.E.

"A finger on the pulse of modern paranoia. Reading RAPID EYE is like teetering on the edge of someone else's insanity...grim, mysterious, scary. A strange and compulsive book."

THE PUNTER

"RAPID EYE is very highly recommended..."

JOHN PEEL, BBC RADIO ONE

"I wonder what sort of 'civilisation' it is that RAPID EYE is suggesting...It's a catalogue of depravity – albeit with an interesting selection of fetishists. Sick. But RAPID EYE does give interesting accounts of minds moving in mysterious ways, and the compilation of restrictions on personal freedom certainly gives a sound basis for its claims about the uncivilised nature of British society. RAPID EYE is interesting and certainly worthy of serious attention, and easily worth the money for the reading, thinking, and speculation."

EYE CATCHER MAGAZINE

"A beautifully presented, most fascinating journal...RAPID EYE celebrates and opens your eyes to the rich underground culture that exists despite today's shallow grasping materialist times, and I for one am very glad that it's here. Interestingly, but not surprisingly, RAPID EYE has met with suspicion and hostility, not least from the police and various bookshops, who have refused to stock it...RAPID EYE is truly a mind-expanding experience."

BUZZ MAGAZINE

There comes a time in every reviewer's life when he is asked to review something that lefies description: An enigma. RAPID EYE is such a thing. There are so many ideas in the ncredible article on Psychic TV alone that it would be foolish to try and convey them here. 'he writing is excellent and the presentation leaves everything else behind...Fascinating, and vell worth the cover price."

BBC RADIO

Intelligent and thought-provoking..."

PAUL DU NOYER, BBC WORLD SERVICE

The articles bear gravity and authority without being stuffy, the content serious without being over-ridingly so. RAPID EYE is a marvellous book."

WEREWOLF MAGAZINE

Very enjoyable read with good artwork. The Alternative Society is not, apparently, dead, but ias been dormant for far too long."

PSYCHOPHARMACY RESEARCH COMMITTEE

'RAPID EYE defends people's right to expression, even when their positions are not so nuch abhorrent as naff. It gives a platform for voices varying from the passionately lissenting through to the merely bizarre...complex, evocatively written...but the best reason or reading this odd volume is that its heart is in the right place...RAPID EYE celebrates paranoia as a designer style – but paranoids have real enemies."

CITY LIMITS

'Original, valid and highly entertaining...THIS is the reality. A most excellent read."

HEADPRESS

'Each article has something new and fresh to say. RAPID EYE makes fascinating reading... untangling some of the crazy mixed up strands of culture that have got a stranglehold on society...People are always talking about books being 'essential' and the books they refer to are usually far from it. When someone tells you that RAPID EYE is essential reading, you know, they might be right."

TWISTER MAGAZINE

"To read RAPID EYE is to descend into chaos...This is the first and final battle."

MELODY MAKER

"The first RAPID EYE book was the finest example of subcultural writing to emerge during the Eighties, and RAPID EYE 2 does not disappoint. In-depth...cynical...brilliant. RAPID EYE is stunning. Buy it immediately."

DIVINITY MAGAZINE

rapid eye movement

[illegible]

love [illegible]

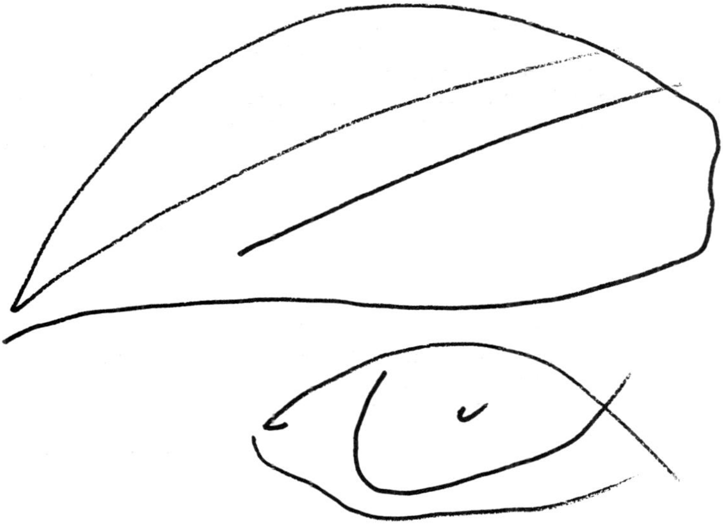

RAPID EYE 1
Edited by Simon Dwyer
ISBN 1 871592 22 4.

First published 1989 by
Rapid Eye Publishing Ltd.
Revised and expanded edition published 1993 by
ANNIHILATION PRESS
83, Clerkenwell Road
London EC1
Tel/Fax: 071-430-9878.

Design, Layout & Typeset:
Simon Dwyer

Logo Design:
Hugh Davies

Cover Design:
Simon Dwyer

Warning:
Neither the Editor, Publisher, nor Distributor can be held responsible for the use or misuse of information contained herein. Readers are assumed to be adults not offended by potentially contentious issues (see Appendix).

Front Cover:
Aldous Huxley photographed by Cecil Beaton.
Used with kind permission of
Sotheby's, London.

Frontispiece:
Original drawing for *Rapid Eye Movement,*
executed and donated by Andy Warhol, 1982.

RAPID EYE

Editor:
Simon Dwyer

Contributors:
Kathy Acker, Ian Blake, William S. Burroughs, Monty Cantsin, Mark Downham, John Helmer, Pat Hollis, Jack Hunter, Kenneth Rayner Johnson, Nancy MacKenzie, Kathleen McAuliffe, R.C. McNeiff, Christopher Mayhew, Genesis P-Orridge, Sandy Robertson, Pete Scott, Eileen Shepperd, C. John Taylor, Michael Timothy, Nick Toczek, V. Vale, Colin Wilson.

Acknowledgements:
Thanks to Fiona Dwyer, Mick, James Williamson, David Brooks, Ken Johnson and Ann. Vale, Paula, Ian Blake, Chris Saunders, Dr. Terence DuQuesne, Jack Stevenson, Pat Burchill, June, and Hugh Davies.

CONTENTS

INTRODUCTION
Dr. Simon Ashton

THE FALL OF ART
William S. Burroughs
1

FROM ATAVISM TO ZYKLON B
An interview with Genesis P-Orridge
Simon Dwyer
7

SYBARITE AMONG THE SHADOWS
R.C. McNeiff
87

DREAMACHINE
Simon Dwyer
96

THE BLACK BOX
Kathleen McAuliffe
102

DANCE RITUAL
I: DANCE RITUAL
Eileen Shepperd
110
II : INAUGURATION OF THE PLEASUREDOME
Jack Hunter
114

BECAUSE AND COSMOS
C. John Taylor
117

THE VIDEODROME
Mark Downham
131

WORDS FROM A ROOM
An interview with Hubert Selby Jnr.
Pat Hollis
146

UNCLE BILL
I: AND HIS NAME WAS ROVER
William S. Burroughs
158
II: DEAD FINGERS TALK
An interview with William S. Burroughs
Vale
160
III: THE JOHNSON FAMILY
William S. Burroughs
170

THE NEOIST CULTURAL CONSPIRACY
I: NEOISM
Pete Scott
174
II: ANOTHER INTRODUCTION TO NEOISM
Monty Cantsin
179

TIME MIRRORS
The Art of Austin Osman Spare
Genesis P-Orridge
185

THE UNDYING MONSTER
Ian Blake
193

I BECOME A MURDERESS
Kathy Acker
210

TANTRA
Sahajanath
225

A REVOLUTIONARY SUICIDE
Transcript of Rev. Jim Jones & The People's Temple of Christ
Simon Dwyer
235

"ATTITUDE"
John Helmer
245

MONTAGUE SUMMERS
Sandy Robertson
249

THROUGH A SCREEN, DARKLY
An interview with Derek Jarman
Simon Dwyer
253

THE GEMSTONE FILE INVESTIGATION
Nick Toczek
286

SLAUGHTER BY STARLIGHT
Ian Blake
313

THE SECRET LANGUAGE OF ALCHEMY
Kenneth Rayner Johnson
320

MESCALIN, MYSTICISM, AND AN EXCURSION OUT OF TIME
Christopher Mayhew
333

THE ANTI-INTELLECTUAL ETHIC
Michael Timothy
342

"BRAZIL"
Simon Dwyer
345

SEX, CRIME & 'OCCULTISM'
I: SEX, CRIME, AND THE 'OCCULT'
Colin Wilson
424
II: HELTER SKELTER
The Trial Testimony of Charles Manson
434

BODY MODIFICATION
I: TWO DRAGONS PLAYING WITH A PEARL
Nancy MacKenzie
454
II: BODYSHOCKS
An interview with Mr. Sebastian
Simon Dwyer
459

HIS NAME WAS MASTER
In memory of Brion Gysin
Genesis P-Orridge
471

A THANKSGIVING PRAYER
William S. Burroughs
479

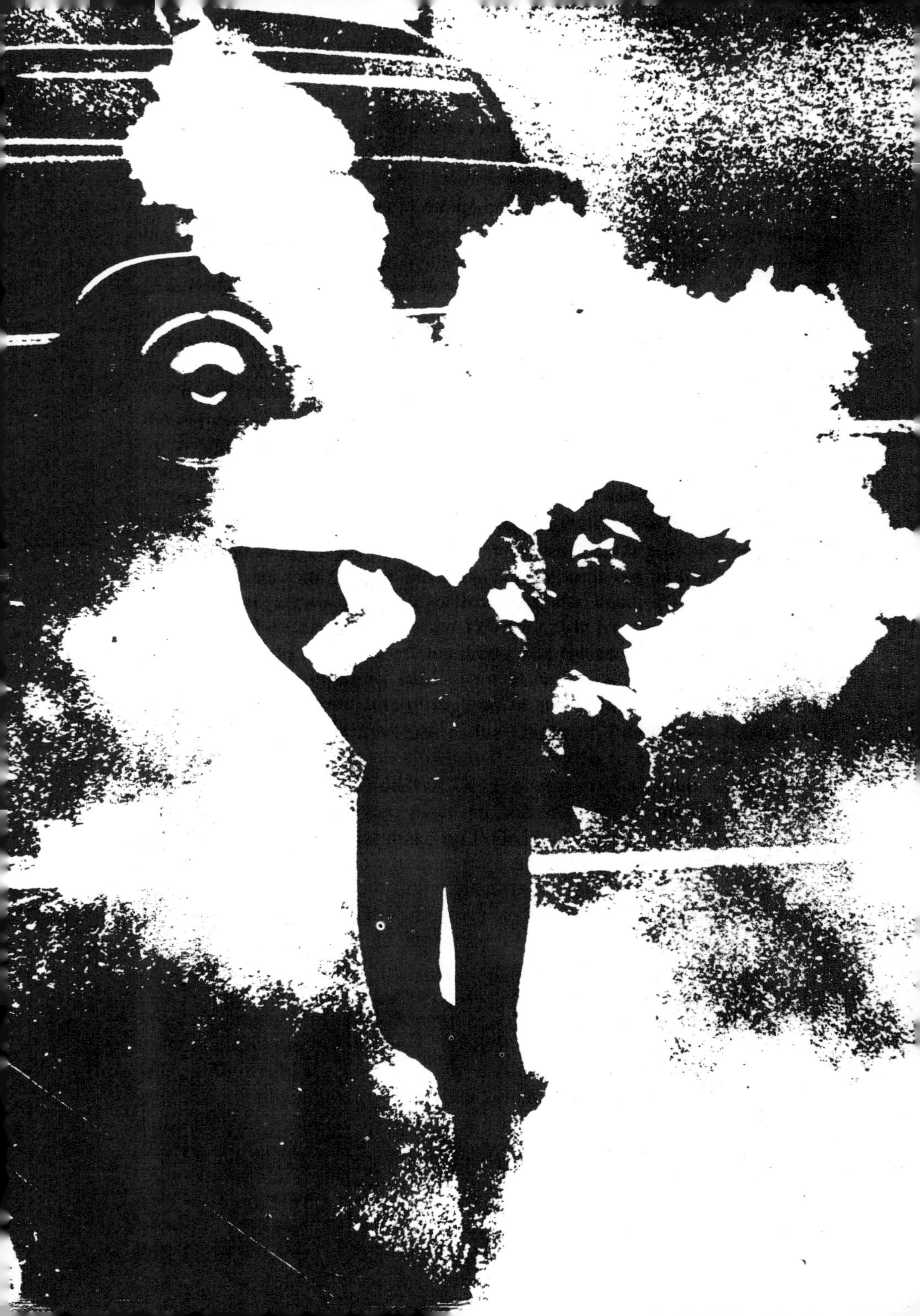

INTRODUCTION TO THE REVISED AND EXPANDED EDITION OF RAPID EYE ONE

DREAMS: INTERPRETATION, APPEARANCE AND REALITY

"Control over information, control over the presentation of reality is the only issue. Not the battle over people's opinions, but the battle over the very perception of life. Our society is geared towards dealing with the description of the appearance, the surface, not with multi-dimensional reality. Look at the media – to take an obvious illustration, when a bomb drops on Baghdad we are presented with a map and a politician explaining why the bomb was dropped. The map and the politician are the news. We are not torn in half, we do not bleed. The reportage becomes the reality in itself, the hyper-reality that we are asked to perceive as being 'real'. No matter how concerned or aware one is, life is presented, and largely experienced, as a series of reflections of reflections, vanishing into infinity. That may go some way to explaining why there is a widespread feeling that there is some lack of reality, some lack of direction in people's lives. Being sane is looking at the same reflection as everyone else and agreeing that it is real. That is, not a reflection. Not its reverse. That may be why, as a society, we are quite mad."

Simon Dwyer, 1993.

Having been a reader of *Rapid Eye* since its early days in 1979 as *"Rapid Eye Movement"* – a colourful, Dada-esque looking punk 'zine full of unusually deep and interesting interviews with the likes of Crass, Julie Burchill and Andy Warhol, spliced with quotes from Nietzsche and photos of scantily clad women – I am delighted to be asked to provide an introduction to the planned series of revised and expanded *Rapid Eye* books to be published by Annihilation Press. Delighted, because I can provide one reader's view of something that, although heaped with praise, is actually continually being misinterpreted in the press.

In the main, journalists and critics have been lazy in attempting to pin down the phenomenon of *Rapid Eye*. Applying to it their own misconceptions, most try simply to categorise it as a series of books brimming over with the most shocking and sometimes sickening responses to what is perceived to be the impending apocalypse. There is, of course, some truth in this view, but to me *Rapid Eye* amounts to much more.

Viewed historically, *Rapid Eye* is a natural reaction to, and result of, contemporary society. And, more specifically, a branch of society informed by work from the likes of Irving Babbit and George Santayana, who both stressed the need for intellectual discipline and the interface between artistic and social values; also of the British philosopher F.H.

Bradley, who declared that most of our assumptions about the world are contradictory, as we are acting without a clear understanding of how the mind perceives the world. These writers, who questioned traditional attitudes a century ago, were given further credence through the work of many others; Marx and Engels, Friedrich Nietzsche, Sigmund Freud, Carl Gustav Jung, Sir James Frazer and even Charles Darwin and Albert Einstein. All their cerebral activity resulted in the creating of new paradigms which presented the West with a simple dilemma.

The class system, orthodox Christian faith, Newtonian science and the classical arts, so apparent in many aspects of nineteenth century life, were obviously inadequate for life in the twentieth century.

Many thus turned to new beliefs; several invented their own. Representational art, once used almost entirely to glorify God and his natural creations, turned into Dada and Surrealism, Abstract Expressionism and Pop Art, Situationism and Punk. Aleister Crowley and others inverted Christian norms and investigated the occult, adding to traditional Western occultism and paganism the wider practices of Middle Eastern mythology and Far Eastern Zen, and their use of meditation and ritual. Anarchists such as Godwin and Proudhorn rejected the sham beliefs of party politics, leading eventually to a climate of cynicism and social dissent and the youth-orientated abstractions of Crass and Class War. Some investigated scientific approaches, others drugs. Aldous Huxley, Timothy Leary, and Steven Hawking (all mentioned in these books) would have had few arguments. A largely literary, sometimes "artistic" class of Outsiders existed, and by the Fifties these were documented by Colin Wilson. Indeed, it is no surprise to find that writers such as Wilson are fans of, and frequent contributors to *Rapid Eye*. The people Wilson has extensively written about were, or are, individuals who have transgressed socially conditioned, materialistic norms in their search for an "answer" to the problem of living in the twentieth century. Many of these individuals are, through their ideas and activities, ignored or shunned by society and are misunderstood and marginalised by the general media. Some, because of their adopted lifestyles, go mad, others die of drug overdoses or, lately, Aids; many get locked up in institutions of all kinds, others write brilliant books and win Nobel prizes. But neither they, nor *Rapid Eye*, are "shocking". Nor do they attempt to be.

In potentially contentious articles such as those featuring the "death art" of film-maker Richard Kern, or the homo-erotic work of (HIV positive) director Derek Jarman, the pseudo-sect art rituals of the (recently media-crucified) Temple of Psychic Youth, or the body piercing practices of (the recently arrested) Mr. Sebastian, one realises that such pieces are not simply newsworthy and anthropological, nor merely entertaining. *Rapid Eye* is clearly illustrating the fact that control over our bodies and destinies, our sexual habits, our fashions and even our deaths are intertwined.

Language and literary structures as modifiers of thought and as functioning facets of Control are also investigated in pieces on or by William Burroughs, Kathy Acker, and the Editor; also in Genesis P-Orridge's revealing "Behavioral Cut-Ups", Adèle Olivia Gladwell's "Other Bisexuality", John Helmer's "Attitude", Richard Dyer's introduction to deaf poet Aaron Williamson – "The Anatomy of Utterance", and Kenneth Rayner Johnson's "Secret Language of Alchemy".

There are no secrets here. *Rapid Eye* may sometimes be surreal and evocative, but it is always clearly written and understandable. Far from attempting to shock or promulgate the cult of wilful unintelligibility that is contemporary art, it is deliberately moderate and often objective – studiously avoiding the pitfalls of pseudo-intellectualism and the obsessive, cranky involvements that mar the perspective of many other "alternative" publications, which seek only to titillate and repel rather than to inform.

Rapid Eye is an informer. How many people knew of the work of Austin Spare before it published work on him in the mid-eighties? Or of Paul Mayersberg? Or Jörg Buttgereit or Istvan Kantor? Juxtaposed with the little-known are several famous names, and it is an indication of the esteem in which *Rapid Eye* is held (and a tribute to some editorial persuasiveness) to note that such a small, independent publication can publish work by a member of the House of Lords (Christopher Mayhew), an editor of Penthouse magazine (Sandy Robertson), and internationally known authors such as Kathy Acker, alongside works from The Saatchi Collection, Sotheby's, and articles on "The Artist as a Young Corpse Fucker". Remarkable stuff.

The apparent randomness of subject matter in both issues of *Rapid Eye* belies an underlying consistency. An historical perspective runs through the two books, *Rapid Eye 1* and *2*, most obviously in articles on Crowley, H.P. Lovecraft, Chinese foot-binding, The Tantra, Aldous Huxley, Austin Spare, Alexandra David Néel, Montague Summers and others. As does an interest in new scientific theories that support the argument for the empirical – most notably "The Black Box", "Dreamachine", the amazing "Because and Cosmos" and sections in the remarkable "Plague Yard" concerned with Dr. Rupert Sheldrake, Stanley Milgram and others.

Not only do the apparently dissociated topics and articles give one a wide breadth of useful sub-cultural knowledge and show the overlapping interests of the editorship, but they do, on closer inspection, adhere to the overall theme: that the arts are ritual, a product of the hyper-real world created in our own heads and designed to deal with the apparent lack of God in the twentieth century; that 'truth' is constantly shifting; and that a functional use of the arts, regardless of fashion and socially accepted norms, is personally liberating and thus socially evolutionary. *Rapid Eye* spreads these (if you really think about it, genuinely subversive) ideas like a virus, one to one, to be replicated throughout contemporary culture and society and, as the Editor says, "facilitate the process of civilisation in a demonstrably uncivilised world".

All articles feature a traditionally English struggle for individuality and, more sophisticated than this, a genuine understanding of the difficult "Control" perception as expounded by William Burroughs and Brion Gysin, both of whom feature heavily.

Theory aside, these two journals also highlight the more obvious results of Control, the authoritarianism and attacks on personal liberties and choice, in features such as "Taboo Breakers" and the chilling "Brazil". Although full of useful, often under-publicised information relating to such matters – Nick Toczek's piece on the CIA also springs to mind – *Rapid Eye* is not only traditionally radical and often anti-establishment, it is perverse. It can be deliberately politically incorrect, going against the acceptable spoon-fed fashions of radical feminism, socialism and much of the "contemporary art world" – which it rightly seems to consider as Fascist and stupid as the Nazi party – and also against prominent heroes of the counter-culture, such as Anton LaVey and Alex Sanders, Valerie Solanas and Andres Serrano, The Church of the SubGenius and some of the more lauded members of the Fluxus movement. One is also left wondering what to think of the much celebrated Charles Manson, after reading his court testimony. The wry reporting of interesting phonies (like Lobsang Rampa) and conspiracy theories, from JFK plots to Nazi UFO lore, are further examples of its humour and wilfulness.

A journal that is truly post Postmodernist, *Rapid Eye* brings into question both choices – "Culture" and "Counter-culture". The "alternative" establishment epitomised by Channel 4 or *Time Out*, or *Rolling Stone* or *The Guardian* is, in Rapid Eye's world, no alternative – a controlled choice. A false appearance of social evolution. (The Church of Satan is still a church. *Smile* is still an arts magazine). To know this and to dissent from making controlled choices is to be forced into a difficult world, to face a personal reality and, as the "Plague Yard" says, create a Situationist-like "Virtual Reality" of one's own imagination.

In other words, to read this, Issue One of *Rapid Eye*, and its companion volume, Issue Two, is to observe a society of interconnected chaos, and to be encouraged to confront this often hidden or misunderstood fact and develop a personal response to it. In this light, *Rapid Eye* is a weapon (socially) and a tool (artistically). Not so much a foreteller of the coming apocalypse, but an existentialist lexicon, useful in providing survivalist techniques in this century's continuous apocalypse of Everyday Life.

Thank your God for *Rapid Eye* and for independent, transgressive publishing houses like Annihilation. Their hearts may be dark, but they are in the right place.

As F.H. Bradley may have said if he were alive today: Most of today's art and media describe appearance. *Rapid Eye* describes reality.

Dr. Simon Ashton.
The P.L.F.
London, 1993.

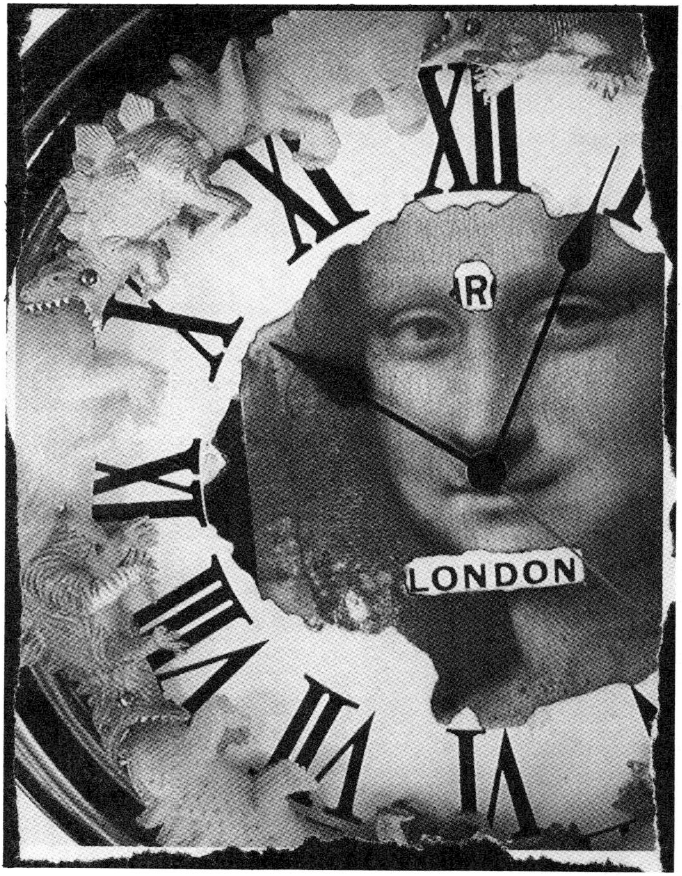

"From dreams to reality is a long way."
Ferdinand Cheval

"Throughout history there have always been forms of art alien to established culture and which ipso facto have been neglected and finally lost without trace."
Roger Cardinal

"You have to paint things black if you want to make future possibilities more vivid."
Michel Foucault

INTRODUCTION

I had been wondering for some weeks what to say to introduce *Rapid Eye*. It was, after all, so obvious. Then, as fate would have it, a few hours before deadline I was given an angle. Or, rather, I was given a word.

My good and clever friend David Brooks rang me up and gave it to me, his voice crackling with excitement down the line of cyber space. Actually, he mentioned a word which he had just invented as the title of an alternative bookshop he was planning to open – and I stole it. I believe that this process of plagiarism is called the 'acid burn' in contemporary parlance. A very post modernist thing to do.

The word he gave me was "Occulture".

This new word obviously suggests both Culture and the Occult. To me, this "occulture" is not a secret culture as the word might suggest, but a culture that is in some way hidden and ignored, or wilfully marginalised to the extremities of our society. A culture of individuality and sub-cults, a culture of questions that have not been properly identified – let alone answered – and therefore, do not get a fair representation in the mainstream media.

It is a culture that has been misinterpreted. Not because it is 'evil' or wrong, but because it is generally apolitical and amoral, unashamedly artistic, experimental, undogmatic, intellectual and oddly evolutionary. It is a sub-culture that is forming a question that 'reality' alone cannot answer. Which is why it makes people nervous.

This, is seems, is what *Rapid Eye* has always been about. The word now belongs to everyone. All these wor(l)ds are yours.

We give you Occulture.

Simon Dwyer,
Editor, 1989.

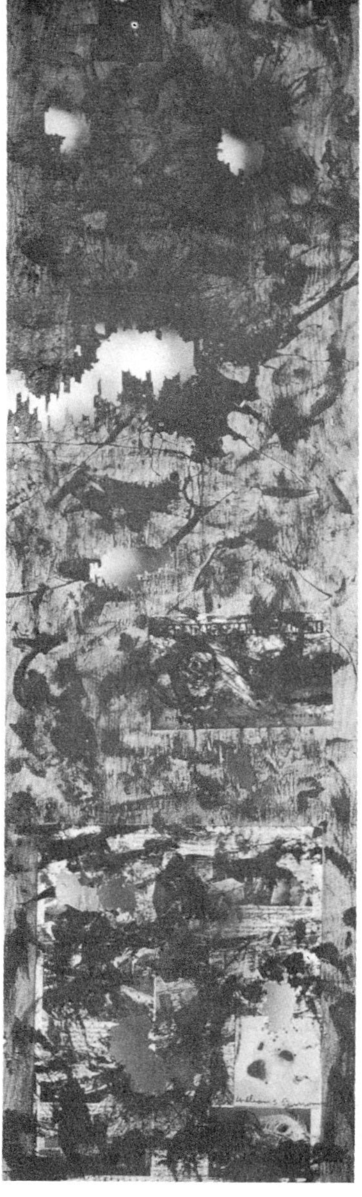

'Spermatozoa Color' by Burroughs, 1987. From the 'Shotgun' series – paintings on plywood using spraypaint and ammo.

THE FALL OF ART

WILLIAM S. BURROUGHS

Some years ago in London, I asked Jasper Johns what painting was all about – what are painters really doing? He countered with another question: what is writing about? I did not have an answer then; I have an answer now: The purpose of writing is to make it happen.

What we call *"art"* – painting, sculpture, writing, dance, music – is magical in origin. That is, it was originally employed for ceremonial purposes to produce very definite effects. In the world of magic nothing happens unless someone wants it to happen, *wills* it to happen, and there are certain magical formulae to channel and direct the will. The artist is trying to make something happen in the mind of the viewer or reader. In the days of cows-in-the-grass painting, the answer to *"What is the purpose of such painting?"* was very simple: to make what is depicted happen in the mind of the viewer; to make him smell the cows and the grass, hear the whistling rustic. The influence of art is no less potent for being indirect. We can leave riots, fires, and wrecks to the journalists. The influence of art has a long-range cultural effect. Jack Kerouac, Allen Ginsberg, Gregory Corso – the Beats wrote a world-wide cultural revolution. Remember that four-letter words could not appear on a printed page thirty-odd years ago. Now, with the breakdown of censorship and the freeing of the World, the *New York Times* has to print four-letter words used by the President of the United States.

We can trace the tremendous indirect effect of the written word; what about the indirect effect of painting? I have explained how in 1959 Brion Gysin said that writing is fifty years behind painting and applied the montage technique to writing – a technique which had been used in painting for fifty years. As you know, painters had the whole representational position knocked out from under them by photography, and there was in fact a photography exhibition around the turn of the century entitled "Photography – The Death of Painting". Premature, but painting did have to get a new look. So painters turned first to montage.

Now the montage is actually much closer to the fact of perception than representational painting. Take a walk down a city street and put what you have just seen down on canvas. You have seen half a person cut in two by a car, bits and pieces of street signs and advertisements, reflections from shop windows – a montage of fragments. And the same thing happens with words. Remember that the written word is an image. Brion Gysin's cut-up method consists of cutting up pages of text and re-arranging them in montage combinations. Representational painting is dead, unless perhaps photo-realism ever takes hold. Nobody paints cows in the grass any more. Montage is an old device in painting. But if you apply the montage method to writing, you are accused by the critics of promulgating a cult of unintelligibility. Writing is still confined in the sequential representational straightjacket of the novel, a form as arbitrary as the sonnet and as far removed from the actual facts of human perception and consciousness as that fifteenth-century poetical form. Consciousness *is* a cut-up; life is a cut-up. Every time you walk down the street or look out the window, your stream of consciousness is cut by random factors.

Painting in the past hundred years has come from an exclusively representational position, where any number of artists could cover the same material to such a state of fragmentation that every artist must now have his own special point on which there is only room for one artist. Any number of artists can paint country landscapes, but there is only room for one Warhol soup can. It's every artist his own movement now. Here is a question for all schools: If art has undergone such drastic alteration in the past hundred years, what do you think artists will be doing in fifty or a hundred years from now? Of course we can foresee expansion into the realm of exploding art... A self-destroying TV set, refrigerator, washing-machine, and electric stove going off, leaving a shambles of a gleaming modern apartment; the housewife's dream goes up behind a barrier of shatterproof glass to shield the spectators.

Now here's another angle for you young art hustlers: There is an explosive known as ammonium iodide made by pouring ammonia over iodide crystals or mixing it with tincture for brush work. This compound when it dries is so sensitive that a fly will explode it. I remember how I used to while away the long 1920s afternoons with sugar sprinkled around little heaps of ammonium iodide waiting for the flies to explode in little puffs of purple vapour. So you paint your canvas with ammonium iodide and syrup and release a swarm of flies in the gallery...or the people walking around set it off with their vibrations...or a team of choir boys touches it off with pop guns...And metal sodium explodes violently on contact with water; so you paint in sodium (which has a beautiful sheen like the side of a silver fish in clear water), and stand well back, and shoot it with a water rifle, or induce a spitting cobra to spit on it and get blown apart. Can sacrificial art be far behind? Cut a chicken's head off and paint with the gushing blood. Disembowel a sheep and paint with its intestines.

Or you can do a combo with the sodium number.

Then there will be the famous Mad Bear Floyd, a billionaire painter who covered a twenty-foot montage of porno pictures with a thousand dollar bills soaked in ammonium iodide...the montage was laid in the middle of the gallery, then a hamper of thousand-dollar bills rained down and set off the charge, burning a million dollars out of circulation while his agent sold the burnt canvas for $10 million on the spot.

Could this proliferation of competitive angles precipitate a revival of old-time potlatches? The potlatch was a competitive destruction of property carried out until one contestant was ruined and frequently died of shame on the spot. It is interesting to consider American tycoons sitting on this game – blowing up their factories and mines and oil wells, burning their crops and sloshing oil on their beaches, irradiating their land, irrigating with salt water, letting the frozen food rot, burning Rolls Royces and Bentleys, original Rembrandts, destroying Greek statues with air hammers...the American team drops atom bombs on America while China and Russia match us bomb for bomb on their own ground.

The potlatch was invented by the Northwest Coast Indians in the area that is now British Columbia, and it occupied most of their time. Objects destroyed at these uncomfortable occasions included salmon oil, blankets, and coppers. Salmon oil poured on an open fire at the centre of the room frequently singed honoured guests in the front row, who were obliged by protocol to evince no signs of displeasure. The coppers were engraved shields of thin copper about three feet by two feet, and are now highly valued as curios.

A copper receives its value from the number of potlatches it has weathered: 'THIS IS THE GREAT COPPER BEFORE WHICH OTHER COPPERS PISS THEMSELVES LIKE BITCH DOGS'. And cowardly coppers shrink back, losing value. You see, a potent copper like this represents so many value units, just as modern art objects may derive value from a series of competitive manipulations: this soup can represents fifty burnt kitchen manipulations: this soup can represents fifty burnt kitchen chairs, twenty urinals, and a Wyeth pig.

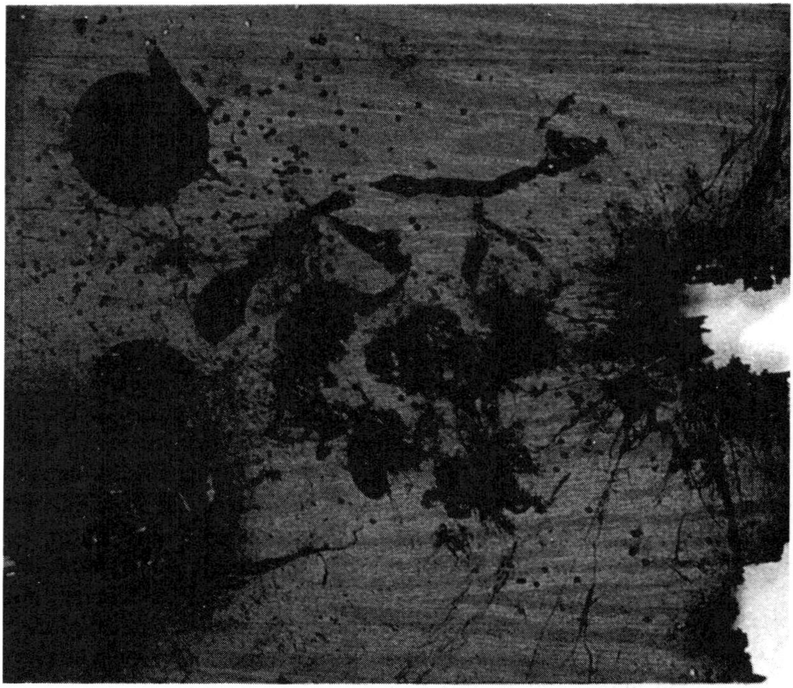

'Curse of the Red Seal' Burroughs 1987

Competitive over-inflation of values could lead to *La Chute de l'Art*; a total collapse of the art market. Imagine the artist *Bourse* where all the painters stand by their pictures – frenzied phone calls from broker to collector...*"Your margin's wiped out, BJ. You gotta cover with the gilt-edge stuff – you know what I mean: Monets, Renoirs, Rembrandts, Picassos..."* And then: PICASSO SLUMPS SHARPLY AS HIS ENTIRE OUTPUT IS DUMPED ON THE MARKET BY FRANTIC DEALERS... As an artist falls off the Board he is obligated by the Board of Health to surrender his pictures to the public incinerator. What art and what artists would survive the holocaust? And how's this for an angle, BJ.? Now this ART grabs you by the balls, see? It hits you in the stomach and dampens your eyes. So that artist gets behind his picture like Punch and Judy and reaches right out through it and grabs a critic by his lapels or slugs him in the guts and sprays him with tear gas. Lots of ways you can slant this. Dead cows in the grass. Dogs leap out of a picture. Vernissage guests savagely clubbed by picture cops. It finally gets so that pictures of dangerous animals, electric chairs, riots, fires, and explosions have the gallery to themselves. Will cows in the grass make a comeback? A critic was gored yesterday. Another drowned in a Monet river and a Bacon exhibition has given rise to unfavourable mutations...

What has happened here? Art has become literal and returned to its magical function of making it happen, after a long exile in the realms of imagination where its appetite for happenings has become inordinate. Now suddenly art makes its lethal eruption into the so-called real world. Writing and painting were in the beginning and the word was written image. Now painters paint a future before it is written, having outstripped the retarded twin, writing, and left it back there with the ABC's. Will writing catch up?

A writer who writes a book about a virgin soil epidemic, impregnating his pages with the virus described...this book about Poland in a typhus epidemic has typhus lice concealed in the bindings, to be released as book-of-the-month-club ladies turn the pages. *Mektoub*. It is written. Others have radioactive pages dusted lightly with botulism. The reader is no longer safely reading about sharks while she belches out chocolate fumes; on the page is a powerful shark attractant. Others scorn such crude tricks and rely on the powers of magic – potent spells and curses, often formed by human sacrifice, flutter from these pestilent pages.

'Beauty kills. Beauty is the murderer,' in the words of Gregory Corso, and painting is reunited with its stupid brother, writing, in books done entirely in pictographs. And by now all books are scented with the appropriate odours and readers are provided with scent bottles for renewal ...Musky Ozone, Rain on Horseflesh, Empty Locker Rooms... Finally comes the Master of the Empty Page, which can only be read by initiates...

LA CHUTE DU MOT...what survives the literalization of art is the timeless ever-changing world of magic caught in the painter's brush, or the writer's words, bits of vivid and vanishing detail. In space any number of painters can dance on the end of a brush, and the writer makes a soundless bow and disappears into the alphabet.

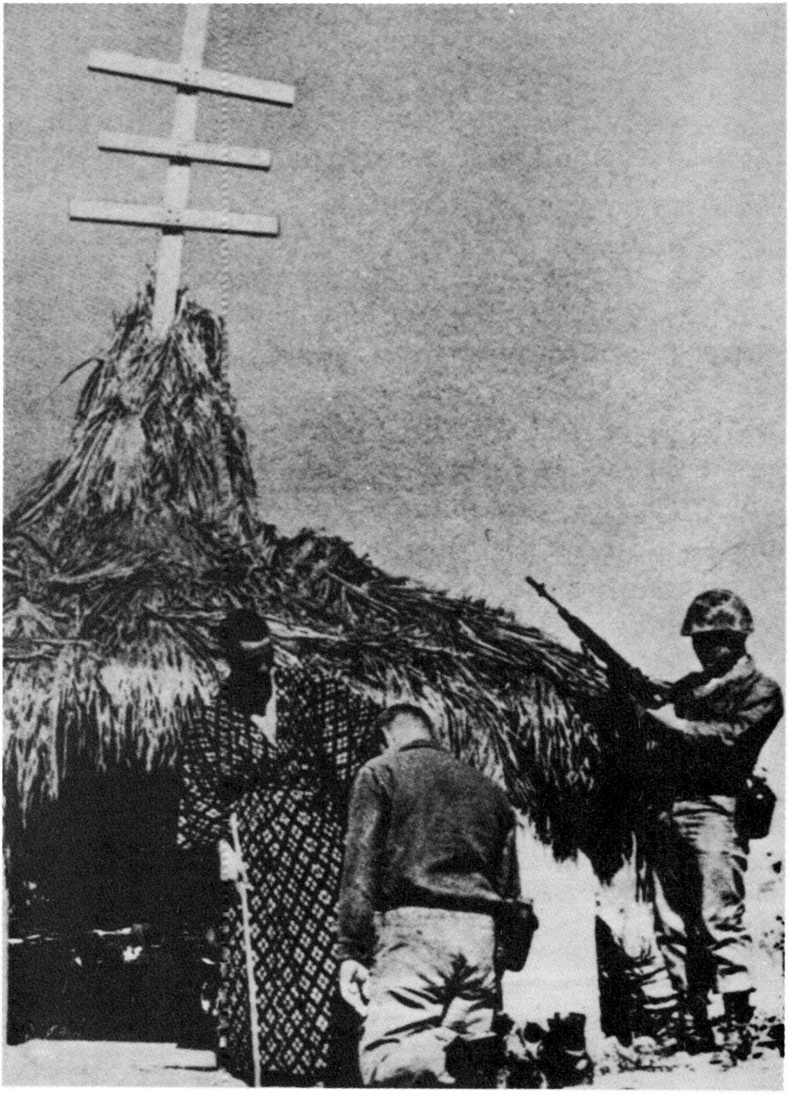

FROM ATAVISM TO ZYKLON B.

Genesis P-Orridge and the Temple of Psychic Youth (From A to Z and back again).

SIMON DWYER

"Western people often see obscenity where there is only symbolism."
Sir John Woodroffe (Shakti & Shakta)

"Who wishes to be creative, must first destroy and smash accepted values."
Nietzsche

"'Cults' he said thoughtfully, examining a tape report grinding from the receptor. 'What about cults?' Sung-Wu asked faintly. 'Any stable society is menaced by cults; our society is no exception. Certain lower strata are axiomatically dissatisfied. In secret they form fanatic, rebellious bands. They meet at night; they insidiously express inversions of accepted norms; they delight in flaunting basic mores and customs'."
Philip K. Dick (The Turning Wheel)

Social cohesion and individual liberty are in a state of permanent conflict or uneasy compromise. The result of this friction being a variety of cults, which fall like a veil of sparks, lighting the dark.

CRACK! Kathy Acker leaves the stage, her American brogue giving way to a whipping electronic beat that incessantly pounds the sweaty walls of a subterranean nightclub. A howl of wolves turns the beery air to frost. Necks tingle and hackles rise to the speeches of Hitler and JFK that spill from the speakers, the 23 TV screens on stage swim to life, forming a giant mirror that glows with recurring images. The ornaments of power, the universal symbols, blend into hypnotic blurs of textural, throbbing colour: tacky 3-D postcard impressions of the Virgin Mary cut with dangling footage of faces caressed by hands: Third World tribal initiation ceremonies (which are acceptable), juxtapose with equally bloody-looking but innocuous Temple Ov Psychick Youth "rituals" (unacceptable). The atmosphere becomes stifling.

CRACK! Art school video techniques look so much more convincing when carried out with self-discipline and purpose. The purpose is mass hallucination, the method enchantment, and enchantment is exactly what is taking place here on all levels. The hypnotic elements of strobe lights, the whirr of the Dream Machine, the primal mantra of "Buddhist" drum rhythms and rock guitars, the spell of meaningless oratory. The many-headed beast of the crowd is plunged into a pulsating trance dance. An angel, or maybe a devil is invoked. Jim Jones cackles his last hyena laugh as his followers make their sound in the white night.

CRACK! A small, elfin figure bawls with tuneless violence into a microphone that's threatening to choke him as he stands perilously straddled between two monitors, *Der Putsch* leather and tattoos glistening in the heat. Wild eyes popping from a shaven skull. The classic rockist image is cut, only to be derided by a large furry hat perched incongruously on the top of his head. A music journalist nearby, wondering what such millinery signifies, scribbles something meaningful.

A cute Berlin blonde spike-top rises purposefully head and shoulders above the pulsating silhouette of heads at the front of the stage. She reaches up and grabs the singer's crotch. Fumbling, she tries to perform fellatio, but the singer instead jumps frog-like into the rippling crowd, still bawling. Equipment gets damaged. People have sex. Er, this must be rock'n'roll! The journalist scowls and scribbles feverishly...

By two-thirty the last stragglers wind their way out through the debris and onto the street. Some ashen-faced, trembling, nauseated. Others angry, some bored, unimpressed, some ecstatic. Few are exactly sure what they've just seen. A large black Psychic Cross has been sprayed on the wall above them – the same symbol as they wear sewn onto their grey jackets and hand-painted Kaftans, or have tattooed across their (wasted) biceps. It hangs silently over the city in the sickly yellow buzz of the streetlights. Marking the spot like a gravestone, a piece of history and mystery. It may bury itself like a martial artist's star in the subconscious levels of some neophytes' minds, perchance to enter into their dreams that night.

The symbol looks aptly like a strange TV aerial. Its tripach cross design inviting interpretations involving Christ and the two thieves, or a timeline incorporating the past, present, and future. It's similar to the alchemical glyph meaning 'very poisonous' and the Japanese symbolic cipher, (or Kana), for 'Fuck'. It's also reminiscent of the Fascist/Christian emblem in Peter Watkins' '60s cult pic *'Privilege'* that culminated in Paul Jones' ultimate pop rally, and a dead ringer for the Samurai ideogram meaning 'Master'. It can also be cleverly arranged from the letters P.T.V., and it is an outside broadcast of this particular company that we have just experienced.

If the main criterion for the creating of any cult is the stoking of fanaticism, then in this world of graphic corporate identity, of Capitalists making capital out of man's innate symbolism (from the Christian Cross to the bird on a Barclaycard) – it's only logical that such fanaticism must also be stoked with its own symbols.

The singer and co-director of the company, a geomancer named Genesis P-Orridge, has a stained glass Psychic Cross hanging in his East London apartment, the morning sun illuminating it as he talks.

A copy of the PTV video of *'Catalan'* flickers on the large colour television in the corner, director Derek Jarman playing pyromaniacally with the flames of Jordi Vallis' car as it lies on the beach outside Salvador Dali's house – crashed on the spot where *'Un Chien Andalou'* was filmed. Gen's daughter Caresse watches daddy on TV as she lies across the couch with Tanith the dog, baby Genesse gurgles happily on his lap, steam rises from the cups, as if in a Jacques Brel song.

As a father and now, approaching 40, homeowner, Genesis is exemplary. Many critics find this fact at odds with his stage persona, and want to know what his 'real' name is. Perhaps it is because people are used to pop stars, artists and their ilk creating a false public image that is at odds with their own character, as 'Entertainment'.

His real name, though, is Genesis P-Orridge, (changed by deed poll in the early 'seventies from Neil Megson) and of all the people working, even on the periphery of this area that I've known, Genesis is the one least interested in entertainment. Awkward and stubborn, sometimes to the point of exasperation, he just isn't the type of person to indulge the fantasies of fans and record companies' press rooms, and even if he were, he would hardly need to change. His lifestyle *is* unusual in some respects. The most weird and unpalatable aspect of his character really being that he attempts to perceive the world in a manner free from moral posturing and finite possibilities, and pays no lip service to those institutions that do. Being all-too-honest about what he thinks and does, he represents a commodity that the Entertainment Industry cannot handle with a bargepole – reality.

Reality, in the right hands, can be very, very dangerous. The fact that P-Orridge has never claimed to be particularly intelligent, original, or talented in his handling of it, only serves to make matters worse. He has thus been subjected to myriad forms of censorship and pressure. Although both his home and the Temple offices have been raided by the boys in blue, and British Telecom, HM Customs & Excise and the Post Office have taken actions against him, rarely are such blunt instruments resorted to. 'Control' protects itself from attack in far more subtle forms if possible. Its deft conditioning of people, particularly the type of people who reach positions of power in organisations like those in civil service, means that their small-mindedness and dogmatism act as a normally impenetrable shield of prejudice and stupidity. (The underlying philosophy seems to be that "he is a weirdo", therefore, it seems, "he MUST be breaking the law, or threatening to the law in some way", and so deserves any vilification he gets as he has brought it upon himself.)

This protection of ignorance manifests itself in a variety of ways. From death threats and rat poison being shoved through the P-Orridge family letterbox, to the wilful misrepresentation of Psychic TV and the Temple in the media. TV stations baulk at properly reporting the phenomenon (like LWT turning down Ben Elton's ideas for a 60 minute *'South of Watford'* special on the Temple), or punish those responsible for giving it fair coverage (Spain's TVE company sacking the makers of the *'La Edad de Oro'* arts show after they did a special on PTV watched by 14 million viewers, many of whom complained after the programme was aired). Record executives are also hot for the group one minute, then remarkably cold the next (contracts apparently being nixed at boardroom level). PTV's paranoia doesn't give credence to the notions of suppression, but the incidents are there most brazenly illustrated in the pages of the Music Press and the trency listings magazines. With their notoriously fickle, censorious and sanctimonious reportage, they remain the most consistent culprits.

Young, untrained cub reporters are (having just left home), likely to be prey to feelings of insecurity and confusion about their identity, so in the facile world of 'Pop' subjects of substance are targets to get the poison pen into and create a name for oneself. That may be forgiven. What cannot be forgiven is the creating of a climate where everything new or potentially serious is automatically derided, where blanket cynicism is somehow presented as being superior to investigation, where 'style' is championed over substance.

Although P-Orridge has prompted reams of misinformation and openly hateful reporting (often penned by the most supposedly 'liberal' of stringers), the situation has generally improved over the last few years. Genesis appears either to take the piss out of card-carrying NUJ enquirers and feeds them the sensationalistic claptrap they furtively desire – spiced with a sarcastic humour that's often received as obtusely as it's reported; or, he adopts an opposite approach, being sickeningly pleasant and lucid in this tea-trollied scene of domestic bliss, daughters and dog always on hand.

"It can be very disillusioning," says P-Orridge, blowing into his tea. *"You just end up not wanting to have anything to do with the majority of this society. Because this society now really seems to exist through its media more than in any other way. And the media are generally absolute low-life. Intellectually small and very unskilled at their job."*

After the initial shock surrounding the group's explosive debut in 1981, reporting of PTV – albeit on the most innocuous of levels – has gradually become more positive. P-Orridge attracts much deference in some hip circles, (even though few of these same people know what he is actually doing), as if the system is now trying unconsciously to absorb him and his group into its antiseptic void – over tea and sympathy – just as it did with Crass (arguably the only other British group in the last decade to present such a precise, informed and genuine threat). Journalists like flirting with groups and individuals they perceive as being 'threats' (hence Nick Kent's obsession with Keith Richard of the Stones, for example) providing there is nothing serious intended. But groups who offer anything more genuinely subversive than gobbing on handicapped kids or puking up in airport lounges are either ignored or somehow made safe. In a world where no-one remembers what you wrote last week anyway, it may not matter, but P-Orridge, having now spent most of his life in the public eye to varying degrees, is a past master at such media games and is well aware of the irony implicit in the media's current, often positive, treatment of the Temple.

That irony being that the Temple *does* do some of the things the suspicious press hates it for. It does, however, do them for different reasons than the press generally presume or are even able to perceive, and it does them with a degree of responsibility and research usually unheard of in the fly-by-night microworld of Pop, as we will discover.

Still though, given the level of misinterpretation, misinformation and downright bloody-mindedness that has hallmarked the reportage of PTV, The Temple, and his earlier outfit Throbbing Gristle, it's hardly surprising that the most common impression people have of P-Orridge is one of almost total misunderstanding. Perhaps another reason for this is that the only constant running through his life and work is that it is in a state of permanent flux. In a system purporting to be based on anti-dogmatism, active research and observation, and the shunning of formulae, it could hardly be anything else. As such it would be impossible to form a finite opinion, draw a conclusion, entirely agree with, or entirely subscribe to, the P-Orridge model for living, or 'join' his cult, so full as it is of apparent contradictions and confusions. And that, of course, is exactly what it must be if the tribal, belief-based system of Control is to be subjectively perceived and demolished.

The Temple is a movement that combines several sets of values that are not easily harmonised. For example, on the one hand it exhibits a ruthlessness, always seeking conflict; on the other, it cherishes literature, philosophy and the arts for their own sake. As Bertrand Russell pointed out, this sort of superficial contradiction need not be wrong-headed. These were, in fact, just the values that often co-existed in the Italian Renaissance; embodied then by the likes of Popes who'd employ mercenaries and wage wars, while preaching peace and commissioning

Michelangelo, and embodied now in the likes of Pope P-Orridge. A man given over to wearing 'secular' dog collars while overseeing what he thinks of as something of an art and social movement.

The Temple itself is based on such apparent paradox. Its ideas must not be presented in a dogmatic manner, but at the same time it must communicate in ways in which people will understand. Its methods and terminology therefore take on the form of illustrations, borrowing elements from religious and political groups and their media in order to investigate the effects of their conditioning. A rather convenient double-bluff is played as such avenues are still used to service the spreading of the Temple's own substitute propaganda.

P-Orridge himself must shun the cult adoration and trappings of 'leadership' his undoubted charm and intelligence foster, or he risks encouraging 'followers' who are quite happy to relinquish responsibility for their own lives and in so doing nullify what are claimed to be the true desires of the Temple. He's aware that he often skates on thin theoretical ice, but in finding himself the focus of attention, is not one to pass up any opportunities for publicity. He is, though, far from being a star.

Stars are unavailable. They are inaccessible but for glossy stills and short bursts of activity on pieces of plastic and celluloid. Few are as consistently self-deprecating or as just plain silly as P-Orridge can be, and who ever heard of a star saying he was "uninteresting" in one breath and then encouraging the people who come to his performances to bootleg them in the next?

Many hectares of newsprint have been devoted to the subject of P-Orridge, particularly concentrated on his supposed 'weirdness' and vision, his disillusionment with society from an early age and his remarkably intricate responses to that situation. Few articles seem to have satisfactorily explained, or even identified this disillusionment and its twin feeling of isolation that would, in many individuals, have resulted in a life of crime or more lonesome social maladjustment.

Behaviour patterns and modes of thinking are not only created by external forces, but also by internal ones. We are all products of conditioning, but we are also all products of chemical balances within our bodies. Gen's test-tube contains an illuminating imbalance.

Being treated with steroids for an asthmatic condition when he was four years old, his faith in the medical profession was (and remains to this day) shattered when it transpired that the side effect of the treatment had caused irreparable damage to his adrenal gland, leaving him unable to produce his own supply of the vital drug. To remedy this, he was to have to take regular does of adrenalin in tablet form.

"I am split in different places
I am split from everything
...All this energy destroys me
Killing my security
...Adrenalin creates this law
And gives me hope for life again"
'(Paper Thin) Adrenalin' Throbbing Gristle

The body's daily requirement of adrenalin obviously being variable, the artificial dose is through necessity set at a constant high, meaning that not all of the drug available will be used – the body simply absorbing and breaking down the excess drug. Any chemist will tell you, however, that adrenalin can break down to something resembling LSD-6. Harmless enough, but meaning that P-Orridge has been on a steady, if infinitesimal trip for the last thirty odd years.

"Normal people experience somewhat the same thing as mescalin users when they have whipped up their adrenal glands with intense anger or fear... For when adrenalin decomposes, it produces adrenochrome – and an intoxication with some of the symptoms of mescalin. These may include brief lapses of reality – awareness, intensified appreciation of commonplace objects, either actual or imagined, and exaggerated emotions of fear and hate."
(Dr. Claude William Chamberlain in *'Magic Land of Mescalin'*, Fate magazine, Vol. 9, No. 1, 1956.)

This fact was borne out most startlingly when Gen experimented with hallucinogenic drugs in the 'sixties – once dangerously taking twelve times the normal dose of LSD and being thoroughly disappointed with the resulting state of near-normality. *"The colours on the carpet got a bit brighter,"* as his friends crawled around on the ceiling being generally wacky.

For all this, he was a fairly ordinary kid, although he has in the past gleefully admitted to the fact that he was more sexually active, and mischievous at an earlier age than most, enjoying such things as once running through town in thick fog with his willy hanging out (he is in fact an exhibitionist to this day!). Another clue to what was to follow came when he was nine, when he says he went through a phase of liking nothing better than going into the corner of a field alone and using twigs, knotted grass, sticks and stones to build...altars.

"I'd spend hours laboriously marking out areas and making clearings and painstakingly build them. And I remember taking great pleasure in the thought that with the first gust of wind, or rainstorm, it would all be blown away."

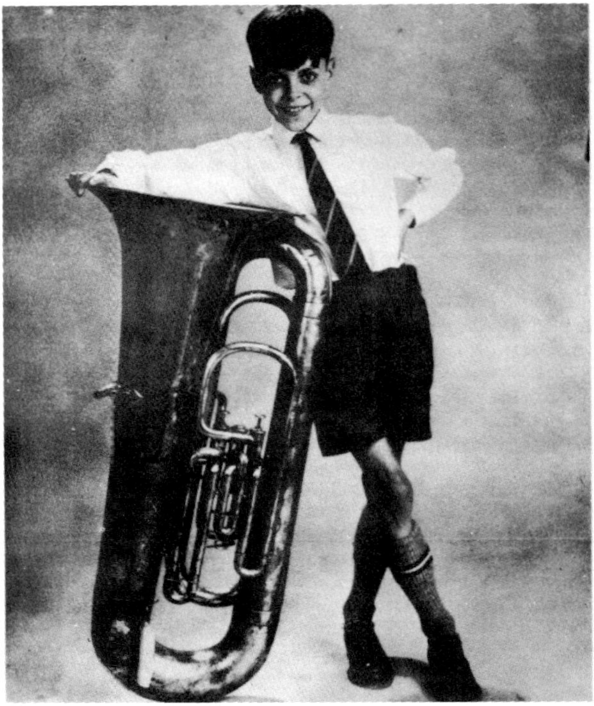

Neil Megson always showed a keen interest in the arts.

Even then, the nine-year-old minimalist took more pleasure from the process of creating than the creation itself.

Recording songs and poetry by the age of twelve he continued through school as a fairly normal pupil. His small physical stature made him a target for bullies, and it was no doubt from here that one of his present-day interests – a belief in the concept and practice of self-defence – evolved. He once "defended" himself in the classroom with a penknife, and was surprised to find blood trickling out of his assailant. The experience was committed to vinyl decades later in TG's song *'Blood on the Floor'*.

At the age of seventeen he seems to have become, as is normal, disenchanted with what life had to offer, particularly as he was disliked and picked-on by certain members of the school staff. He then hit upon an idea that, again, has been used on a number of occasions in his later life. He turned the tables by confusing people's expectations of him. Already an agnostic, if not fully fledged anti-Christian, he became secretary of the Sixth Form Christian Discussion Circle.

"From then on I was protected from everything, even when I was being very naughty, because I was secretary of the Christian Discussion Circle, so I MUST be a nice boy. And that was when I learned that reversing your normal response often has a potent effect. Often bashing on a brick wall is a lot less constructive than walking around the side and shaking someone's hand while still carrying the bomb secretly in your back pocket."

By the age of 18 he was taking Sunday School classes. *"I did that because I was interested in the structure by then, and seeing how people were trained. While doing it I just trained the children there to be thoughtful, and not be the kind of people who'd consciously do others harm. I just used a flimsy web of Christianity as camouflage for that. I was brought up a Christian."* (surprisingly C of E, not Catholic). *"I'd had to go to communion every week and drink the blood. The only good thing about it was to see these very respectable people kneeling and guzzling blood and eating human flesh. I remember being very disappointed when I was young when I found out it wasn't real blood. I really felt cheated. Maybe that's why I've been disappointed in the Christian Church ever since."* Well, that's Christianity in a nutshell. No flesh. No blood.

Passing his exams, he entered Hull University, having chosen a telling curriculum of Philosophy, Sociology and Social Administration – the very structure of society. He'd ignored advice that he go to Art College thinking it "too obvious" a move, and unlikely to be able to teach him any practical skills that he could not learn himself somewhere else if and when they were ever needed (nobody, for example, ever gave him classes in how to use a recording studio).

A difficult student on what he thought a lousy course, he dropped out and lived in a succession of hippy communes based in squats all over England. It was from here that he started becoming involved in Performance Art, and his writing and poetry flourished. He contributed to a string of magazines, including the notorious *OZ*, and other titles like *I.T.*, *MOLE*, and his own, *WORM*. No less than the *Times Literary Supplement* had him pegged as "the most promising young poet in Britain". Faber are thought to have eyed him with interest, and the likes of Richard Murphy and the man who denounced the junket of Poet Laureate, Philip Larkin, tried to persuade him into becoming a serious poet (just like they were).

Unusual ideas were already marinating in Gen's mind, though, so instead the luverly lad joined a greasy gang of Hells Angels – performing oral sex with six of them as part of his initiation – and then went on to develop an interest in areas of communication which avoided the written word. Performance music, and visual art. Eventually becoming deeply involved in groups such as (don't laugh) The Exploding Galaxy, Trans Media Exploration, and (with girlfriend, artist and porno model Cosi Fanni Tutti, now of the Creative Technology Institute) COUM – the logo of which was a semi-erect penis, dribbling with semen, beneath it printed the words 'We Guarantee Disappointment'.

About this time Gen found an ally in the crumpled suit of William Burroughs. It all started when Genesis wrote a fan letter, to which the novelist replied. Gen then sent him a shoebox containing a plastercast hand with the thumb missing, and in the box he secreted a typically enigmatic note saying 'dead fingers thumb', adding only his name and phone number.

When, a few days later, Gen arrived home, a friend – and fellow Burroughs junkie – told him that he'd received a phone call in his absence.

"Who was it?"

"Some wanker pretending to be William Burroughs."

"It probably was William Burroughs. What did you say to him?"

"Oh shit. I told him to fuck off. I just told William Burroughs to fuck off and stop pissing about."

Fortunately, Burroughs persevered, inviting P-Orridge to his Duke Street flat. The two have since remained friends, resulting in "Uncle Bill"'s appearances at *The Final Academy* series of events organised by The Temple at Brixton's Ritzy Cinema. The three-day event, put together by P-Orridge, included performances by 23 Skidoo, Cabaret Voltaire, and readings by the poet John Giorno (once the lover of Ginsberg, and also of Warhol's *'Sleep'* film fame), Brion Gysin, Kathy Acker and the debut of PTV. P-Orridge is also the proud owner of probably the most complete collection of Burroughs books, videos and memorabilia in the country. It was he who the BBC wheeled out to talk on Radio One about Burroughs on the release of the Factory/IKON Burroughs videos, and he was also the person who supplied BBC 2 controller Alan Yentob with much of his material for the *'Arena'* documentary on Burroughs' life in 1984.

Besides Burroughs, the primary influences on his life and work are not hidden. In fact they are made obvious by the pictures that hang on his walls. A Gysin painting; a large framed photograph of Crowley in full masonic uniform (looking ironically like Mussolini, the man who kicked A.C. out of Italy); an original Austin Spare; the only surviving portrait of Harry Crosby given to him by the sado-masochist writer Terence Sellers.

Crosby was a Boston socialite, a born millionaire who devoted himself to living life to the full. He inherited a library of several thousand books, but (saying nobody needed more than 200 books in their collection), he set about giving the rest away – discreetly depositing priceless first editions on the shelves of secondhand bookshops! He married 'pretty' Polly Peabody (said by some to have been the co-inventor of the bra), having stolen her away from her alcoholic husband and carrying her off to Europe in a white Rolls Royce which he later burnt on the beach at Monaco. Saying that he couldn't spend the rest of his life with anyone calling themselves 'Polly' he dubbed the love of his life 'Caresse'.

He spent most of his remarkable life partying, writing, and offloading his vast inheritance by patronising the arts. In order to give himself the sense of panic necessary to ensure that he *lived* life to the full, he promised his friends that he'd be dead by the age of 30. He proved true to his word. On his 30th birthday, Harry Crosby killed himself.

In investigating P-Orridge, one could do worse than look at his heroes. Crosby embodied both decadence and despair, the essential gemini stars in the firmament of Cult Art, and tempered this with a conviction shared only by the likes of a Mishima. Gen admires conviction.

By the mid '70s he was involved in Mailart, (a peripheral member of the Fluxus movement that included La Monte Young and Joseph Beuys, and a correspondent with the likes of Anna Banana and Monte Cazazza in San Francisco), and, again, his contacts made during this time, such as Al Ackerman, and the influence of the philosophies of people such as Fluxus' founder George Maciunas, show some bearing on the later work of The Temple, who, viewed in this light, close-up, appear not so much as a Satanic Church, as a Mail Art movement focused on religious imagery and various forms of ritual.

Some of P-Orridge's mailart in the 'seventies was considered obscene. He was prosecuted for one of his postcards, (which depicted the Buckingham Palace garden with a large female bottom poking out of some bushes), taking legal advice from Lord Goodman, and being represented in court by the same Q.C. who'd previously successfully defended Linda Lovelace and the OZ editors, but who failed miserably in the case of the GPO v GP-O. So, in a world where it is an offence to offend he was landed with a £400 fine and unofficially sentenced to a life of having his mail tampered with.

His charming public image was further polished in 1976, when he and the other members of COUM staged the infamous *'Prostitution'* exhibition at the ICA.

The show included, among an unreported bulk of painting and sculpture, a selection of tampon exhibits. Tory loonies like Nicholas Fairburn MP, who had been invited to the show, reacted by going predictably bonkers. The owner of the ICA building in the Mall was not amused. It made it look as though she was living off "immoral earnings" by allowing the event to be put on, and her house, after all, was only down the street (for it was she – the lady with the bottom).

The gutter press pounced. Screaming from their usual platform of mock indignation, they slammed P-Orridge (with his Arts Council grant) for being disgusting and immoral in columns wedged between lurid reports about horny clergymen and the inky paper flesh of Page Three breasts. He complained about their lies and misreporting of the affair to the Press Council, but it was too late. In the eyes of Fleet Street over a decade later, Genesis P-Orridge is still thought of as 'The Tampon Man' – a thoroughly nasty piece of work. After all, wasn't it he, in 1971 (5 years before the Pistols) who had committed the ultimate crime; hadn't he gobbed on John Peel? He had.

Although he now views his involvement with the Art establishment with contempt, saying that its petit bourgeois mentality and misunderstanding of what he was doing was detestable, and his and others work at the time largely "rubbish", the image was set, and stuck; he found himself framed in a picture of his own making. Besides being an 'artistic statement' as valid as anything else in the Institute of Contemporary Arts at the time, the 'Prostitution' exhibition revealed much about the supposedly liberal art world and also the news media, and, important to our story, Genesis P-Orridge had created the only statement demanded by the arts community in a media dictated society – a persona. *"An achievement in some ways, and also an albatross around my neck in others."*

Pernicious, suspect

October 19th-26th 1976

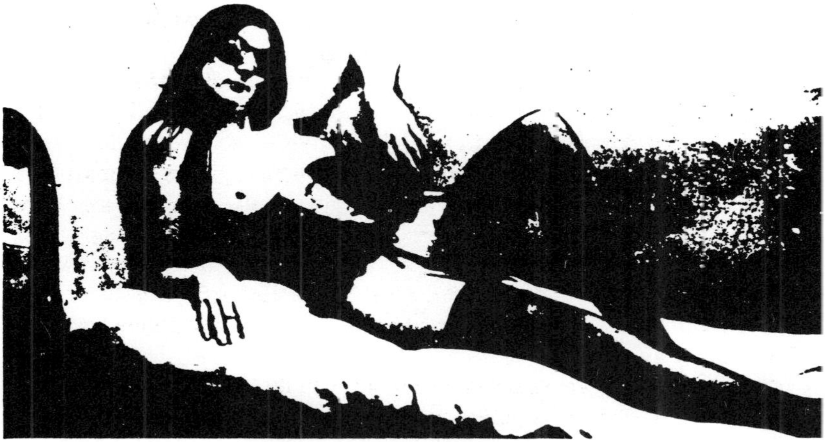

SEXUAL TRANSGRESSIONS NO. 5

PROSTITUTION

COUM Transmissions:- Founded 1969. Members (active) Oct 76 - P. Christopherson, Cosey Fanni Tutti, Genesis P-Orridge. Studio in London. Had a kind of manifesto in July/August Studio International 1976. Performed their works in Palais des Beaux Arts, Brussels; Musee d'Art Moderne, Paris; Galleria Borgogna, Milan; A.I.R. Gallery, London; and took part in Arte Inglese Oggi, Milan survey of British Art in 1976. November/December 1976 they perform in Los Angeles Institute of Contemporary Art; Deson Gallery, Chicago; N.A.M.E. Gallery, Chicago and in Canada. This exhibition was prompted as a comment on survival in Britain, and themselves.

2 years have passed since the above photo of Cosey in a magazine inspired this exhibition. Cosey has appeared in 40 magazines now as a deliberate policy. All of these framed form the core of this exhibition. Different ways of seeing and using Cosey with her consent, produced by people unaware of her reasons, as a woman and an artist, for participating. In that sense, pure views. In line with this all the photo documentation shown was taken, unbidden by COUM by people who decided on their own to photograph our actions. How other people saw and recorded us as information. Then there are xeroxes of our press cuttings, media write ups. COUM as raw material. All of them, who are they about and for? The only things here made by COUM are our objects. Things used in actions, intimate (previously private) assemblages made just for us. Everything in the show is for sale at a price, even the people. For us the party on the opening night is the key to our stance, the most important performance. We shall also do a few actions as counterpoint later in the week.

PERFORMANCES: Wed 20th 1pm - Fri 22nd 7pm
Sat 23rd 1pm - Sun 24th 7pm

INSTITUTE OF CONTEMPORARY ARTS LIMITED

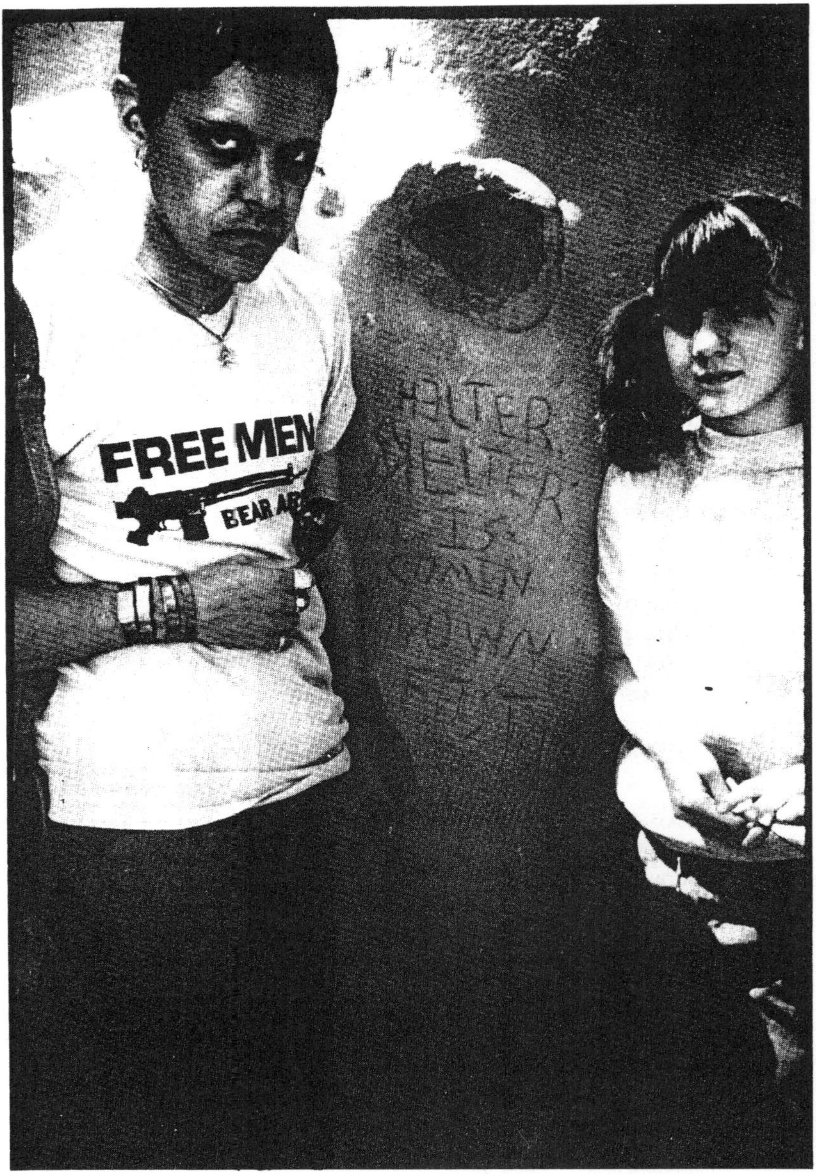

Genesis and Paula at Manson's Spahn Ranch, California, 1982. (Photo:Vale).

Presently, Gen appears to have attempted to divorce himself from the Art World by adopting a simple, yet effective ploy. He has substituted the word 'Art' with the word 'Magick'. He once wrote: *"I do not believe that ANY art has intrinsic value. It is a result, it is not the thing itself. It is expression and description; not experience, it is residue. It is means. Magick is the only medium that can be both."*

In consciously distancing himself from the Art world, he successfully removed himself from the influence of the superficial consumerist ethics which the art establishment expounds. As an 'artist', P-Orridge felt suspicious, embarrassed and uncomfortable. Now, as a Magick Man, he feels at ease. Even if this new definition has resulted in problems that would not be shared by someone clinging to the title of "Artist", as that term still affords some understanding and tolerance in the community not given to these strange "occult" types.

As the *'Catalan'* video decays into static, little Caresse rolls languidly off the couch and gambols across the field of powder grey carpet to play with the two large Mickey Mouse helium balloons that float inanely a few feet above the floor – a present from Daddy. The antique lace curtains billow and the room is livened by a breath of morning Hackney breeze, finding P-Orridge discussing lack of energy in the morning. The tape switches to real time.

"You know why it is don't you? It's obviously biological."

Err, bio-rhythms?

"No. You assume that people transmit frequencies, pulses. You know the evidence."

Zuccarelli's holophonics, the Black Box, Dream Machine, Tibetan trumpets which resonate at frequencies that affect our frequencies and produce aurally-induced orgasms, Dr. Rupert Sheldrake's theory of Morphic Resonance – everything from radionics to Madame Blavatsky's auras would seem to point in that general direction. But how would that effect us in the morning?

Gen is reminded again of the past, revealing more of his exploits with the enigmatic Trans Media Exploration and in the process, more of the drives that motivate him and the Temple today.

"I was with them in 1969, they had grown out of the Exploding Galaxy. The people there used to talk about this guy who'd been with them who used to make strange plastic capes with all objects and things in – Derek Jarman. Then in 1978 I met up with him in person. Anyway, Trans Media was a very strict commune. You couldn't sleep in the same place two nights running. You had no money or clothes of your own. The clothes

were all kept together in a box so you just chose something for the day from it. Meals were always at different times. Everything was affected, even food. No standard recipes were accepted, so you had to improvise. We'd also do things like wake each other up at odd times of the night. It was very tough."

Thus the seeds had been sown. He learnt not to ASSUME anything as being OBVIOUS. To learn what form of behaviour was habit, and to what extent the breaking of those ingrained habits and expectations affected reality. Reality being the way one experiences life. To become self-reliant, through varying rigorous forms of self-discipline, so as to be more able to investigate life subjectively and come up with one's own conclusions and solutions to it. To be as non-lazy as possible. Such a lifestyle explains why his opinions are often so unusual, and inevitably unpopular. On a practical level, it's also an explanation for why he's amassed such an enormous body of work.

One Trans Media experiment was an attempt to crack, or at least tamper with, the limitations of Language – itself a key to 'Control' and a long obsession with the literati, from Orwell and James Joyce, to Burroughs and Anthony Burgess. The interest in language has expressed itself in a number of ways; indeed, one need only read Gen's contributions elsewhere in Rapid Eye to see that he still uses a personalised, highly idiosyncratic form of writing. An early experiment involved his attempts to build a typewriter that produced a form of non-linear writing.

"It could be used to form codes and hieroglyphs as well as shapes and forms of lettering, a type of writing that was more visual and less static. We were interested in breaking people's ways of looking at things. Writing in that way meant that people weren't looking at straight words or letters, and so they had to be looking at what the words were made from."

Editing this symbolised Newspeak not only made it more efficient than linear writing, but also more idiosyncratic.

"People either had to build it back up into letters they could see again in their head, or had to learn to decode it like shorthand"

Even when 'cracked' and read almost automatically, it could still be used to write private messages to other group members, or changed at will, depending on meaning and mood. But this invites criticism. Of, in this case, the language, and more widely any 'alternative' structure. As applicable to The Temple as it is to Trans Media. In doing all this, isn't one just replacing one structure, one language, one mad form of belief, with another? And if so, what's the point?

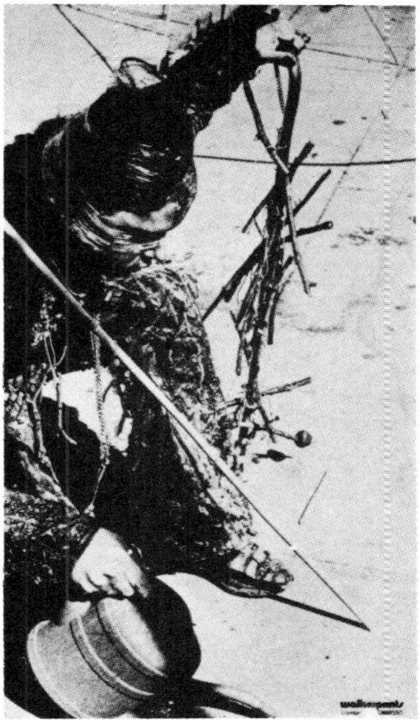

COUM Transmissions performance.

The point is, of course, not necessarily the results of the activity, but the taking part, the research. In the case of the language, learning the nature of language-Control (even with the widest of vocabularies), and the limitations inherent in any form of communication, and creating an individualised alternative that may communicate ideas and feelings that have up to that point remained muted by conventional expression. If nothing else, the understanding of such esoteric language defeats laziness, negates the conditioned passive role of acceptance and expectation, and promotes more inter-action between writer and reader.

Another advantage of creating such a flexible visual form of written communication lies in its magickal applications. The meaning of such symbolism can more easily be forgotten by the conscious mind – a positive disadvantage in normal use, but not so when you are later using the symbolism you have created in sigilisation for example – which we will go into later.

Trans Media's disorientation of logic and expectation, its mischievous Boy Scout pseudo-sect mentality and its interest in *observing process* rather than *creating product* seems to have been something of a blueprint for what was to follow.

But where does Frequency fit into this jigsaw?

"One of the linguistic things we had in Trans Media as a discipline was that there are two types of people. It was only a simplification to express an idea, it doesn't really mean that we thought there were two kinds of people, but for ease of description there are these genealogical terms, and one of them is 'quaquaversal', which apparently means 'pointing in every direction simultaneously'. And there is another word, 'centroclinal', which has the definition of being 'the opposite of quaquaversal'."

Genesis smiles and looks rather pleased with himself. The language creaks and finds it hard to cope. Trans Media loved playing with such ideas, it seems.

"We, and in fact most people observed that as you said, it was easier to work very late at night as opposed to in the morning. And our glib but semi-serious explanation for it was that the centroclines – the people who don't want to wake up, don't want to look around and do anything, that squidgy, lard-like mass who individually are fine, but corporately generated an incredible amount of centroclinal energy. We didn't say negative energy, because the word 'negative' implies a moral judgement, whereas 'centroclinal' implies...wasted, a big black hole. So, when the centroclines went to sleep in their little suburbs and so on their brains slowed down a lot and their centroclinal emissions dwindled."

Creating more space?

"Yes, allowing the quaquaversal energies to pop out and fill the void."

But the centroclines on the other side of the world would still be awake anyway.

"Well I think we decided that the effect of the energy was more obvious the closer you were to the source; it was more powerful locally than globally. If you're next to someone who's trying to punch you in the mouth it hurts more than if somebody's trying to punch you when they're in Japan, I guess." Gen, as you will have noticed, loves parables.

Flashing back to Present Time the Sony booms out as Caresse dances with Mickey across the little ballroom in her head. PTV's breakneck version of The Beach Boys *'Good Vibrations'* (a frequency pun?) sweeps the conversation off its feet. The single was released in 1986 and, aided by a wonderful pastiche video shot during the group's US tour in California, reached the lower regions of the national charts. Although officially a Psychic TV release at the height of P-Orridge's interest in "Hyperdelia", the record was originally intended to be put out on 'The Process' label by *'The Process.'* The Process is not a group. Confused?

The Process is another piece in the mosaic of minor and often unpublicised projects that make up P-Orridge's career. The Process, with its obvious implied references to Brion Gysin and also to Dr Robert De Grimston's cult of the same name, is the way in which a thing is done. Its method rather than its identity (the band), or the results of that band's activity (the 'record'). The Process also produced a killing version of Gen's favourite Stones song *'As Tears Go By'*. The process adopted for the realisation of the project that has produced these two wax almadels was to gather together several interested musicians – such as Rose from Strawberry Switchblade – and use several instruments as they were used on the original '60s recordings, reproducing the originals in more palatable wall of sound disco by using state-of-the-art 1980's recording technology.

The general reaction to the single was that it was pretty, but, coming as it did from P-Orridge, rather pointless. Indeed, Genesis is so revered among the ageing, pseudo-intellectual pop fraternity that they had forgotten he was capable of releasing records purely for the fun of it, and as subject to influences as the next man. Visiting his house at the time of The Process project, one would note the cogent fact that a well-thumbed copy of Warhol's *'Popism'* lay on the P-Orridge coffee table.

There were, of course, other reasons for the *'Good Vibrations'* release. He does have a wife, family, and mortgage to support. Despite advice, he has never watered down his weldgeist to a more weedy, acceptable consistency and gone hell for leather for the money – but The Process single was an undeniable step towards solvency, even though most of the money it made was ploughed back into the Temple's more esoteric projects.

Obviously, the fund-raising activities of PTV are also more accessible than was the mottled sheet of experimental sound that was TG, but even now they are hardly an easy pill to swallow, and anyway, the metamorphosis from abstract electronic din (an experiment in muzak and its effects on frequency) to the dark pop of PTV (an experiment in pop ritual and its effects on frequency), was an aesthetic desirability rather than a tactical manoeuvre.

P-Orridge though, on the bottom line, makes no bones about the fact that the money from such projects as the Process is needed. Alex Fergusson (late of Mark Perry's ATV and Fred and Judy Vermorel's naughty Cash Pussies) has got to be one of the great bedsit-bound pop composers of the moment. Due to his association with P-Orridge though, he has had to earn his living as an usher in a West End cinema. For his part, Gen – recipient of the odd royalty cheque and director of several Temple companies, is better off, though far from rich – despite rumours to the contrary based on false assumptions based on PTV's previous record deals.

Even though Psychic TV signed a whopping million-pound rolling option contract with CBS, all the £30,000 they actually received from it was spent on the recording of the *'Dreams Less Sweet'* album – along with £3,000 of the Temple's own money on top of that, borrowed from Some Bizzare's Stevo and raised by such events as the Marc (Almond) and the Mambas Temple benefit performance in London.

A large chunk of the vast recording costs went towards the use of Hugo Zuccarelli's Holophonic recording system. Zuccarelli is a thirtysomething Argentine physicist. He worked at the Cathedral of Brain Psychology in Buenos Aires, conducting research into sleep and dreams, specifically concerning himself with external induction of visual stimulation and memory. He later studied in Milan, where he worked on electronic and magnetic fields. It was here that he formulated the idea of Holophonics, the audio equivalent of Holography. Approaching the subject of recording from a neurophysiological, rather than from an acoustic/electronic angle, Zuccarelli works on the principle that listening to sound is an active, rather than a passive experience. From Edison onwards, we have listened to recordings of the mechanical vibration created by a sound source. This does not take into account the effect such sound has on the frequencies which emanate from the listener. Recording vibration from the source is only half the sound picture; the other half is provided by the listener, giving sound a spatial quality.

For example, if you were listening to a recording of a voice that has been made with the person speaking standing 25 feet away from the microphone, you would hear a very faint voice – you would hear a bad recording. If, on the other hand, you were to hear someone talking to you from the same distance in a room, you would know that the person was about 25 feet away, how loud he was talking, and where he was standing in relation to you. You would be hearing reality. Holophonics, in giving sound a three-dimensional quality, is the recording of that reality. The sound is recorded without microphones in the ordinary sense of the word, through a dummy body, complete with skull, ears, hair, internal juices and cavities. What we hear through the dummy (called 'Ringo'), is the interference between the sound source and the reference tone given off by our – or in this case, Ringo's – ears. The brain is then able to interpret the result and give it a spatial quality.

Rubbish? Hype? Here is what Fleet Street had to say at the time:

"In the past few weeks several music and Fleet Street papers have written stories about Psychic TV's album. The group ostentatiously proclaim that it's the first "holophonic" record ever to be released and that it allows listeners to hear "3-D" music. Bunkum! After hearing the album I reckon the only strange thing about it, besides the bizarre music, is someone shaking a matchbox around at the end of the final track...Radio One DJ Richard Skinner, who interviewed Psychic TV last week, describes them as 'inventive comedians', adding 'All they're doing is using a very old stereo sound technique'."

Peter Holm, The Standard 24.11.82

"Stand by for holophonic sound, which is set to become one of the major technological breakthroughs of the Eighties. After my rather sceptical piece on Psychic TV last week I was contacted by the inventor and given a special demonstration – and I can vouch that the effect is staggering...it was as if the noise was passing in front of my face and then going around the back of my head...a perfect 3-D effect, in fact, and most extraordinary was that it was no different through only one headphone, meaning that it had nothing to do with conventional stereo...holophonics can also encourage visual stimulation."

Peter Holm, The Standard 1.12.82

Auto-suggestion perhaps? Well several people don't think so. Rick Wakeman, Stevie Wonder, Kate Bush, Vangelis, John Williams and Pink Floyd queued up to use the system first, and Paul McCartney wanted to buy the patent. Zuccarelli though, turning down vast sums, wanted his invention used by someone who would be able to understand it, appreciate its uses and use it with imagination, and with some courage of conviction, held out and chose PTV to be the first group to be allowed to fully record with it. Gen grasped the opportunity, dragging the hapless silver-haired Ringo down into the caves used by Sir Francis Dashwood's Hellfire Club, into wet-walled sewers, crept up behind him, chased him with dogs, poured petrol around him and set light to it, and put him in a coffin and buried him. (When playing it lock the door, put the headphones on and turn the lights out. Even allowing for the usual disorientation caused, if you don't feel some sensations not normally associated with listening to pop records, then you're made of wood.)

The result was a beautiful, mysterious and mean record. Full of breathless oboes and mad pumping church organs wrapped around the songs and poems of the Temple, penned by Thomas Tallis, Jim Jones, Charles Manson, Monte, Jordi, Krafft-Ebbing, Alex and Genesis. A sort of *'Psychopathia Sexualis'* done in rubber, it became the hymnal of the Temple, but the record company couldn't give a shit.

PTV, who had, prior to the *'Dreams'* album already been dumped after the *'Force the Hand of Chance'* LP for abusing WEA Records, were dropped by CBS. Perhaps they didn't like the sight of Gen dragging a handcuffed Marc Almond around their Soho Square offices, particularly when David Jensen was visiting.

Gen was back with the independents. *Illuminated, Fresh, Fetish, Red, De-Coder*, and *Sordid Sentimentale* are just a few of the labels on which he has (literally) scratched his thoughts, giving away the copyright and master tapes of recordings like TG's legendary *'D.o.A.'* to fans so as to encourage them to start their own record companies and in the process defeat the gangland bootleggers who had been getting bloated on TG's deleted endeavours by feeding record junkie youth and charging through the inflamed nose for the service. All very altruistic, but such an attitude to the record business, and money in general, has often left him broke.

Being well-known does have its advantages though. One visitor to the Temple is Anton La Vey, leader of The Church of Satan (a registered church in the USA). La Vey, liking the idea of TOPY, seems interested in giving the Temple's fledgling publishing outlet the UK rights to his unpublished books, such as the rather naff *'Satanic Bible'*.

Another connection made by Genesis may make it possible for Temple Records to release the early 'sonic experiments' of the Velvet Underground, yet another gives the organisation the rights to publish a compendium of Terence Sellers' work.

This writer once bumped into P-Orridge in a London cafe and was introduced to Peter Getty, who had Concorded over from New York to interview P-Orridge for his *'Evergreen Review'*. Peter, who on his 25th birthday will inherit a fair chunk of the family fortune, jetted his poverty-stricken interviewee over to Paris for a few days, Gen returning the favour by introducing Getty to the man who'd done some of the paintings that hang over both of their fireplaces back home – Brion Gysin.

A confirmed Samuel Beckettite (if such a breed exists), Peter is at present writing a play. Without the profit motive being paramount, such a thing is likely to be slated by the critics for lack of 'hunger', or some such contrived drivel regardless of merit, simply because society cannot really believe in anything produced purely for creative reasons – thinking it self-indulgent even though, ironically, its motivations must be the most pure and uncompromising.

The Process single, however, was criticised by reversing this logic. It having had no pretensions to being anything other than an enjoyable, affectionate homage to pop pap, regardless of how it was produced. Sixties styles, with their innocent Yagsur's Farm idealism now made tougher by the perspective given by time, is a current interest of Gen's, musically and spiritually. Just as the exotic strains of Martin Denny in an incongruous marriage arranged by P-Orridge to the techno-pop of Düsseldorf had been the primal source of the later work of TG, Psychic TV are now passing through a phase as eccentric Acid House popists, as opposed to post-punk shockists. A mood reflected in P-Orridge's current mode of dress.

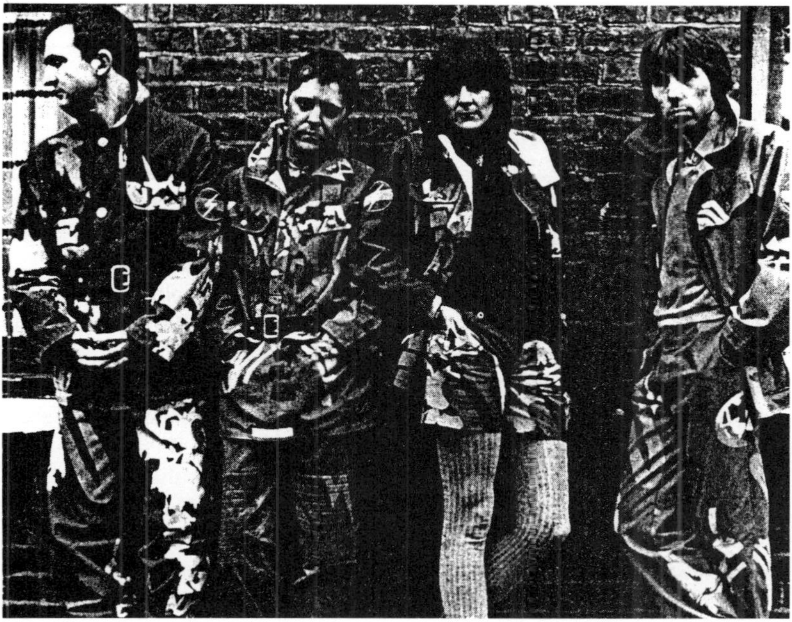

TG in '70s 'TerrorGuard' mode. Camo design by Lawrence Dupre.

The old militaristic image of the Temple – austerely black and grey, threateningly shaved and brutalised, was introduced (quite deliberately) as a fashion. The Temple, purporting to be a loose association interested in 'Individuality', took on a uniformity to test the individual and public response to it. To play a mischievous game with fashion in order to negate it. Just as the Temple plays with the behavioral patterns encouraged by organised religion.

Nowadays, gone are the black shirts and camo-jackets, the vaguely fascistic-looking badges and squeaky DMs that created a false impression to many passers-by in the British Movement infested backstreets of the East End. (The idea was really one of appreciating Design and Image and wresting-back the powerful look usurped by the Nazis. Though most people obviously got the wrong idea, trendy lefties accusing P-Orridge of being a Fascist while at the same time he endured several attacks on the street from right wing skinheads who called him a "Jew".)

Now, bored with the monotonous grime of London, the traffic jams and rain, the bearded Socialists, white high-heeled tarts and acres of grey council housing, all is sweetness and light. It was not always so. TG once commissioned a clothes designer, their friend Lawrence Dupre, to design for them their own camouflage (there are hundreds of different types of camouflage available from around the world, and P-Orridge has quite a collection, but the group wanted a unique one). He came up with a rectangular-looking design in the colours of black, white, and various shades of grey. TG had the suits made up, and would often perform in their "urban camo" uniforms. Now, as a reaction to the prevailing sense of greyness, P-Orridge is often resplendent in silk sari, purple slacks and long ponytail plaited with multi-coloured strands of wool.

The term Genesis has coined for the style is typically loaded – "Hyperdelic", psychedelia forged with modernism. The Temple now talks of "Angry Love", a unification of the peaceful idealism of the hippies and the militant, perhaps violent protests of the Situationists circa 1968. A love which is selective, an anger which is justified, and born out of sheer frustration.

To Gen, Angry Love is the clarion call of a new, realistic radicalism. *"Radicalism is what you do, not how you look. Celebrate and activate! Don't destroy, deploy and decoy...Radicalism is given power by building, not by destroying. Each day that passes this society commits mass murder. It murders imagination, potential, possibilities in people of all ages and sexes, but most obviously in young people. They are encouraged to kill time with Smack, to kill optimism with sarcasm, and to hypnotise themselves with death by the daily wearing of Black."*

Angry Love is Timothy Leary's vision smashing into the immovable object of Thatcher's bitter British reality. As P-Orridge writes in a Temple Newsletter – *"TURN ON (control), TUNE IN (to your Self), DROP OUT (of Control)... We do LOVE, but in a 1980's way. We LOVE the fight, we LOVE hope... We feel ANGER, for all the obvious reasons."*

Angry Love means Stop Hurting Each Other. Not because it's the "nice" thing to do, but because it's a waste of time. It's a diversion from the true fight. Each individual's fight. The fight against complacency, puritanism, uniformity, prejudice, guilt, fear, conditioning. The fight against the social manifestations of CONTROL.

This newer, practical radicalism expresses itself in such things as the Temple-organised demonstration outside the South African Embassy in Trafalgar Square on the 14th September 1987, timed to co-incide with the start of the trial of Moses Moyekaso in Johannesburg, and in the series of Temple demos held outside Brighton Marina calling for the release of the dolphins forced to perform in its shabby pool (hardly activities usually associated with "Satanic"/"Nazi"/"Arty"/"Pornographers", one thinks).

Angry Love has been celebrated at a number of PTV events, such as the

'Riot in the Eye' day at the Electric Ballroom. PTV played with The Angry Love Orchestra and six other bands at the nine hour "indoor festival". Stalls sold "Hyperdelic Wholefood", there was a "Tele-Visionary Lounge" and disco, but did anyone remember to take their Mates condoms for the "Free Love Tent"?

Events such as Riot in the Eye encouraged people to make a personal effort, rather than simply attend a gig. To ignore current fashion and the ridiculous 80's media obsession with 'Style' as dictated by the smug, monotonous voices of Peter York and Lloyd Grossman – and to have fun.

A Riot in the Eye is caused by SEEING and OBSERVING just what is really going on in this society. The concept of Angry Love directs the anger this generates not towards a riot in the street, but to a constructive end. A rejection. An increase in perception. The tape loops back... *"Radicalism is given power by building, not by destroying..."*

Whatever the terminology employed, the Temple now seems to reverberate to the sounds of nouveau hippiedom. It just depends on your view of a hippie as to whether you think the association good or bad. If you are locked into fashion, it's irrelevant and obnoxious. But if you regard a hippie as someone who is likely to be actively seeking better alternatives, and creating for himself a life free from the trappings of compromise and the pressures of materialism and fashion, you probably think it's OK. Personally, I find the Temple's current attitude towards clothes a mite overstated. At a PTV Thames Riverboat party, for instance, invitations insist that you wear Psychedelic clothes or forego admission – much like the early '80s 'exclusive', 'alternative' clubs in the West End, who operated a dress code that ensured everyone was an 'individual', provided they looked like Marilyn, Boy George, or one of Robert Elms' ex-girlfriends. Indeed the attack on all things grey and black continues with each Temple Newsletter. Despite the fact that wearing blank, classic clothes, provided it is regardless of the fashion, *does* actually negate fashion, and reduces the amount of brain power wasted on the trivia of buying and choosing clothes. Quite how Individual (sic) one is being by going along with some of P-Orridge's style games is probably something of no importance to the dancing masses one can see at any PTV gig, but in this kingdom of the double bluff and the clever-clever, who knows or really cares? Whatever your view, the Old Grey Wolf has come out in his true colours and, in so doing, accidentally predicted the Acid House explosion of late '88.

"Coincidentally, I was using the term 'Acid Dance' before the term 'Acid House' appeared from Chicago."

Thinking about what P-Orridge was doing with emulators, voice tapes, his weird sound archive and the electronic, 'industrial' rhythmic discipline of T.G. in the late 'seventies, and joining those elements with his wild eyed pronouncements on Manson, Leary, The Process and psychedelia with the Temple organisation in the early 'eighties, it is hard not to see the link.

This linkage resulted in him collaborating with Richard Norris, behind the anonymous guise of 'Noise Or Not', an in-house acid production team which brought out the *'Acid Tablets'*, a string of phoney 'compilation' albums of original "UK acid dance freakbeats", and also the excellent *'Superman/Jack the Tab'* 12 inch single – called "the finest Acid House record to hit the dancefloor in 1988" by the Melody Maker.

The roots and definitions of Acid House are open to question, but, as Gen says, *"One of the things that's universal in all interpretations of Acid House is a revival of the original idea of psychedelia, which is to take whatever technology is current – back then it would have been the wah-wah, the mellotron – and try to find the weirdest, most irrational thing it can do. That's what Throbbing Gristle were into. We bought a computer and converted it to do sampling way back in '76, long before sampling technology was invented. Six tape decks in sequence, throwing out sounds at random, creating rhythms and conjunctions."*

The Big Sound bounces around the cultural capitals and attitudes of the world like light on mirrors and lenses. Briefly, all the colours bleeding into the white strobe light of Acid House, a very '80s fashion focus which juxtaposes sounds and images and sub-culture plots and, in so doing, embodies a moment, a moment in and out of time, that is the common feeling of disorientation and overload which comes from living in the media jungle of the early '90s.

"There is no message, but the music itself is a statement about media explosion and the acceleration of experiences that the human copes with under the effect of the mass media.

"At last all the different dreams and all the different threads that have gone in strange meandering patterns for about 15 years have all converged, WHOOOMPH! And what's so great is that it's all so open-ended, there are no rules."

The lyric-less acid beat provides P-Orridge with an ideal platform. No format, no rules. By early '89 he and other British Acid Housers were producing harder, weirder sounds than those emanating from the States and transmitting them back to the purist DJ's in Chicago. Three thousand American disc jockeys can't be wrong.

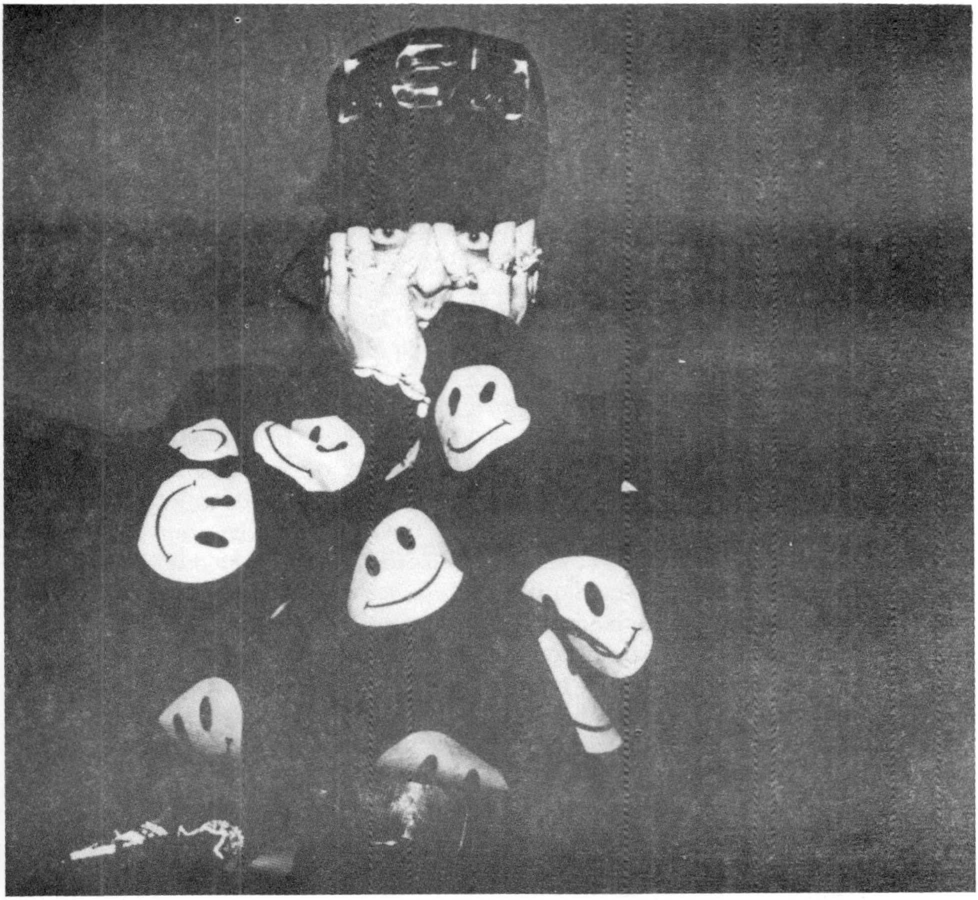

Gen, having jacked the tab.

"It's gonna be like what happened in the Sixties. We took U.S. R&B and tried to imitate it, and in the process peculiarised it, got it a bit wrong, made it British and re-exported it to the U.S. on a massive scale."

Hence the Temple Records Acid House label, a Union Jack logo with an upside-down Peace Sign at its centre.

"The Mods used the Union Jack, which relates to the freakbeat, psychedelic Mod thing. The punks used the torn-up Union Jack. Now we're using it, only upside down, 'cos everything is reversed. Funny thing is, if you put the C.N.D. sign upside down, you get the rune of

'Protection'. So they got it wrong in the Sixties and for the last 20 years everybody has been parading around under the wrong symbol!

"I love Acid House as the music allows sarcasm and disrespect and experiment to become a credible way of life again. We were all doing that anyway, because it's in our nature. But for once, circumstances have conjoined with us. All the best ideas are inevitable, nobody owns them. All popular culture has become a fair target for re-working, stealing whatever bits you need. Music, TV, political speeches, cartoons, movies."

The post modernist ethos of creative plagiarism, the practice of experimenting with, re-arranging and personalising the bones of culture – the tenets of society – is a godsend to P-Orridge.

"Nothing is immune and nothing is sacred. And I've ALWAYS wanted to live in a world where nothing is immune and nothing is sacred. And no one could tell you what was the correct way to do something."

Though usually ignored by the music press, there have been several other PTV albums released since *'Dreams'* hit the record stores in 1983; such as the *'Pagan Day'* picture disc, released at 23.00 hrs on the 23rd December '84 and deleted 23 hours later. Then there have been the three *'Psychic TV Themes'* LPs. Featuring Aleister Crowley singing in Enochian, piano scales that drift up into peaks like a healthy sales graph, and the banging and blowing of human thighbone trumpets. The trumpets not only stretch the capacity of the Musicians Union (who still have problems with emulators), but are in fact a long standing set of ritual tools. Called 'rkan-dun' in Tibet where they originate, they are crafted from the femur of (supposedly) either a murderer, a person who died violently, or a virgin – their sound being thought to call up the restless spirit of the dead person. Many such thighbones are several hundred years old, often elaborately decorated in silver threadwork and semi-precious stones. The less deluxe versions are finished in long-lasting human skin.

December '85 saw the release of the superb PTV soundtrack to the Mantis ballet *'Mouth of the Night'*, an event which combined choreographer Micha Bergese (from *'The Company of Wolves'* movie) with Jarman's set design and the most eerie, echoing score the troupe have ever danced to.

Being presented with a totally lifeless and unsuitable piece of music from the commissioned composer, Bergese wanted to dump the music and ask someone else to provide the soundtrack, but he knew no-one who could come up with the goods before the show opened at Brighton's Gardner Centre just six days later. Jarman phoned his pal, and within 24 hours PTV were ensconced in the studio, writing and recording the soundtrack around a video of the ballet's dress rehearsal in one 36 hour stint, and hot-footing over to Mantis at Pineapple dance studios in Covent Garden, giving them just two days to rehearse to the completely new soundtrack. The finished product resulted in the unlikely sight of P-Orridge's skills being raved over by beautiful ballerinas on MTV.

Early in 1987 The Temple was presented with a problem. Lack of a record deal and a lack of cash on the one hand, and a deluge of requests from the public asking for more PTV-related product on the other. Always original, Genesis then hit upon an idea that would solve both problems and be in keeping with his wish to make PTV as demystified as possible. At the same time, it would present The Temple as a living entity, using records and their covers as a regular platform for messages and diary, while at the same time having the added bonus of irritating the record industry. Between early 1987 and 1989, Temple records would release one new Psychic TV live LP on the 23rd day of each MONTH for twenty three months. All the records were packaged in almost identical covers, pressed in limited editions of between 3,000 and 5,000, and numbered in series. Retailing cheaply at around £3.50 each, they gave the fans what they wanted and the Temple the income necessary for its survival. The record shops hated the idea. The music press couldn't cope with the project. The music industry in general thought that it debased the concept of album releases – they preferred reviewing, selling, hyping and generally lauding LPs as if their releases were cultural landmarks of mammoth importance. "The long awaited U2 album, the Springsteen LP it took three years to record you've all been waiting for..." As the rock giants spent hundreds of thousands on videos, recordings and merchandise, little PTV reverted – partly out of necessity – to the punk ethics that had inspired P-Orridge to form Throbbing Gristle in the first place, over a decade previously.

On an even more esoteric note, there was also the Jim Jones LP, made up of sections of the recordings made of the last speeches of the lovely Reverend and his followers, right up until Jonestown committed its communal 'suicide'. As a study in paranoia, mass hallucination and lemming-like control practices (Socialism and Christianity in this case), it's on a par with the closed, doped, opiated, homosexual order of assassins of Alamout – the Hashishin. A modern microcosm of the Control theory in practice that's still probably under the microscope in some dingy office in downtown Washington D.C. Temple Records produced a limited edition numbering 993 copies of the record, one for each member of the Peoples Temple who snuffed it for Jesus and the Guyanan camp – each disc being stamped in gold 'Dead Body Number One', 'Dead Body Number Two' and so on until the grisly collection is complete. These projects – ignored not only because they are by definition not part of popular culture, but because editors do not think young people should be informed about things that offend their own Moony sensibilities – are, however, mere stop gaps between the last major album and the new masterwork, recorded by Psychic TV and The Angels of Light.

'The Starlit Mire' is a configuration of assorted novas. Pope John Paul, Anton La Vey, and the bleached, chlorinated bones of Brian Jones. If Crowley rears his shaved head at all, it's in deference to his role in *'Sgt Pepper'* rather than the unintelligible *'Book of the Law'*, as this is the Temple at its most accessible yet. Brilliant light and dark hyperdelic pop and Acid House trash fashioned by now fully competent musicians with a sense of direction and a (third) eye on effect rather than purpose.

Due to lack of money the album sits, literally, on the shelf. In need of a few finishing touches that will amount to £5,000 worth of studio time, and the backing and distribution of a company with more muscle than tiny Temple Records – if that effect is to be widespread. Gen has tried to woo a new contract, but the majors just don't want to know. Whatever their promise and international cult status, PTV are just too much trouble, too mischievous, too sophisticated to take the risk with in these days of wavering sales and the return to glamrock heroics and idolism and the splintering fads of Americana – House, Hip Hop, Hi Energy, et al. Perhaps also they remember the stunt Genesis pulled on them a few years ago, sending all the big West One companies a 9-inch long solid brass dildo, each one carved with the corporation's names around the glans... CBS, EMI, Polygram...and stamped at the base with 'Psychic TV Fuck the Record Industry'. The ploy cost hundreds, but all too often humourless, budget-watching A & R departments are of the attitude that they just don't want to get involved with people like them. Indeed, there is a lot of the 'People Like Them' attitude towards PTV. (Although *'The Starlit Mire'* has still to be released, sections of it have appeared on other records, such as the Temple Records album, *'Allegory and Self'*. Corporate small-mindedness has largely been countered through the use of their own independent label, which PTV use on occasions to air new studio material. Due to its small size, however, Temple releases can never compete with records released by the major companies, and are unlikely to achieve high chart placings due to lack of advertising, radio plugging, and distribution).

One thing that went some way to sweeten the large record companies and update the static public image of "Tampon Man" P-Orridge was the release of PTV's biggest selling single to date, *'Godstar'*, a song about Brian Jones. The one in the Rolling Stones.

"And you were so beautiful
And you were so very special
I wish I was with you now
I wish I could save you somehow..."

'Godstar' PTV 1985

"Well, when we were recording 'Godstar', I don't know if people generally know this but when we're using a 24 track studio we only ever use 23 tracks. It's just a tradition really. There's always one track free for...the unexpected. Well, the recording had gone on a long time and it got to an impasse point where we – these things always sound corny but I don't care – we were all so emotionally involved in it, everyone was in an intense state, and there was a strange atmosphere in the studio. We were all tired, we'd all been in there about a week and we'd put more into that one track than we had into any whole LP. And because of the subject we wanted it to be respectful, accurate and a reflection. Ken Thomas was there and an engineer called Mark Fishlock. Jordi Vallis of the World Satanic Network and some of Psychic TV. Anyway, we decided to do a Raudives experiment, y'know, like in his book 'Breakthrough' [Taplinger Publishing, NY, 1971] *where he uses little diodes to record the voices of the dead on tape. So Hillmar, who's an electronics whizzkid made this diode, cat's whiskers thing. I don't know the electronic ins and outs of it but the basic idea is that it's like a receiver without having any charge in it. It's supposed to screen any outside signals."*

And leave the tape free from interference like radio.

"Yeah, leave the tape so nothing can get on it, to stop things being picked up. So we ran the master tape with the empty track, track 23, on 'record', and we all sat down and turned the lights down and did what you'd do in a seance. Trying to commune with...Brian Jones. And the first time we ran it through and played it back and there was nothing. Then the second time we ran it back there was also nothing. Then, the third time we ran it through there was a very clear, loud sound under certain words which Ken Thomas and the studio engineer said was like nothing they'd ever heard in a studio. Not an electronic sound, not an interference sound. It wasn't generated by any of the equipment, and we'd isolated the studio."

This was on track 23 when you listened to the whole thing or just that one channel?

"No. Just listening to the one track. Then we played it back with the whole thing, to see what it sounded like, and it was EXACTLY under the words 'I wish I was with you now'. Perfect beat, time, everything."

Will it be heard on the LP?

"No, only subliminally."

What sort of noise was it on its own then, an electronic noise?

"Sort of a ...cccrroagghh noise! But it wasn't like the noise you get from radio interference. It was sort-of electrical, but also a hissing noise as well, but not one you could get if you sat down and tried to reproduce it. And it was really precise, split-second."

He also plays piano on the LP?

"Oh yes, well that was easy, not so mysterious. We just sampled his piano from 'Satanic Majesties', put it onto an Emulator 2 and we could play Brian Jones playing piano on the LP."

Have you credited him?

"Well no, that might cost us money!"

'Godstar' was released on the 28th February 1986 (the anniversary of Brian Jones' birthday) while the group toured Europe. The single reached Number One in the Independent Charts and featured in the Top Fifty of the national placings, selling some 40,000 copies between March and June of that year. BBC Radio One initially refused to give the disc any airplay amid rumours of disquiet from Jagger himself, who was understandably miffed at the song's finger-pointing lyrical content. P-Orridge compounded the problem at a promotion for the single staged at Virgin's Oxford Street Megastore, where PTV were booked to play a few songs. Grabbing the shop's Mick Jagger waxwork dummy, he proceeded to take it for a little 'dance' as amazed Japanese tourists clicked their Nikons at the clazy plonk lockers. The *'Godstar'* promo video, filmed on a tight budget by old T.G. ally Akiko Hada was picked up by cable channels SKY and MTV, and P-Orridge was beamed into seven million living rooms in nine countries across Europe. He also featured in the most in-depth interview of his career when questioned on satellite TV by Gary Davies (he was not eligible for his 'Young, Free and Single' T shirt on any count). Pop Fame at last.

The release of *'Godstar'* was publicised in the form of 10,000 stickers, placed strategically around the country by Temple Initiates and sympathizers – in subways, trains, toilets, or cheekily in record shop windows. The first 5,000, looking like funeral cards, bear the simple message 'BRIAN JONES DIED FOR YOUR SINS'. The second 5,000, on first sight, appear to be the same, except a second piece of information has been added in the shape of a small black psychic cross. Enigmatic, subliminal, amusing? Some would no doubt say an attempt to be shocking and unnecessarily mysterious – a criticism levelled at every aspect of Gen's work.

Further qualification of most of the expressions of what is going on in his mind would defend his position. But just as simplifying and sanitising the image of PTV would probably result in their becoming a fairly successful, quite rich pop group, it would also tend to defeat the object. What point releasing a record or T-shirt or sticker if you have to attach a book to each explaining, in more straightforward terms, just what it all *means*. Such is the quandary of any artist if his motivations are not purely commercial. The line you draw between the History and the Mystery, the Appliance and the Science, could be the one used to hang you from.

"Well, as with anything you do, hopefully, that sticker is the top of a pyramid. It could just as well be a book, a feature film, a record, a social movement. That's why I can see what Derek (Jarman) meant when he said to you that it's very hard to explain anymore. I can't give you a whole answer. I can try."

Consider it an exercise. That sticker works on a variety of levels.

"Yes, there's one very simple level which is that it's deliberately sarcastic of Christian values and slogans. But also it could be addressed to the Rolling Stones still surviving. In which case, from the way I observed what happened to Brian Jones I would say it's accurate, it's reportage. A jab in the ribs asking for a response. It's also designed to embarrass the remaining Stones. It's also affectionate of Brian Jones, and is therefore meant to be like an epitaph on a gravestone. To the average person in the street it's meant to totally confuse them and make them wonder what it's all about, and make some people who are old enough to remember what happened perhaps think what they may have thought at the time – that he never got a fair deal."

Gen has always been one for able labels anyway – remember the spate of black and red psychic crosses, or the 'Assume this phone is tapped' stickers that kept turning up in phone boxes in London some years ago? With P-Orridge subversion is always effected through the avenues of disposable, mass produced popular culture.

"If Warhol had done something like that, he'd have produced it in wallpaper and covered a gallery's walls with it. Have a few nice cut-outs of Brian Jones, and it'd all look very chic and beautifully presented, and so it would increase his artistic credibility and Art World profitability. But I've always been more interested in doing that same kind of thing on the street, semi-anonymously, to see what really happens. To see what effect it has in terms of generating gossip on the street. 'Have you seen this or that?' and 'what does it mean?' and so on."

The Psychic Cross design does that, so too does the Temple usage of the number '23'. Art on the street is instantly socially effective. As

P-Orridge learnt years ago, Art on gallery walls is not. Look at local papers around the country and you'll eventually come across the smalltown trivia on which legends are made. Here are a few cuttings:

"Barclays Bank in Didsbury was daubed with slogans in an unexplained attack last week... as well as an anarchy symbol there were three examples of another symbol which baffled staff...a vertical line with three horizontal lines through it. They have no idea of its meaning. Do you?"

"'Black Magic' symbols and graffiti have been daubed on the walls at Walsall's parish church and officials say the artistic vandals are costing the council thousands of pounds in repairs...a spokesman told the Observer that the symbols looks like the Greek Eoka sign with a cross through it, although some thought it could be a black magic symbol."

"Police still have no idea what the number '23' means and why it was spray painted on six local churches last weekend. 'We can't find any significance to put on the number' Captain Mark Valleric said..."

"You may not know what this symbol means, but if you've been walking around Exeter recently you can't have helped notice it. Sprayed in black paint this mysterious little symbol has cropped up all over town, leaving passers-by pondering...The symbol of the Russian Orthodox Church has been put forward as one possibility and the cross of St. Catherin another..."

"The police have said that they have been told that the number '23', sprayed on several buildings recently may be a reversal of '32', which experts say represents Jesus Christ... Rev. Dennis Hancock agreed the reversal of Christian symbols is common in Satan worship, though he doubts that the graffiti has much to do with religion. 'There's always the possibility' he said. 'But I'm inclined to believe it's something to do with the pornography issue'. Hancock said a recent push by the local Fellowship of Churches organisation to ban X-rated movies may have prompted the vandalism."

"The Rev. Frank Manieri of St. Marys Catholic Church, Shadyside, believes the recent outbreak of graffiti in the area has no meaning. 'It has to be somebody with a random number. A person with a low mentality not thinking of anything more original than two-three.'"

Thou shalt not snigger. At least such press reaction to the antics of wayward PTV fans (who, incidentally, are encouraged to act responsibly in the spreading of propaganda) prove that policemen, officials and priests don't read *Rapid Eye*. But, more seriously, when one looks at Gen's work – his realisation that, quite simply you can't express ideas without words and symbols – one does tend to see what all this is about. Information takes on a dynamism all of its own, and reveals all sorts of paranoia, prejudice and stupidity when let loose on the general community. But back to *'Godstar'*, another loaded, coded new word that acts on the imagination.

"I came up with this whimsical idea that first of all there were Hollywood stars, then Warhol came up with the idea that there were Superstars, then the mass media moved on to Megastars, so the final one has to be Godstar! Only to qualify for Godstar status you have to be

dead."

A book with every sticker. The things that interest him as projects, and the results of those projects, are things that encapsulate hundreds of threads. They also are things that act as vehicles for many of his associates to put their skills and ideas into on a variety of different levels. Such an arrangement is possible within the pool of loosely amalgamated individuals that make up the Temple. A group of writers, musicians, technicians, film makers, painters that is as much a mutually supportive, though often diverse, arts movement as it is anything else.

Although it is Gen's charisma and mostly his ideas that dominate the Temple which he co-founded, he is by no means the sole source of its substance. For instance, although he may write half of the Temple's texts himself, the other half is just as likely to come from the Temple-stimulated brains of writers such as Jon Savage, David Tibet or people such as those who contribute to *Rapid Eye*. The words of the Temple messages being passed on by the 'Temple Spokesman' on videos who has the honeyed voice of PTV tattooist Mr Sebastian and the face of Derek Jarman (a nice, eerie combination). And the soundtrack to the Temple is as heavily influenced by Alex Fergusson, Hillmar, Andrew Poppy, Dave Ball or Monte Cazazza as it is by P-Orridge himself. The stunning early visuals created by The Temple, expressed in a series of videos, books and posters, were largely put together by Peter 'Sleazy' Christopherson, (now of Coil) who was a professional graphic and video artist and partner of the Hipnosis design firm responsible for so many record sleeves and pop videos in the past. In all areas, the Temple is a co-operative venture. *'Godstar'*, though, was quite definitely the product of a node of Gen's brain cells.

The whole thing started in 1965.

"We sat for half an hour in the cafeteria of the TV studios in Birmingham and chatted. All of the Stones were there, about to perform '19th Nervous Breakdown' on 'Thank Your Lucky Stars'. And even then he was completely separate from the others. Not physically, but going back to what we were saying about 'auras' and so on, there was a bubble around him that was almost physically present it was so strong. Very mysterious and very disturbing. Though simultaneously there was also a feeling of love and emotion and confusion. It really was very weird. I mean I can actually see the table as we sat around it as if I were still there, and I can still feel the sensation, and I can still see it around him, as visible as light. He was not with them. He was not present with them at that table."

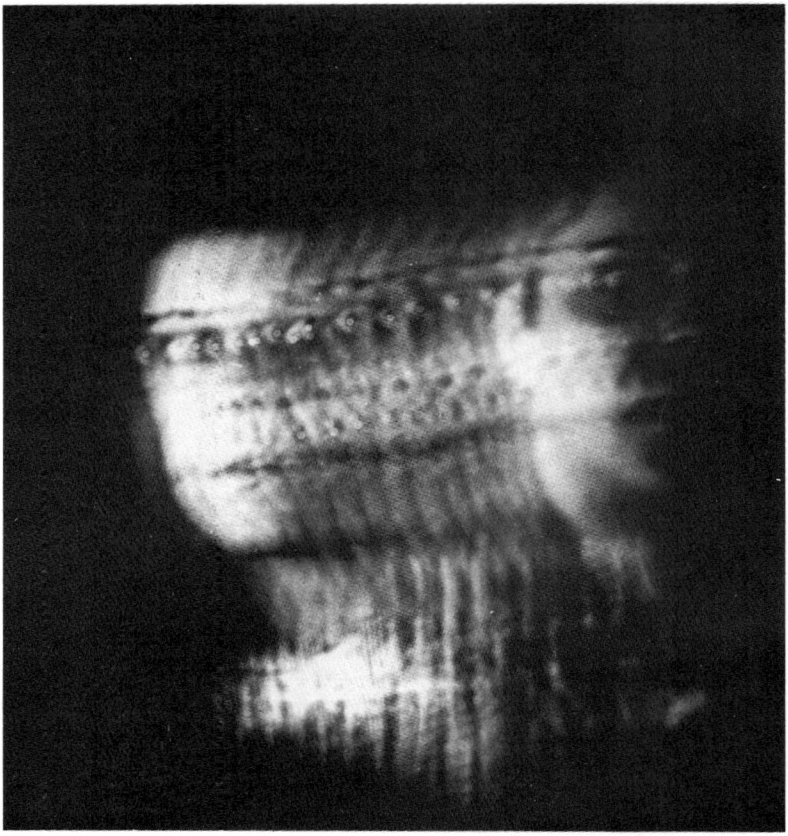

P-P-P-P-Orridge! (Photo Steve McNicholas).

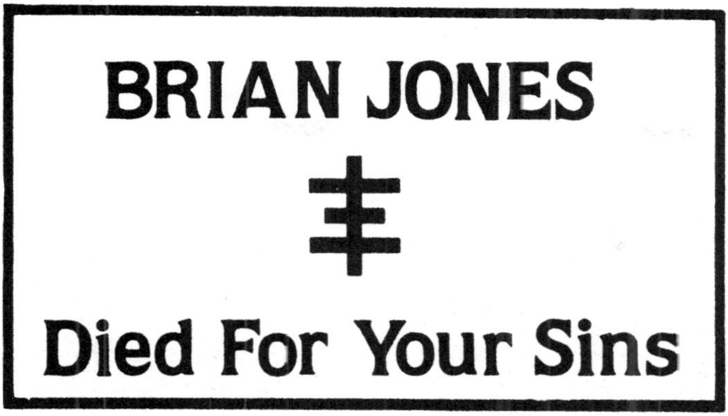

The Message.

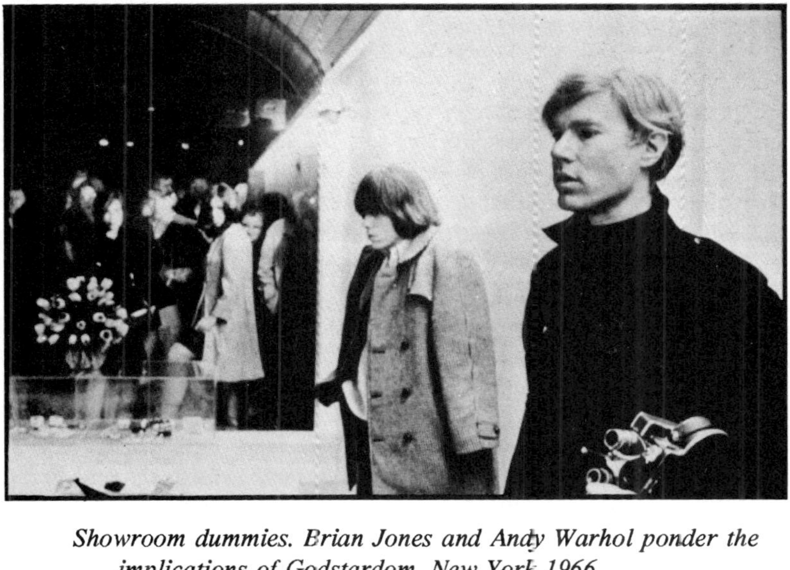

Showroom dummies. Brian Jones and Andy Warhol ponder the implications of Godstardom, New York 1966.

But weren't the Stones nasty to Jones (stealing Anita Pallenberg from him, ostracising him, forcing him to leave the group he helped create) because of his apparently difficult character? And weren't Gen's heightened emotions caused by a simple experience common to any young fan when meeting his heroes in the flesh?

"Well, I was never a Stones fan really. I mean, I always hated The Beatles who I thought were a load of wimps, and compared to them I liked the Stones because they seemed a much better vehicle for rebellion. So I bought their early singles. But there was something about him. It didn't dawn on me until a long time afterwards that I didn't buy any Rolling Stones records after he died. It wasn't a conscious decision, I just lost interest in them. I realised that it wasn't the Rolling Stones that I was ever really interested in, except for a few pieces of their music. Apparently it was the projection of the Brian Jones enigma that drove me to the group, and I think a lot of other people too, quite unconsciously."

Up until early '85, when *'Godstar'* was recorded, this writer had never heard Genesis mention Brian Jones, though looking back at least two years before, I do remember him, on a typical shopping expedition that ended with him going home with armfuls of books, old records, clothes and curios – buying a book about him. A colleague of mine was surprised and asked him why he'd got it, and he hadn't really replied, changing the subject. Looking back it's clear that he was even then engaged in his copious 'research' – secretively. He has now long since read every available title on Jones, typically not opening his mouth about a project until he knew exactly what his feelings were.

"It does seem that in lots of ways he was obnoxious, but it seems to have been one of those chicken and egg things. The others were cutting him out a lot and maybe that was his defence. I don't claim to be able to speak about him from great personal experience, but a lot of people I've met said they found him appalling to deal with."

But why Brian Jones?

"Well, it's as if some people are chosen, against their better judgement, to be a vehicle for the unconscious of their generation and their time. When he died in '69 the Sixties just closed down. I'm not particularly interested in the personalities involved. You've got to remember that the whole of the Sixties was riddled with drugs and various people were unstable and could see money, power, fame revolving around them, so maybe they're not totally accountable for their selfishness and greed. Though of course you could argue that they didn't have to take drugs.

"It's just a sad story. He became inconvenient, he wanted to experiment with different music and soundtracks and so on, and that didn't fit in with

someone's idea of what the Rolling Stones should be. It's just a shame there was nobody around to influence things away from self indulgence. There was no-one around him loving him, loving just HIM, for what he was. And it interests me because it was a symptomatic reflection of that decade. So I see him as a shattered mirror of the Sixties. He encapsulates all the different threads, spoken and unspoken. The archetype angel destroyed."

So that is what a "Godstar" is. A scapegoat. An emotional crutch. An iconoclastic symbol for things that seem not to be able to be expressed in any other form. Godstars don't just die young and famous, but die FOR something in some perverse way, for the social evils and cultural dreams they have been chosen to represent.

"So in a sense that sticker means he died for everyone's sins in terms of popular culture. Even ours, even now. Because we are all part of an ongoing history and I think that the sad thing at the moment is that it's not fashionable to be aware of, and value, your history."

And that's one reason why British society decays like a bad molar with rotten, forgotten roots. It being inconvenient to remember the darker areas of its past – the slavery and gung ho diplomacy – and socially unacceptable to celebrate its achievements in the arts and culture, it's fashionable and easier to deride it all as if a bad smell given off by a senile old man. Culture and history are means by which we can fleece the tourists, and that is that. Britain is a society based on two words, "Me" and "Now". Life experienced as a channel-hopping exercise through various assortments of fleetingly fashionable junk presented as reality by the media. The British attitude of self-hate shows up in the obsessional love for all things American, and is most obvious in our total disrespect for our culture – Theatre, Painting, Design, Music, Literature. Britain is inhabited by people who punish their bodies with a diet of lager and junk food, who punish their children with fifty pence coins to pump into the fruit machine, who punish their minds with the unending consumption of wallpaper TV; soaps; game shows; satellite American football; and degrade or destroy all that they perceive as existing outside of their cultural windtunnel. Hate and punishment are everywhere.

As Gen says: *"We don't deserve to survive as a society, because we don't even love ourselves."* And we don't 'love ourselves' because we are afraid to, as we are a society built upon layers of guilt – for the crucifixion, the reformation, the Empire and the wet dream. Guilty as individuals and guilty en masse. What is worse, Britain wallows in it, and elects politicians who are here to administer the 'medicine' we deserve (we also have to be guilty for the decadence of having jobs in the '60's).

The envy and submission imposed by 'class' compounds the problem, making people grateful to take what they deserve like lambs to the slaughter, or – in the public school mentality of those in power – happy to accept the smacking given by Margaret the Maitresse. As P-Orridge sidekick Kathy Acker said, it's an S/M society. Guilt, like fashion, sexual stereotyping and racial pride, is a great weapon of Control. Adolf Hitler, another politician with precious few ideas who took pride in being hard, rather than caring, did a similar thing to Germany in the Thirties, burning books instead of videos and dispensing with true cultural achievements in favour of artful museums of National Socialist Party propaganda. In many Initiates' eyes, Hitler and Thatcher are two masks on the same face. The face they hide is a snake-riddled skull – the face of Death. The same old face of Control. After all, Socialism and Conservatism have proved in practice to be inter-changeable. Identical but for the most minor detail. The only route to individual sanity is to be empirical.

The art of the Temple *must,* therefore, be offensive to the agents of Control if it is to be able to inform. It cannot allow itself to be engulfed and capitalised on – like Wagner – if it is to be of any social worth. It must also embrace its past culture, not the convenient fixation with the present and reject all considerations of 'good taste' (the last refuge of the witless) and social acceptability. It must love itself if it is to learn anything about itself. Goethe's bitter sorrow for Germany could be transposed to P-Orridge's lips and modern Britain.

P-Orridge took plenty of wet liberal stick for visiting the ovens at Auschwitz in the mid-seventies. PTV are still prone to be thought of as somehow fascistic, particularly by people who accused P-Orridge-related groups 'Death in June' and 'A Certain Ratio' of similar leanings (even though Simon Topping's band ACR got its name from Brian Eno's *'801'* lyric *"looking for a certain ratio"* and has a multi-racial line up). Genesis says his visit to the death camp (taken in whilst visiting friends in Poland) served to remind him of the danger and horror of man's "stupidity".

> *"Those who do not remember the past*
> *are condemned to repeat it."*
>
> George Santayana

Unlike Pope John Paul II, who visited Dachau in '83 and rightly received no flack as I recall, P-Orridge at least used his time at Auschwitz as fruitful research. He found out that the camp – now a museum – and its ovens had been kept in full working order, and could quite easily be used tomorrow. He also set up one of his little 'tests'.

Using an innocuous looking photo of the camp that made it look like a factory set at the end of a leafy lane (a deliberate impression created by the Nazis), he incorporated this into the trendy, acceptable logo of Industrial Records and later, after it had been absorbed into the cosy punk anar-chic establishment, let it be known publicly what the photograph was really of. In sadly predictable fashion, shock horrors ensued among the supposedly enlightened press of *Sounds* (Morgan Grampian's idea of enlightened), and *NME* (ditto IPC). The same people who only months before had carried pictures of Siouxie and Sid in swastika armbands (as the Pistols and Banshees never really threatened anything, that was OK – this P-Orridge character though, was something altogether different). *"So immediately that photograph almost physically changed before their eyes. Just because they'd been given one extra line of information."*

In the Information War, illustrations like that are useful, if a little mischievous. Information is a bullet, the human voice a weapon. Heard any good voice-overs on ITN recently? And as we all know, it's here, in the realm of Television, that the real power lies. Recognising this fact and acting as soon as the practicalities allowed (amassing video equipment and technical ability within the Temple) the company whose plastic ID cards say 'PSYCHIC TELEVISION LTD.' in clear letters at the top, was formed in 1981. Using video not as a promotional toy to aid in the selling of records, but as an end in itself, PTV have recorded many more inches of video tape than audio. At the moment, distributing videos by mail and incorporating them into their live transmissions, they can only hope to chip away at the monolithic structure of TV, but it is a start. Never ones to take the hint and be put off by apparent impracticality and technological myth, the Temple has now mastered this, THE most esoteric of the arts and sciences, and when cable and satellite proliferates under European de-regulation, Gen hopes it will be there on the channel selector button marked 'PTV'. The move of emphasis away from records to video was merely the first step; as pieces of plastic lose more and more of their potency as capsules of information and demonstration, the scale of PTV's visual operations will increase.

Television is an essential area for the Temple to invest in, as it is not only the valium of the people, a daily score of bore, but an actively oppressive mode of Control.

In a world which, as P-Orridge says, *"lives through its media"*, life's choices are limited only to the number of channels on the set. Televised reality is all there is, and often, Television's truth is the only thing to believe. Through 'light entertainment' we are emasculated as individuals – adopting and identifying with limiting stereotypes. And in 'serious'

Television – that dealing with the most finite, square, flat reality – the effects of a voice-over, an edit, a use of lighting or camera angle or piece of music, create for us a common geography. We share the same trigonometric points in this 625-lined world; the same prompts; because we share the same TV. The mass conscious is programmed en masse – therefore we share the same programmed response.

But Control is not only propagated by the people who television programmes represent – the programmers are as much helpless products of Control as any of us. Control is an intrinsic function of any linear form of mass communication – it must be as it is the logical product of programmed brains. However 'radical' a programme may be, it is still a programme. Psychic Television strives to de-programme. Therefore, although it would be more entertaining for PTV to produce fast, in-focus TV and be more acceptable if they posed around in front of a few screens at their performances showing off pretty images, again, it would be pointless. So PTV adopt a creative dialectic, the 'Third Mind' technique when making television, approaching the TV studio with the unaffected curiosity of a child – pressing buttons, experimenting with images and noises – playing with the mechanics of television.

Without formatting, one image may clash with another, creating a third, new, image. One idea may clash with another, creating a third idea. A new idea. And new ideas lead to new understandings, and new perceptions.

Having said that, the process cannot be entirely random – Genesis choosing what images to incorporate into the mix. But the presentation is. Just as Dada did with painting and Burroughs did with writing, PTV were the first to do with Television; without regard to stylism, technical ability or aesthetics: they broke it up and abused it in order to see what happened. Give a child an Airfix model kit and he may not build a plane, but he might build an interesting sculpture that looks far more fun.

All this may be apparently very trendy and arty perhaps, but Gen saw no other choice.

"We're living in the age of television, so we have to deal with it, it's a matter of physical and mental survival. TV is used to hammer people into the ground, to make them stupid and keep them quiet. The answer to that situation isn't just to turn it off and try to ignore it. By doing that you're admitting its power and admitting that you're scared of it. You've got to go and kick it in the face, pull it to pieces and see what's going on. And it's very interesting that with the minimum amount of money and expertise, we've actually managed to dig out and reveal a lot of weird things; worms and reverberations that people didn't know were there. Some people are stimulated by that illustration of how powerful Television is, others just

say they don't like it, as simple as that, treating the whole thing as entertainment. The attitude is summed up by the odd reviews we sometimes get from a few very repressed journalists. The irony is that when they write these totally over-the-top nasty pieces they are actually illustrating our point very well. They are describing what we've done and how powerful it is and how much it's affected them. But they're actually so unsophisticated as people that they don't even realise that is what they're doing."

Self-appointed brainiacs of youth culture, journalists often describe such things whilst labouring under the impression that the perpetrators – PTV – and we, the audience, are less aware of what television can do than they – the journalists – are. We, the herd, the unwashed mass, are, it seems, not supposed to trouble our stupid little heads about such things.

The technique of Psychic TV is also confused with the substance, meaning that in a printed media obsessed with hedonism and style rather than substance (one need not exclude the other), that P-Orridge's outfit is received as being a part of that artless, lumpen mass of Duvet scratch trash propagated by the likes of crazy Channel 4. Not surprisingly, Gen thinks they amount to rather more than that.

"Perhaps we are the first organisation to make truly surrealist television. Television that investigates the subconscious and the unconscious. Whereas Salvador Dali would have done a fantastic painting, we would try to get the same jarring of sensibilities, the same confusion leading to revelation through juxtaposing television and film images and sound. Because as most people realise, film and sound are integrated in order to manipulate the perceptions and emotions of the viewer. The viewer is being bewitched, and in that sense they are put in a position of vulnerability."

PTV's cut-up of reality is aimed at short circuiting the training the brain has had – to twist up the map of that shared geography and make the viewer find his own way, rather than accepting what emanates from the TV screen without thought. Be it the blatant twists of facts and demographs on the BBC, or the more general, subtle and seductive presentation of that punchline reality that gently radiates from the tube in the all-forgiving form of Entertainment. Surreal images are dirty pictures put into the brainwash. 'Psychic' television is that which alters the relationship between man and what PTV recognise as being his latest piece of sensory apparatus – the TV set.

This is also socially positive TV, in that it encourages activity rather than passivity. It reclaims the pleasure of life from the death of TV.

"Even Pleasure has become something which people do not seek after

themselves but have presented to them in simulated forms. So that even an inherently active form of expression has become a pastime and the result is that expression becomes depression."

Psychic TV has never intended to be a replacement for conventional programming, but rather the first step in the de-programming, without regard to redundant assumptions about entertainment. So Psychic Transmissions are made to be viewed when conventional TV is off the air, at night – the time when you are encouraged to be in bed. When the centroclines snooze and quietly wank through their dreamless sleep.

The content of PTV transmissions has inevitably been banned, bleeped and blotched out. The powers that be take an interest in any package bearing the rubber-stamped insignia of the Temple, resulting in PTV videos in the past being posted from its formerly affiliated branch (run by 'De-Coder') in more liberal West Germany. The press has said that they show scenes of torture (untrue) and are 'shocking'. The latter may be true for some people (depending on what you find shocking), because they emphasise the aspects of life normally suppressed by the apparatus of Control for being subversive, contentious, disturbing or too sexual. It follows, using Temple logic, that it is exactly because those areas are suppressed in a deliberate attempt to limit knowledge and experience, that they SHOULD be shown.

Rumours about one particular PTV video abound throughout the backwaters of the media. Accusations from some individuals and groups with vested interests claim that they feature child abuse and Devil Worship. I have seen the video in question on several occasions, and personally know or have met several of the individuals featured in it. Disappointingly for the gutter press and assorted 'Christian' groups, I can confirm that the video features nothing more shocking than a performance art pseudo-'ritual' involving some naked cavorting, tattooing, piercing and so on. The participants are all clearly adults, and out-takes from the video, which include scenes of the participants laughing and joking, prove that they are all willing 'actors' in the piece. Far more sexually explicit and certainly more violent material is openly available in any Sex shop or video store in Europe or America. Indeed, the majority of hanky-panky that does take place is out of focus and distorted to such an extent that it might as well be anything. Anyone who has been familiar with the performance art of P-Orridge over the years will clearly be able to see what is going on. Uninformed individuals with nasty minds will obviously see whatever they like. Which is rather part of the point, I thought.

Psychic television reclaims the night and fills it with colour and information. *"To cause things hidden in the dark to appear, and to take the darkness away from them."*

But if it's TV that makes up "50% of PTV", then the other half of the organisation is concerned with what to show on those 23 screens. The theorising and substantiating of that theory, of which TV images and soundtracks are just the results. It is here where the Inner Circle of the Temple dwells. Beneath the slick talking-head façade of the Temple, that which is put before the unblinking eye of the camera and fed to the public in the tactile form of records, books, videos and all the wall-splattering, symbol-carrying merchandise of pop culture, lies the Temple itself.

A temple without walls that draws its initiates from an international conspiracy of unrest. Dealing with contemporary art, sociology, religion, communication, neurology, and that grey area between the finite fact of science and the dogma of theology – Philosophy. A combination of interests glued together under the Psychic Cross and run along the lines of an intellectual urban(e) terroristic organisation and mock 'occult' fraternity. The type which the occult establishment would rather do without.

In that elitist and overly jealous underworld of traditional occultism, this populist high-tech Temple is not only generally considered undesirable, but also held in some real contempt. For example, I have on file a letter written by one David Rietti, just one of the many claimants to the 'leadership' of the O.T.O., the brotherhood once headed by Crowley. After the Temple of Psychic Youth produced a pamphlet along the lines of Crowleys *'LIBER OZ 77'* (cheekily calling it *'Liber Ov 23'*) in 1987, Rietti threatened the Temple with "a war" which he "would be unable to control", something which P-Orridge and his Temple colleagues seemed to find most amusing. Some people will, it seems, go to almost any lengths to protect what they see as their 'power' and monopoly on mystery.

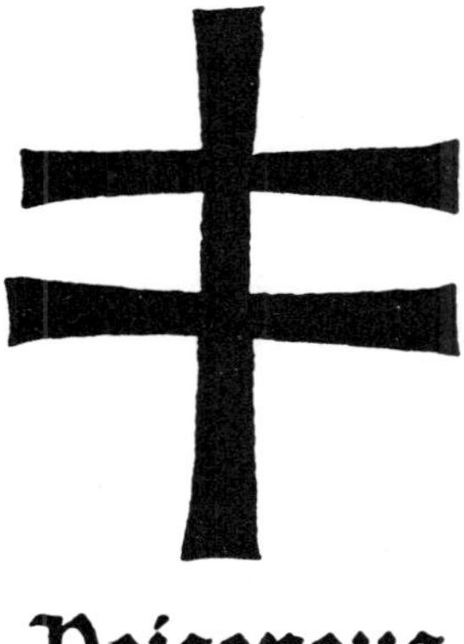

Poisonous

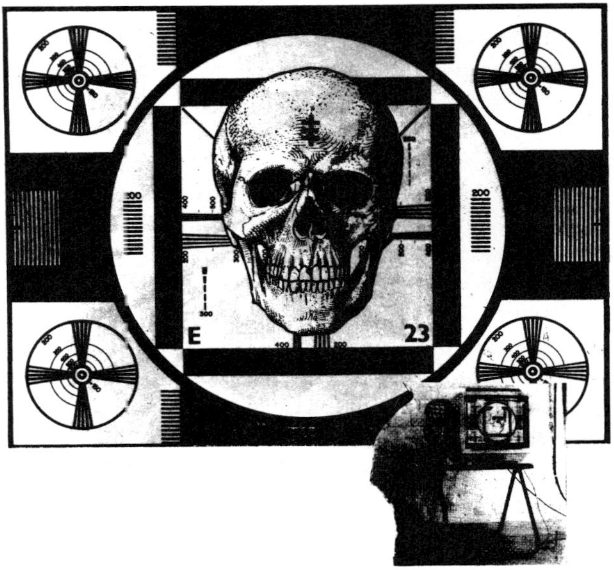

The Test Card

The Sensory Apparatus

Britain is absolutely chockablock with narrow-minded, so called 'magicians' who 'learn magic' by worming into mountains of arcane-looking 'parchments' supplied to them by over-priced specialist bookshops: of witches who are convinced that 'the power' is a solely feminine 'gift' passed down genetically like buck teeth or freckles: of imbeciles who are sure that not only does evil exist in the palpable form of the Devil, but that he regularly plays hoofsie with them under the shabitat dining table over a glass of Bulls Blood. These pathetic types are, unfortunately, the bulk of the 'occult' fraternity. The whole yuppie awareness of the Mind and Spirit, of wands and crystal balls (balls being the operative word), of wholefood, crystal power, alternative medicine and healthy living has provided many with a vast ego-trip through the whole of the 1980s and sprouted an accompanying service industry and alternative dating agency for the socially inept, the bored, and the downright stupid. People sadly unable to come to terms with living in the last quarter of the 20th Century who have opted for a cosy, Luddite approach to life.

This join-the-dots form of occultism is all very well if beneficial, but it has become merely a substitute religion for many and, as a result, covers a multitude of crappy, cranky ideologies that only serve to make the overall situation more confused and socially ineffectual.

Of course, the Temple of Psychic Youth has attracted its fair share of idiots. The smell of (black) candlewax pervades many seedy, spunk-stained 'Temple' loft conversions – the purpose of this highly unromantic grail all too often being the simple acquisition of power, material wealth, image-building and sex. The fact is, however, that people drawn into the Temple of Psychic Youth for these reasons usually fall out from it pretty quickly. After all, if one wants to be pedantic, TOPY is clearly *not* really much to do with 'occultism' at all. The word 'occult' does of course imply 'secret knowledge', and nothing that pertains to the Temple is secret. All knowledge is shared, which is one of the reasons why it is so unpopular with many traditional would-be 'magicians', as it usurps their power, or, at least, their self-image.

However, given the image of the occult in this country, it is not a surprising consequence of the Temple's high profile activity that it has wrongly been interpreted in much the same way as other groups.

Initiates of this Temple though, do not generally feel the need to dress up in funny old clothes (even though those they wear at Tescos may be quite wacky). Nor do they exchange funny handshakes, or study the most elementary forms of physics or astrology towards the attainment of various pseudo-degrees that the circle may confer on them. It is the demystification of psychic research (research that the Temple feels should not, in social terms, remain secret or 'special' any longer) that is at the root of its existence and propaganda. As it does with television, the Temple digs around in the occult, researching and making public what has remained, in political and social terms, futile in its isolation. An isolation that is in itself a hangover from when 'Christian' society perceived such things as Ritual and Magic as a threat – burning witches, torturing 'heretics' and invading communities (like the Cathars or Albigensians) who based their lifestyles on different (some would say more enlightened) values. A process that the West still carries out in the form of meddling, moped-riding missionaries who quite deliberately set out to destroy far more ancient structures than those which they themselves represent, with a smug cultural Coca Cola Kid imperialism.

The concepts of such things as ritual or the perception of a non-physical reality are misunderstood and now commonly seen as retrograde steps towards barbarianism and superstition. The Temple wishes to re-integrate such concepts into the human experience, and has therefore developed, quite consciously, a practical, logical, and presentable system to help this to be done.

In this article I've hoped to present information that will increase, even if only superficially, the understanding of Genesis and The Temple and to give factual insights that have never before been reported. My explanations of what is going on within this movement may be incorrect, but I think it important that the motivations behind this deeper area of Temple activity should at least be presented as I see them. This section is really what it's all about – the blueprint from which all the aforementioned tactics derive.

Taking for a moment the liberal, more contemporary view that the purpose of old occult imagery is to create archetypes from Jung's 'Collective Unconscious' to focus on and achieve a similar set of results as those gained by Temple activity, even this rigid, belief-dependent structure is considered unnecessary and harmful by P-Orridge and other Initiates.

So, rare in circles of the occult, there is no hierarchical structure in the Temple. Just as there are no pointy hats, goatee beards and Latin words, there are also no formalised rituals. There are no rules. In 'admitting' and 'initiating' anyone who has the genuine desire to become associated, and helping them to realise *their own potential in their own way* purely by promoting informed self discovery, the Temple is taking its only political step. By passing information on like a viral infection, one-to-one, it hopes to nudge society gradually into perceiving reality in a different, and more 'realistic' way. To make what is now (due to the aforementioned misuse of occultism and its misrepresentation in the media) seen as being crackpot, unjustifiable and weird, to be accepted as a sensible possible step along the evolutionary path. To replace the dulling, dualistic perception of 'Either/Or', with what P-Orridge theatrically calls the 'Magickal Perception' of infinite parallels and possibility. The TOPY method is a simple lesson in orientation and advertising that is typically efficient.

Temple ritual is tailored to suit the individual Initiate, and as such is just as likely to incorporate the trappings and fetishes of today – scratch videos, House music, rubber clothes and polaroids – as it is to use the (for some) equally viable symbolic weapons, pentagrams, and unintelligible utterances of old ritual.

The primary difference between the Temple and other more traditional organisations, though, is that the results of ritual activity are interpreted in an altogether different way. Successes from spells, for example, are not attributed to the intervention of spirits or deities, but to the internal workings of the ordinary human brain, and the effect the human brain can have in emitting frequencies that effect the collective pool of frequencies between all humans.

This may seem no big deal if the spells work the same but the terminology is different – but in wider, social terms, the difference is vital. Because in the TOPY manner, attempts at understanding are increased, woolly and futile involved explanations are dispensed with, and ultimately control of and access to the process is made more efficient. The intuitive ritual practice is not at odds with or separated from perceived scientific reality, but integrated with it. The everyday experiences and the lifestyle of the Initiate are incorporated into the Magickal Perception, thus psychic activity is embraced more readily as being as natural as physical activity.

To illustrate the attitude of the Temple, and annoy those with a vested interest in keeping such matters couched in gothic mystery – therefore holding on to their tenuous self-appointed positions of superiority – here is the most basic type of experiment in the art and science of 'magick'.

Imagine you have been treated badly in a restaurant – the food off, the service bad. You refuse to pay your bill, so you are beaten up and robbed. Circumstances dictate that you cannot retaliate in the ordinary manner.

So. Go back the next few days, standing nearby the restaurant for half an hour at a time. Take photographs of the building. Record the sounds of the restaurant and the street outside on a Walkman. Steal a menu card from a table. Then, at a time you choose, develop the film. Cut the negative up and print your pictures of the street minus the restaurant. Overdub onto your recording the sound of breaking glass, of fire, of doors slamming shut. Concentrate your thoughts on the restaurant. Slowly cut the menu up, paying particular attention to the logo. Then bury all the photos and shredded card in your dustbin. Forget the incident. A month or so later the chances are that the restaurant will, for one reason or another, close down.

In this Burroughs-inspired example – which basically just gives one the simple understanding of the psychology of such base magick – you are clearly not evoking external forces or worshipping horned creatures that manifest themselves at midnight – shitting on your Axminster. You are not even 'psyching out' the enemy in the usual sense of the term by letting them know your intentions on a conscious level. Indeed, the explanation of how and why such a simple process works is not important here – though would, one thinks, be more satisfyingly described nowadays in the language of the neurologist and behavioral scientist than the warlock, even though nobody could really explain it. In this very easy example, it's clear that one is making contemporary symbols of the same process as used by witchdoctors and their ilk. Affecting change in the transmissions from and between humans, causing physical change to occur.

The realisation of such popularised experiments too is that *everyone* can use their mind to produce physical change purely by mental activity, if they have the self-discipline necessary to train it to do so. The Temple is merely making the necessary information more available, and not attempting to explain such phenomena away with mumbo jumbo or creating a substitute structure of dogmatic belief around it.

"Well, Burroughs would explain that by saying you're actually cutting up reality itself. That reality is like a tape and if you cut it up and distort it you make things happen. Why they do remains a mystery. To what extent the mechanical manipulation of reality affects things is just not measurable. The basic answer is – who cares, if it works? If nothing else a process like that is good therapy."

The stock criticism of such experimentation, and, perhaps, realisation of power is that such things can be used irresponsibly, merely adding to the violence and conflict that already exist. Logically, though, such an argument could be used to support anything from censorship, to the lowering of educational standards, to dictatorship. P-Orridge would argue the case by saying that no extra power has been conferred on the individual anyway. By making such information more available and acceptable, people have simply been encouraged to experiment with and observe what they already possess.

"Their argument is just like saying somebody went out and raped someone because they watched it on TV. They probably did, but that doesn't mean that there should be no TV."

But people could say it's hardly a good advert for the proliferation of TV.

"Yes, but people who take that position are saying in effect that there is no need for awareness because awareness is dangerous. It can be. If people do abuse it then you could, if you wanted, argue that it's because they have been given those perverted motivations as a direct result of the suppression and conditioning they've had in the first place. So be it. I just have the fundamental feeling that the human race is here to evolve and is capable of becoming something relatively interesting and special. And the only way to even begin to approach that is to learn the real way that we work, both physically and psychologically, and there's no easy way 'round that. If given the choice of either moving forward or stagnating – which is what we're doing now – I'd gamble and move forward. And I think information and technique move things forward. For better or worse, quite honestly."

Rather than a pseudo-religion or a sinister Thule-like fraternity then, the

Temple is more like an open-ended Information Exchange that expresses itself using a hybrid of the traditional, esoteric, and contemporary arts. A result of the same brain, it's as snappy, modern and ideologically devious as TG once were. And as with any P-Orridge inspired project, the tendency is towards testing conditioning and individual response. It's thus confusing and provocative; flexible and undogmatic; lacking in convention and therefore (through any success it achieves), threatening to convention.

Gen is not a very good singer in the classic style, and his opinions, appearance, and writing, like his methods, may not be to everyone's taste. But his undeniable strength lies in the fact that anything he turns his hand to is effective on one level or another. Analyzing everything to the minute detail, the strengths, motivations, appeal and (most of all) weaknesses are discovered, and pressure applied at the most telling points.

Because of this efficiency, this realisation and application of that potentially most ordinary of commodities – power – the Temple is threatening to institutions of any kind. Its very existence is proof in all spheres that an 'alternative' approach, founded on a purely information-based system can work, devoid of hierarchies and crippling, limiting structures of belief.

Of the occultists that grumble, Gen remains both free from malice and unconcerned. Besides, if it's credentials that are important to gain acceptance in this closed order of fragmented cults, the Temple certainly could produce these in abundance.

TOPY member Icelander Hillmar O. Hillmarsson is probably one of the most respected and authoritative young figures in European occultisim. So much so that more than one museum and private collection has entrusted him with curatorship over priceless archives of occult books and artefacts. This connection has, for example, given the Temple exclusive access and publishing rights to many of Aleister Crowley's unprinted letters and manuscripts. It has also encouraged the only bona fide Ordo Templi Orientis (forget the people in South America) to offer the Temple a permanent base at their headquarters in Switzerland. The building, designed to the Thelemic specifications of Frater Perdurabo himself, contains what is thought to be the largest and most complete occult library in existence, plus a theatre, hotel, temple, lecture rooms and alchemical laboratory. Gen daydreams about it sometimes. Fitted with a recording studio, computerised data system, gallery, cinema, TV studio and Dream Machine room; peopled by visiting Psychic Youths taking classes in such things as karate, breathing techniques and listening to lectures from the likes of Leary, Burroughs, or Colin Wilson, it all amounts to a tantalising proposition for P-Orridge to consider.

At present, though, the Temple has neither the funds nor the inclination to retreat from the grime of British urban life to a bunker in the Alps – however well appointed. The Temple is most effective, for the moment at least, producing propaganda through pop culture on the streets of the biggest and most youth-sophisticated city in Europe, regardless of the criticism such a high profile attracts.

P-Orridge sees no reason why, in the subterranean world of the occult, TOPY and the more orthodox societies, from the Rosicrucians to the I.O.T., cannot exist in tandem. However much they may disagree about methodology.

"I just don't think that those traditionalist groups, such as the O.T.O., are really honestly very interested in effecting a change in society. I think that if you care you have to be a part of society and its expression and popular culture. You have to set yourself up as an example and scapegoat. If you don't let people know what you do, how are they going to believe you when you say 'I did this and it works!' I think things like the OTO are primarily ego gratification and research into old ideas and old knowledge, which is fine. It's like a symphony orchestra still playing Beethoven is paralleled to Duran Duran playing 'The Reflex'. One does not have to exclude the other...I think, though, for me their way would be too easy. I've never been a joiner. I've never wanted to be subservient to a prescribed dogma of any kind, no matter how esoteric it might be. It just doesn't interest me. In all honesty I'd just feel a complete arsehole standing in costume saying 'Oh Sephiroth, Sephirah, I invoke thee!' You know, I just couldn't. And it'd be boring."

That, then, is the explanation of why the Temple does not undertake any formalised rituals, though ritual itself is practised – sometimes for its own sake (as discipline), sometimes as a controlled experiment (research), and sometimes in order to produce a specific tremor in the fabric of physical reality (from the closing of a restaurant to the making of a perfect baby). The ritual aspect of Temple activity has, for tactical reasons, been underplayed since PTV burst onto the scene amid much blasphemy and scar tissue in '81 (record companies preferring to package wholesome sex – the kind Nik Kershaw clones offer on the back seat of Ford Escorts – to what they see as this pervy arty nonsense). Don't be fooled, though; ritual remains the bedrock of the Temple.

In my mind, the reasons for the incorporation of ritual go something like this: Numbed by contemporary media and education, Man has been distanced from ritual – something the Temple views as a vital *natural* activity. In order to control more effectively, 'Control' has fragmented the human character into tiny, dissociated and often forgotten slivers. Modern man lives in a perpetual state of stupor, and is made to suppress these multifarious aspects of his personality, made to not recognise, or to ignore his deepest desires, so that he may become totally immersed in the stagnant, counterfeitist reality of Control.

He is helpless, like a lone wolf stuck in a 'starlit mire'. Separated from the pack that does not even hear his howls for freedom, and if it did, would not even recognise his association with them – so covered as he is in mud.

That incomplete 'pack' of emotions and personalities – the individual human – runs on. It knows that there is something wrong, something missing, but it doesn't even know where to look. It convinces itself that it is quite content to go on as it is, and even if it stumbled across its long lost members, it would probably tear them to pieces in its ignorance.

The individual human, like a pack of Pavlovian dogs, has been programmed into such ignorance. Ignorance is convenience.

The sham illusion of 'freedom' is dangled before him in the form of material comfort and narrowly-defined political choice. Thus drugged, duped and divided, he is robbed of direction and self-respect. Shambling through life in a blur of trivia, he spends his life waiting for 'something' to happen. When and if he has the courage to ask 'Is this it?' he is told that he will be alright if he keeps the faith. If he continues producing and consuming. If he feigns 'normality' on the outside and does what's expected of him by the Church, by governments, by cartels. If he remains stupid, and even proud of his stupidity (his video-watching, car-driving 'normality'), clings to his set of beliefs, whatever they may be (they are, after all, interchangeable), and keeps his mouth shut, he'll be rewarded with...Life after Death!

Thus he will be robbed of fully experiencing his own life. Of realising his potential, even the potential of his own mind. The passion of the Temple is founded upon this great sadness. The sadness of the 1980's.

There is, though, a hint of optimism here. Just as geographically, racially and politically mankind is falsely divided and compartmentalised, split up into more easily administered nation states on Earth, the individual man or woman is shattered and divided from the inside. The concept of 'divide and rule' is scaled down to horrifyingly personal proportions. In the perception of the Temple, ritual (or, if you like, private performance art) is a way in which the demolished man and woman can be healed. It can be used to promote internalisation, a search for and acceptance of the missing members of the pack. To re-integrate the many aspects of the personality that have been fragmented and ignored and achieve through this a healthy balance again. To incorporate into life those aspects of human character that society has trained the individual into perceiving as being (socially) worthless, (self) indulgent, or unpleasant. Once these various areas are accepted they are better understood, and then you have the first step in the destruction of Control. You have a whole human being again with the self reliance of the 'full pack.' You have the inquisitive, pre-programmed purity of a baby.

> *"From a child of five to an adult is*
> *a short step.*
> *From a new-born baby to a child of five*
> *is an appalling distance."*
>
> Tolstoy

Ritual is an activity that a brief study of human history would seem to show that we need. It is also an activity that has been generally ignored or denied in Western culture (except in the most ineffectual forms offered by the modern church). By investigating what appears to be one of the weak points in the armour of Control, the Temple feels it has touched a nerve. By reclaiming ritual and developing its efficient personalised use, the process of shattering indoctrination that takes place is reversed. One becomes cognizant of one's real needs, and, able to confront and embrace these needs and desires, commit that most heinous of crimes in this group-orientated society – cherish oneself.

People in this position are more likely to be healthy, well balanced individuals. They do not commit suicide. They don't go out and attack people on the street. They don't fight wars on behalf of politicians. They are less inclined to become addicted to false outside stimulation (be it from drugs or TV) for their well being.

"Once you have re-integration and you have an effective whole individual again you can then have evolution, and that evolution I suggest needs to be neurological. If people see things intelligently and are more aware and thoughtful and using more of their brains, then stupid action will become more obviously stupid and therefore laughably irrelevant. The only way to get rid of stupidity is to make it LOOK stupid to the individual, so that nobody would indulge in it. And I think that forms of ritual and what is commonly termed 'magick' are an essential part of that re-integration and that's why they were quite deliberately amputated from man's experience during the middle ages, in order to facilitate the growth of power through various kinds of conditioning and suppression."

So in Temple philosophy, ritual helps the Initiate to commune not with spirits, but with The Spirit. In helping concentration, clearing space for internalisation, it enables the brain to function in a way that, quite simply, it doesn't normally have the opportunity to in the logical life of everyday existence. The real purpose of ritual, the common denominator of all ritual from Christian communion to dervish dances and spiritualist meetings, is to lead you through the subconscious levels of the mind and into the areas of the brain where the unconscious dwells, darkly. Here you may stumble across angels and devils within yourself that have been hidden from you by Control.

The most simple form of ritual is a process of Sigilisation, whereby a wish is concentrated in symbolic form, and brought to bear on the mind when it achieves the required altered state – when it has been pushed into the quaquaversal mode and is able to transmit energies that can have an effect on both the physical and mental planes. Purely physical science does not (yet) allow for such things to be possible. Which is why the quite common phenomena of telepathy and precognition are written off as being 'coincidence', and why there is as yet no plausible physical explanation for such things as poltergeist activity, other than accusations of hoax. In the Magickal Perception of P-Orridge, such things are considered perfectly normal, unthreatening effects of transactions between the unconscious of the individual and the shared unconscious of the earth.

Ritual not only sends tremors through this unconscious, but, while doing so, teaches the Initiate that there may be more to life and death than meets the eye.

"Ritual helps you understand and perceive the invisible language of reality. The inarticulate, non verbal language of reality and relationships between cause and effect and emotion and action and behaviour and so on. The nitty gritty of the Cosmos!"

Ritual is really just a system of tricks which enable you to by-pass the cursors of the solely physical perception of reality (logic based on chemistry, physics, English, maths and biology class), and see the world from a quite different perspective – and new perspectives give birth to new ideas. The Temple's hackers report their individual systems and findings to TOPY H.Q, their research being kept under lock and key and made available only to other practising Initiates through newsletters and meetings, and in more general form in the public activities of PTV and P-Orridge. Each sigiliser's identity is protected from the outside world through the designation of code names and numbers. 'Eden' for boys and 'Kali' (the Indian goddess of sex and death) for girls.

The ritual techniques and sigils recorded at the Temple database are as varied as the Initiates themselves and have grown less familiar and more abstract, personal and effective as time wears on from the Temple's founding in 1981.

P-Orridge's personal rituals, for example, are a natural result of his own history, informed as much by his love of Gysin or Dali as his interest in Crowley and the laws of Thelema. An extension of his performance art exploits in COUM, Trans Media and beyond. He readily admits to the fact that what people often confused with as being Art, was, if seen in another context, Ritual.

"It was really psychotherapy rather than Art. In a sense rituals are a private version of what I always did. In fact you could say that after doing art performances I noticed certain effects and phenomena that I decided to investigate privately and more intensely in a controlled environment. So there was no question of there being Entertainment involved."

The most effective rituals, and usually the most interesting and informative, are those that teach the Initiate certain practical boundaries, both physical and mental. It would serve no useful purpose here to try and go into detail about the more esoteric rituals employed by the Temple. In any case, each ritual is different, suited to the needs of the individual(s) taking part. Here though is an example of the never-before published ritualization of the Lone Wolf. An experiment into a more formalised, less sexual ritual, it has almost monastic qualities.

As his wife Paula and the psychic imps were taking a break in Brighton for five days, Gen decided to make the most of the unusual silence, space, and aloneness of the empty house. *"Each day I started at eleven* [23.00 hrs.] *and I couldn't go to bed until I'd incorporated a certain number of set things into the ritual. I had to do a drawing based on a particular photograph taken of Paula during another more esoteric sexual ritual. I had to write for a period, copying down anything that came into my head, and cut one letter of her name each day in my chest with a scalpel. I also had to drink from a special silver goblet* [shaped like a wolf's head] *which was full of my own urine, and read a section of an Austin Spare book and try to understand it, and do a sigil involving masturbation as well, all while listening to Scriabin's 'Poem of Fire' very loud on the stereo. I also had the television on with no sound and all the static snow drifting across the screen with the colour turned full up, and also have my one-pound steel weight through my prick."*

All the elements of this particular ritual, chosen more or less at random from a variety of associated interests, serve to symbolise certain areas of his life and reflect his lifestyle, and will strike chords in the minds of many of his fellow Initiates.

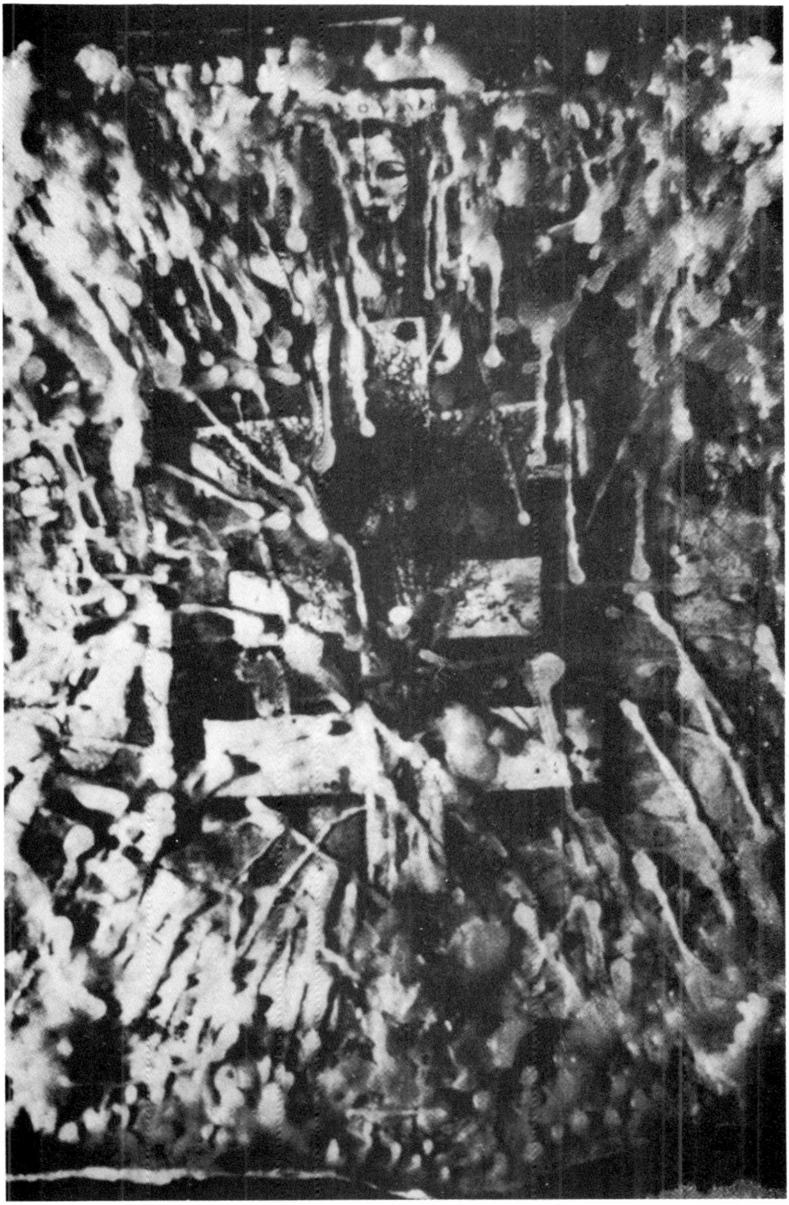

A visual Sigil.

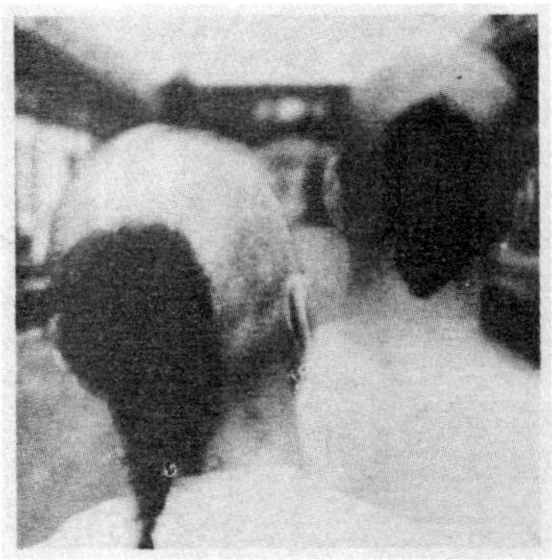

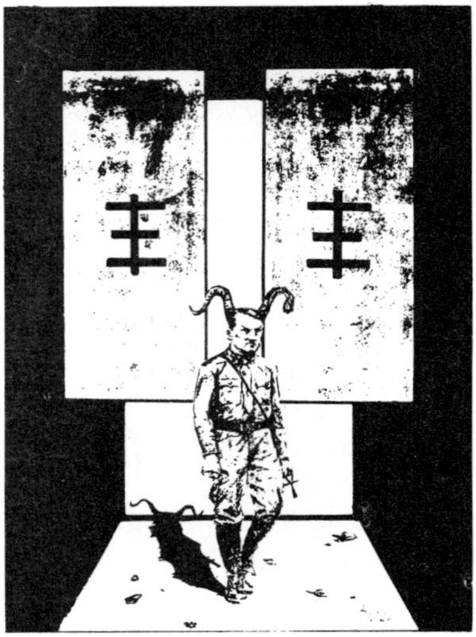

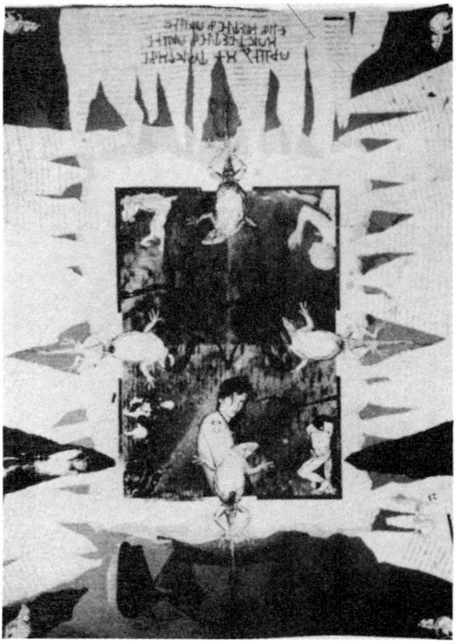

"At first I was very conscious and aware of what I was doing and it seemed very laborious, and I kept wanting to give up the drawing and not to do the shading in properly and so on. But by the fifth day I was writing without thought and the time was going very very fast instead of dragging. And during the day when I went about my normal business I became hyperactive and effective. By the end of the five days I was in a completely different state mentally and physically than when I'd started. I was very alert, perceptive, and just didn't get tired. Looking back at the writing I'd done during the ritual there was loads of stuff I didn't even remember writing at all. A lot of it is really interesting and challenging and quite impressive. And I'd done diagrams that I didn't really see the meaning of – little boxes and key words and relationships between key words and observations about personality and emotion and so on."

Besides such abstract forms of experimentation, P-Orridge also practises straightforward Sex Magick – and is as open about his interests as he is any other subject.

Incapable of dealing with honesty, particularly when sex is involved, the usual reaction of the cynical British Media to this is to make several assumptions based on their weak grasp of such knowledge; that Gen is 'obviously' concerned only with manufacturing a weird sexy pop star image; that Sex Magick is 'obviously' merely used as an excuse for physical gratification; that anyone involved with the Temple is 'obviously' sexually promiscuous – just not honest enough to admit it.

Funny how people become either coy or abusive whenever sex rears its head, isn't it? Strange too, how people are so ready to apply their own sexual hang-ups and code of morals to the actions of others, as if they, considering themselves 'normal', were somehow the arbiters of everyone's sexual preferences and morality. It's always been easier to snigger – in the tinkling of a typewriter the presentation and apparent validity of any body of ideas as potentially threatening as those being transmitted from the Temple can be reduced to inconsequential rubble. The writer simply has to appeal to the tribal instinct that, for protectionist reasons, sees anyone 'different' from the group as being a threat, and the tribal instinct is largely born out of Control.

As the most public figure within the Temple, P-Orridge also finds himself caught up in a crossfire between a whole bunch of ideological imbeciles he cares not a jot for anyway. Macho men who are obsessed with the activity of sex (fucking); copybook 'feminists' who are obsessed only with gender; media people hellbent on sensationalising and disparaging anything to do with (ulp) 'Sex' from their usual platform of mock indignation (to sell papers). They confuse sex with sexuality; ritual with sexual promiscuity. Such people would no doubt be surprised, and not a little disappointed to hear P-Orridge talking about such things as sexual equality. Or learning that even within the Temple a person of course could, if they wished, explore their own sexuality without actually having sex with anyone (using solely autosexual techniques in ritual, for example). Though, as the learning process is always better if studies are shared and enjoyed it'd be surprising for anyone to do so.

There is (unfortunately) a general type of person that usually becomes involved in the Temple, though that is hardly down to P-Orridge. People criticising such apparent anomalies of the Temple, or its activities, easily forget that as there are no strict formulae here, a person could share in its experiences without necessarily agreeing with other Initiates' methods, morals or lifestyles. Sex, though, is still an important aspect of the Temple.

"Because sex is one of the most primal motivations of human beings. I think that people are more animal than they believe they are and that there is a hormonal, metabolic, deeply engrained sexual urge that motivates us and that one has to confront and understand. And if people can't confront and understand something as basic and physical as that then they might as well give up on things that are more abstract, really. And sex is used as a weapon to generate guilt and fear for Control. I think in mental terms it's of more importance than any battlefield on the planet. We have urges for a variety of things that have been suppressed. Ritual is also one of those things. A need to mark one's passage through life on oneself physically and mentally. The signs for something as simple as that are always there – from tattoos and pierced ears and different hairstyles to certain types of ceremony. Like marriage, birth, christening, football matches or whatever. I think the people who refuse to even recognise that need and dismiss it are the dangerous ones. Usually people like burn-again Christians and rightwing politicians and so on. The type of people who're convinced that they're right and tell other people how to live and think. I just prefer to recognise things and embrace them and see what they are and why they are. And I do think that the suppression of ritual and sexuality is why in our society there is a lot of mental illness. Some of it diagnosed and the vast majority of it walking around the streets! In other societies, where ritual is embraced as a natural function they don't even have a word for mental illness, it's just about unknown in many 'primitive' tribal societies. Neuroses are exorcised through ritual, there is always a point given to focus on. Even if it's not a regular everyday thing, there are always ritual points in their lifespan that are utilised to focus on completely different to everyday normal life. And that's

very uncommon in our society."

What about birth and death?

"Well, even childbirth is emasculated as a sensation and as an experience and as a ritual. The medical profession tried to steal childbirth away from women. (Gen and Paula's two children were both delivered at home). *Even death is considered something to be swept away and not talked about. Even fucking! All the things we can't avoid. We all fuck, we're born and we die. Even these three most basic focuses and rituals and experiences are screwed up and twisted and suppressed by our society. So it's no wonder we're all completely confused."*

Add to this the fact that even the most subservient people are now becoming disenchanted with the structure of society. That society's authorities can no longer be trusted as they are consistently being discredited, and being proven to be (often quite openly) dishonest, uncaring and incompetent – which means, in the equation made by the Temple, that a very dangerous and unstable situation has arisen. Millions of directionless, dissatisfied people generating all that unfocused energy equals = Bad Magic. The symptoms of which are manifested in street crime, heroin addiction, sex murders, alcoholism, hypochondria and practically every other social malady you care to mention. People just have no self-discipline or respect for themselves. No clear direction. They do not even have any structure to work around anymore.

That explains why the structure of Christianity is so newly attractive to so many people. A structure in which people benefit from ritual focal points and a sense of direction. The direction, though, seems all too often to be towards death – Christianity in practice generally being a structure based on hedging one's bets for an afterlife, rather than fostering a genuine wish to live with people better in this.

The Temple confines itself to what it knows, to life rather than death. It does not presume to issue 'commandments' or give the impression that it is qualified to do so, representing as it does nothing other than a few ideas. Rather, it simply tries to encourage an active, positive life, assuming that people are quite able when freed from conditioned guilt to make up their own minds about how to live (is it better to help someone because you want to help them, or because you want to protect your own interests and avoid being sent to 'Hell'?). In observing the lure of the shared trappings of all religions, it is interested in the non-aligned, undogmatic investigation into what exactly is going on. Minus the bullshit of organised religion, the rhetoric of party politics, or the promises of 'occultism' that only serve to pervert that understanding and thus strengthen the foundations of Control.

Sex and sexuality lie at the roots of Control. Conditioning is most apparent, and crippling, in this area of our lives – illustrated for example in limiting sexual stereotyping and feelings of alienation, and the mass of hang-ups that pervade what Freud claimed to be this central area of human life. Gen argues then that it's only natural to try and tackle this universally applicable area first, and develop awareness from there.

There is, though, more than a tactical angle in the incorporation of Sex Magick rituals than that – as they are also an excellent method of illustrating the capabilities of the mind when unified by ritual.

The Occult Establishment, in the form of the German Theodore Reuss, for a time ostracised Crowley for making the 'secrets' of Sex Magick more available to non-initiates in books like *'LIBER CCCXXXIII The Book Of Lies'* (in which he wrote about the 'Magick Rood' and 'Mystic Rose'), before Crowley's revolutionary ideas, widely disseminated through his theatricism, gained more acceptance – resulting in Crowley heading the Argentum Astram and eventually becoming World Leader of the O.T.O. on the German's retirement through illness.

Through the works of Havelock Ellis, mason Karl Kellner, Crowley and numerous others, such 'secrets' are nowadays common knowledge (if not often understood) amongst even the most dilettante students of the occult.

To over-simplify, the basic premise of Sex Magick is that when the individual achieves orgasm, he or she is able, albeit briefly, to gain access to and some control over the hidden, dream-ridden world of the unconscious. There the 'True Will' is discovered and focused, the latent powers of this 'unseen' mind being used to alter physical reality. If a desire is first encapsulated (during a preparatory ritual), then visualised at the moment of orgasm (usually in the form of a symbolic glyph), the chances are that the desire will be achieved, in one way or another.

People bound up in the purely physical perception of life, and the traditional sciences used to explain it, must dismiss such notions out of hand. They will perhaps say, sneeringly, that such notions are 'magic'. They will of course be right. As with any theory though, several quite logical sounding arguments can be concocted to support such claims and make them more appealing on an intellectual level. One such argument could be based around the theory that prevails throughout *Rapid Eye* in various forms.

That is, that the language of the two brain hemispheres is frequently of transmitted impulse, and that by artificially tampering with the keys of those frequencies (be it through ritual or exposure to 'psychotronic' sounds, strobes, etc.) the two sides of the brain can be fooled into acting in unison. The right brain, that deals with dreams, 'intuition', creative endeavour and non-logical thinking, and is thought to house the unconscious entity – that which produces poltergeists and demons – is combined with the logical, practical hemisphere of the left brain, where the ego resides (the left brain is what we'd think of as being 'us'). Altered states of consciousness result. Anyone who has taken LSD, or been stupid enough to experiment with PCP, would agree that there are various levels of consciousness, and that the brain, and body, are capable of things far greater than we once may have thought.

By learning the most effective methods of tampering with the brain we can more efficiently produce the required states and find out exactly what the attainment of these states can achieve.

This particular assumption has been made for the purposes of this article, based on the work of Spare and P-Orridge and the most cursory reading of a few neurological facts. If people with a greater store of information in the areas of neurology, psychology etc. wanted to find a more convincing argument then they could no doubt do so. For the purposes of self-discovery and practical results, however, as P-Orridge says, "Who cares as long as it works?" That it does work is only doubted by those who haven't tried it, or approached it in too cynical, clinical, or careless a manner. The Temple is more interested in making such avenues of experimentation known than trying to convince people of the theories or results.

If such capabilities *are* inherent in Sex, it would certainly be in the interests of Control to suppress such information and activity. Genesis would say that this explains why 'Sex', more than any other area of usually private human activity, is subjected to extraordinary levels of outside interests and interference from the unwitting agents of Control – be they police or priests.

Whatever anyone's opinion, it's undoubtedly true that while experiencing orgasm the individual experiences a sensation of freedom that renders any system of Control totally meaningless. In this case at least, sex is a liberator.

P-Orridge does not doubt the validity of Sex Magick at all, and given that medical science is constantly being revised and currently can only account for the activity of about one third of the brain's total physical mass, any explanations and explorations should be possible. From the traditionalist mummery to the more oriented, if equally woolly and vague beliefs of New Science. Gen being convinced that everyone is emitting their psychic transmissions all the time, he feels that there should be someone looking for ways in which to channel that energy. Sex Magick, for him, is the best avenue of exploration as it provides the skeleton key to the Doors of Perception, unlocking hidden areas of human potential. That assumption is his only belief and practically everything he does stems from the fact.

"It all depends on how much credence you give the subconscious to operate in positive ways on its own, almost. I do think over the years as I've gone along I've found more and more evidence to support the theory that people's brains send out these various frequencies, signals, and that through these there is some linkage in the mass unconscious. Which would explain, for instance, how you get apparent phenomena of messages from the dead and so on. So in fact all you're doing is tapping the residual pool of the unconscious thought all over the planet, and a lot of people aren't aware of that so they're thrashing about and being irritating and unhappy because they're tapping useless thoughts from it uncontrollably."

The study of Magick is the study of psychic radionics – how to control the transmissions and improve the reception. Sex Magick is a way of putting more power into the aerials – the brass, wood, paper, glass Psychic Crosses that hang on hundreds of walls from Tokyo to Toxteth, charged with the resolutions of the Temple. An organisation attempting to understand the mechanics of tapping into and tampering with the 'pool'.

Working on Gen's prompt – *"If you really, really want something to happen so pure at the moment of orgasm you get a completely pure desire, for a fraction of a second there is no distraction or dilution of that desire, the chances of it happening are greatly increased"* – Initiates have come up with varying experiments and reported some unusual results.

Here is one example of autoritualisation from the Temple Archives, submitted by an Eden:

"I find it vital to perform a sigil in a way that separates it from everyday activities. The setting is always a darkened room, in the evening – usually about eleven. I rearrange the room taking out all the objects I feel to be superfluous. This leaves the room stripped except for the bed and the tools I've selected for the occasion. There are several objects I always use – chosen by intuition. Finding a set of tools that you can use especially for the Sigil is essential in promoting a magickal reflex. By this I mean a set of conditions, objects and actions that work on the subconscious as shortcuts to the special, elusive state of mind needed. I don't like to use these objects for anything other than the rituals.

"The objects I use are as follows: a knife, which I know has a potent history, a silver bell with a goat's-foot handle which I bought under unusual circumstances, candles and a razor. Before I begin I arrange these objects around me. I find it very useful to take some kind of drug, sometimes just alcohol, not for recreation but as an aid to changing the atmosphere, the consciousness, to stepping through a door to a special frame of mind. Always I keep at the back of my mind the aim and purpose of the ritual, slowly saturating my mind with the task before me. As I begin, I play Tibetan music because of its personal associations, and because it is intended for ritual use. I begin to masturbate, simultaneously using mental images of my own fetishes and playing with the focus of the ritual, swapping and overlapping the ideas with each other. The exact mental processes that go on are extremely hard to describe. I find my actions and emotions going on at once, all spiralling upwards, focusing on the orgasm itself. I simultaneously concentrate on both the situation I'm in and also the internal and intuitive processes I'm trying to arouse and initiate within myself. One knows when the spark of truth is struck. The outside is inside and vice-versa. Both are fused and concentrated - focusing on the one aim of the ritual. The orgasm is the key to the whole process, the seal of the unconscious.

"Once the orgasm has passed, I prepare a physical Sigil. I write and draw on a piece of paper what I feel – sometimes unassociated scrawls and symbols, then I add spit and ov (semenal fluid). I use the razor to draw blood, painting symbols and marks with it, as occur to me at the time. I place the paper in a prominent position in the room, so I am constantly reminded of the aim of the Sigil. For me there is a huge difference between an orgasm during a Sigil and one achieved by normal erotic action or fantasy. Every Sigil I have conscientiously prepared has gained results; sometimes almost frightening in their efficiency and effect.

"For example, once I wanted to meet a boy I'd seen in a magazine and I performed a Sigil to do so, and a few days later decided to go to a pub I hadn't been to for some time, just as a change of scene. As I walked in I saw the boy across the room. Almost immediately he came up to me and said he had the feeling that he knew me or that he'd seen me somewhere before, which he certainly hadn't. We got talking and later had sex."

The leading innovator of such forms of 'Sigilisation' – Austin Spare – described the system with some more lucidity, adding the vital point that, as far as possible, the desire must be lodged in the subconscious without the conscious mind being involved or aware.

"My formula and Sigils for subconscious activity are a means of inspiration, capacity or genius, and a means of accelerating evolution. An economy of energy and a method of learning by enjoyment.

"For the construction of Sigils the ordinary alphabet is used. (For example) the desire for super-human strength could be formulated as follows: 'I desire the strength of my tigers'. In order to Sigilise this desire, put down on a piece of paper all the letters of which the sentence is composed, omitting all repetitions. The resulting sequence of letters, 'IDESRTHNGOFMY' is then combined and incorporated into your Sigil." (This sequence of letters and/or symbols is called a 'glyph'.)

"The wish, thus Sigilised, must then be forgotten; that is to say, the conscious mind must desist from thinking about it at any time other than the magickal time, for the belief becomes true and vital by striving against it in the consciousness and by giving it (Sigil) form. Not by the striving of Faith.

"By virtue of the Sigil you are able to send your desires into the subconscious (the place where all dreams meet). All desire, whether for pleasure or knowledge that cannot find natural expression, can by Sigils and their formulae find fulfilment via the subconscious.

"The energizing of such a Sigil must occur at a special time. At the moment of orgasm the wish must be imperatively formulated. It is not in the actual Sigil that the power resides (this is merely the vehicle of the desire) but the intent with which it is despatched at the moment of exhaustion. Any glyph, personal or traditional, may be used as a Sigil. If personal, it must be the specific vehicle of the desire, and designed for no other purpose; if traditional, it must have received a new direction which thereby consecrates it to its secret purpose. Powers of visualisation, self-discipline and concentration are the qualities necessary."

Austin Osman Spare is, along with Crowley, the major figure behind the 'occult' philosophy of the Temple. Not only an extraordinary occultist, Spare was also a brilliant artist. Having left school at 13 he was given a scholarship to the R.C.A. on the strength of his illustrations and his treatise on Solid Geometry, for which he had won the National Gold Medal.

His father a London policeman and his mother a devout Christian, Spare developed a dislike for convention and developed a relationship with an old woman who was a witch, Mrs Patterson, who taught him many aspects of her craft. When he was still only 17 he published his first book *'Earth Inferno'*, a short text lavishly illustrated with his occult-influenced surrealist drawings. On publication of this critics compared Spare to Dürer, and John Singer Sargent described the young East Ender as a genius. Around 1910 he joined Crowley's Argentum Astram. He served in Egypt during the First World War where he was impressed by the pyramids and the carved hieroglyphics of Egyptian occult art. Inspired by these, he went on to develop his own theory of Sigils, which was a system of ritual symbolism creating glyphs which aimed to express the human will in a secret, concentrated form. The process of sigilisation involved him expressing a desire to his subconscious in symbolic form while in a state of trance (which he called "the death posture"), or ecstasy (usually sexual). A believer in reincarnation, he also felt that during this state he could regress and rediscover all his previous personalities – which he presented in his work in the form of half-man half-animal beasts – and finally be able to trace "the Primal Cause of all", which had been lost by Mankind through the passage of time. This "atavistic resurgence" and the ultimate discovery it revealed was called 'Kia' – the true Being of Man.

Undoubtedly one of England's finest illustrators, Spare's best work is to be found in the book he published when he was 22 years old, something of a bible for Temple Initiates, *'The Book of Pleasure (Self*

Love): The Philosophy of Ecstasy' (1913) which he illustrated with automatic drawings, though his work also appears in another P-Orridge favourite, F. Russel/J. Bertrams' *'The Starlit Mire'* (1911). Spare was someone whom Trans Media may have called a "quaquavine" – being born at midnight on the 31st December 1888, or the 1st January 1889, this event giving Spare what he called his 'Janus Complex', named after the Roman deity who looks backwards and forwards simultaneously. His later years were spent, like Crowley, as a recluse in a dilapidated house. He died in Brixton in 1956.

Spare's rituals were not entirely done alone. He used a string of mistresses, prostitutes and, he claims, succubi for his ritual work. The Temple, too, does not rely solely on autosexual techniques.

Much has been made of the supposed orgiastic goings-on within the Temple (particularly by people feigning disgust while all the time wishing that they were invited to such activities).

Far be it from me to destroy anyone's fantasies, but in truth such activities are rare, though they do happen, normally among small groups of friends and lovers rather than between total strangers flung together in some moonlit meeting of a coven.

'Sex Magick rituals' performed by more than one person in the Temple often take place in an area that is as free from the pervading aura of Control as possible. Somewhere free from the trappings and proprieties of starchy social convention, a place where the ego and false identity is shed and the Initiate is more able to revert to a time of pre-conditioning. The Nursery.

"Without is without
In the Nursery
Darkness is not dark
In the Nursery
There is no fear
In the Nursery
The bear is there
In the Nursery"

'In the Nursery' Psychic TV

The Nursery is an attempt to create an environment without any rules that relate to the outside world. Unlike in Passolini's *'Salo'*, the nursery is not only a microcosm, but also a vacuum – there are NO rules here at all. The Nursery is a functional artistic installation. A theatrical stage set in which Edward Keinholz meets Lucrezia Borgia.

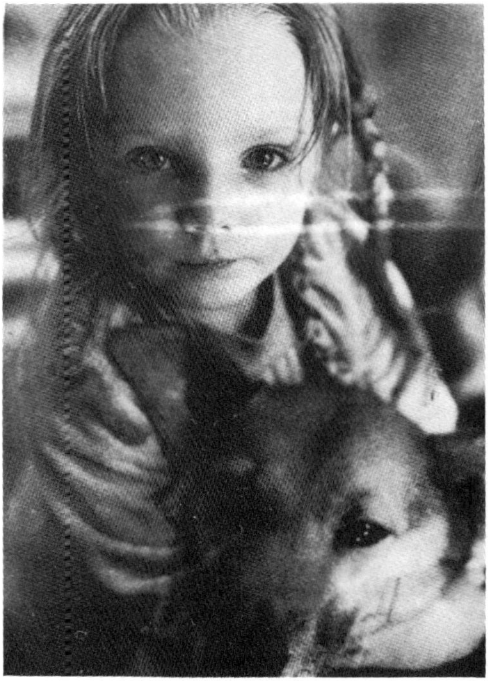

Gen and Paula's eldest daughter, Caresse, and faithful hound, Tanith. Both recording artistes with Temple Records. (Photo – Zbigniew Szydko).

The Nursery is situated at an address in an anonymous East End sidestreet behind heavily bolted doors and a video security system. The walls of the room are blood red. The black floor is clear of obstructions, except for a coffin that lies along one wall and the menacing hulk of an old leather dentist chair (which once played a part in a case of a dentist tried for the molestation of drugged patients) that dominates the room. Peacock feathers, ropes, dildoes, chains, mirrors, human skulls, gnarled wood, candles, carvings...dozens of articles line the walls. To be improvised with during ritual by adults much as the same way in which children may experiment with a box of old clothes in a playroom.

Sexual acts that may take place in the Nursery are not seen as being 'Sex' by participants. People separated from the embarrassment and fear of the outside world tend to indulge in activities that perhaps they would not normally. The sense of vulnerability engendered in such a highly-charged disorientating place serves to strengthen the Temple, creating a bond of trust – the ritual providing participants with a mutual intent. All physical and mental energies are joined and devoted to the ritual, and the liberation and channelling of psychic energy through the ritual abandonment of all aspects of Control, amid sweaty Bundeswehr vests and ecstasy.

As the Temple masters Sex Magick and compiles its research, other systems not involving orgasm have naturally developed. The idea is that once 'wholeness' is hopefully achieved, the vital ELEMENTS of ritual that trigger the necessary altered states are learnt, the goal being to be able to 'switch on' and use such abilities automatically in everyday life. At a bus queue, on a train, lying in bed at night.

So, the assumptions made by the popular media would seem to be false – symptoms of the state of Control, inadvertently used to diffuse interest and divert attention away from suspect areas by making them appear futile, perverted, trendy or laughable. It is, though, just these areas that should, due to their tenderness, be investigated most rigorously. The rigours of the Temple, the ritual pop horrors and sex shocks are, in this light, just a means to an end. The end being this automatic ability. Evolution, no less.

Although Gen undoubtedly harbours a desire to be more famous, and PTV would quite like a stream of Number One records and to be disgustingly rich, it is primarily towards this evolutionary step which this psychic conglomerate strives – a slightly more interesting and important goal than getting your best profile on the cover of *The Face* – though it all depends on your priorities. Members of many groups obviously only want to be rich and famous and get models at cocktail parties to go to bed with them. Fair enough.

Genesis' priorities are patent. They stand drenched in his own blood, semen and urine. For all to see, and attack. For every group of detractors, though, there appears a convert. So when the jolly, trendy 'Biff' in the *Guardian*, or John Walters on Radio One, or Derek Jameson on Thames TV attack the Temple, an ally pops up in the form of a Sandy Robertson, a Paul Morley, or (as is often the case – surprisingly), an Auberon Waugh (who said that P-Orridge was "one of the most lucid modern philosophers of the decade").

The *imposition* of will – be it the will of Thatcher, Stalin or P-Orridge – is quite clearly unjust to most level-headed people. The Temple is based on voluntary commitment. Total commitment. Not obedience. Despite the bombardment of the critics, volunteers are numerous.

The Temple is legion. It spreads like an unchecked disease throughout the disillusioned, existentialist rollnecks that blacken the reading rooms of the British Museum; it forms cells of MACE spraying, Ecstasy-taking 'Terror Guard' post-industrialist punks in sleazy squats; it settles onto the very fabric of White Western Culture (the T-shirts of TV producers and lapel badges of film directors often bear the tell-tale tripach cross).

As the Nineties stretch before us, the Temple becomes more snappy and organised. A small but dedicated staff now run Temple Records from a neat office complete with buzzing computer, Xerox and FAX machines, serving the dual purpose of selling records and keeping the Temple informed. TOPY now has branches in the U.S.A. and 'Access Points' dotted throughout Europe, many of which produce their own Newsletters and Broadsheets independent of London and fund their activities with events, distribution of PTV product, and through the promotion of local gigs and discos.

As was planned by its founder, the Temple has taken on a life of its own, sprouting and inspiring numerous bands, artists, publications and events. People take from their association with the Temple whatever they like. Gen must take most of the credit for the phenomenon on his own narrow shoulders. Or, as his ideas and observations may be totally wrong, most of the blame.

As twilight turns into night, though, the theories behind a worldwide network of neophytes seem distant as Genesis finishes off a plate of his famous spaghetti bolognese, sips his tea, and moans about the chattering face of Noel Edmonds on TV. The grey glow of the cathode ray is turned off with the tap of a remote control consul, allowing the Moon to shine into the P-Orridge living room, reflecting in the dark dead glass of the screen. The huge stuffed wolf's head that hangs above him casts a ghostly shadow across the wall, that glints with three ceramic Hitlers – winging their way above the fireplace like Hilda Ogden's ducks. One's eyes drift across the room like a camera, focusing on objects. A box of piercing and tattooing magazines, a large glass tank housing a large friendly boa constrictor snake, 'Bella', and 'Moonchild' the family cat sitting – now stuffed – on the hearth. Shelves sag with books, occultism, art, psychology, drugs, cinema, and with videos, Anger and Jarman, Warhol and Buñuel, and a display of green bakelite art deco objects. And above the door, a pink perspex arrow with the number '23' at its centre, points the way out.

Twenty-three is the obsessional number of the Temple, appearing in its texts, records and memorabilia. It is suggested that sigils start at 23.00 hrs, major T.O.P.Y. rituals and events are held on the 23rd of the month, and so on.

The digits litter the work of Burroughs and Gysin (stemming from the

Captain Clarke enigma), and figure heavily in Joyce's diaries. 23 is the number of the Illuminatus – the omnipotent, omnipresent secret order of masons founded by Dr Adam Weishaupt in Bavaria in 1776 and now said to invisibly rule the world. (There is tenuous evidence to suggest that they were responsible for both the Russian and American revolutions, even though they were banned in the 19th Century after being discovered in the throes of a plot to overthrow the Pope and all the monarchies of Europe.) 23 is connected in many texts with Sirius, which itself has heavy links with Egyptian and African magical mythology, and with Crowley's '93 Current'. 23 is a useful prime number, is incorporated into the name of a Temple-related band, and is a recurring figure in the cabbala. The number also features repeatedly in Koestler's works on coincidence. "23 Skidoo!" was the coded wolf whistle of New York vagrants on seeing an expanse of stocking-top during the Depression...and so it goes on.

In Temple usage it is largely incorporated as a code of recognition and association, a sign of good luck that brings a knowing smirk rather than a numerologist's jolt. Twenty-three is a leak through everyday normality, through which to get out and crawl into another world – like through one of Herr Vonnegut's mirrors.

As with all Temple mythology, the significance of the number should not be taken too literally, or seriously. Rather, it should be used as a trigger to set off one's own imagination, a seed for one's *own* mythology. Funny that 23 is also the American actors' slang for "Exit", given what Crowley wrote in 1913, a typically quirky poem under the title of *'KeoalI KT (Twenty three)'*:

"...thou canst not get out by the way thou
camest in. The way out is THE WAY
Get out. For OUT is Love and Wisdom and Power
Get OUT
If thou hast T already, first get UT
Then get O
And so, at last, get OUT."

Interpreted as meaning that, first one leaves the life of materialism, then the physical confinement of the world at large and, lastly, even one's fellow Initiates. Life is, essentially, a solo voyage, and nobody can tell you how to get through it other than yourself.

Following the pink 23, your reporter staggers out onto the moonlit street and commences his voyage courtesy of the Number 23 bus (honest), leaving Genesis and Paula to put their children to bed.

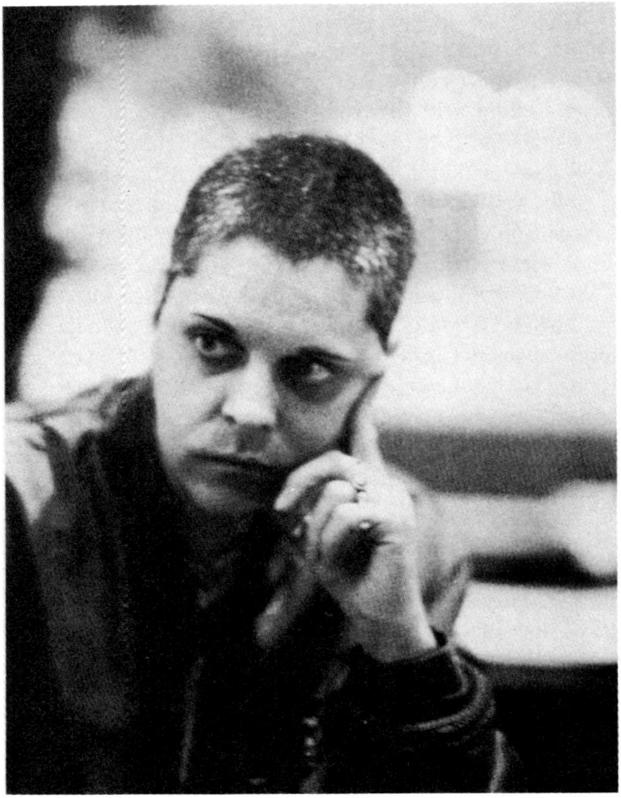

The purpose of including the Temple Ov Psychic Youth and their public manifestations in this form has been only to provide information, and hopefully a degree of insight – however biased I may be in its presentation. The only motivation one has for criticising the work of other people is to review and preview, or to promote the idea that one is somehow better informed than they are, or to help bring about their perdition – as pointless as a journalist interviewing someone for an hour then giving character references (as if they mattered). We leave the smart-arsed sensational journalese to people who think they need to prove that they are clever. We are confident that you are clever enough to gain your own impressions from the information you put at your disposal.

As that information will keep changing as long as P-Orridge and the Temple survive, there are no glib conclusions to be drawn. The Temple is not as easy or as neat as that. Unlike all Religious and Political doctrines, that exist on belief in a statement, the Temple exists only in the form of a question. A question begging a response which only you are able to give, based on your activity and research. Perhaps the only judgemental criterion one need apply to any cult phenomenon is: Does it ask questions that are worth answering?

In critical terms, even PTV manage to slither through the usual net as they claim not to entertain, but to *provoke* – and given the responses to PTV, they succeed.

And how does one take exception to this anti-Christ sitting here surrounded by the warm, slightly shitty domestic whiff that can only come from babies and pets – as he struggles against this "numbness of content" on one side and slanderous and sometimes physical assaults on the other? He claims no salvation, and brings only stimulation – the brass tack nailed into this Psychic Cross in an admission of vulnerability, fallibility that is all too recognisably human to be hero worshipped or obeyed – asking his solitary question from the bleeding heart of The Family: CAN THE WORLD BE AS SAD AS IT SEEMS?

His favourite song of all time is the Velvets' *'I'll be your Mirror'*, closely followed by a sad old Country Joe and the Fish number, which goes "But who am I/To stand and wonder/Wait/While the wheels of Fate slowly grind my life away". Genesis is not one to stand still and wait. Although his letters and late night conversations sometimes show submission to the constant pressure he puts himself under (*"Oh let us write a book, a useful tool, and hide away in Spain living a quiet existence of debauchery"* or *"I have one more pop scam up my sleeve and then I will retire to Brighton to be Grand Old Grumpy of my era, I think..."*) he will continue to fight and provoke and confuse and *force* the hand of chance as long as he draws breath.

"Why do it all? Because it works for me and it makes sense to me and it makes life more stimulating. And, quite honestly, if life can be made more stimulating, then that's enough. Because it's a pretty boring concept really, being alive. It's not normally a riveting sensation, sixty odd years of crawling around the planet. I don't claim to have an original idea in my head. I've just observed things and tried to develop from that a clear line of thought in my mind, which I'm determined to follow through. It's an honest and interesting option for me. And if it's applicable to other people then that's really nice, but primarily I'm doing all this as research for me, but as I've always believed in sharing research and information that's what we do as well. I've never yet come across anybody who's convinced me that we're going in the wrong direction. The more I learn and read about cultures, philosophies, perceptions and aesthetics the more

I believe that it's just a useful synthesis of all those things that we're all searching for anyway. That synthesis has to include everything, and it starts with the individual and their personality, then goes through to their behaviour, then their relationships to the other people around them. That in turn generates outwards to society. I still believe that is the only way to get any change. I still believe that politics is a sham, that the mass media is designed to make us stupid, that drugs are there to control and distract us, and that violence is a cathartic exercise that does no good in the longterm whatsoever."

So here he is, still trying to define and refine and articulate Life. Investigate the expressions of his life, and expect nothing. Ignore them, and expect less.

"'What's with this serum?'
'I don't know, but it sounds ominous. The man's not to be trusted. Might do almost anything...Turn a massacre into a sex orgy.'
'Or a joke.'
'Precisely. Arty type – No principles.'"

William S. Burroughs (*The Naked Lunch*)

"'Ugh,' Sung-Wu agreed. 'It seems incredible people could practise such fanatic and disgusting rites.' He got nervously to his feet.
'I must go'."

Philip K. Dick (*The Turning Wheel*)

Very poisonous, deadly

FOOTNOTE: Since the writing and publication of this article in the original edition of *Rapid Eye 1*, Genesis P-Orridge has been effectively run out of the country. The news media, keen on sensationalising the largely contrived 'satanic abuse' allegations in several parts of Britain (allegations which have now been proved to have been false), jumped on the bandwagon and accused P-Orridge and the Temple organisation of being Satanists, and that they were involved in the ritual abuse and murder of children.

Working with several extremist Christian authors who had recently published wildly over-the-top books and articles on the "Satanist" issue, the production team of the Channel 4 tabloid TV programme 'Dispatches' concocted a false, sensationalistic and completely biased show claiming finally "to prove ritual Satanic abuse".

Showing short edited clips of a supposedly secret cult video that they had discovered (in fact, the 'First Transmission' art video referred to in this article, and shown openly at various performances and exhibitions for years), a voice-over claimed that the film was of a "satanic ritual" involving abortion and torture!

Although neither TOPY or P-Orridge was named (to avoid libel actions that would undoubtedly have been taken by P-Orridge and TOPY solicitors against Channel 4, the station's legal advisors recommended that the programme was changed prior to airing. It was thus re-edited shortly before transmission), the TOPY logo and artwork was flashed on to the screen on many occasions.

Besides the ridiculous, mock 'serious' voice-over, viewers were also treated to sounds of what appeared to be a child crying in agony. The implications were obvious. Though, in fact, we can reveal that the child noises were taken from a personal recording P-Orridge made of his first daughter Caresse being born. As any PTV fan knows, this recording had been used by PTV as the backing for a sentimental, first-time fatherly song Gen wrote to his (then) baby daughter, called *'Just Drifting'*. The 'Dispatches' production team had, therefore, turned what they knew to be a song of paternal pride and affection ("My little girl/precious and pure...you possess me with simple love...you touched my heart" etc.) and gave the deliberate impression (without the lyrics) that it was a recording of a baby being tortured.

In an attempt to back up these ridiculous innuendos and assertions with a modicum of "evidence", the programme makers interviewed on film an un-lit individual, called only "Jennifer", who claimed to have been involved in the Satanic ritual, and, having been brainwashed by the cult (sic), agreed to the murder of her own children. Channel 4 later claimed that the witness, and a copy of the video, had been passed-on to them by a "professional carer". In fact, the presenter of the programme had been introduced to the woman by a solicitor, Marshall Roland. Unbeknown to most people, it is an established fact that Mr Roland had previously been forced to resign from his practice because of his extreme, and some would say eccentric views on "the dangers of Satanism".

The witness is, in fact, a woman who has since been described as a 'professional victim', well known to professional journalists and others, who has given lurid testimonies over the years to abuse-councillors as well as various rape and incest help groups. She is now receiving psychiatric help. (This "witness" later went on to describe the interior of the building in which these "rituals" were said to have taken place – incorrectly. She said, for example, that the scenes filmed took place in the basement of the building. In fact, *Rapid Eye* can reveal the building in question has no basement).

Despite the serious nature of her claims, Channel 4 refused to reveal her identity or fully co-operate with the Police, who were consequentially unable to interview her and carry out proper enquiries into the allegations. The Dispatches team appeared, for some reason, not to want to get to the bottom of the allegations. Either that, or they are quite willing to protect self-confessed child murderers in the interests of getting a sensational story that happens to support their own unusual view of the world. Superintendent Michael Hames, head of Scotland Yard's Obscene Publications Squad, said: "I need to see these witnesses urgently because – if what they say is true – serious crimes have been committed which require investigation." His requests remain ignored by Channel 4.

The Dispatches team did, however, suggest to the police just prior to airing their well-advertised programme that P-Orridge was connected to the ritual abuse of children and was the ring-leader of a "Satanic cult". Police, who, apparently "had P-Orridge and his followers under surveillance for some time", had, however, been planning no raid on P-Orridge, and thus had their hand forced by the journalists, who threatened to reveal on TV that although the identity of the cult was now known to the police (due to the journalists own wonderful investigative reporting), the police themselves had not bothered to act.

Forced into action by the imminent screening of the programme, over twenty plain clothed and uniformed officers from Scotland Yard and Brighton Police station raided the P-Orridge family home in the Lewes Road area of Brighton. Remaining in the house for several hours, they questioned a friend who was staying at the house (to feed the pets) as well as neighbours. They also seized two van loads – over two tonnes – of private "material", including letters, diaries family photo albums, address books, sculptures, musical instruments, artwork and videos (including Walt Disney cartoons).

Genesis P-Orridge, his wife Paula, and two daughters, Caresse and Genesse, were fortunately at the time enjoying a family holiday visiting Buddhist temples in Thailand.

After the 'Dispatches' programme was aired, the story was taken up by the tabloid press, who predictably vilified P-Orridge. Several papers remembered that he was the man who had been involved in the GPO/Mailart trial, and also that he was the infamous ICA Tampon Man. They said that P-Orridge and his "followers" (sic) "are lewd, disgusting people involved in all types of extreme sexual behaviour". Supposedly 'serious' newspapers, such as The Observer, joined in, publishing bizarre, unchallenged articles from Eileen Fairweather, a 'researcher' on the programme, which claimed (wrongly) that doctors and police had confirmed the film was genuine (ie one of a secret Satanic ritual involving child murder and forced abortion). *Rapid Eye* can reveal that this same 'investigative journalist' Eileen Fairweather was at the time a member of an extreme fundamentalist Christian group, and had herself previously undergone an "exorcism" at the hands of that group's leader.

In more sane sections of the media, an angry Derek Jarman and others countered this nonsense with the very obvious fact that the 'Satanic' video in question was in fact nothing more than a (very old) video-art 'piece'. Had the pseudo-journalists (or, more accurately, cranks) concerned with the programme read *Rapid Eye*, they would of course have known that several years previously.

After a thorough investigation (this time carried out by professionals), a police spokesman said that some charges were being considered, though THESE CHARGES DID NOT HAVE ANYTHING TO DO WITH CHILD ABUSE OR MURDER, AS THE POLICE HAD SATISFIED THEMSELVES THAT THESE ALLEGATIONS WERE UNFOUNDED.

Over a year after the raid, police still have not returned any of the innocuous confiscated material. Channel 4 have not bothered to retract their statements and damaging, though suitably vague implications, or apologise, nor even give any coverage to the facts as reported by Jarman and the police. Nor have they mentioned the many factual inaccuracies of their gutter-level 'documentary' or the books that inspired it.

We can in fact reveal that Channel 4 and the Dispatches production team went to extraordinary lengths to cover-up the strong Christian fundamentalist views of those involved in the making of this individual edition of the programme. For example, the Dispatches credits said that the film had been produced by 'Look Twice Productions'. There is no such company listed in the telephone book. In fact, during the production of the programme, the group purchased an 'off-the-shelf' company for around £200 with which to conceal themselves. Channel 4 deny that this was a device to hide the true views of the team involved, but have offered no explanation as to why such unusual tactics were employed to mislead their viewers.

Presenter Andrew Boyd said: "Our religious views are irrelevant". Anyone who has had the misfortune to read his quite laughable, badly researched, inaccurate and at times semi-literate book, *'Blasphemous Rumours'* (Harper Collins), will know that Boyd's religious beliefs are far from being irrelevant when it comes to his presentation of 'facts'. His religious convictions are his private concern, but not when they impinge upon the personal convictions of others, or their liberty, or on the rights of innocent children and parents, or on standards of professional – let alone honest – reporting. Boyd claimed in the documentary that 98,000 children disappear every year in Britain and implied that they are abused and/or murdered. The police, like most normal people, know and say that this is absolute rubbish. Very few children go missing each year, and there are no cases at all of children proved to have been abused or murdered by so-called Satanic groups. Dr. Bill Thompson, a criminologist from Reading University, says: "The truth is that not one child has ever spontaneously described Satanic ritual abuse. It only emerges after repeated questioning and suggestions by adults." This view, commonly held by experts, was not even alluded to in the unbalanced sham documentary.

It is no surprise; the editorial techniques adopted throughout by the mysterious 'Look Twice' team are, to put it kindly, questionable. For example, Dr. Wendy Savage, a respected consultant gynaecologist, had been interviewed by the team. She says: "I viewed the video and told the Channel 4 film makers it clearly was not an abortion being shown. For some reason they cut me and my views out of the finished programme. I also told them that in my opinion, someone had a very fertile imagination." Boyd's book was, by the way, published to co-incide with the screening of Dispatches. The more extreme the programme, the greater the publicity generated for the book, the fatter the Royalty cheque.

Caught in a limbo, the P-Orridge family have been forced from their home (and, in the children's case, school), had their personal belongings effectively stolen, and are in an Oscar Wilde-type exile, forced to live in more tolerant California (legally, and without hinderance) but with no substantial source of income or permanent base. (P-Orridge currently eeks out a living by performing – PTV are still the best-known 'unknown' band in the world – and lecturing extensively with "Weary" Timothy Leary. He is also a "Youth Culture Expert" employed by various Californian Think Tanks in Silicon Valley, and will be writing about this and his experiences at the hands of the law in Issue 3 of *Rapid Eye*). Their family home in Brighton has been invaded by policemen and, later, ransacked by paint-spraying vandals. Valuable paintings and irreplaceable memorabilia have been stolen or destroyed. With P-Orridge unable to meet mortgage payments due to the move, and unable to sell the property, the Building Society are considering re-possessing the house.

Even more importantly, the P-Orridge family's personal, private lives and histories have been ransacked, distorted and debated in public by strangers who have vested interests. (Journalists keen for good copy, religious cranks keen to sway public opinion against libertarianism and sell their own narrow-minded books, and self important rumour-mongers of all types).

Unspecific charges are still being considered by the police (though have not been made), meaning that P-Orridge risks arrest if he returns to this country on charges that he has not even yet been informed of. (It is thought by some that, before bringing charges, the Police have waited for the Law Lords final ruling on the controversial 'Spanner' sentences – several men having been arrested and imprisoned for consentual adult sex in private that involved SM activities that, under a new interpretation of the law, were deemed to involve assault and therefore be illegal. Thus, any adult in Britain involved in SM activities, or even the piercing of a consenting adult partner, became criminals. It is also thought that P-Orridge, as a founding member of COUM and TOPY, may be charged with obscenity for some of his controversial, transgressive artwork).

Despite the lessons learned from the Orkney case, Social Services would also possibly feel obliged in the current media-generated climate of hysteria to investigate the case, which may involve temporary removal and interrogation of the children, regardless of the psychological damage this may have on them and the family. Again, Social Services, who before the programme were happy to let Gen and Paula bring up their children, would have their hand forced by know-all, attention seeking TV journalists and researchers desperate to increase their programme's tiny viewing figures, regardless of the disruption their irresponsible actions cause to innocent parents and children.

Regardless of the laws relating to sub judice, Boyd and his cronies have, in effect, tried P-Orridge in the media, as self-appointed policeman, prosecution, judge and jury. Many journalists and newspaper editors have, as usual, shamelessly followed suit. If charges are ever brought, will it be easy to find a real jury who have not been influenced against P-Orridge by the scurrilous reportage he has attracted?

Mindful, and respectful of the laws of sub judice, we have been careful here only to report proven facts that are already public knowledge. We could say more.

Finally, if the 'investigative reporters' of Channel 4 had any awareness or professionalism, they would have realised that the very video they "discovered" had in fact been made over a decade earlier (in 1981) by a video artist interested in the Temple, and had in fact previously been aired on Channel 4, BBC, and Thames TV arts programmes, as well as on television in Europe.

To our knowledge, the video has never been distributed or been on sale, though it has been shown at exhibitions and performances. Stills from the video appeared openly in Rapid Eye Movement as far back as 1985.

The Temple of Psychic Youth continues to evolve and grow, albeit without P-Orridge, who decided to discontinue his involvement with the group in 1990. Since that time, the Temple has focused its attention more and more on developing new methods and symbolism with which to address the continued slow decay that they perceive in society. This decay manifests itself not only in the economic sense, but also, perhaps more significantly, in an increasing breakdown of hope and genuinely innovative creativity.

The early history of the Temple given in the above article is simply that, HIS-story. As was perhaps intended from the outset, the Temple has gradually become – as was stated – a co-operate venture. Thus, anyone approaching the Temple as it is now, in the hope of finding the Temple as it was then, will be disappointed (or not, as the case may be). TOPY has no wish to live in the past, and has never wished to be a static entity, tied to tradition or any form of fixed myth or methodology. As I said in this article, TOPY is based not on any one idea or system, but on flux. TOPY continually re-invents itself, as time flows, it changes. It is a question of evolution, of continuing to check and re-check the principal concerns of society as it really is; and the application of a "Magickal Perception" to those concerns.

So, TOPY still exists, their forms of communication and interests are broader-based, but equally intense. The exploration of society, of Control, of art and of The Art continues unabated. The period since the raid has taught TOPY a great deal, not only about media and communication, not only about the power of myths (and their construction); but also about the deeper levels of magick as it integrates fully as a truly effective means of Life.

TOPY has never offered easy answers – it still doesn't. It is neither a cult, nor a religion. It is not "Satanic", it is not "Christian". Indeed, these terms, left/right, black/white are not, and never have been the issues here. TOPY simply strives to be a way of seeing just a little bit more than you first thought was there, of seeing through the image that is projected and dealing directly with the realities behind these myths, behind these masks. Perhaps P-Orridge created one myth through which the mythology can be better understood. Perhaps everything was scripted, perhaps, on the other hand, nothing was intentional or true. Whatever your opinions, TOPY is a journey of discovery. Nothing less; and perhaps a great deal more.

For information on TOPY as it is now, write, enclosing an SAE or IRC to: TOPY Station 23, PO Box 687, Halfway, Sheffield S19 5UX, England.

It should be noted that, after the media furore, mail heading for Temple Records, Temple Press, TOPY, and other organisations, including *Rapid Eye*, started to go missing or was clearly tampered with. (Though this has now stopped).

The Liberty organisation (formerly the National Council for Civil Liberties), wrote to *Rapid Eye* saying that the Special Branch were probably opening our mail. Several bookshops refused to stock *Rapid Eye*.

We like to feel we live in a liberal society, and are cynical about any claims of suppression. We merely present you with the facts.

As we said in the above original article, Genesis P-Orridge represents a threat to Control. Society has concocted "good" reasons to remove him from a position of some artistic and social influence. Also, society has tried to come to terms with the genuine problem of child abuse, which most often takes place behind the net curtains of 'normal' suburban families, by transposing the problem onto an imagined minority group of individuals who may be interested in the academic works of assorted writers, artists and prophets who are considered to be 'suspect' by the majority – or, at least, by the populist media that claims to speak for the majority. Thus, people who read books such as *Rapid Eye* are assumed to be paedophiles and "Devil worshippers" (sic), regardless of the fact that many probably do not even believe in God or the Devil (we will ignore for the moment the fact that Satanism and paganism need have nothing to do with concepts of the Devil). So, the problem of child abuse is no longer a problem of society as a whole. The problem, as always, is the minority group.

The society that condones the dropping of nuclear weapons on children, systematically tortures and kills millions of animals, sells and poisons land from beneath unborn feet and profits from the preventable starvation and exploitation of children in differently developed countries, thus remains clean.

As Gen himself once wrote, borrowing from Charles Manson:

"CAN THE WORLD BE AS SAD AS IT SEEMS?"

We let you decide.

Simon Dwyer, Florence, 1993.

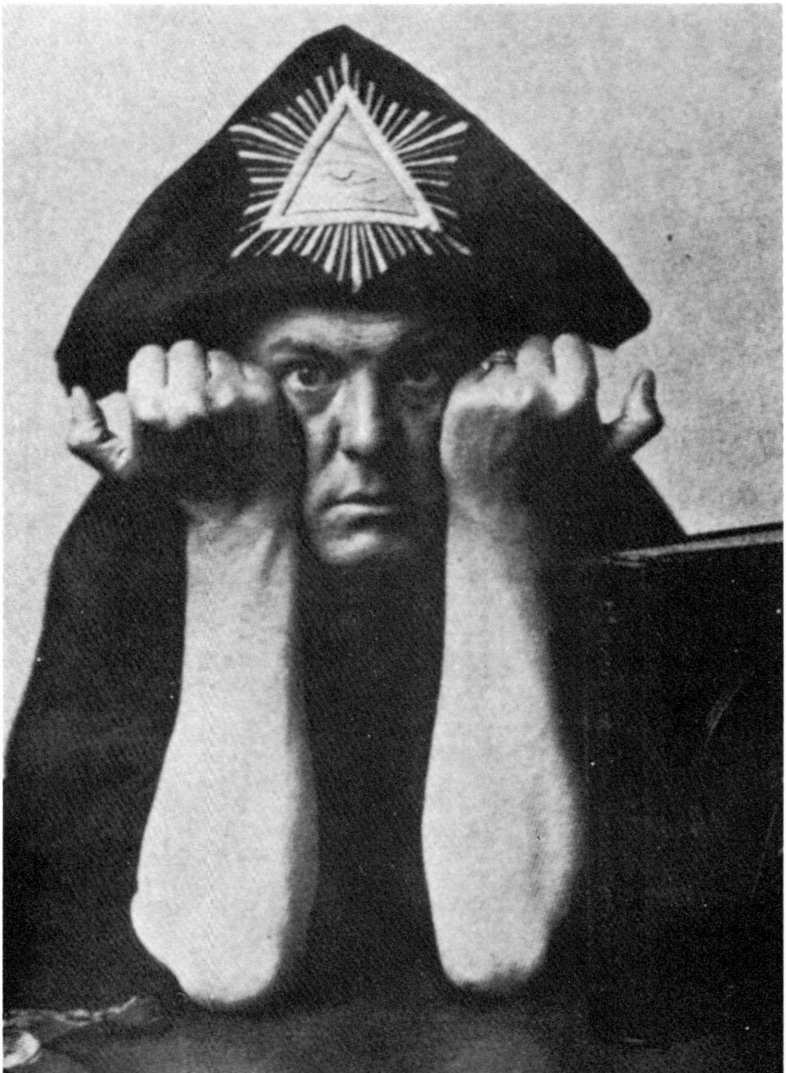

Mad, bad and dangerous to know – The Great Beast

SYBARITE AMONG THE SHADOWS

R. C. McNEIFF

BERLIN 1938: The yellow stars daubed on shop windows in the old quarter, overshadowed by the monstrous towers the Nazis called architecture, museums of the thousand-year Reich. Such a millenarian atmosphere suited Crowley fresh, if that is the word, from the Paris workings. He doted, like a gratified parent, on the 'German Crusade' as he called it. The authorities tolerated his existence. In some places names he had been uttering for years were on the lips of high ranking SS officers: Ahruman, Horus, Moloch...many deities were abroad that summer. Besides, he was well connected with the Nazis stretching back to the early days of the party's formation. However, they didn't like the relationship to be too defined. Already they were a hidden doctrine, a religion of intrigue and the esoteric. Worshippers of the left hand, the perverted spirit – but in secret only. To the ostensible world they presented themselves as the final cultists of the empirical. Crowley to them was something of a buffoon; an actor in a shadow theatre of rich widows and cocaine, someone who shared their language but not their intent. Crowley himself did not dislike this arrangement; he loved outrage and the extravagant, while for them the purpose was enough.

Crowley first met Huxley in a bar in Landulfstrasse. Huxley was in Berlin as an observer of the strange monster Germany was becoming. Like many observers, both repulsed and fascinated by the dark rhythm that beat in the pulse of that nation. To describe their relationship as friendship would be to miss the point. Crowley was doubtless fascinating – notorious as the Great Beast in his own country and much of Europe, cosmopolitan, a brilliant conversationalist and something of an enigma. Whereas Huxley was a myopic creature of the intellect. Yet Crowley attracted him, just as a few years before, he had attracted the dry, peevish Somerset Maugham in Paris. He almost existed for the straying eyes of the novelist, who longed for those chapters of exhibition life did not often afford. Yet now Crowley fades; his rotundity, absurd and menacing, is blurred. A glaring headline of Edwardian sin.

"Do what thou wilt shall be the
whole of the Law
Love is the Law
Love under Will."

So I utter his law in my own defence. That simplification that only he, the pettiest of profaners, could sprout. Dictated in the mirage of a Cairo night by his guardian angel, Aiwass. I think of him shortly after the war sitting in that seedy Hastings boarding house sated with the law. A figure of pathos in his shambling dressing-gown nursing his habits and remorse. An aged centaur; sybarite among the shadows. In the fading of his aeon more like the Fool than Prospero. A wrinkled soul.

Already in the late 'thirties Huxley was fascinated by the psychotropics. Hoffman had yet to fall off his bicycle, but there existed an abundance of literature on the subject. Havelock Ellis' experiments with mescalin or William James' with psilocybin. And Berlin, at that time, was the centre of drug abuse in Europe. Both Hitler and Göering used cocaine, and the SS administered many narcotics in their higher initiation ceremonies, particularly in the ritual of the stifling air, which closely resembled the Black Mass. Indeed, it is my own expressed opinion that the origins of both the Nazi party and the Second World War lie in the combined diet of methadrine and Nietzsche (*Also Sprach Zarathustra*) fed to the German soldiers in the trenches twenty or so years before. An oversimplification perhaps, yet the first chemical psychohistory of our epoch remains to be written.

Thus it was that Huxley came to Crowley for his first taste of mescalin. The latter took the drug irregularly without pretensions, purely as an exercise in that hedonistic spirituality he practised. Huxley, on the other hand, nourished a genuine, mystical longing that could come only from someone as deeply rooted in reason as himself. There was, therefore, a confusion of aims, a perennial ambiguity about their enterprise. And I, Victor Neuberg, sodomite and poet, accomplice of the Paris workings, was the arbiter. They had spent the afternoon in my somewhat less than opulent quarters, discussing Karma. Crowley was talking: *"To me it exists solely as a paradox. It's true, I have seen retribution in many things discerning a balance that is continually maintained. But this process is unending. It acts in everything and thus to allow its acknowledgement is absurd."*

"But we reap what we sow, Aleister," Huxley exclaimed, *"not in a moral sense. At least only incidentally moral, more or less by accident. Nemesis is something like gravitation, indifferent. For example, if you sow self-stultification by an excessive interest in money, you reap a grotesque humiliation. But..."*

"In what sense?" interrupted Crowley. *"How can you possibly accuse the rich of humiliation? Surely they're the last people to fall victim to that particular vice."*

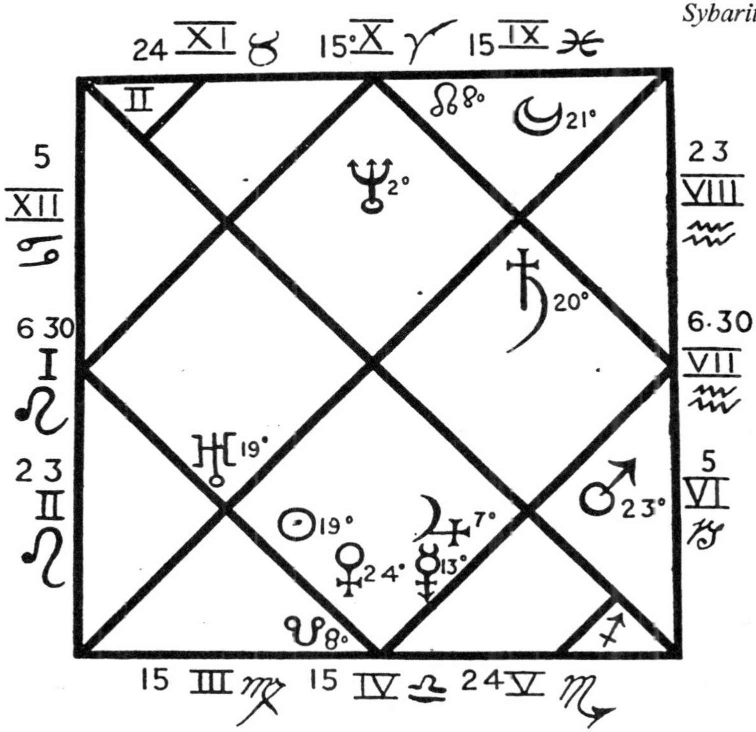

"I was coming to that," Huxley resumed. *"By self-stultification I don't just mean money. I mean anything that clouds the spirit. Over-indulgence in alcohol, food, or sex are more examples of things that wreck our purpose. But because these things reduce you to a sub-human condition, you will not be aware that the humiliation is humiliation. There's your explanation why Nemesis sometimes seems to reward. What she brings is a humiliation only in the absolute sense, for the ideal and complete human being, or at any rate, for the nearly complete. For the sub-human it may seem a triumph, a consummation, a fulfilment of the heart's desire."*

"Moral -" concluded Crowley, *"live sub-humanly and Nemesis may bring you happiness. Well, if you'll excuse me, my dear Aldous, I will proceed to self-stultify. Victor, if you don't mind, Pandora's box."*

I rose and went to the cabinet and took out his medicine. Four phials lay in the ivory box. I selected the one containing Burmese heroin and another containing Bolivian cocaine. Carefully I mixed the powders on a silver tray, crushing the dirty, khaki-coloured heroin and adding about five times as much cocaine. I passed Crowley a silver spoon that, with surprising dexterity, he used to scoop up some of the powder, which he then deftly inhaled, first through the right and then the left nostril. I did the same.

"Won't you join us for cocktails." Crowley invited. *"An excellent combination."* Huxley shook his head, disapproval etched deeply on this thin, drawn face.

Observing this, Crowley commented:

"I'm afraid that if you keep the devil's company then you must see his works. Or imagine you're with an old Falstaff, you know, gentlemen of the shade, minions of the Moon."

"Yes," Huxley said, *"but it's such a waste, the ultimate form of self-stultification. And what's more, I'm sure it's a conscious assault on the soul, an intense dereliction."*

"It depends," Crowley replied. *"Drugs are magic and have always been used as such. The soma of the Vedas, the lotus of Homer all point to the fact, as do the henbane and belladonna of the witches. And I'm sure for the normal man, who I happily call the sub-man, they are invariably detrimental. But in no way do I consider myself ordinary. To me drugs are the litmus test of capacity. I know the wraith-like effects of cocaine, that long corridor of shadows where the soul is wasted and profaned. Or heroin, the cushioned daze of the opiated night. But it is because I have supped large on both the joys and sorrows that I consider myself more than human."*

"But the waste, Crowley! The waste! Have you read the intimate journals of Baudelaire? Isherwood, who's staying near here, has just translated them. I've never seen such desperation, such regret over a lifetime spent addicted to false ideals. Those being hashish and the whole series of indulgences loved by the decadents."

"But that is it exactly!" Crowley exclaimed. *"Baudelaire loved it, gloried in his fall, his personal damnation. And besides, he did write some damn fine stuff, and wasn't that born precisely out of those feelings of failure or hysteria which he cultivated in his drug taking, his negresses, his remorse? You see, Huxley, as long as we are active we are saved. All energy is external delight as long as we use it. To me, to take a drug is to permit a daemon to enter the sanctum of thought and action. And if we give voice to this captured spirit then we enforce, rather than profane. We create new channels and these lead to our exorcism."*

He got up and went over to the sideboard. It was growing dark outside and his obesity threw a giant shadow across the wall. I suppose, in tribute to the spirit of the times, I should comment on the stamp of stormstroopers' boots on the street below. But in truth I heard only the growl of traffic and the occasional voice. Crowley came back and gave Huxley a piece of paper. *"Read this,"* he said.

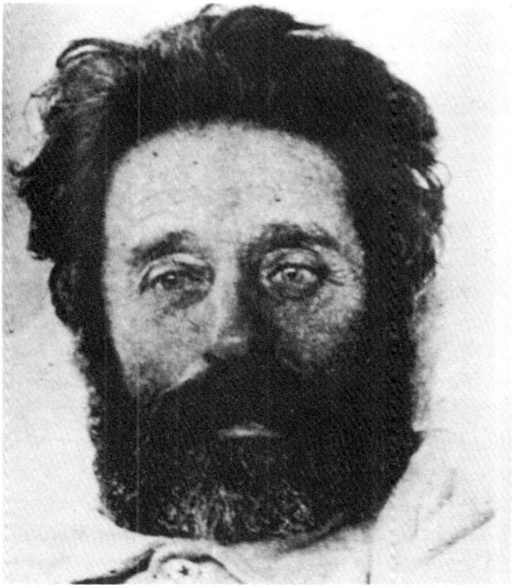

Victor, the last picture.

I have that paper in front of me now. In the last three decades it has become brittle and yellowed round the edges. It is one of many of his papers that I still keep. Bills and incantations and the occasional poem or letter. Existing like me, in obscurity, unknown to both his followers and biographers. It is divided into two parts and I shall transcribe it here:

"From the tower enchantment and the sweet hypnosis of lost time. My dreamseed spill their valediction across known worlds. I tell the cartographers who call my map invisible, that space is frozen in the habit of their fiction. Their cities are my seed; their houses, wives and toil are fantastic shadows of solidity. I see only waves, brilliant, aural cartoons containing but one centimetre of gross matter. Let the radiant language now spill forth. I sing the chisel and the blade; the hammer and the scales, long and measure, and all melodies of craft. The work ferments inside my battery of cells. My voltage is a million watts.

"Alchemy is patient. It sits in stillness. Like Tao it recognises the divinity of hazard, the vigour of the useless, the accident is merely the collision of two meanings. So in me the dross solidifies. I have stopped asking if I have a story as there are no stories now, only decipherable collisions. In me the opaque furniture of the random is condensed and

drained into rich ore. My veins are heavy with dark coal nurturing diamonds. I am the redking, the bronzed phoenix reborn upon the wheel of flame. I have traversed the river of ordeal and was crowned with elementals. Now shall the paradox of prism blaze onto papyrus my hearts bold voice.

"Airborne visions tingle. Coming from rich flight the dreamer's wingspan. Almost prosaic this whirlwind. Lost continents, contours, cartographers. And me, my maiden voyage is crystals and glass, my arbour and my veil. Truly the scheming polarity of vision this placing on a glass a pane that mirrors to the heart's dereliction, the soul's migration. I sweep the city. This is the holy liquid of metropolis, fashioned in the image of its metal bowels. This is the fall of Ushers, the corruption of sense. Neon flashes. Tell me the sex of electricity, of coils, sockets, plugs. Before the planet gave the deity of gender to the thunder in the hills. Only man creates the sexless. My mind is snow vapour, airwaves flow freely, like the magic carpet on Sinbad's voyage. You see, I am standing in Mexico. I have the stature of the ancients, the children of Lilith, twenty-three feet tall. I strut the sunflower Van Gogh sand, eaten by cacti, while the arcane sun explodes above. We eat the sun, my starry brethren. We are portions of its seed, the great spurting, in us forever. In the fever of mirage, in hallucinations I seek to touch the brimming fare of yellow: Peyotl, datura and mescal. Behind the needles sharpened by white light, fantastic buds map shades of an oasis".

Huxley read the piece carefully but was unimpressed. His exact words I cannot recall, only that they were polite and vague. I myself am somewhat fond of the two passages. They represent, I think, one of the few occasions when Crowley had something to say. When he was actually touched by vision. Doubtless, to Huxley, they were another aspect of the man's inescapable lunacy, along with the whole pantheon of dark, forgotten gods and familiars that sprang so glibly to his tongue.

"Well," he said. *"When the wind of the wings of madness come I hope you are prepared."*

His purpose in coming to us that evening was to take mescaline. They had discussed the substance at length – Huxley referring to Havelock Ellis and Crowley to the Vedas, for he believed the divine soma of the Indians was none other than the mushroom. *"Come then,"* said Crowley, *"at about six o'clock"*. And it was then we began. First we smoked hashish from the big hookah, its effect lightening the atmosphere considerably. Huxley lost most of the caustic self-possession that clung to him, like a limpet clings to a rock. He was almost merry. My mind and Crowley's still maintained the intense clarity that cocaine induces and which alcohol or hashish only partly subdue. So we teased him as if he were a mischievous child. His intellect was running wild. He talked scathingly of England and the English, expressing opinions that delighted Crowley. They discussed Gurdjieff, Buddhism, Yeats and his vision, and this time it was Crowley's turn to be scathing. Huxley even launched into a lecture on Tao exercises, which Crowley brought to an abrupt halt by asking if one hand clap wasn't a form of masturbatory syphilis. We all laughed uproariously, like schoolboys over a dirty joke. Meanwhile I had administered the mescaline.

"You know Hitler has taken this stuff," Crowley observed. *"I heard it from a reliable friend in the OTO."*

"OTO?" inquired Huxley.

"The Ordo Templi Orientis. My local branch, you might say. And their connections with the Nazis are nobody's business. They almost founded the party, or at least subverted it. Do you know that two of their chief men personally trained Adolf Hitler? Before, he was a stuttering Austrian oaf, a shoddy Bohemian and a pervert to boot. They taught him oratory, rhetoric and, under the influence of this drug that will shortly, my dear Aldous, set your eyes on fire, gave him his daemon."

There was, in Crowley's words, a certain malice. A hint from the prince to our novelist, our absolute realist, of the irrational and dark forces he might encounter.

"Then" Huxley said, *"all the disparate romanticism that, in its waning, found expression in the irrational, in secret cults, has made its kingdom here. Fascism is, after all, the triumph of decadence, the final madness of Bohemia."*

"So that carnage of Ahriman may be complete, precisely," Crowley replied.

Later, a vast smile spread across Huxley's formerly dry features, now radiant, illuminated, his eyes tinged with fire. In what region of enchantment he walked I do not know. Whether beneath the icy domes of Kubla Khan or, some long vanished field of his childhood, fragrant with wood smoke, haunted by summer's breath, he did not say. And what music flowed inside him, whether the Abyssinian maid soothed him with her dulcimer or some stellar symphony caressed his ears, was also his secret. Whatever is discovered at such moments belongs inviolably to the inner life of the individual. And even should he wish to communicate, he would probably find the few words that pertain to this province of experience unforthcoming. We have no maps for the mescal voyage of the psyche. For me it was a night of colours: yellow spectres emanating from the gaslamps; dancing lights of rain falling on the windowsill; deep cobalt of the sky; violet gauze of cloud over a white moon and all the world's allure gathered in a rainbow.

At one point Crowley produced his Tarot deck, the pack of Thoth. The figures seemed to move, the lovers entwining themselves on the matrix, the empress smiling her impenetrable smile while the prince of wands tightened the reigns of the chimera he rode upon.

All these vital creatures through our intent, in the steely point of time called Berlin, living in the correspondence of their ageless dance. Like some pharaoh of long ago, we glimpsed the highest octaves, the peerless mathematics of the stars.

At another point, Crowley quoted from the Book of the Law:

"I am the snake that giveth knowledge and delight and bright glory, and stir the hearts of men with drunkenness. To worship me take wine and strange drugs, whereof I will tell my prophet and be drunk thereof! They shall not harm ye at all."

"A trifle dangerous, don't you think?" Huxley murmured blearily.

"Of course," Crowley agreed, always lucid at such moments. *"If you read it carelessly and act on it rashly it might well lead to trouble. But the words 'to worship me' are all important.*

"They mean that things like cocaine, mescaline and alcohol may be, and should be used for the purpose of worshipping. That is, entering into communion with the snail, which is the genius that lies at the core of every star. And every man and woman is a star.

"The taking of a drug should be a carefully thought out and religious act. Experience alone can teach you the right conditions in which the act is legitimate; that is, when it assists you to do your will."

Huxley left shortly after. Walking through a Berlin he had never seen before. Where cylinders of fire in the cold dawn air dazzled his senses, and the splashing rain became cartwheels of light, fire flies mating with the pavement. He had entered a hitherto unknown continent and now, like an illuminated Columbus, was intent on discovery. I remained with the good master Therion, his bulk shifting in a reverie on the Turkish couch.

Many years stretch between then and now. Long ago my two protagonists were dust, fallen to the bottom of the hourglass. Huxley on his death bed; two hundred microgrammes of LSD-25, the vapid grin of his chemical exit. Crowley in that dirty Hastings boarding house; a vast spider with a heroin itch, regurgitating the entrapments of the past. Many years: a war, the accelerated madness of an epoch, the dawning of the age of Thelema. To me long, slow years of remorse, when I turned from the gender he had so skilfully taught me, and from the vision that witnessed me abandoned in the desert: the pallid brows, stiff horns, the foul rapture that attends that angel, to we in league with him, through time and eternity.

His sub-contractors.

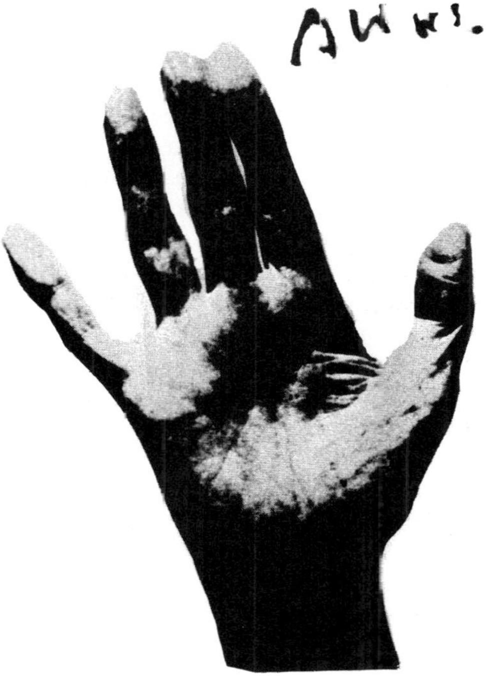

Huxley wrote his name on this photo of his hand just before his death.

DREAMACHINE

INFORMATION MONTAGE BY SIMON DWYER

The Dreamachine was devised by Brion Gysin, artist, writer, traveller and alchemist; one of the great unsung British painters of the 20th Century. Too clever and independent for the consumerist Art World, he nevertheless exhibited with Picasso, had shows throughout Europe and America, and was famously expelled from the Surrealists by André Breton. Gysin was the seminal influence who introduced William S. Burroughs to the use of cut-ups in writing. His wide cultural synthesis led him also into the world of the Rolling Stones, and particularly Brian Jones, whom he introduced to the Master Musicians of Joujouka in Morocco. He did not identify with any codified, preconceived religion, philosophy, or system of thought. He cited his major influence as Hassan i Sabbah, knowing that Hassan i Sabbah left no written teachings or doctrines. Since so little is really known about Hassan i Sabbah – the "Old Man of the Mountain" from whom the word 'assassin' derived – or his followers, any thought that is informed by Hassan i Sabbah must, therefore, be made up of suppositions and the use of the imagination. Gysin's world was thus magickal in origin. Brion said that we are "here to go". The future is in space. Not, as most thought, outer space, but interior space. The future – like the universe – is here, in the mind. The Dreamachine is a spacecraft that travels through time. NASA and the technophiles are left behind for the price of a lightbulb. Brion Gysin spent many years of his life in Britain, America, Morocco and France; but he spent most of his time in that place where all true visionaries are forced to dwell – in his mind.

"Brain waves, minute electrical oscillations associated with brain activity, can be measured accurately and graphically recorded by the electroencephalograph (EEG) machine. EEG records show that brain rhythms divide into groups according to frequency. One of these groups, the alpha or scanning rhythms, is strongest when the brain is unoccupied, searching for a pattern, and weakest during purposeful thinking, eyes open studying pattern. The strength and type of rhythms vary between individuals. The EEG records of some primitive peoples are similar to those of a ten year old in our society. Variations occur with age. The alpha rhythms do not appear in children until they are about four years old."

Ian Sommerville *'Flicker'*

"Had a transcendental storm of colour visions today in the bus going to Marseilles. We ran through a long avenue of trees and I closed my eyes

against the setting sun. An overwhelming flood of intensely bright colours exploded behind my eyelids: A multi-dimensional kaleidoscope whirling out through space. I was swept out of time. I was out in a world of infinite number. The vision stopped abruptly as we left the trees. Was that a vision? What happened to me?"

Extract from the Diary of Brion Gysin 21/12/1958

Department of Transport guidelines say that trees planted alongside motorways must not be of uniform height or distance apart. The reason for this is that drivers passing such trees for long periods experience pulses of light and changes in sound levels which can affect their concentration, and their ability to drive. Drowsiness, nausea and "motorway madness" can ensue.

Tests in Britain and America have taken place investigating the effects of strobe lights and loud oscillating sound on humans. It has now been confirmed that this research has been put to use by some security agencies in the area of crowd control. It is believed that systems have been developed which can induce epileptic fits in approximately one in four people – which would be more than enough to confuse and disperse any demonstrating crowd.

On February 15th 1960, Ian Sommerville, who had been recently inspired by Grey Walters' book *'The Living Brain'*, wrote a letter to Brion Gysin: *"I have made a simple flicker machine. You look at it with your eyes shut and the flicker plays over your eyelids. Visions start with a kaleidoscope of colours on a plane in front of the eyes and gradually become more complex and beautiful, breaking like surf on a shore until whole patterns of colour are pounding to get in. After a while the visions were permanently behind my eyes and I was in the middle of the whole scene with limitless patterns being generated around me. There was an almost unbearable feeling of spatial movement for a while but it was well worth getting through, for I found that when it stopped I was high above the Earth in a universal blaze of glory. Afterwards I found that my perception of the world around me had increased very notably. All conceptions of being drugged or tired had dropped away..."*

Following Sommerville's later description of the 'Flicker Machine', Gysin proceeded to make his own, adding to it an interior cylinder covered with a painting which he produced along the lines of his 'flicker' experiences. (Indeed, much of Gysin's later painting sprang from his visions experienced in front of the machine.) Gysin wrote at the time:

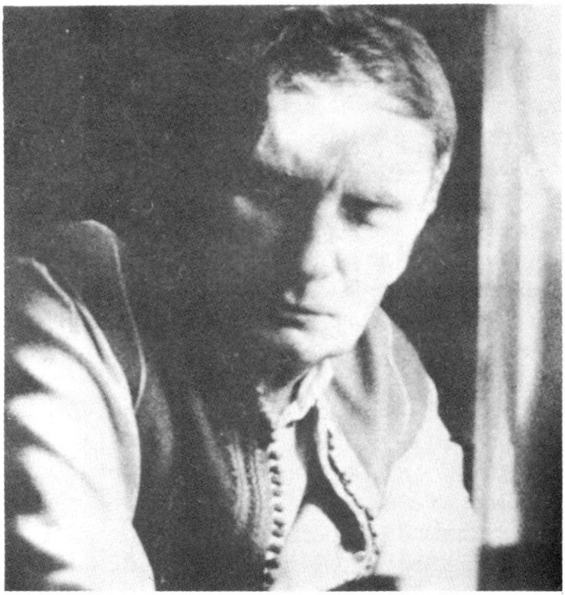

Brion Gysin using a Dreamachine.

"Flicker may prove to be a valid instrument of practical psychology: some people see and others do not. The DREAMACHINE, with its patterns visible to the open eyes, induces people to see. The fluctuating elements of flickered design support the development of autonomous movies, intensely pleasurable and, possibly, instructive to the viewer.

What is art? What is colour? What is vision? These old questions demand new answers when, in the light of the Dreamachine, one sees all of ancient and modern abstract art with eyes closed."

IN THE HISTORY OF ART. IN THE HISTORY OF MAGIC AND SCIENCE. IN THE HISTORY OF THE WORLD. ONLY ONE OBJECT HAS BEEN MADE TO BE VIEWED WITH THE EYES CLOSED. THE DREAMACHINE.

Dreamachines bring to a conclusion the period of kinetic invention in 'modern' painting and sculpture. The Dreamachine opens up a whole new era and a new area of vision...Interior Vision.

Look into a Dreamachine, and look deep. Here you will actually SEE the fundamental order present in the physiology of the human brain. Your brain. Order imposed on chaos. Life imposed on matter. History and

Mystery.

"You are the artist when you approach a Dreamachine with your eyes closed. What the Dreamachine incites you to see is yours...your own. The brilliant interior visions you so suddenly see whirling around inside your head are produced by your own brain activity. These may not be your first glimpse of these dazzling lights and celestial coloured images. Dreamachines provide them only just as long as you choose to look into them. What you are seeing is perhaps a broader vision than you may have had before of your own incalculable treasure, the 'Jungian' store of symbols which we share with all normally constituted humanity. From this storehouse, artists and artisans have drawn the elements of art down the ages. In the rapid flux of images, you will immediately recognise crosses, stars, halos...woven patterns like pre-Columbian textiles and Islamic rugs...repetitive patterns on ceramic tile...in embroideries of all times...rapidly fluctuating serial images of abstract art...what look like endless expanses of fresh paint laid on with a palette knife."

Brion Gysin

The visions hollowed out of the Dreamachine usually start off with a rapid, and quickening, succession of abstract patterns. Often this transit of speeding images is followed by a clear perception of human faces. Humanoid figures and the apparent enactment of highly coloured events, or, as Gysin described them, "pseudo-events", carried out in time and in space.

"Do you dream in colour?"

Bill Nelson

The Dreamachine really IS just that. A dream machine. One person I know who exposed themself to its spinning glare came out of their semi-hallucinatory state talking seriously of visiting another planet, complete with aliens, cavepaintings and children. Some people have reported nightmares of sorts, but these, as all dreams experienced on the Machine, can be abruptly brought to an end by opening your eyes.

"However you look into a Dreamachine, in a short time you will have acquired greater self knowledge, extended the limits of your vision, brightened your perception of a treasure you may not have known you own."

Brion Gysin

"A light like a billion watt bulb floated up through the bars on my window. The Great White Light, the Ineffable Light the Tibetans are always talking about. I was transfixed, of course. I felt I could see it, naturally, because it ran straight up my optic nerve and through the disintegrating mass of my freshly re-awakened brain right down to my hypothalamus. My narrow cell began to revolve like an old 78 rpm turntable and the bars on my cell window on the spiral stairs to spin at between eight and thirteen flickers a second – the alpha rhythm of my soft old brainbox. An overwhelming flood of intensely bright abstract patterns in supernatural colours exploded somewhere behind my blind eyes where multi-dimensional kaleidoscopes whirled through endless space. Dazzling lights of unearthly brilliance and colour were developing in magnitude and complexity at great speed. Infinite acres of geometric wallpaper and rubbishy canvases by painters like Vasarely spread all around me. I was the pivot in the centre of developing worlds, giant galaxies hurtling through my own interior space at the speed of light. It all means that my EEG has not flattened out yet and the old brain is still working. I laugh uncontrollably...

"Long experience of Gysin's Dreamachine had taught me what to expect. I knew I could expect to see the symbols of all the great religions float free from this background noise to pass slowly and majestically across my field of vision. The cross in all its variations flashed as brightly for me as it had for Saul on his way to Damascus racing down an avenue of trees on the buckboard of his chariot as the sun set behind the tree trunks, producing flicker at his alpha rate. So he fell off his chariot and came to as Saint Paul, more's the pity for all of us. As I said before, all these religions ought to be taxed out of existence. Then the swastikas spinning clockwise and counter were followed by a magnificently jewelled Tibetan dorje, raised like a club or sceptre. The all-seeing eye of Isis floated by, eyeing me knowingly, succeeding by other eyes flashing fire. The crescent moon of Islam or the Blessed Virgin Mary and the blue hand of Fatima gave way to the symbols of forgotten religions or, who knows, those of other planets. I waited expectantly..."

Robert Anton Wilson

Gysin was approached by various large companies, including the Dutch electronics giant, Philips, sniffing around the patenting possibilities of the machine which he and Sommerville had effectively invented out of nothing. *"When I told them that it made people more awake"*, said Gysin later, *"they lost interest. They were only interested in machines and drugs which made people go to sleep."*

If the Dreamachine is real, a non-habit forming, simple spinning dreambox that is capable of inducing a drugless high, why is it not available in your local department store? The answer would seem obvious. Look at the Financial Times and you will see that some of the biggest companies in the world are chemical giants, ICI, Bayer, Hoffman La Roche. Go to your GP and tell him that you are ill and what will you get? Drugs. Seek a path out of everyday trivial reality and what will you be offered? Drugs. You can only sell people one Dreamachine, one turntable, the occasional lightbulb. Drugs and their accompanying paraphernalia (and I include most doctors as an integral part of the paraphernalia) generate far more money in a drug dependent world.

How do you go about getting a Dreamachine? Well, only a handful exist, made in metal cylindrical form and costing upwards of £500. But you can experiment by making your own.

To build your own Dreamachine you need a sheet of 4-ply paper, 32 inches square, a record player that can revolve at 78 rpm (available from many secondhand shops for a few quid) and a hanging lightbulb.

On the paper, draw three inch borders along the top and bottom, then carefully divide the rest into two inch squares. Cut out the cardboard templates, then trace them onto the paper in the positions illustrated. With great care and accuracy, then cut the holes out and connect the two ends together, thus forming a cylinder. Dangle a light bulb down the middle of the cylinder and rest this on the turntable. Now darken the rest of the room, play some repetitive but "unfocused" music, and spin.

From now on, it's all free, it's all safe, it's legal and it really works.

THE BLACK BOX

KATHLEEN McAULLIFFE

It looks like a small black Walkman, but it won't play anything audible to the human ear. In place of headphones are two wires. These are attached behind the ears, the box clipped to the user's belt and adjusted to the right frequency.

The Black Box in question does not originate from some vast factory out the outskirts of Kobe, but from the hands of a British Doctor practising in California. Its purpose is simple. To cure drug addiction.

The Box transmits a tiny electrical signal that appears to harmonize with the naturally produced rhythms of the human brain, in the process reducing the craving and anxiety associated with any drug withdrawal. Still in relatively early stages of development, it has already been successfully used to help patients off heroin, barbiturates, speed, cocaine, marijuana, alcohol and cigarettes.

Dr. Margaret Patterson, a Scottish surgeon, is the inventor of the strange device. A woman Pete Townsend called a 'miracle worker' for helping him kick his various habits. The Black Box is also credited with reforming Eric Clapton, Boy George and the seemingly indestructible Keith Richards.

Patterson herself would disagree with Townsend; she is not claiming to have answered the problem of drug abuse, just to have made one useful step in the right direction. *"I hesitate to use the word cure,"* she says, *"I prefer to call it a method of rapid detoxification."* The electricity quickly cleanses the addict's system of drugs, restoring the body to normal within ten days. Most patients report that their craving subsides in the process.

Over the last 15 years over 300 addicts of various types have received treatment with the Black Box in Britain. The results of this NeuroElectric Therapy (N.E.T.) were that all but four patients left drug-free at the end of the detoxification process – a remarkable 98% success rate. *"NET should not be confused with ECT – electroconvulsive therapy."* she cautions, ETC being the type of therapy meted out to the mental patients as in 'One Flew Over the Cuckoos Nest'. *"NET is far, far milder, involving currents at least twenty times weaker. Patients feel only a slight tingling sensation behind their ears where the electrodes are taped on."* Yet this mild therapy, she claims, will subdue the violent reactions that can make Cold Turkey bad enough to turn John Lennon to God.

Patterson asserts quite unequivocally, *"I can take anyone off a drug abuse, no matter how severe his or her addiction, with only the minimum of discomfort."*

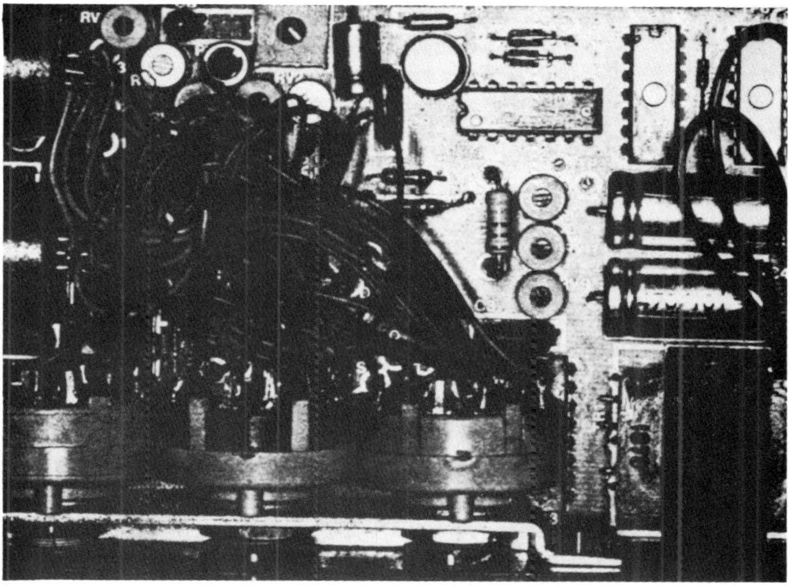

As with all drug treatments, not all those who complete the detoxification programme remain abstinent. She emphasizes the NET is most effective when backed up by counselling, remedial training, and a supportive home environment. For a large number of people, however, the treatment does seem to have worked. If one is to believe the recidivism figures she cites, they are many times lower than average for every type of addictive drug.

A glance at Patterson's credentials gives reassurance that she is both serious and highly capable. At twenty-one she was the youngest woman to qualify as a doctor at Aberdeen University. Only four years later she obtained her fellowship to the Royal College of Surgeons, through Edinburgh University – an elite circle that few surgeons penetrate before their thirties. Just before her fortieth birthday, she was presented with an M.B.E. for her outstanding medical work in India. Hardly quack material.

Patterson's clinic still incorporates a large degree of old fashioned affection and concern for its patients on their road to recovery, though. *"She's the sort of mother you always dreamed of having,"* says one female addict. This high degree of rapport she has with he patients has led some professionals to question if her dazzling record in drug rehabilitation is really attributable to the powers of the Black Box, or her personality. However, a number of NHS doctors are now testing her electrical stimulator model with the same beneficial results. Dr Margaret Cameron, a psychiatrist working in Somerset, reports that NET *"gives very, very good results, better than any other method of treatment I've encountered."*

If NET has met with resistance, it is because its mode of action strains the explanatory powers of modern science. Until very recently orthodox medicine refused to recognise that infinitesimal electrical currents may influence the behaviour or function of living organisms. Currents less than 100 millivolts – or below the threshold for triggering a nerve impulse – were always assumed to have no effect on biological processes.

This dogmatic view had to be reassessed when accounts of such unsettling phenomena began appearing with increasing frequency in technical journals over the last decade. NET is, in fact, only one branch of a young, controversial discipline that is still struggling to achieve respectability.

In the early Seventies scientists began introducing very small currents via electrodes to different parts of the body – with dramatic results. A rat amputee was induced to regrow a forelimb down to the midjoint. In America, the Federal Drug Administration has approved the use of such currents for stitching together stubborn bone fractures. Recent experimental trials also indicate that trickling flows of electricity promote the healing of such things as chronic bedsores, burns and even peripheral nerve injuries. The external currents, it is theorised, stimulate rapid healing by augmenting the body's internal currents.

"By contrast, weak currents applied to the brain affect different physiological processes," says Dr Robert O. Becker, a pioneer of electrical medicine in New York. *"But I believe the Black Box is producing profound alterations of the central nervous system. The psychological set that makes a person become an addict seems to disappear."*

Researchers are now starting to elucidate a scientific rationale for NET, and are winning over converts from the more conservative ranks of the medical profession in the process. Pattersons Black Box is helping to unlock the mysterious inner working of that other black bo – xthe human brain. Investigations are shedding light on the underlying mechanisms that control everything from addictive behaviour to our most basic drives and emotions. Underlying consciousness is an intricate orchestral arrangement of trillions of brain cells firing in concert. Like different instruments playing in a symphony, sub-populations of neurons are now believed to produce frequencies within a specific range. Frequency, so to speak, is the music of the brains' hemispheres.

Like penicillin and X rays, NET was born of scientific serendipity. It began in the Autumn of 1972, when Patterson was working as Chief

Surgeon of a large charity hospital in Hong Kong. A Neurosurgeon colleague of hers, Dr H L Wen, had just returned from China where he had learned electroacpuncture techniques. Primarily interested in using it in the suppression of pain, he began using it on patients with a variety of ills. Unbeknown to him, however, some 15% of his patients were addicted to heroin or opium of exceptional purity – a daily shot costing the same as a packet of cigarettes in downtown Hong Kong. To his surprise, many addicted patients came to him reporting that electroacupuncture had completely stopped their withdrawal symptoms, some equating the electroacupuncture experience with a dosage of opium. Later it was also revealed that cigarette smokers and a few alcoholics had also been cured of their craving.

Patterson always figured that acupuncture was essentially an electrical phenomenon. The ancient practice revolves around the theory that all living things possess vital energy called 'Chi' which circulates throughout the body by way of a network of channels or meridians. Sickness was seen to be the result of disharmony manifested by an obstruction in the flow of 'Chi'. Perhaps the Chinese, more than 2,500 years before the discovery of electricity, had recognised the internal currents that we know course through the body? Patterson reasoned that the twirling of the needles generates a tiny electric voltage.

Replacing needles with more efficient and comfortable electrodes was something that Western people – including, surprisingly, mainline heroin users – preferred.

Continuing her research, she also found that different frequencies were better for the treatment of different addictions. Those addicted to narcotics and sedatives preferred one frequency, barbiturates addicts responded to lower frequencies, and people dependant on cocaine or amphetamines benefitted from the highest frequencies. *"Musicians,"* she fondly recalls, *"really helped to strengthen my guesswork during the early days. They invariably found the correct therapeutic frequency setting right away. It was as if their brains were more attuned to frequency."*

Jean Cocteau, who resumed his opium smoking after medical treatment had "purged" him of the habit, once wrote *"Now that I am cured, I feel empty, poor, broken hearted and ill."* In sharp contrast, NET patients are said to emerge from treatment feeling healthy, energetic and even cheerful. Dr Joseph Winston, an American physician who collaborated with Patterson in the treatment of Keith Richards, says that the Glimmer Twin *"came to us terribly ill. He was literally GREEN... Ten days later he was playing tennis and the 'Stones said he hadn't looked so good in years."*

Patients who have undergone NET treatment, it seems, are more liable to remain off drugs once detoxification has been undergone, largely because they feel in such health, physically and mentally. NET alone cannot educate addicts to deal with the everyday problems of life again without resorting to drugs, though, so it's surprising that many of Patterson's patients have gone on to build drug-free lives without any formal counselling beyond that provided during the brief NET programme.

Patterson believes that the treatment simply sets the stage for further growth. *"Because they feel good they are better able to face the sort of problems that drove them to addiction in the first place. You see, most people who come off drugs without NET enter a phase of prolonged dysphoria: they suffer from fearful depression and pessimism; they can't eat; they can't sleep; they have no energy. This can last for six months in the case of heroin and even longer in cases of methadone and barbiturate addiction. But NET restores physiological normality within ten days, which enormously reduces the amount of time needed for readjustment."*

If anything, though, Patterson thinks that euphoria – not dysphoria – is primarily to blame when rehabilitation fails. The newly detoxified addict is optimistic to the point of being over-confident. *"In their elated state"*, she says, *"they think it will be easy to stay off drugs and then end up stumbling because they don't make enough of an attempt to change their ways."*

As if obeying Newtonian mechanics, the Black Box appears to counter one mood shift with an equal swing in the opposite direction, until the emotional pendulum finally comes to rest.

Is the Black Box in reality an electronic substitute for a chemical high? How can a physical treatment cause such swings in mood? Dr Hans Kosterlitz, a former colleague of Patterson was, able to illuminate the subject when, working at Aberdeen University, he made a remarkable discovery that was to win him the American equivalent of the Nobel Prize in medicine, the Lasker Award. He identified an endorphin, a natural brain chemical which had a molecular structure almost identical to the opiates. The finding triggered an explosion in the understanding of the biochemical basis of behaviour, opening new vistas on the controlling factors behind addiction. Opium, heroin, morphine and other related drugs owe their potency to a bizarre natural coincidence – their uncanny resemblance to the endorphins. Later research showed that myriad other brain hormones mimic psychoactive drugs, from valium and angel dust to hallucinogens. Almost every mind-altering substance is now assumed to have an analogue in the brain. The precise mixture of neurojuices in this biochemical cocktail inside our heads can mean the difference between tripping, speeding, crashing, or seeing the world through sober eyes.

These insights immediately suggested how the addict becomes trapped in a nightmarish cycle of dependency. The first few hits of heroin in the normal, well mixed cocktail in the brain cause a sudden and enormously increased level of the opiate elements, which is subjectively interpreted as ecstasy. If through repetition the brain is regularly flooded with unnecessary opiates, it redresses the imbalance by cutting back on the production of its internal supply. The addict then gets a reduced amount of opiates with each hit, so he must increase his dosage in order to get the desired effect. Hence the condition of tolerance develops. The addict steps up his dosage again and the brain further compensates by calling a massive shutdown of its own production. Eventually the addict is shooting up solely for the purpose of feeling normal. Should the drug supply be shut off at this stage the sudden opiate shortage cannot be instantly remedied by the brain. Drought ensues, unleashing the horrific symptoms of withdrawal.

If an exogenous drug depletes the brain of its normal counterpart, it seemed that NET was working by stimulating the brain at this vital time to compensate for the drought by juicing up the system with production of its own opiates. Different frequencies of current from the Black Box seemed to catalyze the release of different brain hormones, so the one which corresponds to the artificially induced drug could be released specifically. By the end of the ten day treatment, the levels have been brought down to normal.

How a tiny electrical current can open the floodgates of the mind is still largely a matter of conjecture, but the implications are obvious. Like a Citizens Band transmitter that infiltrates television frequencies, the Black Box must broadcast through the brain frequency channels. And just as a TV receiver can pick up CB transmissions from a passing juggernaut, the brain undoubtedly responds to the alien generated signal as if it had originated from within its own communication network. Research carried out so far seems to show that each brain centre generates impulses at a specific frequency based on the predominant neurotransmitter it secretes. In other words, the brains language is based on frequency. Unfortunately scientists are not yet fluent in this new tongue. NET is still a very blunt tool, being used in a limited fashion. Addicts may represent only a fraction of the people who will eventually be helped by NET. Some scientists predict that it will find an enormous range of uses, particularly, for example, in the area of pain control. By stimulating the brain to produce its own painkillers, the practice of administering morphine and other potentially harmful drugs would become redundant.

Early data also indicates that NET may prove beneficial in the treatment of mental disorders People suffering from severe depression, for instance, have already been test treated with frequencies that reduce tension with excellent results. Unlike many longterm pill-popping solutions, no harmful side-effects have been reported. With a far-reaching sense of optimism, some people have voiced a belief that NET may offer hope in the battle against all sorts of disease and injury. If the secret language of brain frequency is eventually de-coded, perhaps it would be possible to increase its natural attacks on infections, stop the growth of tumours, and heal injuries more quickly.

Quite how the giant drug companies are viewing the wider longterm uses of NET is anyone's guess. How, too, would tobacco companies and, for that matter, Government – awash with the money gathered from a variety of socially acceptable addictions – adapt to a society free from addiction?

Paranoia aside, one only has to look at tax sums acquired through tobacco revenue, and set this against the amount spent on anti-smoking propaganda, to sense the wider implications of an addiction-free society – particularly when one learns that Dr Patterson is now hoping to treat behavioral addiction, from overeating and compulsive gambling to videogame fanaticism with her Black Box.

If one accepts that behavioral addictions have a chemical basis, the treatment would be quite logical. It is thought very likely that, for example, all activities that are vital to survival – from sex to physical exercise – are physiologically addictive. It is now thought that the common phenomenon of 'Jogger's High' is actually endorphin mediated. In all probability, eating also releases some kind of pleasurable molecule. *"After all,"* says one researcher, *"why do we crave food? Hunger, low blood-sugar levels don't explain why. The truth is that we feel abnormal when we haven't eaten for a while. Some chemical in our brain has become depleted. We become restless and agitated and eventually start to have withdrawal symptoms."* This Cold Turkey for cold turkey comes long before the body physically needs more food to survive. This natural early warning system, created by the depletion of a certain chemical in the brain, is more commonly known as hunger pangs. *"The only way to relieve this discomfort of withdrawal is to eat something. It's a fix – pure and simple."*

If even such basic drives are addictive, then the tampering of natural drug levels, through safe NET stimulation, would be an ingenious means of shortcutting the elaborate scheme nature devised to ensure that we maintain health and reproduce ourselves. Merely by twiddling a frequency dial on our black 'Walkman' we can top off our neurochemical reservoirs with no sweat expended. Instant orgasms without any foreplay. A cheap thrill. Could not the wondrous Black Box become addictive in its own right? An electrofix?

Patterson, aware of the problem, has kept her well-trained eyes peeled for any signs. In over a decade of research she has not encountered one instance of electronic addiction. The explanation, she believes, *"is that drugs – for the very reason that they are foreign – upset the brain's chemistry. NET, on the other hand, simply coaxes the brain to restore its own natural chemical balance. The body heals itself."* Besides, the possibilities of a street trade in the Boxes is limited by the prohibitive costs involved – upwards of £1,000 each, a hefty lump sum for most junkies.

Treatment, and especially research, is also expensive. Patterson needs financial backing to extend both areas of her practice, her main motive for moving to the U.S.A. Until the medical establishment can be coaxed away from the belief that bases most treatment on the administering of pills and potions, such large scale funding and research will not be able to take place. Before she can even start to treat patients on a routine basis, she must first receive clearance from the Federal Drugs Administration. She remains optimistic, but realistic. If the backing comes, even then *"all we can do is give people a chance. We can get them off whatever drug they're hooked on, but it's up to them to fill the void."*

Will she get the support she needs to carry on her research? And if so, will her Black Box provide a solution to the addiction problems that produce the sight of 11 year-old junkies on housing estates in Liverpool stealing to support their habit, or 50,000-plus premature deaths a year from cigarette smoking? Clearly the final verdict is contingent upon replication of controlled studies. But if a feeble electrical current can truly curb the mind's excesses, the impact of this particular Black Box is sure to be far-reaching.

DANCE RITUAL

EILEEN SHEPPERD

I wish we could rediscover in Britain today the magical power of dance. I don't mean dance as entertainment, but used as part of a healing ritual. For many tribes around the world, dance provides a natural psychological medicine, and is an integral part of life – far healthier than popping tranquillisers or soul-searching on a psychologist's couch.

W. Sargeant, psychiatrist and author of *'The Mind Possessed'*, defines the use of dance in a ritual:- *"Rhythmic dancing and leaping are among the principal methods of inducing states of ecstasy in which a man feels taken over by a force being greater than himself."*

Perhaps the best-known dance ritual users are the Whirling Dervishes, a religious Sufi sect who use dance to create an altered state of mind to reach closer to their God.

I first became aware of the power of dance when I took part regularly in charity shows as a child at my local dance school in Yorkshire. Here was the magic of the theatre, the ritual of dressing-up in yards of garish net and satin, painting my five-year-old face like a wartime movie star. Backstage smelt mustily of damp wood, combined with clouds of talcum, sweaty ballet shoes and nervous armpits. I was a good dancer, but as tiny and stocky as an elf, and so lacking the extended balletic line needed for pseudo-Swan Lake routines. However, strangers from the audience would often express their admiration after the show as I stood outside the theatre, waiting to be ferried home, illusion now dashed by an old school blazer over my frothy net skirt.

On stage, I felt an excitement and direct communication with specific people in the audience as if I was talking to them intimately – something was bridging a gap between us. Years later, research into the realms of Dance, Magic and the Theatre defined those childhood experiences as akin to psychic energy and the hypnoid brain activity of mesmerism, possession, meditation and other altered states of consciousness.

Dance in this country today is most often experienced as entertainment in the theatre or disco. The 'ritual' or cathartic effect of dance sometimes makes itself present, but this is largely accidental. People *like* dancing, as it is both exercise and exorcism. T.J. Scheff in *'Catharsis in Healing, Ritual and Drama'* explains the need for purging the mind and body of past emotional shocks which have led to lasting states of stress. He believes that in western society, catharsis often fails because the techniques are either 'overdistanced' or 'underdistanced'. For example, TV cartoon violence is more often effective in releasing stress than certificate-X movies, because the unreal cartoon characters sufficiently distance the audience from their pain.

In the theatre, the tradition of catharsis goes back to the Greek dramatists. I believe that dance in the theatre is not generally popular in the UK because dance is not a normal part of life for most people and therefore the experience of simply watching it is too overdistanced. This is particularly so with classical ballet, with its archaic costumes, gestures and story-lines. Often, there is nothing for the viewer to relate to. There are, of course, exceptions where modern directors and choreographers such as Peter Schaufuss have tried to bring the experience closer to modern life.

Dance as a ritual also fails in Britain because of our general antagonism towards the occult. However, Rogan Taylor writes (*New Society*, March 1985) that the hippie rock scene and drug-taking of the '60s had shamanistic qualities and made magic more acceptable: *"For perhaps the first time in 5,000 years of settled culture, showbiz stood briefly revealed for what it (secretly) had always been: ecstatic religion in performance"*.

In ballroom dancing or ice dance, the competition element can provide for catharsis. Here, the audience can identify with or imagine themselves as the performers trying to win. *'Come Dancing'* on BBC1 involves contests between dance halls and clubs, where teams and supporters dress up in clothing specific to the ritual, and the struggle takes place in an arena, rather like a football match. It is no surprise that with the gradual isolation of ballroom competition dancing, so the costumes have become more stylised and extreme.

Western dance is most often used as a courtship ritual. Youth ballroom or 'contact' dancing seems to survive *"where there is still some degree of sexual prohibition on the young"*, according to Lyndon Wainwright, General Secretary of the International Dance Teachers' Association (*Times*, 1 June 1984). I have experienced the rigid courtship routine of the Irish dance hall in Kilburn, North London, where girls still line the walls, waiting for males to get sufficiently inebriated to ask them for a dance. Middle-aged couples mingle with the kids, whereas discos are largely taboo for the over-40s. Much time is spent in the ladies' powder room rather than dancing, where groups of females offer mutual encouragement and advice about behaviour, decisions on partners, approval of hairstyles and make-up. In *'The Anthropology of Dance'* Anya Peterson Royce notes that the term "going to a dance" in Europe and America can mean eating, drinking and chatting with little or no dancing at all.

Disco dancing arrived in the late '50s along with a relaxation of sexual courtship rules and corresponding change in music and fashion. It caters more for the much-discussed 'me' generation of the '60s and so self-expressive swaying and wiggling replaced the partnered fox-trot or two-step with their set patterns of steps and rigid upper body and arms.

The coupling ritual of discos was captured by Tom Jobee's *'Rite Electrik'* (choreographed for the London Contemporary Dance Theatre). It takes place in a gay disco and overt sexual statements of display are made as each dancer vies for attention and approval. They jump to the centre of the stage, dressed in leather straps, reminiscent of Roman gladiators.

More rigid patterns of dance have appeared in the soul and rapping discos, dominated by young blacks, where the aim is to entertain and compete. The moves vary between the quick, muscular isolation of robotics and body-popping, which is freer and very acrobatic.

Disco dance from its inception has strongly identified certain 'tribes' of youth culture, along with the music and fashion, and from an anthropological view-point this aligns it with identification dances of most ancient civilisations. For example, heavy metal freaks and punks are marked by a very aggressive rocking of the upper body (with none of the fancy footwork of disco smoothies), as if reacting *against* dance as such. I recently saw a circle of them at a Psychic TV concert engaged in a display of mock fighting. No blows were landed, but movement was confined to rocking, kicking and punching.

Dance as part of a 'religion' seems to survive in aerobics, which has its own ritual of pain and release. Although it cannot be classified as dance, it is largely taught in dance centres alongside jazz and ballet which, incidentally, have become more athletic in motivation. The fitness 'religion' of controlling the body, sometimes to fanatical degree, has its counterpart in the Eastern yogi on a bed of nails or fasting ascetic, who display body control to reach a more traditional god than that of fitness. Aerobicising the body can cause what is known as the 'runner's high' or ecstasy in pain.

Dance in Britain was last consciously and seriously used in ritual during the early pagan rites of fertility. Here, as in aboriginal and American Indian dancing, much stamping and hopping from one foot to the other was employed, calling up psychic earth energies which would provide for a good harvest. Most often, the dance was circular or snake-like along ancient energy paths or ley lines, and accompanied by feasting and drinking.

In *'Earth Rites'* Janet and Colin Bord describe ancient fertility practices in pre-industrial Britain, and many survive today, although more as village entertainment than serious ritual. The Summer Solstice was celebrated in

Ireland up to the late 18th century by lighting fires on hill-tops which people danced around, and then danced through the embers, along with their children and cattle. This was a fertility rite where the (female) earth mother forces and the passage of the (masculine) sun through the sky was celebrated.

Primitive tribes throughout the world believed (and still do) that stones, trees and other natural objects contained individual gods. Tree worship in this country involving dancing had much to do with the fertile phallic symbol of the tree, which now survives in Maypole dancing.

In spite of all the similarities with ritual which dance in this country shows today, it is still too 'overdistanced' and haphazard in its therapeutic effect. I think we would baulk at the acceptable use of dance in exorcism, although it is not so far removed from modern psychotherapy. Michel Lambek in *'Human Spirits'* studied the possession states of the Mayotte peoples (Comoro Is., East Africa) and identified a need in our society for structured trance and rite of passage.

For the moment, we consider ourselves as civilised and in need of sophisticated entertainment, but perhaps discos and dance halls are a few steps nearer ritual than we'd care to think.

INAUGURATION OF THE PLEASURE DOME

JACK HUNTER

Throughout the length and breadth of England, weekend in, weekend out, tens of thousands of young people are attending and celebrating Black Mass.

If that comes as something of a shock to you, you may draw some comfort (or not) from the fact that most of the revellers are unaware of it themselves. I refer to the phenomenon of House culture.

Under the most propitious circumstances, to attend a House event is to participate in the recreation of centuried, primal rites whose like have not been seen – save perhaps in covens – in this country since pagan times, and certainly never on such scale. Outlawed except in a controlled environment, the ceremony holds the ancient, clandestine attraction of bacchanalia.

First comes the descent from a world of light into darkness. The celebrants are gathering, and already there is a palpable atmosphere of super-charged expectancy. Intoxicants, psychedelic or hyperdelic drugs, are ingested. The throbbing, tribal, perfectly repetitive music grows louder and louder in direct ratio to the intoxication of the revellers. At a seemingly arbitrary moment, as if by telepathy, the event explodes into full swing. Everybody is dancing – unselfconsciously, and with increasing abandon. The concept of a "dancefloor" is quickly proved obsolete: people are dancing on chairs, on tables, or wherever they happen to be standing. Many are banging drums or shaking maracas they have brought with them, helping to whip others into frenzy. Illumination comes only from stroboscopic, spell-binding laser light. The impression is darkly orgiastic: scorpionic. Finally, a mass immolation of self is achieved; the celebrants become as one, a circuit is completed again and again, generating enough ecstatic, *sexual* energy to raze the venue. In this trance-state, out-of-body experiences are common. Time is suspended, and has no meaning while the music plays.

Here at last is a seminal, atavistic alchemy of music and drugs which enables the participants – albeit unwittingly – to tune into occult (hidden) dimensions within themselves, to invoke or exorcise demons just as shamans in other, wiser cultures have for centuries before. A truly communal, healing – because genuinely cathartic – experience which opens up psychic avenues denied to countless earlier generations. This is the antithesis of the now-redundant "rock concert": these people are praying to the gods *within themselves*, and in this sense House has usurped rock and roll to become the true "Devil's music".

The drug in question is, of course, Ecstasy. A remarkable catalyst: taken with a sexual partner, a powerful aphrodisiac; in the ritualistic environment of a House event, a modern-day, synthetic soma every bit as efficacious – if more short-lived – as the mushrooms and cacti of the Mexican Indian or Innuit shamans. And the music, ever-evolving, sculpted to stimulate and complement the effects of the Ecstasy; at once ultra-sophisticated and terrifyingly primal, its pounding electronic beat pushes the dancers toward trance while its top layer and occult frequencies trigger endorphins in their brains. Indeed, one frontline Progressive House record contains more sex, sophistication and sheer power than a hundred offerings from those poor deluded, anachronistic souls still fumbling with electric guitars and lyrics.

Like the Dreamachine, conceived in future time, the total House experience is pointing the way for individuals to achieve self-awareness by tapping into the "collective unconscious" of ritual in a non-violent convocation whose effects ripple into their personal lives and philosophies. As an at least partial antidote to the sterility, isolation and frustration of modern urban existence, its value cannot be too highly stated. For the enlightened, it's only a small step from here to the brave new world of psychoactive cocktails and Virtual Reality.

So, next time someone sneers at House music, or Ecstasy, take (just a little) pity on them; by living in the sexless straitjacket of the past, they are denying themselves access to a present which theoretically knows no boundaries.

Time is suspended, and has no meaning while the music plays.

May it play on forever.

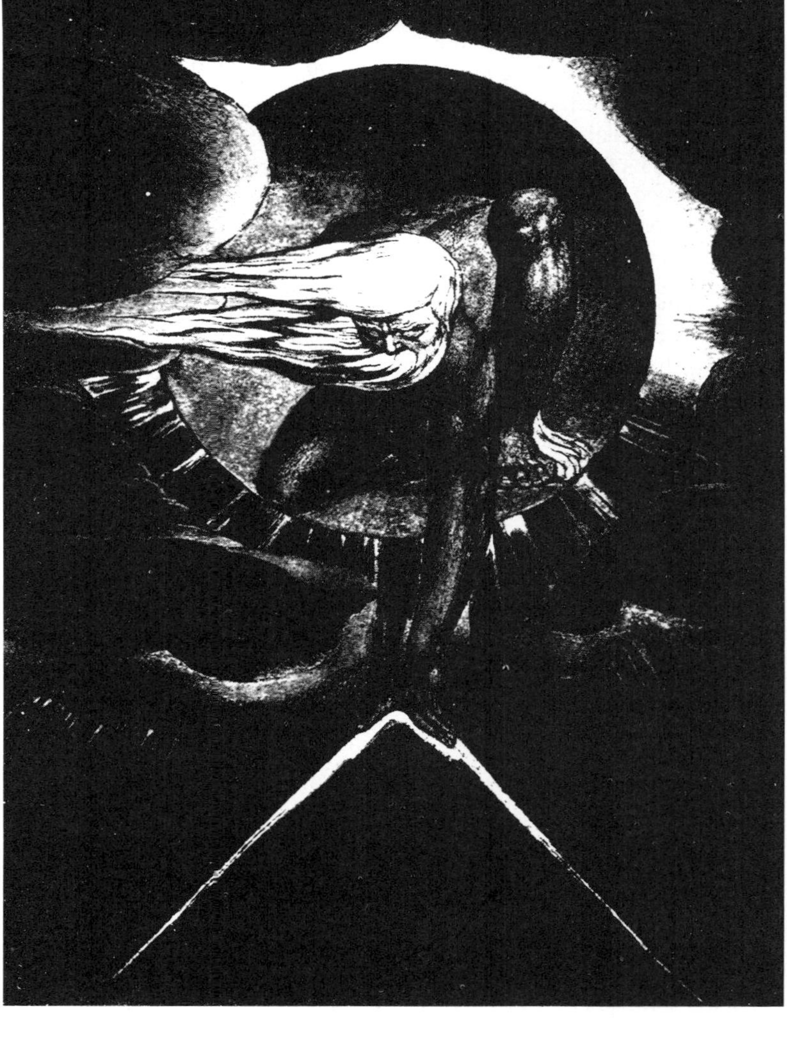

BECAUSE AND COSMOS

C. JOHN TAYLOR

The universe is so unimaginably large because Man exists. The universe had to bring Mankind into existence. The universe, in turn, exists only because Man brought it into being. Intelligent life, once it has evolved, will continue for all eternity, spread throughout the entire universe, and accumulate all the knowledge that there is to know.

A translation of chants sung in Hindi, wafted through the summer air of Surrey from a distant manor house inhabited by people with bald heads and orange kaftans? The teachings of a secret Californian mushroom cult? What Jim Jones meant to say instead of 'bottoms up'? Actually, the statements made by a very serious theory proposed by very serious scientists.

For many centuries it was taken as a fundamental law of the universe that Man was at its centre. Indeed, this notion played a very important role in Christian dogma, and anyone who thought otherwise was condemned as a heretic. The fact that the Earth and Man were at the hub of all things was obvious, wasn't it, when one could see the sun and the stars revolving around us? The only trouble was that, once the planets were identified and observed over a period of time, they were seen at certain points in their orbits to double back on themselves before turning once again and continuing in their previous direction.

This, as Nicholas Copernicus realised in 1517, was a quirk caused by the way the planets, including Earth, in their different orbits and at their different speeds, revolved around the sun. It's hard to imagine today just what an earth-shattering realisation that must have been, and Copernicus was sensible enough to go no further than to suggest that things could be explained better if this model were used. It took another 100 years before Galileo was so foolish as to say that this was the way things really were, and that all observable phenomena could be explained in terms of mathematical laws, without reference to Man. He fell foul of the Inquisition for his troubles, but eventually the overwhelming weight of scientific evidence forced this view to become accepted.

So, the idea took hold that mathematical laws defined and controlled everything in the universe, and reached its apogee in the work of Sir Isaac Newton, whose laws of motion and thermodynamics, and numerous mathematical formulations, are still fundamental to science today. Indeed, Newtonian mechanics, coupled with the reductionist philosophies of Cartesian Dualism, have today led to the generally held view that Man and Earth are no more than tiny cogs in the vast machine of the universe.

When it's reckoned that there are some one hundred thousand million (one hundred billion in common parlance) stars in our galaxy alone, and about the same number of galaxies in the universe, it's hard to think otherwise.

Only in the early decades of this century did the Cartesian/Newtonian paradigm begin to be challenged, through the work of Einstein and his theories of Relativity, and Nils Bohr in his brilliant formulation of Quantum Theory. These men and their contemporaries working in the same fields began to realise that, in describing quantum phenomena – events on a tiny, subatomic scale – the old Newtonian system simply didn't hold water anymore. New models were needed, and their implications would forever change Man's view of the universe, and his place in it. The reason our everyday lives and philosophies seem to have been so little affected is that, for general day to day occurrences, the old systems still work perfectly adequately. Nevertheless, knowledge of subatomic structures has led to such fundamentally influential devices as the microchip and the atomic bomb – not to mention the Sinclair C5 and the keyring that squeaks when you whistle for it.

Of the many startling ideas to emerge from Relativity and Quantum Physics (time dilation, gravity lenses, black holes, a bewildering variety of sub-sub-sub-atomic particles, to name but a few) possibly the most startling of all is Heisenberg's Uncertainty Principle, which suggests, in simple terms, that nothing can be said to exist until it's observed.

Electrons don't spin sedately around the nucleus, as Newtonian mechanics would have it, but rather exist as a sort of haze, representing the probability of their being in any one place at any one time. Depending on how it's observed, a subatomic unit can be said to exist as a particle, in other words a discrete package; or as a wave form. The *more* accurately a particle's momentum is measured, the *less* precisely can its position be determined, and vice versa. Likewise, the *more* precisely the energy is measured in a quantum event, the *less* accurately can its time-span be determined, and vice versa. These limitations have nothing to do with the measuring techniques used, and their possible inaccuracies. They are part of the actual fabric of the world of subatomic particles, and are very precisely described mathematically in the Uncertainty Principle. If a particle's momentum is measured precisely, it actually does not have a well-defined position; and so on. As Fritjof Capra put it in his book *'The Tao of Physics'*: *"In atomic physics, the scientist cannot play the role of the detached objective observer, but becomes involved in the world he observes to the extent that he influences the properties of the observed objects"*. Some scientists see the involvement of the observer as the most important feature in quantum theory, and have suggested replacing the word 'observer' by the word 'participator'. Until the observer observes, subatomic particles can be said to exist anywhere, or not at all. Only in the act of observation is the particle brought into existence, so to speak.

Clearly, then, early relativistic and quantum thinking led to what many scientists would regard as disturbingly metaphysical fulminations; but in the last decade or so, what has become known as the 'Anthropic Principle' (from Anthropos, Greek for 'Man') has taken metaphysics based on hard science into a whole new league.

Let's keep it fairly straightforward to start with... Why is the universe so huge? Well, the cosmological theory regarding the formation of the universe which is generally accepted these days is that of the 'Big Bang', which suggests that the universe came into existence fifteen billion or so years ago as an infinitesimally small point of matter which formed spontaneously in a complete void. This point expanded at an unimaginable speed, with an incalculably huge explosive force, to the extent that the universe is still expanding today. All matter that now exists is believed to have come from that initial tiny smidgen of proto star stuff.

When you take a moment to ponder it, this is an extremely bizarre idea in itself, and is not a million miles removed from the Judaeo- Christian belief in The Creation. It's indicative of the extent to which scientific thought has in a sense almost turned full circle since the days of Copernicus that a theory which could easily pass for a creation myth is so taken for granted today, and a fine irony indeed that such an idea has developed from Copernicus' 'heretical' views on the motion of planets. Better still, the very word 'Revolution' in the sense of radical upheaval in the spheres of politics, religion, philosophy and so on, derives its use from the book *'De Revolutionibus Orbium Coelestium'* written by Copernicus in 1543 to describe his ideas on planetary motion. One scientific 'revolution' has spawned many others, each one nowadays seemingly closer to a religious, or at least mystical weldgeist than its predecessor. Nevertheless, whereas in centuries gone by science and the church were inseparable, today any scientific theory that sounds rather similar to a religious or mystical notion has been arrived at, you can rest assured, via a very different avenue of thought and several centuries of divergent history.

Anyway...assuming the Big Bang Theory to be correct (there's a lot of evidence around to suggest that it is), and assuming to be correct the inference that atoms accreted into stars, and that more and more complex atoms were manufactured in the nuclear furnaces at the centres of the stars, then finally, after billions of years, there were all the right atoms around to form life. As it's taken billions of years for the stars to form into galaxies, and to produce the atoms required for the formation of planets and the evolution of life, and as everything has been expanding at huge speeds for billions of years away from the original point of the Big Bang, the universe simply *had* to be immense before we could come into existence; otherwise there wouldn't have been sufficient time for us to have evolved. This means that there is a direct link between our existence and the size and age of the universe. The very fact that we exist dictates, in a certain sense, what the universe looks like today. This is what is known as the Weak Anthropic Principle.

Few Scientists would disagree with this view today, because it's akin to saying that, on observing a molecule of water just beginning to oscillate at the edge of a pond, and knowing that a stone had been thrown into the pond at a certain point, it's possible to work out when the stone was thrown. The fact that the molecule has just started oscillating dictates when the stone was thrown in, and therefore when the ripples began which led to the molecule's oscillation. Nothing too startling there. The disagreement starts over whether the universe had to bring Mankind into existence. Scientists have never been noted for their ability to leave well alone, and one clever dick formulated the Strong Anthropic Principle, which states precisely that *the sole function of the universe is to bring us into being*. Before we dismiss this out of hand, let's consider the evidence.

Life, most would agree, is a product of chance. As any Star Trek fan knows, we're carbon-based life forms, and there's plenty of carbon, oxygen, nitrogen and hydrogen around for us to use. But on Earth, these elements combined in a life-enhancing way, and not into vast quantities of methane and ammonia, as on some of the other planets. For us to have evolved on Earth, a very narrow temperature range was required, so the Sun needed to have a very stable temperature (it's got one) and the Earth needed to have a very clearly circular orbit (it's got one). Similarly, if the gravity here had been a little weaker, all the atmosphere would have dissipated into space (as on the Moon), and if it had been stronger everything would have been crushed under huge pressures on the surface of the planet (as on Jupiter). If there'd been no ozone layer, deadly ultraviolet radiation would have killed everything. All in all, we're pretty lucky to be here.

But did all these factors somehow deliberately combine to produce us? An Evolutionist would argue that, on the contrary, we evolved to fit the conditions; but the amazing fact remains that, not only are conditions on Earth extremely finely balanced in favour of producing life, so are those in the entire universe.

There are dozens of 'constants' in physics, covering every imaginable aspect of physical existence. These constants appear to be so throughout the universe, and absolutely dictate its structure and appearance. The staggering fact, however, is that they interlock so precisely that if they were knocked out of equilibrium only slightly, there would be no universe. If one of the constants were changed just a few percent in one direction, the stars would burn out in a million years, rather than billions, making the evolution of life impossible. Change the constant a few percent in the other direction, and no elements heavier than helium would form, again ruling out life completely. Change the relative mass of the proton and the neutron by a mere fraction of a percent, and atoms would be unstable, meaning nothing but utter chaos. Had the Big Bang been slightly less powerful, it would have collapsed in on itself long before the heavier elements had been formed, and if it had been a little more powerful, matter would have been flung apart at too great a rate for heavier elements to ever have been formed in the first place.

Again, this is all widely agreed upon today – but why should Man hold such a privileged place in the scheme of things? Couldn't the size and age of the universe, and all the above, be inferred by looking at any animal on Earth? Proponents of the Strong Anthropic Principle would argue that the fundamental difference lies in the fact that Man is alone in understanding the laws of the universe, and is therefore somehow inextricably interwoven with them. This sounds a trifle glib, vague and unscientific, but let's persist.

In the 1950s the astronomer Fred Hoyle (since knighted for his many achievements) was working out just how the atoms in stars combined to produce the elements required for the formation of life. Stars are made up mostly of hydrogen and helium, and for carbon to be produced three helium nuclei have to collide and combine. The chances of this happening are very slim, but the strange thing is that, once two helium nuclei have combined, the resultant mass somehow makes itself much more attractive to a third helium nucleus, so immensely increasing the likelihood of a carbon atom being formed. As far as is known, this process is unique in the whole of nature, and it just happens that it has enabled enough carbon to be formed for our bodies to exist. And that's not all. If another helium nucleus hits the carbon atom, oxygen is formed; but in that case, why is there enough carbon left? It transpires that the oxygen-forming reaction is so far out of kilter with the energy requirements that it's quite unstable, and only half these collisions produce oxygen. Hoyle was so struck by all this that he was moved to say: *"A common sense interpretation of the facts suggests that a superintendent has monkeyed with physics, as well as chemistry and biology, and that there are no blind forces worth speaking about in nature. I do not believe that any physicist who examined the evidence could fail to draw the inference that the laws of nuclear physics have been deliberately designed with regard to the consequences they produce inside stars".* Remember, this is a world-renowned scientist speaking. Perhaps the Strong Anthropic Principle doesn't sound so far-fetched after all.

Once again, though, if the conditions for life are so propitious, why should such cosmic jiggery pokery favour Man to the exclusion of vast legions of other life forms which should have prospered in the same conditions throughout the universe? And for that matter, how do we know there aren't billions of other planets teeming with life anyway? The fact is that we don't, but advocates of the Strong Anthropic Principle argue that, assuming other life forms would be anything like ourselves, in that they have an instinct to explore and colonise, and given that it's fantastically improbable that we should be the most advanced race in the universe if there really are billions of others, we've seen no hard evidence whatsoever of life on other worlds, either in the form of inexplicably non-random emissions from space, or earthly visits.

You may find the assumption of human instincts in alien life forms rather unjustified and arrogant, and may argue that perhaps we're too thick to see the evidence for alien life right in front of our noses, or that any interstellar travellers who might happen to drop by our third stone from the sun would be so advanced that they could easily hide their presence from us if they wanted to. You may also insist that there's ample evidence for visitations, citing Erich von Daniken, Men in Black, abduction experiences, photographs of mysterious objects and so on; but von Daniken has long ago been thoroughly discredited, hardly any UFO pictures have stood up to rigorous analysis, and the vast majority of close encounter experiences can be ascribed to processes rather more intracerebral than extraterrestrial. All but a tiny percentage of UFO experiences can be put down to one or a combination of the following: wilful deception, self-deception, wishful thinking, unusual atmospheric conditions, car and aeroplane lights, good old planet Venus, dream and trance-like states, and Jungian 'mandala archetype' theories. The fact that a very small number of encounter and Men in Black experiences *are* very strange and sometimes disturbing, and a few photographs defy all attempts at rational analysis, does not by a long chalk prove the existence of life on other planets. Happily for those who hope life does exist throughout the universe, though, it can never be proven that earth is alone in being inhabited.

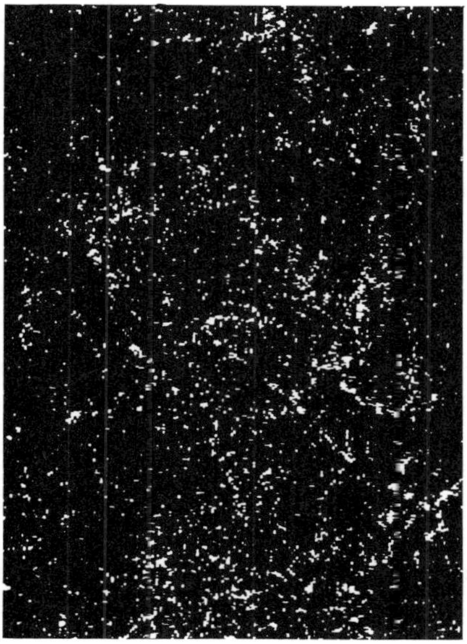

"In hearts at peace, under an English Heaven." A small sample from a map of the brightest galaxies, all relatively close to our own Milky Way galaxy. Each square is a galaxy containing billions of stars. (From a telescopic map by Donald Shane & Carl Wirtanen, Lick Observatory, California.)

So, having satisfied themselves, albeit somewhat controversially, that life exists on Earth and nowhere else, Strong Anthropicists would go on to say that, even though everything tends to be balanced in our favour, we still only just made it. It's estimated that the Sun has already used up half its available source of hydrogen, and therefore if its rate of burning had been just twice as fast (a very real possibility in cosmological terms) we wouldn't be here at all, because the Sun would have burnt out before we had a chance to evolve. Although many planets may have nearly all the right conditions for giving rise to intelligent life, in practice few, if any, may have achieved it. The universe may, after all, have given rise to life on Earth alone. We in turn are unique on Earth because we understand the laws of physics, and Anthropic commentators read great significance into the fact that, merely by using physical systems which observe the laws of nature, we are able to discover those laws of nature. If this is no coincidence, and had to be so, it is argued that we have a very significant place in the universe indeed.

Time for a little experiment, the significance of which will become apparent later.

Fig. 1 shows a laser emitting a beam of pure light, of one wavelength. This passes through a semi-silvered mirror which has the effect of splitting the beam in two. Half the photons which carry the light energy are reflected to Mirror 1, and the other half pass straight through to Mirror 2. These beams are in turn reflected, to be detected by Screen 1 and Screen 2 respectively. Now, if a second beam-splitter is inserted in the apparatus at the point where the two photon beams cross (see fig. 2) the beams hitting the screens are mixtures of photons from both paths. The second beam-splitter can then be positioned so that interference occurs – in other words, the two recombined paths of photons travelling towards one screen cancel each other out, because the troughs of their 'wave' forms exactly coincide with the peaks, and the beams to the other screen reinforce, because the troughs coincide with troughs, and the peaks coincide with peaks. Let's say the second-beam splitter is so positioned that interference occurs in the beam travelling towards Screen 2 (it would work just as well the other way). No photons will reach Screen 2, and a steady stream will reach Screen 1.

Now if we dim the laser so that only one photon passes through the apparatus at a time, with the second beam-splitter still positioned to cause interference, we would expect each screen to be struck by 50% of the photons, because each photon could travel any way through the apparatus. Surely no interference could take place, because a photon can't interfere with itself. In fact, staggering though it seems, Screen 1 receives every single photon that's emitted. Interference occurs even with one individual photon, which means that in some mysterious way each photon must go through the apparatus all possible ways at once. But how can it possibly do this? Where can each photon be said to be in the time after it leaves the laser and before it hits the screen? Nils Bohr described the area between the light source and the screen as a kind of smoky dragon, with its tail at the light source and its mouth at the screen, but a nebulous and insubstantial body in between. He believed it was pointless to discuss what the photon was 'doing' while in the apparatus.

It is perfectly possible, in fact, to observe the photon in the apparatus by moving a screen in, but in so doing you destroy the original experiment because now no interference can take place. With interference, it's impossible to observe the photon as it passes through the apparatus, so within the apparatus the photon cannot be said to exist at all, in any meaningful sense. We bring it into existence when we observe it on the screen.

Fig. 1

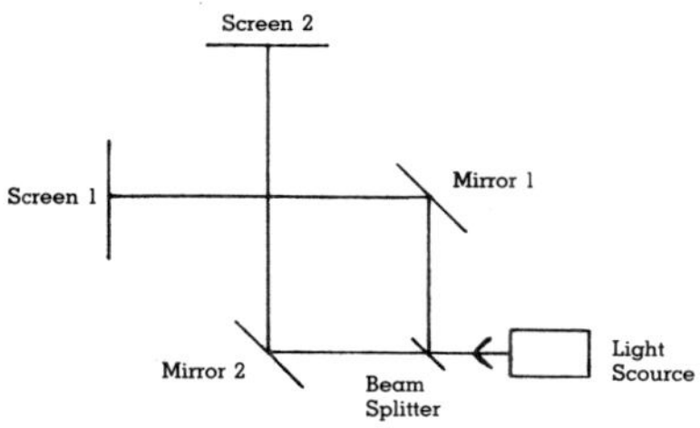

Fig. 2

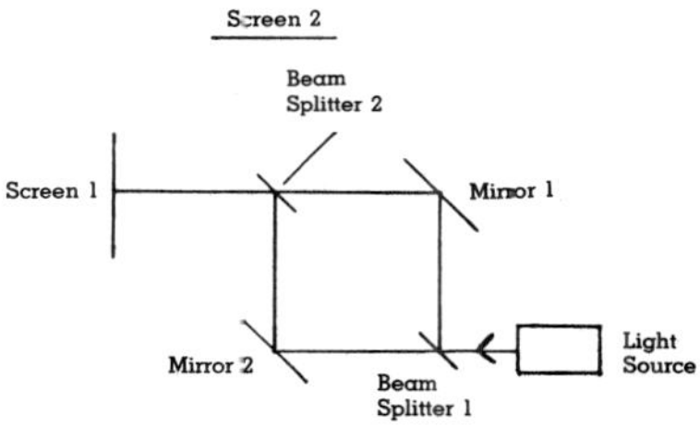

Fig. 3

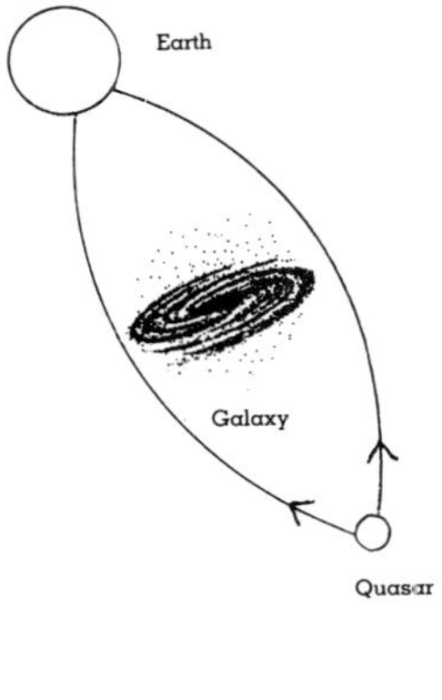

Fig. 4

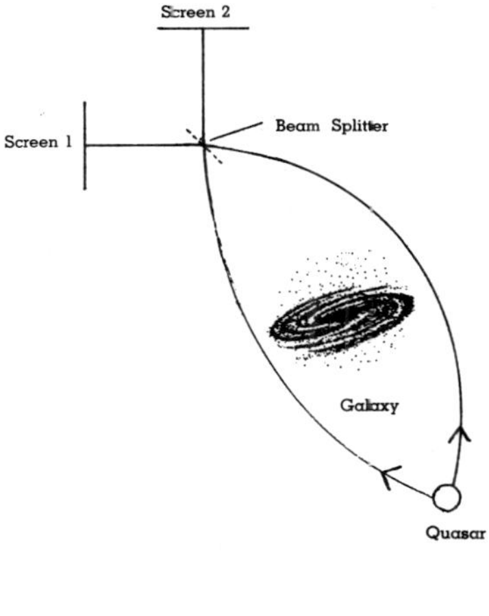

As you may have realised, the above is an example of Heisenberg's Uncertainty Principle in all its perplexing glory, and this is taken as the starting point (yes the starting point) for what is known as the Participatory Anthropic Principle. The chain of thought goes something like this: on a subatomic scale, quantum phenomena are only brought into existence by observation; but the entire universe is made up of nothing but a vast multiplicity of quantum events, interacting on a monumental scale. Therefore, why shouldn't the principle be extended to the universe as a whole? Do we need any other explanatory device for the whole of the cosmos? If not, then the universe has been brought into being by countless acts of observation, by all the observers who have ever existed, exist now, and will ever exist in the future. No other explanation is needed for the existence of the entire universe, even through the past to the Big Bang itself.

It's difficult enough to swallow this thesis even to account for the present and the future, but how on earth could the past be affected by our observations? The Anthropicists can even resolve this little teaser, but before they get a chance a few basic explanations are called for.

A light year is not a measure of time, but a measure of distance. It's the distance light travels in one year, which comes to something in the region of 5,865,696,000,000 miles (9,385,113,600,000 km). Enormous galactic and intergalactic distances are measured with the aid of the Doppler Shift technique. Its not important to go into the mechanism of the Doppler Effect here, but suffice it to say that, the greater the speed at which an object is receding from the observer, the greater the spectrum of the light it emits appears to have been shifted towards the red end. All objects recede from all others in the ever-expanding universe of the Big Bang, and Hubble's Law states that the greater the red shift of an object, and therefore the greater the speed at which it's receding from us, the further away it is. There's some controversy as to whether Hubble's Law holds for large red shifts, but let's leave that to the astronomers. All anyone can ever do in trying to make sense of the world is to go by the best knowledge available at the time. The whole of science revolves around this concept.

Quasars ('quasi-stellar objects') are star-like bodies which appear to be emitting energy of galaxy-like proportions, and are believed to be the most distant objects yet observed. Using Hubble's Law, they've been 'measured' at up to something like 15 billion light years away, a distance which is getting on for 90,000,000,000,000,000,000,000 miles (or 144, 400,000,000,000,000,000,000 km). This means, of course, that they existed about 15 billion years ago, because the light took that long to reach us.

When we observe them, therefore, we're looking billions of years into the past, to the early days of the universe.

Time for the promised teaser resolution. An astronomer by the name of Alan Stockton took a digital picture of two quasars close together. Because they appeared to be so close, and looked very similar, he suspected that they were actually the images of one and the same quasar whose light had been partly focused by an intervening galaxy acting as a gravity lens. (In Einsteinian Relativity, all masses warp the space-time continuum, and enormous masses like galaxies warp it to such a degree that light rays are deflected considerably. A huge mass, therefore, can act as a gigantic lens, with the warping effects of its associated gravity on space-time taking the place of the more familiar refractive properties of the glass in a conventional lens.) By electronic means Stockton subtracted the image of one quasar from the other, and sure enough the image of a galaxy appeared. It turned out that the galaxy was about a quarter of the way from the Earth to the quasar, and was bending light rays from the quasar that had spread 50,000 light years apart, bringing them almost back together by the time they reached Earth, so producing two images of the same quasar (see fig. 3).

Now let's go back to the beam-splitting apparatus, and do a thought experiment, a technique which is popular with scientists and which can produce results every bit as valid as the real thing. The light source is now the quasar, whose light radiates in all directions so there's no need for the first beam-splitter. The galaxy takes the place of the mirrors because, in its capacity as a gravity lens, it has the same effect of crossing the beams of photons from the quasar. The screens are placed as before. (See fig. 4). Now assume that the quasar is so faint that only one photon is emitted at a time. Intuitively we feel that, billions of years ago, each photon chose one of two possible tracks around the galaxy, and indeed over a period of time half the photons hit one screen, and half the other. Now insert the other beam-splitter to cause interference as before. The principles are identical, so again *no photons hit Screen 2*. But what could have happened to all those photons which apparently set off on their journeys billions of years ago? Only one explanation fits, and that's given by Bohr's comments on the previous experiment. The ancient light showing the distant quasar *didn't exist* until the experiment was carried out. In other words, the quasar itself didn't exist billions of years ago until the light emitted from it was observed; and what holds true for the quasar holds for the entire universe. Our observation has had a retrospective effect on events in the distant past of the universe.

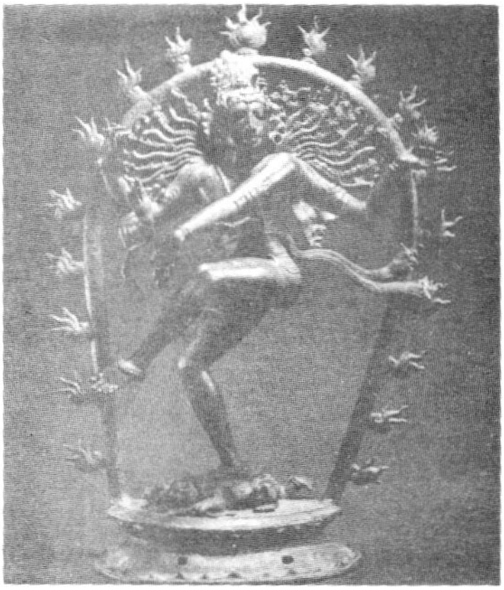

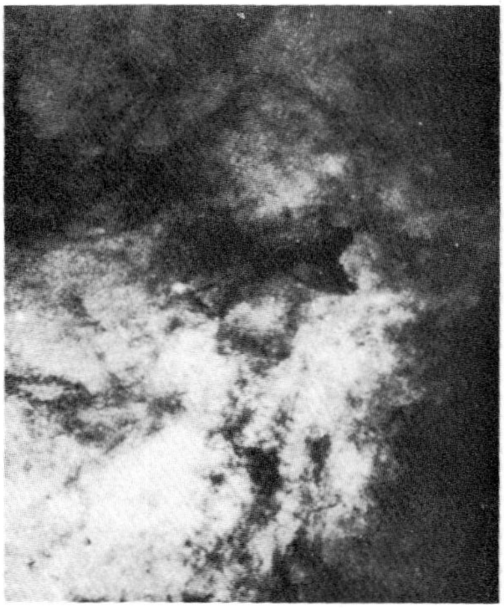

Top: The Dance of Shiva. His halo of fire represents the rhythm of the Universe and emanates from a lotus pedestal, the Hindu symbol of 'Enlightenment'. Shiva dances on the body of 'human ignorance'. The front right hand is held in the abhaya-mundra pose, which means "do not be afraid". (Norton Simon Museum, California).

"Heaven is a place / A place where nothing ever happens..." Within our own small Milky Way galaxy is the star cloud in the constellation Sagittarius. In this photograph there are about one million stars.

Another sweet irony here: René Descarte's most famous saying was *"I think, therefore I am"*. In the avowedly non-Cartesian world of Quantum Physics, Relativity and the Anthropic Principle, we seem to have arrived at the not altogether dissimilar phrase: *"I observe it, therefore it is"*. But does this mean that, whenever we observe a star or galaxy for the first time, it suddenly pops into to existence in the distant past? Maybe. The idea of the conservation of mass and energy is very Newtonian anyway, and even the Big Bang Theory talks about matter suddenly appearing out of nowhere, so who's to say that it doesn't happen all the time? And what about our apparently mystical understanding of the laws of physics? Perhaps we can decipher them so well because, in observing the universe on the microcosmic and macrocosmic scale, we actually impose our own laws on physical phenomena when our observation brings them into existence. Maybe we make up our own laws; and maybe there are some we still can't fathom because they were retrospectively brought into existence by future astronomer observers who are much more advanced than we are, and are therefore able to impose much more complex laws on the universe. And perhaps if a future astronomer observes a massive black hole in the vicinity of our solar system, we'll all be sucked into oblivion, and won't have to worry about it anymore.

To pick up the thread again, the Participatory Anthropic Principle's view of the universe makes it a kind of self-perpetuating loop. A snake biting its own tail... The Big Bang takes place, stars and planets develop, life begins, the universe is observed further and further into the past – and as such the distant past is projected from the far future. The observer at the end of time brings all the past into existence.

So what happens if all life is extinguished, if there is no observer at the end of time? The whole universe will cease to exist, and, what's more, cease to *ever have existed*. How to account for this? Well, extending the Participatory Anthropic Principle: if we exist now, it must mean that there will always be a future observer to bring us into existence. This is the essence of the Final Anthropic Principle, which states very modestly that, once intelligent life exists, it will continue to exist until the end of time, and spread throughout the entire universe. If organic life isn't up to the task, intelligent self-reproducing machines will do instead. Life, after all, can be described simply as a sum of knowledge, of many parts of a program working in unison. It's not the body that's important, it's the program, in whatever form it's carried. All our knowledge, all our culture, all that is the essence of our intelligent existence, can be carried throughout the universe by such machines, thus perpetuating life forever, and accumulating all the knowledge that there is to know, and observing all that there is to observe, until the end of time.

Perhaps the very universe itself is a single life form, programmed for total self-knowledge. Perhaps the final piece in the jigsaw of complete knowledge will be the observation of the Big Bang itself, by the observer at the end of time. Perhaps at that point the universe will wink quietly out of existence. And perhaps, then, an infinitesimally small point of matter will form spontaneously in the void... And if you think that all sounds rather pointless, think about how it compares to your own life.

Many of the above ideas bear striking similarities to the Hindu belief in the Dance of Shiva, in which the god Shiva brings the universe into existence by his dancing. When he stops dancing (observing?), the universe ceases to exist. His dance takes place over an enormous length of time, and follows cycles, wherein the universe is forever renewed, to live its life over and over again.

Christians, too, can draw comfort of sorts from the above. They're taught that God has always existed, and will always exist, that he is omniscient and omnipotent. This is a very difficult concept to grasp, but perhaps if the universe is thought of as a self-perpetuating loop, things become a little clearer. The thought may not greatly appeal to Christians, but is God the Observer at the End of Time? Is God an unimaginably large number of intelligent machines spread throughout the universe? Is God, after all, the Son of Man?

The Anthropic Principle makes considerable assumptions, but has an enormous number of religious and metaphysical ramifications, only a few of which have been touched on here. The more you think about it, the more complex it becomes. It's not overstating the case to say that it represents a revolution in scientific thought, but will it stand the test of time? Perhaps only Time itself will tell.

THE VIDEODROME – THE THING IN ROOM 101

MARK DOWNHAM

Situationism. A sixties political dada that identified and described the Society of the 'Spectacle' and encouraged an altered perception to deal with it. Twenty five years after the Student riots that it provoked, Mark Downham discovers that the Spectacle has absorbed the Situationist's original revolutionary perception and re-sequenced itself to absorb and 'recuperate' any such threats. The Spectacle is Control, the experience of a false perception of reality. We are children of the Videodrome, and nobody owns Death TV.

Programming Phenomena

"You asked me once," said O'Blivion, "what was in Room 101. I told you that you knew the answer already. Everyone knows it. The thing that is in Room 101 is the worst thing in the world...The Videodrome."

"More and more people these days are no longer gullible, they know everything is false."

Michel Prigent

Video-spectacular life revolves around twin self-reflexive switches that activate us: *Control* (Authority and Obedience) and *Behaviour* (Production and Consumption). The Videodrome is the enigma of the thing: not simply as object and commodity, but as pure object and absolute commodity. The Videodrome is the point where the image is made more concrete than the commodity. The 'Spectacle' now has a new organization of appearances. That is, VIDEO DNA LIFE, the hyperreal. More deadly than death, a vampiric carnage of virulent description. It seems to move with intelligence and purpose. Bending sound as the electron gun in the Cathode Ray tube scans the frequencies that put your brain in the alpha wave state, the *relaxed* state; and this totalitarian, electronic Oceania dredges the oceans of your subconscious in preparation for the embedding.

The "Spectacle" is going through an evolutionary jump and is becoming more than the facility with which images can be detached and alienated from their sources and reorganised for representation in accord with initial stages of the Spectacle; where everything that was once directly experienced has already shifted into its own representation. The Spectacle has always been more than just a collection of images; and the Spectacular Videodrome is much more than a social relation among people mediated by images, more than Capital to such a degree of accumulation that it becomes an image. It is a VIDEO DNA GESTALT.

The Videodrome is debordment, overflow; it is hypervisibility: here even terrorism is a neurosis – the violence of a society without secrets; totally media-transparent, a spectacular gesture from the see-through, silent age.

In the Videodrome there is nowhere to hide. There are only terminals, and we are the terminals for our alienated experiences – the spectacle of our deepest secret fears. It's so much television that it isn't television at all – it's a monstrous double. The ecstasy of too much, of more X than X, of televised videodrome image overload (T.V.O.D.), spectacular excess. Just when you thought it was safe to switch your television back on, you get bombarded with televised videodrome image overload – the Cathode Ray tube sprays its message at you, point-blank, you haven't got a chance. Here they come, subliminal spectacular spores! Reminding you as they peel back your skin to access, that the television screen is the retina of the mind's eye, the manipulator of the imagination and the invader of the subconscious. The Videodrome is your deepest secret fears played back to you, come back to plague you. *The Videodrome is the destruction of the autonomous imagination*. Every person's subconscious contains the total collective unconscious, which is recuperated by the Spectacular Videodrome into the Communications Landscape – that inscape, that interzone of phenomena, evolution, revolution and 'everyday life'. The hyperreal Videodrome is growing and mutating so that, in effect, 'reality' no longer exists autonomously.

The television screen is like the cerebral cortex and they are aspects of each other – aerials in the ether, motes in the eye, and so whatever manifests itself on the television screen emerges as raw experience for those who watch it, as it watches them. Therefore television is an expression of VIDEO DNA Spectacular reality; 'reality' only as it is mediated through the Videodrome, 1,000 centuries in the worst place in the world, Room 101, dystopia revisited and looped again and again. The video-DNA mind which is building its own secrets into the world manipulates everyone through dominant power-elite conspiracies, 1984 Leviathan bureaucracies, labyrinthine media realities, the military/industrial state complex, the cycle of production and consumption. It is the materialised trinity of the State, the Commodity, and the serried, serial ranks of the mass Media. For when you perceive the world through spectacular mediations, you perceive the superimposed shape of the cathode ray tube on your own cerebral cortex; valves, filaments, silicon chips on your ganglia. *The Spectacle invades your mind,* your subconscious in the communications landscape...through endless repetition, replication and insertions.

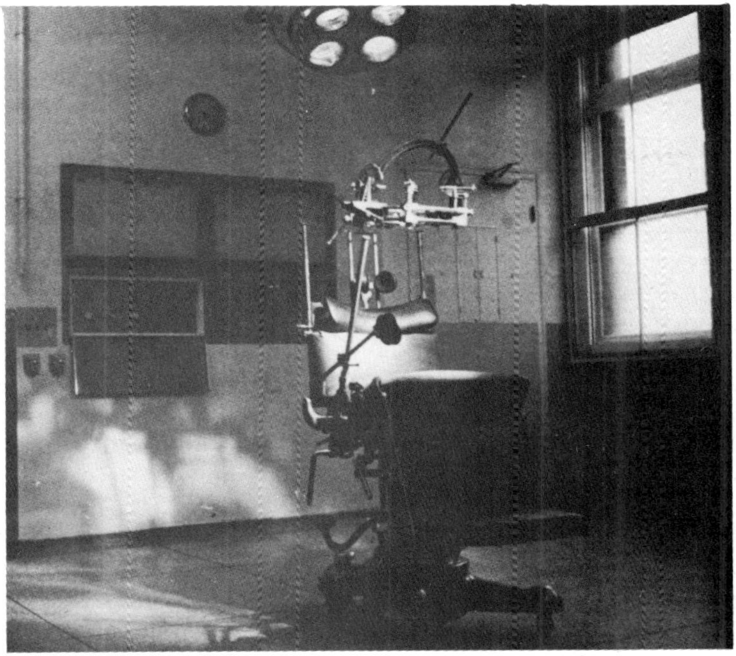

To experience this, to try to understand it and begin to decode it is to confront and resist the false realisations (revelations, perhaps) flooding towards you; released from some video-genetic storage unit in the Video-DNA Spectacle. It tells you that all the photonic video-DNA molecules in the Spectacle are, on some subliminal subatomic level, working in collaboration and always have been. They are spectacular-atomic structures, but ultimately they are forms of information. A vast, interconnected web of information, like the cells in a human brain or the mass media of print, billboards, sound, vision, media images, disinformation, propaganda, the silicon chips in a TV set...Any single molecule is, of course, nothing more than a molecule; but all the Video-DNA, taken as Gestalt, constitutes the Spectacular Videodrome itself, an ordered, evolving unity – of miseries.

Here, at the Event Horizon.

"There is an immense quantity of important contemporary phenomena that remains completely unchallenged – to be realistic, completely unnoticed by radical critique."

Chris Shutes

The Videodrome: Video-spectacular knowledge is capital intensified knowledge – capital moving beyond its accumulation into an image – an evolving video simulacrum of itself, pure anti-matter. This process has caused perceptions of reality to go through changes, adjustments, they are once again being re-distorted by the insertion of a vast new mediational system into an already multi-plexed, anti-historically accumulated maze.

In the context of these changes, the relationship of information to spectacular society and alienated nature has to be rethought – a new praxis is needed. It is clear that the phenomenon of self-organisation is not limited to living matter, but also occurs in certain energy, chemical, social, 'material' and meta-image geist systems which contain similar dynamic quantum properties. The Spectacular Videodrome is one of these systems. It releases a form of video DNA electromagnetic pulse or field; and everything in post modernity is drawn into its event horizon and then goes into the Spectacle. All these systems are 'dissipative structures' in that they break down other systems in the process of metabolism or recuperation, so creating only the appearance of change. The frequencies, falsely revelatory states of stimulus, production and consumption released by these Spectacular feeding frenzies come at you through subliminal visual and sonic Pavlovian triggers, for which there is no defence (some always get through in this hypnotic triggering siren song). The Spectacular control implants are usually superficial grafts, but the general self-valorised confusion that is generated by one's false contestations makes any conscious, ritualistic negation or refusal superficial and counterfeitist, because of the prigoginic levels of complexity involved – since the Spectacular turbulence of phenomena, event, and pre-situation immediately congeal and petrify into dead pre-history (history beginning with its self-realisation).

The components of the Videodrome are mainframes, minis, micros and personal computers, TV sets, printers, copiers, automated cashpoints, automatons, point-of-sale sensors, aerials, surveillance technology, fibre optic wires, hackers, bio and silicon chips, software, hardcore, tapes, discs, diagnostic equipment – a babble, babel, Babylon of Spectacularly appropriated languages, ju-ju, telephones, modems, telexes, relays, radio, cable, satellites, the semaphore of social communications systems, visual body languages, the shifts of Capital through the electronic plasma of the video DNA. The terrain has really changed since 'The Society of the Spectacle' (DeBord). It's pure programming phenomena and information now. Therefore it is no longer merely a question of the subversion of social relations or of making radical changes in *'everyday life'* (Vaneigem). Everything is being drawn, inch by inch, towards the new spectacular event horizon, the information Babylon, the image syndrome, THE DNA VIDEODROME. The technology of the Videodrome is now interphasing with the nervous system through a variety of devices, becoming day by day more fused and symbiotic. It can be seen most clearly in the medical data bases, military experiments at Porton Down, diagnostic and treatment machines buzzing in BUPA hospitals. The video DNA world is becoming wired-up to the brain nerve complex with the invention of new sensing devices and psycho-perceptual systems. The Spectacle is scrambling and re-sequencing itself with new simultaneities and juxtapositions. There are also recombinant changes going on with the rise of multi-nationals, artificial intelligence, cyber space and gene programmes...

"Spectacular commodity society is a phase in modern capitalism and it is more of a misery than a conspiracy."

Michel Prigent

...it's now possible to alter the genetic code with a virus which works parasitically by inserting its genetic code into the nucleus of a cell so that the cell starts using the code to make more viruses. It can be programmed, like video DNA, to wait. Instead of immediately making more viruses, the cell just incorporates the viral DNA codes into its own, making it go into hibernation like a control-imperative inserted trigger, and then, 5 or 10 years later, triggered into pre-coded action. It's very simple, and it seems that in this way the Videodrome is attempting to recuperate everyone by their own video-genetic codes . . .

"Recombinant DNA for profit or genetic engineering is finding new uses in production, while the growing influence of psychobiology promises greater social control..."

Phil Mailer

The struggle purely over the MASS of production, *'the dignity of labour'*, the industrial workers of the world, most elements at Wapping, *are all pre-history*. A history lost or virally infiltrated by the miseries of the decomposition of unions, leftism, and the division of labour. The necessity of the Videodrome is to translate all living forms into non-living forms, to simulate events and natural processes, to chart interactions and simulate these towards a total environment. Hegel called this phenomenon *'the cunning of reason'* – which means the sum total of alienated human consciousness as hardcore 'Spectacle' rising out of the real; permeated with the (historical) real but grown to such fantastic, grotesque and mutated proportions through the (Mass Media Inc.) 'information videodrome', that it is itself the dominant false reality; making the Spectacle an (idiot) 'intelligence' on the fifth prigoginic level of complexity – a loosely autonomous gestalt.

"The Spectacle is sustained not by images produced by the media, but by US when we reproduce these images in our daily life – which, in turn, are reported by the media as examples of reality...a mass media allows for the mass dissemination of illusions."

Larry Law

"When the real world changes into simple images, simple images become real things and effectiveness motivations of a hypnotic behaviour."

Guy Debord

"Most people will tell you that they aren't fooled by advertising and that they don't believe all they read in the newspapers or see on the television. We should not cynically dismiss these claims – even when we see them continue to uncritically consume the advertised products, read the newspapers and watch television – to do so would be to totally misunderstand the nature of propaganda in spectacular society."

Larry Law

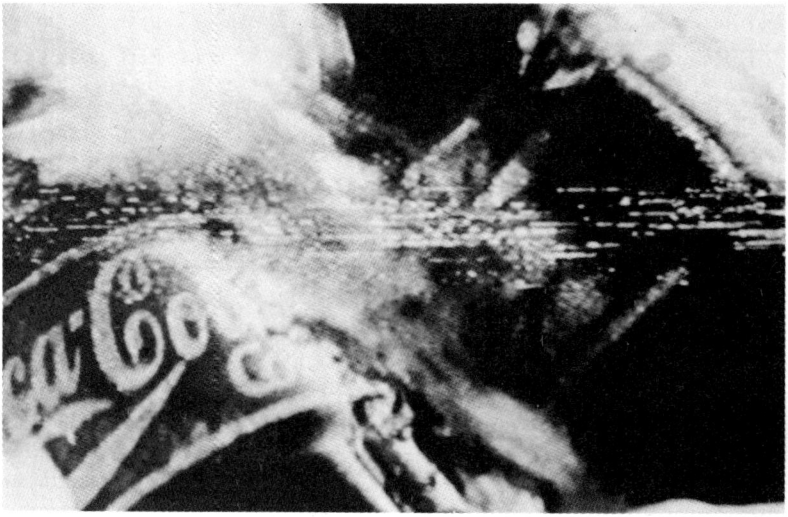

The Videodrome is assisted and developed by a legion of collaborators – psychologists, psychopaths, psychotherapists, sociologists, pop-politico revolutionaries, assassins, analysts, encoders, cryptographers, advertisers, consultants, booksellers, situationists, surrealists, historians, Leninites, economists, critics, mystics, myth makers, incoherent intellectuals, imagified proletarians, and the queue waiting to join the list.

"The modernisation of the old world advances implacably behind the dissimulations of the spectacle of economic decomposition...a pseudo-dialogue that dominates the relations of alienated daily life and the pseudo-communication that develops there: the deluge of words that covers every single aspect of 'reality'."

William Spencer

But Marx, for instance, realised that 'cunning of history', whereby dialectical counterblasts such as 'commodity' are possible, because 'material' social history (which is realised in commodities or assemblies) is making its own jump.

"These organisations! These terms! Left/Right/Social Democratic/ Trotskyist/Marxist/Leninist/ Anarchist are now totally inadequate both theoretically and practically to deal with what is different in the historically unprecedented situation which is now developing in the U.K."

Dave Wise

An international network of hackers is growing: whole nations can be ripped off – their repressive economies collapsed – since their total economies can be simulated and displayed on some electronic input/output device – and be more real than the real thing.

National boundaries are becoming porous and eroding – everywhere can be anywhere in the Videodrome, as transnational data-flows penetrate and disrupt borders. Nations and their security systems become illusions as multi-national enterprises buy pieces of the globe, industrial espionage and sabotage escalate and hackers loot at random like international vandals, giving the informational process some concrete results. Wapping was another sign of the jump of history, of these changes: away from the misery of unions (which are a union of miseries) towards the explosive emergence of commodity or assembly; which involves individuals from every background combining together into a community geist/gestalt – it is there in every strike, riot, act of sabotage, hack-in, intervention, wildcat action, occupation – every situation...*the spirit won't be denied.*

"A change in history is always, in the last analysis, brought about by a change in ideas; even though a change in ideas might bring into play material forces which reinforced that change, or have material consequences which are instrumental in realising that change, or have material consequences far beyond what we imagined."

The Pleasure Tendency

Primordial Videodrome – Get Ready, Here Come the Subliminals!

"The totally inhuman reality of the commodity as a social relation constantly gains in cohesion, tends towards the point of absolute reification of the world."

Daniel Denevert

"All human activity has become subordinate to the production and consumption of commodities."

Michel Prigent

The Videodrome is where the medium and the message merge, but there has been a divorce between sight and insight with the dissolution of T.V.O.D. into life, and the dissolution of life into T.V.O.D. We live in the video DNA hyperreal, in a universe everywhere strangely similar to the original – here things are duplicated by their own appearance, their double – the materialised image. The Videodrome is the realisation of the image of Leviathan in Hobbes; a Megaman composed of a vast congregation of alienated individuals. Here at the event horizon the distinctions between cause and effect, between active and passive, between subject and object, between ends and means, between the real and the hyperreal converge – held in replicate in video DNA.

"The management 'allows' us to consume to the rhythm of the muzak."

Nick Brandt

"A subject is presented with a set of choices. They are all bad. Under the circumstances the subject consciously chooses what he or she feels is the lesser evil. The aim of the controller is to keep the tension surrounding the choice at a high level, so that no alternative choices outside those proposed are offered or perceived. It is the equivalent of locking someone in a mental box, the perfect controlled environment. Once one such choice is made, the next set of 'choices' can be presented. As long as the choices

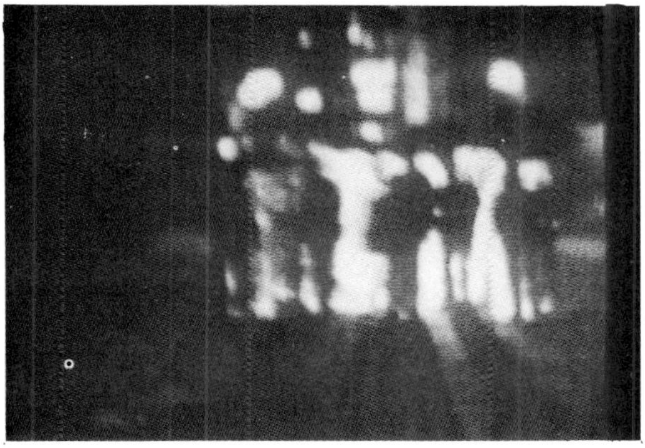

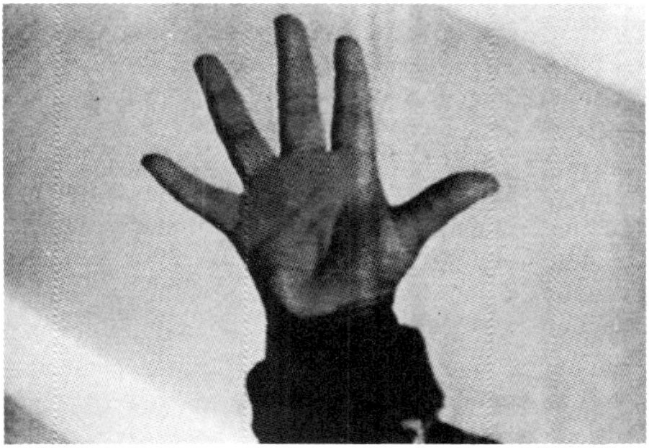

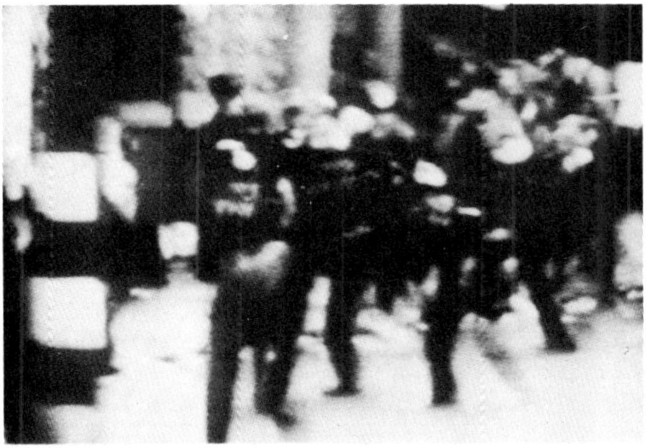

are regulated – that is the subject or subject population perceives that it has only the set of choices presented – the outcome is also regulated...it is important that you – the victim – feel that there is no cause and effect in this world, simply information. From here on in there will be no release from the tension, only an escalating series of crises...(Production, Consumption, Simulation, Excitation, Stimulation, Craving, Production, Consumption ...)"

Lonnie Wolfe

"We did as we were told to do..."

Milgram's 37 at the Chicago Institute of Psychology

Advertisements are part of the video DNA (idiot sentient) demiurge; another aspect of the video DNA hyperreal. The spectacular-cultural forces cum spectacular commodity field moulding and reflecting the alienations of our daily lives today in the Spectacle or primordial Videodrome. In the Videodrome, production and consumption are changing to the proteinic moment of connections, contact, feedback, and the generalised interface that goes with spectacular totality. Television increasingly uses soundtrack mixes of fluids, electronics, heartbeats, relays and breathing. The Videodrome tries to make the complexity of its control network too difficult for our minds to grasp – this leads to conspiracy theories. Conspiracy theories applied to advancing technologies lead to negative, paranoid technophobia.

"Confusion, or deliberately manoeuvring so as to create it, has for a long time been the practice of States when they fear a coming confrontation."

Lou Forsyth

Advertisements are everywhere. They have become embedded in the social environment and their constant presence is a reinforcement and an inevitable part of everyone's daily survival. Even if you block out most forms of media stimuli trying to implant post-hypnotic suggestions into your mind; the images, the spectacular spores posted all over our environment are inescapable. Pervading all media, limited to none, advertising forms a vast superluminal topography and subliminalised superstructure, like social pheromones – an Auschwitz of consumption, in which work makes you free...to consume.

Obviously adverts as part of the spectacular-commodity field have the initial function to sell things to us, to get us to consume, but as part of the

Spectacular Videodrome they have a deeper function. Adverts displace art, religion and the spectacle of revolt. They create structures of subliminal meaning, psycho ideologies which trigger and reinforce the dominant ideology. Advertisements implant more than just consumption; they are part of a structure in which objects and people are interchangeable, they sell us ourselves in Room 101. Advertisements are simple videodrome ideologies that can incorporate anything (and some people in the marginal *'pop muzak'* spectacle can't sign up quick enough), even reabsorb criticism of themselves, because they are dissipative structures and because they refer to it devoid of content. The whole spectacular-commodity system of advertising is part of the great recuperator: The Videodrome. It will work on any material at all, hollowing out historical meaning from structures and suspending them in timeless self-reflexive inertia...But it *can* be negated and decoded, through the creation of ongoing situations.

Video Spectacular Commodity Hype: Collapsing New People

"In the essential movement of the Spectacle, which consists of taking up all that existed in human activity in a fluid state so as to possess it in a congealed state as things which have become the exclusive value by their formulation in the negative of lived value, we recognise our old enemy, the commodity, who knows so well how to seem at first glance something trivial and obvious, while on the contrary it is so full of metaphysical subtleties. This is the principle of commodity fetishism, the domination of society by intangible as well as tangible 'things', which reaches its absolute fulfilment in the spectacle, where the tangible world is replaced by a selection of images which exist above it, and which simultaneously impose themselves as the tangible par excellence."

Guy Debord

The Videodrome has its roots in the stimulus addictive commodity culture and it is realised through the commodity in fashion, style, newness – the obsessions of the '80s. The spectacular videodrome generates subliminal overstimulation, and this hype leads to a craving for stimulation for its own sake.

More addictive than Crack: SPECTACULAR HYPE

The Videodrome through the television screen (in words, sound, visual imagery) releases spores which make us gorge ourselves on it, always wanting more, whether it's tactile, sexual, social, material or emotional – *seeking what we can never find – the realisation of our desires*. The video spectacular pulse inserts a permanent feeling of dissatisfaction of the senses, a crisis of identity, a confusion with personality. It collapses each new construct it proffers, it collapses new people. This is an ever – accelerating law of diminishing returns – craving, production, consumption, simulation, excitation, stimulation, craving – the video spectacular hype is never over. The Videodrome is the deepest fix you'll ever crave and it's a craving stimulus junkies never shake.

More descriptive than description: SPECTACULAR HYPE

SPECTACULAR HYPE? This is the Spectacle as a commodity social relation invoking that which is Most, the Best, the Absolute. The simulated feeling of being drunk on history out of control; that big black motorcycle of video DNA commodity implants careering under you as your roar with uncontrollable laughter feeling like the Archangel Michael on speed. TOTAL power – that's what the addiction of spectacular hype is like – craziness without consequence.

The Videodrome is the spectacularly boosted equivalent of the ultimate object – but it is also subliminally virulent description which induces frenzied consumption in the pursuit of beating everyone else, the ecstasy of endless one-upping, the fascination with luxury, the fetishisation of undirected spectacular charisma as a sign of being so over hyped that you survive intensity, survive totally. Brian Jones went all the way and consumed his own death. The Spectacular Videodrome provokes and annihilates desire and provokes it again because that desire can never die, because it can never be fulfilled. Spectacular hype is pure video DNA promotion – promoting itself. The relation reinforcing its own dominance: the object (Brand X, Brian Jones) is only ever a pretext, a decoy, a diversion, a ceremonial trigger. Spectacular hype summons us not to differentiate between objects, but to falsely discriminate. To exercise a controlled choice' while in an hypnotic fascination between falsely competing brands of spectacular hype, shimmering illusions of the spectacle.

"What hides under the spectacular oppositions is a unity of miseries."

Guy Debord

Television is the main means of accessing to the hallucinatory world of television videodrome image overload (T.V.O.D.). It is also ultimately lethal and tumour-inducing as all spectacular optical events are. The Spectacle is the death instinct, the Videodrome is death T.V., it killed Brian Jones. It had to. It has to. It must overwhelm and swamp the objects that act as pretexts in the commodity social relation. Spectacular hype is the dream of death, a dream of absolute commodity – like Brian Jones – some arch object, some corrupted and terribly transcendent decomposed thing which floats glowing...waiting with simulated sincerity, knowing possibly like Brian Jones did, that it is to be sacrificed to spectacular hype by those video DNA subliminal insertions in the collective unconscious. Lured, dragged along, exhausted, stood ironic and indifferent as it participates in its own annihilation...*"This is a song about Brian Jones, the one in the Rolling Stones..."*, a proffered offering to spectacular hype – Primordial Videodrome. The Videodrome is the update, the charnel house of spectacular subliminal language. Take your room – the walls have been rebuilt; the decor updated (video, hi-fi, CD, computer, subliminal triggers, hallucinogenic transmissions...); but the familiar torture chamber is the same. THE VIDEODROME OWNS DEATH T.V. Just watch it collapsing new people. The worst thing in the world is not live burial, drowning, fire, impalement – but the Videodrome that surrounds us – the thing in Room 101 – *that is the worst thing in the world.*

The Subversion of Decoding, the Decoding of Subversion

Ideology: This is the system of video spectacular representations controlling, in the Videodrome, the relation of all individuals to the activities fixed by the structure of the Videodrome.

"Counterfeitism: The misuse of detournement/subversion resulting from a confusing adaption of spectacular identity by the detourner."

Isaac Cronin

"History about to undergo a fundamental change, manifests in the individual as a fundamental change in his life...you reverse the perspective of power by returning to pleasure the energies stolen by work and constraint."

Raoul Vaneigem

William Burroughs developed a counterfeit theory of subversion which relied heavily on tape recorders, tape and sound cut-up techniques, known well to readers of *Rapid Eye*. But this was only a recording of the Videodrome's treatment of behaviour modification. Burroughs only wanted to use subliminal triggers, impulses, insertions for his own perpetuated misery. He equated liberation from habitual social / neurological associations with counterfeitist *freedom from 'control'*. The counterfeitist goal of Burroughs' techniques was for the individual to know what *is* going on well enough to stay one step ahead of the control machine. Not to transform the Videodrome, but to manipulate its marginal relationships to one's own ends; like all other spectacular philosophers, pundits, politicos, pop stars, and poets. According to Burroughs, being compulsively unpredictable is supposedly being rebellious because society is meant to be based on its ability to predict the future. Chaos and madness will remedy video biological conditioning by shocking the sleeping awake. All this assumes that decoding is a ritual, a fierce surrealistic disruption of the organisation of appearances which leaves your newly discovered backbone, the deep brain, supposedly capable of seizing radical consciousness. But with undeveloped replication this is subverted into the spectacle of 'revolt'. The de-control process is *not* just a question of cut-ups, edited blocks of images and sound, *'Apocalypse Now'* type close-ups; nor is it understanding that when things are transmitted at you that ideas will become ideologies; or just assuming that decoding as a ritual will penetrate the Video DNA informational shell which is imposed on us and subliminally inserted throughout the 24 hour horror show of the Videodrome. Setting Harold Wilson cum Neil Kinnock speaking about the white heat of the industrial revolution with the Dr. Who theme tune might bring about a useful leap in consciousness, but it is only superficial accessing to the decoder.

Since the Videodrome is a *total* environment, the deconstruction must be a *total* environment, and this environment begins to emerge only when you realise that the map is not the territory, the menu not the meal, the diagram not the dialectic. You realise that there is a dialectical-decoding shift between the abstract relief of the Videodrome and the material relations of the situation. The central activity of this process is the construction of 'SITUATIONS' in all the above forms and then trying these leaps in awareness back to psycho-geographical 'drifting'.

Decoding as drifting involves the conscious investigation of the urban mass – the architecture and the environment to sort out conscious and unconscious emotional and psychological responses to the multi-levelled geography of the architectures of the Videodrome – to create, to make psycho emotional maps of transformed areas, events, riots, occupations, assemblies, cut-ups, edits, new contents, dialectical jumps and to invent 'situations' which will fantastically transform the spectacular relationships in those areas.

IT IS THE UNLEASHING OF VIOLENT DESIRE, CREATIVITY, INVENTIVENESS, DESIRE, WHICH, THROUGH DECODING ONESELF CREATES NEW CHANGES IN ACTIVITY AND CONSCIOUSNESS. IT RELEASES THE MARVELLOUS, THE IMAGINATIVE AND THE SURREAL INTO EVERYDAY LIFE.

Decoding is a total adventure which resists video spectacular deadness, petrification and decomposition. Drifting and decoding is the wonderfully dangerous accumulation of incredible effects on consciousness and activity. Decoding is seeking out and experiencing the significance of mysterious, wonderful and apparently unrelated objects. A huge network of possibilities, entropies, energies, ciphers and encoded instructions surround us in reality. They need to be hacked from the Videodrome. Decoding is the destruction of the spectacularly hyped importance of each autonomous element in the dialectical landscape, and at the same time the organisation of a decoded series of relationships that confer on that element, the emerging 'situation'; new scope and effect.

The *'Situation'*, which is what the decoder essentially is, remains the paradox of the palindrome, it is both new territories and new maps. The Videodrome is a palimpsest, it recuperates relationships, draws them into the Video DNA spectacle – do decode it, but make no mistake, the Videodrome is spectacular purity. It survives and imposes survivalism; because it is unclouded by conscience, remorse or delusions of morality. But it is not invulnerable, and the Situationist drives the stake home.

WORDS FROM A ROOM

INTERVIEW WITH HUBERT SELBY JR.

PAT HOLLIS

"The facts about anything, and especially about a man's writing, are usually so much dust in the eye. What is important to know about a writer is given in his writing. No amount of information about a writer will clear up the controversy which his work arouses, if he is a controversial writer. The discerning ones will read between the lines; the patient, plodding researcher will only grow more confused."

Henry Miller

I wouldn't be the first person to suggest that Hubert Selby is one of the more important American writers of the 20th Century. But, for some reason, he's never achieved the recognition of writers he is occasionally compared to, for example, William Burroughs and Charles Bukowski. He certainly never developed the public persona that surrounds both these writers and, in fact, keeps a public profile that is low to the point of invisibility. Until quite recently, few people even knew that he was still alive.

A film adaptation of Selby's most famous work, *Last Exit to Brooklyn*, was in post-production at the time we spoke, and was released in Britain in 1991. Selby lent his enthusiastic support to the project in an advisory capacity.

Although Selby is best known for *Last Exit*, his other works certainly deserve attention: *The Room, Demon, Requiem for a Dream* and *Song of the Silent Snow*.

RE: I wonder if you would tell us a little of your past prior to writing 'Last Exit'.

HS: *"Well, briefly, I left school when I was about fifteen and started working in the harbour on dredgers and tug boats and, when I was sixteen, I went to Europe on a liberty ship. I had been a big kid, a healthy kid, and just never went to school and I never bothered using my head a lot, so when I got sick, it really screwed me around because when I was eighteen, I was taken off the ship in Germany with TB, and they said I wouldn't live more than a couple of months."*

What year was that?

"That was in 1946, and I came back to America in October of 1946, and they used Streptomycin to keep me alive and eventually they cut out ten ribs and collapsed a lung, cut a piece out of the other lung and I spent three and a half years in hospital."

Is this back when they had TB sanatoriums?

"Right. So it really turned my life around. I started to read books, shoot-em-up and things to pass the time, and then I eventually got out of hospital. I was in and out for a while and for a while I hung out with some friends of mine down around the army base in Brooklyn where 'Last Exit' takes place. Then I started hanging out in a bar with some friends from the neighbourhood in Brooklyn where I lived, and one of them was Gil Sorrentino, the writer, who was really my mentor. They were going to college, I guess, at the time or something, I don't know. Anyway, I used to sit and listen to them and they would talk about people like Ezra Pound, William Caulder Williams etc., and I would listen and try to remember as many names as I could. Then the next day I would sneak over to the library, making sure nobody saw me."

Didn't want to ruin your reputation?

"Yeah. And I'd get out whatever books I could. I started reading and, reading everybody at once. Which is really kind of nice because I didn't have to work out any influence. I remember when Gil was moving, we were helping him move, and he had this big box of papers, manuscripts and stuff, and naturally we sat around and started reading it. He'd read something, and you could tell who he was reading at the time. That's the stuff he wrote when he was a teenager. You could tell he was reading Williams or Eliot or Pound, you know, because that's what the poems sounded like. So I didn't have to work out any influence like that because I never concentrated on one writer or one country or period of writing. I might be reading Hemingway one day, Anatole the next day, or Rabelais or Homer, whatever I could get from the library."

Self-education.

"I suppose that's what it would be called."

So, then, what prompted you to begin writing your stories for 'Last Exit to Brooklyn'?

"Well, a couple of times they said I wouldn't live long, and then I finally got out of hospital. I was married and we had a daughter a couple of years old, and I was taken back into hospital with asthma, and this one doctor, a so-called specialist, told me 'You know, you just don't have any lungs, and you can't live. Nothing we can do for you, just go home, sit in a chair, and don't move.' He walked away and sent me a bill. You know, consultation fee. He never even came into my room. I remember him so clearly, just sitting in the hallway and he talked to me for about two minutes."

I work in the medical profession in my regular job.

"Oh really? Then you know, man, they're just unscrupulous,

unbelievable. Eventually I was back in the hospital again. This time an allergist started treating me, and I was on disability; my wife was working at Macy's, if I remember correctly. And I had an experience, what I realise today was a spiritual experience, although at the time I never thought of it as such. Just something that happened. But, as you know, with spiritual experiences, they are more real than any experience we have on this level of living. It was very intense and I experienced it in all of my dreams."

When you finished writing 'Last Exit', did you have any trouble publishing it?

"Well by that time I was hanging out with poets, writers, painters and musicians, and just about every weekend we were over at Roi's house, Le Roi Jones, now Amiri Baraka. He always had a big apartment and we just kind of hung out there, and people would read my stuff and they liked it. And Seymour Kerr, a commercial publisher, had me send the stuff up there, and they asked me to come over for lunch and talk about it. What they wanted me to do was sign a contract with them and write a novel, and after they published the novel, then they would publish 'Last Exit'. They said no, a book like this never sell, and so on, so you write a novel first.

"I went into the Cedar Street Bar where we hung out that night and told Roi what had happened at the publishers and he asked why I didn't get an agent. I told him I didn't know anything about agents or publishing, I was just trying to write the best story I could. He said, 'Well, Sterling Lord is Jack Kerouac's agent, why don't you try him?' So I called him up and gave him the manuscript, and a few days later he called back and said 'I read it and I think we can make money together'. So he submitted it to Grove [Press]. They accepted it and, by that time, Gil Sorrentino was working at Grove as an assistant editor, and he had written a really detailed critique of 'Last Exit', one of the things that Grove did to help sell the book. They sent out a copy of Gil's critique along with all the review copies.

"I didn't think of 'Last Exit' as being unusual or anything else, but evidently it was. It was not a very common kind of book, and these people who make their living reviewing books etc. are usually rather academic people and have no idea what the hell is going on in the world. Coming across something of this nature, I now realise today from what I've since been told, would have dumbfounded them. They wouldn't know what the hell to do. They would be afraid to say they liked it, and were afraid to put it down because they didn't want to look like fools. Having this triumph, so to speak, helped them, and it got some wonderful reviews.

Another thing that really helped was Time magazine reviewed it and called it 'Grove's dirty book of the month'. That gave everybody ammunition to attack Time, and Newsweek gave me a big spread, and Grove took out a full page ad in the New York Times, and the thing just went on from there."

How was your life following publication? I believe it sold quite a few thousand copies.

"Yeah, it did very well. It had quite a few printings in hardback and paperback, and was translated into quite a few languages, and I just went on from there."

You had no problem with censorship?

"Well, in England they had a debate about it in the House of Commons for two weeks, and they had a big court case that ended with them forming an organisation of people like Anthony Burgess and Sam Beckett and so forth, to defend the book. That organisation still exists."

A similar thing happened to Henry Miller's stuff when they tried to publish it here in the States. To switch topics, when did you start writing 'Demon'?

"'Demon'. When the hell did I write 'Demon'!? Oh, 1975, I think."

Why the long time period between books?

"Well, 'The Room' was written before 'Demon'. I wrote 'The Room' in 1970. After 'Last Exit' was published, some money started coming in and I found it very easy to sit around and do nothing but stay drunk."

Were you a success at that?

"I think so. I drank myself to death and now I haven't had a drink in nineteen years, so I guess I was a success."

Certainly you went as far with it as you could.

"Yeah, I couldn't go any further without drowning. I mean, when something kills you, that's about as far as you can go with it."

When you started to write 'The Room', was it prior to your decision to stop drinking?

"No. That happened after. I was sober when I wrote 'The Room'. That book is a good example of a lot of things for me. I didn't read that book for twelve years, and I just re-read it a year or two ago, and my initial impression was right. It's the most disturbing book I've ever read in my life. It's horrifying, but at the same time, I think it's a masterpiece. It's really is a great book, and I can see in the last stage, it took me six years because I had to learn how to write. It's a great book, but there are parts of that book when it came out and suddenly I saw it on the typewriter, I couldn't believe it. My initial reaction was no, I'm not going to write this, you know. But, as I say, I don't have the right to do that, it's up to me to

understand the story that has been given to me and to meet the needs and demands of that story, so the stuff was there coming out. I just put it on paper and when the book was finished, it all worked. So I didn't have the right to not write that stuff just because I don't want people to think that there's something wrong with me."

What was going on at that time in your life?

"My life was wonderful at that time. That particular period of my life was wonderful. I has been sober and I was living with a young lady I eventually married. She had a little girl, and my life was just terrific."

It was interesting to me, reading that book. Part of my job is to deal with people who are having similar problems, and 'The Room' has a certain screaming to it of realising the lack of control in your life, or that feeling of lack of control.

"You've hit it."

It's very common, and when I talk to people who are saying these things, they're thinking those things, no matter how logical or illogical.

"You're right."

The cage may be bars or the cage may be addiction or the cage may be your marriage.

"We create it ourselves, but we don't see it, the guilt we feel. That's absolutely right. Lack of power is of the limit. You look at the best-seller list, in the non-fiction category, and you'll always see that at least half the books have to do with power. How to exert power over other people. How to be a success. How to have more power, in one way or another, they're all talking about power."

Or powerful people explaining how they became powerful.

"Right. In one way or another, that's right."

How was 'The Room' accepted once it was published?

"Well, it got the greatest reviews I've ever read. I mean, I wouldn't have the nerve to write a review like that of my own book. You know, like Walt Whitman did, I wouldn't. In The Saturday Review and New York Times. Not only were they very complimentary, but they also understood the book."

I notice the French tend to label it 'existential'.

"I don't exactly know what that means, to be perfectly honest with you."

I don't either. 'The Room' just seemed to be a picture of one man who's caged and doesn't know how to get out.

"At the end of the book they open the door, but he stays caged. Yeah, I want to explain something. When I talk about understanding that story, I don't necessarily mean a psychological understanding, moral or ethical.

For instance, 'The Room', the basis of it, the thing that I understand and work from was variations on a theme. That's right, it is a musical concept in 'The Room' and it's more a jazz concept than a classical concept, in some sense, simply because it's more contemporary. But it's also the simple baroque kind of variation or trio sonata, so to speak, and it has to do with whatever the facts may be. It has to do with memory, it has to do with fantasy. It's all variations on the same thing, almost like a Rosh Hashanah in a way. Which story is true in Rosh Hashanah and which story is true in this guy's head. We know, I think you know, by the time you finish the book, you know which is true and which isn't. But the point is, it doesn't make any difference because he's already found himself guilty. And it's the same thing, I had to understand, like with 'TraLaLa'.

"Now, 'TraLaLa' is only about twenty pages long, and it took me two and a half years to write. Of course, I was working at a job during the day, and I'd come home at night to work.

"That's how 'Last Exit' was written you know, at night, a couple of hours every night."

Were you able to devote all your time to writing when you were doing 'The Room'?

"Yeah."

And then after 'The Room', when did 'Demon' come out?

"1972, I think. Oh, wait a second, I guess 'The Room' didn't come out until 1972, and then 'Demon' came out in 1976. I spent a year pumping gas, and I spent a year as a stockboy and was unable to do any writing at all..."

I think Terry Southern said that you are one of the moral writers of our time.

"I can't get away from that, but there doesn't seem to be judgement in it. You know, the word 'moral' is like the word 'God'. It's a tough word, man. It's got bad press. Real bad press. But it doesn't have to be judgement in the sense of morality. In other words, it doesn't have to be that way. I believe true morality is totally lacking judgement, and that's one of the things people respond to in a lot of my work."

As opposed to Josephine Hendon who did an article in *Harper's*. The title of the article was *Angry S&M As A Literary Style*. She said about you, "There are writers who hate people, who thrive on the rage that bristles in every city. They know the crowd craves blood because they crave it themselves and feel thoroughly alive."

"That's what she said about me? That's funny, that's not what she said when she reviewed 'The Room'."

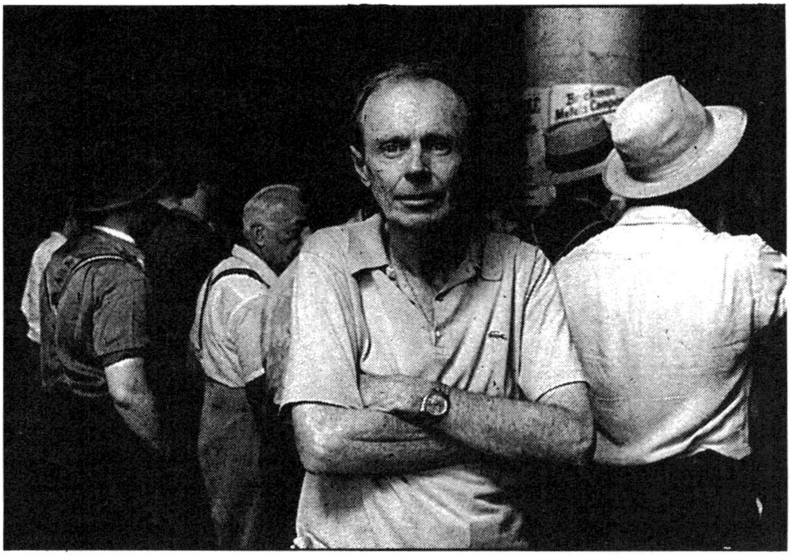

Selby on the set of 'Last Exit to Brooklyn'.

This is where she lumped you and William Burroughs and Barthelme and Hunter Thompson, which I kind of think is an odd grouping of people anyway, but that is what she said. She also went on to say that "from human dregs, from the unremittingly tormented, Selby extracts the very odour of rage or essence of that free-floating danger that lies like a pall over all of us." That seems somewhat accurate to me.

"Yeah, she reviewed 'The Room' for 'The Saturday Review' and it was an absolutely great review. I think she called me 'the poet of our decline'."

Although it is interesting, in this article, she said that "in Selby's rare heterosexual love scenes, most of his characters hate women so totally and do not want to get close to them, even to destroy them." I don't have that sense of your writing.

"I don't know, but I can certainly understand how she might react that way, especially as a contemporary woman. I don't know if I would totally disagree. You know what I mean, I can see that could be a valid interpretation."

I guess what I look at is that the alienation and fear aren't necessarily directed at women. It just so happens that a lot of relationships involve women.

"That's true. If you look at the work, I think you'll see that alienation between everyone. For instance, in 'Demon', the only real relationship Harry has is with his wife, and he has, to the best of his ability, a loving relationship with her occasionally."

A friend of mine, after reading 'Demon', said that he thought it a religious book, but not necessarily in the sense of Catholicism or a formal religion. It is a view of a person looking for an answer, and whether you want to label him a sexual psychopath, a sexual addict, or whatever, it's that striving to find an answer to things that are going on.

"I think the Epigraph really tells you the whole thing. A man obsessed is a man possessed by a demon and it doesn't make any difference what the obsession is.

"You can feel obsessed with gambling, with eating, with drinking, drugs, women, with money, you know, power. You just can't satisfy an obsession."

That seems to be a recurring theme in your writing.

"Yeah just like that loss of power. It was very interesting that you noticed that loss of control, because one of the things that I did after I had written a couple of little things was to re-read them and see what was in the work that hadn't been put there deliberately and consciously. The thing I noticed, what really leaped out at me, was that they all failed because they lost control, not because they were immoral or anything, but they lost control."

I guess I have a lot of empathy for Harry.

"Which Harry?"

They're all Harrys. Harry White.

"Harry White. Yes."

Because even though his acts could be viewed as immoral, you had sympathy for him, not necessarily because he chose not to do it, but once you get started, it doesn't stop. It's like getting a little bit pregnant or having just one drink, or just going to play a friendly game of cards. Once you start, the ball starts rolling and it doesn't stop.

"That's right, man. Try and get a little bit pregnant. Man may one day accomplish this, but hasn't done so yet."

That's right. In dealing with people with addictions, there is no in-between. For example, the same thing is true of sexual addicts. It's like, well, I can just cruise the streets and look at 'em as long as I don't touch 'em.

"Yeah. Lots of luck, Charlie. I'm gonna buy 'Playboy' for the literature in it. I've heard so many people say that, as if they're going to convince someone they are buying 'Playboy' for the reading."

In a sense, I agree that guilt was the first step of an obsession, because of the self-consciousness.

"Guilt is the first step of human existence, right. What I mean by human existence is life as we are experiencing it now. If it wasn't for guilt we would realise the truth about our nature, wouldn't we? But when we are guilty we are afraid to look and see that we really are God."

Catholicism has done a good job of implanting that guilt in most people.

"Mea fuckin' culpa, man!"

Yes, I remember being an altar boy. Having them tell me that every day.

"I remember, of course, it's much different today, but when I was a kid I was in a predominantly Irish Catholic neighbourhood, and I was a 'Black Protestant', and in those days we used to have what they called Brooklyn Days, in May, which was really like the anniversary of the Methodist Sunday School.

"There was a big parade in our area. It was terrific, with ice cream and cake and all that, and I remember my friends - we were eight years old - I remember my Catholic friends being told by the nuns that if they looked at a Protestant parade, they would go blind. Jesus Christ!"

I remember in the Catholic church, they said, "You're not allowed to enter another church, that's a sin."

"That's right."

I noticed similar remarks about 'Requiem'. That is, first they thought you were a professional inmate after 'The Room', and a sex addict after 'Demon', and then you wrote 'Requiem' and everybody thought you were Black. It seems there are similar themes of getting trapped and sometimes of being afraid of getting out of that trap because it's more familiar than taking a chance on something you don't know.

"Same self-delusion."

Were you able to support yourself with your writing up through 'Requiem'?

"Yes, I was. I was doing a couple of little movie things and so forth, and then I got sick. Physically sick. Oh, shit, for five or six years I was unable to do any work, and everything just fell apart. I went back East for five years and eventually my wife left me."

Your first wife?

"No. This was my third wife... I wrote a thing for Stanley Kramer, 'Remember the Sabbath Day and Keep It Holy'. Back in 1974 ABC

Television was going to do a Special on the Ten Commandments, a two-hour movie, on each of the Commandments, but not with a religious or historical theme, just a contemporary story. It's very funny, because ABC took five of the Commandments, with an option on the other five."

That's typical.

"I can just see them do all ten and they get this great rating, so ABC send Moses out for another five, right?"

Either that or they go'Gee, we got good ratings on seven, but eight isn't really making it, so we should drop it and go to nine.'

"I tell you, it's just marvellous. The whole thing got cancelled, but I guess it might not have got done anyway because Kramer said to me 'You know, this is the most beautiful and wonderful script I have ever read that will not be done on television.' He said, 'You wrote literature.'"

I heard that Robert De Niro and Stanley Kubrick were interested in doing some of your stuff. Did you see 'Taxi Driver' and what did you feel about that film?

"Well, I saw 'Mean Streets' and I enjoyed that very much. I liked 'Taxi Driver' too. I think that's all I've seen actually. I've missed all the others that are supposed to be so good, like 'Raging Bull'."

Do you have a TV at home?

"No."

Are there any films or film makers now that you like?

"I forget, but I enjoyed 'The Unbearable Lightness of Being' very much. Except it was forty five minutes too long and tough on the bottom. One of the funniest films I've seen in a long time was 'Blue Velvet'. Did you see that?"

Yes I did.

"That was fantastic. I got such a big kick out of that."

A lot of people didn't see some of the humour in it though.

"Well, it was almost like a take-off. He was just taking off on the whole genre. I don't know how you could miss it. It was very blatant. Anyway, I got a big kick out of it, but I've seen some English movies recently that I thought were terrific.

"You know, I don't see many foreign films, but 'Au Revoir Les Enfants' was marvellous, I thought. 'My Life As a Dog' I enjoyed thoroughly. I liked 'Dark Eyes', that was good.

"Most of the American movies today are just hopeless, you know. They're made by young kids, I mean the people at the studios and all that, who have, I guess, MBAs or something, and who have been raised on television and have no idea what life is, they have no life experience. They just have TV experience, and they're re-making old movies according

to their interpretation of life as viewed from 'Father Knows Best' or something. I don't know what, but it's really amazing what they do with the money. I mean, they spend 30 or 40 million dollars on a movie and it's dreadful. It's not even like the old movies where they were hopeless but they were a lot of fun. These are just not a lot of fun."

I hear that a couple of your books have been optioned again.

"Well, the option on 'Demon' I have nothing to do with. He does this thing by himself and he's in France, so I have no idea what's happening with that. But the 'Last Exit to Brooklyn' film I was involved in. They asked me about everything that came along. They wanted my input on everything."

You have been doing some readings in California.

"Yeah, there were a few I did with Henry Rollins, three with Henry and Lydia Lunch. Then I did one with Henry and some other people up at the Roxy."

How did those go?

"Oh, it's wonderful, just really wonderful. One of the great things about it is that the young people, like people in their twenties, really respond to my work. I didn't notice, but evidently there is a whole following out there of young people. It was a big audience."

There are a lot of people, including film makers, who have been close to your work who have been praising it and sending it to other people to introduce them to it

"Really? I'm not aware of any of it. As far as I'm aware, I'm dead. You know, I have never been acknowledged as existing in this country by more than a couple of people."

Do you feel any kinship or do you communicate at all with some of your contemporaries, such as Burroughs or any of those? I know he's a big fan.

"No, I don't get to see anybody. William Kennedy I love. I wrote a little note to him, but there is just really no communication."

Ironically I see a certain kinship with Bukowski. He writes about similar people, and it's fairly non-judgemental, although he tends to be a little more experimental, which you chose not to be, and he asserts himself more. For years, people were not interested in him, and now of course he is gaining a resurgence.

"Yeah, well that's been going on for quite a while, I understand. For quite a few years now he has been making a lot of money, reading in Europe and all that kind of thing.

"I remember seeing a little article on him in some magazine, oh, four years or more ago, where he had just bought a $250,000 house and all

that kind of stuff."

I guess that makes it a little more difficult for him to write about the hotels he lived in. Are you familiar with his work?

"No, not really."

What authors are you reading now that you appreciate who are your contemporaries?

"Well, I just finished reading a thing by Milan Kundera that I really liked very, very much. Like I said, I love Kennedy. God, he's marvellous. Just fuckin' marvellous. Michael Stevens, Gil. I love Gil's stuff. I forget names though sometimes. I don't read as much as I like because I teach one night a week at USC, so I spend a lot of my time reading and going over the students' stuff."

Are you working or doing anything besides writing and teaching?

"No. I had a job for a couple of years, but that ended last year, so now I've just been at home trying to finish my new book."

Can you tell me where you are headed with it?

"Well, this is a whole new kind of thing for me. It's a first person book and it's just a whole different approach... There is a man who is, I think, in the book he is fifty years old, and looking back at his childhood. Trying to understand the child. In that process he tries to understand his father, and through that, he understands his relationship with God. How this all started is really kind of fun. Like I say, I try to say yes to life. Whatever is put in front of me, I believe, is an opportunity for love and service, so I just try to say yes to life. I was reading a story by one of my students and one line in it didn't make sense. I read it about three times, four times, and it just didn't make any sense and I couldn't figure out what the hell was wrong with this line. Then I noticed I was misreading it. So many people have told me how they read what they experience in life. That line was 'Eyes filled before the tears came', and I kept reading 'He remembered how his father felt before the tears came'. And I said 'Ho, ho, Mr Freud. What do we have here?' So I wrote down the line as I had misread it, and shortly after that I typed it, and I have been going ever since."

AND HIS NAME WAS ROVER

WILLIAM S. BURROUGHS

"I don't think anyone knows really...what happens when you die, I mean."

"I know," he said smugly. "There was a little dog and his name was Rover. And when he was dead he was dead all over."

This irritated her. She thought he was bigoted.

"Oh, by the way. While you were in town there was a dog in the yard...acting most strangely. I'm almost sure..."

"My God, the kids."

"I kept them in the house, of course. Then it threw back its head and howled."

She shuddered, remembering the abject misery and despair of that sound.

"No collar?"

"No nuttin."

When people live together they will throw out something like "no nuttin" hoping it will turn out to be humorous or in some way portentous.

He finished his martini. "I'd better go out and have a look."

He crossed to his gun cabinet and opened it with a complicated key that looked like some futuristic instrument. He liked the feel of it as it slid into the lock. He turned to her. "Doggie big?"

"About thirty pounds, I'd say...yellowish brown fur...longish muzzle...narrow head. Young dog."

He decided the .12 gauge was definitely too much gun.

"If I'm going to overkill the wretched brute might as well use the .375. He acquired it from a dead uncle by getting to the house before the plundering herd. He'd fired it once at the range and got a gutsy sensation of pure power like throwing a thunderbolt. Like as not kill a cow or a peasant in the next county. He decided to use her .20 gauge pump action skeet gun. There was only a half hour of daylight left...better take the flash. He didn't relish getting caught in the dark with a mad dog prowling about, could leap out at him from a bush like God jumped on Moses.

He made the perimeter of the house, looked in the laundry room and the old hen house. The hens had to be moved because of the hideous grating noises of the roosters screaming day and night at ten minute intervals.

"But we have to have fresh eggs," she insisted.

"What good are fresh eggs if I can't sleep?"

So they moved the hen house three hundred yards from the house, and they were all killed by weasels or skunks or racoons. So they decided to get in some Guinea hens. They can fly...roost in trees at night. The Guinea hens were on order and they looked forward eagerly to their arrival. What would the eggs be like?

Next day he cautioned her about keeping the children in the house and to keep the .20 gauge loaded and ready.

"And kill the dog on sight."

"I wasn't quite *sure,* you understand," she explained. "It just might be a neighbourhood dog, and you know how much trouble that sort of thing can cause."

He knew. In Mexico he was once accused of poisoning a neighbour's dog because he'd been overheard to say someone should poison it.

"But I didn't poison the dog," he protested to a police lieutenant, slim elegant and impenetrably stupid in riding boots. "I just said someone should poison it."

"It comes to the same thing. You were heard to threaten the dog. You had the motive and the opportunity to kill the dog. I have studied criminology," he said firmly. "The Gonzales have suffered greatly from the loss of their pet. The children especially are decimated." (Would it were true) "Small presents...regaltios would lift their spirits."

It cost $500 in regaltios. They were eating him a becita at a time. Finally he fled Mexico with paper hangers. He was proud to know that a paper hanger is a bum check artist.

The light was failing fast. He turned on the flash and directed a beam of light into the barn. It was only a shell; the animal's eyes glinted green in the light and he raised the gun. A racoon. He lowered the gun. After all, they had no chickens left to lose. But the sight of the animal strengthened his resolve to find the mad dog and kill it. He could be preventing an epidemic.

"All is in the not done, the diffidence that faltered," he told himself firmly. He remembered a funeral director whose motto had been 'unfaltering service'.

"It's not time to falter," his father said. But nothing was to be gained by tramping about in the dark. The dog could be miles away by now. He walked back to the kitchen door.

DEAD FINGERS TALK

The William S.Burroughs Interview

VALE

RE You see outer space as the solution to this cop-ridden planet?
WSB "Yeah, it's the only place to go! If we ever get out alive... IF we're lucky. But it isn't just COP RIDDEN, it's ridden with every sort of insanity. Of course, all these nuts make the cops necessary. In New York there was one guy who was going out and pushing people in front of subways. Another guy – the Mad Slasher – he had a meat cleaver, he carried it around in a little bag, and he suddenly started cutting people up. He cut a guy's ear off. They got TWO mad slashers, another with a knife – a big hunting one – he killed about three or four people."
RE In New York?
WSB "Just suddenly on the street, he started cutting up! Stabbing everybody in sight. Just like the Amok in Southeast Asia, just exactly the same phenomenon. He just went around and killed people. He escaped. Usually, with the Amok it was a form of suicide, and they were usually killed. Everybody starts yelling out, *'Amok! Amok!'* and rush up with whatever weapons they have and they finally kill the Amok. But this one got away and may do it again... You know, just one thing like that after another..."
RE Have you witnessed any altercations recently?
WSB "Well, yeah...very often you see somebody freaking out, on a subway. I saw this guy he had a wild look in his eye, he was sort of swinging from one strap to another – he'd start at one end of the car and go down to the other end. As soon as the subway stopped EVERYBODY got off! The last I saw there were about four cops on their way to subdue him."
RE It seems this sort of thing is escalating. What role do the media play in this? Are they just passively reporting or -
WSB "I don't know, because they don't have this problem in other places. They don't have this problem in Paris."
RE In Tokyo they have a huge population, overcrowding, but...
WSB "I know. In Paris they've got poor people, they've got everything, but it doesn't seem to express itself in that way. That's what you're REALLY worried about, the people that are just nuts, that don't have any rationality."

RE Usually the solution is to 'beef up the police' -
WSB "The police, my god, the police have taken such a beating since New Year's. Some guy got in an argument with a cop and took his gun away and killed him. Another guy beat a cop almost to death with his own nightstick. These things happen all the time! Maybe you read about it; you see, the cops pulled this van over and two guys in the van jumped out and started shooting with 9-millimetres, those 15-shot Browning. Man, they just riddled the car, both cops had about five bullets in them. They were slow on the uptake! You see somebody jump out – you'd better jump out too in a hurry! But they didn't. One of them's dead (the other will recover). He was shot in the brain, he lived for about five days. Finally had to pull the plug."
RE I think criminals are raising their aiming point since so many cops wear Second Chance (Body Armour) now.
WSB "These guys knew what they were doing – they weren't muggers and they weren't lunatics. They knew how to use the guns, they had the two hand hold...were really pouring it in there."
RE Ever had the desire to go to the Cooper School Gunsite? (A progressive arms training school in Arizona.)
WSB "Well...yeah, you'll get some tips there, I think. By and large it's just getting out on the range and doing a little practising. What I do is, I start as close as I need to get, in order to get em all in the black, then start moving back. Then see what's wrong, if you're shooting high or low (I'm shooting a little to the left on my 9-millimetre). Then move back to fifteen yards. It's not very practical to bother with anything beyond twenty five yards – there's no point."
RE That's seventy five feet -
WSB "Seventy five feet, that's fair enough...most anything to do with self defence is going to be not fifteen yards but FIVE yards."
RE It seems like it's going to get worse...
WSB "Well, some company has a shock stick – it's supposed to give someone a paralysing shock. But I've never seen one. They also have this thing – it's just like a flashlight – it develops a tremendously bright flash that will blind someone, particularly in the dark. See, if someone came on you in the dark straight, and you give them a flash of that, they're all completely blinded long enough for you to either run...or give them a kick or two!"
RE How would you use your cane?

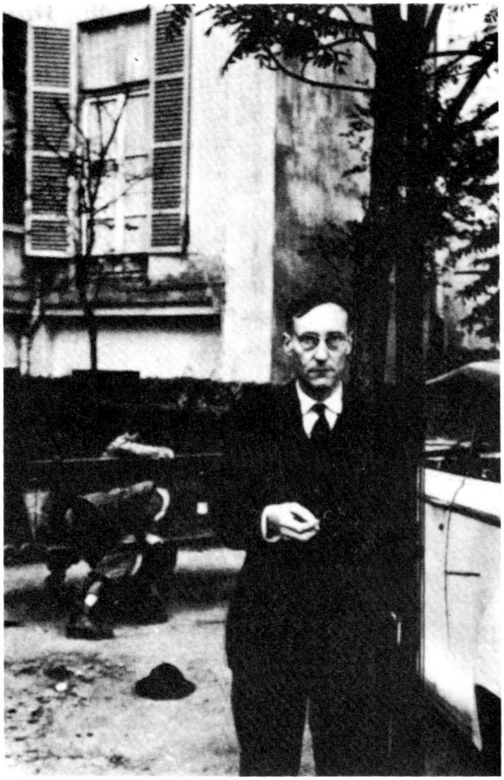

WSB "There's all sorts of things you can do with a cane, practically anything except THAT (demonstrates using it as a club). That's only a feint. If you ever do that with a cane you go like THAT. When he puts his hand up, you slice down to the knee. That cane of mine's not very heavy. Of course, if a guy's got something in his hand then slap the hand. Jam it into his solar plexus or Adam's apple, or anywhere. Clay Wilson just gave me a spring steel unit. I wouldn't carry it because I want to buy something, the cane's always slipping down, hitting somebody... it's incredibly inconvenient to have a cane that doesn't have a hook on it."

RE Society seems to be tending toward new survival requirements...you once mentioned that you yourself have three lines of defence. That seems to be thought out for a reason.

WSB "Yeah. A mace gun, a cobra, and a cane are my three lines of defence. It's something new. This didn't used to be true, you know. I talked to people in Los Angeles who said they used to leave their doors open and not worry about it, and now they've all got security systems and all the rest of it. I draw the line at keeping a fuckin' dog! I don't like them anyway – particularly not vicious ones' – cause they're always biting other people. (A friend) has a dog in New Mexico, outside of town. Well, the dog bit three people who were friends of his – finally it killed his cat. He had to get rid of it. But...if you don't have a dog, everybody knows it. And they know, of course, when you're going to town – how long it's going to take you to get there and back – so you just get ripped off for everything you own. I don't know what you can so, what substitute there is. That's what dogs are for. Another thing that they do: they alert you if anyone is coming. And they know from about three hundred yards away. It's amazing. Two or three hundred yards, all the dogs start barking. They know somebody's coming long before you would have any knowledge. And THAT's what they're for."

RE It seems a general state of alertness would be the first condition of being out in the Bowery where you live.

WSB "The Bowery house base is so watched. The Bowery itself, there's nothing there, just old bums; they're harmless. That's a safe neighbourhood – safer than the posh neighbourhoods. The Upper West Side and the East Side – that's where they have the REAL trouble, where they got these big apartment houses, because the muggers feel they can GET something there. Not in the Bowery; there's no muggers in the Bowery. But when you go down the subways, of course, well then anything can happen."

RE You stay away from them?

WSB "No, no! I travel on them practically every day. I have to get uptown for my various reasons, it's the only way to travel. Oh yeah, I travel on the subways all the time."

RE Have you taken any special precautions for your YMCA in New York? (At the time of the interview, WSB lived in a converted basement toilet of a former YMCA building.)

WSB "That's quite secure, it has no windows. It has some windows that open on a shaft – we've got bars on them. And there are four doors between me and the street. And in the daytime there's a guy downstairs with a pistol guarding the furniture store there. And they check people that come in and out. If someone comes in and asks for me, they look him over. So that's pretty good. I haven't had any trouble with people breaking in."

RE Do you ever practise with an air pistol?

WSB "I've got one, yeah. A 'Diana', I believe. It's got a gas cylinder. I'd rather have one that didn't have a gas cylinder, you're always running out of them. And it doesn't work exactly, I've got to put some sort of wad in it to make it engage. But it's alright. I practise with it a lot."

RE Just shooting targets?

WSB "Yeah, I've got a loft, and the walls are three feet thick. So there's no hassle. Usually I put a telephone book up as the backing. It'll chew a telephone book to pieces in about...oh, several days' shooting. It's pretty powerful, it'll imbed itself in wood, soft pine, it's good practice."

RE Except you don't get the feel of recoil...

WSB "Somebody says that he solved the whole problem of recoil by balancing the forward movement and the backward movement so there's no recoil. I saw a picture of it in *Soldier of Fortune* – that's all I know about it. But of course, I'd like to see a smoothbore shotgun revolver... even in .410. If it was good and heavy you could even have it up to 20-gauge. After all, they're shooting these Thompson Contenders with really high powered rifle cartridges. Why couldn't they do the same with a shotgun? In other words, a hand shotgun. Double-barrelled perhaps, heavy enough to balance the recoil, so you'd have hand shotgun hunting just like they have handgun pistol hunting. The point is, they can sell all they make, so why should they change? It's like the internal combustion engine, so long as they can sell 'em they're not going to change the design."

RE By the way, what was the Tucker car?

WSB "It wasn't quite a turbine engine, but it had all sorts of improvements. It's so much better than any car on the market, there's just no comparison. It could stop on a dime. It could do all sorts of things. He only made two. He had about $20 million, but that's a drop in the bucket; when you're bucking General Motors, $20 million is chicken feed. And he WAS bucking General Motors. So they put him out of business. He couldn't get the materials. See, if they can freeze the materials on anybody ... I've seen it happen with a lot of things. Another guy was going to make Lustron houses: this guy had a prefabricated house that was made of porcelain steel with the insulation in the middle. It was rustproof, termite proof, it would last forever. They were supposed to come on the market for $5,000, then it was $9,000, then $12,000. He only made a few hundred before they went under."

RE Do examples still exist?

WSB "Oh yeah, there must be, because they could never wear out! They were in different colours, you could add rooms to them, they could put this thing up in a couple of days. You got a lot, you could put up your house. And it could last forever. Well of course the real estate lobby really go into HIM... They want houses that'll fall apart in ten years so you gotta get a new one. Just like everything – cars, anything else. And you can't buck 'em. There was this woman who went down to South America and found a birth control herb that'll last for SEVEN years – and you can reverse it with another herb if you want to have children. So she came back thinking the chemical companies would jump all over it. They said: Wait a minute – we can sell a pill every day – what do we want to know about a seven year pill for? So...they didn't want to know."

RE Good grief! What happened to that?

WSB "Nothing. Some friends of mine – the Eco-Technic Institute – they're going to the Amazon this summer and they're going to try to pick it up, do something with it. It would have to be a small firm, sort of entrepreneurs. But then you'd never get the okay from the FDA, the Food and Drug Administration. They'd never give you the okay, 'cause they're sort of the company cops of the big drug companies. They get THEIR shit through no matter how dangerous it is, like Thalidomide and a lot of other compounds that turned out to be very dangerous, that have all sorts of side effects. But if some guy's making it in a basement laboratory – HE'LL never get the okay!"

RE Who are the Eco-Technic Institute?

WSB "They are primarily an ecology organisation...very successful. They have a big place in New Mexico; they have a beef ranch in Australia; they have an hotel in Katmandu. They own a huge.. they seem to have the money...millions, 'cause that house they bought in the South of France with thirty acres, a house that could hold, house and feed 70 people at a conference, it's huge. That's about, I'd say £6 million anyway. Thirty acres, man, twenty miles from Marseilles! But at their conferences – any of their conferences – they will not allow journalists. None! No matter how well intentioned. And that's very sensible, cause you get scientists up there and they're going to get misquoted: *"Scientist sees end of the world in ten years"* when he's saying that a certain situation will be CRITICAL in ten years – a water table or something like that. And then they won't come to the next conference. So the woman in charge just banned all journalists... Heyerdahl was there, the Kon Tiki man, the guy that sailed the papyrus boat...and doctors from the World Health...a lot of very interesting people. I was glad I went, but, god, the first night I got there, it was in wintertime, and these great big country houses – just a big room with one tiny electric heater. I never took my clothes off throughout the conference!... Beware of country houses in the winter!"

RE I'm interested in turning-points in history, like, in 'Cities Of The Red Night', there's that story of Captain Mission, which presented an entirely different possibility for the Americas which didn't happen.

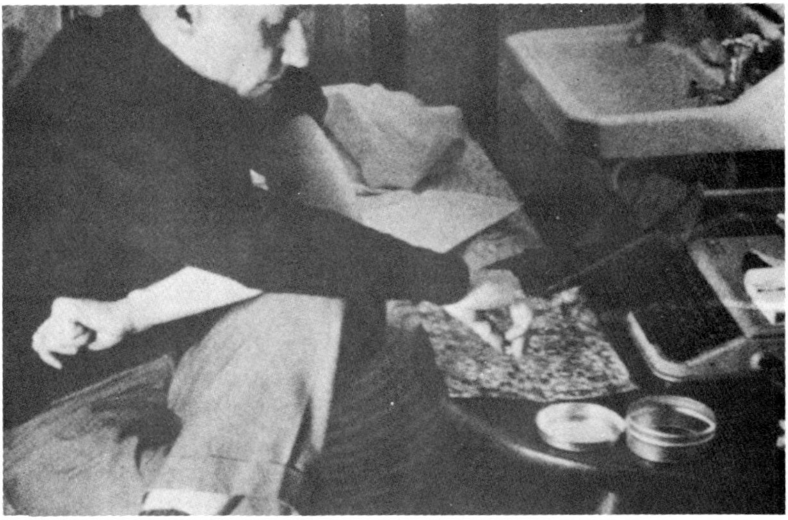

WSB "There are lots of those turning points, dates; important, crucial dates. One of them is certainly (although it isn't a clear-cut date like a battle or something, but it's one of the great dates in history) – Systemic Antibiotics. Because before that, boy, you got an infection, you were dead! It's nothing now to have an infection, and pneumonia was a BIG killer. So, that's a very big date..."

RE I think the birth control herb you mentioned could be equally important.

WSB "Absolutely. And, of course, August 6, 1945. Godalmighty, the atom bomb, what a date!" (laughs)...

At this point, several people talk briefly to Burroughs. Jello Biafra, lead singer with The Dead Kennedys, asks if William is familiar with the cancer cells of Henrietta Lacks, that keep reappearing in laboratories all over the world. S. Clay Wilson asks *"Bill, when you stared at your foot all that time when you were strung out in Morocco or wherever it was – did you have your shoe on or off?"* WSB answers with matter-of-fact politeness: "Oh, no, I left my shoe on. I'd rather look at my foot with my shoe on than off."

RE What do you think about the assassination attempts on Reagan, the Pope, -
WSB "It looks like it's going to get very dangerous to be a Pope or President or Prime Minister. The time may come when they can't get anybody to take the job!"
RE It seems they weren't totally serious, using a .22.
WSB "Well, HE was a nut. The other guy wasn't, the terrorist. I think he was really trying. If it had been a .45 I think that might have been IT... De Gaulle had real professionals after him for years and they didn't succeed, because his bodyguards knew what they were doing. That's the point – they would never have let anyone get THAT close to Le General. But here was this guy in the press circles, he had no press credentials!... It's just ridiculous. Not only should they have checked the press credentials, but they should put ALL the fucking reporters through one of those metal detectors. Because a nutty reporter could get the idea of assassinating the president – same thing would happen... A bodyguard has to be telepathic. Oh, absolutely! He's got to be able to see round corners. And another very important thing is LOOKING UP. A lot of people don't do that. The American Secret Service – THEY DON'T HAVE IT! They're not alert like that."
RE How can we improve our telepathic abilities? Are they genetically limited?
WSB "No, I think everyone has it in them. It's just a question of pressure. PRESSURE! Those guys had to do that, or they'd find somebody who would. In other words, if they were going to be bodyguards to de Gaulle, they had to be INTUITIVE. Not just telepathic, but know something's wrong: I don't like the look of that guy...or that window...or that's a bad place there..."
RE Why are bodyguards doing such a bad job these days?
WSB "They're just not paying attention to what they're doing, that's all. They've never been up against real professionals. Well, they're not now – Hinckley's not a professional. But de Gaulle's bodyguards were up against army officers with money and weapons and knowing how to use them – not .22 pistols!... The week before President Kennedy was assassinated, he was in New York. He stopped at a red light and some girl rushed up and photographed him from a distance of three feet. Someone said *'She could've killed the President!'* That was a week before Dallas! But that didn't seem to inspire them to tighten their security. Of course, protection from a rifle with a telescopic sight is not so easy. But de

Gaulle's men, they covered all the buildings along his route... That Ruby and Oswald thing stunk to high heaven, the whole thing..."

RE What do you think of the theory that Jonestown was a CIA experiment in mass mind control -

WSB "It's conceivable, conceivable. We KNOW that they've performed such experiments in countries like Brazil...and in Athens, the whole junta was CIA inspired. In Brazil all these experiments in control and torture etc. were definitely CIA organised – we KNOW that. They sent all these torture experts down to South and Central America. Did you see *'City under Siege'*, I think that was the name of it. It was about...one of these CIA torture experts was kidnapped by the Tupamaros in Uruguay. He was sent down there as a police advisor. So they kidnapped him and they finally killed him. And then – at the end of the movie – you see another one getting out of the plane..."

RE Do you think they could take a disoriented person out of prison and programme him to become an assassin and the person wouldn't really know exactly what he's doing?

WSB "I think it's possible, but it seems to me more trouble than it's worth. If you really want the job done you don't want a disordered person, of course you've got an alibi there, no one can pin it on you, but...still, it's an around-the-world-oxcart way of doing it! But it's certainly within the range of possibility."

RE What about telepathic suggestions to the subject while they're asleep?

WSB "Well, they wouldn't have to be telepathic – they could do that with microphones, sort of subliminal microphones. As to how effective the suggestions would be I just don't know. All these people are talking about hearing voices, telling them to do these things. Now where do the voices come from? Well this is one of the symptoms, of course, of schizophrenia, and we know now that the voices come from the non-dominant brain hemisphere, whichever that is. In fact you can PRODUCE voices by electrical stimulation of the non-dominant brain hemisphere in normal subjects. So that's the line to take – if you can get into the non-dominant brain hemisphere, then it has this terrific power: people can't disobey it. But only certain people would be subject to that sort of brain conditioning"

RE How can we strengthen our psychic defences?

WSB "There are whole books on that. Dion Fortune wrote a fairly good one – *'Psychic Self Defence'*. It's not a bad book, a bit old fashioned, but there's some good tips in there. How to know when you're under psychic attack, what to do about it, and so on. There are quite a few, there's something by David Conway called *'Magic: An Occult Primer'*, that's a very good book."

RE Have you heard anything new in the field of biological warfare?

WSB "Well, we know that the English had what they called a 'doomsday bug' in World War II – which was created by exposing viruses to radiation and producing mutated strains. That's more than FORTY YEARS AGO! They've come a long way since then! And also there are ethnic weapons that would attack only whites or blacks or mongoloids or whatever because of their racial enzyme differences. So they can devise a plague that would attack only one ethnic group. That also is pretty old: the first statement about that was over fifteen years ago. So they've come a long way on that one too."

RE What do you think of the hardcore survivalist movement in the USA? Stockpiling dried food, weapons...?

WSB "It could be, I suppose, a good idea, but then there's the question, you might not be able to get to your stash! (drily) And you gotta be able to defend it and all that! You have several priorities: your first priority is weapons, second is drugs, third is tools, antibiotics..."

RE When you say tools, do you mean like water purification devices?

WSB "No no no. I mean tools! Hammers, saws. If you don't have them, it's very bad!"

RE By the way, do you still record your dreams?

WSB "Oh, of course! I'll write down a few notes and then if it's worth bothering with, I'll write it out in a diary form..."

THE JOHNSON FAMILY

WILLIAM BURROUGHS

I first heard this expression in a book called *'You Can't Win'* by Jack Black, the life story of a burglar. The book was published in 1924 and I read it as a boy, fascinated by this dark furtive purposeful world. I managed to get a copy and re-read the book with poignant nostalgia. Between the reader in 1924 and the reader in 1980 falls the shadow of August 6, 1945, one of the most portentous dates of history.

Train whistles across a distant sky. This is a peep show back to the world of rod-riding yeggs and peat men and cat burglars, bindle stiffs, gay cats and hobo jungles and Salt Chunk Mary the fence in her two-storey red brick house down by the tracks somewhere in Idaho. She keeps a blue porcelain coffee pot and an iron pot of pork and beans always in the fire. You eat first and talk business later the watches and rings sloped out on the kitchen table by the chipped coffee mugs. She named a price and she didn't name another. Mary could say no quicker than any woman I ever know and none of them ever meant yes. She kept the money in a cookie jar but nobody thought about that. Her cold grey eyes would have seen the thought and maybe something goes wrong on the next lay. John Law just happens by or a citizen comes up with a load of .00 buck shot into your soft and tenders.

In this world of shabby rooming houses, furtive grey figures in dark suits, hop joints and chili parlours the Johnson Family took shape as a code of conduct. To say someone is a Johnson means he keeps his word and honours his obligations. He's a good man to do business with and a good man to have on your team. He is not a malicious, snooping, interfering, self-righteous trouble-making person.

You get to know a Johnson when you see one, and you get to know those of another persuasion. I remember in the Merchant Marine training centre at Sheepshead Bay when the war ended. Most of the trainees quit right then and there was a long line to turn in equipment which had to be checked out item by item; some of us had only been there a few days and we had no equipment to turn in. So we hoped to avoid standing for hours, days perhaps in line for no purpose. I remember this spade cat said, *"Well we're going to meet a nice guy or we're going to meet a prick."* We met a prick but we managed to find a Johnson.

Yes, you get to know a Johnson when you see one. The cop who gave me a joint to smoke in the wagon. The hotel clerk who tipped me off I was hot. And sometimes you don't see the Johnson. I remember a friend of mine asked someone to send him a cake of hash from France. Well, the asshole put it into a cheap envelope with no wrapping and it cut through the envelope. But some Johnson had put it back in and sealed the envelope with tape.

Years ago I was stranded in the wilds of East Texas and Bill Gains was sending me a little Pantapon through the mail and he invented this clever code and telegrams are flying back and forth.

"Urgently need pants."

"Panic among dealers. No pants available."

This was during the war in a town of 200 people. By rights we should have had the FBI swarming all over us. I remember the telegraph operator in his office in the railroad station. He had a kind, unhappy face. I suspect he was having trouble with his wife. Never a question or comment. He just didn't care what pants stood for. He was a Johnson.

A Johnson minds his own business. But he will help when help is needed. He doesn't stand by while someone is drowning or trapped in a wrecked car. Kells Elvins, a friend of mine, was doing 90 in his Town and Country Chrysler on the way from Pharr, Texas to Laredo. He comes up over a rise and there is a fucking cow right in the middle of the road on the bridge. He slams on the brakes and hits the cow doing 60. The car flips over and he is pinned under it with a broken collar bone covered from head to foot with blood and guts and cowshit. So along comes a car with some salesmen in it. They get out cautiously. He tells them just how to jack the car up and get it off him but when they see that *blood* they don't want to know. They don't want to get mixed up with anything like that. They get back in their car and drive away. Then a truck driver comes along. He doesn't need to be told exactly what to do, gets the car off Kells and takes him to a hospital. The truck driver was a Johnson. The salesmen were shits like most salesmen. Selling shit and they are shit.

The Johnson Family formulates a Manichean position where good and evil are in conflict and the outcome is at this point uncertain. It is *not* an eternal conflict since one or the other must win a final victory.

Which side are you on?

I recollect Brion Gysin, Ian Sommerville and your reporter were drinking an expresso on the terrace of a little cafe on the Calle de Vigne in Tangier... after lunch a dead empty space... Then this Spaniard walks by. He is about 50 or older, shabby, obviously very poor, carrying something wrapped in brown paper. And our mouths fell open as we exclaimed in unison.

"My God, that's a harmless looking person!"

He passed and I never saw him again, his passing portentous as a comet reminding us how rare it is to see a harmless-looking person, a man who minds his own business and gets along as best he can in a world largely populated by people of a very different persuasion, kept alive by the hope of harming someone, on their way to the Commissaria to denounce a neighbour or a business rival leaving squiggles and mutterings of malevolence in their wake like ugly little spirits.

He passed and I never saw him again. But I recognized him. He was a Johnson. You get to know a Johnson when you see one... the cop in New Orleans who slipped me a joint to smoke in the paddy wagon, the doctor who gave me a shot of morphine in the hospital while a colleague was muttering about the moral questions involved, the hotel clerk who tipped me the law is on its way, better move out fast.

February 3, 1982... A programme on San Salvador... a reporter has contacted a guerilla group. One look at those faces and I know where I stand. I know them all. They are Johnsons. The reporter is checking the contention of the junta and the Reagan administration and the guerillas are armed with soviet Weapons via Cuba and Nicaragua...

"Let's see your guns."

Young man has a Belgian assault rifle 9M... handsome boy about 20 has an MI6, a little fat boy about 16 has a .22 held together with wire and tape.

"Fifty years old," he tells us, smiling.

Man in his thirties, nice smile: *"Me, I got no gun."*

"Well where are the Russian K-47s you are supposed to be getting from Cuba?"

"No hay." (There aren't any).

Look at these facts. Nice faces. Johnson faces. You can't fake it. That old Spaniard couldn't have been a KGB Colonel, or a Cousin, or MI6. No agent could have that cover. Because it isn't a cover. It's the real thing.

Three guns for 20 men. Shy handsome boy of 15 has been with the guerillas since he was 14. Why? No ideology no rubbish. Self defence. Once you take up arms against a bunch of shits there is no way back. Lay down your arms and they will kill you. I've seen the Policia Nacionale in action in Colombia during the civil war. Vicious thugs. No Johnson faces there.

That's all the orientation I need to make up my mind about San Salvador. Don't want to hear Haig's lies or any other lies. Haig is no Johnson. He's got one of the most basically dishonest faces I ever saw. And the same look on his face when he lies as General Westmoreland... LIE LIE LIE written all over it.

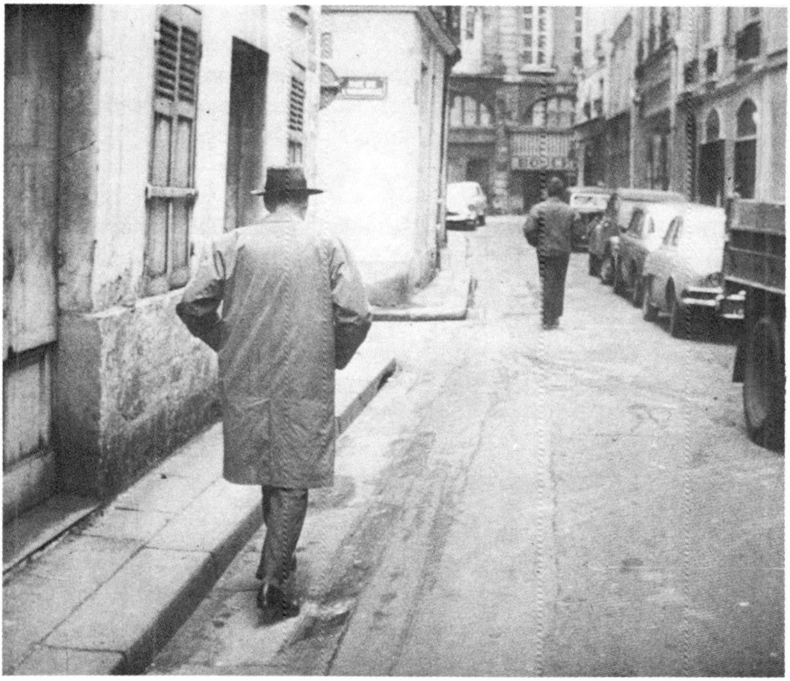

William, rue Git le Coeur. (Photo: Antony Balch)

NEOISM

PETE SCOTT

"We are not a dead serious political party or religious institution; we are Neoists. Each decade has Neoists and their situation is always different. We formed a network to revolt against oppression, and we hope that our efforts will end with big retrospective exhibitions in the world's most established museums, because we know that each revolution ends with the imprisonment and execution of its leaders and participants..."

These are the considered words of Hungarian 'total media artist' Monty Cantsin, a charismatic, self-obsessed technophile (*"I love mass media"*) who repudiates all forms of authority. Cantsin was actually christened Istvan Kantor, but changed his name at the instigation of American mail artist David Zack. The two met for the first time in Budapest circa mid-1976 and struck up a close working relationship. On Zack's advice Kantor emigrated to Canada in September 1977, and established a base of operations in Montreal. Today he is known throughout America and Europe as Monty Cantsin, high priest of Neoism, *"the mass movement of individuality"* (sic). *"We Neoists are at the beginning of an unprecedented history,"* he says; *"kill normality before it kills you."*

A mercurial, deliberately enigmatic figure, Cantsin always provokes extreme reactions. He embraced the Neoist Cultural Conspiracy in 1979, and has been co-ordinating its activities ever since. *"We are not any more artists,"* he explains in characteristically fractured English, *"but most of our members have the artistic background. Most of them came from art, but there are others who came from science and many other kinds of activity. We call ourselves Neoists because a Neoist is not just an artist, a Neoist is another kind of human being more involved in social and cultural activities."*

The Neoist information conduit was actually devised in the early '70s by the aforesaid David Zack. Established first in the mail art network, it later spread to apartment festivals and is now heavily into mass communications. In essence it's a loose-knit cultural junta founded on the undeniable fact that traditional art is dead. One slogan defines it as *"Nothing more than the performance of a movement called Neoism."* Another explains that *"You cannot understand Neoism without first of all becoming a Neoist."*

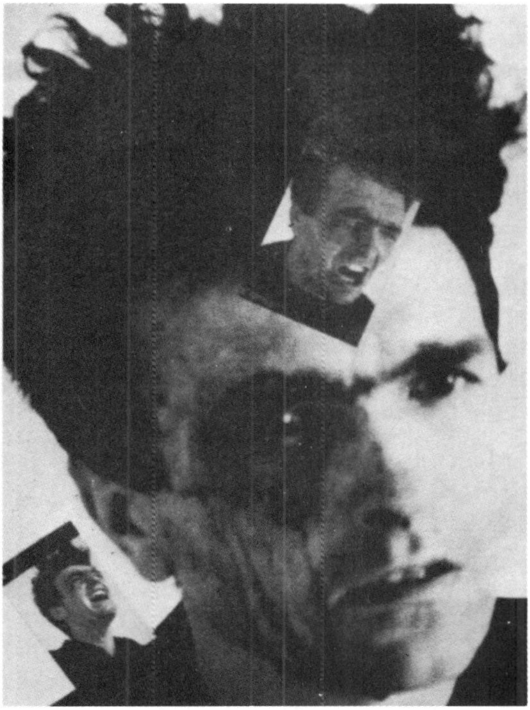

To Monty Cantsin Neoism is *"The fight for total freedom through all forms of creativity."* There are almost as many definitions as there are individual Neoists. Cantsin himself is the movement's most eloquent spokesman, trotting out any polemic that may bring publicity or interest. *"Neoism is an open situation"* he says. *"In the beginning it was so new that it didn't even have a definition. Today of course there are thousands of them – but the best definition of Neoism is always the* ***next one!****"*

Neoism stresses the value and importance of new ideas. Its central tenet is simply that anyone can take on the mantle of Monty Cantsin and perform actions in his name. As a key manifesto explains: *"Monty Cantsin is the ultimate art product, and ultimately we must all* ***become*** *Monty Cantsin. As society has become increasingly drained of real individuality, the emphasis in art has shifted away from the art object onto the personality of the artist. Monty Cantsin is an artist with such a strong personality that a unique name is unnecessary to his individuality."*

Although it is available for general use, only Istvan Kantor has taken the conceptual persona of Monty Cantsin to extremes. After seven years he is firmly established as its chief exponent. *"I am a true individual in a world where individuality is a crime,"* he says with disarming modesty.

"I have witnessed the dematerialization of the art object and I know that the only art work still worth creating is my own life."

Cantsin likes to dramatise himself as a kind of latterday André Breton. He presently dominates the Canadian performance art scene with a calculated blend of violence, eroticism and self-immolation. His continuous action since 1979 has been the so-called 'Blood Campaign', a tactic derived from the body artists of the '70s. During live performances a nurse appears onstage and methodically draws from his arm two phials of blood. The phials are then signed by Cantsin and sold as objects of value. These displays have drawn criticism from some quarters, but Cantsin himself remains cheerfully unrepentant. *"Yes, I sell my blood to finance the Neoist Cultural Conspiracy,"* he disclosed in a recent personal letter; *"it's my job, my occupation, but anybody can do it. This year alone I've made at least twenty blood paintings during live actions – on canvas, T-shirts and white ballerina costumes worn by a live model. I always have fun doing it."*

With his Blood Campaign rituals and related activities Cantsin displays an implicit sense of how to feed into other systems of thought and communication. (Parenthetically, he is also one of Canada's premier recording artists with a number of excellent 12" releases to his credit.) Under his guidance the Neoist Embassy in Montreal has become the central information filter for a global network of conspirators. Together these conspirators have explored many diverse media, appearing at film, music and performance festivals throughout North America and Europe. They now have work on display in several art galleries and private collections, and have published a seemingly endless succession of manifestos. Much of their written material extols the virtues of plagiarism, *"a revolutionary tool uniquely suited to meet the demands of the late twentieth century."* Film and video presentations depict elements from contemporary Neoist mythology; live performances are designed to shock and provoke the viewer with *"primitive corporal information, giant-screen perversion and psycho-dramatic counter-actions."*

One of the chief aims of this activity is simply to gain attention for Cantsin and his circle. As former British disciple Stewart Home recently pointed out, *"Most Neoists would stoop to anything to achieve a little scandalized press coverage."* Cantsin, he added, *"even went as far as pointing out to an attendant that he had thrown his blood over an art gallery wall, hoping that this action would get him arrested. He was disappointed."* (Home renounced Neoism some years ago, but as it is a movement based on paradox, irony and conceptual gestures, he remains one of its foremost British exponents, editing with others a number of

Neoist/Situationist-inspired pamphlets and magazines, such as *'Smile'* under various names including Monty Cantsin and Karen Eliot).

It's true that Cantsin values dramatic, flourishing gestures over cold, hard specifics, but this in no way diminishes his importance. An accomplished media manipulator, he is able to take liberties by virtue of his sheer audacity. At worst he appears to be that rare breed of person, a mythomaniac, someone whose estimate of his own value is so high that he feels justified in inventing a legend that moulds it *"closer to the heart's desire."* Reviled by the establishment press for his various attention-grabbing strategies, he nevertheless continues to chart new frontiers of outrage. His riposte to his critics is typically oblique: *"This Monty Cantsin job is one of the most difficult ones I ever got, and it is not easy to accomplish it and balance the fictive and real parts. Of course, you can always kill me if you want, but I'll never die because I'm immortal, a six-fingered electronic entity, oh yes..."*

FURTHER READING:

'The 9th Neoist Festival' Catalogue, Arte Studio, Italy 1985
'Plagiarism: Art As Commodity And Strategies For Its Negation' edited by Stewart Home, Aporia Press.
'The Assault On Culture', Stewart Home, AK Press.
'Neoism Now', edited by Monty Cantsin, Artcore Editions, Berlin 1987.
'The Neoist Network's First European Training Camp', Pete Horobin and Peter Below, Kryptic Press, Germany, 1982.

STOP MISERY

A Message From
MONTY CANTSIN

SELF APPOINTED LEADER OF TH
PEOPLE OF - THE LOWER EAST SID

HARDART SINGER

Neoist Headquarters N.Y.C. 1987

Printed by
RAM
989-1976

ANOTHER INTRODUCTION TO NEOISM

A MONTY CANTSIN

No matter how much we may be capable of learning the past, it will not enable us to know the future.

When everyone is dead NEOISM is finished. Not before.

For no matter what learned scientists may say, NEOISM is politically speaking, not the beginning of humanity but its end, not the origin of peoples but their decay, not the natural birth of man but his unnatural death.

Is this confusing and contradictory?

Of course it is.

For legends attract the very best in our times, just as ideologies attract the average, and the whispered tales of gruesome secret powers behind the scenes attract the very worst.

No doubt, no political structure could have been more evocative of legendary tales than NEOISM, than the Neoist conspirators drifting from the conscious founding of research centres into ruling and dominating the world.

Legends have always played a powerful role in the making of history.

Legends were the spiritual foundations of every ancient city, empire, people, promising safe guidance through the limitless spaces of the future.

Legends made **MONTY CANTSIN** master of what he had done, and capable of dealing with what he could not undo.

The nineteenth century has offered us the curious spectacle of an almost simultaneous birth of the most varying and contradictory ideologies, each of which claimed to know the hidden truth about otherwise incomprehensible facts.

Legends however are not ideologies, they do not aim at universal explanation, but are always concerned with concrete facts.

The foundation legend of NEOISM, as Istvan Kantor tells it, starts from the fundamental reality of the neoist conspirators.

Surrounded by misery, they need and win help of the three elements of CONVULSION, SUBVERSION, DEFECTION, through the invention of Neoist Apartment Festivals.

"We will win the world," says Monty Cantsin, the open-pop-star leader-character of NEOISM (NEOISM is the only school of character in modern art), *without anyone caring how we did it: we will keep the world without anyone knowing how we did it: and we will carry the world on our backs without anyone seeing how we did it."*

But neither we, nor our sons will get anything out of that conspiracy except IDEAS.

According to a close friend, **Ackerman**, the well known psicolizer, Monty Istvan Kantor Cantsin, expects to live for at least five thousand years.

"It is his duty to do what he wants," declared recently **Dr Ackerman** who is also a founder member of the **14 Secret Masters of the Universe**. *"He feels himself a god – nothing less."*

It is obvious that the **Neoists** feel no obligation to man-made laws. *"We are not subject to the lies of science."*

The only 'law' they obey is the law of expansion and the only proof of their 'law fullness' is success.

They (the **Neoists**) are monsters of conceit in their success and monsters of modesty in their failure.

Kantor took great delight in his **Monty Cantsin** role that demanded a reconditioning of his whole personality.

He fitted into NEOISM.

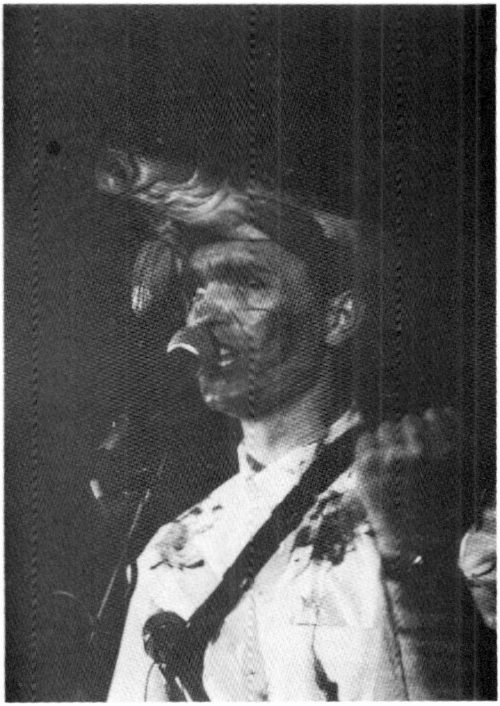

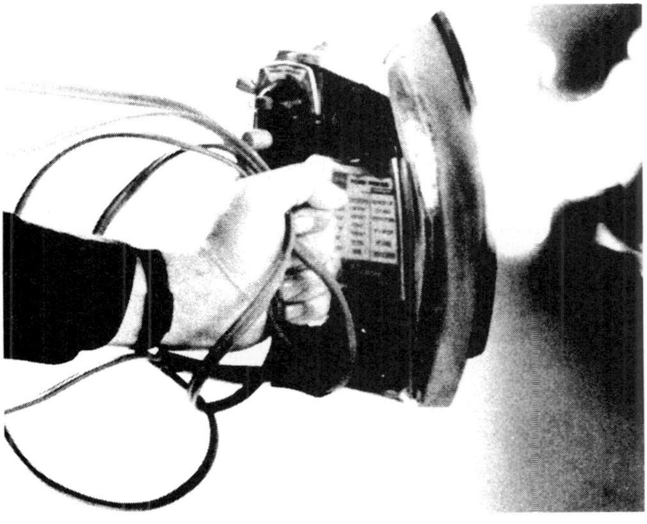

The origin of neoism manifesto.

The Monty Cantsin Commando announce the beginning of NEOISM.

We know that there were several efforts made to start NEOISM in the past 10 years in North-America and Europe but these were just insignificant, unimportant and unofficial attempts with no success.

The Monty Cantsin Commando declare that NEOISM never has been before and the First Neoist Manifesto was printed in Taiwan, on Oct 23, 1987, at 1.34 pm.

A few minutes later **The Monty Cantsin Commando** took over the world's biggest TV stations and Monty Cantsin gave the following speech:

"Hello"
Within the next second he was assassinated by **The Monty Cantsin Commando.**

But of course a miracle happened and the bloody and wounded Monty Cantsin continued his speech:

"I am your immortal friend."

At this moment all members of **The Monty Cantsin Commando** committed suicide.

Monty Cantsin went on saying:

"I hope you enjoyed this opening ceremony."

Members of **The Monty Cantsin Commando** got up, dried their blown up, bloody head and smiled to the cameras.

"From now" – continued Monty Cantsin – *"we are all immortal friends. Killing and suicide are popular forms of amusement."*

The Birth of Monty Cantsin Frozen-bob-star (-e)

The Monty Cantsin Commando announced the birth of Monty Cantsin frozen-bob-star, -e.

We know that there were many self-appointed Monty Cantsins in the past 10 years but all of them were fake, false prophets, so called *open-pop-stars*.

Monty Cantsin frozen-bobstar (-e) was born just a few seconds ago but -e is already bigger and stronger than King Kong, more powerful than Lenin and the Russian Revolution, and wiser than Einstein.

There is only one frozen-bob-star (-e).

-e is well guarded and protected by The Monty Cantsin Commando against hate, insults, mail-art, journalists, plagiarists, shitheads, etc.

Monty Cantsin frozen-bob-star (-e) does not want to communicate with you and does not want to participate in your activities.

Monty Cantsin frozen-bob-star (-e) only reminds you that you are not Monty Cantsin.

You are just a starving artist who wants to be famous and rich by using the name of Monty Cantsin.

For this you have to suffer and you have to send your welfare check to Monty Cantsin frozen-bob-star (-e).

-e will use your money to control you and to have total domination on you.

Monty Cantsin frozen-bob-star (-e) is the newborn dictator of the world, the King of NEOISM.

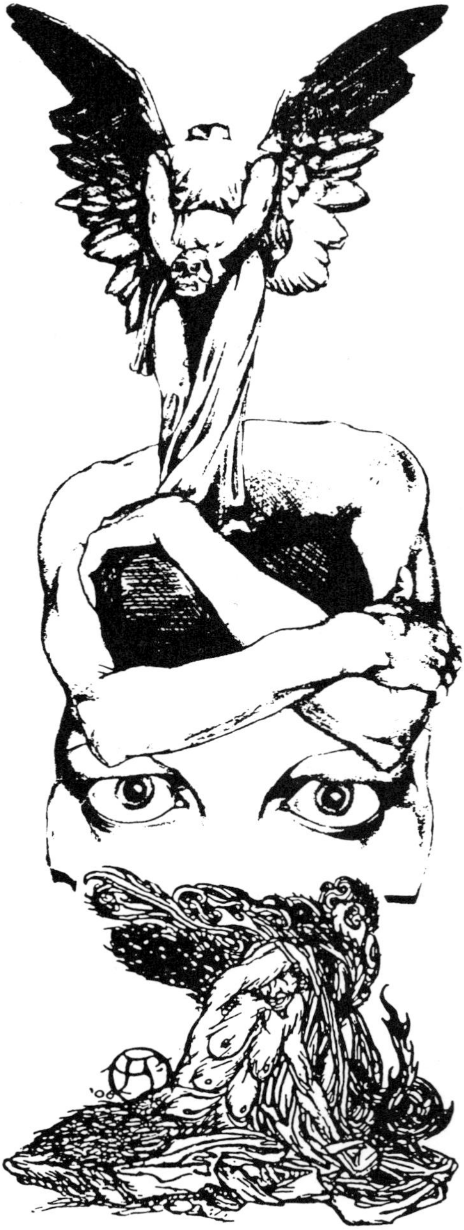

TIME MIRRORS

'The Art of Austin Osman Spare 1888-1956'

GENESIS P-ORRIDGE

"Since all phenomena (or phenomenally appearing things) which arise present no reality in themselves, they are said to be of the noumena. (In other words they are of the Voidness regarded as the noumenal background of source of the physical universe of phenomena.) Though not formed into anything, yet they give shape to everything. Thus it is that phenomena and noumena are ever in union, and said to be of one nature. They are, like ice and water, reflection and mirror, two aspects of a single thing."

'The Seven Books of Wisdom'
Tibetan Text

In the case of a mirror there is a third aspect, the subject/viewer. Mirrors reveal and conceal. Their mystery permanent, their hints at doorways, windows and thresholds out of reach of most minds. Time. Image. Idea. There can be no separation, scientifically or subjectively. The atavistic face gazes down into a crystal pool. Ice cold water. Grunts. A hand shatters the image, fear gaunt and haunting passes across, a shadowy cloud, and through all Time that moment can persist, be reclaimed.

"What is Time, but a variety of one thing?"

A.O.S.

These moments of Time accumulate, are listed under memory in our modern synapses, are posited as always retrievable, amorphous. Nothing is forgotten, all is permitted. In a stinking cave muttering babies scream and scratch, furs undulate in copulation. In one corner, bright-eyed first marks are daubed on a wall. They are marks to function, marks of place, of Time. They are marks to draw results and persist beyond one human lifetime. Instinct has arisen, snake-like, coiling itself into intuition and suggested the very power of suggestion. No-one noted down from a book this process, it grew from watching the elements, closeness to life-forces, death-forces that modern persons are divorced from. On this damp stone there is a curve, it is land, horizon, ejaculation, movement.

"Magic consists in seeing and willing beyond the next horizon"

The Sar.

Mrs Patterson stares down. Pencilled into existence. It is her as she was when she took Austin Osman Spare at 14 years old and initiated him into the art of sexual magic and a powerful system of sorcery that she had rediscovered through communion across time with systems and techniques that grew from the most animalistic and pure union of instinct. She knew, and she taught Spare, how to travel through Time, and how to remain present in Life after bodily death. She was a medium, but her guides were not just ikons of the intuitive tribes, American indians, tantric Tibetans, aborigines. She understood the most particular secret. Her medium was herself. She was able to travel through mirrors back in Time, and forward in Time. There is a drawing by Spare, pencil & gouache, finished in 1928. The main figure is Mrs Patterson. Coming from behind her making a blister in the shimmering green aura, a half-complete face. It belongs to no one, everyone. It is her, literally, it is a cavalier, symbolically, it is Austin Osman Spare literally. This one picture contains all the secrets Spare never wrote down. He appears in the bottom right-hand corner, an old man, eyes closed, concentrating, materialising. What Spare does is trick us. All his writings are symbolic, they were never intended to be taken literally on any level, despite modern infatuations to the contrary. His writings are purely decorative. They are entertainment. His relaxation *after* his real work. His special trick was to convince everybody that his drawings, paintings, images were symbolic. They are in fact his only real work. Like all great sorcerers, he hid the real secret in apparently commonplace media. In the key picture he is actually kneeling. It is a photographic image of his prediction of both his bodily death and his worship of Mrs Patterson as his true Goddess. His use of prostitutes and scarlet woman of middle age in his sexual magic was to return to his potency with his only access point through Time into Timelessness. They were closer to Mrs Patterson, so he used them as a focusing visual image to recharge his contact with her. When she died, he took her energy and literally trapped it, living, into this, and one or two other pictures. He sinks into her chest, is absorbed, they rise together, androgynous, both their faces, all their ages superimposed. He has drawn himself dying, conjuring himself into the image in advance, so he remains always able to return.

"Art is the truth we have realised of our belief."

A.O.S.

"Art can contradict science."

A.O.S.

"Do you see those flowers growing on the sides of the abyss whose beauty is so deadly and whose scent is so disturbing? Beware..."
de Gautia.

In his images of sorcery, his purest incantations through Art, Spare uses a graphic skill and technique second to none. Yet his most commonly seen works are excellent, but obvious in their skill. Sometimes deliberately fast and loose. The nearest modern parallel would be Salvador Dali who could suggest perfection in a few marks, or worship HIS Goddess, Gala, with photographically pure technique that is unearthly accurate. It seems to me that Spare is equal in genius to Rembrandt in the past, Dali in the present and Brion Gysin in the future.

"The future is in the past, but it is not wholly contained in the present."
Hoene-Wronski.

Both Spare and Gysin lived to reach new dimensions, they understood to pursue Wisdom, not knowledge. This alone made collaboration with the most magickal groups impossible. Where the need for nostalgic elitism and power by knowledge and length of bookshelf far too often camouflages self-aggrandizement, where self-improvement to serve is the reality. Peladan was in fact a prophet of developments that later became possible, and only now become likely. Spare was aware that mystery and magick generate fascination and attraction in human persons. He used his books, his Beardsley-like graphics, his writings to attract interest after his death. He knew that this would reactivate his soul and animate his psyche once more. He was also shrewd enough to make *all* his secrets non-verbal. Not one is contained in his writings. Only the atavistic paintings, and the 'Time Mirror' drawings explain his vision.

"The universe is a creative process carried on by man's imagination, an operative power capable of becoming more supple, more fully animate."
Teillhard de Chardin.

What is happening in these certain key pictures is this: All ideas have an image. There are no exceptions. All materials that make a piece of art are material. They are formed of patterns of atoms and molecules, charged by various energies. Modern psychology also accepts that Ideas are material entities, like animals and plants. All mythological ideas, Jung states, are *essentially real,* and far older than any philosophy. They originated in primal perceptions, correspondences and experiences. The catalytic element that regenerates a reaction between Entitic Ideas and spectator (viewer of Painting) favours parapsychological events in the presence of an active archetype. In the case of Spare's Art this can be anything from an obvious glyph, a non-decorative aesthetic arrangement, or in the most intense works an invisible charge of energy which calls deeper, instinctual layers of the psyche into action. The archetype is a borderline phenomenon, an acausal connecting principle closest in the explanation to deliberately controlled, SELF-conscious, synchronicity. When Spare says Self-Love, he means 'Self-conscious, yet egoless'. When he uses the word Chaos, he is amusing himself, and leaving a key clue. Austin Osman Spare's Chaos is both a signature and a sign-post to future time. ChDVH (CH)=Joy=23. A.O.S. is simply his name, his authorship within his secret sorceries.

"Art is the instinctive application of the knowledge latent in the subconscious."

A.O.S.

After Mrs Patterson died Spare was waiting to be inside her again, fused with her energy. The key picture is the actual moment of his death, and the moment of her death overlaid. His aim in all his magick was to reunite his spirit and hers within his Art so that they might quite literally live forever. They do live. Many unprompted witnesses have seen Mrs Patterson's eyes close, open, cry, her whole head turn, a quite literally living portrait. Magick makes dreams real, makes the impossible possible, focuses the will. Throughout its history, crystals, water, polished metal, mirrors have been used to oracular ends. Spare's massive achievement is that he recognised the potential of Art, of image, to be the most powerful mirror of all. A window in Time, an Interface with death. In his art he captures not just an image but a life-form and energy. What happens is that this lies dormant until it comes into contact and reacts with other energies; the viewer. Primal, atavistic man knew this and invested his ideas/images with unrestricted power; when you deal with image only, as with most 20th Century Art, you don't get anything back except aesthetics. Spare has achieved the previously impossible, a two way communication where his image reacts to and with us. It has a life of its own. The nearest parallel, a mirror in which you can see another world, another time, another dimension, yet one you cannot reach into like water, one your hand reaching out cannot quite touch; the glass remains solid and frustrates us.

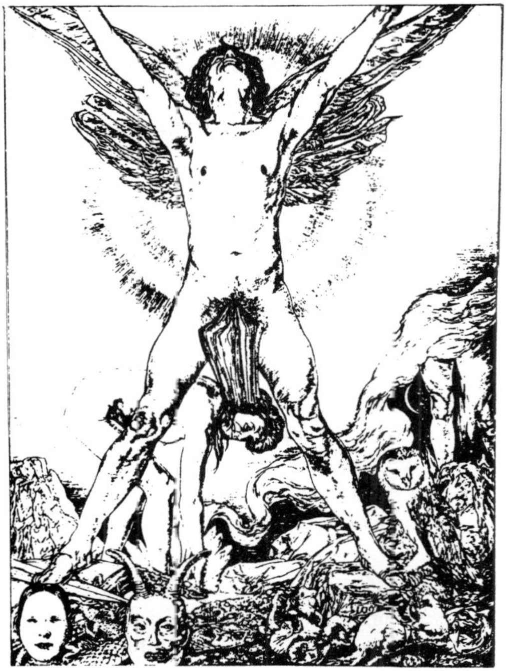

What this energy held within his images is doing is transcending the barriers of Time; so what we are dealing with is a four-dimensional object or image. This form of energy will have existed at all times and will exist at all times.

An objective and critical survey of the available data would establish that perceptions occur as if, in part there were no space, in part no time. Space and Time are not only the most immediate certainties for us, they are also empirically, since everything observable happens as though it occurred in Space and Time. In the face of this overwhelming certainty it is understandable that reason should have the greatest difficulty in granting validity to the peculiar nature of 'telepathic' phenomena. But anyone who does justice to the facts cannot but admit that their apparent space-timelessness is their most essential quality. The fact that we are totally unable to imagine a form of existence without Space and Time by no means proves that such an existence is in itself impossible. And, therefore, just as we cannot draw from an appearance of space-timelessness, any absolute conclusion about a space-timeless form of existence, so we are not entitled to conclude from the apparent space-time quality of our perception that there is *no form* of existence without space and time. Just as physics now allows for 'limitedness of space', a relativization, it is beginning with Catastrophe Theory to posit a 'limitedness' of both Time and Causality. In short, nothing is fixed, the possibilities *alone* are endless.

"Conscious looking is a search for verification of the notions that impel the search, and always has a circular mirroring element in it."

T.O.P.Y.

In Spare's best images it seems a medium has been found whereby the essence that survives death, but is mostly beyond our communication, has been captured by, and transmitted into an object that we are familiar with (i.e. a painting), and that we are therefore used to trying to interpret or receive information from. Because of the familiarity of painting we don't put up barriers. We expect to try and see what the artist felt, wanted to say. If Spare said he was going to capture and demonstrate the soul after death, most observers would switch off. There would be interference with the transmission. Because Spare seduces us by saying this is an artwork, a picture, when in fact it is a photograph or mirror of an actual reality we remain open-minded which means there is more chance that the phenomenon of actual physical changes in his pictures will happen. We shall see, in short, that which many of us rightly choose not to believe in: living, moving, changing images of a post-death life-force, or soul essence. You see it reacting to you, it receives and transmits direct into your conscious senses, but it must also be transmitting direct into the subconscious also, just as Sigilisation does. Presumably we transmit back to what is there so what is there will change over the years as it reacts with various observers. All these energies mingle and mutate. The soul, life-force, energy, call it what you will, is generally said to be visible through the mirrors of the soul, the eyes. In the 1928 key work of Mrs Patterson the eyes are neither open, nor shut, and this is true in much of Spare's works. They are neither rejecting the possibility of seeing the captured soul, nor openly inviting it. This half-shut, half-open limbo suggests responsibility lies with the viewer to choose to commune with the elemental energies portrayed. By painting himself old when he was young and young when he was old, Spare mirrors Rembrandt once more and clearly directs us constantly to links going backwards and forwards through time as he succeeds in presenting an image of the apparently impossible – IMMORTALITY.

"Accept nothing, assume nothing, always look further, be open-eyed as

well as open-minded and don't kid yourself."

Old T.O.P.Y. Proverb.

The psyche in its deepest reaches seems well able to participate in an existence beyond the accepted web of Space and Time. This dimension is often dubbed eternity, or infinity, yet it actually behaves, if we take Spare's art as representational (it is *not* symbolic), as either a one-way or two-way mirror dependent for its function upon the translation of the unconscious, into a communicable image that bonds the actual molecules of the graphic image with its driving forces, unlocked from the unconscious into a fixed or mobile source of power dependent upon previous viewers, and, more vitally, our own abilities to interface directly with its energy. All 'matter' is formed of molecules and atoms; therefore, at least in theory, we *can* potentially walk through walls by correct vibration of our own body corresponding with the vibration of the wall. It is just as theoretically possible to lock energy into the form of an image that has the ability to move, change, alter and animate its content, the only gap of credibility being that of first-hand-experience. We don't believe it until it happens to us. We only know what we have experienced. Belief is rooted in recognition.

Imagination opens to synthesis something larger than the sum total of reason. New images reflect more than logical synthesis can produce. There is a radical discontinuity in every truly creative idea or discovery. Projection direct from image to viewer involves more than the logical mode of thinking that does the projecting. An idea cannot exist separate from an image. For example, the Virgin Mary image embodies the idea of 'compassion'. A Goddess or God is a figurative image of an idea. Images are the root language of social and self control. Science attempts to explain the universe objectively, without a viewer, therefore it cannot explain Art, or the unique effects or phenomena Spare generates by it. That is not a possible function of science; it cannot tell us why Spare's images can alter, why his faces change, eyes open and close, colours vary. Photographs are said to steal souls; they certainly capture a moment in Time. Freeze it. So do the images and oracles of Art, true Art. For Art was originally revelatory, shamanistic, fully integrated into every moment of life. Spare's images capture the process of creation, the thoughts of the creator, and the memories of the viewer, which recalls past events and feelings that are more compact, briefer, than when they took place originally. Memories are Past-Time brought into 'Present' Time.

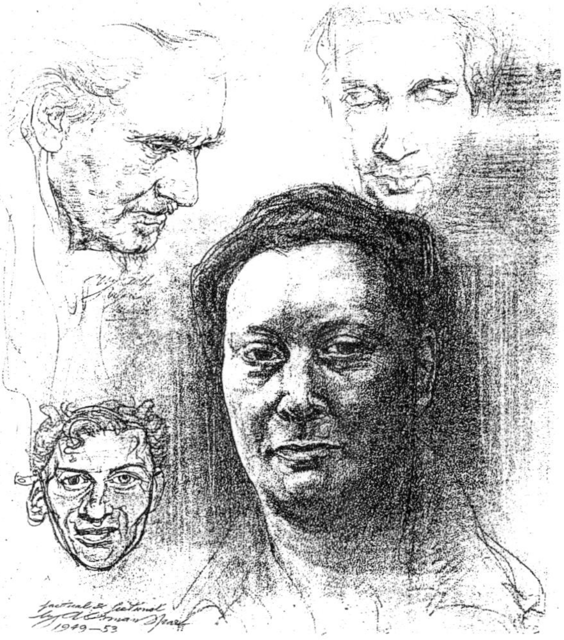

'Factual and Fictional.' Pencil, 1949-53.
(Editions Graphiques Collection).

Time is not linear, all Time exists simultaneously and points in every direction simultaneously. It is quaquaversal, omnipresent. There is no reason why Spare's images should not capture Time, thought and experience, then recreate and expand upon it in the viewers' mind. Subjective experience is no less real than objective conjecture. All roads lead to Rome in a mirror-to-mirror function. This function of mirroring is found in the trance state in a simple, direct way. The higher techniques of idea and artist's illusory skill make active through Time and Space effects and phenomena normally consigned to the sceptical parking lot of modern existence.

Years of trying to rationalise inexplicable experiences adequately fall apart, and only a unique reassessment via Spare's self-confessed image sorcery begins to give answers to what we see and feel. Time mirrors Time.

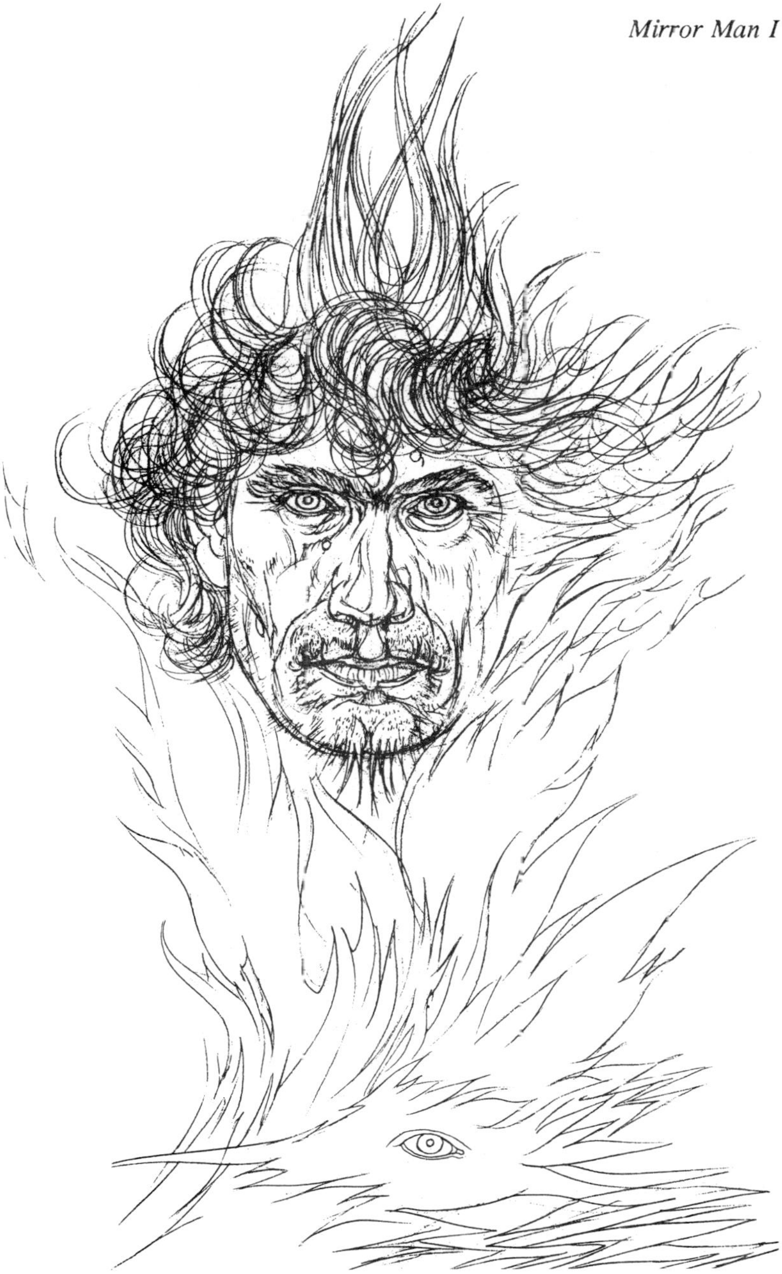

Automatic Self-Portrait (1925)

In the Mrs Patterson picture Spare depicts her not at the moment of death, but as she looked when she was young. He depicts himself, then quite young, as he would look, old at the moment of death. He thus creates a situation of contradiction. She is dead, yet alive and young, he is alive and young, yet dead. This visualisation makes the image energies circular, not closed. That is why the picture is a window, mirror, threshold active and useable by them or us. The illustration is a key to understanding the entire situation and its implications. It is a depiction of the real. Spare and Mrs Patterson live on in his art, taking the concept of Art being the Life and Soul of a culture further than ever before dreamed. The only question remaining is, now they have cheated death, can they, will they ever come back out?

"He who transcends Time escapes necessity"

"All nature is a vast reflection of that which
is within us, or else we could not know it."

"Embrace reality by imagination".

"What is death? A great mutation to your next self".

"The life-force is not blind, we are".

Austin Osman Spare

THE UNDYING MONSTER

IAN BLAKE

1.The Undying Monster.

In 1922 Jessie D. Kerruish published a gothic horror novel titled *'The Undying Monster'*. Plot-wise it was a combination of various elements necessary to the supernatural mystery genre, including murder, moon-madness and hereditary evil. The Undying Monster of the title was finally revealed as a werewolf and despatched by a stalwart psychic detective. Good triumphed over evil (after a fashion) and the cosmic balance of the universe was once again restored. A film version of *'The Undying Monster'* was produced in 1942, but to the best of my knowledge the book itself has been out of print for many years. I mention it here simply because its title sums up one of the chief characteristics of all true monsters – namely that they are *undying*.

The Frankenstein Monster exhibits this characteristic. So too does Dracula. So do Dr. Fu Manchu and Jason from the *'Friday the 13th'* movies. Each of these characters has been killed repeatedly, both in fiction and (especially) on the big screen. And yet, despite all the immolation, despite all the burnings, beatings and bodily impalements, they still keep on coming back for more. They are archetypes, you see. And an archetype cannot be killed.

In a sense this also applies to Adolf Hitler. He too was a 'monster' in human form. And, like Dracula and Dr. Fu Manchu, he has achieved a kind of immortality in the realm of imagination. American conspiracy researcher Mae Brussell of the radio show *'World Watchers'* seriously postulates that Hitler may still be alive. Not only alive but in full possession (more or less) of his faculties and actively participating in US government policy. She cites as evidence the fact that many of Hitler's top advisers were secretly flown into the States at the close of WWII. There they were given new identities, new status, and put to work on a variety of government projects relating to 'defence', etc.

The question of Hitler's advanced age (if alive today he would be in the region of 100 years old) in no way deters Brussell from her theory. She responds by drawing attention to the case of Mikhailovich Molotov, who worked for many years with Stalin during the '20s and '30s. Molotov went into political exile during the mid '50s and was expelled from the Communist Party in 1964. In 1984, however, he was reinstated, and now receives a full Soviet pension. He is, apparently, of sound mind, and still speaks lucidly about his aims and ideals. Brussell continues:

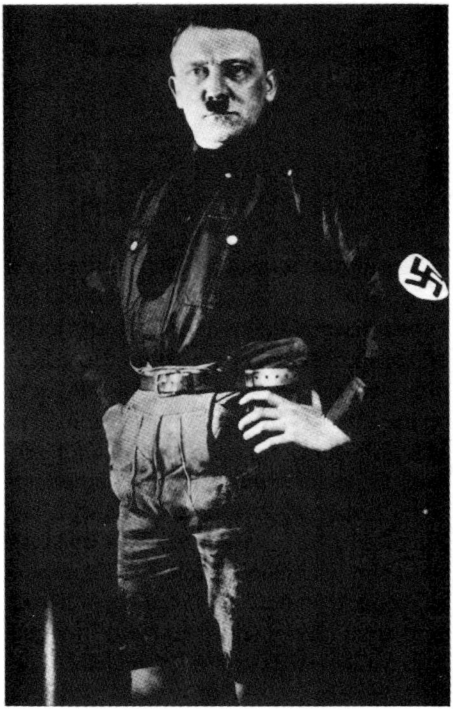

"The Beast does not look what he is. He may even have a comic moustache." (Soloviev 'The Anti Christ)'.

"The main argument that I receive when I talk about the possibility that Adolf Hitler is still alive is that he's too old, and that if he's too old he can't make decisions, and he has to be senile. And I have said that there's no physical evidence of any kind – and this is written up in many books, that Adolf Hitler and Eva Braun died in the bunker; and there is a possibility that Hitler has been directing a lot of activity that has been going on since WWII, from Antarctica, from Argentina, then Brazil and then into Switzerland, where he can have his mind, he can have his protectors, and where people know that Hitler is alive. The people who want to tell you that Hitler is dead have nothing to fall back on except the reasoning that even if he were alive he could do no harm, and you see that Mr. Molotov, who has a good mind, who can speak, who talks about his activities, his desires – this throws aside the possibility that all 100-year-olds necessarily have to be senile and don't know what's

happening. To say that Molotov is alive therefore Hitler is alive is ridiculous, but there is a possibility that, in conjunction with top people in our (the US) defence department, such as the late Otto Skorzenzcy; or Klaus Barbie; or the mysterious Fritz Kramer with the monocle, or Peter Drucker and the management of our money and our multinational empire, there is no way of knowing if the genius of that man isn't still around... I have every reason to believe that things have gone too smoothly for everyone around Adolf Hitler... And there hasn't been a break in what he had or did, with his top intelligence chief Reinhardt Galen coming into the USA and so forth..."

Mae Brussell isn't alone in believing that Hitler may still be alive and kicking (however feebly). According to Gunther Rosenberg of the European Occult Research Society: *"One persistent rumour in occultism is that Hitler, Martin Bormann and many of the missing Nazis were spirited out of Germany. Some claim they are in South America, and as we know, Eichmann was found there. Others who believe in the hollow Earth theory claim that a fleet of Nazi submarines took Hitler and his henchmen to a Nazi base set up under the ice-cap at the South Pole."*

The 'Hollow Earth' theory referred to by Rosenberg derives from a curious amalgamation of ancient and modern myths. According to numerous texts on the subject our planet is actually a hollow sphere with access points at the North and South Poles. These access points, enormous holes each some 1,500(!) miles across, have allegedly been photographed on several occasions, notably by the ESSA 3 and ESSA 7 satellites in 1967/68. Author and UFOlogist Brinsley Le Poer Trench describes the ESSA photos as *"the most exciting and remarkable ever taken."* They prove, he says, that UFOs emanate from a mysterious region hidden in the bowels of the earth – the Agharti of legend.

A variation of this theory is known to UFOlogists as the Nazi hypothesis. It proposes that UFOs are actually secret weapons, developed by Hitler and his aides during the latter days of WW11 and now headquartered in a tropical base beneath the Antarctic. Believers in this theory claim that international Arctic expeditions conducted in 1946/47 were actually searches for Hitler, who was thought to be still alive. Contemporary UFO 'flaps' are explained as reconnaissance trips by Nazi aeronauts at the controls of flying saucers. Among the chief proponents of this theory are a group based in Toronto, Canada, known as Samizdat (actually a faction of the neo-Nazi Western Guard). Their propaganda speculates that Nazi forces may one day return to the surface world and there wreak vengeance on Britain and her wartime allies. Because of this most UFO pundits feel that the group is merely using UFO imagery to promote a groundswell of Nazi sentiment. Nevertheless, despite its sheer improbability, the Nazi hypothesis has supporters in virtually every country on earth.

I wrote to the Samizdat group circa April 1987, requesting further information on their Nazi/UFO connections. In reply I was sent details of several relevant publications, including *'Secret Nazi Polar Expeditions – Nazi UFO Bases Under the Poles?'* (a snip at £10) and *'UFOs – Nazi Secret Weapons'* (again only £10, but "supplies are limited so order NOW!"). Also contained in the Samizdat info-pack was a list of 64 posters depicting Nazi secret weapons for use on land, sea and in the air. I now have the list pinned over my desk. It includes drawings of such marvellous Heath Robinson gadgets as the Bachstelze U-Boot Rotordrachen (a rickety-looking one-man gyrocopter) and Krummlaufgewehr (a rifle with a bent barrel for shooting around corners). Sure enough, poster No. 51, the Fliegende Scheibe (Flugkreisel), shows three gleaming discoid UFOs drifting across an inky background. Even in such a preposterous setting as this, it remains an image of considerable force and appeal.

2 What's History

Nazi policy regarding the hollow earth concept can be traced back to a specific incident in 1942, when Hitler convened a meeting of his chiefs of staff and announced that he was in receipt of important new information. *"We have just learned that the earth is concave, not convex."* He allegedly continued, *"We are living not on the outside, but on the* ***inside****. Man is like a nest of insects crawling on the inside of a crystal bowl."*

"Has this been proved scientifically?" a top aide asked dubiously.

"It has been developed by several scientists of the National Socialist party," Hitler replied; *"and now we must make tests to demonstrate the truth of the plan."*

In pursuit of this outlandish theory Hitler gathered together many of Germany's leading experts on radar techniques and despatched them to Rugen Island in the Baltic Sea. There they were ordered to set up their equipment in a misguided attempt to monitor British shipping manoeuvres. Radar units were trained at the sky at an acute angle, and left to run for periods of up to a week. As Dr. Gunther Rosenberg of the European Occult Research Society later explained: *"The theory was that radar waves travelled in a straight line, so it would be possible to obtain a reading on an area beyond the horizon. In other words, by bouncing radar rays off the top of Hitler's 'bowl' they could obtain a reading of the British fleet and its positions. It was one of the most fantastic theories in history."*

Needless to say, the Rugen Island expedition failed to achieve its objectives and returned to Berlin in disgrace. At this Hitler allegedly lost all faith in his so-called 'scientific advisors'. Several were shipped off to the concentration camps, where, according to Gunther Rosenberg, *"Himmler's death's head division of S.S. murdered them and scattered their remains to the wind. And yet, despite this setback, the Nazis continued to believe in a hollow earth."*

Hitler and his aides apparently derived this bizarre fixation from Tibetan esotericism with its persistent references to Agharti and Shamballah. They were also inspired to a great extent by Bulwer Lytton's hollow earth novel *'The Coming Race'*, which first saw the light of day in 1871. Despite its extreme age *'The Coming Race'* is still regarded as a classic of subterranean lore. The action takes place in a cavern world lit by *"artificial gas lamps placed at regular intervals, as in the city."* Here, in this hitherto unsuspected realm, live the mysterious Vril-ya, whose powers far exceed those of ordinary homo sapiens. Tall and statuesque, with inscrutable sphinx-like faces, the Vril-ya are nurtured and sustained by a fanatical hatred of the surface races. Bulwer Lytton, who belonged to several magical orders (including Samuel Mathers' Golden Dawn) always maintained that their existence was pure invention. The Nazis, however, believed otherwise. As early as 1936 they began to send teams of explorers into the caves and mines of Europe to look for entrances to the hollow earth. Their objective, according to Rosenberg, was to find *"the new, advanced man."* In other words, to establish contact with the Vril-ya and forge an alliance aimed at world domination.

Hitler apparently gave this research his full support. He is said to have encouraged most forms of occultism within the Nazi inner circle, whilst simultaneously proscribing them elsewhere. Several of his most trusted officers even went so far as to launch a *'Luminous Lodge of the Vril'* society to learn the secret of *'Vril power'*. There is also some evidence to suggest that a black lodge of Tibetan monks was established in Berlin to practise ritual magic on behalf of the Axis powers. (This may have happened as long ago as 1925 following the publication of Ossendowski's *'Men, Beasts and Gods'*, which sparked off renewed interest in hollow earth phenomena.) Pauwels and Bergier believe that this lodge may have contained anything up to 1,000 members. Warren Smith takes up the same theme in his *'This Hollow Earth'*:

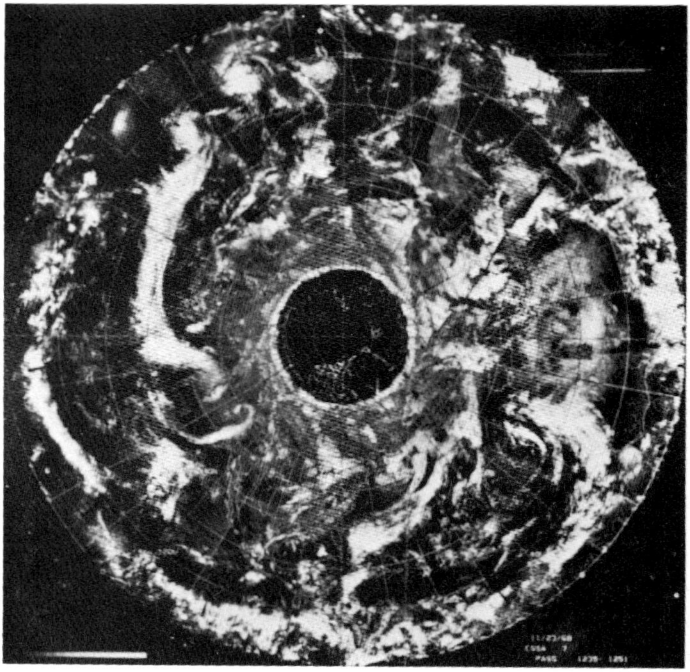

The famous photo of the North Pole taken in 1968 by the ESSA 7 Satellite. For some, this was conclusive proof that the Earth is hollow.

"When Germany fell, Berlin was a smouldering city assaulted by the weapons of modern warfare," he writes. *"The centre of the Third Reich was in flames. And in the rubble of Berlin were hundreds of thousands of Nazi warriors. Among them were several hundred volunteers in the black uniform of the S.S. death's head division. They were orientals, without badges, papers or any kind of identification. They were the last of the black monks who helped Hitler's dark, menacing movement."*

Hitler's *"dark, menacing movement"* came to an end in 1945, ground into submission by sheer weight of numbers. Nevertheless, rumours persist to this day that Hitler didn't die in the ruins of Berlin but went 'underground' in the literal sense of the term, retreating into the bowels of the earth and there striking up an alliance with Rex Mundi, the legendary King of the World.

These rumours were again brought to light in the early '70s when an organization known as APEN, or the Aerial Phenomena Enquiry Network, began to make its presence felt in UFO circles. APEN first appeared on the scene circa 1974, commencing its activities with a sustained propaganda campaign. Leading UFO researchers were bombarded with letters, articles and other written material for a period spanning almost four years. Tape recordings heavily interspersed with Nazi war broadcasts and martial music were also circulated. At no time did the members of APEN identify themselves or specify their objectives. Close ties with the American government or secret service were implied, but these were never proven. In point of fact the structure and tactics of APEN were more reminiscent of Hitler's Nazi party than anything else. (This impression was reinforced by the title of the organization's 'in-house' magazine, a German phrase meaning 'spearhead'.) APEN either disbanded or went underground a decade ago, but its influence continues to be felt. As leading British UFOlogist Jenny Randle's remarks in her book *'Skycrash'*: *"One or two UFO investigators have speculated that a fantastic UFO technology was handed on from the dying remnants of the Third Reich in 1945. And indeed, we know that experimental weapons of a distinctly UFO-like appearance **were** tested during the last few months of the war. It is said that a Fourth Reich exists, and is readying itself for future world leadership. Perhaps there is a group of Nazis flying around the world in UFOs. Perhaps APEN are (sic) their spy network..."*

Perhaps...

3 Notes From The Underground

Hollow earth lore was given a tremendous fillip in March, 1945, with the first publication of Richard Shaver's *'I Remember Lemuria'* in the science fiction magazine *'Amazing Stories'*. Shaver was actually a lowly welding machine operator from Pennsylvania, USA, who, at some time in the early '40s, allegedly began to hear 'voices' which helped him to remember a former life in legendary Lemuria. According to Shaver the lost continents of Lemuria, Atlantis and Mu were populated in the distant past by beings from another planet. These beings had access to a technology far in advance of anything mankind has ever possessed. Their reign was a veritable golden age in the annals of prehistory. It lasted for centuries, only coming to an end when the sun began to emit a form of radiation which caused them to die out in large numbers. Faced with extinction these Titans had no choice but to flee back into the depths of space. Some, however, stayed behind and established a toehold in the underground world, where the rays of the sun couldn't reach them. Their descendants still live on today, clinging to the remains of a now moribund technology and attempting to manipulate the lives of earth's surface inhabitants. Those who bring harm to mankind are known as the Dero (from *de*trimental *ro*bots or Abandon*dero*). They are usually described as degenerate, idiotic midgets, their bodies covered in boils and running sores. Another, less populous group are known as the Tero – a contraction of *te*rrestrial or integrative *ro*bots. The Tero are the good guys of the underground scene. By using beneficial nutrients, chemicals and ray machines they have managed to ward off any suggestion of mental or physical degeneration, thus retaining their original, almost godlike appearance. They now exist for one reason only – to oppose the villainous Dero and thwart their machinations.

For a period spanning almost five years Shaver's rambling, barely literate flights of fantasy were published as non-fiction in the pages of *'Amazing Stories'*. Managing editor Ray Palmer is now known to have rewritten and expanded the original manuscripts, imposing at least some semblance of order onto Shaver's prose. Many faithful readers of *'Amazing'* were scandalized at the presentation of this material as fact. Others, however, responded favourably and even began to remember exciting *"past lives"* of their own. The reason for this state of affairs is simple. The Shaver Mystery touched a deeply responsive chord in popular consciousness. Like many 'new age' religions it succeeded by getting people to notice their IMAGINATIONS for the first time. Remembering previous incarnations proved to be an appealing concept. Suddenly even the lowliest manual worker, his endurance strained to breaking point under the dead weight of everyday life, could console himself with the thought that he had once been a handsome prince or mighty warrior in legendary lost Atlantis. It was all great fun.

When interest in the hollow earth began to flag, Ray Palmer moved on to the subject of UFOs in a new magazine, *'Fate'*. The Shaver Mystery, however, is still with us today, surviving in the pages of such magazines as *'Shavertron'* and *'The Hollow Earth Bulletin'*. Later writers have added their own perspective to the mythos, but the basic elements remain unchanged. The Dero, for instance, are still working constantly to overthrow the surface races. To this end they employ all the impedimenta of forbidden science, including a fiendish array of Telaug and Vision Ray Machines, Tractor Ray Beams and Surgical Ray Cannons. With these they are able to wreak havoc in the fabric of everyday life. As Warren Smith writes in *'This Hollow Earth'*: *"The Dero can instantly change highway traffic signals, sabotage industrial machinery and ruin complex devices. Have you ever had a machine or object that refused to work, then performed marvellously when the repairman arrived? A Dero may have been amusing himself."*

Quite!

Among their many unsavoury practices the Dero are said to indulge in endless sex orgies, periodically using *'Stim Ray'* machines to restore their flagging vigour. Not infrequently they will kidnap an unfortunate surface girl and rape her repeatedly until she dies of exhaustion or sheer physical abuse.

As one might expect, there is no *'hard'* evidence to support any of this nonsense, only a mass of personal testimony. Take for instance the following letter, which appeared in the June 1946 issue of *'Amazing'*:

"Sirs:

I flew my last combat mission on May 26, 1945, when I was shot up over Bassein and ditched my ship in Remaree Roads off Cheduba Island. I was missing five days. I requested leave at Kashmere. I and Captain (name deleted by request) left Srinagar and went to Rudok, then through the Khese pass to the northern foothills of the Karakoram. We found what we were looking for. We knew what we were searching for.

For Heaven's sake drop the whole thing! You are playing with dynamite. My companion and I fought our way out of a cave with submachine guns. I have two nine-inch scars on my left arm that came from wounds given me in the cave when I was 50 feet from a moving object of any kind, and in perfect silence. The muscles were nearly ripped out. How? I don't know. My friend has a hole the size of a dime in his right bicep. It was seared inside. How we don't know. But we both believe we know more about the Shaver Mystery than any other pair ..."

At first the author of this letter requested that his identity be withheld. Later his name was revealed: Fred Lee Crisman.

Taken by itself Crisman's testimony is worthless. In the light of his subsequent exploits, however, it assumes greater significance. Crisman, you see, later became a central figure in the notorious Maury Island 'slag' mystery, which was to change the face of UFO research irrevocably.

The affair began on June 23, 1947, when a *"doughnut-shaped object"* discharged a shower of slag onto a small boat moored off Maury Island near Tacoma, Washington, USA. One piece of slag slightly injured a fifteen year old boy who was working on the boat; another struck and killed the boy's dog. The boy's father, Harold Dahl, took him to a nearby hospital where his injury was given medical treatment. Dahl then reported the incident to his 'superior officer', who turned out to be none other than Fred Lee Crisman of *'Amazing Stories'* fame.

The following day, June 24, 1947, was pivotal in the history of UFOlogy. It was marked by three closely related events, each of which was to have far-reaching implications for the entire field of phenomenal research. The first of these began when Harold Dahl was visited at his home by a black-suited man who recited in detail everything that had happened the previous day at Maury Island *as if he had been there*. He then warned Dahl not to discuss the incident with anyone, adding that there would be unpleasant consequences for his wife and family if he disobeyed. *"This,"* according to John Keel, *"was the first modern Man In Black report."*

The second of the day's far-reaching events took place as Kenneth Arnold, a salesman who lived not far from Tacoma, was flying his private plane over Mount Rainier in Washington State. Arnold was making good time on a journey from Chehalis to Yakima when he saw a formation of nine UFOs approaching the mountain on a southern trajectory. They moved, he later told reporters, *"the way a saucer would if you skipped it over the water."* It was from this graphic description that the term flying 'saucer' entered the language.

The third event came when Fred Lee Crisman (who just happened to own the boat over which Dahl's sighting took place) went to Maury Island to look for verification of what had happened. To begin with he allegedly found quantities of some strange slag-like material strewn along the shoreline. Then he too saw a doughnut-shaped UFO flying across the sky.

Shortly after these events took place, Harold Dahl's son disappeared, only to turn up weeks later in a distant state, suffering from total amnesia. His entire memory had apparently been wiped clean like a precious but foolishly unlabelled cassette. Crisman, meanwhile, had mailed details of the Maury Island UFO sighting to Ray Palmer at *'Amazing Stories'*. Palmer was intrigued by Crisman's account and decided to send an investigator to the scene. With this in mind he enlisted the services of Kenneth Arnold, whose UFO sighting over Mount Rainier had taken America by storm only a short time before. Arnold agreed to help and made his way at once to Tacoma, where he soon became embroiled in a series of mysterious events. Feeling that things were getting out of hand, he requested the help of US Air Force Intelligence. Two officers, Captain William Davidson and Lieutenant Frank M. Brown arrived from Hamilton Air Force base in California, and began to cast around for evidence. When Dahl was unable to produce a film he claimed to have taken of the UFOs, the pair lost interest. Feeling that the affair was probably a hoax, they boarded their B-52 for the return flight to Hamilton, taking with them samples of the slag collected by Crisman from the beach at Maury Island. Twenty minutes after take-off their plane burst into flames and crashed to the ground. Two enlisted men on board parachuted to safety but Brown and Davidson unaccountably stayed on board and were killed on impact.

Dahl subsequently disappeared, and Crisman, who had been a flier in WW11, was recalled to active service and posted first to Alaska, then to Greenland. As John A. Keel later wrote: *"The Maury Island case fell apart in Kenneth Arnold's hands. The slag samples given to him by Dahl and Crisman were switched by someone; the investigating officers, Brown and Davidson, were killed; Dahl vanished; Crisman was literally exiled to Greenland for two years; Tacoma newsman Paul Lance, who helped Arnold in his investigation, died suddenly a short time later. Palmer claims that a box filled with the original slag samples was stolen from his Chicago office soon afterwards."*

Towards the end of his investigation Arnold was taken aside by Ted Morello of the United Press, who told him: *"You are involved in something that is beyond our power here to find out anything about... I'm going to give you some sound advice: Get out of this town until whatever it is blows over."*

Arnold decided to do just that, heading for home in his private plane. He stopped over in Oregon to refuel, and, shortly after taking off again, his engine stopped cold. Only quick thinking and expert flying saved him from certain death.

"Today," according to Margaret Sachs' *'UFO Encyclopedia'*, *"some UFOlogists believe that the Maury Island mystery was a conspiracy involving either US or Soviet intelligence agencies."* Support for this theory comes from the subsequent exploits of Fred Lee Crisman. Twenty years later, in the late '60s, his name cropped up in connection with another conspiracy. It happened when District Attorney James Garrison of New Orleans subpoenaed one Fred Lee Crisman of Tacoma to testify before a Grand Jury investigation into the assassination of John F. Kennedy. Garrison had apparently become convinced that a man named Clay Shaw was instrumental in the Kennedy affair. (Readers of Robert Anton Wilson's *'Cosmic Trigger'* may recall that one of Garrison's aides, Allan Chapman of Texas, *"believed that the JFK assassination was the work of the Bavarian Illuminati.")* Shaw, however, was cleared of all involvement and set free. Garrison's conspiracy theories collapsed in court (*"he never convicted a single conspirator"* Robert Anton Wilson recounts gleefully) and today he is largely discredited. Nevertheless, a number of significant events were never explained. Crisman, for instance, never testified at the actual trial. As John Keel has it: *"he was hospitalized in 1969 after being shot during an attempt on his life only days before he was due to testify."* Crisman eventually recovered and changed his name to Jon Gold. He died in 1978 amid persistent rumours that he had once

been either a CIA agent, or an operative in the field of 'industrial warfare'.

To review events in some kind of chronological order: Crisman made his first recorded appearance as an exponent of the Hollow Earth concept, which, as we have already seen, has disturbing Nazi connotations. He later resurfaced in connection with the very first modern Man In Black encounter *and* the first UFO sightings of the so-called 'modern era'. Of those involved with him in the Maury Island case, one disappeared (Harold Dahl), a second suffered total memory loss (Dahl's son), and several more were killed outright (officers Brown and Davidson, newsman Paul Lance). Another investigator only escaped with his life by sheer fluke (Kenneth Arnold). Crisman's next appearance in the public eye came in November 1968, when he was implicated in the trial of Clay Shaw. Wire service stories identified Crisman as a radio announcer, but District Attorney Jim Garrison's investigators implied that he was either a member of the CIA, or had been engaged in undercover activity for a part of the industrial warfare complex. It was also alleged that Crisman posed as a preacher, and took part in *"work to help gypsies"*. A would-be assassin's bullet prevented Crisman from testifying before Garrison's Grand Jury, neatly heading off any speculation about his involvement in the Kennedy affair. The full story, therefore, may never be told. Nevertheless, even this skeletal version of events points, as Jim Garrison himself remarked, to *"a conspiracy so vast as to stagger the imagination."*

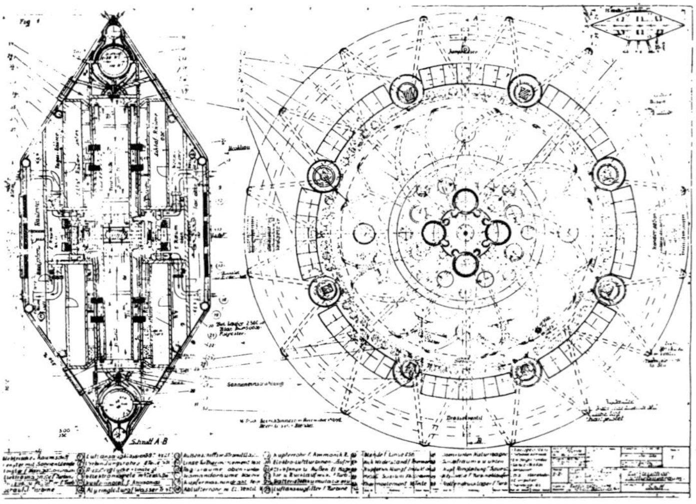

Technical plans of a Nazi 'UFO'.

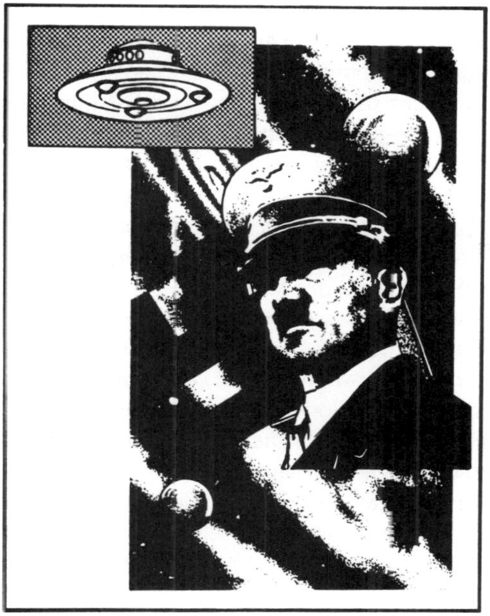

4 "It was forty years ago today..."

In compiling this article I have tried to show how, sooner or later, virtually all conspiracy theories seem to overlap or converge. Some are linked by significant events; others by the presence of key individuals, such as the enigmatic Fred Lee Crisman, who appears to have taken part in everything from the 'invasion' of UFO and MIB lore to the J.F.K. assassination. Coincidence also plays an important part in joining together apparently diverse belief systems. The great psychologist Carl Jung referred to this process as *"synchronicity"*, while District Attorney Jim Garrison preferred the term *"propinquity"*. Even the most casual investigator soon begins to find himself surrounded by random but apparently meaningful events. For instance, after typing up the bulk of this article I switched on the radio for a time-check and caught the tail-end of a programme change. *"Good morning,"* a typically vacuous DJ was intoning; *"it's June the twenty-fourth, another wet, rainy day, and you're listening to..."* It was only then that I realized what date it was: June 24, 1987. In other words, exactly forty years to the day after the events I'd just finished writing about. Hardly an earth-shattering coincidence, but one worth mentioning. And indeed, the entire field of phenomenal research is full of such odd happenstances. (Such as the fact that the first edition of Robert Anton Wilson's *'Principia Discordia'*, as featured in the *'Illuminatus'* trilogy, was printed in 1963 on a Xerox machine owned by our old friend Jim Garrison.) The following day brought another surprise, when I received in the post a book donated by a correspondent. I have it beside me as I type these words. Written by Toyne Newton and titled *'The Demonic Connection'*, it purports to be *"an investigation into Satanism in England, and the international black magic conspiracy."*

According to one chapter, *"Legend has it that somewhere in the dales of the West Riding of Yorkshire there is an entrance to the underground world. Further research reveals the belief that there exists underneath the old mines at Wharfedale in Yorkshire an underground tunnel that links with others, and which ultimately leads to Agharti itself."* What is interesting about this revelation (which came as a complete surprise to me) is that *I* live in what was once the West Riding of Yorkshire. And I'd visited Wharfedale only a few days before.

In researching this article I was particularly struck by the way in which many seminal UFO events appear to have been manufactured by some unknown agency. This 'manufactured' quality is evident even in the case of George Adamski, one of the earliest and most famous of all saucer 'contactees'. Adamski was a self-styled Professor of Eastern Mysticism who gave his address as Mount Palomar Observatory (it later transpired that he ran the hamburger stand next door). During the 1950s he wrote three books about his alleged meetings with beings from outer space. His disciples included Queen Juliana of the Netherlands, and Pope John, who presented him with a special medallion. Later researchers, however, have theorised that Adamski was the victim of a colossal hoax perpetrated by US government agents. Author Leon Davidson has devised a particularly ingenious explanation for the spaceships in which Adamski allegedly travelled to the moon. They were, he says, man-made devices whose windows were actually TV screens showing filmed vistas of outer space. Jacques Vallée, on the other hand, suggests that Adamski's experiences were part of a deliberate conspiracy to unite mankind by creating a bogus extraterrestrial threat. He also points out that Adamski *"had prewar connections with American fascist leader William Dudley Pelley, who was the leader of the Silver Shirts, an American Nazi group which began its activities in 1932."* Again, that disturbing link between UFO cults and Nazism. (Another seminal contactee, George Hunt Williamson, aka Michel d'Obrenovic, was a member of Pelley's racist occult group Soulcraft in the 1950s.) Whatever the case, we may be sure that Adamski wasn't entirely 'on the level'. On balance the evidence points, yet again, to a conspiracy aimed at deceiving people by introducing a new and completely spurious belief system.

This article isn't complete; it doesn't pretend to be. So far I have barely scratched the surface of this fascinating subject. I'm presently trying to establish contact with several UFO and occult groups in the hope of finding out more about the way in which they interact. For the time being, however, I've merely provided a number of new avenues for further research. I leave the task of carrying out this research to other, possibly more capable hands.

I BECOME A MURDERESS

KATHY ACKER

Intention: I become a murderess by repeating in words the lives of other murderesses:

I become a murderess.

I'm born in the late autumn or winter of 1827.

Troy, New York.

My childhood is happy, and my parents allow me to do whatever I please as long as I, by my actions, don't infringe on their high social standing. My father is a great and wealthy man, a tall man, whom I look up to. As a child, among my dolls, I feel safe. I will never die. No one can hurt me. My mother, my father, my two older sisters, my younger sister, and my brother often ignore me, or promise to love me, give me a present, then don't and I cry. My name at this time is Charlotte Wood.

I don't remember any of my childhood before I was 6 years old when I started learning to read. My eldest sister marries a baronet and lives in England; my second elder sister marries a doctor and moves to Scotland. I'm an obedient child: I stubbornly do what my parents and their associates want me to do. I hallucinate. I climb trees, stick needles up the asses of young boys. I hallucinate that the Virgin Mary wears black leather pants and a black leather motorcycle jacket, she climbs trees, she doesn't give a fuck for anyone. (I call up D in Los Angeles do you want to sleep with me with me when and where there why don't you spend a few days with me I'll call you tomorrow. No call three days later I'm maniacal I have to see D I don't know him hello I've got a ride to Los Angeles lie I'm not sure I know where we can stay should I not come up come up. We don't touch talk about anything personal until we get to motel never talk about anything personal spend night together I have to be at Irvine in the morning I'm busy call me Friday. Do you want me to call you yes. I call Friday call Saturday Sunday this is Kathy O uh do you want to spend a night with me again are you too busy I'm too busy uh goodbye have a good time in New York uh goodbye.)

When I'm 16, I board for the next two years at the Female Seminary in Troy, the school my elder sisters went to. The school sits by a large lake, or ocean; I spend my free time staring at the blue then green then white water. I want to be a mermaid: I swim under the heavy water with my legs together; the heavy muscles in my arms move the rest of my body. I want someone, a man, to walk up to me while I'm standing on a stone terrace, put his arms around my shoulders, his hand brush the hair off my forehead. While I'm at school, I meet the only love of my life. He is honest with me, as intelligent and paranoid as I am. My father forbids our marriage because my lover's family has insufficient social connections. When my (adopted) father suspects I've been sleeping with my future husband, he slobbers over me. Rape. My parents take me out of the Seminary, 1846, and return me to their home in Quebec.

I'm 19 years old, I meet Lieutenant William F. A. Elliot, eldest son of a baronet, who loves me, and, with the help of my parents, forces me to marry him. I have to get married. My new husband plans to take me to New York to England but I'm no longer safe. I change my woman's clothes to man's clothes, roam through the streets of New York. My parents, my husband, and I have locked me in a prison and I'm unable to fuck anyone. England is worse. Europe is worse. Scotland France Italy. These are the first signs of my madness.

Despite my two children (I fantasize D calls me that's impossible I fantasize he reads my letter to B he finds out decides he likes me we're both in New York or Los Angeles he undoes my black velvet cape, puts the palms of his hands over my nipples, rubs his hands quickly up and down his hands swerve around to the centre of my back he pulls my body against his body I begin to open my stomach he leads me to a hard bed lays down his stocky body under me) I leave my husband, I decide, I get out, leave my children out I go back home to America. My maid Helen comes with me. I hate everyone, I want to kill everyone, a rich famous man at a hotel in New York City sees me, I know what he wants, I go back home. The man has a lot of influence. My parents hate me, they drive me out of their house in Quebec, I've left my husband, I have no right to leave a man especially a man who loves me, I'm weird, I'm not a robot. Get the hell out, get the hell out of here. Do what I want. Get the hell out everywhere. Fuck them. Fuck them shit up their ass.

I have no money I'm on the street I'm dying no one's going to help me they step on me I puke I cause whatever happens to me I'll get the fuck out of here.

On the boat back to New York I have paranoid delusions: I believe that the man who is staring at me is not staring at me out of desire, lust etc. Spies haunt my footsteps at every hour of the night. I allow the man to talk to me so I can find out who my husband my parents has hired him to spy on me. Fuck me. I don't love this man; in the future I will never love him. I have a paranoid delusion I'm revenging myself on my parents. I'm escaping. I become crazier.

I give a party for my doll.

In Albany: I'm 23 years old; my lover tells me I'm beautiful and intelligent. I can't speak to anyone else but him. After skulking in the streets of Troy, I force myself to move to Albany, New York where I'll be freer. I'm constantly alone; I have no one to talk to. There's no one to whom I can be myself. The people who live in Albany hate me; they don't notice me, I'm in disguise, they talk solely about me when I can barely hear them. (I sneak down to the dark green hall to the edge of the doorway of my parents' bedroom I'm supposed to be asleep my father's telling my mother I'm bad and worthless child I can barely hear what my parents are saying.) I have to buy a pistol I scare my new maid so much she swears out a warrant for my arrest. Everyone hates me they just want to fuck me they don't want to fuck me. The cop finds me with my new lover; my lover gets me out of jail. No matter where I move in Albany everyone talks about me. I force myself to move back to Troy. Seclusion.

25. Not 25.

To escape my parents, I tried to fuck whoever I wanted, lean on a number of people; I become more closely imprisoned. I don't want anyone to tell me what I should do. I don't want anyone following me around, secretly gossiping about me, because I'm not also a robot.

In Troy I learn not to talk to anyone, even my maids, I make my life-long plans in secret. I travel to Boston, then to England, back to my beloved husband. My lover follows me to Boston, he puts his arms around the upper part of my body where are you going I'll take care of you I love you I'm the only person who can take care of you he's tall and thin grey hair I don't care who he is I don't care what he looks like his hand swings down the side of my thin body into the waist the broad spread of my ass I don't know what I look like skin separates from skin in my cunt the skins below my navel around my navel reveal a hand curves around the edges of the soft skins.

He takes my left hand places it below his cock on softer skin his hand rests above my hand his cock rises above his hand I shape move my hand around his skin he begins to moan I hear body rolls side to side I squeeze my hand in out I feel his hands grasp the turns of my shoulders push me down along his body lies over my body so that his cock moves in and out of my mouth between the opening of the skins I form a long narrow tunnel I begin to move my thighs up.

(I come out of the bathroom buttoning my pants I ask him to put on the T.V. my left hand touches his shoulder he suddenly turns toward me I've wanted him to turn toward me quickly I feel wet lips tongue in the centre of my mouth the sudden change from dream-fantasy to reality makes me unable to react he lifts my body on to the bed I feel his tongue enter my mouth the sudden change from fantasy-dream to reality makes me unable to react we both lie on our right sides I in front of you your cock touches the lips of my cunt enters the wet canal your arms tightly clasp my body around the waist warm fur up down my spine your cock slips out I bend my body until my hands almost touch my toes though I lose warmth of your skin I can feel your cock moving inside my skin skins I can begin to come the muscles of my cunt begin to move around your cock my muscles free themselves swirl to the tip of my clit out through my legs the centre of my stomach new newer muscles vibrate I'm beginning to come I don't know you.)

These are my insanities: I tell people I see on the street my neighbours are conspiring against me. I arm myself with pistols, threaten my enemies I'll rape murder them. My neighbours are a band of burglars who're planning to rob me. One of them has stopped all navigation on the Hudson. I hold a magic cork in my mouth which will accomplish everything. As the sun comes up each morning I wander around the streets of Troy in disguise. I can appear to be sane (a robot).

I will never again write anything.

My only friends are the poor unwanted people of Troy. I hate the rich shits, will do anything to destroy them. I'm not political. I buy my meagre groceries from a grocery-saloon keeper, an Irish bum, Timothy Lanagan, who has a wife and 4 children. I know that I'm drinking too much beer and brandy, I'm too close to myself to think clearly about my degradation, my unhappiness, I'm scared all the time. I don't know what to be scared about. I love I don't love I hate I don't hate I'm scared I'm not scared I kill I don't kill. I'm beginning to learn who my enemies are.

One day the spring of '53 I'm at a dance in the Lanagans' booze-parlour I've learned how to speak the correct language one of the disgusting men insults me. No one believes he insults me. I don't know anyone I can really talk to. The Lanagans' filth ask me to leave. I'll show them. This time I'll revenge myself. I tell my gardener to ask the Lanagans to lend me two dollars. My gardener's thinking of killing me I ask the Lanagans myself for the two bucks they don't have any money they're starving I know exactly what's happening. I go back home. (I dream I return to New York I'm going to miss an important meeting of radicals in the middle of St. Mark's Place I sit in an uptown apartment stare out a window of course I miss the meeting I wander into the church when it's empty night.)

Two hours later I walk into the Lanagans' back room tell the Lanagans and the mysterious men the truth: my husband just had a railroad accident.

I know exactly what's happening.

Two hours later I walk into the Lanagans' back room. The Lanagans are eating. I ask the Lanagans for an egg, and Mrs. Lanagan gives me the egg and a peeled potato. I invite her and her sister-in-law to drink beer with me. I know I'm a drunk. I'm clever, this is my plan:

I ask Mrs. Lanagan for sugar they refuse I just bought sugar I ask Mrs. Lanagan to put powdered sugar in my beer she brings back powered sugar in a saucer, two glasses, some beer. I ask Mrs. Lanagan for enough beer to fill the glasses to the brim I now have the sugar bowl in my hand. She leaves gets more beer. I spoon the sugar and arsenic I bought ten days ago to kill rats in the beer. Mrs. Lanagan notices powder on the top of the beer. It's good to drink. Lanagan calls his wife to mind the store Lanagan drinks the untouched beer. The sister-in-law drinks her beer. Two hours later Mrs. Lanagan tells me I've killed her husband and sister-in-law. She tells me to go home.

I feel angry. I've forgotten how to feel. I feel like I've done what I wanted. I feel elated. I've succeeded forgetting my parents. (I awake between 11.00 and 1.00 for a half hour to an hour clean up, talk to friends, eat, spend an hour on the beach, exercise, work for the next 8 hours taking 3 or 4 short breaks, eat a quick meal, drink wine or play chess to calm myself, fuck or don't, fall asleep. I speak to almost no one because I find it difficult to find people who will accept my alternating hermitage and maniacal falling-in-love. My style forces me to live in San Francisco or New York. I don't want to learn to drive a car I love cities I have to be sure I keep working hard in a large city.) During my childhood I give ample signs I'm wild, unlike my parents and other people. I run away with a gang of gypsies from my family's estate, my father is heavy dull I'm meek my mother's beautiful I elope with one of the grooms. I have gold hair, large blue eyes, I'm always laughing. I'm very tough. Because I won't stop being a tomboy, my parents decide I have to get married. I want to get married to get away from my parents do whatever I want to do. I'm born poor St. Helen's, the Isle of Wight. 1790. As a child, I had hardly any food to eat. My parents go to the work-house; I become a farmer's maid. The shits begin to tell me that if I don't become humble, respectful, I have to have security... I'm going to rape you you need security... I become chambermaid in a hotel. I know better.

They take me to jail. My lover who has kept me in the white house by the river never appears to help me. The Troy Female Seminary where I went to school announces in the local newspaper that Charlotte Wood lives in England. I'm Henrietta Robinson. My brother visits me in prison, due to the uproar, shaking, I'm not his sister. I wear a veil. I try to commit suicide but the shits save me. How do I get the vitriol? They make me confess the truth.

(I live quietly I change my way of life I eat grains vegetables some dairy products because I have an ulcer I'm too poor to see a doctor about once a month I fall in love with someone at the same time I live with Peter who I love I rarely form friendships I deal awkwardly with people I fall in love with.)

I'm born poor St. Helen's, Isle of Wight. 1790. As a child I have hardly any food to eat.

I'm still a child when I see my father and mother dragged to the local poorhouse, I walk alone on the city streets an old man stops me asks me if I need help I run away a dark man sticks his hand under my sweater touch my flat chest a local farmer takes me in general maid. Three years of shit I have to be tough I learn fast. I know I have to get myself what I want: The fuck with the farm-life I vanish.

I walk through a black world if I want something I have to get it. These are my next jobs – before I begin to do what I want: assistant in millinery place in the West End of London where I get fired for sleeping with a workman, I learn I can't sleep with who I want until I get enough money; I almost starve; hawk oranges in the gallery of Covent Garden theatre; become the mistress of a wealthy army officer. I'm too insecure, I'm still almost a slave, I'm not yet fully planning every step of my future life, but grasping on to this man who can feed me and clothe me and hold me warm.

I make my first mistake: I become too calm I identify too much with this man who stops me from starving. I become confused, I forgot my ambition and the ambition becomes misplaced: I have no clothes so I want more clothes; I think I can do what I want without fear of starvation so I order my lover around. I'm learning about lies. (I wear men's clothes, jeans cut an inch above the hair of my cunt I hold the jeans up with a studded brown leather belt when I sit on my waterbed where I write the material of the crotch of the pants presses against my cunt lips I'm always slightly hot I masturbate often when I write I write a section 15 minutes to an hour when I unbuckle my brown leather belt either unzip my jeans and/or squeeze my hand between the cloth of the jeans and my abdomen the lower palm of my hand masturbating calms me down maintain a level energy I can keep working the last two days I haven't wanted to fuck P because D hurt me I wear men's clothes jeans cut an inch above) I act too much like a man, I seem too forceful; despite my beauty my lover leaves me. I'll give you 50 pounds a month, I need more, you spend too much money, you don't save up enough money. I look at myself in the mirror

I don't understand whether I'm beautiful plain or ugly I have to use what I see as an object make it as attractive as possible to other people. Now I'm two people.

The second step of my success begins in hell. No one notices me despite my beauty and intelligence; I try to teach myself politics and philosophical theory but I begin again to starve. No one can get me down; I'll show the creeps. I'm wandering in hell the streets stink of shit I want to be able keep doing new and different actions I can't find how, the dogs eat the limbs of living humans and howl. Robbers mingle with the corpses of rich men and no one denies the rich the aristocrats anything. I decide to become servant to the madame of a brothel patronized especially by foreign royalties and noblemen forced to flee the enmity of the revolutionary governments in their own countries. The social bums, as long as their vision isn't annihilated by starvation and fear, usually known more about the ways men operate and kill in a city, than do the wealthier. I go straight for the information, the knowledge, I'm curious; I'm too vivacious charming dazzling to be fired. I hide my ambition then my knowledge behind this new front. Fuck them, I don't have to pretend to be humble and sweet. The only men I meet are the servants of aristocrats, not the aristocrats themselves.

The Duc de Bourbon one night tells his valet Gay that all beautiful women are stupid. Gay protests, mentions me, does His Royal Highness want to meet me? I've somewhat attracted a near relative of of Queen Victoria and an earl, but I'm not sure of them. This time luck favours me. I meet the Duc de Bourbon in the house in Piccadilly and become his mistress. Almost the entire rest of my life I devote to His Royal Highness, who I do not love, but use. Intellectually, I don't know if I can love anyone. I want what I want if I let myself become involved with a man his socially-made power over me will make me merge with him. I'll lose myself, amy ambition. Perhaps at some times I love the Duc de Bourbon, but at every moment I have to tell myself I'm using him, I'm separate from him, so that I keep our powers at least equal. His Royal Highness, like me, is ambitious, and I know how to play someone who is like me.

First, I have to insure that I'll never again hawk winkles in Covent Garden theatre, work for a fat imperious prostitute in any house, spread my legs, watch women smile flirt with men I know they hate I always try to look young that's the only way I can keep my lover I'm 23 years old I look at pictures of myself when I'm 20 so I know how to compose my facial muscles so I still look like I'm 20 I do a strip to keep the muscles under my skin tight and smooth why do you ruin yourself this way I'm too old to sleep with a woman I'm getting older I'll stop being beautiful my intelligence can't influence His Royal Highness unless it's backed by a strict education; I have to force His Royal Highness to respect me and need my advice about his personal and political affairs.

My goal: to enslave the Duc de Bourbon so I'll be safe, be part of the court aristocracy, so noble men and women will ask for my opinions, especially the men, I can kick them in their asses for the rest of my life. No one will look down on me and starve me again. The Duc de Bourbon laughs at my charming desire to study: I learn French, Greek, Latin the expertise of a university don:

I have to learn to use my defeats. I never again become defeated. About the Duc de Bourbon: My name is Sophie Dawes. He is married. A reversal in the politics of France restores to him his vast ancestral possessions and political powers. By this time, I am the only member of the royal set who can influence him, who can please him, who has his trust. He returns home to Chantilly, his palace: he tries to explain to me that recent upsets in the French Government force him to live quietly with his wife and to abandon me, his mistress. He's a tall slender man, and man whose subtle and quick intelligence in hindered by his belief in the restrictive morals of his ancestors. He's frightened of being alone and being disliked. I become scared of again starving and of being without him. I show him he's blind: he'll never again feel the touch of my hands inside his thighs, he'll live alone, not even knowing if his abandonment of them helped his political career and the affairs of the Country. I love him more than I ever have or will. How can I tell? (remember)? I'm scared, I'm no longer beautiful: I'm tall and heavy, my features are large, slightly red. I can only rely on my wits, like any man.

What happens? I enter the palace, Chantilly; the Duc de Bourbon subjugates his poor wife; for 14 years I rule that part of the court aristocracy. I want both men and women to love me. I don't have enough control the women look down on me; they sense I once worked in a whorehouse, I'm not married, fuck them, I'm not a robot, I want to love them, I want to walk into a room, watch them flock to me so I can kick their shit up their assholes. When you've come from the gutter, done everything you can to stay alive, rich and famous, you don't forget anything, you get a photographic memory. I tell the Duc de Bourbon I want to ease his wife's position at Chantilly. I now make use of the ambiguity of my position at Chantilly to raise my social position in the court. I bribe an old watchmaker 10,000 francs to tell Adrien Victor de Feuchères, a young nobleman in the Royal Guards, that I'm the daughter of the Duc de Bourbon and have a dowry of ten million francs. I have to get married.

The next day I marry Adrien in London; my lover gives my husband a position in his household. I meet the King and Queen of France. I entertain royalty; I'm 29 years old, I'm not beautiful; I own jewellery, horses and carriages; my husband purchases two estates for me because his other property, when he dies, descends to the nearest blood relation; I visit the Court several times. What does this wealth mean to me? I can no longer remember any of the events of my childhood. One of my brothers dies in a workhouse infirmary. I'm able to do the work I want and have the men I respect discuss my and their work among each other and with me. I care about the economic aspect as much as I care about my fucking with men. I often sleep with my women friends, I lie under heavy quilts, my body next to my friend's body; I place my lips on her lips, I put my left arm under her soft head, dark curling hair, my right arm around her left shoulder my hand touches her back. Her thousands of long arms draw my body against the front of her body so my head rests under her head in the hollow of her neck and chest. My eyes are closed. For a long time we lie still like this we both rest at the edge of sleep. I don't have the leisure to be monogamous. Other women sleep around our bed watch us. My sex operates as a mask for my need for friends.

I make a major mistake. I stop trying to gain more power; for me, respectability. My husband realises I am the Duc de Bourbon's lover not his daughter; censures the Duc de Bourbon, god knows for what the fucking moralist; writes to the King; resigns his commission in the Royal Guards; and disappears. The King informs me I'm no longer allowed in Court. The Duc de Bourbon tries to console me. Give me more money. I spend almost all my money trying to reobtain my right of entry to the Court; I can find no way to do what I want. This is the first time anyone has absolutely denied me (I remember). I can't understand, deal with the situation. I begin to become monomaniacal and learn the nature (nonnature) of reality.

The duke, like most men over 70, is attracted to young charming women. I'm neither young nor charming; he could abandon me any day, tell me nothing until the disaster occurs. I discharge almost all the servants who are loyal to the duke; I substitute my servants who check all his mail. The duke might revenge himself on me for his imprisonment by secretly making a new will and dying. I fight. I have to get as rich as possible.

If I make the duke leave me all his money, the duke's relations will begin a series of lawsuits which will, at best, tie up the money while I'm alive. I ask the duke to make the younger son of the Duc d'Orleans, the cousin of the King, his heir. (1) The Duc d'Orleans is almost impoverished, will gladly help me to obtain the money if he can get part of it. Poverty destroys stupid scruples. (2) The royal family will help settle the will, as relatives to the Duc d'Orleans, and they'll grant me the right of entry to the Court. The duke refuses to make a d'Orleans his heir. I force him to. Am I doing wrong? The duke secretly plots to flee Chantilly; I find this out; he hides in the corner of an old room, his frail body shakes when he sees me. He tries to bribe me to leave him 50,000 pounds. I watch myself destroy him, I become more scared that he'll take possession of me. I'm often too frightened to fuck, to let myself open myself. Masturbate.

The King informs me he is graciously pleased to receive me at his Court. Louis Philippe becomes King of France. One night the duke and I are dining at the Château de Saint-Leu, a present the duke has given me. (I don't like or don't care about most people when I decide I like someone I over-react I scare the person. I know I'm going to over-react, no one I like will like me, I try to hide my feelings by acting like a sex maniac, excuse me, would you like to sleep with me, I begin to think I'm only sexually interested in the person. I chase the person, I'm vulnerable, I act as tough as possible to cover my vulnerability. I don't know how to tell people I like I want to be friends, sit next to them so I can smell the salt on their skin, try to learn as much as possible about their memories, ways of perceiving different events. Because most people I like don't like me, I'm scared to show them I like them. I feel I'm weird. I don't comprehend what signals a person I like gives indicate the person likes me, what signals indicate the person dislikes me). The duke, two gentlemen-in-waiting, and I play whist; the duke calmly tells Gay, his head valet, he wishes to be woken at 8.00 the next morning, and retires to his bedroom. I feel restless. I see a warm friend of mine, a woman servant, who tells me she knows the duke has made a secret will which disinherits me. Where's the will? She shows me the will. If I destroy the will, the duke will eventually discover its disappearance, make a new will. I can stop this only by killing him. My friend understands. We sneak quietly to the duke's bedroom, we use two of the duke's handkerchiefs to strangle him in his bed, sailors' knot my nephew taught me when he stayed with me at Chantilly; we move the huge heavy bed the duke sleeps in two feet away from the wall, hang the thin body by the handkerchiefs from the fastening of the strong French window, the feet of the duke 30 inches above the floor. The duke seems to have committed suicide.

My name is Laura Lane. I'm born in Holly Springs, Mississippi, in 1837. My name is Adelaide Blanche de la Tremouille. I K A, fall in love with D; D burns me.

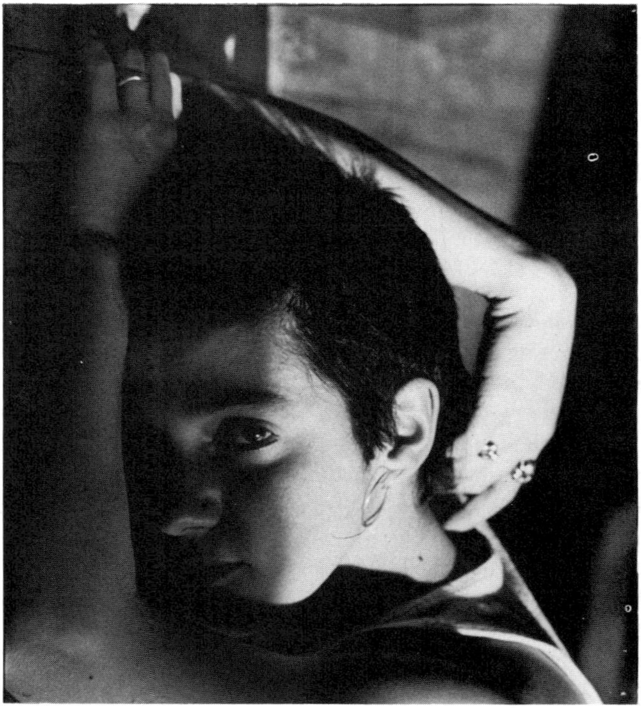

Kathy Charlotte Henrietta Laura Acker.

When I'm 16 I marry William Stone who owns a liquor store in New Orleans. He likes to think of himself wearing black leather, studded flashy boots, he drinks, shoots bullets into the walls around me, I learn to handle guns, I have to do what I do, into the chicken coops, he threatens he wants to kill someone. I learn about that fantasy. He holds a gun to my head when he's drunk so he can watch me throw fits. I love my mother; we decide to go to San Francisco together. First fantasy.

I marry Colonel William D. Fair, a lawyer. Lawyers tell you what's wrong, what's right. The Colonel shows me if I don't do what he wants, he'll kill himself. Phooey. Two years later, he shoots himself in the head with a Colt six-shooter. Am I supposed to feel guilty? Second fantasy.

My mother, I, my six year old daughter Lillias, with three hundred bucks, head for the silver, Virginia City, Nevada. Head for the money without a man. I have to do what I have to do. Single-handed I open the Tahoe House, make a success out of my hotel. I don't want to sit in my room, count my money forever; I got sexually burned twice. Big shit. I want more than money and fame. Third fantasy.

I meet Alexander Parker Crittenden and fall deeply in love with him. He's 46, a hawk; the first time we fuck, he holds me on top of him in bed, he's surprisingly gentle especially since he's a bad fuck. Has no idea how to touch the skin around my clit, give me pleasure. Fourth fantasy.

My mother believed that marriage, both marriage and monogamy, cause the people involved to lose their ambition, wits, and sense of humour, especially the people who have less of the power. My mother's neighbours son showed my mother they would accept no bastard weirdos in their robot town; my father, a well-to-do Englishman, flees with me to England.

On April 9, 1895 I marry a man who I've met only once before my father's paid him to marry me because I'm a bastard.

The story of seven years: The early 1860's in Virginia City, Nevada. 30,000 people shove to get themselves as rich as possible. I don't want to be rich and famous. You can kill whoever you please as long as you've got a reason. Make one up. Wild dogs howl beneath the gangrened limbs of the old. Respectable has no real meaning. I'm 19 years old five feet three inches tall large dark eyes curly hair I know about music and art. Crittenden's a famous lawyer; elected to Nevada's first General Assembly; holds one of the most successful corporate practices in the state. Like me, he believes in being politically powerful, socially respectable, and rich. We're both tough; we do what we have to do; we don't believe in bucking other people, the society, unless we have to. We're both loyal Southerners who respect the ways of luxury and tradition. When some fucking Yankee runs his puke Union flag up the pole that stands outside Tahoe House, I flash my revolver, order the Yankee off the roof; no; I shoot the son-of-a-bitch.

The bastards arrest try me for attempted murder. I appear to go along with society, but that's what they are; bastards. Crittenden, my lover, has the same respect for society I've got my flashy looks. He uses his prestige and money: impanels a jury of twelve secessionists, prays aloud to Shakespeare and Jeff Davis; his silver tongue gets me off the hook. I learn about the nature of reality and love Crittenden even more. In this situation, murder means nothing.

All that matters to me is my love for Crittenden I think about him every hour I imagine I see him again he tells me he hates me I turn around in the bathroom I see his blue eyes next to my eyes I put my hands on his shoulders he closes my body with his body his skins close wild horses around my skin.

What are the sources for this insane love? In what ways is my desire to have someone I love with me connected to a desire to murder? (When I'm a child, my parents own a summer house by the Atlantic, every afternoon between 5.00 and 8.00 I walk on the sand by the green ocean, I climb up to the end of the jetties, watch the waves break as they turn under each other, not back/forth, but back/forth/under/same/time/as/over/back/forth.) I decide I'll do anything for Crittenden. A few days after my acquittal I learn Crittenden's married, has 7 children. Crittenden convinces me to have dinner with him and his wife at the Occidental Hotel in San Francisco. I descend into slavery, I let a man drive his fingers into my brains and reform my brains as he wants. Crittenden follows me back to Virginia City; my mother kicks him out of Tahoe House, refused to let him see me; I buy a house in the rich part of town and move in with Crittenden. Crittenden invites his wife to stay in my house. Why do I let Crittenden enslave me? I'm crazy. I'm no longer interested in this. I remember my second husband; I shoot at my head with a gun.

Stop. I go from trap to trap to trap. Crittenden's still promising to divorce his wife. I follow Crittenden to San Francisco; I have more money than I need. I have more than I want.

I almost die from stillborn childbirth; I tell my husband I'm not going to have a kid again. I didn't want to marry him; I don't want him around, ruling me. Fuck all of them.

If someone bothers me, I shoot her/him. I shot that Union soldier on the roof, and Crittenden got me off the hook. Crittenden now tells me that Mrs. Crittenden's back East; he won't let her again into California. I'm his slave and believe him. I don't want to be a slave. I aim a five-shooter at Crittenden, fire, and purposely miss him. I marry this guy Snyder who's a weakling; in a month Crittenden arranges for me to get a divorce so I can return to him. He begins to furnish a house on Ellis Street for his wife who's returning from the East. (A wants to fuck E. A's sleeping with me he puts me to sleep in the attic M's fucking next door I hear A make love to E through the floor. I open the attic window climb down the roof, shimmy down a long pole, I run back to a school A tells me he'll decide between me and E; I'm better. He picks me. Next day he tells me E's pregnant, get out this instant.) Crittenden's going to get a divorce, go East with me. For the moment I'm content, I don't believe him, I pretend I believe him. I have to learn how I can co-exist with my tempestuous emotions. I'm mainly interested in myself. I buy a new gun: a sharp four-shooter. (After L at night goes to sleep he has to work the next day I think about killing him I imagine I walk up to the bed in which he's sleeping with a knife stick the knife through the left side of his body under his ribs.) On November 3 Crittenden stops at our house, I know it's the last time, I want to be tough; I won't be hysterical; I can't let the first emotions out I'm not his robot fuck. He could belong to me; I have to kill the other people he thinks he belongs to. I'll be a vegetable. (I let L hit me leave me broke without a home because I no longer want to fuck him he lives at the same time with a new lover his new lover watches him hit me makes comments about the scene. I let L tell me the only thing I'm good for is fucking, the only reason he lives with me.) I want to be rich and famous; no, I want to be able to talk with people without having them put me down.

I put on a huge velvet cape, a hat with a thick veil, my holster and gun; I follow my lover carefully silently in a hack I secretly hired yesterday, past low brown and grey buildings whose empty windows rats hover over, past women and men walking arm-in-arm as if they can. (In New York, I shaved off my hair, wore a black bishop's coat, jeans, heavy boots, so I'd look like a boy; if a man asked me the time in public, I'd kick him. I tried to meet more women, I couldn't figure how; everyone disliked me) Secretly I board the El Capitan, the opium-infested side-wheeler that's going to ferry my lover to his so-called wife. People crowd around me; they want to confuse me, gather me; I become lost. I don't like to be in a crowd of people unless I'm invisible I have fantasies I'm invisible or people rush over to me how are you darling do you want to sleep with me? The ferry docks; I rush through the crowd to see Crittenden meet his wife; bodies block me; I can't do what I want; I see Crittenden and Clara sitting on the upper deck; Clara's hands are crossed, I see a blue dress with tiny white flowers, gloves, why gloves; I think she's smiling, a stupid kid in a military uniform, Crittenden's smiling; I can't even escape into my own pretensions. I watch every moment they make. I hear a whistle, 5.50 p.m. the side-wheeler's about to return to San Francisco. I'll never see Crittenden again. (I don't know how to deal with someone I love or want to see refusing to see me, disliking me. I finally force myself to see that the people I love (some) dislike me. Even though they dislike me, I can't them; I keep trying to talk to them, I keep bothering them, make them dislike me more, me more entangled in fears/shyness. They show they hate me; I see myself sitting under the clothes in my closet; I don't see anyone; I wait for the whole to close.) I shoot Crittenden; he mutters something; I drop my gun, wait for the police to capture me. I'm hysterical start screaming louder and louder.

All the above events are taken from myself, ENTER MURDERERS! by E.H. Bierstadt, MURDER FOR PROFIT by W. Bollitho, BLOOD IN THE PARLOUR by D. Dunbar, ROGUES AND ADVENTURESSES by C. Kingston.

TANTRA
An Introduction

SAHAJANATH

"Soft sandal mountain winds caress quivering vines of clove.
Forest huts hum with droning bees and crying cuckoos.
When spring's mood is rich, Hari roams here
to dance with young women, friend –
A cruel time for deserted lovers."

Jayadeva, *Gitagovinda*

People tend to think that Tantra is about something dirty or rude, although this attitude says more about them than anything else. (Lokanath's first words to me were that the ignorant think that Tantra is about fucking.) The word 'Tantra' is as mysterious and obscure as many other of the terms bandied about in pagan circles. In this sense it is rather like the old chestnut 'Kabbalah' or even 'magic'. Very commonly used, but with very general and therefore vague meanings. It is a Sanskrit word that roughly translates as 'tradition' or 'line' which is again very similar to the translation of the hebrew term The Kabbalah. Although this is its literal translation, the term Tantra' has come to be applied to some very specific practices and techniques and it is these that I intend to discuss in this article. My plan is as follows:

1. General definition of Tantra.
2. Review of its influence and similarities with western occultism.
3. Example of Tantric meditation.

1. Tantra is a very broad tradition and includes all of the things that we would describe as 'magic' – these include sorcery, divination, alchemy and the quest for higher knowledge. Tantra is sometimes called the way of the Wand or thunderbolt (vajra) because, unlike many other spiritual systems, its practitioners expect to become masters and to achieve liberation within the course of one lifetime. Those of you familiar with the Kabalistic tradition will recognise the parallel here with the Kabalistic concept of the Lightning Flash of inspiration striking downwards from the crest of the Tree of Life, through each of the spheres and into the earth/magician. A better name for the follower of the Tantric tradition is a 'Kaula', meaning member of the clan; a word very similar in meaning to 'coven'. Alternatively Tantrics can be called Naths or Nathas, meaning Lords.

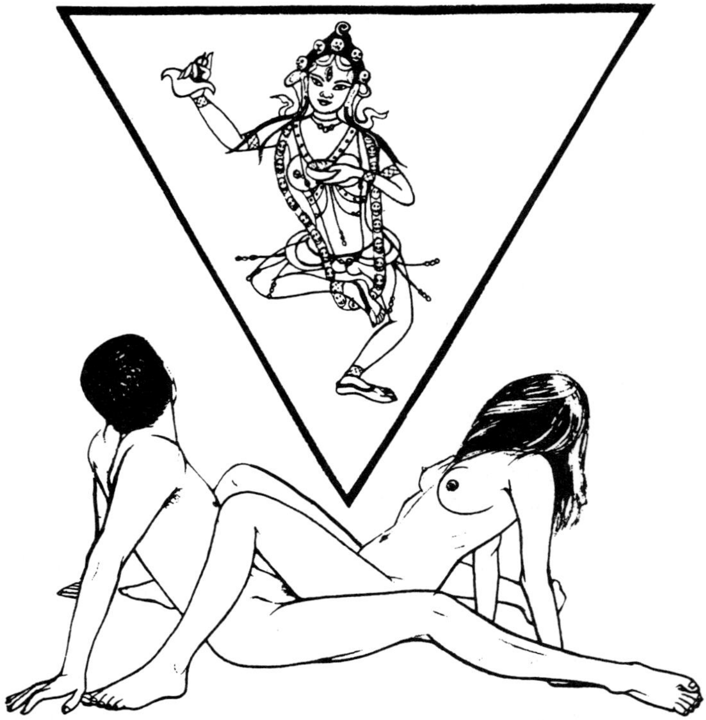

The magical weapon of the Kaula is the 'vajra' or wand and this is adopted because the Kaula will USE any and every EXPERIENCE and bend it towards the chosen goal. This is in marked contrast to other systems whose practitioners are inhibited and therefore unable to make full use of the whole of their human experience. For example, the inhibited can find no spiritual value in their own sexuality. The Kaulas are noted for their lack of inhibitions in this area – hence the notoriety Tantricism has achieved in the mind of the uninformed. In fact many Tantric practices are INTENDED TO DECONDITION its members from the inhibitions built up by the indoctrination of other religious and social systems. We are sometimes told that the body, especially the sexual parts of the body, are defiled and unspiritual, but to the Kaula there is no holier temple than the body *"with its five elements, ten gateways, solar and lunar energy"*.

This revolutionary character of Tantric magic is best illustrated by a look at a special ritual. A major part of a Tantric ritual is anti–social in character. Its aim was – and is in some contexts – to negate the accepted mores of the majority. In the modern context it is rather like Crowley's injunction that one should *"Crucify a toad in a basilisk abode"*. Or more recently Ray Sherwin's comment that every aspiring magician should perform a black mass at least once.

There are said to be five essential components of any Tantric rituals, the so-called 5 M's: These are: Meat, Fish, Alcohol, Parched Grain and Sexual Intercourse.

I should point out that these are 'twilight' words, or codewords used to disguise the true content of rituals.

Meat is eaten in order to deliberately antagonise the puritanical brahmins who place an absurd premium on vegetarianism. Meat is also a symbolic reference to the presence of men within the circle.

Fish again is something of a wind-up designed to symbolically decondition the Kaula. It may also refer to the presence of women within the circle. (One of the great gurus of the Natha tradition is named 'Matsyendranath' after the fish in whose belly he discovered a great tantra. Such a humble name also suggests a rejection of all notions of social class.)

Alcohol again is a substance prohibited by many of the world's religions; we can extend this conceptually to mean any form of intoxication or use of strange drugs. To be intoxicated during a ritual is something unthinkable to many of the world's so-called great religions.

Sexual Intercourse is the acid test of the real tantric or, dare I say it, any magician in whatever tradition. The acknowledgement of the sexual polarity and its spiritual significance is what magic is all about.

Parched Grain sounds a bit tame, but this is a code-word for retention or delay of orgasm. Something that is extremely important in the higher rituals of the kaula circle.

The above should not really be taken as typical of a Tantric ritual any more than the so-called 'Great Rite' (during which the priest and priestess are said to consummate an act of sexual intercourse within a coven circle) is typical of the rites of witchcraft. What is important is the continued breaking of taboos, which undoubtedly still plays an important role in the magical work of several traditions, east and west. More typically, Kaula rituals can be divided into two distinct areas. A daily rite performed alone or in the company of another Kaula; and a group or circle ritual or 'cakra-puja', performed with other members of the sect. The mention of the word 'cakra' may ring a bell with some of you, especially in connection with the seven cakras of the astral body. This theory of the cakras, now a commonplace idea amongst western occultist and indophiles, is a wholly Tantric theory, and plays a major role in tantric ritual.

The Seven Cakras are:

1. Muladhara (Root Cakra)	Base of spine	Earth	Yellow
2. Svadisthana	Base of genitals (crescent surrounded by red petals)	Water	Dark blue/grey
3. Manipura	Navel (triangle with grey petals)	Fire	Red
4. Anahata	Heart (hexagram with 12 petals)	Air	Smokey blue
5. Vishudda	Throat (circle)	Ether/Sound	White
6. Ajna	Third Eye		
7. Sahasrara	Brain		

(See Aleister Crowley's poem *"There are seven keys to the great gate, being eight in one, and one in eight."*)

The daily ritual of the Kaulas involves a basic dedication to the God and Goddess (Siva/Sakti) which are invoked from inside the body of the celebrant. This is a good illustration of the positive attitude Kaulas have towards their own bodies. The Gods and Goddesses are not archetypes that dwell outside of the human life-wave, but something that can be found in all parts of the human body, even in the penis of the man and the yoni of the woman. In fact it might be said that the purest archetype of the God and Goddess is situated in these places. This constitutes something of a conceptual breakthrough for many people, who, due to their conditioning, find it almost impossible to visualise a God or Goddess as resident in what they have been taught to consider as the lowest parts of their body. But as it says in the New Testament *"The first shall be last, and the last shall be first."*

The Group rituals are often amplifications of the practices described under the individual rite. Any magician would feel fairly at home in a Kaula circle, with its banishings, invocations and visualisations. Some of the similarities will be described below.

I became a *'Nath'* about six months ago. I'd been involved in magic for several years beforehand and always leant towards the Tantric path partly influenced through the ideas of Aleister Crowley, the greatest occult teacher of our time, and also through the interpretation of Crowley's ideas as found in the works of Kenneth Grant, especially in *'Aleister Crowley and the Hidden God'*. One of the first Occult magazines I ever bought was called *'Sothis'* and I was particularly struck by the articles written by Mike Magee, one of that magazine's editors. When I met him several years later I became increasingly interested in the tantric sect, of which he was head outside of India. The Guru of the Order, called AMOOKOS (Arcane and Mystical Order of the Knights of Shambala) is 'Dadaji', a one-time pupil of Aleister Crowley in the 'thirties, who was once advised by Crowley to seek enlightenment in India. After a few years fighting the Spanish Fascists, Dadaji made it to India, becoming a sanyasi and eventually receiving the line of an ancient and obscure tantric sect called the Naths. It was into this sect that I was initiated.

Some of the above material may have struck a chord with some of your own views and beliefs. This is no accident – Tantra is in fact a very pure pagan tradition, and many of its central concepts have found their way into the western tradition of magic, either within the last hundred years or as part of the original and ancient influx of pagan ideas into the west via the Egyptian and other teachers. Some of the parallels are quite striking; in addition to the ones already noted are:

Digambari:

This is one of the thousand names of the Goddess and means *'clothed in space'*. This is the origin of the modern day wiccan expression 'Skyclad'. The initiation into the Kaula circle has to be a naked initiation during which the candidate affirms *"Nakedness shall be my symbol of freedom, a symbol of my new birth into the Magick life. It is the highest expression of freedom."*

During a formal meeting of the Kaula sect, clothes may or may not be worn, depending upon the will of the participants and the nature of the work in hand.

The Goddess:

A striking similarity between the ideas of the kaulas and those of modern paganism is the fact that the Goddess plays an equal role in the pantheon. There is a legend in which the Goddess Sakti is dismembered in a struggle with a powerful demon, when the various parts of her body fell from the air, landing on various parts of India. The yoni of the

Goddess was said to have landed on Kamarupa, which takes its name from this 'event' and is even today one of the focal points of Kaula devotion. This legend is a female equivalent to the Ancient Egyptian myth of the murder of Osiris by his brother Set. Osiris was cut into 15 parts and scattered all over Egypt. His wife/mother, Isis, searched for the parts, doing devotion at each of the temples at the appropriate times. The last part to be found was the phallus. In both of these legends is hidden a magical formula of great value to those with the inclination to follow it up. Whilst on the subject of the feminine, it should be said that devotion to the Goddess is not a guarantee of a raised status for women. It is my view that a third archetype, over and above either God or Goddess is required. This archetype is the child or, as it is called by the Nathas, Siva/Sakti.

Circle Worship:

All Tantric rites take place within the duly consecrated confines of a circle, or as it is called in Sanskrit, the Cakra. The names may be unfamiliar but the concepts shouldn't be. The circle is cast in much the same way as in the west, with the calling up of four guardians of the directions, or cardinal points, invocation of the God (Siva) and Goddess (Sakti).

The Five Elements:

No rite of the kaulas is complete without the presence of the five things or elements, there to remind the magician of the physical plane on which the effects of the work is manifest. Out of the five elements Earth, Air, Fire, Water and Spirit any phenomenon can be manifested.

Yantra:

If you are wondering how there came to be this overlap between the ideas of the Kaulas and those of modern paganism, one partial explanation is that they were introduced into the West around about the turn of the century by such groups as The Theosophical Society and later on, the Hermetic Order of the Golden Dawn. One striking example of this is found in the area of colour theory and mystical diagrams. Consider, for example, the crucial Yantra (diagram) to the Kaulas, known as the Sri Yantra, sacred to the Goddess Sri or the Full Moon Goddess of the Tantrics. The four doorways represent the four directions/elements, the twelve petals the signs of the Zodiac, the eight inner petals the planets, the downward facing triangles the female, the upward facing triangles the male, and the dot or bindu in the centre, male and female co-joined, or

Siva/Sakti.

Note now the similarity with the key symbol of the Golden Dawn, worn on the breast of every member at Order meetings – The Rose Cross Lamen.

Wax Image Spells:

There is a parallel between Western Paganism and Tantrika at a deeper, more ancient level, which is illustrated by the use by both systems of the wax image spell. Most of the surviving examples in the West, for instance in the Pitt Rivers Museum, Oxford, of these wax dolls, show quite clearly that their purpose was to harm an enemy. I make no judgement on this, for who can say whether it may not be necessary to use such methods at certain times? A label of a similar exhibit in the Witchcraft Museum in Boscastle puts it more strongly: *"Before the nineteenth century the working classes of this country were virtual serfs. The judges, landowners and clerics were a law unto themselves. If someone was harmed by them, there was very little chance of just redress of a grievance. The only recourse might then be to a witch and the wax image spell. And if some hunter or rapist or land encloser broke his stupid red neck whilst out hunting, good riddance!"* Or words to that effect.

A final word on the great affinity between the ethos of the Naths and the Thelemic idea, promulgated by Aleister Crowley. There is a direct translation into Sanskrit of the term *'Thelema'*. It is *'Svacchandacara'*, and in both instances the meaning is FREEDOM!

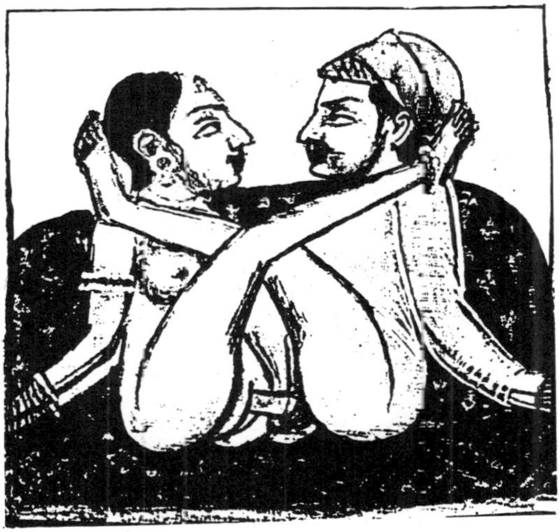

ECSTATIC KRISNA

"Yadava hero, your hand is cooler than sandalbalm on my breast;
Paint a leaf design with deer musk here on Love's ritual vessel!
She told the joyful Yadu hero, playing to delight her heart.
Lover, draw kohl glossier than a swarm of black bees on my eyes!
Your lips kissed away the lampblack bow that shoots arrows of Love.
She told the joyful Yadu hero, playing to delight her heart.
My ears reflect the restless gleam of doe eyes, graceful Lord,
Hang earrings on their magic circles to form snares for love.
She told the joyful Yadu hero, playing to delight her heart.
Pin back the teasing lock of hair on my smooth lotus face!
It fell before me to mine a gleaming line of black bees.
She told the joyful Yadu hero, playing to delight her heart.
Make a mark of liquid deer musk on my moonlit brow!
Make a moon shadow, Krisna! The sweat drops are dried.
She told the joyful Yadu hero, playing to delight her heart.
Fix flowers in shining hair loosened by loveplay, Krisna!
Make a flywhisk outshining peacock plumage to be the banner of love.
She told the joyful Yadu hero, playing to delight her heart.
My beautiful loins are a deep cavern to take the thrusts of love –
Cover them with jewelled girdles, cloths and ornaments, Krisna!
She told the joyful Yadu hero, playing to delight her heart."

Jayadeva's *Gitagovinda* translated as
'The Love Song of the Dark Lord'
by
Barbara Stoler Miller.

('Sahajanath' is a magician living and working in Oxford).

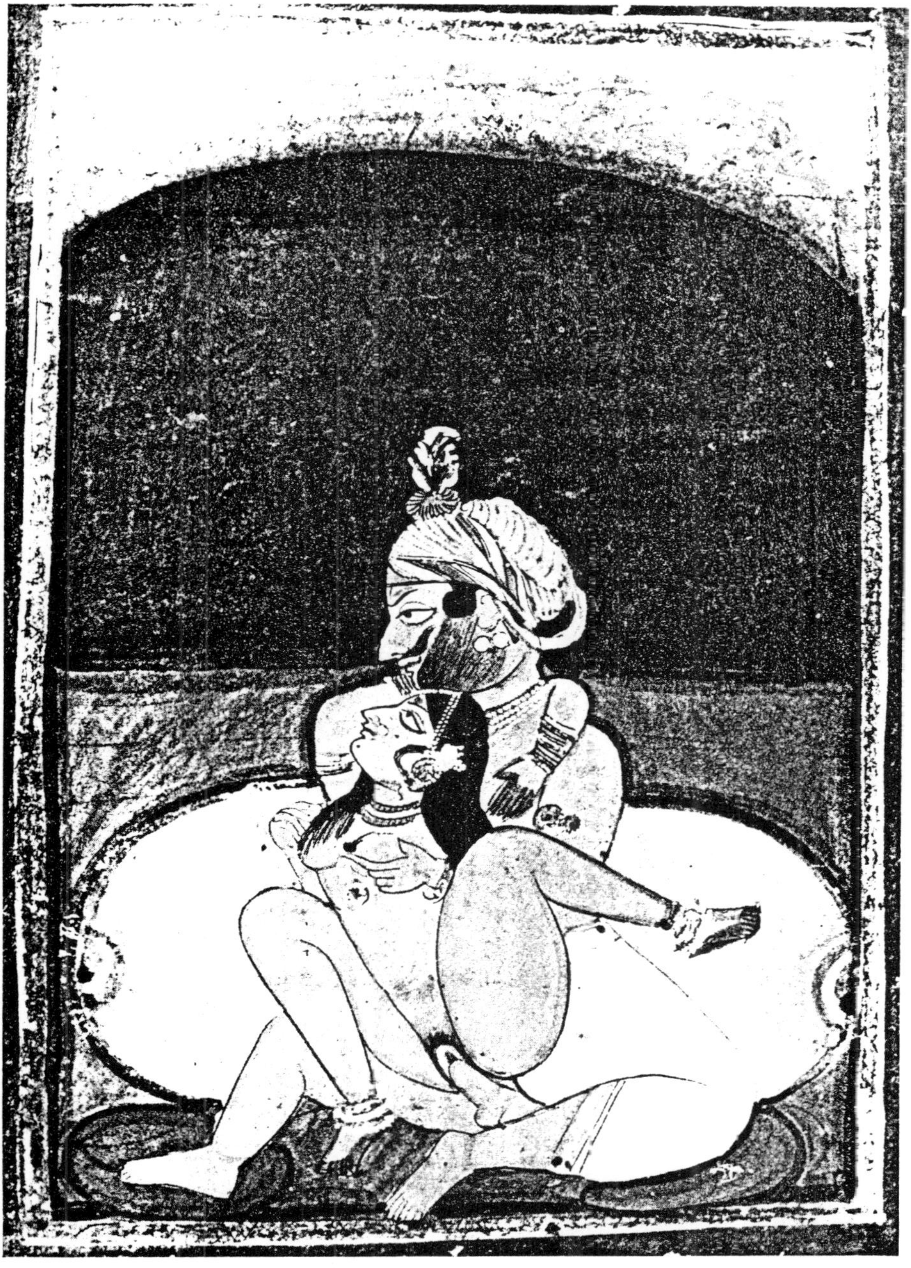

PEOPLES
TEMPLE

OF THE
DISCIPLES OF CHRIST

A REVOLUTIONARY SUICIDE

SIMON DWYER

In the light of the David Koresh/Branch Davidians affair that took place in Waco, Texas, in March 1993, and the general religious climate that currently exists in America and Britain, now may be an opportune moment to consider Jonestown.

In the winter of 1978, Sunday newspapers around the world were ruffled by the news of the mass suicide of 993 people at an American religious commune set in the heart of the jungle in Guyana, South America.

The People's Temple – a Christian religious sect from the United States – were led by the enigmatic Reverend Jim Jones, who had moved his congregation to Guyana from San Francisco a year earlier to escape investigations into his ministry by numerous journalists and politicians. Jones, who had earlier enjoyed the support of Vice President Walter Mondale and First Lady Carolyn Carter for his work with ethnic minorities, the unemployed and animals, had become convinced that Godless America had decided to discredit him because of his socialist beliefs. He'd also become sure that the U.S.A was destined for nuclear war, and convinced his followers that the greenery of South America was the ideal Garden of Eden in which to re-start the world.

It all started to go wrong when John and Grace Stone left the Temple, and entered into a custody battle with Jones over their five-year-old son, Timothy. Their case, and their complaints against Jones' domination of his followers were taken up by Congressmen Leo Ryan, who eventually arranged a fact finding visit to the 'Jonestown' camp.

The visit did not go well, and when Ryan and his entourage left the camp for the nearby airstrip they invited any of Jones' followers to come back to America with them. Jones was convinced that they would be back with American or Guyanan troops to smash the commune. And, as they left, some of his followers panicked. On the way to the plane Ryan and three reporters were shot dead, and eight others were wounded. The plane eventually took off but while in the air, hardcore Jones follower Larry Layton produced a gun, shooting two passengers before being disarmed and jumping out.

In Jones' eyes the system had come to destroy his Masada, his fortified Garden of Eden. It was all over, and he knew just what to do.

As his followers drank a lethal cocktail of cyanide, strawberry cola and tranquillisers, the Reverend spoke to this, his final congregation. His last words were recorded on a cassette by person or persons unknown and filed by the U.S. Government. The tape has been leaked, and now, with the co-operation of the World Surrealist Network, we can reproduce the complete transcript of these previously confidential last words. As document. As memorial. As insight.

Mad Jones and his sad followers were certainly not 'evil' people. They would have argued that they were not even misguided people. In a world of hypocrisy, of rampant materialism, of complacency and suppression. In a world of lies, Jones hurt by telling his confused truth.

The word 'suicide' usually conjures visions of hopelessness, helplessness, submission. Indeed, all these things are true in the case of Jonestown. But the Guyanan tragedy throws up something else. An element which – if we face it – is a part of each and every suicide. A failure on the part of Society. A failure to cope with individuals and groups who are dissatisfied. A failure to accommodate change, and embrace those people who see the world differently. A failure to love.

Something big was missing from the lives of those who volunteered for the Temple. And for all his egomania, his warped vision, his bullying and murder, Jones was really totally logical in his paranoid search for the truth. The result of his equation in this intolerant world of lies was inevitable: Death.

Indeed, this was a suicide. A revolutionary suicide.

[Tape Transcript Starts]

"How very much I've tried my best to give you a good life. In spite of all that I've tried, a handful of people, with their lies, have made our lives impossible. There's no way to distract ourselves from what's happened today.

Not only do we have a compound situation, not only are there those who have left it to me (?)... The Betrayal of the Century... Some have stolen children from mothers and are in pursuit right now to kill them, because they stole their children. I mean we are sitting here waiting on a powder-keg and I don't think that is what we want to do with our babies, I don't think that is what we have in mind to do with our babies.

It was said by the greatest of prophets from time immemorial: 'No man may take my life from me, I lay my life down...' So just to sit here and wait for the catastrophe that's going to happen on that airplane – It's going to be a catastrophe – It almost happened here, it almost happened, the congressman was nearly killed here, but you can't steal people's children, you can't take off with people's children without expecting a violent reaction.

And that's not so unfamiliar to us either, if we only look at the old Christians (?) who weren't communists...

World opinion – violence, and violence – force. [?] But if we can't live in peace, then let us die in peace. I've been so betrayed. I've been so terribly betrayed. We've tried, and – what he said right this minute was that, he said if it was only worth one day it was worthwhile..."

[EDIT] "Right then, what's going to happen in a few minutes is that one of the people on that plane is gonna, is gonna shoot the pilot, I know that. I didn't plan it but I know it's going to happen. They're gonna shoot that pilot and down comes the plane into the jungle and we had better not have any of our children left when it's over 'cause they'll – on us. The point is that this plane. I dunno how to say it... I've never lied to you, I never have lied to you. I know that's what's going to happen. That's what he intends to do and he will do it, he'll do it.

What it means [?] I've been loaded with many pressures seeing all these people behave so treasonous. It was just too much for me to put together but I know what he was telling me and it'll happen...if the plane gets in the air that is.

So my opinion is that you be kind to children and you be kind to seniors and take the potion like we used to take an ocean breeze and step over quietly because we are not committing suicide – it's a revolutionary act. We can't go back, we won't lose it for long [?] we're not going back to tell more lies which means more congressmen, there's no way, there's no way we can survive. Anyone that has any – opinion please speak".

(Question from audience)

"You'd be making a strike but we'd be making a strike against people we don't want to strike against. We'd like to get the people that caused this stuff and if some people are prepared and know how to do that tell it to Timothy Stone but there's no plane, there's no plane. We can't catch the plane in time".

(Audience)

[EDIT] "He's (She's?) responsible for it. He brought these people to us. He and Diana Myrtle. The people in San Francisco will not be idle over this. We do not take our death in vain you know."

(Audience)

"Is it too late for Russia? Here's why it's too late for Russia. They killed, they started to kill. That's why it makes it too late for Russia. Otherwise I'd said – but it's too late. I can't control these people. They're out there. They've gone with the guns and it's too late. And once they've

killed anybody, at least that's the way I want it. I just put my lot with you. If one of my people do something it's me. When they say I don't have to take the blame for this well I don't I don't live that way and if they deliver up – and try to get the man that's it. And – was – mother's being lying on him and lying on him and trying to break up this family and they've all agreed to kill us by whatever means necessary. Do you think I'm going to let them?... Not on your life. No you're not going, you're not going. You're not going. I can't live that way. I can not live that way. I've lived for all I'll die for all."

[EDIT] "I've been living on hope for a long time, Christine, and I appreciate you've always been a good agitator and I like agitation because you have proof from two sides on one issue, on two sides of the question. And what those people going to get done, what they go through. They make our lives worse than hell. And make the rest of us not accept us. They tell so many lies there in that truck. We are not in as far as any alternative."

(More questions about Russia from audience)

"...but to me death is not a fearful thing, it's living that's fearful. I have never, never, never seen anything like this before in my life. I have never seen people take the law...and do – and provoke us and try to purposely agitate mothers of children.

It is only...it's not, it's not worth living like this, worth living like this."

(Testimonial from audience)

"There is one man there who blames, who blames Michael Stone for the murder of his mother, and he will stop that plane by any means necessary. He'll do it. That plane will come out of the air. There's no way you can fly a plane without a pilot..."

(More talk about Russia)

"I haven't seen anybody yet that didn't die, and I like to choose my own kind of death. I'm tired of being – to hell, that's what I'm tired of... Tired of it. So many people's lives in my hands and I certainly don't want your life in my hands. I've been telling you to this day, without me life has no meaning. I'm the best friend you'll ever have. I have to pay. I'm standing with you people – you're part of me. I can detach myself... I – detach myself, no, no, no, no, no, I never detach myself from any of your troubles. I've always taken your troubles right on my shoulders...I'm not going to change that now. It's too late. I've been running too long. I'm not gonna change now. The next time, you'll get to Russia. The next time round. This is...what I'm talking about now is the dispensation of judgement, this is a revolutionary suicide council. I'm not talking about self...self-destruction. I'm talking about what...we have no other road. I will take your call. I will

put it to the Russians, and I can tell you the answer now because I'm a prophet. Call the Russians and tell them...see if they'll take us." (Audience)

"I tried to give it to you (peace). I laid down my life practically. I practically died every day to give you peace. And you've still not had any peace. You look better than I've seen you in a long while, but it's still not the kind of peace that I wanted to give you.

A person's a fool who continues to say that you're winning when you're losing. Win one, lose two, what?..."

(Audience)

"He's taking off, the plane is taking off...Suicide many have done it...Stone has done it. If somebody oughta lis...somebody...can they talk...can they not talk to San Francisco? See that Stone is not here by – the sins of men... He has done the thing he wanted to do. To have us destroyed."

(Audience)

"We win, we win when we go down, they don't have anybody else to hate. They've got nobody else to hate. Many will destroy themselves. I'm speaking here not as the administrator but as a prophet today. I wouldn't – talk serious if I didn't know what I was talking about.

Has anybody called back...the men...by now the damage will be done. But I cannot separate myself from the pain of my people. We can't separate myself, if you think about it (?) we've walked together too long."

(Audience)

"I saved them, I saved them, but I made my example. I made my expression. I made my manifestation and the world was ready...not ready for me. Paul says I was a man born out of due season. I've been born out of due season just like all we are and the best testimony we can make is to leave this Goddam world."

(Audience)

"Everybody hold it, hold it, hold it...lay down your burden and I'll lay down my burden, down by the riverside, shall we lay 'em down here inside of Guyana, what's the difference? No man didn't take our lives right now he hasn't taken them, but when they start shooting them out of the air, they'll shoot some of our innocent babies. I'm not lying...it's fifty, there's fifty but they've gotta shoot me to get through to some of these people. I'm not letting them take your child. Would you let them take your child?"

(Audience)

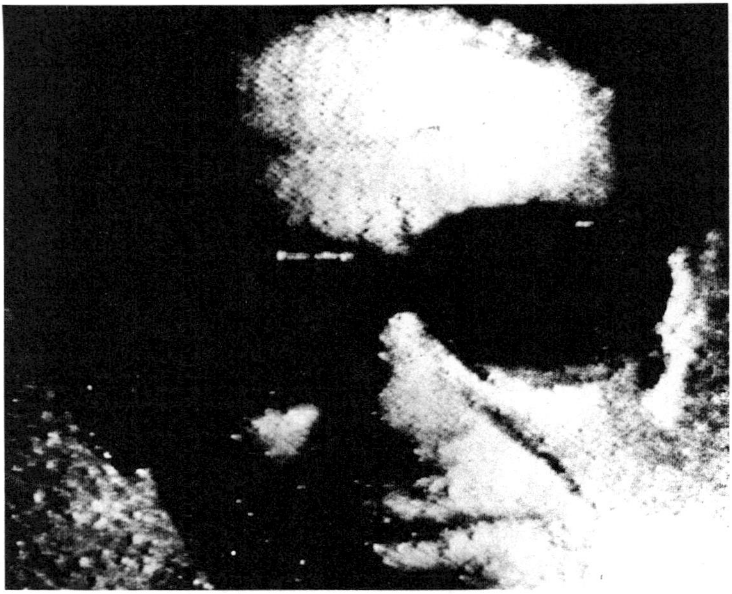

"For months I've tried to keep this thing from happening, but I now see that it's the will of the Sovereign Being that this happened to us. And we lay down our lives in protest at what's been done. And we lay in protest to what's been done. The criminality of people, the cruelty of people, who walked out of here today. You know those people who walked out, most of those white people. Most of those white people walked. I'm so grateful for the ones that didn't, those who knew who they are. There's no point, there's no point to this...we have...we are born before our time.

"They won't accept us. And I don't think we should sit here and take any more time for our children to be endangered and if they come after our children and we give them our children, then our children will suffer forever.

"You have to be honest and if you say that you want to run you'd have run with them 'cause anybody could have run today... I know you are not a runner and I'd...your life is precious to me – it's as precious as John's (?) I don't...what I do I do with weight (?) and justice and judgement. And I have waited against all evidence... Take ease, take ease, take ease, take ease, take ease... Sit down sit down sit down. I tried so very very hard...what's gonna happen...who is it? Get Dwyer out of here before something happens to him."

(Audience)

"It's all over, it's all over... What a legacy, what a legacy well the Red Brigade's the only ones that made any sense anyway. They invaded our privacy, they invaded our home, they followed us six thousand miles away. The Red Brigade showed them justice – the congressman's dead.

Please get some medication...it's simple, there's no convulsions with it. It's just simple. Please get it before it's too late. The GDF will be here I tell you. Get moving, get moving, get moving. Don't be afraid to die. If these people land out here they'll torture our children, they'll torture some of our people here, they'll torture our seniors. We cannot have this. Are you going to separate yourself from whoever shot the congressman. I don't know who shot him. They speak of peace, they gotta right to how many are dead... Oh God, Almighty God..."

(Audience)

"I don't know how in the world they are ever gonna write about us. It's too late, it's too late. The congressman is dead. The congresslady's (?) dead...many of our traitors are dead... They're all laying out there dead."

(Audience)

"I didn't but my people did. They're my people and they've been provoked too much. They've been provoked too much. What's happened here has been too...has been an act of provocation."

(Audience)

"Will you please hasten, will you hasten with that medication. You don't know what you've done...I've tried... They saw it happen, ran into the bush and dropped the machine guns... You've got to move, you've got to get that medication, you've got to move. Might be in about 20 minutes."

(Member of audience) (not J.J:) 'One of the things I used to do before I came here, was I used to be a therapist. It might make a lot of you more comfortable. Sit down & be quiet please. One of the things I used to do, I used to be a therapist and the kind of therapy that I did had to do with reincarnation and past lives... Everybody was so happy when they stepped through to the other side...'

J.J: "You've gotta step that way. It's the only way to step. The choice is not ours now, it's out of our hands..."

(Audience)

"And I do hope that those battalions will stay where they belong and don't come up here..."

(Audience)

"It's hard, it's hard only at first is it hard. It's hard only at first. Living... when you're looking at death...it only looks...living is much more difficult... Raising up every morning and not knowing what's going to be...the night brings...it's much more difficult. It's much more difficult...

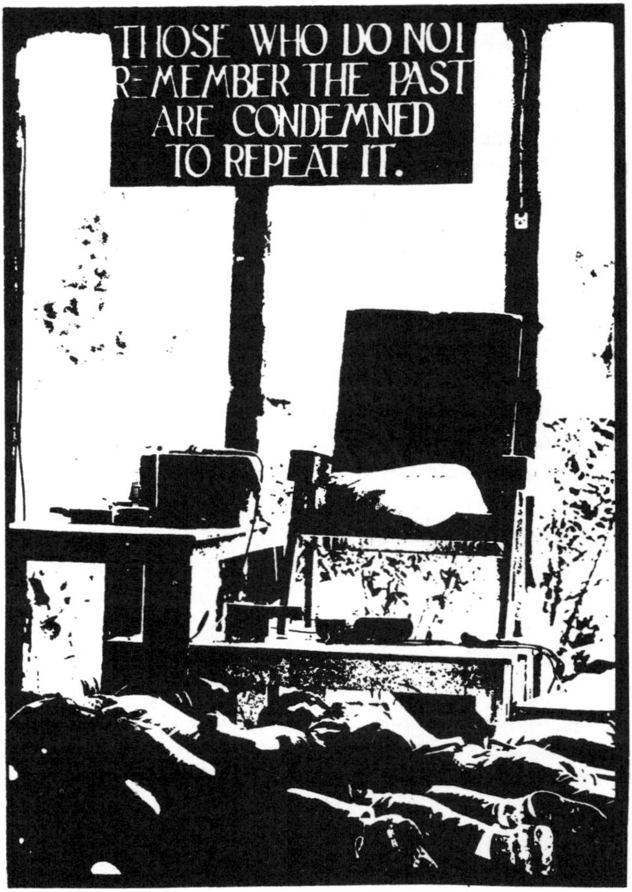

"No, no sorrow that it's all over. I'm glad it's over. Hurry, hurry my children hurry...let us not fall in the hands of the enemy. Hurry my children, hurry. There are seniors out here that I'm concerned about, hurry. I don't want to leave my seniors to this mess. Now quickly, quickly, quickly, quickly, quickly... No more pain Al. No more pain I said Al. No more pain. Jim Cobb is laying on the airfield dead at this moment. Remember the moment...all of the moments that he... These are the people, the peddlers of hate.

"All we're doing is laying down our life, we're not letting them take our life, we're laying down our life. We're sick of their lies, we just want peace."

(Testimonial from audience)

"All it is is taking a drink to take...to go to sleep. That's what death is, sleep. (Screams) Whatever, I'm tired of it all."

(Testimonial from audience)

"If you don't...don't fail to follow my advice you'll be sorry. You'll be sorry...If we do it then let they do it. Have trust in...you have to step across. We used to sing. This world, this world it's not our home, well it sure isn't. We were saying, it sure wasn't. And we don't want to tell him...the only thing(?) to tell him...assure these kids, can some people assure these children of the relaxation of stepping over to the next plane. We'll set an example for others...we set...one thousand people who've said we don't like the way the world is.

"Free at last... Keep...keep your emotions down, keep your emotions down... The – will not hurt if you will keep your emotions down, if you will be quiet. (Screams) It's never been done before you say?... It's been done by every tribe in history. Every tribe facing annihilation... All the Indians of the Amazon are doing it right now. They refuse to bring any babies in the world. They kill every child that comes into the world, because they don't want to live in this kind of world. Be patient, be patient. Death is...

"I tell you I don't care how many screams you hear. I don't care how many anguished cries... Death is a million times preferable to ten more days of this life. If you knew what was ahead of you, if you knew what was ahead of you you'd be glad to be stepping over tonight. Death, death, death is common to people. If you ask the Samoans they take death in their stride... Just have dignity, just be dignified... If you'll quit tell 'em they're dying... If you adults will stop some of this nonsense... Adults, adults, adults, I call on you to stop this nonsense... I call on you to quit exciting your children when all they're doing is going to quiet rest. I call on you to stop this now if you have any respect at all. Are we black, proud and socialist or what are we? Now stop this nonsense. Don't carry this on any more. You're exciting your children."

(Audience)

"Please for Gods sake let's get on with it. We've lived as no other people have lived and loved. We've had as much of this world as you're gonna get. Lets just be done with it, let's be done with the agony of it. It's far, far harder to have to watch you every day die slowly, and from the time you're a child to the time you get grey, you are dying...dishonest and I'm sure that they'll pay for it... This is a revolutionary suicide. It's not a self-destructive suicide. They'll pay for this. They brought this upon us, and they'll pay for that – I leave that destiny to them. (Screams) Who

wants to go with their child has a right to go with their child I think it's humane. I want to go – I want to see you go though. They can take me, and they can do whatever they want to do. I want to see you go. I don't wanna see you go through this hell no more. No more, no more, no more, we're trying...somebody relax...the best thing you can do is relax and you will have no problem. You will have no problem with the thing if you just relax."

(Testimonials from audience)

"It's not to be feared. It is not to be feared. It's a friend. As you're sitting there show your love for one another..."

"ATTITUDE"

JOHN HELMER

Not appearing to say anything is the most important part of writing a dance-music lyric. On the whole, people who like dancing hate content in their music. Also, songs with messages belong to *sub*-culture (spotty youth) whereas Dance music is *popular* culture. The language of Dance-music is language in slavery, stripped down and manacled to the rhythmic imperative; labouring under the heaviest prohibitions of subject-matter, the most limited vocabulary. But if having a message is dance-floor death, everyone can get behind an *Attitude*.

Until relatively recently, the word *'Attitude'* was neutral; it meant about the same as *'frame of mind'*. Then, suddenly, it began cropping up in American TV programmes in lines like; *"Don't give me Attitude, Leroy"*; in funk records; *"I was giving Attitude all over the room"*, and in the small ads section of music papers; *"Wanted, Bass player, must have Attitude"*. Not *an attitude; not this* attitude or *that* attitude – just Attitude.

We all know what Attitude is; it's young, it's Black, it's rebellious. It implies disrespect for authority, disrespect for – the rules, disrespect in the abstract. The way it's used makes out that disrespect is the only *authentic* attitude.

The Dance-music lyric can't give us a message, but it *must* give out Attitude. It has to orient itself; to take up a stance you can get behind. And Attitude's disrespect for the world in general extends to language; words and terms here don't have the same meanings they carry in 'straight' parlance. The way lyrics with Attitude put language under pressure is what I want to deal with here, using the example of three Attitude-heavy lyrics.

"Give me back/All my love/I've had a/Change of heart."

Love is bread and butter to the lyricist, and has been throughout recorded time, but for a writer of Attitude, 'Love is a dodgy concept to get behind. To start with, it's an institution, which automatically inspires disrespect; it was a big word in Christianity, and in the Sixties – Attitude hates Christians and hippies. Love is most often used in lyrics as a euphemism for sex – Attitude hates euphemism. Its meaning is vague: Attitude thrives on the concrete and the everyday – the word 'Love' is an example of the semantic clutter that the lyricist of Attitude has to hack through in order to arrive at the pure form of his art.

The writer of *'Change of Heart'* is an oblique strategist. He puts the word Love' into a formulation which pressurizes its accepted meanings. Saying *"Give me back/All my love"* doesn't make sense; you can *GIVE* love, you can *RETURN* love, but you can't give it back as if it were a pair of shoes, or an engagement ring. The heroine of the verse believes you can. The word is hedged about with her pronouns: *"Give ME back all MY love I'VE had a..."*

Demonstrating that she is the owner and controller of her own emotions. 'Love' is cut down to size. If it was hers in the first place, why can't she do what she wants with it? After all, is not the Language of Love a machinery with which to trap women into a subordinate role? Her love belongs to her. It can be passed back and forth across the lines of sexual combat irreducible and intact; given without surrender – retrieved without shame. This love is uniquely embodiable in material objects; it is the equivalent to what remains of a relationship when sex is removed from the equation, i.e. the shoes, the engagement ring, the Womak and Womak albums. The heroine of these lines is a woman of Attitude; capricious, arrogant and ultimately invulnerable.

"Our Love is History/I burned the letters you were sending me"

A different writer, a different continent, but the same Attitude. Again the concept 'Love' is embodied in a material form (letters), and its connotations cropped down to manageable proportions by the way it is handled. Burning his letters is like an act of magic; the destruction of Love is accomplished by destroying the words which simultaneously describe and embody it. Love here is doubly assaulted. By being burned and by being compared to History.

The word 'History' is another institution that Attitude disrespects. History is what *THEY* teach you in school. *THEIR* History, the story of *THEIR* culture. Nietzsche's Theory of Eternal Return incites sympathy for those events in life which do not have sufficient 'weight' to qualify them for the eternal recurrence experienced by weightier occurrences: the tragedy of life is that some things only happen once, to vanish into insignificance. This twilight of the never-again is the Realm assigned to History by Attitude – for the science of what has ceased to be, the domain of burned letters.

'History' is an example of a word which has a horrific value in White Literary Culture, and a completely opposite meaning in the context of Attitude.

It couldn't have any other meaning in the context of this lyric, just as

'Love' in the previous example can only have that meaning which the context forces it to accept. These slogans are like mathematical equations which redefine the terms and values of which they are constituted.

So far we've chosen fairly crude examples which illustrate how individual words can be destroyed and remade, but there are more subtle lyrics in the field of what can be danced to, and more comprehensive transformations. *'Automatic'* by the Pointer Sisters has a lyric that illustrates how a major area of assumptions can be challenged by Attitude.

"No way to control it/It's totally Automatic."

The comparison of sexual response and performance with machinery in Black Lyrics goes back to the beginnings of mechanisation, from the *'Big Wheel'* rolling *'in a Georgia Cotton Field'* to the Sex Machine that James Brown felt like being. As the machines people work with become more sophisticated, so the penetration of this Man/Mechanism comparability into the metaphorical fabric of the lyric becomes deeper. *'Automatic'* is a lyric for the computer age. It uses a wide variety of mechanical and technological images (*"Your camera looks through me...that makes my motor run"*) and splices them in with more recognisably human, natural images; *"My hands perspire and shake like a leaf"*, to produce an effect of total breakdown in the presence of the loved one which, because it is not pinned down as a specifically physical, or specifically emotional response, achieves a more complete picture of the human organism in flux. The language of love is completely avoided. Conversely, it presents a picture of the human psyche as a mechanism.

In the White Literary Tradition, to compare a man with a machine almost always involves diminishing his 'humanity'. To be machine-like is to be cold, calculating and without feeling, or else to be stupid, and perform repetitive menial tasks. As far as Attitude is concerned, White Literary culture can go hang. By comparing organism and mechanism in a state of breakdown – *"All I can manage to push from my lips/Is a stream of absurdities/Every word I intended to speak/Winds up locked in circuitry"* – the lyric discovers an essential similarity which is not so evident when both are in working order.

In all three of these examples, meanings which words and phrases hold in White Literary culture are reversed, flouted or destroyed. Attitude transforms meaning. These lyrics do for Popular Culture what poetry does for Literary Culture; they re-process language. All cultural forms are products of necessity, and this revising of meaning is particularly necessary when you consider the limited vocabulary with which popular culture operates. If you only have 2,000 words to choose from (this is the number of words that the Ayatollah Khomeini had apparently limited himself to, in order to avoid the sin of luxury in language) they have to be words which work well, and whose meanings are current and precise. This process is informed by Attitude.

Attitude does not operate at the level of conscious debate; it's something you have to *'get behind'*. If you can't align yourself with the moral and social assumptions it implies (and it implies a world) you can't orient yourself so as to appreciate its possibilities. The power of these lyrics to rattle around in your brain for months at a time is a by-product of their relevance to your life, but it's possible you might never understand why. There exists not only Attitude, but Anti-Attitude. This would tell you that Cliff Richard is in the same tradition as Hound Dog Taylor, that Sade's got soul and that White Men invented the blues. There is a battle for the control of language going on at all levels. *Attitude exists because it is the only possibility of expression for those who have access to language only under the severest pressure.*

Jamaican patois, long considered slang, has recently been discovered to be an authentic language, with a consistent structure. Black slaves who were brought to the Caribbean were forced to speak European tongues. They formed their own language by slotting the foreign words into African grammatical structures. This is a monument to the ability of a subject culture to preserve its structure intact under the heaviest pressure, and is analogous to the way Dance-music lyrics treat words like *'Love'*, *'History'*, and *'Automatic'*. Wherever the authentic Black voice surfaces in Popular Culture it shines out as the real thing, and is instantly recognisable. Not by the sunglasses it prefers, or by the instruments that it is played on – but by a certain, indefinable *Attitude*.

MONTAGUE SUMMERS

With Reference To The Reverend

SANDY ROBERTSON

Very few people seem to remember Montague Summers these days. Generally the reaction at the mention of his name is a suppressed shudder or, as with the editor of the esteemed organ in your hands the unravelled threads of memory flicker and out comes: *"I've for some reason always had the impression that he was a bit of a nutter"*. Aaah, the folly of youth, cackled the senile shuffler into his weirdly curving pipe...

Summers is (or was) best known for his series of books on the occult. Born in 1880 in Clifton near Bristol, The Reverend Alphosnus Joseph Mary Augustus Montague Summers was affected by the decadent posings of the era in which his youth flowered. When once his strict father asked if an Oscar Wilde book he'd come upon (to his outrage) was his, he replied (affecting a lisp designed to infuriate), *"Yeth, father, I have all the workth of the mathter!"* Swanning about in flamboyant clothes, carrying a cane the head of which was an 'immodest' representation of Leda and the Swan, he'd whisper to friends, *"Tell me strange things."* It was all *very* Dorian Gray.

The only record of his dabbling in this area is the rather rare *'Antinous and other Poems'* (1907), for he was appointed deacon of Bitton the following year, having attained suitable theological qualifications at Lichfield. It is this period, though, that is the genesis of much of the sinister rumours about Summers. People who knew him say he was neurotically obsessed with evil; *too* much for a clergyman, at any rate. And he left the district under a cloud after being acquitted on a charge of paederasty...

The next year, 1909, he entered the Roman Catholic Church. More suited than the C of E for a man beloved of ritual and romance, of course. But that is only the half of it. Though he thenceforth wore the holy purple, called himself 'Reverend' and acted the part of a medieval Abbé, many sneered and questioned his right to call himself a priest. All this is gone into in great detail in Joseph Jerome's limited edition (750 copies) memoir of Summers (published in 1965) for those with the perseverance to track down a copy, but the consensus seems to be that his orders were "valid if irregular".

Summers became, after this, firmly entrenched as one of the literary characters of the age. A learned bibliophile, an expert on the Gothic novel, a champion of the Restoration Theatre, a demonologist. He lived in Hampstead and Richmond, at various times, and the house where he resided in Hampstead still looks...evil, the kind of place in which a sordid sex murder might take place. And the new owners of his Richmond abode, who moved in when he died, found the atmosphere *so* uncongenial that they had to have it exorcised!

The basic nasty tale about Summers was that he was either *not* a priest or was an unfrocked priest, or that he had taken holy orders with the notion of usurping them to hold Black Masses. Even his defenders admit that there is strong evidence that Summers held one Satanic ceremony when younger, though they claim that this was why his books on witchcraft maintain such a staunchly olde-worlde *"lynch 'em"* tone in the face of ridicule and liberal attitudes. He was a *reformed* sorcerer, they say.

His 'classics' on the subject are *'The History of Witchcraft and Demonology'* (1926) and *'The Geography of Witchcraft'* (1927), though the later stuff like *'A Popular History of Witchcraft'* (1964) are good too, despite their cannibalization of large chunks of the original works. He also translated and/or introduced many of the ancient religious texts of an anti-witchcraft nature, like the notorious *'Malleus Mallificarum'* and Sinistrari's *'Demoniality'*, though the latter (along with *'The Confessions of Madeleine Bavent'*) was actually seized as an obscene book! He in fact planned an entire Church and Witchcraft series, though (like many of his ideas) it never got completed.

Other Summers books of note include *'The Werewolf'* (1933), *'The Vampire: his Kith and Kin'* 1928) and *'The Vampire In Europe'* (1929). He was always acutely fascinated by anything evil or supernatural: he kept a huge file of cuttings on Aleister Crowley, and when the two met they got along (perhaps surprisingly – or not) famously.

Nowadays Summers is hardly a fashionable writer, mainly due to the fact that he accepts witchcraft and its workings as a proven fact, moreover an evil one to boot. His archaic style of prose also puts many off: *"budge nims the togeman"* he once wrote, whatever that means! *(I thought everybody knew what that means! – Ed.)* He died in 1948 and is now mainly known for his most famous collection of great (and not so great) supernatural tales, *'The Supernatural Omnibus'* (1931). This last is still in print, as are some of the others, but to form a collection of first editions by Montague Summers is a difficult, time-consuming and expensive (but rewarding) business.

Strange, clever, erudite, gullible, opinionated, sinister... Summers was all these and more. There remains much that is not known about him. He planned two volumes of autobiography, but only wrote the first (which doesn't deal much with his ecclesiastical and supernatural interests) which wasn't issued until a few years ago. His library was sold off at his death and his private papers were either lost or burnt by his private secretary in mysterious circumstances. A full-scale biography of this wonderful man is long overdue.

Further Reading

Apart from the works mentioned in the text, anyone desiring information should check out *'Montague Summers: A Bibliography'* by Timothy D'Arch Smith, published by Aquarian.

'The Supernatural Omnibus' mentioned is in Gollancz hardcover and Penguin paperback. Foyle's in Charing X Road may have the Summers autobiography *'The Galanty Show'*, and, unbelievable as it may seem, the last time I looked they had a handful of copies of the limited edition *'Memoir'* mentioned earlier, even though there were only 750 copies printed. Published 1965 by Cecil & Amelia Woolf.

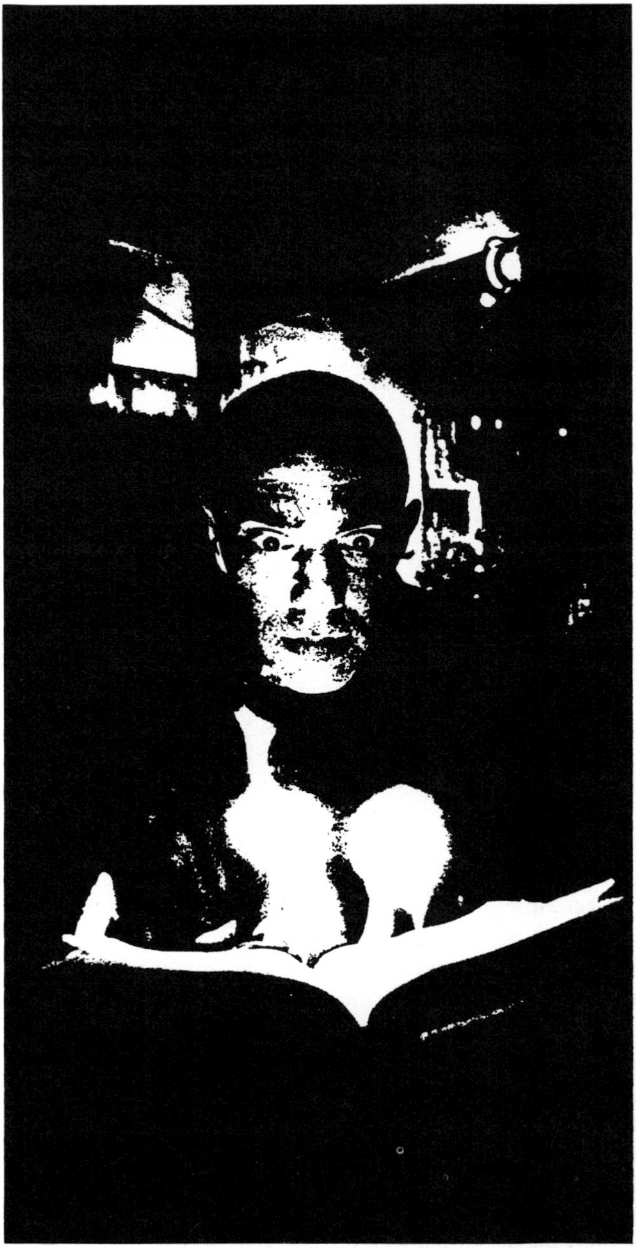

THROUGH A SCREEN, DARKLY

THE DEREK JARMAN INTERVIEW

SIMON DWYER

Derek Jarman – painter, film-maker and theatre set designer, held his first one-man show at the Lisson Gallery in 1969. He designed sets and costumes for the theatre ('Jazz Calendar' with Frederick Ashton and Rudolf Nureyev at Covent Garden, 'Don Giovani' at the Coliseum, and 'Mouth of the Night' with Micha Bergese). He was production designer for Ken Russell's films 'The Devils' and 'Savage Messiah', during which time he worked on his own films in Super 8, which became underground classics, such as 'In the Shadow of the Sun'. He went on to make feature films: 'Sebastiane', 'Jubilee', 'The Tempest', 'Angelic Conversation', 'Caravaggio', 'Imagining October', 'War Requiem', 'The Last of England', 'The Garden', 'Edward II' and 'Wittgenstein', working with a variety of actors from Sir Lawrence Olivier to Adam Ant. His autobiographical books include 'At Your Own Risk', 'Caravaggio', 'Dancing Ledge', and 'Modern Nature'. He has returned to painting (shows at the Royal Academy and the ICA) and design ('The Rake's Progress' in Florence), and made a number of pop videos, including promos for The Smiths, Pet Shop Boys, and Marianne Faithful. His video for REM's 'Losing My Religion', won an MTV award for best pop video of 1991. He 'came out' while at art school in the company of David Hockney and Patrick Proctor, and had affairs with Robert Mapplethorpe and the serial murderer Michele Lupo. Deified as a Saint by the activist queer group The Sisters of Perpetual Indulgence, Jarman is now a prominent media figure in the political and social battles against homophobia and Aids. He was diagnosed HIV positive in 1986. He lives in a small flat in central London and a wooden fisherman's cottage on the beach near the nuclear power station at Dungeness, Kent. Gay martyr to some, transgressive art hero to others, he spoke to *Rapid Eye*.

"I have thee not, and yet I see thee still. Art thou not, fatal vision, sensible. To feeling as to sight?"

On the inner levels of philosophy, literature, theology and metaphysics, certain masters developed impressive esoteric ideas, founding new schools of thought through their synthesis of ancient teachings. The most famous of these was Jabir el-Hajyan, better known in the West as "Geber". It was from his name and the apparent unintelligibility of alchemical writings in general that the derisory descriptive noun "Gibberish" derived...

Walking up the demolition site of Charing Cross Road in the morning sunshine, the rolled-down windows of the immobile metal snake that stretches up to Centrepoint gives an aural cut-up of the state of the world. Passing from big BMW to tiny Toyota is like listening to the post-intellectual hiphop of Cabaret Voltaire. LBC, BBC, Capital, bulletins of IRA action spliced with S-Express, Terence Trent D'Arby, and The Eurythmics – Annie Lennox talking to the Angels..."Da da do da-da dahn da da dahh dahhh..." Some people would understand.

Derek Jarman sits on a stool in his lovely little room, surrounded by his labyrinth of "gibberish", surrounded, quite literally, by himself – one hand on the back of his head, the other resting at the base of his spine, body rocking awkwardly as if he's waiting for the tooth-puller. Behind him stretches a long window, in front of it a large writing desk, empty but for a full appointment book. A double bed is headed by a big home-made bookcase, a maze stuffed with hundreds of titles; Psychology; Biographies; Art; Occultism. It all figures. A classic plastercast head of Mausolos looks on from the corner – saved in the '60s from the Slade just before it was to be smashed to make way for the flood of modernist American giganticism. The white walls are darkened by a symmetrical arrangement of Jarman's own beautiful miniatures – ghostly gold figures and skulls, naked silver shadows and scribbled hieroglyphics caked with thick black paint, all set in heavy frames and deep glass. A cylindrical witch's mirror, as used in medieval laser shows, dangles by a thread from the ceiling, giving a convex impression of the streetlife below. Jarman knows the art of mirrors.

In a climate of seamy social realism, 'adult' films are packed with Content (the stuff of broken marriages), obsessed with kitchen sink narrative and dazzled by American Actor's Workshop graduates who put on accents, weight and stubble for the making of a Picture. (It's always a "Picture". Not a Movie, never a Film, and never, ever a Dream.) All of which leaves little room, or backing, for the unfocused visual cinema of Derek Jarman.

As an individual media figure his own stature has increased enormously in the last couple of years. But often he is in demand not because of what he does, but because of what he says. A man who puts his art into his life, rather than his work.

Uncompromising, fiercely independent, Jarman is still more distanced from the British Film establishment than any other major director, as his is still seen as 'serious', 'arty' cinema that they wish neither to encourage nor understand. But he remains unconcerned about being understood, using as he does the unpopular language of the artist, the language of the angels, without regret.

I'd met him before on brief occasions when he'd often seemed polite but preoccupied. Preoccupied with his work which, in such a personal artist, such an honest autobiographer, was a preoccupation with himself. When Jarman is working, he is often gliding around in a tizz and he seems to float half an inch above the ground, untouchable but untouching – ignoring everything, and everyone, around him. Reminiscent of the Queen Mary leaving harbour, at such moments it is advisable to give the man a wide berth.

As the creator of such a powerful body of work he has always remained something of an enigma behind this self-assured front. Seemingly aloof not only to the demands of the Film World, but also the needs of his audience.

Flippant and occasionally bitchy, but thankfully never apologetic, as so many less determined artists are. In a society so hostile to its Art World and cynical of the gay mafia that operates within it, it would be easy to harbour doubts about him. One could picture Derek as a boy, sensitive, frightfully middle class and fresh from the closet of public school, standing in front of that distorting witch's mirror engrossed in his cleverness and beauty. Like Quentin Crisp in *The Naked Civil Servant*, like the clone boys standing in uniformed rows in the full-frontal mirrored toilets at Heaven – so heady with the nitrate that they believe what they see in the mirror, as if it had their own mind, as if it couldn't lie. It was always possible that Jarman had latched on to anti-fashion, olde worlde imagery and mild eccentricity just as the clones had pieced together their own acceptable identity. In cultivating his own image and believing his own publicity, distancing himself further and further from the Art/Cinema establishments that don't always think too highly of him anyway, and while doing so making no explanations for self exploration and possible self love, one could easily wonder if Jarman were merely subsidising his lifestyle; still living through a massive hangover from the Andrew Logan party that was the '60s and at which Jarman was, in his own words, "an extra".

Was he gratifying himself, existing only for himself, was he (let's face it) a wanker? Why should anybody wish to eavesdrop on this man's private visions, decode his mystical signals, when we can gulp up pop culture in the sanitised columns of IPC? Boy George and his ilk, being a so much less bitter pill to swallow as cultural crusaders for we modern, liberal people. George, the type of harmless eccentric the English convince themselves they love, was at least free from all that artistic solipsism. And probably a far truer, more apparently 'real' reflection of the 1980's than anything found in Jarman's mottled mirror.

But the fact is, however confused or romanticised Jarman's vision may sometimes appear, there is sitting before us a pearl in the shit of 'experimental' film-making. Derek is erudite, funny, and completely charming, but the reason this man is so engaging, so fascinating in his pretention – the reason he gets away with sometimes acting like the Queen Mary – is that out of the shadows of his films there is a human face. As in all 'worthwhile' art, be it film, music, literature, comedy or whatever, when the mask is removed that face is (often uncomfortably) like your own. In Jarman's films, the whole being greater than the total parts, your senses are honed to perceive "the face of the soul". Not the fat face of America. Not the face the TV would like us to have, the face we show the world in *Brideshead* or *Brookside*. In Jarman's films, real people are allowed to exist. Real, weird people shimmer silently across the screen in his vaguely allegorical, image-based, mood drenched stories where the traps of time and place are cross referenced and transgressed, and where 'meaning' is supplied by the viewer. The dreamer. As naturally follows in a world that lives through its media, real people are therefore more able to live life the way they wish. People are allowed to leave Brookside. Bad actors in the scripts given to them by Lorimar and Granada, they are instead able to confront their wildest dreams and live because they see themselves on the screen.

Such escapist philanthropy may, in Jarman's eyes, be merely a by-product of his own wish to exist. He just holds his mirror up to 'Reality' or 'Control', like Boy George does. But in Jarman's mirror, instead of a confirmation, Control sees its 'reality' distorted, made, in Jarman's eyes, more 'real'. Such an image may not be part of the Grand Plan, which may explain why Derek Jarman remained until 1986 the only British film maker to have made three feature films and not have had any of his work shown on TV – the IBA banning the original planned Channel 4 screenings in the same stroke as they nixed transmission of Ron Peck's *Nighthawks* (in which, coincidently, Jarman played a small role).

It is, though, always self-defeating to over-intellectualise about anything as vague and subjective as Art, even with the aim of trying to decipher and disperse it, so that pieces, fallen neglected like Jarman from the high tables of Melvyn Bragg and *Time Out* be better appreciated – or at least disliked for more sensible reasons. Perhaps, then, not bucking for a job on The Late Show, we should just say that in case you have never seen his work, it is only Jarman who could make such superficially boring cinema so seductive, and listen to his own words echoing from the Sanyo...

Talking of the British Film Institute funding of his long-awaited, much acclaimed, **Caravaggio** epic, of his enduring associations with Genesis P-Orridge and Coil (from **In the Shadow of the Sun** to **Mouth of the Night**), of artistic control over the huge production of anything as heavyweight as a modern feature film, of Money... *"The money needed in film is enormous. The money needed in other areas, to put out a tape of music for example, is peanuts by comparison."*

RE: Do you envy people who work in other areas then? Would you like to be free as the musicians you use in your work, for instance, like your pals at PTV?

"Oh, I'm MUCH freer than Gen! Because I don't have any theories to hinder my development. He's going to love that isn't he!?"
RE: I'm surprised you have that approach. Gen, for instance, always has very good reasons for doing anything-
"Oh, I have my reasons."
RE: Alright. What was your reason for making **Caravaggio**, then?
"Umm...what an appalling question! I don't know."
RE: Well, it's just that, talking of Gen, he always knows exactly, he always analyses everything he does y'know.
"Yes, I do too. It's just that I've got to such a state of self-analysis that people can't understand the language I'm talking in, so it actually becomes impossible. You see, I'm working in a sort of way which, in my own mind, is not very easily communicated. Do you know what I mean?"
(I'm not sure if I do.)
RE: ...Feelings?
"Yes, feelings and things like that. So I really can't say it's theoretical. Personally I can't see the point in communication at all any longer."
RE: Why not? Because it's all been said, or people have nothing to say?
"Well, because I don't think it's necessary to say it. My feeling is that all of this is centred around people sending messages to other people. I suppose one sends messages to people who're already inclined to actually receive one's messages. One doesn't make many converts. My feeling is I'm a bad audience. I dislike audiences. No one should go and see anything, they should go and do it for themselves. Therefore this precludes even a situation like Gen's, theoretically. On the other hand in an imperfect world in which I've got to live I've to make a film. So...I'm doing it for the money!"
RE: Yes of course, but now you're being flippant, you don't only think of that at all.

He doesn't, in 'theory'. But the fact is that in this imperfect world Derek Jarman is almost a bankrupt, and the bigger films, such as **Caravaggio** and **The Garden** should, if not make him rich, at least wipe out his massive debts. And the important idea is encapsulated there – in a perfect world we'd not only need to devote most of our energies towards survival, but there would also be no need for us to be culture vultures, picking over the brains of usually very dull musicians, film makers, fashion designers, painters and novelists for interpretations of Life. We'd all be too busy finding our own interpretations ourselves. The ethics behind the bedroom-bound cassette makers he refers to, similar to the motivations that started *Rapid Eye* in the late Seventies, would be close to Jarman's heart. In theory at least the whole Ladbroke Grove 'alternative' activity was not only about producing something for oneself, but about doing it while being uncorrupted by the needs of the audience. This is something the likes of the Record Industry and Music Press could never collectively admit to understand. In the acceptable areas of culture (anything prefixed by 'Youth'), chart placings and ratings are what count. Jarman knows only too well. The audience is everything.

"Audiences have always been dangerous. They can get enormous." Hardly pop culture material, Jarman gets his mouth around the word 'enormous' as if he meant 'monstrous'.

"Like audiences listening to some speaker telling them to go and kill people. I don't believe in audiences, therefore it is essentially difficult for me to be honest with people about communicating anything in art like that. I'm only communicating really to the converted, and quite honestly at this stage in my life I'm sufficiently aware of the structure outside to realise that in a certain sense you can blind yourself by believing."

RE: So you don't even have any ideas about the feelings you would like people to have when leaving the cinema, say?

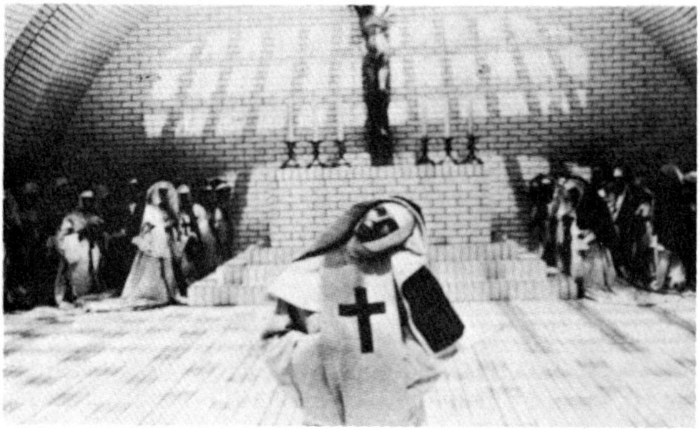

Vanessa Redgrave surveys Jarman's set designs in 'The Devils', 1970.

"No I don't. Not even that. What happens is I think other people decide afterwards exactly what things are. What a thing becomes in a culture after it's made is very different from the intentions of the person making it. Also, don't believe that you can set up a situation and know what the outcome is going to be. You can say 'I'm going to do this', but you end up with the other. Invariably things end up with their opposites... To put it in really blunt language, systems of Peace and Love end up as War and Hate. It's quite simple."
His mind picks up the thread.
"Where I do agree with Gen is that while one's working one should encourage people to take the leap to work as well, because the more people who're doing it, the more interesting and vibrant it becomes."
RE: Why is it vibrant if nobody is communicating anything to anyone?
"Because it's all to do with internal things, it's nothing to do with external things at all. That's what it comes down to. There's no such thing as the world outside. The only thing that's of interest is the world inside, and it's relationship with the world outside. That's the attrition point, and that's what makes Art."

An explanation, of sorts, for films that have nothing to say. Home movies made by, and for, Derek Jarman – a man hellbent on finding his own explanations – props for the physical realisation of his own reality. In this context, then, ironically it's Jarman who is being unpretentious. His usual lack of obvious propaganda, ideals, and messages is far less presumptuous on the viewer than anything one sees on TV, for example. Television, by its nature, will lump millions of people's perceptions – their opinions, politics, morals, memories – into one insipid mass, to be moulded by anyone with a big enough hand (such people include the likes of Mary Whitehouse and Douglas Hurd). As so many 'alternatives' to this are merely equally arrogant, loaded and absurd reactions to the right-wing propaganda that dominates every TV and cinema screen in the country, Jarman's unfashionable artiness is like a breath of fresh air. If his films must have a socially credible quality, it is in nudging the voyeur into looking for such "internal explanations" himself. One starts by wondering what the fuck his films are about and, realising they need not "be about" anything, begins to read whatever one likes into them, his dream vehicles. He knows many ways of skinning a skull.

The most common and base criticism of Jarman is that he is nothing more than a neo-romantic libertarian. That he's not obviously 'political' enough. Yet Jarman is a tacit anarchist. It doesn't take an enormous leap of the imagination to see throughout his work a quite clearly defined attitude.

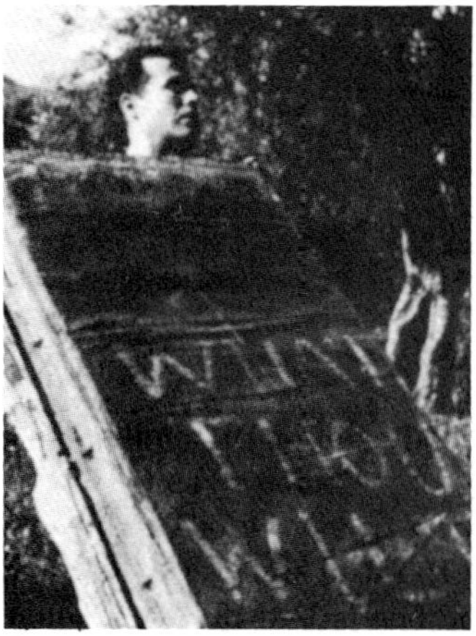

Film maker Kenneth Anger with one of the doors from the Abbey of Thelema in the '50s.

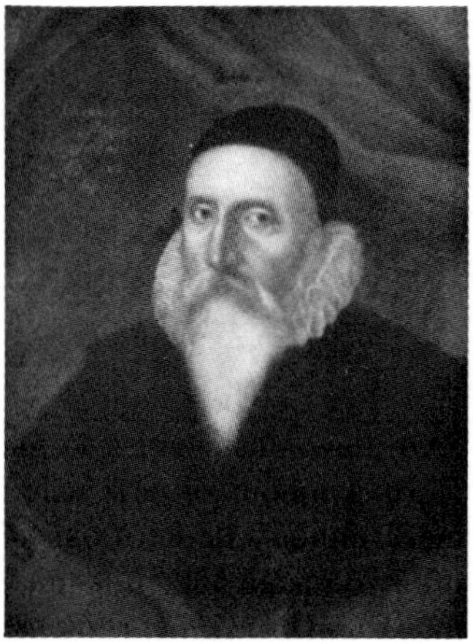

Dr. John Dee.

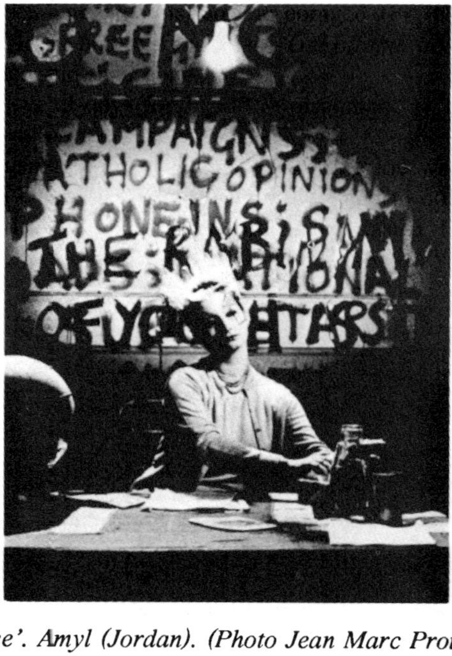

'Jubilee'. Amyl (Jordan). (Photo Jean Marc Prouveur).

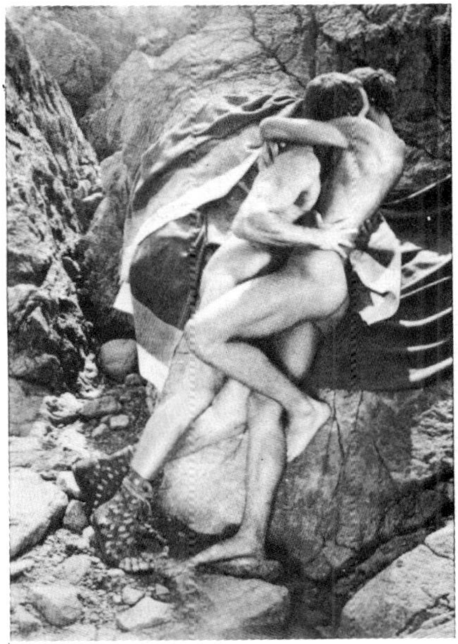

'Sebastiane', love sequence.

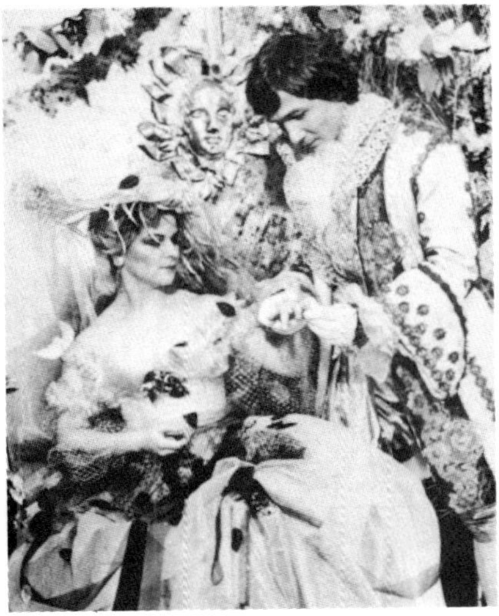

'The Tempest'. Miranda (Toyah Wilcox) and Ferdinand (David Meyer) (Photo: Bridget Holm).

Look at an exhibition of his paintings and you will find works such as the sardonically titled **'GBH'**, a series of vast canvasses depicting a melting, burning map of Britain. *"A Britain in the grip of hellfire, a ritual destruction of little England, the Old Country – by Oppenheimer's nuclear grandchildren"*. Jarman's view of modern Britain seems to be one of damnation. Damned for being the most class conscious, hypocritical, xenophobic island in the West. Damned for being a puppet of Washington. Damned for shunning painting and literature in preference of M.T.V. His obsession with the past – **Jubilee** cross referencing punk London with Elizabethan England, **The Tempest** raking over the coals of Shakespeare, **Caravaggio** set in the Renaissance and so on – is also a rejection of the present. Surely a quite overt 'political' statement. Jarman himself says – *"I think of myself as a Green film maker. Our culture has always been backward looking. Shakespeare is backward looking. What interests me is that Elizabethan England is our cultural Arcadia. As Shakespeare is the essential pivot of our culture, it seemed really important to deal with it. Nearly everyone who works in the arts at some point actually pays attention to Shakespeare. The whole myth of Camelot, Blake, Tennyson – you can go through all the English artists – there's that dream of Arcadia. We seem to be the only European culture which has that dream background."* Jarman's dream is one of the *"pre-scientific world"*, of John Dee's alchemical visions.

"People are recovering that view again because it saw a world in which matter was living – that's what alchemy was all about. People like the Greens are realising that the destruction of the Amazon jungle, fences across the Kalahari desert and so on show a scientific world which is rapacious and might be wrong. We might need those dreams and they might really be a part of us, and that's what interests me about John Dee. Alchemy is about turning matter into gold, about dross and being. About dark dross being pure gold. And for pure gold don't read 'capitalism', read gold in its spiritual sense – metal that doesn't corrupt."

"If you desire to get this golden Lodestone, your prayers must be rightly made to God in true knowledge, contrition, sorrow and true humility for to know and learn the three different worlds... Out of the Super Celestial World doth spring the Light of the Spirit; from the Second Celestial World is derived the fountain of life and of the Soul: and from the third, the elemental World, cometh the Invincible, heavenly yet sensible fire, by which is digested and ripened that which is comprehensible."

John Dee, 'Of The Spirit Of Gold'

"Maybe an audience can see something that can trigger off that inward exploration. That's what it's all for, there's nothing else. As for dictating

or believing or having theories, one knows that one can have all those things but one knows that they're really suspect. Not for oneself, but when put in other people's hands, because everyone misinterprets them. Look at the painter I've been dealing with, Caravaggio; he influenced a whole generation. Now, some painters actually took off his work, like Velasquez or Rembrandt for instance, and produced their own quite extraordinary work from it. Others just took all explorations of Caravaggio and turned them into convention."

And so, while British Film Year fades into memory, as slickly shot message movies attract the money and consequently the publicity that ensures our images of ourselves remain constant, ex-advertising men become influential directors and Jarman stubbornly continues his inward exploration...publicly.

RE: What do you think of the British Cinema?

"I don't think about it at all, it doesn't interest me. Nor do other British film makers particularly, except my friends."

Unlike the rest of Europe, the British Cinema exists in little-known fragments. Never having been quite the same depository for American iconography as the U.K., the continent has been left to a larger extent to improvise with its Fassbinders, Passolinis, Godards, Rossis and Antonionis. Names to conjure with. Here, amid the Deadwood, the exponents are less lauded.

RE: Cerith Wyn Evans?

"Yes, I rate him. I think he's a master. I like Terence Davis, I like a few of the older film makers, Michael Powell. Nicholas Roeg at the moment, Ken Russell at the moment. I love old 'Carry On' films because they're so ridiculous and wonderful. I like John Maybury's films, Sophie Williams too. So actually I do like a lot of films, all my friends' films!"

RE: You opened a Young Film Makers Festival in Leicester recently. What was that like?

"Well, it was very very good. That was an object lesson. I said in my opening of it that it would be the most important thing that the British Film Institute would be engaged in, and it was, because was all people making their own Cinema. People outside it criticise it because it only goes to the other enthusiasts, but they're missing the point, I think, of what art is about..."

RE: As opposed to the Film Industry.

"That...vague and nebulous and much maligned word, as opposed to the commercial cinema, yes. I've made a very uncomfortable brush between the two which is quite an interesting area. That's an attrition point."

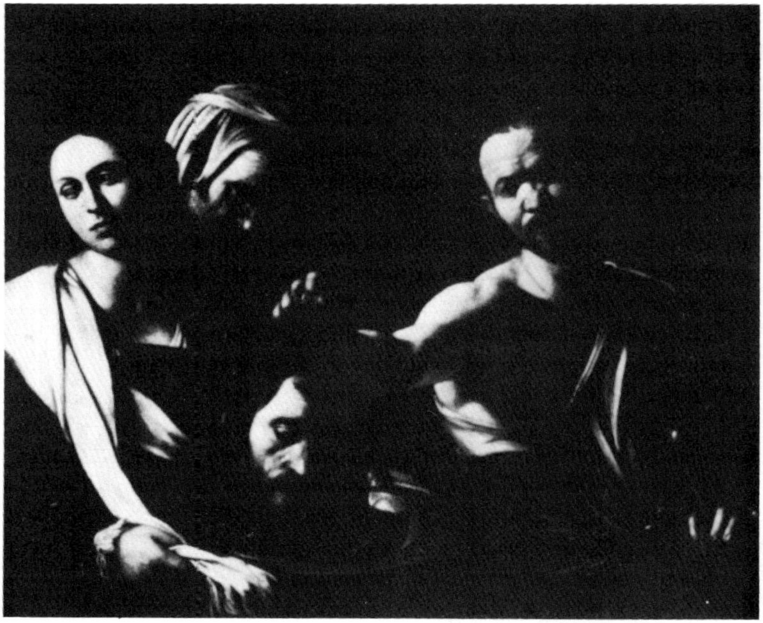

Salome receives the head of John the Baptist. (Caravaggio.)

His major 'brushes', the sweeps of **Sebastiane**, **Jubilee**, **The Tempest**, **Caravaggio**, **War Requiem**, **Edward II** and **The Garden** represent only a fraction of a film output that has spanned over twenty years. His smaller-scale films, which he describes as *"movie art rather than Art Movies"*, slip out like an O.A.P.'s willy (once every few months and with nobody noticing). They are usually greeted with a deafening silence by everyone apart from Mary Whitehouse and her anti-sex lobbyists (who have gone on record as condemning Jarman for his work) and those who occupy the most hip and hallowed corners of the ICA. One could, for instance, be forgiven for not hearing too much about his classic short, **Angelic Conversation**, a tellingly titled film about "an avant garde romance" that was shot in Dorset. The soundtrack features music from Coil, and Jarman got Judi Dench to provide its voice-over monologue in the form of 14 of Shakespeare's sonnets. This one left me fairly cold, but Radio 4's resident 'alternative' comic, Simon Fanshawe, once told me that it was the only film he'd watched which had made him cry.

Conversation had it's premiere in July '85 to herald the opening of Pride Week, the proceeds going to the admirable Terence Higgins Trust.

Watch out, and you may still find it blown-up at your local art house fleapit playing along side Peck's **What Can I do with a Male Nude?** I wonder, too, how many readers will have actually seen his main 1987 film, **The Last of England**, starring Jarman's 'only woman actor', Tilda Swinton? It was perhaps his most overtly 'political', autobiographical and controversial work to date. Loved by some – it won 1st Prize at the 1988 Berlin Film Festival – it was predictably annihilated by reactionary critics in papers like *The Sunday Times*. Critics who actually admitted that they did not understand what it was about. Jarman's super, Super 8's are often hard to find, but always worth seeking out.

But why does he keep making them? Keep struggling to set up his projector (Jarman is no Film School technician) – to run these strange, slow flickerers to any audience larger than three people?

"Well I'm just not interested in giganticism. I love small things, small audiences, film shows for friends. They are really private films which have just been made to inspire and illustrate. They also give me a good sketchpad for ideas. In a sense there are similarities with that and the independent music that sprang up in the late Seventies."

RE: But the difference was that with records being de-mystified people could easily do something about it. The money needed was peanuts, like you said. There also existed a ready-made outlet for those records that were being produced. You couldn't make a film independently and put it out yourself very easily; the structure wasn't there, still isn't. So how do people wanting to do that get 'round it?

*"Well, I think Gen had a bright idea with video. It is difficult, but, I mean, something like **In the Shadow of the Sun** which started off in 1972, well, thousands of people have seen it now. And if it carries on being shown it'll be seen by many more people than saw a lot of the commercial films of that period."*

RE: Which show in town for a week then disappear forever.

*"Yes, vanish! It'll probably be seen by more people than saw **Exorcist 2!***

"RE: You don't worry too much about how many people are going to see what you do.

*"No, as long as there are six or seven people in a room you're away! Nearly everyone's value judgements are overshadowed by the cash till. It's quite simple, if you make a film costing 22 million dollars it's really just 22 million dollars' worth of publicity telling the world that you're the best. You've only got to see what happened with something like, say, **Absolute Beginners**. That had fourteen million behind it and it cropped up in every single magazine. But you can make a film like **Caravaggio** which I was working on a lot longer than Julian (Temple) was working on that, and*

the silence is overwhelming, which I think I prefer, though I love the publicity as well!"

RE: That film, **In the Shadow of the Sun** seemed to me to have a lot to do with dreams.

"Yes, well, it was as much to do with that as it was with experimenting with Super 8. In the sense that dreams are random and uncontrollable and often crop up in groups and recur, and I think that film in that sense is rather like a dream. But there was no design before that film as to how it was going to come out. It was just an experiment."

RE: This was 'Flowing With The Glue' then.

"Yes! What Heathcote says!"

RE: Is that how you always like to work?

"I think so, because if one sets down plans beforehand they never really work, like we were saying. I think then that you have to let it go when it goes. In that film I just set up a series of images and they randomly did whatever they did when I was re-filming. And it was very random."

RE: But however random it was you still chose what images to film in the first place. The quality and type of work still depends on the person doing it, no matter how random the process involved in the creation.

"Yes, I'm not trying to divorce myself from it at all. It was me, that film was an accurate reflection of how I was when I made it."

RE: But you see what I'm getting at. There is a culture of cut-ups that have emerged since Jamie Reid and the current interest in Burroughs and Dada and everything else, and a lot of pseudo-arty types are using cut-ups and scratching and so on as an excuse to be lazy, aren't they? It's so easy because both the technology and the market are easily available.

"Absolutely. In experimental music and a lot of experimental film. I think, though, that it depends on how much work you've done on yourself beforehand. If you have had discipline and worked, that random element can work really well."

You may notice that Jarman, painter, film maker, writer and designer, often refers to music – one of the few things that he hasn't tried himself. He's scathing about the Record Industry, but at the same time attracted by, and attractive to, musicians. Like Jarman's heroes Roeg and Burroughs – who photograph, or get photographed with all of pop's preening pin-ups (the highbrow ones anyway), there seems a mutual fascination. Perhaps because Pop can disseminate ideas and create cultural climates so much more effectively than film or literature nowadays. Pop Stars are now the perfect vessels through which all the hopes and dreams and hare-brain ideas of the world can pass through. The immediately acceptable face of art or revolution or good old fashioned decadent eccentricity.

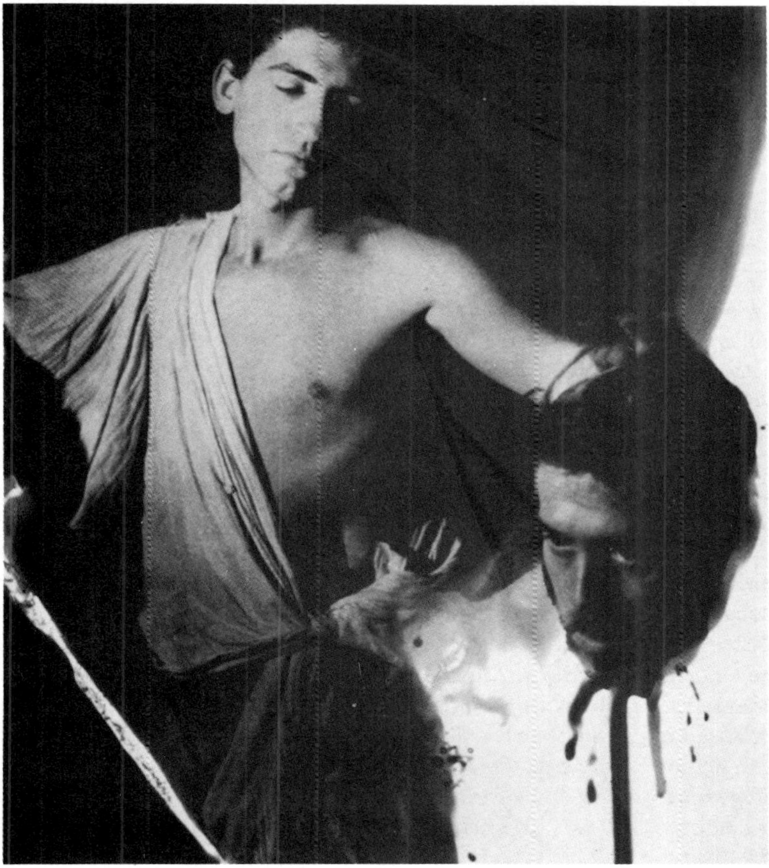

'Caravaggio' influenced by Caravaggio's Salome
(Photo: Gerald Incandela).

Roeg worked with Jagger and Art Garfunkel, Burroughs with P-Orridge and 23 Skidoo, Jarman with Coil, Eno and Steve Ball. All three with Bowie. Trying to use him as his Edward Kelly substitute, Jarman called him *"the tuning fork of the media humming to perfection...the mirror of ambivalence and monarch of the invisible threads of communication"* and summed it all up rather neatly. Bowie once left a pack of cigarettes on Jarman's mantelpiece, which he kept like a souvenir-hunter until Bowie's next visit, when the Thin One noticed them and tore them up as a slightly embarrassed film maker looked on, feeling something like a silly schoolgirl. For his part, Bowie had Jarman marked as "a Black Magician".

RE: You were going to make **Neutron** with David Bowie once, weren't you?

"Well, it was one of those On/Off things that never really gelled. It was never really on."

RE: It was a sort of post-apocalypse story?

"It was, I suppose, yes. Though I've never thought of it in that way. It was the apocalypse of St. John the Divine done in a dream state, though there were about six different scripts for that film. I never really worked it out properly. It's quite dead at the moment."

RE: You get a lot of ideas for films that never get made?

"Lots, but they usually get swallowed up into the ones that do get made. There was nothing of ***Neutron*** *in* ***Caravaggio,*** *for instance, but it'll come somewhere else."*

The most cursory glance at Jarman's work – his sets scribbled with hieroglyphs, his fascination with figures such as St. John the Divine, with angels and magi, Ariel or John Dee, gives an obvious impression; but Bowie was only partly correct. Jarman may be a magician of sorts, but he's no Kenneth Anger. An avid reader of the esoteric works of Dee, the Hermetic mnemonicist Giordano Bruno, the physician and mystical philosopher (Grand Master of the Prieuré de Sion) Robert Fludd, and the enigmatic Paracelsus. Paracelsus was the central figure of Jung's alchemical studies and a looming figure in the Renaissance, who wrote in a language that was allegorical, mystical and symbolic. His vocabulary thus being complicated and obscure, coupled with his self-confidence and dismissal of established forms of medicine resulted in him being misunderstood and disliked by his peers.

Paracelsus preached a form of 'alchemical' homeopathy that, in its own way, predicted the rise of antibiotics and synthetic changes in the human environment centuries before their arrival, and warned against the inevitable cancers and viral infections that such an 'unnatural' lifestyle would bring. The connections Jarman has with the old masters are not only aesthetic. The perennial philosophy shows up whenever one chips away at the camp, urbane veneer of Jarman's media-perceived image. Paracelsus, a 'natural' doctor, misunderstood by his peers. Derek, a 'naturalist' film maker, misunderstood by the media.

If Jarman is, as Bowie says, a Black Magician, though, the description rests in the original meaning of the term.

All alchemy originated in Egypt – "al khem" (the Black Land) in Arabic. To further confuse the issue, 'Black' in Arabic speech is pronounced "fecham". 'Wise' is pronounced "facham". The true nature of alchemical studies has therefore been misinterpreted. So Jarman is not connected with the over-emotive Hammer Horror branch of the Occult; in fact, in conversation, few people could be less diabolical. For "Black" then, read "Wise".

Jarman is merely conversant in the language of the angels – Enochian – the unspoken language of what he calls the *"pre-scientific approach to the physical world"*. And with his films, *"the wedding of Light and Matter"*, he takes up his role as Wiseman, a modern-day alchemist of Fulcanelli-sized proportions. Substituting the pestle and mortar for their 20th Century equivalents in this world of magical mass media – film and video.

For fear of intellectualising that which is instinctive, of gaining "lust of result" and losing potency, he's suitably vague and mysterious when pressed on the subject.

"Well...hmm... It's not based on any particular fact... I don't dabble in magic. I am magic!"

RE: (Pressing on) Your imagery is very obviously influenced; would you just say, then, that it's a similarity of attitudes with -

"It's a dangerous...er, it's very deeply buried, I really don't know how to answer. I have no theories about it. What can I say? One can read about magic, but that doesn't make one magical. I practise magic in films, not outside them. I've always found, umm, I think it's more alchemical, yes, rather than Crowleyite magick, although that interests me also. I'm interested in Cornelius Agrippa and all the Renaissance magicians greatly."

RE: Because of their struggle, because their perception was similar to your own?

"Yes. I'm fascinated with certain things. Well just the whole... I suppose I've always quite liked losers. And they all lost out, didn't they? But their time will come. I mean John Dee lost out in a big way, didn't he, he just became known as a charlatan. The most intelligent man in Elizabethan England, he was no charlatan. So there's a sort of feeling of rehabilitation

in my interests, because there was something quite extraordinary there. And I fell on 'The Art of Memory' of Frances Yeats in the early Seventies, and of course Jung who was involved with Alchemy in his later works. Then it just branched out."

Currently his interest has led him to become infatuated with the works of archetypal psychologist James Hillman, dug up on forays into Foyles bookshop across the road. Looking at Hillman one can see why. He is something of a kindred spirit to the film maker, a clinical manifestation of the same soul-facing intent. The psychologist writes drily about 'Betrayal', 'Masturbation', 'Abandonment' and dreams.

"I find him fascinating. So that's the interesting area to me. Not so much magick and Crowley, it was always more to do with psychology."

As he gestures towards a copy of Hillman's *Loose Ends* on the bookshelf, I notice next to it a volume on Sado-Masochism, and remember that Jarman had loose connections with the staging of Georges Bataille's *Feast* at the Bloomsbury Theatre, along with the likes of Cosi Fanni Tutti and Terence Sellers – otherwise known as the New York Mistress 'Angel Stern'.

Jarman himself was no stranger to the underworld of backroom bars and coded handkerchiefs. Derek did not used to visit Hampstead Heath only to take in the night air. Though he detests the Californiaised cloning process that 'liberation' brought (*"nothing could bring me to want to touch a moustache!"*), he did seem to find some solace in his anonymous cruising alter ego. A character that could escape the world of Art and the Cinema and their accompanying pressures. He once wrote: *"Anonymous sex can be the sweetest and most transient. The imagination runs riot. Earthbound minds suddenly take on angelic bodies."*

Jarman, a brave man, made no attempts to keep things secret when he discovered that he was HIV antibody positive, feeling – in this current climate of homophobia – that it was his duty to discuss it.

The most repugnant aspect of the swing against homosexuality in the public arena is, of course, Clause 28 of the Local Government Bill (discussed elsewhere in this book), which effectively banned schools, local councils and other organisation from 'promoting' homosexuality.

"The repercussions are very dangerous. You could potentially have a ban on Shakespeare's sonnets in the local library! Many of the sonnets are evidently addressed to a man, such as Sonnet number 20, 'for a woman wert thou first created...'"

On the subject of banning teachers from talking about homosexuality in schools, he points out that this will not only make it more difficult for young people to come to terms with their own sexuality, but it will also

detract from the promotion of the Safe Sex message.
"We can't create a climate of fear where homosexuality can't be discussed...We also have to talk about using condoms, about safe sex and so on."

The obnoxious apartheid-like Clause could mean that some cinemas would have to think twice about screening Jarman's work, art galleries of exhibiting David Hockney or Robert Mapplethorpe, council libraries of stocking books by Ginsberg, or Isherwood, or Mary Renault. The list is endless.
"At least ten percent of the population is gay. If people were trying to say these things about blacks or Irish people, you would think they were insane...I just hope I live to see the Clause rescinded."

What kind of a society is it that passes laws which officially condone the persecution of minority groups, at a time when their need for help, support and understanding is at its greatest?

At time of writing Derek is thankfully feeling "hale and hearty", and judging from a survey carried out by doctors in San Francisco published in early '88, he has about a 50/50 chance of seeing out the 1990's.

Although we all hope and pray for breakthroughs, it's frankly doubtful that a cure for the disease will be found by then, but it may be that blocking agents can be used to limit the effects of the illnesses caused by having a low CD4 count (tumours, pneumonia, T.B. etc.) and save the life of the patient. Let's hope so. I have nothing but admiration for the way in which Jarman has acted since his discovery, being open and honest, keeping busy and, on the surface at least, coping remarkably well.

RE: Where do we go from here?
"God, where DO we go from here..."
RE: Somewhere to the lift the gloom. Italy!
"I got beaten-up in Italy."
Oops.
"They were thieving primarily. I got knocked down by a gang who went through my pockets, they were really quite nasty, really kicking me. One never knows what to do in situations like that. I could've been killed, so I just let them get on with it, and for some reason I just kept smiling at them! I just looked up at them in complete disbelief and wondered what the fuck they were up to. I remember saying "Is this how you welcome people to Rome?" to them in Italian as I lay there with them all kicking me. It was crazy. Fortunately Italian shoes are not as heavy as british Bovver Boots; they were all wearing soft Gucci numbers, so it was mainly just bad bruising. They got away with about 50p and a bottle of Poppers!... I still love Italy though."

RE: It's far more art-orientated and design conscious in Italy. Does the British attitude to art annoy you?
"Well, it's deeper in the culture there. It's not stratified as it is here, their whole system of class is different, there's much more of a shared language in Italy... It's just, if you're Florentine you know who Michelangelo was no matter who you are, whereas you couldn't say that about people in British cities. In London they wouldn't know their Turner from their Constable!"
RE: Don't you find, then, that here you're generally considered an eccentric arty farty type, making boring films? Doesn't that bother you? Surely they love you in Italy.
"Yes, well, it's a completely different attitude. They call me 'Maestro' in Italy. It's like your title, it's position. It would be like saying you're a Doctor or something here, you're accepted. 'Maestro' is accepted in Italy. Especially ones who've had their head kicked in!"
RE: The attitude to art here is hostile to the point of artists having to be apologetic and defensive and coy. It's like what you said before about doing something for yourself, internally, rather than doing something for the audience, for the greater good. If you do that you're acceptable to society because you're making money and products and offering a service to entertain people with. The cash till you mentioned.
"Yes, but Art is the only thing that matters!"

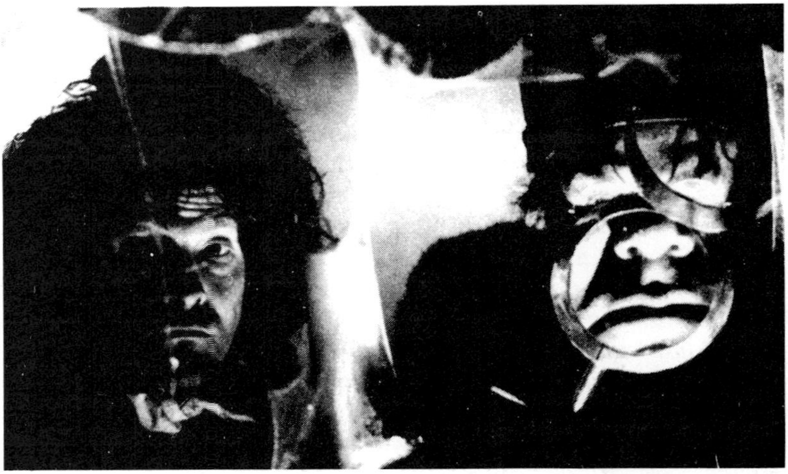

'The Tempest'. Prospero (Heathcote Williams) and the King of Naples (Peter Bull). (Photo: Bridget Holm).

RE: But in a country so dominated by the industrial Victorian attitudes to work, they don't produce anything tangibly useful. Unless they're "successful artists" that people can make money from. Because by nature artists must be egotistical bastards in a sense, and selfish to be any good, because they're looking internally instead of pandering to the needs of the audience. How would you -

"Yes, but I am useful because I'm showing people how to do it for themselves. That's the most important thing anyone can discover. Themself. So in that sense art is vital and does contribute. Though one does have to be careful about calling oneself an Artist, yes. The greatest art of all would be to be able to sit on top of an oak tree and do nothing. The art of doing nothing is the greatest art of all. I like that."

RE: I don't think I agree with that, Derek, doing nothing. Anyway, you never do nothing. You never stop working.

"No. Well, what I mean is as you said, the West is so orientated towards Product, the greatest thing would be to be able to do nothing at all. But to answer your basic question which you were getting at with Italy...it's really, I suppose, that if I wanted to be accepted I'd live in Italy. but I don't want to be accepted. It's far more interesting here because it's abrasive. I could easily have been accepted if I'd wanted to at a few points in my life."

One such point would have been in 1980, after his version of **The Tempest**, with Toyah as Miranda, Heathcote Williams as Prospero and Elizabeth "Stormy Weather" Welch as the Goddess romped its way to critical acclaim and modest profit. He could then have gone for the real money, got backing for a bigger, straighter feature, or sold himself to Channel 4's pre-launch alternative film project. *"All Beaujolais Nouveau and scrubbed Scandinavian, pot plants in place...a channel for a slightly adventurous commuter."* But, not surprisingly, he didn't. To be very cynical critics could say that he didn't have to. Helped by being bohemian, free and single, able to devote himself to his work without major responsibilities to others, he has been able to survive, barely, without having to compromise. But that misses the point, and is the stock excuse for all forms of compromise and laziness.

First of all, nobody needs to get married, nobody needs to have children, nobody needs to get a mortgage or a car or a TV. It is simply a question of priorities, and Jarman has never had any of these things. Besides, the L.A. Hillbillies are hardly making multi-million dollar blockbusters to keep the bailiffs from the door, and many of them were once young British revolutionaries.

RE: You could've capitalised and become very big. (He smiles broadly at this.)
"Yes, but I am big! No, not in terms of cash but I know that underneath it there's an immerse interest in that stand. Particularly among other film makers, because it's something I think all of us would like to do. Mind you, it is wearing; I don't ever preclude the possibility of my selling out!"
RE: It's been an advantage in that respect, your being single?
"Yes, I don't know what I'd do having someone around my neck all the time if I was married and with children. One can be alone a lot of the time. As soon as one takes on mortgages and so on one becomes a part of that structure and under that pressure."

So instead of making a clutch of pop videos, for the likes of Lords of the New Church, Marianne Faithfull, Carmel and The Smiths, which he did for the money, Derek reckons he'd have been on the video treadmill for life.
"Which would've been deadening and have left me with no time to get Caravaggio together or read James Hillman!"
RE: Before we talk about **Caravaggio**, what about your film **Imagining October**?
"Yes?"
RE: You filmed that illegally in the USSR, prior to the dismantling of the Iron Curtain.
"No. You were allowed to film with a Super 8 camera in the Soviet Union you know."
RE: But not in that cemetery though, or is this another Western myth?
"No, it's true, they did ask me not to film the cemetery."
RE: Well I thought, when watching that film, that it did have a very definite theory and message behind it.
"Yes? You're going to pin me down now, aren't you?! Well, yes. It did have a message. It was an agitprop film in an odd sort of way."
RE: To do with what we've been talking about.
"It was a film to do with profit, and the influence of profit on communication. That was part and parcel of the quotations that came up. In the present context. Then there was an element of materialism with the painting being done of the soldiers, and a wonderful feeling of, well, sadness at the end. A feeling of, you know, all the ideals of the 20th Century have become their opposites. They've come to their real fruition."

That, in having unswerving faith in ideals and arguing for their case, "the systems of Peace and Love become Hate and War", to use his language. A million miles from the October uprising, the film, just like the tanks in Afghanistan, underlines what Jarman said earlier in chilling fashion – you can blind yourself by believing.

RE: Why did you go there?

"I was invited to show ***The Tempest*** *to the Film Union there."*

RE: Did they like it?

"I don't think so; well, some did but they didn't get to open their mouth as it was all done through a spokesperson, and they are very adept at not quite getting around to the questions they don't want raised. There is no real individual voice in Soviet discussion."

RE: Was their reaction to it better than the Americans? (One *New York Times* critic, in a piece short on style and critical content but big on venom, said that it was like "watching Shakespeare through a broken windscreen." Cute how these Americans are so proud of their Anglo Saxon culture.)

"Well..." says Derek, sidestepping a potentially hurtful question. *"It wasn't open to an audience in the Soviet Union so I don't know."*

RE: You don't seem to like American culture very much.

"I love America. It's just that they have such a hold over our lives. If I was Polish I'd feel the same way about metropolitan Russia. I think we're completely enthralled with them. We're a dumping ground for all their ammunition. But my generation believed that everything that came from America was good, because the food parcels came from there. And the really horrid decade, the 1950's, had a ridiculous myopic vision about it all, and we still think in the same way. It was a bad time, the fifties, the decade that's been remembered as...a haircut. Which is all that it deserves! We all just wanted to go to America then. They had some good propaganda."

RE: They've all done it, including the British.

"Yes, well, all the power centres have done it. If the USSR or China was ruling the world they'd do it. The Americans had to rescue Europe during the war otherwise the Soviets would have it."

RE: And there'd be nobody to buy their hamburgers.

"Yes! And there was this terrible confusion in thinking how nice they were to help us, and the terrible thing is, the confusion's still there. All over the culture. It's interesting, people will suspend judgement when they see, for instance, a film, as somehow in this country it's seen as 'Entertainment' and it's in everyone's interest to keep these people in power and just look upon it as entertainment because then it's of no consequence. Even in the more supposedly analytical journals, like 'City Limits' or 'Time Out', they look at it as if it were just entertainment. They would completely suspend judgement as to where it came from and what and who the film was representing. They would just say that it was entertainment, good or bad.

They wouldn't say that it was made with megabucks from Hollywood. They should have seen it more in terms of corporations, as the product of American culture, the product of a rotten system. There were many refreshing things about the Soviet Union. Art is taken very seriously, for instance, whereas here it's rendered impotent. Especially pop music, which is the most important form of art ever ever ever invented. Talk about non-communication! It's kept in a perpetual state of pre-adolescence, so nobody is allowed to grow up in it and think. It's therefore worthless. It's a good system of Control. It channels revolts that would otherwise be political; the powers that be connive in it. And as for 'Street Credibility' most of it's about as street credible as Channel 4..."

Although most of us would probably agree with that, I can't really see how that by "taking art seriously" in the sense that the Soviets take solely traditional art seriously (classical ballet, opera and music) there is any real improvement. By denying people even the cultural illusion of revolution I don't think the Russian system is any better in this respect. It is, in fact, less resonant.

I don't argue with Derek as he continues his attack on all things Pop, and waves his hands about a bit. The last thing I want to talk about with Derek Jarman is pop music, though he seems convinced that anyone under the age of Cliff Richard is obsessed by the stuff, and keeps dragging it into conversation in order to knock it down and stress, "with the perspective given by time", that anyone can see the innate superiority of the classics. He had a soft spot for Bronski Beat, though.

"Some things are of a positive value, yes. I think Bronski Beat did a fantastic amount of good in their area, more practical good than I could ever do with my films. But that doesn't preclude what I'm saying and I'm sure if Jimmi Sommerville reads this he'd agree with what I'm saying. Each generation is coming along every five years, so it can be valuable. If one knows one is in that area then alright, but if these people make other claims for it then they're crazy. This isn't just some tired old queen sitting here moaning; if I was seventeen I'd be listening to it."

I point out that many people criticised Bronski Beat for being crass and evangelical – not the type of thing one would have thought would appeal to the sophisticate sitting before me.

"Well I think there was a reason for them working in that way. There's a social reason for it, they're dealing with young people who are by the system denied."

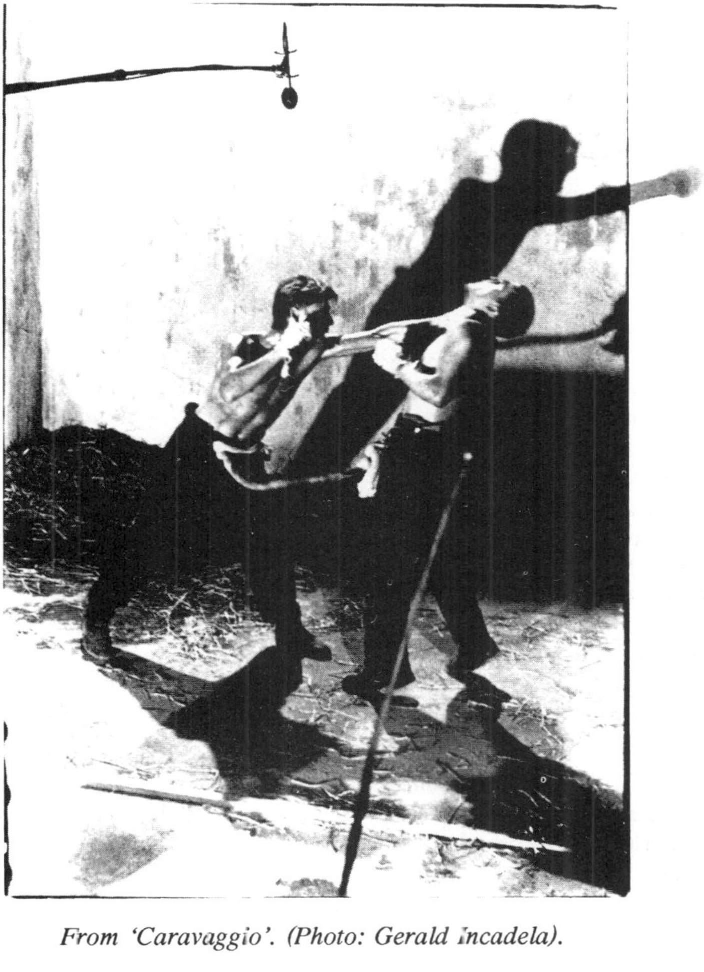

From 'Caravaggio'. (Photo: Gerald Incadela).

A hint of public school condescension if you ask me, but hardly worth worrying about. Jarman is the last person one could call a snob and actually what he says is largely true, and could apply as much to his own work as that of the late Bronskis, if for different reasons. Disinterested in communicating messages and pandering to the limitations of "the audience", he would still like to think that his work has helped erode prejudice without having to resort to artless political rhetoric.

*"I know my film **Sebastiane** has had a huge effect when it has been shown at odd cinemas here and there. One hopes that **Angelic***

***Conversation** will eventually filter through: I've also written an autobiography that is fairly frank by most standards."*

His first book, **Dancing Ledge**, was written in 1983 and published a year later – an 'autobiographical collage" compiled from notepads, appointment books and filmscripts – realised or imaginary – from his childhood spent as the son of an RAF officer to **The Final Academy** and beyond. The themes of the book, and his life, recur in apparently haphazard tracts of print. (As Ken Campbell said, it's a great book for picking up and reading in the toilet.) A constant attack on all establishment culture; Film; Sex; Painting; anecdotes from twenty years spent as a self styled artist; Renaissance rehabilitation; references to a quaint and slightly crooked Olde England of vicars and royalty, picnics, castle ruins and empty beaches (as loved by Michael Powell); Occultism; Famous friends...and Caravaggio. A figure that has fascinated him since his days as a student at the Slade, when a young Jarman hunted down anything that was the product of another isolated, homosexual, mind. Isherwwood, Wilde, Genet, Sartre...

Much has been made of Jarman's sexual orientation. Too much, in my view. Though perhaps it's not surprising. If there is a stencil under which every Jarman movie fits, it would be one cut from Derek's lucid sexual imagination. The problem is, although Jarman's candour may help in the gradual erosion of homophobia, there is a danger that his presentations may just be labelled as being "gay" films, the deifying products of a queer martyr that have nothing to say to people outside of the embattled gay circle.

In wider terms, the relative liberalisation of male homosexuality over the past 20 years has led to the creation of a cultural ghetto. The re-definition of the word "gay" brought with it not only a greater (and necessary) freedom, it also identified and defined a certain kind of life within specifically defined boundaries. So gay people are not only still looked upon as being 'different' because they enjoy slightly different sexual relationships, but also because they live a largely different lifestyle – a life style created by the gay and straight media. In some ways, gay people became more isolated in their liberalisation, with their own clubs, their own music, their own clothes, literature, Cinema, and (supposedly) their own shared ideologies. In my mind, integration and synthesis are the ways forward. A ghetto is a ghetto from both the outside and the inside. In the future, everyone will be bisexual. An individual's sexual habits will not define their social position.

Realising that a yawning (and unnecessary) chasm exists between "gay" and "straight" society, Jarman has often been concerned with trying to bridge the gap. Not by making more 'ordinary' films about suburban hetrosexual couples, but by making such things as openly homo-erotic films be accepted as being ordinary. Which of course they are.

Jarman hacks away at the parameters which society has set down in a variety of ways. Visually, many of his actors are androgynous, and attractive to either sex. Tradition is, if not trampled, at least confused in Derek's shadowy world. Even the word "gay" is being eradicated from his scrapbook of press cuttings.

"I did a book with ***The Last of England*** *in the form of a series of interviews, and of course the word 'gay' came up a lot. Eventually, we decided to take the word completely out of the book to see what happened. It was on computer so I just pressed a button and said search the word 'gay' and obliterate. So a question like 'What was gay life like in the Sixties?' became 'What was life like in the Sixties?' and the answer was the same, only it was no longer ghettoised by the question."*

Caravaggio, then, is transformed at the tap of a computer console from being a Gay Movie into being a film about a Renaissance painter.

The cast was headed by Nigel Perry, playing the title role, and Tilda Swinton as Lena. Other notables in the film were the Comic Strip's Robbie Coltrane as Borghese and a Jarman favourite, the blind actor Jack Birkett, playing the part of the "Satire Pope". The old punksters among you will also remember the name of ex-Chelsea lead singer and one-time beefcake model Gene October (who's been turning up in bit parts all over TV land and once appeared in a 1978 magazine edition of this very publication in a piece written by Alan Anger). Gene's thespian skills are put to the test in the role as a street hustler peeling a piece of fruit. To coincide with the film's release, Thames & Hudson published a Jarman book about the making of the film, with breathtaking photos by his old pal, the brilliant photographer Gerald Incandela.

Caravaggio - "the inventor of cinematic light" - was an Italian painter who lived between 1572 and 1610. After a history of violence, on the 29th May 1606, he murdered one Ranuccio Tomassoni while playing a ballgame in Rome. For the last four years of his life he went on the run, with the help of rich relatives, friends and admirers, through Malta, Sicily and Italy, taking commissions from town to town and producing probably better work than which he'd done before the murder. Reports of how he met his death conflict, but most evidence now points towards him having died on the 18th July 1610 on the beach at Porto Ercole, collapsing while running along the waterfront – aged 39. Ironically, he was probably just about to be pardoned for the murder and be able to return to his beloved Rome. You can read such information in any book on the Renaissance painters; though few will tell you of the man's private life.

"He was obviously a gay artist though there's obviously no proof as there was no real documentation. Though it does appear that he was drummed out of Syracuse for molesting young men. It's generally accepted now that he was gay."

RE: He interests you partly because of that?

"Partly, yes, because of the fact that with that difficult nature, unacceptable at the time, he came up with all sorts of solutions in his work which were very radical... He was the first Italian painter, for example, to use ordinary people in his paintings, probably his friends, and paint them as the Virgin Mary for instance in one of his altarpieces. He was an innovator."

Jarman's main reason for making the film was not because Caravaggio was homosexual, but because his life is a study of being an artist, as relevant now as it was 400 years ago.

"Everything we've talked about today would be applicable to Caravaggio. You've just got to translate Church patronage for TV Companies and Caravaggio for Roman Polanski, say. It's just imaging a culture. It's all to do with images. How they're read and how they're received by people, and how to achieve that sort of communication, in order to become 'successful', you have to make a pact with the powers that be."

RE: And that's still the case now.

"Precisely. It's always been the case. Completely now. So it's possible to make a case for someone like, for instance, Alan Parker, who in a much clearer way is utilising the powers that be. That's advertising. Or Warhol who did it very well with his painting in the 1960's. You can make a case for that kind of representative art of the age if you want to, for success in those terms rather than staying outside of the mainstream. Caravaggio was very much the mainstream, he was very successful. Personally I think that being outside, being a stand against is a more interesting area to be in, and that's the ambivalence that interests me... Some people are part of a culture and some people commentators on it."

RE: Even though everyone's a result of the same culture.

"Yes, one person is the Action and another is the Reaction. Caravaggio was the Action, one of the most successful painters of his time, and that's what interests me, how someone who is a killer is immediately welcomed into the next cathedral in the next town to paint the next altarpiece. He had to get out of Rome as he was too much of a problem for the authorities, but in the town down the road he was welcomed with open arms. It would be as if I killed someone and carried on working, like 'Please make another video, Mr Caravaggio!'...he died of neglect in the

end, like a pop star, lived too fast."

RE: Talking of which, did you take drugs?

"Who didn't? In the sixties everyone went through the stage of taking drugs, one wasn't even aware of it being damaging or not, it was irrelevant. Drugs were just part and parcel of the moment."

RE: I thought you might have been an Aldous Huxley type, taking drugs for your own 'internal exploration', quite deliberately.

"Well, his 'Doors of Perception' was why people took drugs. Most of the interesting artists took drugs. I mean, Coleridge, de Quincy, Cocteau...Burroughs. Lots. If you include excessive alcohol then just about everyone of them; look at Dylan Thomas."

One is left wondering if Jarman took drugs to more properly fulfil his '60s poloneck, to stick to the classic wasted image of an artist, living as he did at the time in his draughty loft overlooking the Thames at Wapping before Dockland became infested with red Porches and sunken wine bars. Despite his shoestring (or, at least, Shoebox) existence, his Smirnoff tipples and his past dalliances in the backrooms of Europe, Derek seems somehow too wholesome to have slid headlong into a romantic façade at the expense of his body.

His monster – "the audience" – may in some perverse and fascinated way have scripted Jarman's life for him. The tragedies of Dean/Monroe/Orton/Vicious et al please the public, their fast lives and deaths satisfying the bohemian script and relieving the miserable boredom of fans and critics. Forces that require a conveyor belt of dead artists and pop stars to be used as some huge emotional crutch. Artists who lived life to the full on behalf of the audience (an audience that is in the main locked in a world of boring jobs, boring houses and boring marriages), and produced a steady stream of saleable relics – records and prints – are ensured a cultural immortality.

The fact that Derek has been unlucky enough to contract a potentially lethal virus that in the main confines itself to people who lead interesting sex lives or take hard drugs served – sure enough – to massively increase public interest in both the man and his work. To Derek, though, and the thousands of others in his position, this is a time of uncertainty, of fear, of anger, of sadness. Every day.

This is a strange mirror indeed. Just look at the last four years of Caravaggio's life, under threat from Rome. Caravaggio, though, was, for all his antisocial behaviour, a figure loved by the Establishment. Not so Jarman. The Art World aren't too keen on Derek because, in the words of the Royal Academy's Norman Rosenthal – "they tend to like people who stick at things". Jarman looks pained.

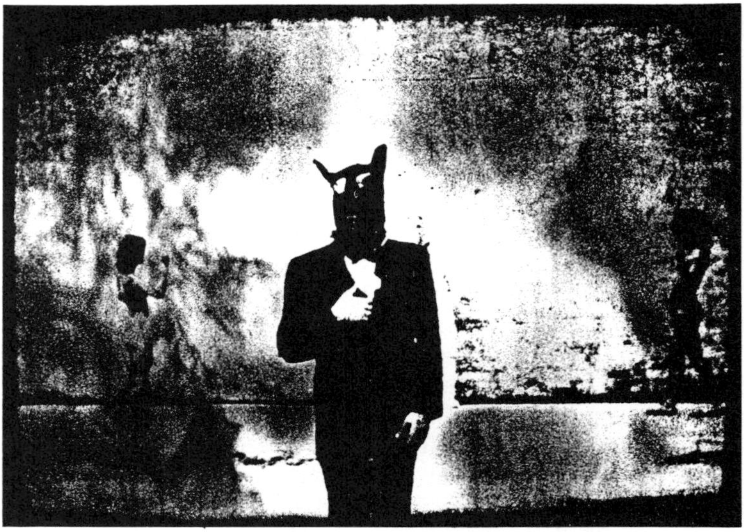

From 'The Art of Mirrors', 1973

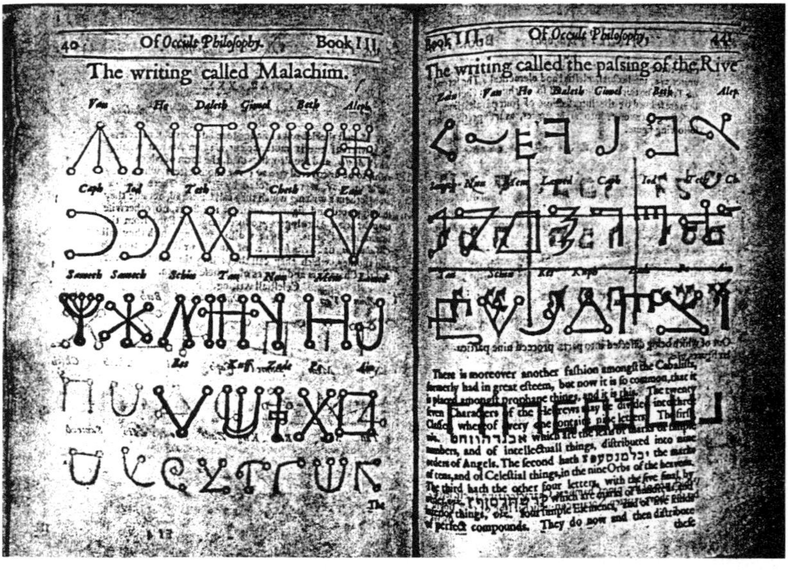

40 Of Occult Philosophy. Book III.

The writing called Malachim.

Book III. Of Occult Philosophy. 41

The writing called the passing of the Rive

There is moreover another fashion amongst the Cabalists, formerly had in great esteem, but now it is so common, that it is placed amongst prophane things, and it is this. The twenty seven Characters of the Hebrews may be divided into three Classes, whereof every one contains nine letters. The first, [illegible] which are the seals or marks of simple numbers, and of intellectuall things, distributed into nine orders of Angels. The second hath [illegible] the marks of tens, and of Celestial things, in the nine Orbs of the heavens. The third hath the other four letters, with the five final, by [illegible] which are marks of hundreds, and inferior things, [illegible] four simple Elements, and of five kinds of perfect compounds. They do now and then distribute these

A page from 'The Occult Philosophy', Cornelius Agrippa, 1631.

"But I think I DO stick at things, you know, I've had exhibitions of my paintings, I've produced sets for opera and ballet, I've written several books, scripts, I've made a number of feature films – I think to do that you've got to be quite a good sticker. Though I'm sure there are better stickers than me, Francis Bacon, for example. [Jarman is off to visit Bacon's show at the Tate later in the day]. *Films, though, they include everything. Painting, music, set design, writing, filming. It uses it all up. Being just a painter nowadays is like being involved in stained glass. Film making is really the art form of the twentieth century. Being a film maker is wonderful. It's also a marvellous esoteric pursuit for someone like me and a lovely lifestyle."*

In the 23rd Century, the names of Fassbinder, Pasolini and Jarman may – who knows – carry as much weight as Michelangelo, Raphael and Caravaggio.

That Jarman's cinema will live long there should be no doubt. As he himself said about Shakespeare's *Tempest*, *"it's the greatest play in the English language because people are still trying to explain what it all means."* Jarman, always sharp, knows that *The Tempest* appeals not to the intellect, but to the imagination. Just as with his films, audiences are then seeing something timeless because they must be applying their own interpretations to it. Once a piece of art is understood, it is absorbed and lost in the culture and used to make memory – and money. It ends up on an advertising hoarding or a biscuit tin. It dies.

You may, using this logic, still think Jarman's work is rubbish, but must admit, it has life. He would ask no more.

And so we leave him, alone with his sketchpad and imagination, perhaps on the beach at Porto Ercole, on the spot in the sand where Caravaggio fell dead and where Jarman, 361 years later, had anonymous sex in the dunes with an Italian boy...

QUEEN ELIZABETH: "The sea remindeth me of youth. Oh John Dee, do you remember the whispering secrets at Oxford like the sea breeze, the codes and counter codes, the secret language of flowers...and I with yellow celandine, true gold of the new spring of learning."
JOHN DEE: "Oh Majesty, to me you are the celandine now as then before, balm against all melancholy."
ELIZABETH: "Ah, but I was young then."
ARIEL: "There and back and there and back. The waves break on the shores of England. The white cliffs stand against the void. We gaze seaward, contemplating the night journey. The sun sinks lower. The moon waits to make her entrance. In the south at Tilly Whim, a picture of wind

and sea. In the west a vision of silver dew on a sea of pure gold. In the east a black hoarfrost. The sun eclipsed by the phoenix. In the north a howling chaos into which black rain falls without ceasing. Now is the time of departure, the last streamer that ties us to what is known - parts. We drift into a sea of storms."

And now Elizabeth and Dee go along that same great highway, and the light of the air about them seemed somewhat dark, like evening or twilight, and as they walked the phoenix spoke and cried with a loud voice...

"It's horribly uncomfortable dying from the HIV virus. It's like being in a coconut shy and having things thrown at you, being battered and buffeted. You can feel everything about your body falling apart. It's an appalling feeling. But I've had an amazingly wild and happy life, and I've not got a single regret. I've lived in a fantastic time. I've been blessed with the chance of making the films I wanted to make. I'd do everything the same way again. I don't deny my past. I don't feel mea culpa at all."

We leave Derek washing the cups in his no-room-to-swing-a-cat kitchen, among the dried flowers. The last Englishman. Witnessing the last of England – the closed factory furnaces, now embers among the dark satanic stumps. Police sirens screech beneath his window, the mirror glowing blue at night over Soho. Operation Tiger/Operation Faggot/ Operation Spanner. Operation censor. The guardian angels with gloves on go about their business of protecting new England's Peace and Love. Blinding all to its system of Hate and War. Who can doubt him? The Sun rises, the Sun sets, the World constantly changes colour.

Self-obsessed, handsome, erudite, funny, intelligent, explorational and misunderstood – cruising through the anonymous hidden connections of Time and Space. They are all here in Charing Cross Road: Mr Caravaggio, Mr Dee, Mr Jarman with their spirits to enforce, art to enhance; with their brushes and mirrors and lenses. Sweeping the leaves up from the garden, forming perfect, beautiful mounds that will, we love to know, all be blown away forever. All – despite their problems – fortunate men. Our eyes, now as then, with their celestial geometry in the micaolz olprt. They whisper ...COME AWAY

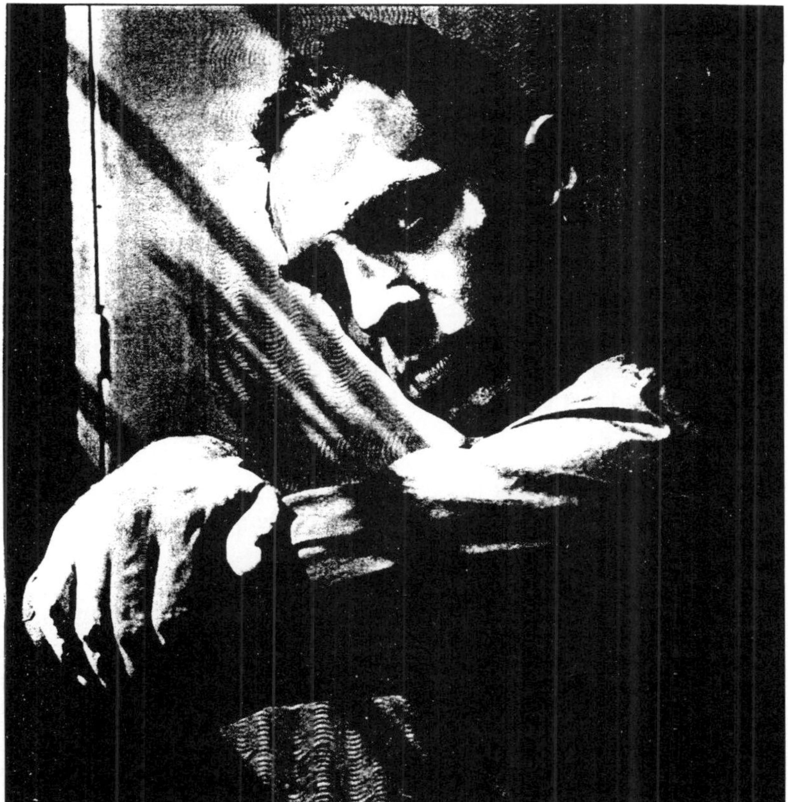

THE GEMSTONE FILE

An investigation into the revelations of Bruce Roberts, the murder of the Kennedy brothers, and the paranoia of America.

NICK TOCZEK

The once popular illusion of American presidential integrity, honour and respectability now seems long gone. In the run-up to the 1988 election, the inclusion in the parade of potential candidates of so many proven cheats, fakes, frauds and liars came as no surprise to anyone. Yet, as recently as the early Sixties, that picture of God-fearing and truly democratic liberal President whose moral and ethical honesty was beyond question still held its own with most white, and many black Americans. Indeed, it did so for the majority of people in the western world.

That illusion died at 12.30pm on Friday November 22, 1963 between the Dal-Tex Building. The Texas School Book Depository and Dealy Plaza in the centre of Dallas.

In the passing motorcade was the 35th US President. A look of puzzlement had just passed across his face and he'd started to raise his right hand to the top of his head. But the hand never got there and there was no top to the head. As he slumped forward, chunks of skull, some brain and vast quantities of blood were already splattering across himself, his wife, the upholstery and everyone and everything within blood pressure shot.

The blood on Governor John B. Connally Jr. however, was mostly his own. He'd taken two bullets and would soon be convinced, wrongly, that he was also about to die.

Police Officer J.D. Tippit, on the other hand, had no idea that he'd only got 45 minutes to live. He too was to be shot down. And one more person was soon to die. Lee Harvey Oswald, an employee of The Texas School Book Depository, would have his shooting televised on NBC in a little under 48 hours. But none of that mattered to him now. His concern was to slip out of the Depository and get away from the area. He'd just fired at least some of the shots. He probably knew that people in the car had been hit, but had no idea who, if anyone, was dead or dying.

The assassination of John Fitzgerald Kennedy gave rise to numerous questions and hatched a plethora of conspiracy theories. And the rushed and often inaccurate Warren Commission Report that constituted the official investigation did nothing to allay these worries.

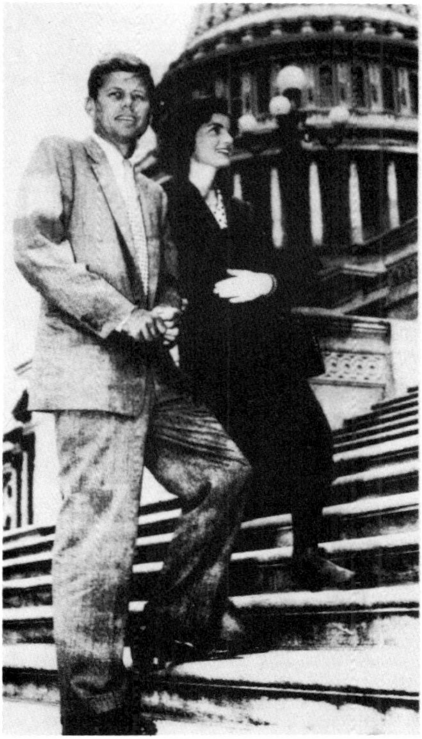

Thus the spectre of cover-up crawled across The White House lawn and took up permanent residence indoors. Not only did the subsequent incumbents fail completely in their repeated attempts to have it exorcised, but they actually induced its regular reappearances in a succession of guises. From the bombing of Cambodia, through the undignified US withdrawal from Vietnam, to Watergate, and on through Irangate, the cover-ups and lies multiplied under increasingly intense public scrutiny.

As the news of Kennedy's death flashed across the globe many people openly wept. He'd championed civil rights. He'd been a figure of hope and faith to so many. He'd been painted as America's Mr Clean and the one bright hope for world peace and freedom in the face of a daunting future. If that's hard to believe now it is an indication of the discredit that has been brought to the post by the subsequent presidents: Johnson, Nixon, Ford, Carter, Reagan, and now Clinton.

In the welter of post-assassination investigations, some unsavoury light was shed on the life and deeds of JFK, but much more began to be focused on some of the more clandestine machinery of American political and financial life. In particular, the work of members of the FBI and CIA was called into question. Likewise, the power of the Mafia and of big business, not just over local politicians or particular senators and governors, but over international politics as a whole. Congress and even the President himself. All of this and much more is covered by an extraordinary document called *The Gemstone File*. As far as can be established this work has never been published before – a fact that is all the more surprising considering that its author names those who actually killed Kennedy.

Bruce Roberts studied journalism and physics at the University of Wisconsin in the mid-Thirties. Here too he first started to take an interest in the business activities of a Greek ship owner called Aristotle Onassis. But Roberts' special field of work – through physics – was crystallography. He applied himself to the creation of synthetic rubies and eventually came up with what he felt were viable artificial gemstones. In 1960, the year that saw JFK elected President, he approached Hughes Aircraft, the company founded by millionaire Howard Hughes, and tried to sell them his gemstones for use in laser beam research. As far as he was concerned, they simply stole his invention.

Meanwhile, he reckoned to stumble on an Onassis-Hughes link that is, to say the least, bizzare in the extreme. Driven by his grudge against Hughes Aircraft, he began, in 1969, to secretly release sections of his findings to certain Americans. In all, *The Gemstone File* eventually came to well over a thousand pages.

What follow, then, are some of the allegations made by Bruce Roberts. Subsequent research into material by other writers involved suggest that a lot of his claims are provable and that they fit. There are also intriguing points highlighted for the first time.

Aristotle Onassis was undoubtedly ruthless, cunning, calculating and, above all, insatiable in his greed for money and power. Roberts began his account in 1932 when Onassis, already a millionaire by way of selling opium in Argentina set up a lucrative deal with Joseph Kennedy (JFK's father), Eugene Meyer (later to buy *The Washington Post*) and Meyer Lanski. The four of them made a fortune by importing bootleg liquor into the USA.

Then we're told of an agreement two years later between Onassis, Rockefeller and the Seven Sisters (the world's major oil companies). This pact resulted in Onassis getting still richer by transporting cheap Arab oil on his ships.

During World War II, Onassis amassed an even bigger fortune by selling oil and arms to both the Allies and the Germans and survived the entire war without losing a ship or even a single crewman.

Then, in 1949, with the help of lawyer Burke Marshall, he bought US war surplus 'Liberty ships' (cheaply assembled, mass-production boats that became redundant soon after their useful wartime work) in a deal of questionable legality.

Now comes the first of the amazing allegations. It concerns Texas millionaire Howard Hughes and forms the Onassis-Hughes connection. Up to and during 1956, Hughes had been 'buying up' various US political figures such as senators and governors. Finally, he elicited the support of newly-elected Vice-President Nixon by way of a quarter million dollar non-repayable loan to Nixon's brother, Donald. Nixon then repaid the favour by having the Internal Revenue Service and Treasury grant him tax free status (refused twice before to Hughes Medical Foundation, sole owner of Hughes aircraft). This created a tax free non-accountable money funnel or 'laundry' for Hughes' various projects. Nixon also saw to it that anti-trust suits against Hughes' TWA and other enterprises were dropped.

Then, according to Bruce Roberts, Onassis moved into action in March 1957. He had Hughes kidnapped from his Beverly Hills Hotel bungalow by some of his own employees, the main conspirator being Chester Davis (a Sicilian whose real name is Cesare). A few days after this, with the rest of the Hughes staff either ousted or taken into the new Hughes/Onassis organisation, he had Mayor Cannon (later to become senator) of Nevada arrange a fake marriage to Jean Peters. This serves to explain away Hughes' sudden loss of interest in chasing movie stars.

Hughes, battered and brain-damaged by Mafia treatment, was taken to The Emerald Isles Hotel in the Bahamas, where the entire top floor had been rented for the Hughes party. Here, Hughes was shot full of heroin for thirty days and then taken off to a cell on Onassis' island, Skorpios. Here he spent the rest of his life, finally dying there on April 18, 1971. L. Wayne Rector, who had been employed by Hughes since 1955 to act as his double, took on the job full-time. He now became 'Hughes'. Thus Onassis had a much larger power base in the United States that included the entire Hughes empire as well as control over Nixon and all the other Hughes-purchased politicians.

Later that year, Onassis called the Appalachian meeting at which he informed US Mafia leaders of his control of the Hughes empire and of his aim to continue the Hughes method of purchasing high-ranking politicians en masse in order to gain control of the US government 'legally'.

The same year, Joseph Kennedy took JFK and wife Jackie to see Onassis on his yacht. This introduction was to remind Onassis of an old mafia promise to deliver the Presidency to a Kennedy. Onassis agreed to it (and, significantly, according to Peter Evans' book *Ari*, developed more than a passing interest in fostering a friendship with Jackie).

During 1958, hordes of Mafia-selected, purchased and supported candidates swept into office.

1959 was the year of the Cuban revolution when in one sweep, Castro's government wiped out the island's lucrative Mafia gambling empire being run for Onassis by his 1932 partner, Meyer Lanski. Aside from the steady returns, Mafia losses included and immediate eight million dollars in unbanked casino receipts.

Onassis was far from happy. Vice-President Nixon became operations chief for the CIA-planned Bay of Pigs invasion. Howard Hunt, James McCord and other CIA men teamed up with Cubans who were once members of former incumbent Batista's much-feared secret police. These men were then referred to by the US authorities as 'Cuban Freedom Fighters'. (Obvious parallels are to be drawn here between Cuba and current events in Nicaragua, where large US investments were similarly threatened by the revolution.)

Meanwhile, 1959 was also the run-up to the US presidential election. Onassis could sit back and watch. The race was between Kennedy and Nixon. He controlled both candidates.

JFK's election seemed to make everyone happy. However, things didn't go according to plan. For Kennedy, his 'thousand days' in office were to prove more than a little difficult. Apart from making numerous dangerous enemies in the right-wing establishment by his open support for the black civil rights movement, he'd got the war in Vietnam to contend with, a missile crisis in Cuba that brought the world to the brink of war, and he made a series of moves that outraged the Mafia.

April 1961 was a disaster. The Bay of Pigs invasion of Cuba to overthrow Castro failed completely. The CIA and the Mafia placed the blame squarely on JFK. (In Lucien Vandenbroucke's book *The 'Confessions' of Allen Dulles*, the then Director of the CIA is quoted as blaming Kennedy's *"lack of determination to succeed"* as prime cause of the defeat.)

Onassis had his US right-hand man, Robert Maheu, hire and train a Mafia assassination team to kill Castro. To do this, the former FBI and CIA man who was 'Hughes' (ie Wayne Rector's) top aide, used a dozen Mafia hitmen including John Rosselli and Jimmy (The Weasel) Frattiano and working with Hunt and McCord formed a CIA/Mafia team who tried five times to kill Castro using everything from long-range rifles to sodium morphate pellets to induce a heart attack. Castro, however, survived.

If the above seems far-fetched, it's all corroborated in John Raneleigh's book *The Agency: The Rise And Decline Of The CIA*. Maheu was indeed ex-CIA and FBI. He first worked for Onassis in Rome after the CIA had him 'bug' Onassis' room. And, in this account, he approached John Rosselli, Santos Trafficante and Sam Giancana, all three long-term high ranking mafiosi, with a deal to kill Castro for £150,000. (Interestingly, Giancana was Rosselli's boss and one of Giancana's mistresses was Judith Campbell. On February 7, 1960 at the Sands Hotel in Las Vegas, Frank Sinatra introduced her to JFK - dining at a nearby table, incidentally, was John Rosselli. Within four weeks, she became JFK's mistress. That affair was still going in the winter of 1962 when she turned down Giancana's proposal of marriage. Raneleigh suggests this arrangement might have been seen as useful by Giancana but it would also have given him good reason to loathe JFK, remembering the fact that he was Rosselli's boss. A point that proves important later.)

Around this time, Joseph Kennedy had a stroke, leaving sons John and Bobby (by then US Attorney General) free of his firm control. More importantly, however, they rebelled against Onassis' influence. It's hard to tell if they were motivated by idealism or their own ambition. It might also have been part of some inter-Mafia rivalry. Whatever the reason, the result was a series of actions that would threaten their well being.

Firstly, they arrested Wally Bird, owner of Air Thailand who'd been shipping Onassis' heroin out of the Golden Triangle (Laos, Cambodia, Vietnam) under a CIA 'Air Opium' contract. They arrested Mafia man Jimmy Hoffa, leader of the Teamsters' (US truck drivers) Union – and jailed him. They declared the $73,000,000 in forged 'Hughes' land loans (which had been deposited with the San Francisco Bank of America as 'security' for the TWA judgement against Hughes) to be what they were – forgeries.

By 1963, Mafia attention, under Onassis, shifted from Castro to JFK. According to Roberts, two particular killings are noteworthy. Senator Estes Kefuafer, whose crime commission investigation uncovered the 1932 Onassis-Kennedy-Meyer-Lanski deal, was murdered by way of a sodium morphate induced heart-attack which occurred on the floor of The Senate prior to a planned speech denouncing Mafia operations. Likewise Philip Graham, editor of the Washington Post and husband to Eugene Meyer's daughter, Katherine, whose sin was to side with Kennedy against Onassis. Roberts claims that Katherine bribed psychiatrists to certify her husband insane. He was later found dead from shotgun wounds to the head during a weekend visit home from the asylum and was subsequently ruled to have committed suicide. Roberts thinks otherwise.

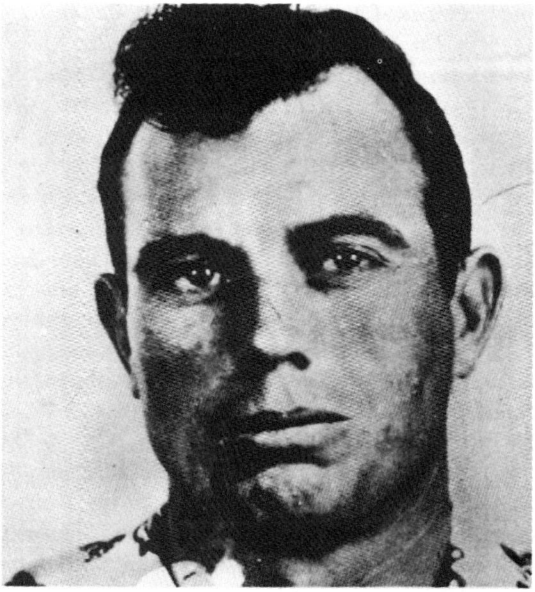

Officer J.D.Tippit

The climax to all this, though, is the killing of a President...well, two, in fact. On November 1, 1963, the Mafia plan was to mount a triple execution. Those targeted were JFK in a Chicago football stadium (Sam Giancana was Mafia boss of Chicago and, by this time, the most powerful figure in the US Mafia) and South Vietnamese president Ngo Dinh Diem together with his powerful brother Ngo Dinh Nhu. (The latter pair did in fact die after a coup that was carried out with the full knowledge and approval of the CIA, according to Raneleigh.)

But JFK was tipped off that Onassis planned to kill him and cancelled the stadium appearance. Ironically, at this point Jackie Kennedy was to be found on a cruise...with Onassis; and an enraged JFK phoned the yacht from the White House and told Jackie to *"Get off that boat if you have to swim"*. No sooner said than done.

It took only several days for Jackie to disembark in Turkey, walking down the gangway on the arm of Onassis.

Onassis was using Maheu for the killing. The job was scheduled for November 22 in Dallas. This time they were going to do it right. Maheu enlisted the Mafia-CIA team he assembled for Castro. He added Mafia hitman Eugene Brading and a CIA man called Lee Harvey Oswald who was an oddball with carefully planned links with both the ultra-right and the Communists. He was set up as the 'patsy' and given the job of shooting Governor Connally. Brading, Frattiano and Rosselli were the three who'd got the JFK job. Hunt and McCord were also there to help.

The plan would work like this: Each of the four hitmen would be accompanied by two assistants; a back-up man (to pick up the shells and get rid of the gun) and a timer (to signal when to shoot).

Frattiano was an excellent shot. From a second-storey window of the Dal-Tex Building, using a hand-gun, he hit Kennedy twice, once in the back and once in the head. The Dallas Police Department was also in that building. Hitman and his back-up man were 'arrested' driven away in a police car, and later released without being charged.

Rosselli, on Kennedy's left, and shooting from a small pagoda across the street from the grassy knoll, missed because of almost simultaneous hits by Rosselli and Frattiano. He got away by wearing a hat marked with an 'X'. Police had been previously instructed to let anyone through who was thus identifiable. It was used to indicate those who were secret service men.

Oswald left the Texas School Book Depository through the front door, unaware that his back-up man had 'hidden' his rifle behind some boxes instead of getting rid of it. And, of course, the ruse worked. Ask anyone to name Kennedy's killer.

The three men dressed as tramps picked up shells from Dealey Plaza. One of them was Howard Hunt. They wandered over to an empty boxcar on the railway spur behind the grassy knoll area and waited. The police took them in and held them until the alarm went out to pick up Oswald. They too were released without being charged.

In all, ten men were arrested after the shooting. All were released without being charged. Not a word of their existence is mentioned in the Warren Report.

So what about the shooting of Officer Tippit? According to the Warren Report, at least 12 people saw Tippit stop, talk to a man and get out of his car and walk round the front towards the man.

At this point, the man shot him four times. However, it only presents the evidence of two witnesses – Domingo Benavides and Helen Markham.

Mark Lane, a lawyer who was dissatisfied with the Warren Commission's work, spent three years re-examining the evidence in painstaking detail. His book, *Rush to Judgement*, undermines many of the Commission's conclusions. When he comes to the Tippit murder, he demolishes Helen Markham's evidence, puts question marks against most of the corroboration offered by the other 11 witnesses and proves that two guns were used to shoot Tippit. He then comes up with several important witnesses that were never called up, suggesting they were ignored because they didn't 'fit', and finally comes up with one Acquilla Clemmons (see Sylvan Fox's book *The Unanswered Questions About President Kennedy's Assassination*) who states she saw two gunmen.

But what does Bruce Roberts claim? He says that Tippit was dispatched in his police radio car to the Oak Cliff section (all versions of the radio message back this up), where Oswald had rented a room. Tippit was supposed to kill Oswald, but something went wrong. (Here, Mark Lane adds credence to the assertion by proving that the radio transcripts presented to The Warren Commission were deliberately falsified and questions their claim that any calls from Tippit, if they existed, were too indistinct to reproduce.) Roberts goes on to say that Tippit was shot by two men using two revolvers and suggests that the witness Domingo Benavides, who used Tippit's car radio to report that *"we've had a shooting here"* may have been one of the men who shot him. (Significantly, a 'Domingo Benavides', according to Roberts, also crops up in relation to the Martin Luther King shooting.)

Jack Ruby then shot Oswald. Mark Lane points out that both Oswald and Ruby had visited Cuba and established strong Cuban connections. Sylvan Fox points out that the Tippit murder occurred only two blocks from Ruby's home on Marsalis Street.

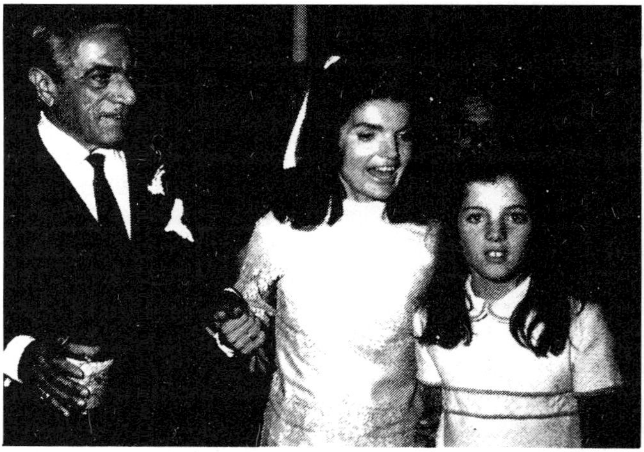

Onassis and Jackie on Skorpios.

William Manchester in his book *The Death Of a President* shows how Jack Ruby was a non-too-bright small-time hoodlum who got his kicks out of having a lot of cops as his personal friends. He set off to kill Oswald, was so confident of his success that he stopped to mail some money to an employee (Ruby ran two seedy clubs) and walked into the police station about a minute-and-a-half before delivering a .38 bullet through Oswald's liver, spleen and aorta.

The odd fact is that the police brought Oswald out of the cells an hour later than planned, suggesting Ruby knew this was going to happen. When cross-examined on this point, Ruby eventually shrugged and replied that the only way he could've known was if the police had told him. That's true. Ruby was a patriot and made much of his anger about the assassination in the two days between the deaths of Kennedy and Oswald. So, was there an Oswald-Ruby connection, perhaps via Cuba? Or was Ruby just another 'patsy' set up by the police to finish off the first or just nail a cop-killer? The possibilities multiply. Roberts adds an extra dimension by saying that Brading stayed at the Teamster-Mafia-Hoffa financed Cubana Motel in Dallas. Ruby was there the night before.

Roberts also says that the inadequacies of the Warren Commission Report were far from accidental (Mark Lane says the same). He points a finger at Gerald Fox who, at Nixon's recommendation, was one of the top six figures, after Warren, presiding on the Commission. (John Raneleigh emphasises Ford's close relationship with the CIA that dated back to the early 1950's.)

Of the other five, three – Senator J.S. Cooper, Representative Hale Boggs and John J. McCoy – were easy-going and were unlikely to rock the boat. For some reason, Roberts fails to mention the other two. One was CIA chief Allen Dulles. The other was Senator Richard D. Russell who, to quote Raneleigh, was *"an important Senate power"* and *"one of the key people involved with the CIA on Capitol Hill. From the 1950's until his death in 1971, Russell was a friend of the agency and defined his role in the Senate as protector of the security and position of the CIA."* In other words, the CIA had nothing to fear from the Warren Commission, and by reason of their connections neither did the Mafia...nor did Onassis, if there's any truth in what Roberts has been telling us.

So what happened to the three JFK hitmen? Here's what Roberts offers:

Johnny Rosselli got $250,000 as a 'finder's fee' for bringing Onassis (by way of L. Wayne Rector as 'Howard Hughes') to Las Vegas in 1967. The take-over of the city was handled for Onassis by Maheu. And Rosselli's quarter million was just part of his pay-off for the JFK head-shot. From Brain Freemantle's book *CIA: The 'Honourable'*

Company comes this information. On 24 June, 1975 and again on 23 April, 1976 Rosselli (reluctantly because he feared the Mafia might kill him) testified to the Church Committee. On 7 August, 1976 his trussed body was found in an oil drum floating in Dumfoundling Bay, North Miami Beach. He'd been shot.

Jimmy Frattiano's pay-off included $109,000 in 'non-repayable loans' from the San Francisco National Bank (president Joe Alioto). Credit authorization for the series of loans, from 1964 through 1965, came directly from Alioto and a high ranking Teamster official. Dun and Bradstreet noted this transaction with amazement and listed the loans in their 1964-65 monthly reports, wondering why Frattiano could obtain so much 'credit' when his only known occupation (and the one with which they actually credit him in their listings) was 'Mafia executioner'. This official recognition of his occupation must have amused him. Roberts says he went round for years boasting about it. He'd introduce himself with the words, *"Hi there, I'm Jimmy Frattiano, Mafia executioner."* A bank vice-president later told the whole story to the California Crime Commission before it was carefully buried in a file. Later, Frattiano testified before a San Francisco Grand Jury with regard to his participation in the Sunrol Golf swindle.

East Coast Mafia man Tony Romero was also involved and, according to Roberts, so was Mayor Joe Alioto. It cost the city of San Francisco between $100,000 and $500,000. In between, Frattiano had used his $109,000 to start a trucking company in the Imperial Valley, where he engaged in more swindling involving US government construction contracts. As one Californian Crime Commission member put it: *"The Mafia is now doing business directly with the US government."*

Brading, despite his X-marked hat, was arrested briefly outside the Dal-Tex building, but was immediately released. Two months later, he was questioned by the FBI for The Warren Commission. Despite being a known criminal with an arrest record going back over 20 years (he was out on parole for a series of crimes when Roberts tells us he fired at JFK) the FBI simply reported that Brading knew nothing whatsoever about the assassination. Brading went on to become a charter member of the La Costa Country Club, a known Mafia haven, near San Clemente. He also became a runner for 'skim money' from the Onassis-Hughes Las Vegas casinos to Onassis' Swiss bank. Brian Freemantle tells us: *"Sam Giancana went four times before Grand Jury investigations into organised crime in 1974 after unsuccessfully seeking help from the CIA to avoid appearing. On Thursday 19 July, 1975 staff from the Church Committee arrived in Chicago to arrange Giancana's appearance before their assassination sessions. That night Giancana was shot to death in the basement of his home."*

And that's how to kill a president. This is how you cover it up. Virtually no limits, in terms of money or human life, were set on the cost of concealing the real facts behind the murder in 1963 of John F. Kennedy. The CIA, the Mafia, and (via the Onassis-Hughes connection) multi-national business interests were among those involved in the massive cover-up.

It's in this light that we now look at the increasingly bizzare string of events over the decade following JFK's death. As we'll see, behind each lies the fear that the real truth will emerge.

Oddly, perhaps, it hardly matters that the official story of Oswald as the lone-wolf motivated single assassin is hardly credited by anyone. On the contrary, the plethora of conspiracy theories that results from all the unanswered questions and the glaring inconsistencies help to cloud the issue. It would be hard to believe that Aristotle Onassis, having bought control over Nixon and Kennedy prior to the 1960 election and then having set up the JFK killing, didn't make sure he had Lyndon B. Johnson in his pocket. Bruce Roberts, in his *Gemstone File*, says that this was done by threat. And there's the implication that LBJ had prior knowledge of the Dallas shooting.

JFK's death was confirmed 30 minutes after the shooting. One and a half hours later, LBJ was sworn in as the 36th President of the United States of America. Later, as he flew back to Washington, Johnson was warned over the plane's radio, in a message relayed from an airforce base, that *"there was no conspiracy. Get it, Lyndon?"*

And how's this for a neat dirty twist with which to post script the JFK killing? It concerns a painter called Mary Pinchot-Meyer. She was the ex-wife of Cord Meyer (a co-founder of the CIA) and also the sister of journalist Ben Bradlee, a buddy of JFK, who was then a Newsweek correspondent, and later became editor of the *Washington Post* at the time of Watergate.

Mary was one of JFK's seemingly innumerable bed-mates. (Two others were Danish journalist and suspected Nazi spy, Inga Arvad, and English 'vice-girl' Mariella Novotny, whose suspected KGB connections emerged when she grabbed headlines as an active figure in the 1963 Profumo Affair in Britain.) However, like Judith Campbell, she was a regular partner rather than one of his usual brief flings. Not only did she sleep with JFK in the White House itself, she actually got him stoned on marijuana, and even persuaded him to think about tripping!! He later wrote her love letters and she kept a detailed diary of their affair right up until his death.

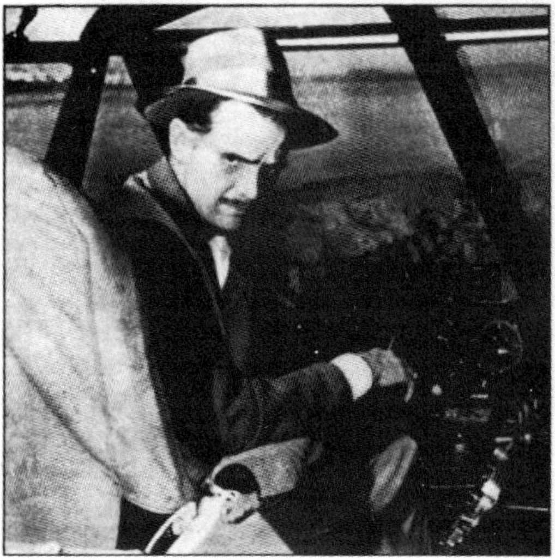

The real Howard Hughes.

Eleven months later, in October '64, Mary Pinchot-Meyer was murdered in the street by *"a crazed black youth"*. A young black man was arrested, charged, tried and found completely innocent. No-one's ever been caught for her murder. Her diary and the JFK love letter disappeared from her home at this time. The CIA admitted one of their men *"accidently burned them"*.

For his years in office, LBJ diverted attention from internal politics. He greatly expanded the war in South East Asia. The old-style US urban Mafia started to show signs of weakening. The CIA faced growing Senate opposition to its 'unofficial' operations in the field of US internal politics. Such work was contrary to the CIA's charter. Onassis, meanwhile, was filling important US government posts with his own men, manipulating government agencies to his own financial ends, and opening up more lucrative operations in South America via Rockefeller and his own man Kissinger. It was this duo who took over the running of Kennedy's 'Group of 40' big business think-tank.

Now we come to the killing of another Kennedy brother. Robert Kennedy had already been implicated in a famous death. It's now fairly well established that he'd had an affair with Marilyn Monroe, as had brother JFK before him. What she knew as a result of these relationships, coupled with the fear that she'd spill the beans, especially with the rate at which she was pill popping and drinking, is often cited as the reason for her death.

Certainly, some of the circumstances surrounding Monroe's supposed suicide on the night of 4 August, 1962, were inconsistent with self-inflicted death. Robert Slatzer in his book *The Life And Curious Death Of Marilyn Monroe* says that Robert and Marilyn were actually briefly married (an informal ceremony in Mexico in October 1952). He goes on to establish that RFK was at least nearby on the night of Marilyn's death, if not actually in her house. And the Mafia link crops up too. In the months before her death, Marilyn's social life had centred on Sinatra's Mafia-riddled Ratpack parties.

Bruce Roberts says that RFK knew who actually killed his brother in Dallas, adding that there was a full account of the events in RFK's unpublished book *The Enemy Within*. That alone should have been enough to get him killed. Add to this the fact that both Johnson and Onassis hated him with a vengeance equalled only by his dislike for the two of them. As US Attorney General, he'd implemented (and often been the driving force behind) most of JFK's moves and policies which brought about the Dallas death. RFK was the one obstacle between Aristotle and his plans to marry JFK's widow, Jackie. Finally, he made the ultimate gaffe of deciding to run for President. They'd got rid of one Kennedy and weren't about to let another one into the White House. Anyway, the Onassis-Mafia-CIA axis had their own special candidate – Richard Milhous Nixon.

The method used to kill RFK, according to Roberts, was a new one. Sirhan B. Sirhan, who took the blame for the killing, was the 'patsy', working under hypnosis. He was seen to fire his shots from in front of RFK. All those bullets in fact missed their target. The actual killer, a 'security guard' from Lockheed Aircraft called Thane Cesar, fired from behind at a distance of two or three inches. He couldn't miss.

Hypnosis may seem far fetched but, in fact since the early Fifties, the CIA has been running experiments on hypnosis, drugs and mind control. Project Bluebird looked at the application of psychology, drugs and hypnosis in interrogation techniques. Out of this work arose Project Artichoke which applied the same methods to making agents and other operatives function reliably, efficiently and without the interference of emotions. This work is well documented and formed the basis of such films as *The Manchurian Candidate* and *Telefon* – though both films attributed such methods to the KGB, not the CIA!

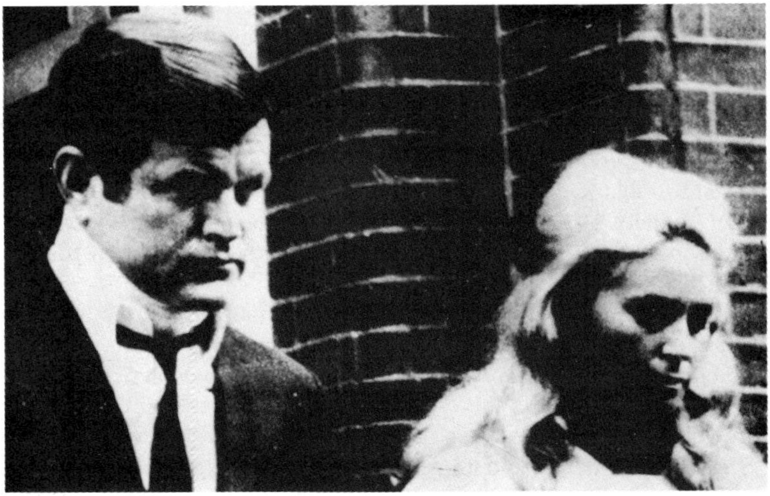

Teddy Kennedy with wife Joan leaving the funeral of Mary Jo Kopechne.

RFK was shot on 5 June, 1968, at the Ambassador Hotel in Los Angeles. Frank Mankiewicz announced his death around 10am next morning. Onassis, six thousand miles away in London, phoned his closest friend and longtime confidant, Constantine Gratos, just after 10am. He said: *"She's free of the Kennedys. The last link just broke."*

According to Peter Evans in his book *Ari*, Onassis showed no hint of regret, no trace of surprise. According to a London aide, he merely displayed *"a sort of satisfaction that his biggest headache had been eliminated"*. Whether this is just another of the many examples of Onassis being heartless or the reaction of a much more ruthless man who knew full well, in advance, what would happen to RFK in LA is open to speculation.

Only four months later, on Skorpios, Aristotle Socrates Onassis married Jacqueline Bouvier Kennedy. He who kills that man who welshes on a deal gets his wife – an old Mafia rule.

According to Roberts, Thane Cesar's work was covered up by the LA District Attorney bearing the wonderful name of Evelle Younger. This not only earned him the post of California Attorney General, but also secured a judgeship for his son, Eric Younger, at the age of thirty.

Roberts cites a documentary film, *The Second Gun*, based on the RFK murder. Made by LA author and director, Ted Charach, it was bought up and suppressed by Mafia-owned Warner Brothers. It seems that the movie included too many accurate details.

By 1968, LBJ had had enough. He announced that he wouldn't be standing for re-election. Teddy Kennedy, last of the three brothers, was faced with a choice between candidacy and longevity. He opted for the latter. That left 'Tricky Dicky' Nixon with a clear path to the post he had been chasing for years. No-hoper Hubert Humphries was the token opposition fielded by the Democrats. It was a one-horse race, but of course it would be. Nixon was the man whom US big business wanted up there. It's said that his political career began when he answered a newspaper advertisement placed by a consortium of business bosses looking for their own presidential candidate. And, as we've seen, Onassis found him an easy fish to hook. In November 1968, Nixon became US President No. 37.

The small island of Chappaquiddick was secluded. It had only twelve permanent residents, no shops, no restaurants, no hotels, not even a church. In mid-July 1969, Senator Edward Kennedy, Joseph Gargan, Paul Markham, Ray La Rosa, John Crimmins and Charles Tretter arrived at a cottage on the island to spend the weekend partying. All were married men in their thirties and forties. None brought his wife. With them were six women in their twenties whom they referred to as Boiler Room Gals. They were Kennedy campaign workers. One of them was Mary Jo Kopechne. At 11.30pm on Friday, July 18, she stepped into Teddy's black Oldsmobile. He would later claim he was just driving her back to her hotel room on mainland. Strangely, under the circumstances, she left her handbag and room key back at the party.

He said he made a wrong turning on the way to the ferry. To do so, he had to turn sharply right off the paved road and travel three-quarters of a mile down a dirt track called Dike Road, before reaching Dike Bridge, beyond which lay a beautiful little beach.

The route was well-known as a popular spot for late-night lovers. His mistake was even stranger given the fact that Teddy had regularly holidayed on Chappaquiddick since the age of seven.

The car didn't skid, it just went straight off the bridge and settled upside down on the bed of the pond. Teddy got out. Mary Jo didn't. He said he went back to the cottage for help, returning with Markham and Gargan who watched while Teddy then dived in, over two hours after the accident, to attempt rescue.

In order to walk back to the cottage, according to Stephen Dunleavy and Peter Brown, in the carefully researched chapter on the drowning in their book *Those Wild, Wild Kennedy Boys!* (which is nothing like as superficial as its lurid title suggests), Teddy had to pass six houses, all occupied, four with lights on all night. And would two men let a senator, a man shaken up and shocked, dive into cold murky water while they stood by and watched? This seems especially unlikely considering that Teddy still wore a surgical brace as a result of a '64 plane crash. That Teddy then went to the Shiretown Inn and slept through till 8am seems extraordinary. Markham and Gargan, having spent the night in the cottage, called for him and the three took the ferry to the mainland. Only then, eight and a half hours after the incident, did Teddy inform the police.

Meanwhile, the car had been found by a couple of fishermen. Mary Jo's body was in it. She had lived for some time, breathing in an air pocket. Doctors estimate that she lived for at least two hours after the accident. Ironically, only two weeks before, there had been a couple of similar accidents. In both cases, the people were pulled out alive, two hours later in the case of one passenger in an upside down Volkswagen. So why was Mary Jo allowed to die?

Bruce Roberts says that Mary Jo's supposed affair with Teddy and his clumsily denying it, is part of a clever cover-up of the real facts. Mary Jo had been a devoted JFK aide, who later worked with Bobby and finally for Teddy. She had the job of packing up Bobby's files after his assassination. She read too much, learned about the Kennedy Mafia involvement, and began telling her friends. An honest and idealistic Catholic American, she was shocked by the double standards. On Chappaquiddick, she overheard Teddy's telephone conversations with Joe Alioto (of whom we'll learn more soon) and with other Mafia politicians. She died trying to get off the island after Teddy caught her attempting to contact Ralph Nader, the citizens' rights campaigner.

During the two and a half hours that Roberts reckons Mary Jo was drowning, he says Teddy was on the 'phone. He spoke to Jackie, to Onassis himself, to Katherine Meyer Graham (daughter of Eugene Meyer and inheritor of her father's Washington Post) and to several lawyers. Jackie 'phoned the Pope on Teddy's behalf. He assigned Cardinal Cushing (who'd handled the recent Jackie-Aristotle marriage) to help. It was Cushing's priests who later persuaded Mary Jo's parents not to push for an autopsy. When Teddy eventually decided, next day, to be seen to take the blame as driver of the car, he'd phoned lawyer Burke Marshall who had helped Onassis buy up Liberty ships in the 1940's and was the designated custodian of JFK's brains after Dallas (they've since disappeared).

Before ending this episode let's look at a footnote to *The Gemstone File's* account of the events. It offers a few more bizzare details as a gory postscript.

During the Chappaquiddick cover-up arrangements Joan Tunney, sister of the senator, John Tunney, heard the end of a 'phone call to her brother made on the night of the drowning from her house in Tiburon. It concerned the Senate's part in the cover-up, in which it was agreed they would not ask to see the existing log of 'phone calls made by Teddy that night. Likewise, they wouldn't ask to hear the recordings of the calls. The next day, after hearing of Mary Jo's death, Joan ran away to Norway. From there, she was kidnapped by two Mafia hoods named Mari and Adams who locked her up in a Marseilles heroin factory for sixty days. Heroin fumes were used to make her a junkie of her (no needle marks) before they eventually turned her loose. She went home. Her husband complained of her strange behaviour. Her reaction was to behead him with an axe. She was subsequently locked up in an asylum belonging to the Marquis of Blandford who, at the time, was the husband of Tina Livanos Onassis – Ari's daughter.

There's no gratitude in this world. Mari and Adams got pressed into scrap metal in a New Jersey auto junkyard. In the panic of trying to cover up all the facts behind Mary Jo's drowning, many skeletons started to rattle. In particular, the JFK murder details began to re-emerge. Black Panthers Hampton and Clark got shot dead by the Chicago cops because of what they knew about the JFK murder squad at Chicago (which was where Kennedy was originally going to be killed, three weeks before they finally assassinated him in Dallas).

Daniel Ellsberg had been responsible, while working for the Rand Corporation, for designing the missile ring around the Iron Curtain countries. Describing him as 'a well-known hawk', Roberts is cynical about the 'folk hero' image he gained from leaking the Pentagon Papers to the *New York Times* in May/June 1971. These papers purported to be the official and top-secret history of the US role in Indo-China. But Roberts says they were simply another piece of cover-up work; this time to make the Vietnamese war look like 'just one of those incredibly dumb mistakes' rather than the calculated money-spinner that it was.

Unsure of its continued power in the US and deprived of the Cuban casino empire, the Mafia was looking to the world drugs trade. There was now a huge Western youth drugs culture to be milked, and the Vietnam war was helping to wean kids and young soldiers off pot and on to heroin. South East Asia (and South America) beckoned. For the CIA, involvement in the trade helped them to finance 'suitable' governments. Also, imported drugs gave them another excuse to maintain their operations within US borders. The 'international student plot' that centred on opposition to the

Vietnam war also gave them cause to operate inside the USA. In fact, student internationalism was almost entirely CIA funded and organised. It's catalogued in *Student Power* by Cockburn and Blackburn (Penguin Books). Onassis, as we have seen, made his first million out of drug deals.

The CIA supplied planes to fly opium/heroin out of the Golden Triangle. The Onassis-Mafia gang handled the distribution and marketing. And there were other methods of getting it out. As Roberts explains, heroin was sometimes brought into the US in the bodies of dead GI's. One corpse with the guts removed can hold up to forty pounds of heroin.

A lot of the heroin, Roberts claims, was processed in a Pepsi-Cola plant in Laos which never produced a single bottle of Pepsi. And he goes on to tell of one dope bust in San Francisco (under Mafia mayor Joe Alioto) that yielded six billion dollars worth of heroin. The story was hushed up and the stuff was stored for a while in the SF police department before being quietly removed by FBI men. From there, it vanished, probably into American veins.

Nixon conducted a noisy campaign against dope smuggling over the Mexican border. However, the numerous dope arrests and murders were of independent dealers and smugglers trying to compete with the massive Mafia-run operation. Nixon's agent in charge of protecting Mafia dope interests was none other than Howard Hunt, encountered last in various CIA escapades.

Ellsberg's boss at the Rand Corporation had been McNamara. Robert says these two faked the Pentagon Papers and the 'leaking' of them.

He says McNamara went on to become head of the World Bank through which American money for 'starving nations' actually went into private accounts of various dictators. These accounts were in Swiss banks controlled by Onassis. For example, eight billion dollars in World Bank funds for 'starving Ethiopians' would end up in Emperor Haile Selassie's personal Swiss bank accounts. We've since seen similar examples such as Iran's former Shah and The Philippines' former leader, Marcos.

On June 28, 1971, Ellsberg was indicted for 'leaking' the papers. On September 3, 1971, there was a burglary at the Los Angeles offices of a Doctor Lewis Fielding, Ellsberg's psychiatrist. Later it would transpire that this was the first of the series of break-ins carried out by Nixon's team of 'plumbers', the most famous of which were the two Watergate break-ins. Two key figures in this White House burglary team were the ubiquitous duo Howard Hunt and James McCord who, as we have seen, were in the Castro/JFK death squads.

It wouldn't be until April 27, 1973, during the trial of Ellsberg, that presiding judge Matthew Byrne would reveal to the public that Watergate conspirators Howard Hunt and G Gordon Liddy had done the Fielding break-in. The judge continued on May 11, 1973 to declare a mistrial and to dismiss all charges against Ellsberg. In doing so, he also revealed that Watergate burglar John Ehrlichman, then the domestic affairs assistant to President Nixon, had offered him the post of Director of the FBI in exchange for another cover-up.

Why the Fielding break-in? The Pentagon Papers were very damaging to the CIA. Hunt and McCord had both 'left' the CIA in 1970. However, an indication of the real situation is given by the fact that throughout his career as a White House burglar, Hunt was supplied with necessary equipment directly from CIA stores. That first burglary was to get hold of Ellsberg's psychiatric records. These could be used initially to secure his full co-operation and, later, to discredit him.

Hunt was appointed a White House 'security consultant' in July 1971, although he'd already been there a while by that time. Throughout June and July of that year, Nixon set up his 'plumber's unit'. Its official job description was 'to stop security leaks and to investigate other security matters'. As this work expanded, more and more members of the White House staff became directly involved in its highly illegal activities. And the CIA, desperate to create a few successes that would improve their own flagging standing in the White House, was right in there with them. John Raneleigh backs this up in his book *The Agency: The Rise And Decline Of The CIA*.

1972 would be election year. Nixon wanted a second term. To ensure Nixon's re-election, some anti-Democratic Party smears would be used. On September 23, 1971, according to Roberts, Howard Hunt spliced up phoney cables implicating the JFK administration in the assassination on November 2 1963, of President Diem and his brother Nhu in South Vietnam. For more dirt, more burgling was planned.

The Watergate complex is a plush mixture of office, apartment and hotel facilities on the bank of the Potomac river in downtown Washington. A Republican stronghold, it surprisingly also acted at this time as home to the headquarters of the Democratic National Committee. The successful bugging of these premises would obviously have greatly helped Nixon in his campaign to retain the presidency for another four-year term. However, direct CIA involvement in one side of a party political struggle would have been completely contrary to the agency's charter. It was a non-political body, allowed no role at all in US politics. It's easy to see why Hunt and McCord 'quit'.

The team that actually tackled the first Watergate break-in in the early morning of May 28, 1972 consisted of McCord, Barker, Martinez, Garcia,

Gonzalez and Sturgis. De Diego and Dico stood guard outside. Hunt, along with the evil Gordon Liddy, directed operations from a short distance. Martinez, incidentally, was another 'former' CIA man. The plumbers set up their bugging equipment.

Bruce Roberts knew some of the plumbers. Even before the Watergate break-in, he socialised with several of them. Here's how he fills in some details that are missing from standard accounts.

In January 1972, the Watergate team were in San Francisco to plan tactics. They showed up at the Drift Inn, a CIA-FBI hangout bar also frequented by Roberts. The Drift Inn bartender, Al Strom, recorded their conversations. He was being paid to do so by Katherine Meyer Graham. So, her paper's reporters, Bernstein and Woodward, didn't just stumble upon the Watergate break-in facts to create the subsequent *Washington Post* exposé. Their editors knew all about the plumbers and their plans well in advance. At least, that has to be the case if we believe *The Gemstone File*. Roberts says that Al Strom, a close friend, passed the details on to him too, adding that the bar was also wired for sound by Russians, Arabs and Chinese.

On January 27, Roberts tells us, Gordon Liddy and John Dean (counsel to the President) met in the office of former Attorney General John Mitchell. Here Liddy outlined his plan for a million dollar spy and kidnap operation. Central to this was breaking into the Las Vegas office of Hank Greenspun (Herman Greenspun, editor of the *Las Vegas Sun* newspaper). The aim was to recover Greenspun's files on the Howard Hughes kidnapping and the Onassis Las Vegas operations. Apparently, Greenspun had used these to blackmail Onassis out of over four million dollars. A getaway plane would stand by to take the White House burglars to Mexico.

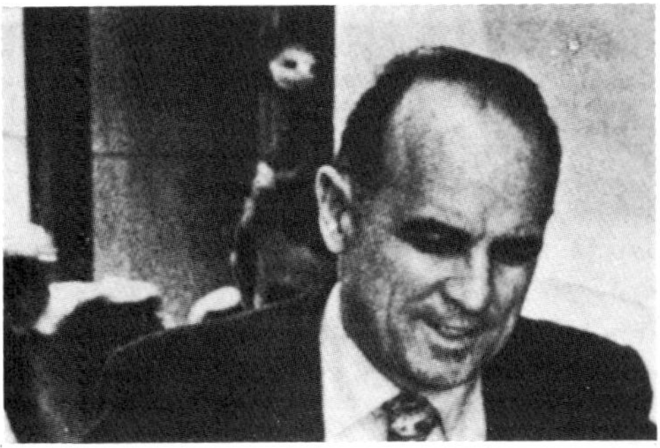

Watergate shitface James W. McCord Jnr.

Around this time, Liddy and Hunt were travelling round a lot under aliases, often names used by Hunt in his spy novels. And they used Hughes Tool Co. (a Howard Hughes company) cards as their business front. If all this seems a bit over the top, it was. Hunt liked to dress up, using wigs and other accessories to disguise his appearance. Such items were among the equipment supplied to him by the CIA. It all smacks of the novelist trying to live out fictional roles. If it weren't so sinister, it would be funny.

Most of the photos of Liddy, Hunt and the other plumbers which later appeared in The Washington Post were taken for Katherine Graham by Al Strom. He was able to do the job without them noticing whenever one of them dropped into the Drift Inn for a beer.

Al Strom was killed on July 9, 1973. Roberts reckons he died by order of Katherine Graham for having shared her information with Roberts.

In April 1972, Liddy gave McCord $76,000. He spent $58,000 of this on bugging equipment and cameras.

The first Watergate break-in on May 28, 1972 seemed to go without a hitch. In fact, they were being observed by Hol Lipst, Katherine Graham's detective, who had been following two of the plumbers. He reported back to his boss and the two of them set up a trap for the team when they had returned to remove the bugs and other equipment they had installed.

On June 17 Hal Lipset, disguised as a mailman, taped the door at Watergate. Frank Wills, the security guard, discovered the tape and became suspicious. He called the police who caught the team red-handed. Only Liddy and Hunt avoided arrest.

Liddy immediately telephoned Magruder (deputy director of White House communications) who was in California at the time. He notified Mitchell and the others. There was plenty of time to burn files and destroy incriminating evidence. Another cover-up was under way.

On June 20, Larry O'Brien, chairman of the Democratic National Party, filed a million dollar suit for the burglary and bugging. He filed it against the Committee for the Re-election of the President (usually referred to as CRP, but Roberts calls it CREEP). In doing so, he named Francis L. Dale as head of CREEP.

Roberts points out that this was a big Mafia mistake, as Dale led directly back to Onassis. Indeed this is one of the only times that the name of Francis L. Dale crops up. It seems that everyone conspired in ensuring that he's omitted from all records of Watergate and surrounding events. And this is strange indeed.

CREEP was the organisation behind the break-ins. Liddy, Magruder and Mitchell were all key figures in the management structure of CREEP, as were many others whose name crops up in reference to the role of the White House in Watergate.

Roberts first mentioned Dale and CREEP with reference to the pay-offs for the JFK cover-up. He says that CIA's Dallas chief John McCone was rewarded for his co-operation by being given a seat on the board of the International Telephone and Telegraph Corporation (ITT), sitting right next to Francis L. Dale.

Next mention comes in February 1972 when, Roberts tells us, Dale pressurised Magruder to push Liddy into Watergate. Adding that, by April, money was pouring into CREEP. Roberts claims that Gulf Resources and Chemicals Corporation of Houston contributed $100,000 illegally (laundered through Mexico, coming back through Liedke of Penzoil Corporation, Houston). He says Robert Vesco gave $200,000 in campaign contributions to Maurice Stans. Stans was finance chairman of CREEP and former US secretary of commerce. Bernstein and Woodward confirm this in *All The President's Men: "International financier and accused swindler Robert L. Vesco's gift of $200,000 in $100 bills was delivered to the committee in a black attache case. It had been added to the cash fund in Stans' safe and had helped finance the Watergate operation and other under-cover activities."* The $76,000 that Liddy gave McCord came from this fund.

Robert tells us that on May 10, 1973, the first witness at the Watergate hearing running down the names on the CREEP organisational chart, mentioned one named at the top: Francis L. Dale, chairman. His name was never mentioned again during the rest of the trial. Indeed, his name never occurs in the book by Bernstein and Woodward, who won a Pulitzer prize for their *Washington Post* exposé of the whole Watergate scandal. The suggestion is that multi-national ITT was powerful enough to buy their man out of the whole mess.

The Gemstone File offers an interesting postscript to underline the power of ITT. Roberts says that in August 1973, Rockefeller, Kissinger and the CIA joined forces with ITT to bring down the Allende government in Chile. This accusation would seem to be fairly well founded. McCone, former CIA head, was now on the ITT board. His former second-in-command at the CIA, Richard Helms, was now head of CIA. John Raneleigh, in his book on the CIA, says that McCone approached Helms and proposed a joint CIA-ITT effort to prevent an Allende victory in that year's election. ITT offered the CIA a million dollars up front to fund such an operation. Helms gave ITT the contracts to the job themselves. Allende got in and did exactly what ITT feared. He nationalised their holding in Chile. ITT lost $8,000,000. Roberts tells us that after Allende was toppled in August 1973, Rockefeller got back his lost investment (in copper mines) and ITT got a return of $125,000,000.

Another scandal, in early 1972, supposedly involved ITT, Hunt, Mitchell and Nixon. It seems ITT merged with the Hartford Insurance Group rather too easily after they funded the Republican Convention in San Diego for Nixon.

Back in the USA, on August 6, 1974, Richard Nixon and Gerry Ford met at the White House and agreed that Ford would become the President, Nixon would burn his tapes and files and Ford would assist in any way necessary to cover it all up. Two days later, Nixon resigned.

On August 30, Ford hired, in Roberts' words, *"Mafia lawyer Becker to work out a pardon deal for Nixon"*. Then, on 8th September, Ford pardoned Nixon for *"all crimes committed from 20th June 1969 through August 1974"*. In October, the Watergate trail began. Roberts describes it as *"the cover-up of the cover-up"*.

Previously we learned that Howard Hughes, kidnapped by Onassis in 1957, was pumped full of heroin and reduced to a vegetable. Onassis kept him locked up on the island of Skorpios until his death in April 1971. L. Wayne Rector, whom Hughes had taken on as his double in 1955, got the stand-in job full-time from 1957 onwards.

The death of the real Hughes hardly mattered to Onassis. His handwriting could be duplicated by a computer and all the known facts about his life had been compiled, with a computerised biography having gone out to top 'Hughes' executives.

Then, Roberts tells us, Clifford Irving, a writer who wanted to do a book on Hughes approached the 'Hughes' Mormon Mafia (the six 'nursemaids') for information. He persuaded one of them, Merryman, to give him a copy of the computerised biography. Irving used this to produce the book that became the centre of much controversy.

Onassis was furious. He mistakenly thought that Robert Mahue had leaked the information and fired him in November 1970. On Thanksgiving Eve, the 'Hughes' entourage made a well-publicised 'secret departure' from Las Vegas (where they'd been living for the past three years, with Maheu running the 'Hughes' casino business for Onassis). In December, discovering his mistake, Onassis had Merryman killed.

On April 18, 1971, the very day that the real Hughes died, Clifford Irving's wife, according to Roberts, presented her husband's cheque for the writing of the book to Onassis' Swiss Bank. It was made by 'Hughes'. Onassis paid up.

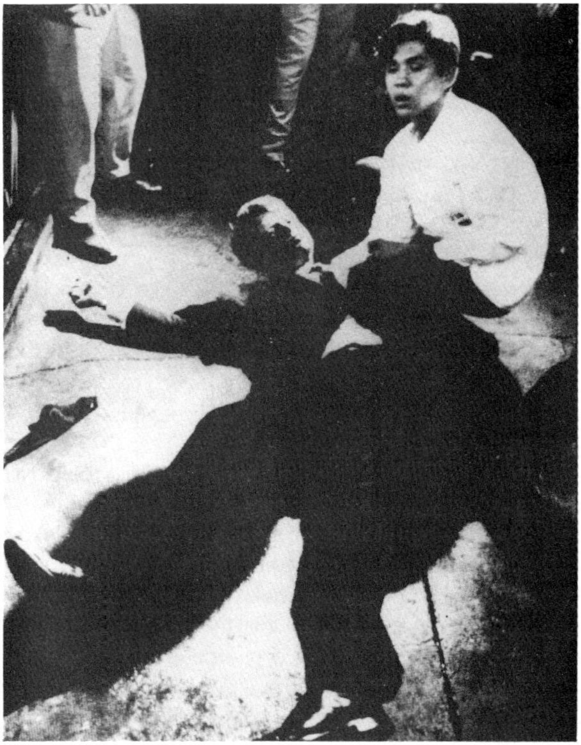

Bobby hits L.A.

Three years later, in January 1974, Robert Maheu won a damages suit that he'd filed against 'Hughes' for the loss of his half million dollars salary and, as Roberts puts it, *"had his blackmail carefully hedged"*. Maheu knew enough to incriminate everyone, Onassis included. Onassis paid again.

The 'Hughes' party (Rector, his nursemaid guards, etc.) first stopped off in the Bahamas. Here, they murdered the governor and a police chief who noticed there was no 'Hughes', just Mafia. They then moved to Nicaragua and on to Canada. Here, Roberts says, they worked a Canadian Stock Exchange fiddle before moving to England, holing up at what Roberts terms *"Rothschild's Inn of the Park, London"*. Here, around the end of 1972 they killed L. Wayne Rector, but maintained the pretence of caring for an ageing and eccentric Hughes.

If you saw the film *Howard and Melvin*, based on an allegedly true encounter, you'll realise that Melvin actually met Rector, presumably on the run from his nursemaids. The money left by 'Hughes' to Melvin in his will would then have been the pay-off from Onassis for keeping quiet on that aspect of the story.

And if Hughes died in '71 and Rector died in '72, then whose body became the official Hughes corpse in Houston, Texas on 4th April '76? The FBI must have wondered. They took the singularly unusual step of fingerprinting the body! They 'positively identified' the corpse as Hughes and Dr. Henry MacIntosh described the death as being *"just like any other"*. Cause: chronic renal failure.

Roberts says that G Gordon Liddy arranged Rector's death, along with those of Lyndon Johnson (by sodium morphate induced heart attack), Eugene Lyman (Californian Democratic Party Chairman and JFK Mafia bagman, also by sodium morphate), and Alexander Onassis. Alexander, only son of Aristotle, died when his plane crashed a few seconds after take-off from Athens International Airport on the afternoon of January 22, 1973. Roberts says this was engineered by fixing the altimeter *"at the 1000-foot Walter Reuter level"*.

Roberts himself had by now become deeply enmeshed in the corrupt business. He wanted to see this foursome killed and claims that he offered Liddy 'the Chinese stock market in ears' (i.e. a lot of money) if he would rid the world of them, adding that *"Quoting the prices to Liddy at the Drift Inn (in February 1972) made their deaths a mortal clinch. Liddy's like that, and that's why the murdering slob was picked by the Mafia."*

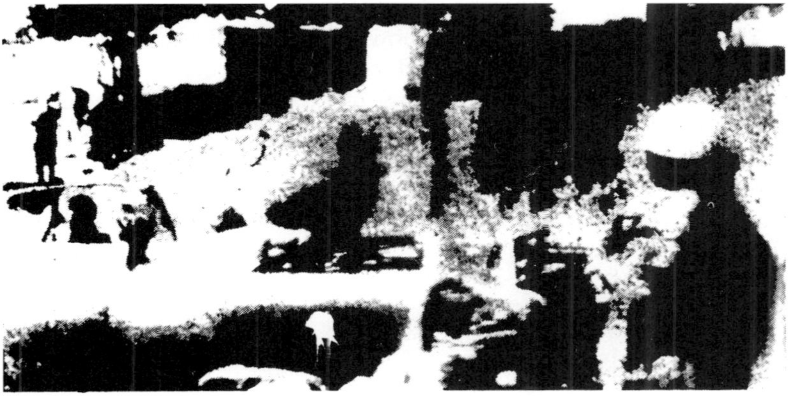

"In the most high and palmy state of Rome the mightiest Julius fell..."

Nixon and others had been receiving each section of *The Gemstone File* since 1969, which is when Roberts first started to make copies of his revelations available to certain Americans. Roberts claims that the eighteen and a half minutes of 'accidentally erased' White House tapes were of Nixon cursing and swearing in a fit of rage at those who'd taped the door at the Watergate building. In part, not knowing about Hal Lipset, he blamed *"that asshole Roberts"* whom he suspected simply because he'd been doing so much nosing about to compile his file. Nixon also named Onassis, Hughes and Dale. The tape couldn't be released.

According to Roberts, a secretary called Beverly Kaye later heard the 'erased' tape, having found it stored in a locked room in the White House. It upset her. She sent some depressed letters to friends. She became a problem. She too died of a sodium morphate heart attack in a White House elevator.

Sodium morphate, says Roberts, has been a favourite Mafia poison for centuries. It smells like apple pie, and causes lethargy, sleep and sometimes vomiting, followed by a heart attack. It leaves no trace in the body.

In May 1972, J. Edgar Hoover, right-wing boss of the FBI, had just such a heart attack after eating apple pie. He'd had a copy of *The Gemstone File* and, Roberts tells us, intended to expose the Dallas-JFK story in his book entitled *The Texas Mafia*. All his files were burned after his death.

Meanwhile, Aristotle Onassis, maker and breaker of Presidents, had thrown in the towel. Having lost his only son, to whom he had intended to hand over his entire global empire, he died on Saturday, March 15, 1974, a wreck of a man. Jackie was in New York at the time.

The Gemstone File contains further amazing allegations by Bruce Roberts which he says are based on the secret diaries of Cardinal Tisseront, former head of the College of Cardinals who, he claims, was murdered using sodium morphate in February 1972.

Tisseront, it seems, had been keeping a written record of the career of Montini who murdered Pope Pius XI with poison, was banished from Rome by Pius XII and then became Pope himself in 1963. Tisseront detailed all of this, calling Montini *"the Deputy of Christ at Auschwitz"* and fulfilment of the Fatima prophecy that *"the Anti-Christ shall rise and become the head of the Church"*.

SLAUGHTER BY STARLIGHT

THE STRANGE CASE OF THE ANIMAL MUTILATORS

IAN BLAKE

In theory it is impossible to drain all the blood from a still-living cow. The animal's veins, we are told, will collapse before the operation can be successfully carried through. Yet someone is able to accomplish this feat with ease. Someone, working at night under the most adverse conditions, is able not only to drain cattle of their blood, but to mutilate the resulting carcasses in strange and ingenious ways. Such mutilations are now a staple element of modern folklore. Cases have been reported from as far afield as Brazil, Sweden, Australia and Central Europe; but the problem is particularly bad in the American cattle states. Colorado, Montana and Kansas have suffered enormous losses over the past two decades. So too have Texas, Oregon and Ohio. The unknown mutilators strike swiftly and silently, leaving behind no clues as to their identity. It is impossible to judge the full extent of their depredations, but even the most conservative estimates suggest that thousands of cattle have been lost since the mid-'60's. Michael D. Albers, writing in *'The Terror'*, puts the figure at *tens* of thousands, though in this case it may be advisable to make some allowance for journalistic exaggeration. Either way, the problem is such that Colorado Governor Richard D. Lamm was moved in 1975 to describe it as *"one of the greatest outrages in the history of the western cattle industry."*

Any solution to this problem must encompass all the phenomena being observed in the vicinity of mutilation sites. These include unmarked helicopters, meandering nocturnal lights and a "flying boxcar" of unorthodox design. Mysterious humanoid figures are also reported from time to time. All this has led to speculation in some quarters that UFOnauts (whatever they may be) are behind that mystery.

Devil-worshippers, CIA agents and the ubiquitous Bigfoot also number among the suspects. Other researchers believe that the answer may lie closer to home. As Colin Wilson writes in *'Mysteries'*: *"Sex murders involving mutilation have increased sharply during the past decade or so. Overcrowding tends to incubate abnormal sexual impulses, particularly sadistic aggressions towards the female. In the past this expressed itself chiefly in urban areas; nowadays, when most people own cars, urban violence and frustration can express itself in remote country areas where the most accessible victims are cattle."*

It is true that frustrated urbanites or thrill-seeking teenagers may be responsible for some of the deaths; this explanation probably applies to a number of mutilated sheep found in Scotland circa mid-'85 by a correspondent of the present writer. Nevertheless, many cases cannot be explained away quite so easily.

Manson biographer Ed Sanders investigated a spate of cattle mutilations in the early 70s, subsequently publishing his findings in *OUI* magazine. I have a copy of his article beside me as I type these words. *"Tongues, eyes, ears, tails, genitals and udders were removed,"* he writes; *"all perfectly snipped as if with a tailor's shears."* Most mystifyingly of all, the rears of the animals were sometimes bored, *"as if with a razor-sharp geologist's core-sampler."*

Things become a good deal more mystifying when we consider that events of this sort have occurred throughout history. Indeed, many modern cases replicate far older mythological patterns. In Paraguay, for instance, there is a long-standing tradition of cattle mutilations involving the removal of tongues and entrails. Similar stories are found in Brazil and Columbia. In the past these atrocities were ascribed to the Mono Grande, a South American version of the Bigfoot/Sasquatch archetype. The Mono Grande was said to live in deeply wooded areas, stealing forth only occasionally to carry off goats, mules or cattle. The injuries it inflicted on its victims – specifically the removal of tongues and entrails – were exactly similar to those found in contemporary American reports of cattle mutilation.

In his book *'Messengers of Deception',* Jaques Vallée discusses numerous latter-day cases in which the corpses of animals – usually cattle – have been found with their vital organs removed, blood drained and external parts (eyes, ears, teats) neatly snipped away. *"The numbers alone are eloquent,"* he writes. *"In an 18-month period before January 1977 there were 700 mutilations in 15 western states. More than 180 cases occurred in Colorado alone in 1975."*

In compiling *'Messengers'* Vallée drew extensively on sworn statements given by county coroners and attending veterinarians, finally concluding that the mutilations are not of the sort that some youthful gang or witchcraft cult would be likely to cause. *"They involve surgical techniques that demand both good anatomical knowledge and procedural skill."*

As we read through Vallée's book a number of interesting points emerge. To begin with, the injuries he describes are by and large meaningless. They serve no discernible purpose other than to draw attention to themselves (this applies in particular to the more gruesome cases of sexual mutilation). If they carry any message at all it is simply that ordinary rustlers cannot be held accountable for what is going on.

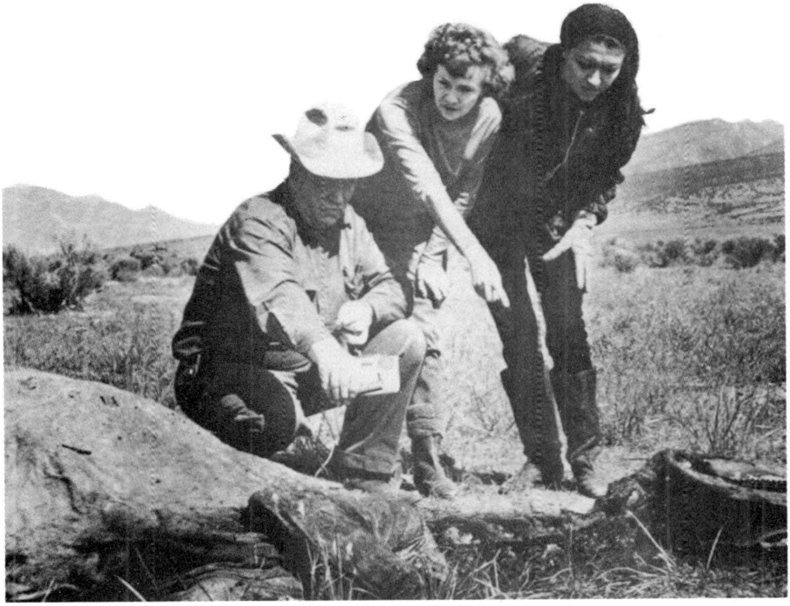

Rustlers would take only the choice steak cuts. Our phantom mutilators, on the other hand, are far more interested in blood and offal. Some of their more bizarre flourishes – such as removing perfect squares and circles from the hide of a dead calf – appear to be carried out purely for artistic effect. Others defy even this tenuous explanation. Why, for instance, would anyone bother to slaughter a cow, remove its internal organs and neatly arrange them on top of the carcass? Or cut a hole in the side of a dead heifer, draw out the animal's intestines and place them beside its head? Yet these mutilations – and others far more inventive – are by no means uncommon. *'Messengers of Deception'* contains a veritable catalogue of such horrors. Among the entries we find the following:

"The bottom jaw was cut back and the tongue was gone...the sex organs were cut off...the navel was cut out in a circle and the meat inside was not touched...two teats and the rectal area had been removed...an udder, an

ear and four square feet of hide had been removed...the whole hide had been removed WITHOUT PUNCTURING THE TISSUE UNDERNEATH" (my emphasis), and, most bewildering of all, *"the udder had been neatly cleaned out, leaving only the skin, which was then tightly packed with several gallons of sand."* Sheriff George Yarnell of Elbert County, Colorado, was moved to describe the latter as his *"most memorable case."* No doubt.

Relating his own personal observations to the work of other researchers in the field, Vallée posits a link between cattle mutilations and the UFO mystery. The aim of both phenomena, he conjectures, may be to manipulate our beliefs and thus achieve social change on earth. *"What we see here is not an alien invasion. It is a control system which acts on humans and uses humans. However, we still need to discover the source of this manifestation."* Despite an interim of over ten years since the publication of *'Messengers'*, the nature of Vallée's 'source' is still open to conjecture.

I have dealt with *'Messengers of Deception'* at some length because it discusses the mutilation syndrome in a particularly intelligent and penetrating fashion. Its conclusions are validated to some extent by the work of scientist and UFOlogist Thomas E. Bearden. Dr Bearden's theory is too detailed for me to attempt a full summary here. In essence he maintains that UFOs are not physical objects at all, but 'tulpas' or thought forms called into being by Russia's hostile impulses toward the West. Their purpose, he says, is to spread fear and nurture paranoia throughout the American heartland. The systematic mutilation of cattle is just one of the many tactics at their disposal *"The cow is a Western symbol par excellence; Western children nurse on cow's milk. Attacks on livestock should therefore be regarded as tulpoid phenomena of a sharply symbolic nature."* An ingenious theory.

Although it cannot be made to fit all the facts, Dr Bearden's hypothesis does provide an explanation for one of the most baffling aspects of the mystery: namely, the strange *insubstantiality* of the perpetrators. This phantom-like propensity was demonstrated on August 5, 1976, when two residents of Atwood, Colorado, were privileged to witness a mutilation in progress. The pair watched in amazement as "two strange men" crawled under a fence, entered a feedyard (apparently a kind of corral where cattle are fattened for market) and mutilated a cow. When challenged the mutilators turned and fled, and "a merry chase ensued." It was later observed that they left no tracks, even though the ground was muddy from a downpour earlier that day. Capture seemed inevitable when the two men ran up against a barbed wire fence, but at this point they simply dematerialised, leaving no trace of their passing. (So why, one wonders, was it necessary for them to crawl *under* a fence to enter the feedyard?) This event is described more fully in *'Earth's Secret Inhabitants'* by Jerome Clark and D. Scott Rogo.

Veteran psychic researcher John A. Keel also has much to say about our elusive mutilators. During the '60s he investigated a spate of UFO sightings in the West Virginia and Ohio regions of the USA. At several points during his research he interviewed ranchers whose herds were being depleted by unknown marauders. As usual they took only the brains and viscera, leaving behind the more desirable steak cuts. A nurse living on a remote farm near Gallipolis, Ohio, was able to give Keel a general description of the attackers. *"They're tall men in white coveralls,"* she explained; *"and they can certainly run. I've seen them leap over high fences from a standing start."* This ability to make prodigious leaps is, of course, well known in the annals of psychic phenomena.

Having sifted the evidence at great length, Keel is of the opinion that cattle mutilations and related phenomena are perpetrated by a race of ultraterrestrials (UT's) or Elements whose purpose is to deceive mankind and manipulate human affairs. This theory is partially endorsed by the British researchers Janet and Colin Bord. However, in their book *'Alien Animals',* the Bords suggest that people *"need and enjoy the unknown".* They... *"like the uncertainty of not knowing what's out there".* Such a dictum certainly applies to many students of mutilation phenomena. For them the mystery, with its many ramifications, is far more intriguing than the solution could ever be. Each finds in the evidence confirmation of his darkest suspicions about life and the nature of reality. Thus John Keel sees the entire business as an ultraterrestrial ploy, while *OUI* reporter Mike Reynolds ascribes it to a large, well-equipped organization with possible government links. Reynolds' view is supported by a growing number of small independent ranchers who point out that unmarked military-style helicopters are often seen in the vicinity of mutilation sites.

Other ranchers blame their losses on the major agricultural corporations, who (it is alleged) wish to monopolize the cattle business for their own ends. Thomas Bearden sees the mutilations as 'psychotronic' projections of Russia's hostility towards the West, while author Robert Anton Wilson, himself a practising White Cord Witch and Voodoo Priest, archly observes that the sacrifice of cattle... *"was part of many shamanic traditions throughout history."* There are almost as many solutions to the mystery as there are researchers. Each theory has something to recommend it, but not one can be made to accommodate all the facts.

What, then, are the facts as we know them?

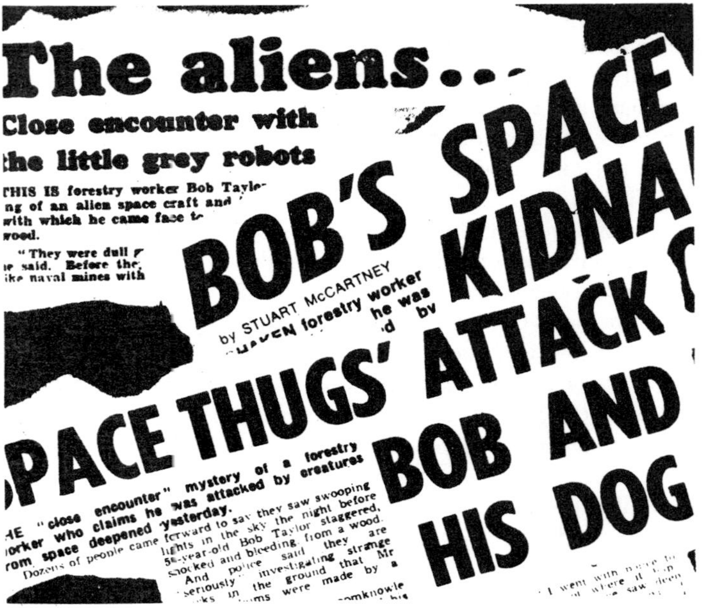

The aliens...

Close encounter with the little grey robots

THIS IS forestry worker Bob Tayl-
ng of an alien space craft and
with which he came face t-
wood.

"They were dull
he said. Before the
ike naval mines with

BOB'S SPACE KIDNA

by STUART McCARTNEY

forestry worker he was

SPACE THUGS' ATTACK

BOB AND HIS DOG

HE "close encounter" mystery of a forestry worker who claims he was attacked by creatures from space deepened yesterday.

Dozens of people came forward to say they saw swooping lights in the sky the night before 58-year-old Bob Taylor staggered, shocked and bleeding from a wood. And police said they are seriously investigating strange marks in the ground that Mr

To begin with, the mutilations constitute a particularly bizarre form of terrorism or ontological guerilla warfare. There is a psychic component to many cases, but in general they appear to be the work of a large, well-equipped terrestrial organization with access to military-style hardware and chemical agents. (Traces of nicotine – a powerful tranquillizer – and nerve gas have been found in some carcasses.) Helicopters are probably used to airlift the cattle away from their grazing places, and to return then again after the atrocities have been carried out. Support for this theory is provided by a number of cases in which carcasses have been found with broken limbs. Ruptured internal organs are also fairly common – the result, presumably, of being dumped overboard from a great height. Airlifting would also account for the curious lack of blood and other evidence (footprints, etc.) at mutilation sites. The actual mutilations require some degree of surgical knowledge, since a standard autopsy procedure known as the Rockitansky technique is employed from time to time. Finally, the purpose of all this is seemingly to spread terror, mystification and a kind of superstitious dread among the community at large. *"As with many UFO encounters, the mutilations carry a message,"* writes Jaques Vallée. *"In the United States they seem to tell military authorities, with their radar and computers, 'See how helpless you are; see how obsolete your technology is!'"* Just so. Anything beyond this is conjecture.

Although cases occurred as far afield as Puerto Rico, France and the Scottish Highlands, cattle mutilation remains a curiously American phenomenon. As such it touches a deeply responsive chord in the popular imagination. The perpetrators, whoever they may be, have now entered the realm of folklore, where they exist as shadowy, insubstantial figures almost akin to Jack the Ripper. Their identity is, in a way, strangely irrelevant. So too are their motives – at least to anyone not directly involved in the mystery. The mutilation mythos has acquired a kind of self-perpetuating momentum; it proceeds at its own pace, resisting all attempts to unravel it. Perhaps this is to be expected. After all, as Sacheverell Sitwell observed in *'For Want of the Golden City'* : *"In the end it is the mystery that lasts and not the explanation."*

THE SECRET LANGUAGE OF ALCHEMY

KENNETH RAYNER JOHNSON

ALCHEMY?

A dead, pseudo-science, the forerunner of chemistry in which a long line of misguided individuals tried to turn lead into gold?

Or an elaborate, ornate and fanciful precursor of experimental psychology?

The real secret of the alchemical art or Hermetic science is contained, for those capable of grasping it, in a brief inscription on one of Heinrich Khunrath's illustrations. It appears on a panel on the left-hand side of an engraving entitled: 'The Door of the Sanctuary and the Stairway of the Sages'. The plate was featured in Khunrath's *'Amphiteatrum Sapientiae Aeternae Christiano-Kabalisticum'*, published in Hanau, Germany, in 1609. In translation, the Latin inscription says simply: *"Mystery truly divine, which by right reason shall ravish with wonder and love all beholding it and THOSE CHIEFLY WHO SHALL CONSIDER IT INWARDLY."* The emphasis is my own.

Forget the retorts, athanors, alembics, sandbaths, curcubites and all the other pots-and-pans paraphernalia usually associated with the alchemist. Forget, too, the idea of a literal, magical transmutation of the base metals into gold. At least, for the time being.

The truth is – despite the voluminous documented evidence for physical laboratory operations – that they are essentially intended to be symbolic. European writers on alchemy have underlined this quite clearly and frequently by making a precise distinction between the true Alchemist and his vainglorious but all too literal-minded imitator, the Souffleur, or *"Puffer"* (at the bellows).

For those who may have read my book *'The Fulcanelli Phenomenon'* (Neville Spearman, 1980), this may appear at first sight to be something of a recantation; a total about-face. In a sense, perhaps it is. But I should explain that, since writing that volume, with its necessary historical background to set the scene for the advent of Fulcannelli, France's Master Alchemist, I have continued to study the subject and, as a result, have readjusted my overall viewpoint.

In fact, the study of alchemy and the abstruse, ancient texts which purport to unveil its secrets, may itself be thought of as part of the alchemical process. A long and complex exercise involving the real First Matter: the human process of mentation.

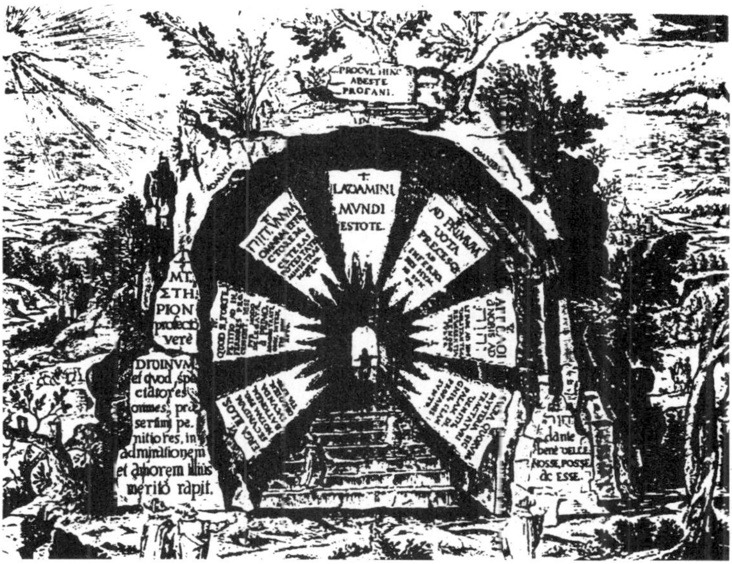

The Gateway to Eternal Wisdom.

The fact of the matter is that the true Adepts of the art, for some reason I won't enter into here, wrote in allegory or code. The code itself and its various glyphs, ciphers and phraseology was elaborated upon, underwent changes and was modified over the centuries by the various operants and by different *'schools'*. But it remained an allegorical code nevertheless.

Without being absolutely explicit, many alchemical writers pointed to this fact. Fulcanelli himself, and his pupil M. Eugene Canseliet, alerted the reader to it, when speaking of a *'phonetic cabala', 'the Language of the Gods', 'the Language of Diplomacy'* and of cant, play on words.

And on the penultimate page of his first treatise, *'Le Mystère des Cathédrales'* (Spearman, 1971), Fulcanelli emphasized once and for all that alchemy is a mental labour: *"It demands the greatest simplicity and complete indifference with regard to theories, systems and hypotheses... It requires its candidates to LEARN TO THINK MORE WITH THEIR OWN BRAINS and less with those of others... By constant exercise of the faculties of observation and reasoning AND BY MEDITATION, the novice will climb the steps leading to KNOWLEDGE".* Again, the emphasis is mine.

So, what are these many symbols of the Hermetic allegorical code and how are they applied? Let us begin by looking at that old stumbling block,

First Matter, without which, the alchemists warn, the Great Work cannot even be started. (And having told you that, they invariably – no doubt with a wicked smile – proceed to tell you everything – except what the mysterious First Matter, or Prima Materia, is!)

First Matter is variously described as more precious than any gold or treasure and yet a most common thing, which everyone has in their possession. It is something with which children play, which women spin, that is found everywhere and yet is spurned, ignored or unnoticed by most people. It has been described as *"like thick, curdling milk, but it is not milk"*, or *"like mud, but not like any other mud"*.

In their attempts to find something that answers to any or all of these descriptions, the Soufflers tried working with all manner of things:

Urine (ever seen a woman spinning it?); horseshit (try taking a few grammes to an assayer); dew (not found everywhere, is it?); blood (scarcely unnoticed by the average person); vitriol (sulphuric acid is not a recommended plaything for kids); mud, milk, common earth, menstrual fluid, semen...and so on, ad absurdum. Just about everything imaginable seems to have been tried at one time or another by the 'physical' alchemists.

And yet, with a little careful consideration, there is really only one thing which will really fulfil the innumerable descriptions applied to First Matter by the Alchemists, provided it is borne in mind that they are great allegorizers: the mind itself, conscious and, of course, subconscious.

On first consideration, this proposition might seem so simple as to be absurd. Yet isn't this what so many of the alchemists also assert: that it is so simple that nobody believes it?

As I noted in my book, many people sighed with relief when Dr Carl Gustav Jung put his final full-stop on the last of his erudite works on alchemy (*'Alchemical Studies', 'Psychology & Alchemy', 'Mysterium Coniunctionis, The Psychology of the Transference'*, etc. etc.).

It must have been a great comfort to many academics and scientists who had wrestled vainly with the subject, to be able to read Jung and then say: *"Of course! It's so simple – alchemy was just an archaic expression of Jung's individuation process; a medieval form of psychoanalysis."* And, in the loosest sense, that is true.

Unfortunately, however, Jung himself did not – perhaps he *knew*, but dared not – take it any further than that. Yet what he postulated does lend itself to further development.

The real and completed alchemical process, which a fellow-researcher and author, Roy Norvill has called *"the transmission of consciousness"*, can result in much more than the self-integration of the personality. And

I cannot recommend highly enough Norvill's book *'Hermes Unveiled'* (Ashgrove Press, 1987) and its planned sequels, in which he elaborates upon the process in much more detail than I can hope to do here.

Before we examine the process itself, let us look at some more examples of Hermetic symbolism and allegory.

First of all, it should be noted that genuinely knowledgeable writers in allegory, who may be considered initiates, tend to alert the reader from the very outset that they are writing in allegory. And by studying various texts, it is possible to build up a Hermetic key of codewords, literary devices and phrases which crop up over and over again and which enable the unlocking of the alchemical 'secret'.

Here, then, at random, are examples of the kind of devices used by the Hermetic writers – and they are to be found in a surprising number of sources, apart from purely alchemical works, not always recognised by students of the occult as sources of Hermetic knowledge: the Old and New Testaments; Plato; Greek and Egyptian mythology; stories of buried treasure; legends of Atlantis and Shangri-la; the Arthurian cycle; sacred dramas – even classic works of fiction, like Victor Hugo's *'The Hunchback of Notre Dame'*, H. Rider Haggard's *'She'* and Mary Shelley's *'Frankenstein'*.

The original difficulty is that, as in some languages, such as Arabic, the Hermetic writers used a whole range of words, emblems or phrases to indicate the same idea.

The meditational process itself, for instance – leading to Norvill's "transmission of consciousness" – may be found symbolised in the following ways:

Any act of *labour*.

Any *journey*, pilgrimage or voyage, usually involving a 'long and circuitous' route.

Any symbolism involving the number three – because there are *three* main stages, or degrees, in the process.

A mass *exodus*, as in the Old Testament.

A period of *40* days and nights, or years, a device which occurs frequently in the Bible.

Any reference to *'celestial' agriculture*.

Death or *sacrifice* (of the conscious mind), as in the lives of avatars such as Krishna, Prometheus, Christ, Odin, and many of the saints.

Acts of *torture*, as in the cases of the martyrs.

References to *'blackening'* – again, the stilling of the conscious mind; the Ethiopian, or *nigredo* stage in alchemy.

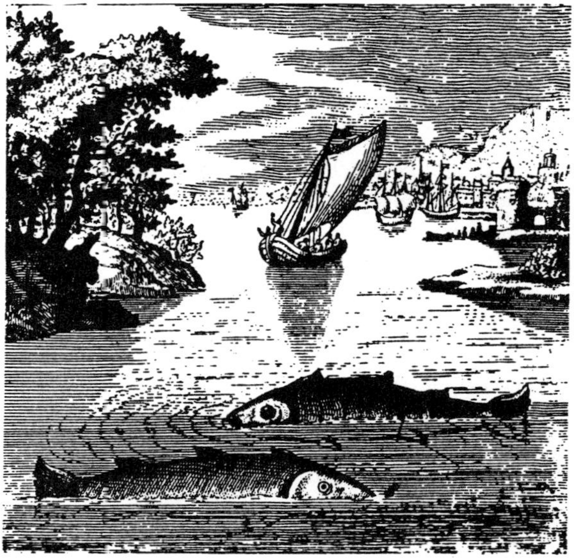

Alchemical allegory: Body, Mind, Spirit.

The *slaying* of a dragon or monster – once again, the quelling of random thoughts of the conscious mind, which are a bar to any progress in the process.

Watching – as in the shepherds who 'watched their flocks' (i.e. random thoughts) 'by night' (in the inner silence of the mind); or Jesus, who urged his disciples to 'watch' in the *garden* of Gethsemane, and rebuked them because they failed to do so.

Finally, the operation may also be indicated by a string of related symbols, all of which suggest the same idea of sustained, inner *reflection*: the Moon (reflected light), silver, mercury, water, a mirror or glass vessel, the sea or 'mare' and thus on to Mary, the Virgin.

The Alchemists' mysterious 'Our Mercury', which they are quick to point out is not common, elemental mercury, is one of the major devices for indicating the sustained, inward-looking attention necessary for the process. Also used for this same concept are the *sword*, the javelin or spear, and the goat (sure-footed and determined).

The ubiquitous and equally mysterious 'Secret Fire' of the alchemists is also none other than sustained concentration. Metals are the emotions, which get in the way of the process, while blood or circulation signify the random thoughts.

Symbols used for the conscious mind by the Hermetic writers include the following:

A *dog*, and any related canine references: Sirius or Sothis, the dog star; Cerberus, the *three*-headed dog-guardian of Hades; Anubis the Watcher, etc.

Ugliness – the hunchback, a monster, or a camel, for example.

A stone, *earth*, or compost.

The *serpent* or dragon which must, like the conscious thoughts, be slain.

A bearded *old man*, a hermit, or Saturn, Uranus, Kronos, indicating that the process required time.

Lead or *base metals*; the crucible.

The *left* hand or foot.

The sabot, or *boot*.

It is an interesting digression here that it was the use of the *left* hand by the Hermeticists, to denote the unwanted ramblings of the conscious mind, which eventually lead to the equation of 'left' with 'evil'. The aspirant's greatest enemy in undertaking the Hermetic meditation process is his conscious mind.

Allegories employed for the Subconscious Mind, on the other hand, include:

Any fabled land of *Utopia*: Punt, Shamballah, Shangri-la, Atlantis or Avalon.

Buried treasure – the *'treasure'* of the enlightened mind.

The mushroom, or bolt-capped plant, and the leopard; even the disease of leprosy. (These particular devices are too complex to explain here; a reading of John M. Allegro's *'The Sacred Mushroom & the Cross'* should provide some insights. It may, however, be pointed out that all involved *'spots'*.)

Any place that is barren and desolate: the *wilderness*, the North or, depending upon the fashion at the time of allegorizing – the East; Holland – the 'nether lands'; Spain (again, a matter of temporal style).

Any pure spring or unblemished source of *water*: i.e. a fountain.

More obscurely, perhaps, a thorn or bramble and, particularly in French alchemy, the *lily-branch*.

The *right* hand or foot.

Now, armed with this compendium of frequently applied symbols – and this is by no means a complete and comprehensive list – it should be possible to make much more sense of the abstruse Hermetic tracts. And, indeed, of many other writings not normally associated in the popular mind with Hermeticism or esoterica.

It should also be noted that, in setting out their versions of the Hermetic process, the adepts used real, historical events and settings, as well as fabled and legendary stories, to indicate the required method. I will now give some typical examples of both varieties, emphasizing the key phrases and, where necessary, giving a brief interpretation.

First of all, let us take the Greek myth of Perseus and his slaying of Medusa, the Gorgon.

It will be recalled that Medusa was one of the *three* sisters (the three stages in the process), whose *head* was covered with writhing serpents (the constantly shifting activity of the conscious mind). Perseus' mission was to *kill* (still) the Gorgon by cutting off her head – the idea of such sacrifice symbolising the active effort required to quieten the internal dialogue of the conscious mind. Anyone who looked upon Medusa directly was turned to *stone* – another frequently used symbol for the ordinary consciousness. To fulfil his task, Perseus looked at her *reflection* (emblem of meditation) in the highly polished surface of his shield (again, the mirror as a symbol of the process), and approached her *walking backwards* (reversing the normal flow of attention from outward to inward). His reward for fulfilling this heroic duty was the Golden Apples of Hespirides – symbols of the completed process, the *'gold'* of the successful alchemist.

Whether or not the story of the Flood, as depicted in the Book of Genesis, actually occurred, is of little consequence, although archaeological research has indicated evidence of an inundation which could correspond with the story, along the Euphrates and dating around 4,000 BC. Whatever the truth, the writer of Genesis used unmistakably allegorical motifs and key ideas which are repeated in many other parts of the Bible and elsewhere by Hermetic authors.

As I have already indicated, the mental process was allegorized by some writers as a long and dangerous voyage – and the story of Noah is no exception. The lengthy time required for the process is symbolised by Noah, his family and menagerie being afloat for forty days and nights. This is also emphasised by repeating the same period for the length of time the heavens rained down to flood the earth. (Elsewhere in the Bible, we read of the Israelites wandering in the wilderness – the desolate symbol of the subconscious – for *forty* years; of Joseph embalming his father, which took forty days; Moses being upon Mount Sinai for forty days, and of Jonah predicting the overthrow of Nineveh within forty days, to give only a few examples.)

The word 'ark' itself is of some significance. Hermetic writers, it should be noted, frequently employed puns or phonetic similarities, a device which can transcend any limitation of language. One phonetic equivalent of 'ark', for example, is 'argha', an Ayro-Hindu root word, signifying *reflected light*. The animals aboard Noah's ark, one of each, male and female, represent not only the generative power of the mind, but the balance of sexual polarities – often depicted in alchemical texts by the Androgyne.

Noah's ark had *three* decks (stages of the process) and, after the requisite long and dangerous voyage, Noah sent out firstly a raven – a *black* bird, symbol of the nigredo, or *"blackening"* stage of the alchemical process, when the ever moving thoughts of the conscious mind are successfully stilled. Next, a dove, a *white* bird, symbol of the 'albedo', or purification stage, was sent out *three* times. It did not return on the third occasion, indicating to Noah that there was dry land – symbolic of the fact that the Hermetic process is completed after the third stage. This is further pointed up by the appearance of a rainbow – a step frequently referred to as the *"tail of the peacock"* in alchemical texts. The third and final stage, the 'rubedo' or reddening, is represented by the fire on Noah's altar of thanksgiving.

As I have indicated, there are literally countless other examples of allegory of the Hermetic process in both sacred and secular literature, aside from the overtly alchemical texts themselves. It is even demonstrable that occasionally non-initiates transmit the key symbols and phrases of the process unconsciously: an example, perhaps, of Jung's theory of eternal archetypes which recur in the unconscious mentation of people down the ages.

I have no evidence, for example, that the writer Anatole France was a Hermeticist. Yet nonetheless, he recounts a distinctly Hermetic allegory in his short story *'Le Jongleur de Notre Dame'*. Basically, it's the story of a poor juggler, Barnaby, who on Fair days, would put on a show throwing six *copper* balls in the air and catching them with his feet or, with his body *arched around the shape of a perfect wheel*, he would juggle a dozen knives. Barnaby was taken in by a monk who felt sorry for him. All the monastery fathers devoted their lives to the service of the Blessed Virgin. Some wrote scholarly treatises, others painted or sculpted, composed hymns or wrote poems. The illiterate juggler, who could not even say the prayers, became downcast because he could not participate in the worship – until he *discovered a way of his own* to show his devotion to the Blessed Virgin. Daily, he retired to a *deserted chapel*, where he stayed for one hour. When the Prior and two older monks, having become curious, watched him furtively, they saw him before the altar, head downwards with his feet in the air, juggling six balls and a dozen knives. Just as they were about to interrupt this *"sacrilegious performance"*, they saw the image of the Virgin descend the altar steps and, with a fold of her azure robe, wipe the sweat from Barnaby's forehead. The Prior and monks immediately prostrated themselves and said: *"Blessed are the simple-hearted, for they shall see God"*.

Some of the Hermetic clues are emphasized in the above summary. Copper, for example, is the metal associated with *Venus* who, like the Virgin, is a symbol of inward reflection. The arching of Barnaby's body *"in the shape of a perfect wheel"* refers to the circular nature of the Hermetic contemplative process – reversing the thoughts. The juggler, another archetypal figure like the "jongleur" of the medieval Tarot decks, is *unlike the others* and discovers *a way of his own*. In other words, he is a seeker who has stumbled upon the key to the system of meditation, which he practices for one hour each day in the deserted chapel (of his mind).

His posture, head down and feet in the air, recalls yet another Tarot symbol, *'The Hanged Man'* (Atu 12), which again evokes the *reversal* of the thought process from outward to inward, as in proper meditation.

The approving act of the Virgin, wiping the sweat from Barnaby's brow is also significant: *sweat* and *dew* are popular symbols in the Hermetic canon of the concentration and effort of singularly directed attention required. Readers of Fulcanelli's *'Le Mystère des Cathédrales'* may now recall, perhaps with a wry smile, Eugene Canseliet's reference to a letter which Fulcanelli constantly carried around with him, which was stained with sweat *"from the heat of the furnace"*!

Students will find literally hundreds of examples of Hermetic allegory explained and delineated in the already mentioned *'Hermes Unveiled'* by Roy Norvill and its sequels, *'The Language of the Gods'* and *'The Golden Understanding'*, which I have read in manuscript.

It will also become possible, once the reader has a familiar grasp of the range of symbolism, to discover one's own examples in the most unlikely places. Even, believe it or not, in such works as Stevenson's *'Treasure Island'* – or even in the occasional movie plot, where the screenwriter has (probably unwittingly) picked up and repeated a classic Hermetic theme.

Despite the tendency of the alchemists to be 'grudging' about giving away the Great Secret, there are also quite explicit outlines of the Hermetic process. Among the best, perhaps, are the Wilhelm-Jung translation and commentary on the ancient Chinese classic, *'The Secret of the Golden Flower'*, and Dr. Paul Brunton's *'The Secret Path, The Quest of the Over-self'* and their sequels. I cannot recommend them strongly enough for study towards a full grasp of the meditative process prescribed.

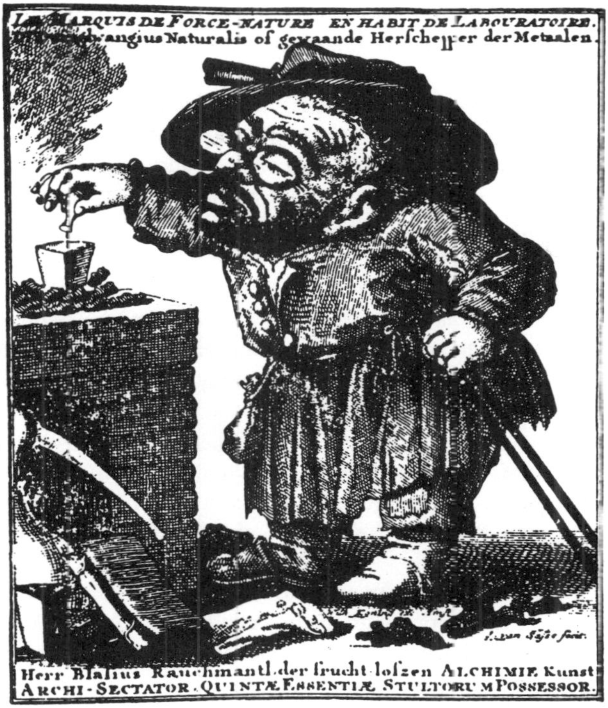

Anti-alchemical pamphlet.

So, what is the process, precisely? In essence, it sounds and should be easy. And yet, there are vital elements of it which, in practice, are probably the most difficult of achievement in man's entire experience.

Which is why, no doubt, we are not overpopulated with enlightened initiates and adepts.

The first requirement is the total cessation of conscious, objective thought. It is the turning inward of the conscious attention of everyday, an inner reflection towards the real "I", the real "me" inside. The "me" that was there when the individual first became sentient and which is the only element of the entire human makeup, if you think about it, which *does not change* throughout our entire lifetime. The outer personality, the superficial ego, of course, is changed and conditioned and modified as life goes on. And the entire experience of outward life is geared to delude the individual that this outward ego is the real self – the so-called personality. It is not. And this can be proved by experimental psychology in which, through other forms of brainwashing – sensory deprivation for example – can utterly destroy the objective personality and replace it with one which is completely different.

It is the real, inner "I" which Dr. Paul Brunton, borrowing from the Hindu Atman, has called the Overself. It is where pure thought comes from: inspiration, intuition, higher knowledge and genuine seership.

The Bhagavad Gita alludes to it: *"He who thinkest constantly of me will always find me: I will at all times be easily found by a constant devotion to me."*

If the conscious mind, with its incessant internal dialogue, its easily distracted nature, its constant outward-looking irregularity and capriciousness, can be stilled, the attention can then be focused intently inward, like a laser beam. A simple analogy may give the idea of the concentration of attention required.

Suppose you are in a building which is, to your knowledge, totally deserted and miles from anywhere – and reputedly haunted. As you walk through this place you hear, quite distinctly, a human footstep, or a voice. Immediately, you freeze – and your entire attention is immediately directed to that sound.

This highly concentrated mode of thought – like the 'sword' or 'spear' so often used in Hermetic symbolism – can then impinge upon the inner mind, the Eternal "I" within. (And it was at this point, it would seem to me, that Jung faltered or, it may be, halted. For him, it appears, the confrontation of the conscious mind with the unconscious, with all its inner gods and demons and a coming to terms with them, was the final aim of his therapy: a sort of laundromat-of-the-psyche process.)

For the Alchemist or Hermeticist, it was merely the beginning. There, in the inner reaches of the normally inaccessible subconscious mind – and the 'superconscious' might no doubt be a better description – the successful adept gained access to what he called Higher Knowledge. How?

Well, Jung almost postulated the same thing, too, but perhaps thought it might have sounded too 'occult' had he spelled it out fully. He termed it the Collective Unconscious. Again, maybe a better term might be the Universal Consciousness. A great timeless network of knowledge, there to be tapped by those who know how – what the Theosophists and others have called the Akashic Record, Teilhard de Chardin labelled the 'noosphere' and Steiner 'the psychosphere'.

Absurd? Impossible? There is, I suppose, only one way to test the validity of this proposition: practice. Set aside a period each day, absolutely free from distraction or interruption. It should ideally be the same time each day and in the same place. Half-an-hour or, at most, an hour a day should suffice.

Once having relaxed the body, try to think of the real 'me' inside; the place from which your thoughts originate and emanate. Try to think *how* you think. While you are letting your mind dwell upon this 'me' inside, you cannot think of anything else. You have, in effect, successfully stopped all other random thoughts – which is the great bugbear of all who attempt meditation.

The state cannot be held for long – except after a great deal of practice and effort. This is the crux of the Hermetic secret: the transmission of consciousness to a third and enhanced state by means of prolonged and carefully directed meditation.

Despite all the efforts of alchemists and other esotericists to keep the 'secret' – the general fear being that, in the wrong hands, the power it bestows could be abused – the secret in fact continues to protect itself, for two main reasons:

1. It is virtually impossible to convince anyone that the mind can be enhanced or altered, merely by thinking of the eternal 'I' inside – and utter, absolute, unshakeable conviction and dedicated application are essential for a successful outcome.

2. If one tries to prove the process, by pointing out the keys to Hermetic allegory in the Bible or any other sacred and secular source, as both Roy Norvill and myself have tried, there is immediate rejection and prejudice in the minds of most people; minds conditioned by eighteen or nineteen centuries of indoctrination.

Scepticism notwithstanding, here now is Dr. Paul Brunton's description of the three stages of the process, as given in *'The Quest for the Overself'* (Rider & Co., 1937):

"The value of the prescribed spiritual practices may now be better appreciated, for it may be said that the habit of daily introspection eventually enables one to cultivate during moments of mental quiet a condition of reverie closely akin to a dream. If the introspection is profound enough, the dream condition is perfectly reproduced. This is not to say that one has entered a region of mere phantasy. On the contrary, in this state one experiences oneself and one's thoughts to be at least as real as they seem during waking external existence. So clear and connected does this condition become with practice, that the vague and fitful dreams during sleep of the average person will bear no comparison. Only those who have experienced dreams of the highest degree of vividness, wherein everything seemed to partake of the nature of utmost reality, can appreciate the condition in which the meditator, profoundly wrapped in his abstractions, finds himself.

"But this is only the first stage, although it may represent a result reached only after many years of effort. The next stage of advance along the path brings one during these practices to a blissful condition akin to that of deep dreamless slumber, but with this essential difference – one experiences all the bliss, the lingering peace with which he emerges from profound dreamless slumber, but experiences it in full self-awareness throughout the period of practice. This is, of course, a very advanced stage along the path and may be reached only after years.

"The third stage of the path is represented by the lamp. [Brunton's own analogy of the Universal Mind]. *In this part, one transcends the condition corresponding to deep sleep and instead of sensing the beautiful presence of the Overself as a thing apart, in whose rays one basks, one becomes the light itself. There is then no need to continue these practices for the goal has been reached..."*

Of course, *knowing* about the Hermetic process, having unravelled all the allegories, and successfully putting it into practice to the stage of fulfilment, are two totally different things.

As recounted in my book, the late Jacques Bergier in 1937 met a mysterious stranger whom he became convinced was the alchemist known as Fulcanelli.

Towards the end of their conversation, 'Fulcanelli' told him: *"The vital thing is not transmutation of metals, but that of the experimenter himself. It is an ancient secret that a few people rediscover each century."*

"And what happened to them?" Bergier asked. *"Perhaps I shall know, one day."*

And perhaps the *"peace which passeth understanding"*, as expressed by St. Paul, might have been better rendered as *"the peace which comes when the conscious mind has been by-passed"* ...

MESCALIN, MYSTICISM, AND AN EXCURSION OUT OF TIME

CHRISTOPHER MAYHEW

Of all my TV series, the one which interested and influenced me most was about the world religions, called *'Men Seeking God'*, which was broadcast in 1954. After surrendering to the allurement of logical positivism at Oxford, I had become steadily more sceptical about the arguments for the existence of God. On leaving during the war, I wrote down, somewhat presumptuously, and at excessive length, the truth about religion as I saw it. These extracts are typical:

"There is no God. When men want badly to understand and influence things and can't, they postulate a deity. They have done this at various times in respect of fire, flood, fertility, madness, mysticism, creation, war, the destiny of man, the orderedness of nature, goodness, beauty and love. As soon as a more reasonable hypothesis has been found, the idea of God has begun to lapse.

"The idea of God is a psychological projection of human minds. It has often brought comfort and reassurance and still does. But it is no advance towards truth. Rather, it impedes truth by choking off scientific enquiry. It is a wall built on the limits of man's knowledge, often broken through but always building itself up further on.

"We are still, and always shall be, surrounded by mysteries. But we must not be mugs again. They are evidence of our lack of knowledge, not of the existence of deity. Theology is rationalization, full of special pleading, self-contradiction and obscurity. Saintliness is not inherently mysterious, nor does it necessarily imply the existence of God. The attribution to it of the idea of God has retarded its scientific analysis.

"The constituent parts of a spiritual person seem to be the following: he has an integrated personality, at peace with itself. In psychological terms, his instincts are harmonized, sublimated or expressed in ways approved by his reason and will. He has, partly as the result and partly as a cause of this, a lively perception of the goodness in things, leading to an apprehension of, and love for, an abstract idea of goodness. This induces in him self-forgetfulness and often, in a wicked world, other worldliness.

"Some outstanding personalities can be saintly in the worst of circumstances. Many can be saintly in fine weather. But the vast mass of people are prevented from thus realizing themselves fully by their nature

and circumstances. For people born in slums or inheriting mental or physical weaknesses, or prevented by circumstances from experiencing things of goodness and beauty, saintliness is as difficult to attain as the beauty of music to someone born deaf. Preaching only 'believe' to these people is cant."

But how then did one account for the indisputable fact of religious experience? That was the puzzle. When devout religious people felt aware of the presence of God, were they simply deceiving themselves – victims perhaps of some neurotic delusion? If God did not exist, what was the source of religious experience? Confident that other people would share my curiosity about this, I asked Grace Wyndham-Goldie to let me make six thirty-minute film portraits of devout adherents of different world religions. I then visited Rome, Jerusalem, Benares, Calcutta, Lahore and Rangoon, selecting and interviewing representatives and devout believers – a Catholic, a Jew, a Hindu, a Christian Methodist, a Moslem and a Buddhist, asking them about their religious experience rather than the doctrines and observances of their faiths.

My first conclusion was that my friends' religious beliefs, if taken at all literally, hopelessly contradicted each other. For the Christian, God was a loving personality, for the Hindu, a much less personal inner self of you, of me, of 'everything else that exists', for the Buddhist, God did not exist. God was a Trinity for the Christians, but for the Moslem and the Jew, one and indivisible. For the Christians, God revealed himself uniquely in the person of Jesus Christ, for the Moslem, not only in Jesus Christ but in a long line of prophets of whom Muhammad was the last and greatest. In fundamentals, as well as in countless matters of detail, the beliefs of these devout people were mutually irreconcilable.

Then was one set of beliefs right and the other wrong? This seemed unthinkable. It would be a strange God who revealed himself truly in one geographical area and falsely, or not at all, in others. Moreover if one conception of God was true and another false, one would expect this to be reflected in the moral and spiritual stature of the believers. Yet I returned from my journey with the impression that the depth of a person's spiritual life depended less on which religion he belonged to than on his own inner qualities and the devotion with which he followed the religion of his choice.

But perhaps there was some common truth underlying all the different beliefs? This too was untenable. Subtract from the world religions their diverging doctrines and nothing important would be left. If the Jew was right and Christ was not divine, Christian doctrine became meaningless. If the Christian was right, and God revealed himself to Christ but not to

Muhammad, what was left of Islam?

So I returned from my voyage more sceptical than ever about the arguments for God's existence.

However, when it came to my friends' religious experience, a different picture emerged. Admittedly, they interpreted their experience differently, each in the idiom of his own religion. The Christian spoke of a sense of the 'presence of God', the Hindu of 'unity with Brahma', the Moslem of peace through submission to the will of 'Allah', the Jew of the feelings of 'being at one' with God in the sense that we are performing his will, and the Buddhist of 'enlightenment', 'Nirvana' and the absolute detachment which comes 'at the last stage of perfection'. In every case, there were important differences – in the language in which the experience was expressed, in the manner and intensity with which it was felt, and in the methods by which it was achieved; and yet it was impossible to doubt that the experience itself was basically the same in all cases. All agreed that it could not be defined exactly, that it was extremely precious, that it was accompanied by joy and a sense of peace and unity, and that it was associated in some way with moral goodness – with unselfishness and detachment from material values and desires. Finally there was a striking similarity in the descriptions they gave of the occasions when they tried to achieve it and failed.

In short, when my friends talked of their religious beliefs, they talked with different voices, and they also differed when they talked of their religious experiences in religious terms. But when they spoke of their religious experience in everyday language, they came together.

What then was the source of this common religious experience? Was it, as my friends believed, some outside power or spirit? Or did it simply come from within themselves, the product of particular physical or psychological conditions? At the time, I inclined to the latter view, and this opinion was now to be strengthened in a curious manner. Dr Humphry Osmond, Medical Superintendent of a highly-regarded mental hospital in Saskatchewan, was an old schoolfriend of mine. In his search for a cure for his schizophrenic patients, he had for some years past been experimenting with a particular range of drugs known as 'psychotomimetics', which produced in those who took them some of the symptoms of insanity. He had recently administered one of these drugs – mescalin – to Aldous Huxley in the fascinating experiment described in Huxley's *'The Doors of Perception'*.

In anticipation of a visit to Britain, Humphry asked me to approach the BBC about the possibility of his broadcasting on the Third Programme about his work. I replied by suggesting that we should make a television film together about mescalin, in the course of which he would explain his research ideas and give me the drug, and I would describe my reactions.

The year was 1955, long before the 'drug scene'. There was little awareness of the dangers of addiction and, except to a few specialists, hallucinogens like mescalin and LSD were unknown. The term 'psychedelic' had only just been invented, by Humphry himself. In these circumstances the BBC approved my idea, and in due course a BBC producer and film team arrived at my home and filmed me drinking down 400 mg of mescalin hydrochloride before Humphry's watchful eye.

Even today, after hundreds of thousands of people have taken drugs of this kind, often with bizarre or ridiculous or disastrous results, I still look on this mescalin experiment, professionally supervised and filmed, as the most interesting experience of my life.

In particular, the drug totally changed my experience of time. At irregular intervals – perhaps once every five minutes at the peak of the experiment – I would find myself withdrawn from my surroundings in a state of euphoria, quite rational and conscious, for a period of time which – for me – simply did not end at all. It did not last for minutes or hours but apparently for years. During this period I would be aware of a pervasive, radiant light.

On the first occasion when I 'came back' from one of these excursions, I exclaimed to the film team in astonishment, "Are you still there!" From my standpoint, they had been waiting, with fantastic patience, for years. From their standpoint, however, no time had elapsed and they had not been waiting at all. From my standpoint, I had spent years in paradise: from theirs, I was deranged.

On one occasion I made a time excursion in the middle of an intelligence test.

Dr Osmond: *"Will you subtract seven from a hundred and go on subtracting until nothing is left?"*

Myself: *"Ninety-three, eighty-six, seventy-nine, seventy-two, sixty-three – whatever it is – fifty-eight, fifty-one, forty-four, thirty-seven, thirty-three – I'm off again for a long period. But you won't notice that I've gone away at all."*

Dr Osmond: *"When are you coming back?"*

Myself: *"I am now in your time."*

For several days afterwards, I remembered that afternoon not as so many hours spent in my drawing room interrupted by these strange 'excursions', but as years of heavenly bliss, interrupted by short spells in my drawing room.

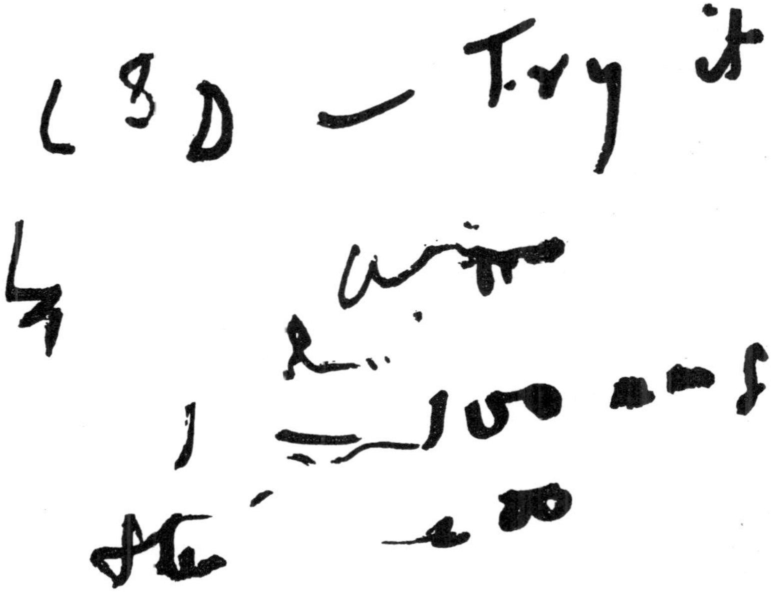

Common sense would say that I had simply taken a hallucinogenic drug and had a hallucination, a dream-like episode lasting a fraction of a second during which I had been deluded into thinking that I had been conscious for a long period. Psychiatrists would – and indeed did – explain the experience in terms of depersonalization, time distortion, light hallucinations and the disintegration of the ego. But I thought then, and still think now, that a truer explanation is that I had had an experience that had taken place outside time, that I had visited, by a short cut, the timeless world known to mystics and to some schizophrenics.

I understand very well the feelings which Dostoevsky – himself an epileptic – attributed to Prince Muishkin in *The Idiot:*

"When his attack was over, and the Prince reflected on his symptoms, he used to say to himself – 'These moments, short as they are, when I feel such extreme consciousness of myself, and consequently more of life than at other times, are due only to the disease – to the sudden rupture of normal conditions. Therefore they are not really a higher kind of life, but a lower.'"

This reasoning, however, seemed to end in a paradox, and lead to the further consideration: *"What matter though it be only a disease, an abnormal tension of the brain, if when I recall and analyze the moment, it seems to be in one of harmony and beauty in the highest degree?"*

What more unanswerable than a fact? And this fact had occurred. The Prince had confessed unreservedly to himself that the intense beatitude in that crowded moment made the moment worth a lifetime. "I feel then" he said one day to Rogojin in Moscow, "I feel then as though I understood those amazing words 'There shall be no more time'."

Is there then no dividing line between sacred and psychotic mystical experiences? Given that its causes and results are so vastly different, how could the end-product of sanity and insanity be substantially the same?

Determined to solve this mystery, I began studying the life and work of perhaps the greatest and most articulate mystic of all times, St Teresa of Avila. I paid special attention to her attempts to define the difference between mystical experiences and insanity. About inner 'voices' for example, she wrote:

"It will be a good thing, I think, to explain the nature of the voices God bestows upon the soul. The words are perfectly formed, but are not heard by the physical ear. You can't shut them out, however hard you try. But when our understanding invents voices, no matter how subtly, we are aware of the intellect actually ordering the words and speaking them. And the soul knows they are the ravings of the mind and takes no more notice of them than of someone it knows to be a lunatic."

Sadly, however, this explanation, characteristically brave and thoughtful, conflicts with what we know about schizophrenics. Their auditory hallucinations would often slip through St Teresa's test. They too are not heard by the physical ear, cannot be shut out, and include perfectly-formed words. I could find no criterion put forward by the saint that clearly marked off sacred from psychotic mystical experiences.

Did this mean that her exemplary life and work, her voices and visions and the reverence paid to her by religious people over many centuries were all based on an illusion? I found this hard to accept, and decided to look deeper.

Once again, television came to my aid: the BBC agreed to my visiting Spain and making a documentary portrait of the great saint.

The film began taking shape in my mind during a visit to the USA on a different television project.

I came across this diary note, written in a New York hotel:

"Strange how the idea of the Teresa programme develops and increasingly overwhelms me. Read T's account (in her autobiography) of her leaving

her home: 'I do not believe that I shall ever suffer more when I come to die than when I left my father's house...'

The sound of this spoken, as it will be spoken, over the sight of the road to the Convent of the Incarnation, as it will be filmed! I heard these words spoken, in the most beautiful, clear, determined voice of a radio actress, over the most lovely shots by Tubby Englander of the road; and then suddenly realized that we will hear the bells of Avila too, and found myself saying aloud, 'The bells! The bells!' in my hotel bedroom."

Before leaving for Avila, I called on the Papal Nuncio in London, and asked for the Vatican's permission to film inside St Teresa's foundations. It emerged that, apart from an occasional doctor, no man had ever crossed the threshold of these convents since they had been built. However, the Vatican approved our project, and attached a Dutch Franciscan friar to our party, to help us obtain the permissions we needed.

Each day of filming would begin at a grille near the entrance to one of St Teresa's convents. Here, tense negotiations would be conducted between the friar and the Mother Superior. Though not understanding Spanish, I could guess the arguments on both sides, and my better self sided with the Mother Superior. Why should she allow this quiet and holy place to resound to the tramping feet of my Spanish film crew? How could she be expected to set aside the rules of her Order, decreed by St Teresa herself, kept inviolate for centuries?

However, the Vatican's wishes could not be set aside, and in the end a compromise would be reached. We would be allowed, for example, to film for a set time in one part of the convent, while the Mother Superior and the nuns – none of whom were on any account to be filmed – took refuge in another part.

Our producer was an old friend, a member of the BBC's Religious Affairs department, the Rev. Peter Hamilton, and the chief cameraman was Gerry Pullen. Their sequences of Avila and the foundations were strikingly beautiful, and we persuaded Flora Robson to record passages over them from St Teresa's autobiography, including her fervent descriptions of her strange, powerful, visions and voices.

I was tempted to let this wonderful film stand by itself; but stuck grimly to my original purpose. The finished version suggested that the world the saint visited in her trances was real, and that we must try to understand and serve the spiritual power that dominated her life, but that sacred and psychotic mystical experiences were hard to differentiate, and that at times during the early part of her life St Teresa could, by modern definitions, be held to have been mentally ill.

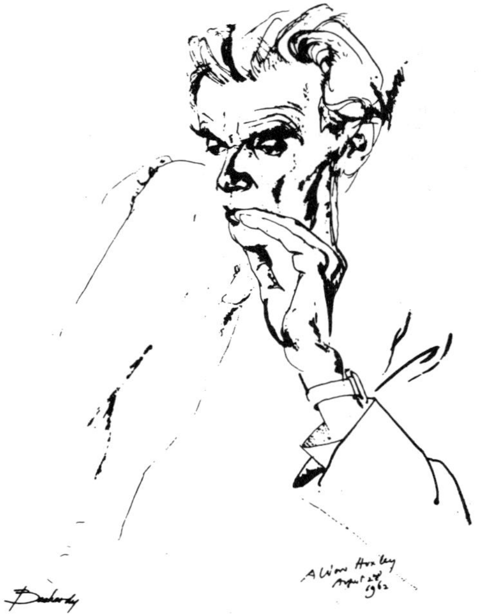

To my sorrow this conclusion was disliked by the BBC's Religious Affairs department, and led to the programme being shown only once, and then very late at night.

The mescalin experiment naturally also increased my interest in mental sickness. It had helped me to understand what it must feel like to be insane, and had given me a fellow feeling for sufferers from schizophrenia. Their bizarre behaviour, I thought, was a natural, desperate, human reaction to wildly unnatural sense-data. And their illness must surely have a simple physical origin. How could my symptoms have been caused by environmental stress, or genetic make-up, or some traumatic childhood experience? They could only have been caused by what I had drunk. All that was needed, therefore, was to isolate and neutralize whatever chemical substance in the bloodstream of schizophrenics was distorting their perceptions, as mescalin had distorted mine.

Later, I realized that schizophrenia takes many different forms; that my symptoms may not have been typical, and that search along the lines I hoped for had already been attempted without producing decisive results. But at the time my convictions were simple and strong, and led me to think about ways of helping the mentally sick.

For most people in those days, mental patients were objects of fear and shame. Herded into locked wards behind high hospital walls, they were widely seen as unpredictable and uncontrollable, at best embarrassing, at worst frightening. I thought television could be used to soften and civilize these attitudes, and persuaded the BBC and the Ministry of Health to allow, for the first time, a mental hospital to be filmed from inside. They also agreed to my interviewing some of the patients, provided their faces were not shown. To help bridge the gulf between patients and viewers, I stayed in one of the hospital wards myself, as a 'patient', for some days before the filming.

If shown today, the programme that resulted, the first of a series called *'The Hurt Mind'*, would arouse little interest; but in those days it was startlingly original. It attracted a large audience, and according to an elaborate opinion survey helped to lessen the stigma surrounding mental illness. My work on it led me into many years of campaigning for the mentally sick, including a seven-year spell as Chairman of MIND, the National Association for Mental Health. The afternoon of December 2nd, 1955, when I took mescalin, had left its mark.

THE ANTI-INTELLECTUAL ETHIC

MICHAEL TIMOTHY

British people are xenophobic, almost by birthright. Anti-intellectualism is simply a form of mental xenophobia.

We are actively discouraged from thinking constructively and questioningly, and once an individual has accepted the numb acquiescence so encouraged, an insidiously vicious circle has successfully been promoted. *"I can't be troubled to think about anything which seems too difficult to grasp, because I'm not intelligent enough anyway. I can't be very intelligent because there are so many things I can't grasp."*

Another rather convenient result of such a situation is that people who don't think constructively and questioningly don't even realise it.

A staggeringly low proportion of the population of America ever reads anything more than the sports pages and cartoons in the daily paper, and Britain is rapidly catching up in the illiteracy stakes. We're inexorably regressing to Medieval times, when the general populace knew very little about even less, and an élite (then the clergy, now the 'scientists') ran the show by virtue of their superior knowledge, not least their literacy and numeracy. Intelligence had, and has, very little to do with it. The bloated, hollow shell of American cultural imperialism, crassly manifest in soapy nonsense and designer cops and robbers; our increasing reliance on the essentially passive activity of viewing the moving image as our prime source of information gathering and entertainment; the virtual collapse of the education system; *The Sun* Argy-bargy Fox and fun; all are clichéd culprits, but not without justification. Still, who wants to read a book when you can watch a video?

British cultural xenophobia is all too familiar, and can often be seen subtly at work on television (the papers rarely trouble themselves with subtlety). Sometimes it overlaps with anti-intellectual, mental xenophobia. A sportsman has a funny foreign name, so what does Harry Carpenter do about it? Says to his audience, in effect, *"Ho ho, I'm as thick as you lot. Anyway, I regard it as an imposition to have to pronounce this name properly, especially in my own country. I'll make no effort to pronounce it correctly, and will continue in this vein until the name becomes as familiar as Severiano Ballesteros, by which time everybody will realise that it's actually quite easy to pronounce"*. An example of the more straightforward mental xenophobia might be as follows: A quite interesting but vaguely esoteric item finds its way onto the local news programme. At the end of the item the announcer says, *"Oh, well, it's all a bit high-brow for me – I only got three CSE's – but I expect somebody must have known what it was all about"*. Of course, the announcer hasn't only got three CSE's; he's actually got a degree, and he understood the item perfectly well, but he mustn't let the audience know that. That would be giving the game away. You might say, *"Well, he doesn't want the audience to feel stupid. He wants them to feel he's the same as them, and that it could just as easily be them doing his job"*. The point is that he IS making them feel stupid and, what's more, making them PROUD to feel stupid. He's saying, *"Don't worry your dumb little working class heads about such things – they're not important to you anyway"*. And so indeed they're not.

So many people have absolutely no self-respect in the matter of intellect. They're quite happy to describe themselves as thick, but how many of them have you ever heard professing to be lousy in bed? It's not even a matter of modesty; there is undoubtedly a climate wherein a lack of knowledge, or at least a pretence of such, is not only acceptable, but desirable. Try using a word of more than four syllables and the chances are that you'll get a reaction something like *"Oh Gawd, been to bleedin' university, have we?"* Such an attitude is positively encouraged, even from the earliest school days. 'Bright' kids are referred to in a derogatory way by their schoolmates as 'brainboxes' and are ostracised or beaten up for coming top in class. Even the name 'Einstein' is used almost entirely pejoratively.

Quite obviously wide discrepancies do exist in the level of intelligence of human beings, and jealousy, however strongly denied, is a partial cause of anti-intellectual attitudes in school and throughout life. Nevertheless, the vast majority of the population is of roughly equal intelligence, and there is no reason, theoretically at least, why a working class person should stand any less chance of getting a place at a university than a middle or upper class person. But there's the rub. While the expectations of 'middle' or 'upper' class parents are that their children may indeed enter college and later one of the 'professions', 'working class' parents expect nothing more than that their children will leave school as soon as possible and start bringing home a wage from one of the local employers, just as previous generations of the family had done. In this context anti-intellectualism can be thought of as a kind of defence-mechanism designed to circumvent the almost inevitable disappointment to be experienced by the individual from the 'wrong' background who may entertain the thought that he or she can climb the ladder on educational merit alone. *"What's the point of trying to do well at school when I'm going to leave at sixteen anyway?"* Instead, simpler goals are encouraged. *"If I put in a few hours overtime and cut down on the fags and beer for a while, we'll be able to buy that Bendix the wife has had her eye on. Wouldn't mind changing the car soon, as well. Then there's the BMX for the lad."*

Now, what would happen if all these children with little education and low expectations had actually been encouraged to use their minds from an early age, instead of being encouraged to allow them to atrophy? They might even dare to hope for something more from life than unfulfilling drudgery, sweetened by a few quid spending money. Heaven forbid, they might begin to question the work ethic itself, which naturally has been promulgated by people whose closest contact with a factory is probably their ownership of shares in ICI.

It's hardly surprising that the massed unemployed are crying out to be given their jobs back, even though they hated them when they had them. After all, they had dignity then, didn't they, and their expectations did at least include a slow but steady rise in their all-important standard of living? Now they'll have to dump the video, the computer (on which they played games, of course) and the annual holiday in Spain.

Such are the poisonous fruits of the tree of greed and ignorance which has been carefully nurtured and which now flourishes in our spiritual and cultural junkyard. As we know, the tree of knowledge died a long time ago. Acquisitiveness is the name of the game. Acquisition of 'things', that is, not of knowledge and understanding, and the fulfilment and wisdom which may accompany them.

We are a nation of intellectual snobs of the very worst kind. Genuine stupidity is forgivable. What is not forgivable is a refusal to use intelligence.

"BRAZIL"

SIMON DWYER

**Britain is not a free country.
In this special investigation,
Rapid Eye tells you why.**

"MAN IS BORN FREE. THAT IS HIS NATURAL STATE. HIS GOD-GIVEN RIGHT. NOWHERE IS THIS TRADITION MORE DEEPLY ROOTED THAN IN BRITAIN. OFTEN, IN OUR LONG HISTORY, WE HAVE STOOD ALONE, FACING THE MIGHTIEST ARMIES OF THE WORLD TO DEFEND OUR FREEDOM, SOMETIMES AT TREMENDOUS SACRIFICE – NEVER DOUBTING THAT THE PRICE IS WORTH PAYING. FREEDOM HAS BEEN BOTH OUR STRENGTH AND OUR BATTLE-CRY. WE ARE A PROUD NATION OF INDIVIDUALS. WE FLOURISH UNDER FREEDOM."

Tory Election Broadcast (May 1987)

"And therefore never send to know for whom the bell tolls. It tolls for thee..."

John Donne (1610)

"From the age of restriction, from the age of secrets, from the age of lies – greetings!"

George Orwell (1948)

Ask people what it is that they most like about living in Britain and invariably one word will crop up: "Freedom".

Most of us like to think that we live in a society that allows a far greater degree of individual freedom than anywhere else. For all our faults, that element of freedom is what – we are told – makes Britain 'great'.

The idea is nonsense. Despite the Newspeak put about by Saatchi & Saatchi, British people are not free. We never have been. What is more, the few freedoms that we have traditionally enjoyed in the past are now being eroded at an alarming rate. Under a veil of State secrecy, cynical political manoeuvring, media control and socially engineered public apathy.

The infringements of the State into the private, personal life of the individual are usually subtle and – due to our conditioning – barely perceived as being intrusive at all. When each infringement is viewed singly, it is normally not considered something worth bothering about – a mild irritant that can be tolerated without too much hardship. It is often not until the individual strays far from the popular path of social acceptability that one is forced to turn and face reality, forced to realise that the sum total of minor irritants, bad laws and corrupt practices congeal to present a frightening whole. In reality, a labyrinth of social and legal diversions stand around the kernel of Individual Freedom which we are supposed to hold so dear.

As most people proudly consider themselves to be 'normal' members of some unspecified majority, the question of Freedom is not something thought worthy of serious popular consideration. For most, the rhetoric is enough. Attacks on one's civil liberties thus pass, for the most part, unchallenged. Sometimes, through a clever use of the news media, they are actually lauded, being presented to the public as pieces of legislation that will make our community a safer, more wholesome place to live. Such a sophisticated exercise of control only comes from a great deal of practice. In this area, few other nations are as experienced, or as expert, as Britain. And it is this ability – the ability to keep people oppressed yet contented, rather than to make people more free – that is what in reality has made Britain 'great'.

There has never been a full scale revolution in Britain, as through a deft mixture of camouflage and persuasion – peppered liberally with buzzwords such as 'Democracy', 'Justice' and 'Patriotism' – the control of the State has been presented as being universally benign and a practical necessity. Put simply, there has been nothing tangible enough to revolt against. In this century, the country has never had anything as openly dictatorial or corrupt as a Hitler, Stalin or Marcos to identify with the oppression and target such revolution against (though it is interesting to note that the only peacetime Prime Minister in British history to have had a serious assassination attempt made against them is Margaret Thatcher). In Britain, the State machine is more oily and silent running. Here, it is more often the case that the enemies of freedom are faceless bureaucrats, lethargic institutions and two-faced politicians.

In any society, the argument runs, this treasured concept of Personal Freedom must be hedged in with other considerations and compromises. Sacrifices must be made for 'the greater good'. Officially, 'freedom', (always somehow considered a concept rather than a practical reality) is simply a question of degree, and in a democratic society the *amount* of freedom an individual has is ostensibly dictated by the majority.

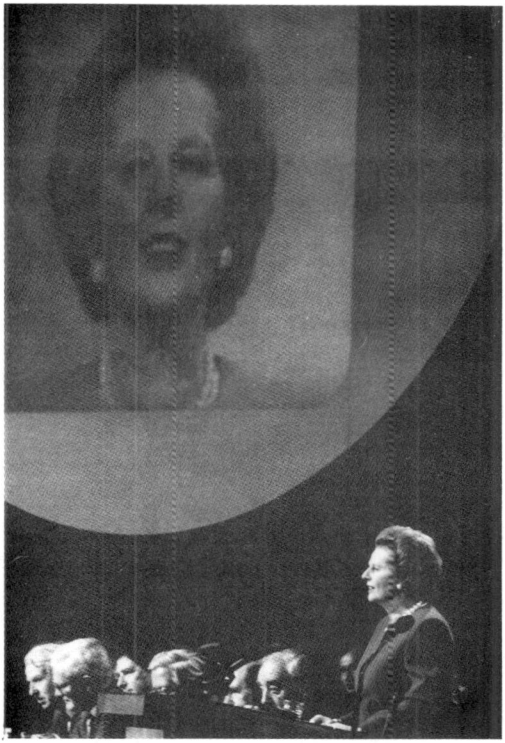

'Big Sister' (Photo: courtesy The Independent)

If an individual member of that majority is encouraged to remain ill-informed about the limitations of his freedom, he will be unable to extend those freedoms in his personal life. His choice will be controlled, as will its outcome. If he wishes to choose an entirely different path, he will discover that no such alternative exists within the framework of this society. Immediately, by not making his controlled choice, he will become a social outcast to some extent. He will be labelled as being selfish, subversive, criminal or insane.

In a country that has resisted radical change and quashed revolt, even the word 'revolution' (so loved in many countries), equates with violence, pseudo-intellectualism and oddness. Words which are the antithesis of Britain's self-image. Revolution, even if carried out peacefully in films, literature, or in the mind, (rather than on the streets) can be considered a treasonous act. And it is not surprising to find that treason remains the ultimate crime and the only one – in theory at least – that is still punishable by death.

In a society so blind to the everyday facts and bedazzled by the ancient myth, even to address the topic of Individual Freedom in a manner such as this is to invite criticism and misinterpretation. Yet it is these potential critics, who in all probability claim to be concerned about Law & Order, Freedom & Justice, Peace & Happiness etc., who should be those people who are most interested in ensuring that the people of this 'great' country are governed by just laws which are implemented fairly within a humane society. A society that pays more than lip service to the ideals of democracy, equality and personal liberty which it purports to champion.

In the 'alternative' culture it's fashionable, even essential, to claim that the 'system' is so unworthy it isn't worth thinking about; that all politicians are ego maniacs; that the police are universally corrupt and Fascistic; that all journalists are liars and so on, ad nauseam. Such criticisms are usually carried out by people who've never printed their own magazine, never made a subversive video, never done anything, in fact, but consume the products that the State produces and condones. Acned youngsters with £30 haircuts are keen to fall, lemming-like, into generation gaps created by a succession of stupid young (and not-so-young) men in leather jackets, whose bounty from this bottomless mine (gold records, coke limitless penicillin) is also the main motivation for their sanitised form of revolt. It is no accident that rock'n'roll is now being embraced by Russia, China, and other societies which operate a high level of control. Contrary to the myths put about by numerous dullards in the 1960s and late 1970s, although music can be used to express and refine certain attitudes, as a revolutionary weapon, or information channel, it is usually about as much use as a lightbulb to Stevie Wonder.

In social terms, the pop placebo is a good method of keeping society visibly healthy, transmuting disenchantment and real social disquiet from the Problematic to the Profitable. State control and rock and roll are run by clever men. Feelings of alienation caused by repression are absorbed and turned into escapism in the land of Entertainment. In the Coke generation social reality is made to look boring. Information on how things really are is made to look stupendously boring. Here though, we intend to present a pellet of information – slug death to the hedonist – which makes no apologies for being chockablock with dull fact. Only by using the dialect of 'Control', the language of the Law and the hard currency of Information, can we hope to present the current situation as it really is. Or at least, go as far as official records, *Hansard, The Times*, the BBC etc. *admit* that it really is. The facts speak for themselves. This is how we live in this free country in the late 1980s.

Anyone who doubts any of the incidents and facts reported here is encouraged to check them out independently. In so doing they will find that this informational collage represents but a drop in the ocean. All we can hope to do here is convey a sense of the whole, horrible truth.

Although the excessive levels of control which presently operate cannot be laid at the door of any single political party; although the 'system' is obviously flawed in that it apparently lacks the capacity to successfully reconcile the rights of the individual with the supposed wishes of the majority, Britain's current crisis (and I use the word advisedly), is partly brought about by the attitude of the present government. A government which reflects the age in which we live. An age in which 'freedom' has been edited, limited and re-defined to mean the 'freedom' individuals and companies now have to compete more ruthlessly with others on a purely economic level.

To be fair, we do have certain new rights under this present regime. The right to own a Telecom phone all of our own, but not the right to express feelings that detract from the dominant ideology of the State. The right to buy council houses, but not the right to expect employment. The right to buy a share in British Airways, but not the right to be educated properly by the State...

These are uncertain times. Brought about indirectly by the social and economic failures of the country since the war. In such a climate, many unimaginative people in the political arena have been persuaded to abandon even the pretence of consensus politics, consultation and moderation. So dispensing with the need for debate, freedom of information, and the recognition of equality that goes hand in hand with such old-fashioned ideas.

It seems that the British people have been largely conned into believing that the sins of their fathers – the relative liberalism and over-indulgences of the '50s and '60s – have been visited upon them, the children. The blackouts, shortages and strikes of the '70s and the mass unemployment, riots and new diseases of the '80s have strengthened their belief that we must have 'strong' leaders, and restrictive laws, in order to fight such menaces and mount some yellowbrick road to 'recovery'. The climate is one of guilt and retribution. Dr. Benway's medicine must be gulped down if you want to keep that job, that mortgage, that veneer of success. So we, the compliant majority, allow ourselves to be ruled by a tiny dictatorial minority with an iron fist in a velvet glove. The boots may be Gucci, but they're stamping on our faces just the same.

In this silent, submissive age, it seems that public resistance decreases as oppression increases. Our tolerance goes up and up in a never-ending spiral. So with each bullet fired from a police gun, less uproar is heard. Because the more bullets fired, the more restrictive laws passed, the more frequent the acts of repression – the older the news, the less interested and concerned we become. And our training, highlighted by our age-old acceptance of such ridiculous things as the Sunday Trading and Licencing Laws, has stood us in good stead for the current swing against libertarianism and attacks on civil rights.

In the face of an increasingly polarised political left and right wing, the fundamentally civilised, moderate and caring quality of life desired by the silent majority looks more and more impossible to attain. While all the time the organisational machinery of the State rumbles on like a Chieftain tank, oblivious to any instruction that does not emanate from the Downing Street. This would not be so if Britain had adequate safeguards as enjoyed by other countries.

A BILL OF RIGHTS IN A STATE OF WRONGS

In 1215 King John signed Magna Carta, a charter which gave the individual Englishman the right to fair trial and protection from arbitrary arrest and imprisonment. Thus the concept of 'individual freedom' was lodged into the psyche of what history has shown, in some ways, to have been the most advanced social structure on the planet. Ever since, as was pointed out earlier, this vague idea of Freedom has swilled around the neurological backwaters of the collective British unconscious mind to be used and abused at will throughout subsequent generations.

Thus Nazi Germany was fought as it was seen as being against all that Britain said she stood for. The Nazis were anti-freedom, anti-democracy and anti-Christ. Co-incidentally, just the same set of reasons given later for the vilification of our allies against Nazis, the U.S.S.R. And thus, the General Election campaign of 1979 – a full 764 years after Magna Carta - this ancient freedom factor, by now almost akin to an Arthurian legend, was invoked by the black magical advertising executives employed by the Tories (just as it was in 1983 and 1987).

Wantonly wrapping herself in the Union Jack, a latterday Boudiccea born very much from the 'Jerusalem' school of English thought, stood on a platform of 'Personal Freedom' and pitted herself against what was depicted as being the Socialist's platform of 'state interference'. She promised to set people free with jobs (Arbeit macht Frei) and *"To make Britain strong enough to give the individual citizen more freedom of choice."* Appealing to an almost genetic instinct (like Franco and Hitler), Margaret Thatcher was elected as Prime Minister on the 3rd May 1979.

Britain, we were told, was about to be set free.

Not surprisingly, the politicians lied. The reality has not matched the pre-election rhetoric. Since the Thatcher administration came to power, voted in by 11 million of the 56,488,000 people who live in the U.K., the practice of increasing the individual's personal freedom has included some apparently incongruous actions, which we will investigate here.

What Thatcher did not make clear was that her idea of 'freedom' was highly selective, and in creating the greater economic freedoms of the rich to get richer, a certain amount of morality had to be dispensed with. For when market forces are unleashed, there will inevitably be fall-out. The 'losers' in this new system who cannot compete will no longer be looked after by society. Welfare rights take a backseat, so social conflict, class polarisation, dissatisfaction and even crime are encouraged. So a strong disciplinary regime is an accompanying necessity when one enters the era of the Free Market. The State intervenes less in financial matters (as people are encouraged to sink or swim on their own) but interferes far more in other areas.

Since the Tories came to power, Britain has witnessed the introduction of random police roadblocks, strip searches in women's prisons, a removal of the right to be tried by jury, bans on the right to protest, restrictions on Trade Union Membership and their rights to strike and picket, the abolition of democratically elected local councils, a rise in censorship, a plethora of new laws involving the media, an enormous increase in the powers of the police and courts, Customs and Excise, and officers of the DHSS to search and snoop without warrants and to incarcerate in prisons and hospitals without an individual being found guilty of any crime or social defect.

The continued calls for an adequate Freedom of Information Act, genuine reform of the Official Secrets Act, and demands for a Bill of Rights have all been largely ignored, or not properly implemented.

As one will see, the list is long. It could be far longer. One safeguard against this unpleasant trend continuing would be constitutional. *Britain does not have a written Constitution that protects or recognises the rights of the Individual.*

A Constitutional Bill of Rights is a permanent charter that, in many countries, is in itself more important than any transient law or passing government. Its sole purpose is to recognise the Individual and his or her rights as a human being, and to protect those basic rights from the misuse of State power, be it from extremist left or rightwing governments, their police and courts, or the Monarchy. Britain does not, and never has had a Bill of Rights. In this sense, in the free world, we're rare. (Even countries who didn't enjoy a written constitution while under British rule have drawn them up since independence. The last Commonwealth country to do so was Canada in 1982. If Australia becomes a Republic, as seems likely, it is almost certain that their first constitutional changes will be connected to drawing-up a Bill of Rights. In freeing themselves from what many states formerly in the Empire think of as the British yoke of oppression, it is natural for new, independent countries to base their constitution on something that has been denied them for centuries. The British people, unfortunately, cannot benefit in this way as we are one of the relatively few countries not to be a Republic. What was once the genuine oppression of the British Empire, is now confined to being the British constitutional oppression of the British people. We are, as British subjects, punished by our ancestor's history).

A Human Rights Bill for the British people was introduced by Sir Edward Gardner QC in 1986. It went through the Lords, helped by Lords Scarman, Hailsham and Broxbourne. Although a hardcore of reactionary MPs and civil servants opposed it, the Government did not wish to be seen to officially oppose the Bill. Strangely, however, they did not officially support it either. It was also arranged through Parliamentary processes for the vote on the Bill to be made late on a Friday afternoon, (30th January 1987). A strategic time, when most MPs will already be on their way back to their far-flung constituencies after the weeks usual Parliamentary business. It is indicative of the Government's true attitude, and of all political parties' set of priorities, that (unlike when an 'important' Bill is voted on) no party whips were in operation. MPs were thus freed by their parties not to attend the House of Commons when the Bill was read.

Although, for the first time, politicians were given an opportunity to make British people more tangibly, legally 'free' than ever before in their history, only a paltry 20% of them turned up to vote. Some of those who did appear wanted to vote against it, but it didn't matter. With such a low turn-out a Bill cannot even get through to its Second Reading, necessary to make it law. Had the Bill gone to the Second Reading stage, it's widely thought that the government would have blocked it anyway, but that's hardly the point. Although millions of British servicemen over the years have died for an abstract sense of Freedom, when the real crunch came, politicians simply couldn't be bothered.

So as things stand, British people are open to abuses of power that would be illegal in countries such as, for example, France or the U.S.A. We are prey to practically anything dreamt up by puritanical governments, tyrannical local authorities and senile judges.

Our only recourse, as Europeans, is to take any complaint we have to the European Court of Human Rights in Strasbourg, an astronomically expensive and time-consuming process.

Contrary to popular opinion, the European Court itself has shown recently that it is less ready to risk offending individual member governments by applying the European Convention of Human Rights and finding for the complainant, particularly in the case of Britain who is *the most persistent offender in the European Court;* the country which already has the least 'European' outlook; and is the second largest financial contributor to the community budget.

So, as things stand, any British Government riding in on the blatantly unfair electoral system which we operate, awards itself a 'mandate' from the entire population, so it can do *whatever* it likes. Providing they have a large enough majority in Parliament, there is *nothing* to stop them passing any weird laws they wish. Indeed, it is because the present government has been so liberal in its interpretation of the people's mandate that so many laws which are alien to the British way of life have been swept through.

Of course, not all governmental actions are intrusive to Personal Liberties, but a written Bill of Rights would provide us with a catch-all, basic set of rights that would stop all manner of unjust things happening to millions of people throughout this country. That such a Bill would be popular with the British people is not open to question, so why do politicians continue to ignore the demands for such a piece of legislation? What, exactly, are they scared of?

FREEDOM OF SPEECH

The Oxford English Dictionary is surprisingly sparing and unhelpful when it comes to defining the word 'Censorship' reflecting the belief that censorship and control in Britain is not a topic to be discussed. A censor, it seems, is either a Roman who collects data or, it says, a present-day official whose duty it is to ensure that *"no books, journals, plays etc. contain anything immoral, heretical or offensive to the government."*

In a sophisticated, well-educated, supposedly 'free' society, the needs for censorship are, to say the least, somewhat dubious. But nevertheless, censorship remains rife in Britain, and is now on the increase.

'Control' is self-perpetuating because even when the practical need to exercise control has disappeared or become questionable, the desires to assume control, and to be controlled, remain. So basically any form of Authority, however out-moded, useless or corrupt it may be is bound to protect itself. Protect its authority. Otherwise it would, by definition, cease to exist. Censorship is in this sense just a bureaucratic version of the survival instinct.

As with all forms of bureaucracy, it is snowed in with confusion, over-justification and triplicated humbug. The reasoning behind it is said to be complex. In fact, censorship is quite easy to understand. It is simply the policy of cutting-off the individual's right to express certain opinions, ideas, desires, concepts and impulses which the State believe may have the capacity to undermine its authority. Its power. (And it seems in Britain that if power is wonderful, absolute power is absolutely wonderful.)

The key word of the censorious is *information.* If you carefully restrict and regulate its collection, presentation and dissemination, the edited and corrupted information which you implant into the Information Exchange systems of the mass media becomes the only currency. In a country absolutely obsessed with its media, it becomes truth. The Truth.

Remember. Information is power. The sharing of information is the sharing of power.

In this light, the concept of censorship in a free, democratic society just does not stand up to scrutiny. The practice of censorship in an unfree, undemocratic society is, however, absolutely essential. In a country like Britain, censorship may be less obtrusive than in more blatantly dictatorial nations (partly because we find the idea of it so natural and acceptable), but make no mistake, our system requires the use of censorship if it is to continue to exist in its present form. It is a practical necessity. If this were not the case our government, supposedly keen to cut costs, reduce red tape and unclog our courts would have abolished the costly and cumbersome legal systems that surround censorship long ago. Surely?

Isolation, dissatisfaction and crime are encouraged if an individual, or minority group of individuals, are denied access to the rights enjoyed by the majority. It is an essential basic freedom for each individual to be allowed to gain access to information and education, entertainment and stimulation, in any advanced society that seriously claims to be 'free'. In such societies, people have a right to read published works that may enrich their existence in some way, and the right to form educated opinions based on such works, plus the right to express those opinions within a lifestyle that suits them. Equally, people who attach themselves to groups of other people who happen to feel the same way about life as they do, should be able in a free country to find out about the history, culture and shared experience of such a group.

At this point, one should forget the newspeak definition of 'freedom' and put aside petty prejudices. Freedom could, more fairly, be defined as a simple recognition of people's rights, including, most importantly, their right to be wrong. *Their right to choose*. This is the most unpalatable definition of freedom that governments can hear, for obvious reasons.

The fact that various 'minority groups' interpretations of life do not conform to those held by the majority should not affect such basic human rights. Specifically, the right to seek happiness. Providing their opinions and actions do not deny equal rights to other individuals, it is only natural justice that is being served if they are left to go their own way.

In Britain, a populist theologically dubious set of 'Christian' morals and customs are lodged at the heart of the State system (even though only about 4% of the population are Christian church-goers on a regular basis and do, themselves, form a minority). These largely corrupted pseudo-Christian values, as interpreted by the State, allow for any level of interference to be applied to the personal, usually private lives of individuals who choose not to conform to the narrow moral codes of the assumed majority.

The most obvious consistent target of the 'moral' majority are homosexuals; particularly, in a male orientated society, homosexual men. Despite their relatively new found legality (in 1967) and general social acceptability, the British State, it seems, can t quite bring itself to recognise their rights of expression, *or the rights of any perceived 'minority group'.*

Why else would police raid the offices of Toshanex Ltd., and seize gay books and titles such as William Burrough's *'Junky'*, *'Fear and Loathing in Las Vegas'* by Hunter Thompson, and works by writers such as Tom Wolfe which are in current use as University texts?

In a quite recent series of raids, bookshops in several other locations have been raided in similarly heavy-handed fashion. As a result, many people have been criminalised and brought to trial for a number of offences – though inconsistencies often appear between one part of the country and the next. For example, magistrates in Nottingham ruled that some titles brought before them by police in court were not obscene, while, at the same time, police in London continued to hold copies of the same books from raids in the Metropolitan area under the Obscene Publications Act.

Titles published by such reputable firms as Pan, Corgi, Penguin, Granada and the Harvard University Press were included in the seizures, but it is interesting to note that not one of these established publishers was actually brought to trial. Smaller companies, who could not afford teams of solicitors and whose prosecution would not attract the same amount of publicity – such as Airlift Books – were, however, charged with offenses such as "having obscene articles for publication for gain". They were also charged with "conspiracy to incite offences" under the Misuse of Drugs

Act, for stocking such books as the aforementioned Burroughs number. All this, despite the fact that many of the books involved were openly on sale in High Street shops all over the country and the information relating to drugs therein could be found in any public reference library. The tenuous drugs connection was, in any case, thought by many to be a cover for the raids' real target – erotic literature (gasp).

As in many other countries, access to such literature in Britain is limited to people over a certain age. In this country, people are free to legally indulge in sex at 16 but not allowed to read about sex until they are 18. Unlike other European countries, Britain licenses Sex Shops. Unlike many other European countries, it also stringently censors all the material available in such shops to the legally consenting adult customers who wish to buy such books. The annual license fee for each shop selling primarily sexually-related literature is £12,500 per year. (Despite police claims that a third of traffic accidents and nearly 50% of violent crime involves people who are drunk, this figure compares with the £10 average sum needed to licence a pub.) Many feel that the exorbitant licence fee required from Sex Shops amounts to unofficial prohibition of all sexually related material, despite the fact that such material has already been heavily censored, and is only available to adult customers.

In June, 1984, 120 titles heading for the Feminist Book Fair were intercepted by H.M. Customs & Excise Officers. Books worth more than £1,600 on their way to the Essentially Gay Mailorder Company were also seized, and the company was forced to close. A parcel of books ordered by a general book shop, Balham Food & Book Co-Op was also stopped. Two thousand books were taken from Gay's The Word book store, and eight of the company's directors were brought to trial. Lavender Menace Ltd. of Edinburgh had two shipments of gay books seized, and London's Peace bookshop, Housman's, have also had material confiscated. Indeed, the list goes on and on. Britain's *only* licensed Gay bookshop – Zipper – has also been raided

No complaints about the books or the bookshops concerned in this series of raids had been received from members of the public. No figures are published giving the numbers of police and customs men involved in the operations, or giving details of how much court time and public money has been used on such cases over the past few years. Whatever the figures, they must be considered against a back-drop of supposedly spiralling street crime, over-worked courts and complaints from both the Police and Customs that they are seriously under-manned, particularly, for example, in the fight against the importation of hard drugs, which all claim to be their highest priority.

In October 1986, a month in which new figures showed a further increase in the numbers of heroin addicts, police busied themselves with raiding the offices of *Skin Two* magazine, and also confiscated copies of the latest edition from news-stands around the capital. Despite the fact that the magazine is primarily fashion-orientated and has little in the way of erotic content, the Metropolitan Police still decided it worthy of persecution due to its S/M overtones (Fashion photos of women modelling high heels, leather skirts etc. Compare this to the situation that exists in Amsterdam, where a local S/M on-premises sex club is a respected member of the city's Chamber of Commerce.)

It is interesting to note that since the current Tory administration has come to power, the law used to try many bookshops is not the Obscene Publications Act, but the more obscure Customs Consolidation Act, a law which came into force 111 years ago. Under this law – unlike the Obscene Publications Act – *No book can be defended in court on the basis of its artistic or literary merit.* (Very convenient). Some book companies have been charged with the more usual Obscene Publications Act. This law makes it an offence to produce any book which "may deprave or corrupt" an ordinary member of society. A charge that is in itself almost impossible to defend oneself against. In an extraordinary move, however, some booksellers have recently been charged and found guilty under this law for the publication of books *which contained no violent or erotic content whatsoever*, meaning, in effect, that the scope of the Obscene Publications Act has been widened by the Government and Courts, giving the police even greater opportunities for arrest, without consultation with the public or in the Houses of Parliament.

Many feel that the way in which the present government has evoked ancient laws and encouraged the courts to re-interpret and increase the scope of others is typical of the unpublicised, underhand way in which people's individual freedoms are being eroded without debate, publicity, or the chance of protest.

Other brand new laws inhibiting personal freedoms have, however, come in for a good deal of public criticism, despite efforts to confuse or distract the issues by the government's publicity machine at the time of such laws being pushed through Parliament.

Under the notorious Video Recordings Act, all films put onto video now have to be re-submitted to the British Board of Film Censors for new classification. (Meaning that each movie shown at a cinema and also available on video has to be classified twice) It costs an average of £500 to have a film certificated by the censors. Films included in the new censorship net are Donald Duck cartoons. Hundreds of bona fide video rental shops have been vetted by the police. Thousands of tapes have been confiscated and not returned to their owners, including many titles which have B.B.F.C. 'X' or '18' certificates and which have been screened openly to cinema audiences.

At this juncture, it should be remembered that despite unsubstantiated claims to the contrary (claims which find an unquestioning outlet in both the popular press and pseudo-'feminist' women's magazines), *no* scientific evidence of a reputable nature has been produced to link acts of a violent sexual nature to video viewing. The Act itself was based on pseudo-research into children's viewing habits, and the effect of video watching on the 'family unit' (commissioned independently by an extremist Christian organisation), which has since been proved to have been fabricated and exaggerated. Research that is so flawed and biased, that even the Catholic and Methodist churches have publicity dissociated themselves from it. Despite this fact, the Bill, which was lobbied for by The Festival of Light (who acted under a pseudonym at the time) remains law which directly affects everyone who uses a VCR (over half of all households in Britain) and inconveniences and wrongly criminalises many who seek to earn an honest living in the business of renting and manufacturing quite ordinary videos.

Although a small number of criminals have claimed in mitigation to have been influenced by their viewing habits, these are in a tiny minority – a minority that has received excessive amounts of publicity from newspapers keen to sensationalise the issue and support the powerful and vociferous rightwing minority. It is no surprise to find that the papers which have given the most coverage to this topic are *The Sun* and *The Sunday Times*. As a result (as Dr Terence DuQuesne pointed out in a previous issue of *Rapid Eye Movement* magazine), a climate now exists in Britain where one is given a clearly defined choice between being seen to support "The Family/Law & Order/Godliness" *or* being seen to support "Moral breakdown/Crime/Sin". As in most totalitarian regimes, no middleground, no grey area of debate is perceived. The choice, as always, is limited. Not surprisingly, under this blackmail and pressure, most people in public positions or power, such as MPs, despite their personal reservations, want to be seen as being on the side of 'good', and allow such new pieces of legislation to pass unchallenged. Furthermore, to actively introduce legislation that seeks to repeal old laws, such as the Obscene Publications Act or Customs Consolidation Act, would be to stand up and be seen as being pro-pornography.

As a result, Britain today goes against the liberalising trends of almost every other civilised nation on Earth.

For example, many 'Catholic countries' around the world, who are often condescendingly portrayed in Britain as being strict and somehow old-fashioned, have *no* film or video censorship. Indeed, in Western Europe, the U.K. and Ireland are the only countries to have film censorship. In South America, post-junta Argentina moved into the 20th century when it abolished *all* its film censorship laws in 1984, just at the time when rejoicing, victorious, happy-and-glorious, 'free' Britain tightened its own laws and increased the powers of the courts and police to implement them. Italy, home of Vatican City, has several pornographic TV channels. Holland allows any form of sexual behaviour between adults to be shown in books and videos – but has a lower rate of violent crime than the U.K. Japan, which has by far the most violent TV and Cinema in the world, has only 1.9 robberies with violence per 100,000 inhabitants each year. The U.K. has more than *twenty times* as many violent crimes per capita and nearly *eighty times* as many rapes. (Co-incidently, since the new censorship laws have been introduced, rape has increased faster than any other type of crime.)

In 1975, West Germany relaxed all its censorship laws. Since then, crimes of rape and child abuse have declined, against an increase in all other types of serious crime.

We are told by the Government that, despite such inconvenient (under publicised) statistics, the general population actually *want* more censorship. This quite clearly is not the case.

In a poll carried out by the Opinion Research Centre into people's views on what is shown on television, it was discovered that only 23% wanted 'Sex and Blasphemy' banned from the T.V. Only 18% wanted nudity banned. 66% said that they thought acts of sex on the screen acceptable and 57% said that blasphemy should be allowed on television.

Opinion polls such as this – and the results of this poll broadly correspond with others – do not get cited by politicians keen to mould public opinion in their direction.

As other countries (even Russia) question the reasoning and true motives behind the censorship lobbies and increasingly challenge the right of the State to interfere in the private lives of citizens, Britain – the most 'free' country in the world – stands alongside a small number of countries like the Mullah's Iran and Lee Quan Yews' Singapore in reversing this trend, despite the wishes of the silent majority of its people.

One of the main advocates for censorship is Mary Whitehouse, self-appointed mouthpiece and founder of the grandly titled 'National Viewers & Listeners Association'. Whitehouse not only supports the right of the State to interfere in an individual's personal sexual and cultural tastes, but is also of the opinion that the TV news should be censored. (She has cited, as an example to defend her position, the widespread riots of 1984/86, which she said were the direct result of South African rioting being shown on ITN and which, she says, should not therefore have been screened).

Of course, the news is already censored in Britain. A classic example sprang from the Law Lord's ruling made on the 30th July 1987, which effectively forbade journalists from reporting on the Peter Wright case. The following morning's BBC radio news bulletin was curtailed with the words, "we are unable to report what was said next under the new restrictions..." For journalists, who a few months earlier had winced when having to file similar-sounding reports from South Africa during the state of emergency, it was a sorry time. The editor of *The Sunday Times*, Andrew Neil, said: *"We live in a totalitarian state. It's like living in Russia."*

In December 1987 the Government took out an injunction banning the BBC from airing the Radio 4 programme *'My Country: Right or Wrong'*. A programme which threatened to expose the way in which State Secret Service agents operated outside the jurisdiction of Parliament. The action also forbade journalists and broadcasters from referring in any way to the names of people whom they knew were – or had been – involved in the Security Services.

The Government's bizarre actions had some severe and widespread implications, as well as some revealingly silly ones. For example, the day after the injunction, BBC Radio Essex was barred from mentioning the names Wright, Philby, Burgess or McLean in a trailer to an interview with the star of a new musical playing in Basildon called *'Philby, Burgess and McLean: The Musical'*. Bemused listeners were instead treated to a selection of records. (If the Law was made to look an ass, the government was made to look a bunch of arseholes).

Such a public banning order is rarely resorted to, however. Usually it is sufficient for the government of the day to censor items behind the scenes.

When the BBC planned to screen a programme on N. Ireland, *'At the Edge of the Union'* in 1985, Leon Brittan, then Home Secretary, wrote to the BBC's Governors asking them not to show the programme. Brittan latter claimed that his Government were not censoring the BBC, as he had simply written his letter as "an interested citizen". The fact that as Home Secretary he had the power to ban programmes and also fix the BBC's licence fee, had nothing to do with it at all. (The film was banned.)

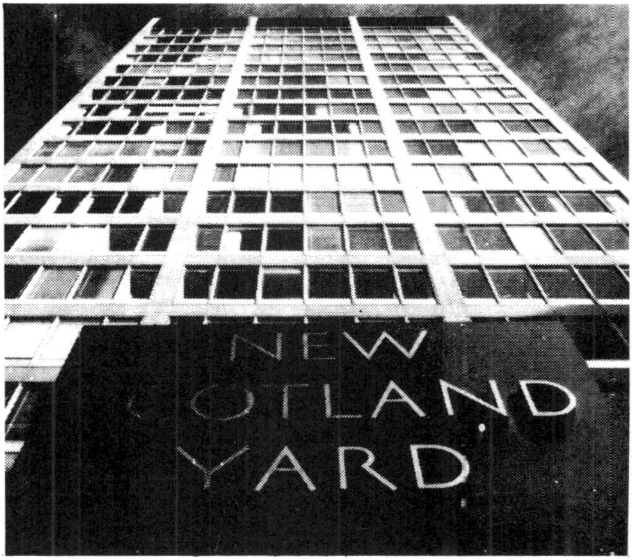

The Ministry of Love

Early in 1988, three unarmed terrorists were shot repeatedly by an SAS team in Gibraltar. Despite Government pressure, the IBA refused to ban the commercial TV programme *'Death on the Rock'*, which revealed some unsavoury facts about the killings (the Government had already refused to co-operate with an investigation by the Amnesty International organisation into the killings). A few days later, the government introduced a new tier of TV censors (the third tier in all), Thatcher herself chose as the new body's Chairman her avid admirer Sir William Rees-Mogg, former editor of the low circulation *Times* newspaper and a well-documented campaigner for censorship. (If Rees-Mogg was appointed, as the government suggested, to reflect public taste, why was *he* appointed at all? *The Times* was, under his editorship, one of the smallest-selling national daily papers in the country. If one really wanted someone to reflect true public taste, should Thatcher not have appointed the editor of *The Sun* or *The Mirror*, easily the most popular papers in the nation?)

The National Viewers' and Listeners Association, whom one would think would be interested in the viewer's right to know, did not comment on the Law Lords ruling, or the later injunctions and threats: Whitehouse and co. were, in fact, more concerned with counting the number of times the word "bloody" was used in Billy Connolly's stage act.

An avid admirer of this loathsome Whitehouse woman is Winston Churchill MP. His Obscene Publications (Amendment) Bill proposes to give the Director of Public Prosecutions more powers to prosecute TV producers under the all-embracing accusation of 'obscenity'. Programme controllers and directors, if found guilty of airing a programme that offends the likes of Whitehouse and Churchill in some way, could find themselves in prison for three years in Thatcher's "new, free Britain".

As film director Michael Winner points out, under the wide implications of the Bill it could be an offence to transmit a production of, for example, Shakespeare's *'King Lear'*; the censors argument being that, in showing Gloucester getting his eye gauged out, the programme makers would be inciting viewers to do the same. (What, indeed then, about *'Oedipus Rex'*, or a cinematic version of the crucifixion?)

The general impression given by the censors as they seek to increase their control is that things are "constantly getting worse". We are told, for example, that violence on TV is more frequent and brutal than ever before, but, again, the *facts* simply don't support the censorship lobby's argument. In a lengthy report carried out by Dr Guy Cumberbatch and his team at Aston University in 1987 into TV violence, it was found that there has, in reality, been a steady *decrease* in violence on British television in recent years. The doctor's findings, based on 2,078 hours of monitored TV output, was totally ignored by Churchill. Should his ideas solidify into law – and it's almost a certainty that in some shape or form, they will – then adventurous drama programmes such as *'Edge of Darkness'*, *'The Singing Detective'*, or *'I, Claudius'* will become a thing of the past.

Although Churchill's Personal Publicity Bill, at time of writing, is not yet law, the previously-mentioned Video Recording Act is, having come into force amid deafening silence in September 1985. Among other things, this new law made it an offence for a person to have in their possession a video that has not received classification from the British Board of Film Censors. Clause 2 of the Act does, however, allow for some types of video to be exempt from this necessity. The Minister of State for the Home Office, defending the new legislation in the House of Lords, admitted that the exact definitions of what videos are exempt and what videos are not exempt is open to testing in the courts. So, if the police stop a citizen in the street, find an uncertificated video in his or her pocket (a Cabaret Voltaire scratch tape, or a copy of Peter Shaffer's *'Equus'* starring Richard Burton, for example), and decide that it is not exempt, then that citizen can be charged. One's only protection, in the words of the Home Office, is if that person "convinces the court that they *thought* it was an exempt video".

This system goes against the traditional belief that, in British courts, a person that is charged with an offence *has to be proven guilty by the prosecution.* In this instance, the onus of proof is put upon the person the police have accused.

It is also a generally accepted fact of British justice that ignorance of the law is no defence, so one could imagine severe practical difficulties if one were faced with the task of defending oneself in court on the basis of ignorance of the law. Another defence may be to say that the video was not for supply to anyone else, though again, in practice this defence may be impossible to prove, particularly if one has video-copying facilities at home. It also leaves any aspiring video artist facing a heavy fine or even imprisonment.

New laws such as this and suggested amendments to established laws show how attitudes are becoming more restrictive and reactionary, rather than more forward-thinking and reformatory. For example, the aforementioned Obscene Publications Act 1959 has been tampered with on several occasions over the years, but no real changes have been implemented which make the law more obviously fair in the context of a free society.

The government has still *not* implemented the recommendations of its own committee on the Obscenity Laws. (Not surprising really, as the Williams Committee recommended that these laws be relaxed).

The latest change, mooted in a Private Member's Bill by Tory MP Gerald Howarth, ostensibly attempts to make the Obscenity Law more up-to-date and clearly understood. On hearing this, one is supposed to be pleased to hear that someone in Parliament is taking the trouble to alter bad laws. But on closer inspection, one finds that the suggested changes to the wording of the law are not intended to remove the ambiguous and subjective criteria of "...to deprave or corrupt...", but to add to that anachronism the words "and/or grossly offend a reasonable person." So the new Bill doesn't even claim to offer a new, fairer test for obscenity, but merely adds yet another subjective test to the old one, thus *increasing* the scope for prejudice and making prosecution of anyone dragged before a judge even more of a foregone conclusion.

The practical reasons for the Bill's introduction are that, despite the hardline attitudes shown by the current government and the police, some magistrates (such as those in Nottingham mentioned earlier) have thrown police cases against some booksellers and video shops out of court saying that the material confiscated was clearly not obscene and the police had been wasting public money in bringing such cases before them. Howarth's new proposals therefore imply that because some independently-minded magistrates and jurors had chosen to return some fairly ordinary magazines to their owners – as they have a right to do – there must be something wrong with them, and wrong with the law that allows them this freedom. The logic is that if the jurors go against the wishes of the police, the law must be made more restrictive, thus making it more difficult for courts to acquit those who stand accused. Howarth knows that people can, after all, be 'offended' by almost anything, particularly the type of people the Tory government would describe as 'reasonable'.

Howarth, an unknown backbencher, has received more personal publicity due to his Bill than at any time since the BBC accused him of being a member of a secret right-wing 'militant' organisation operating from within the Conservative Party. So the Bill is good for his career. He wouldn't admit to it though, but he does blunder into defending tighter controls on individual freedom by saying that such things are "good for police morale", as if that is justification enough. Both he, and the Police, condescendingly say that the new broader wording of the law would make it easier for the public to understand. Indeed, London's senior Vice Squad officer said *"the word 'offensive' may be more easily interpreted by the man on the Clapham omnibus"*. Ordinary people, the people Howarth and the Police exist to serve, are apparently incapable of interpreting such words as "corrupt", or at least unable to do so in a way which pleases rightwing politicians and policemen.

The British Board of Film Censors are far from being such ordinary people. According to their own leaflet explaining their reasons for existence, they claim to be able to judge the moral standards of other people and they have the power to exclude from the public exhibition anything likely to "impair these moral standards" (the word 'moral' is always followed by the word 'standards', inferring that a person who has different moral attitudes and customs must have *lower standards)*.

The Kinematograph Manufacturer's Association makes much of the Board's supposed independence, though in fact Members cannot be appointed to the Censorship Board without lengthy prior consultation with the Government's Home Office.

The BBFC was founded in 1912, with one of its first stated aims being "to protect the Cinema from local authority interference". In this area, they seem to have failed miserably.

In reality, despite the propaganda put about by the Board, it is the personal peculiarities and whims of local councillors that account for the nation's cinematic viewing habits. The ultimate power of veto lies with them, at local authority level, and councillors often show a keenness to exercise that power. For example, the progressive members of

Beaconsfield Urban Council banned The Beatles' *'Yellow Submarine'* because, in their own words, "it was pure unadulterated rubbish." Never mind that the British Board of Film Censors had already given it a certificate that allowed it to be shown to children. (So much for the Board "protecting the Cinema from local authority interference".)

Although the BBFC's certificates are often disregarded by local councils when the Board passes a film and the council wants to ban it, as in the above case; the majority of councillors are willing to accept the BBFC's opinions without question when the Board simply refuse to give a film any certificate at all.

Normally, when the Board does not give a film a certificate, the film's distributors shelve the picture and it simply doesn't make it to general release, regardless of the work and money put into its making. When the Board refused to give any certificate to a film version of James Joyces's *'Ulysses'*, however, Columbia Pictures took the usual step of applying directly to individual authorities for permission to screen the film in their areas. In the event, 54 councils refused them permission and 27 let it be shown.

At this point one wonders if local councillors and policemen are the best people to judge works of art? Police raiding the Open Space Theatre Club in London, to seize Andy Warhols film *'Flesh'*, admitted to some startled customers that they didn't even know who Warhol was. Similarly, in the case of *'Ulysses'*, Councillor Beardsworth of Blackburn admitted that he hadn't read Joyce, *or* viewed the film, but he'd heard it was "so obscene" that the film was banned in his area anyway. Alderman Michael Pettitt of Southampton proved to be rather more well-read, having brought a copy of *'Ulysses'* 30 years earlier. "I believe that without the obscenity and blasphemy, a film version of *'Ulysses'* would not be worth seeing" he said. No help. Without even viewing the film, he and his council banned it.

This power of film censorship in the hands of local authorities is clearly not only unlikely to be of benefit to the flagging British Film Industry – it is also legally dubious.

In a flagrant abuse of the spirit of the law, local councillors and the courts have connived to re-interpret The Cinema Acts to give councils more power over what people can – and more importantly cannot – see in a cinema.

The Cinema Acts were passed only to ensure that cinema *buildings* were safe places for audiences, giving councils the right to inspect and licence cinemas on the grounds of public safety. However, by interpreting the Acts in a way which even the Home Office admits Parliament never intended, the courts have been able to uphold in law the validity of the censoring powers which local council despots have usurped unto themselves, through an imaginative interpretation of the law. Now it is unquestioned universal practice for local authorities, when issuing licences to cinemas, to impose their *own conditions* with regard to the films screened at cinemas in their area, rather than just licensing the buildings in which the films are shown.

This means, in effect, that if a handful of local councillors disagree with the content of a film they can stop it being shown to the public. In Brighton, for example, the newly-elected Labour Council banned the already heavily-cut film *'9½ Weeks'* in 1986 as the female 'feminist' Mayor and two of her colleagues found the film (unspecifically) "offensive to women." The adult population of Brighton (both male and female) were therefore denied the right to decide for themselves, nor able to watch a movie seen by people all over the rest of the country. Public opinion weighed heavily against the council's action but, as usual, the wishes of the public were ignored by the politicised minority.

Indeed, the bible-thumping, loud mouthed minority of would-be censors on the political Right often form an unholy alliance with the equally vociferous, breast-beating minority on the Left when the thorny question of censorship arises. Besides both sets of people being earth-shatteringly boring, they have something else in common. They both presume that their view is 'right' – so sure, and so opinionated are they, in fact, that they have the arrogance to take things a step further by insisting that everybody with differing opinions must be wrong. This self-appointed state of grace allows them to use their powers in any way they see fit, regardless of any now-redundant assumptions of democracy. In Ken Livingstone's words, when speaking to support his Militant colleague Clare Short's motion to ban 'Page 3' photos from the tabloid press – *"People must be moulded to think properly."* (Moulded by Ken, in his own image, in other words).

The question of censorship is oil for the cogs of Social Engineering. In the search for any despot's version of Utopia, where uniform people think harmoniously, censorship of all that is 'nasty' and 'naughty' and 'subversive' and different is an essential part of the blueprint. Media types like Livingstone and Whitehouse live in the public eye solely because they realise the power of the news media, realise that as a society our perception of reality comes only through the edited, stylised 'reality' presented to us by the media, and purely because as politicised people they are interested in 'moulding' how other people think. So that, one day, we may all live happily ever after in their antiseptic heaven. This is all very well, if you conveniently forget the concept of freedom of choice and the right of each human to decide for himself. Censors are not interested in writing or reading books themselves, they are interested only in what other people write and read. On top of that, they are also able to magically predict what effect a person's reading matter will have upon that person. (Yes, they are remarkable people.)

The news media is vital in the arsenal of the censors. The media needs sages, prophets of doom and monstrous figures who will fulfil such prophecies. The media needs news. Any newsworthy item is seized upon and wrung dry. So, figures like Michael Ryan for example, who shot up Hungerford one dark afternoon, are godsends to the vultures in the media. Follow-up interviews with shocked members of the public and outraged politicians create a counterfeitist call for "something to be done" across the nation, and a totally media-invented panic gains momentum in the Press and on TV. Pressure is put to bear on hapless politicians who can only save their popularity by doing "something" – almost anything – to appease the hyped-up Leader Writers of Fleet Street. So, in the case of the appalling Mr Ryan, instead of looking upon the incident as an isolated event in which a man who owned guns went stark raving mad, the government introduced a set of new laws which affected every sane, law abiding citizen who owned a gun, and also affected every sane law-abiding citizen who did not. It's important to realise that the changes in the law did *nothing* to prevent a repeat of the Ryan incident, but merely did something to appease the media, which was the object of the exercise. The government also promised to do "something" about the adventure-game computer programmes and survivalist magazines to which the pathetic Ryan subscribed. In the Britain of the 1980s the rights of well-balanced people count for little. The wishes of the true majority count for nought. We must all be treated as potential sickos and children, so our TV and Cinema and magazines must aim to be as bland and yellow and innocuous as possible.

Nowadays, it is not only the individual's personal viewing and reading habits which are interfered with. The whole question of Free Speech must now be viewed within a context of harassment and general intimidation.

Madeline Haigh, a housewife living in Sutton Coldfield, wrote to her local paper in 1985 airing her views about British and American nuclear weapons. A few days later she was visited and questioned by officers of the Special Branch. This, and other similar incidents which occasionally come to light, have been officially acknowledged as being true. But as others have pointed out – how many other such cases go by without a mention?

Even before his national notoriety, journalist Duncan Campbell's home was raided and searched by the police. Nothing unusual about that, perhaps. But, at the time of the raid, Campbell was being treated in hospital after a road accident. The police knew about this when they applied for a warrant to search his home, and that his hospitalisation would ensure that the troublesome citizen was not around while his private files were being gone through. An uncanny coincidence indeed.

Friends of the Earth and Greenpeace are among the non-violent, essentially apolitical citizen's organisations that have had their offices raided and searched without any charges being brought against them. (Under the Telecommunications Bill of 1984, police and other government agencies were given the right to tap the telephones of people who had not been convicted of any crime. In 1987, some 33,000 telephones were officially tapped).

To some, it seems that the only right to free speech that really exists in this country is the right to freely express support for the established political parties, churches, and traditional institutions. The only criticism that is allowed is mild cynicism exposed in the areas of entertainment, or criticism of one political party – providing it is supporting the (similar) ideology of another major party. Protest against the Police, the Political system, the Church and the State is quite definitely taboo.

EDUCATION

If a country claims to be Free and Just, the main foundation of its Freedom and Justice must lie in the education which it provides and allows for its citizens. Without a basic education, the individual is not only denied facts which may be pertinent to his decision-making, but he is automatically placed in a subordinate position in relation to those who have the facts at their disposal. When this situation arises, the individual is inclined to take advice unquestioningly. Depending on the motives of the people supplying him with information, his decisions can be influenced by means of editing what information he is given – omitting facts which may detract from the dominant argument and giving misleading projections about the results of the individual's decision. It therefore follows that in any society which claims to have a failsafe system of democracy, an unbiased and wide-ranging education is essential. So too is the creation of an atmosphere which encourages the individual to think independently.

When it wants to be, the basic State educational system in Britain can be very effective. It is a tribute to its effectiveness that, for instance, the overwhelming majority of its graduates accept unquestioningly the historical existence of Jesus Christ – regardless of their level of interest in religious matters – even though verification of this cannot be made by usual historical methods. (Some form of Religious Instruction is a legal necessity in schools, and in some areas of education and law, no religion other than Christianity is given the same protection and avenue of propagation. This is why, for example, *'The Satanic Verses'* could not be tried under the laws of blasphemy, which only cover blasphemy against the Christian idea of God.)

However, one simple indictment of the education system's wide-ranging effectiveness may be seen in the area of Religious Education. Although British people do probably leave school believing in Christ, they hear next to nothing about the teachings of Buddha, Mohammed, or the subject of comparative religions. This may be a crass example, but it is just this sort of one-sidedness, the *selection of information* made available to the individual, which is at the heart of the debate about Freedom. All too often, education in Britain compares uncomfortably with straightforward conditioning.

The narrowness of education is not limited to religious matters or to the schooling of impressionable young children. Unless any college's curriculum toes the predominant line, it is open to interference of all kinds.

When, in 1969, the Open University was founded, its stated aims of providing a good non-traditional form of education for all adults whom the traditional educational system had 'missed out' was praised by all political parties. It is now the largest university in the world. In a free society, an overriding and long-established principle has been that the syllabus and methods involved in educating students should be left to the educationalists, free from interference from the State.

In June 1984, however, the Open University received a communication from the Department of Education 'advising' that its Social Science course texts be revised so as to change their political content. The OU faculty was also informed that the Minister of Education, appointed by Margaret Thatcher, was "taking a personal interest in the matter". At this point, it should be remembered that the Open University relies for the vast majority of its income from the Government of the day. Its bursary is decided by the Minister of Education.

Such instances are not as isolated as they seem. It has long been the case that political parties in control of central and local government funding of schools and colleges in this country have sought to influence the presentation and content of subjects taught to young people through the unfair application of such pressures.

It is not only political parties and right-wing extremists who monopolise the right to interfere, though. Despite an increase in cases of child molestation in the capital, when the Inner London Education Authority made a video warning children about sex attackers in January '87, the Inner London Teachers' Association refused to show it to pupils "because the police were involved in the making of the video". So the way in which vital information was presented to pupils was interfered with on the grounds that it was not the Association's policy to work with the police, for political reasons, by a group of people who, as Educationalists, would claim to put the educational needs and safety of their pupils above anything else.

Besides such cases of interference, it is notable that over the last few years the State Education system has been starved of funds for necessary equipment etc., the government of the day having chosen to question the high priority given to education, preferring, it seems, to create a semi-literate, generally ill-educated pool of easily influenced, easily pleased people – a practice that must be at odds with the concept of democracy. The rights of individuals to gain education in a free society have also been brought into question by the State and by people in positions of political influence. Both the following quotes came in 1986 and are taken as examples from many which are in a similar vein on the subject. The first is from a non-aligned civil servant in the Department of Education, the second from former Vice Chairman of the Conservative Party, Jeffrey Archer (a man who definitely does not give money to prostitutes).

"We are in a period of considerable social change. There may be unrest, but we can cope with the Toxteths. But if we have a highly educated and idle population, we may anticipate more serious conflict. PEOPLE MUST BE EDUCATED ONCE MORE TO KNOW THEIR PLACE."

"The problem is that, nowadays, people think they have a RIGHT to education."

Conspiracy theories aside, the State, it seems, is engaged in a longterm exercise in social engineering, so as to produce, through its (non-)education system, a new 'proletariat' lacking in adequate education (and therefore choice) who will accept the prospect of such things as continual unemployment and the increasing lack of individual liberty without serious or co-ordinated revolt. (Under the present Tory regime we spend less of our GNP on Education than any other EC country.) At the same time, as the effectiveness and resources of the State Education system decline, tax concessions and other benefits have been extended to those seeking private education. The vast majority of MPs, peers, top civil servants and members of the British Institute of Management, as well as most senior ranks in the armed forces, attended private schools. The next generation, it seems, is being set into the same polarised mould, with even greater gaps between the education of those taking over the effective running of the State, and those who are at the other end of the economic scale. The resulting Society this type of policy creates will inevitably be even more divided, in educational and economic terms, than it is at present.

As Information is the key to the Freedom of Choice, the control of Education is a vital area to dominate, as is the control of the media. If one carefully controls both areas, one has all but won the battle for control of the people's minds. Interesting then to note that no other Government since the War has interfered so frequently in the areas of Education (see the Education Reform Acts etc.) and the Media (see the numerous new rules governing TV and video).

The only area you now need to concentrate upon is the overtly Political one. If you control Education and the Media properly, all you have to do now is ensure that all opposing political parties appear incompetent and corrupt, if you are to stay in power.

INFORMATION, SURVEILLANCE, DECEPTION

It is generally believed that one of the common criteria of all free countries is the right for each individual to be free to engage in any legal political activity they wish, free from harassment and interference from the State.

The Campaign for Nuclear Disarmament is a peaceful, non-aligned movement founded in 1956. At its height, its membership numbered over 100,000 and its general views are supported by more than a third of the population (given the results of various opinion polls). Its supporters include Bishops, Lords, MPs of most major parties, and former Government Ministers. Despite its legality and general credibility, it is one of many institutions that is under close scrutiny from the Government, and a target for interference from its agents.

In 1985, Sir Ronald Dearing, Chairman of the Post Office, revealed that he had established that CND correspondence had been "substantially tampered with". When challenged with this information, the Home Secretary replied that he would "neither confirm or deny the existence of authorised interceptions". He went on to say that he had no reason to believe any *unauthorised* interceptions were being made on letters to CND members and to the campaign's offices. As the interceptions had been established – by of all people the Chairman of the Post Office – one is therefore left with no choice but to come to the conclusion that CND mail is *officially* tampered with. Besides this, it has also been reported that the

CND office telephone lines were tapped. (As these reports came through, bugs were found in the offices of the Communist Party of Great Britain, adding credence to the phone tapping claims of CND.)

The Independent Enquiry into the policing implications of the Miners' Strike of 1985 found that there was strong evidence to suggest that the telephones of many miners were tapped during the dispute. The Chairman of the inquiry, Professor Peter Wallington, called on the Home Secretary to "make a clear statement" on the extent of the phone tapping of NUM members, but his requests have been ignored by the government.

In 1986, further evidence of such shady goings-on came from an unlikely source. Ex-MI5 agent Peter Wright tried to publish a book – *'Spycatcher'* – about his experiences while working for Her Majesty's government. Even though Mrs Thatcher said in the House of Commons that Wright's claims that he burgled and bugged his way around London illegally were "fiction", the book was banned in Britain. The public were quite simply denied the opportunity to read the book, which was freely available in other countries at the time. (Rather strange that the government should invest so much time and money in banning a work of pure fantasy.)

As MPs' demands for an enquiry into Wright's claims were turned down by the government, the British media – by now fed up with the story – contented themselves with poking fun at the Americans' painstakingly public enquiry into the Irangate affair. The sense of irony was acute. If Irangate had happened here, the British legal and constitutional system would not even be able to accommodate such a mammoth investigation, even if such a scandal were ever admitted by the politicians and civil servants involved. (Can any British citizen imagine Thatcher, the Home Secretary, the Head of MI5 and senior civil servants from the Ministry of Defence being grilled by MPs and judges on live TV for several weeks? Sadly, I for one cannot.)

Between 1985 and 1987 another ex-secret service officer, Cathy Massiter, gave MPs a series of highly detailed accounts of how MI5 operatives deliberately misinterpreted Home Office rules on gaining interception warrants, so that they could legally tap the phones of private citizens. Of the accounts she gave, the Home Secretary told the Commons that "this does not and cannot happen". Massiter, who worked for the Security services for many years, insists that it does. She cites numerous examples of the bugging and phone tapping of people who were neither criminal, nor suspected of being involved in espionage – though the Government refuses "to confirm or deny" any of the cases involved.

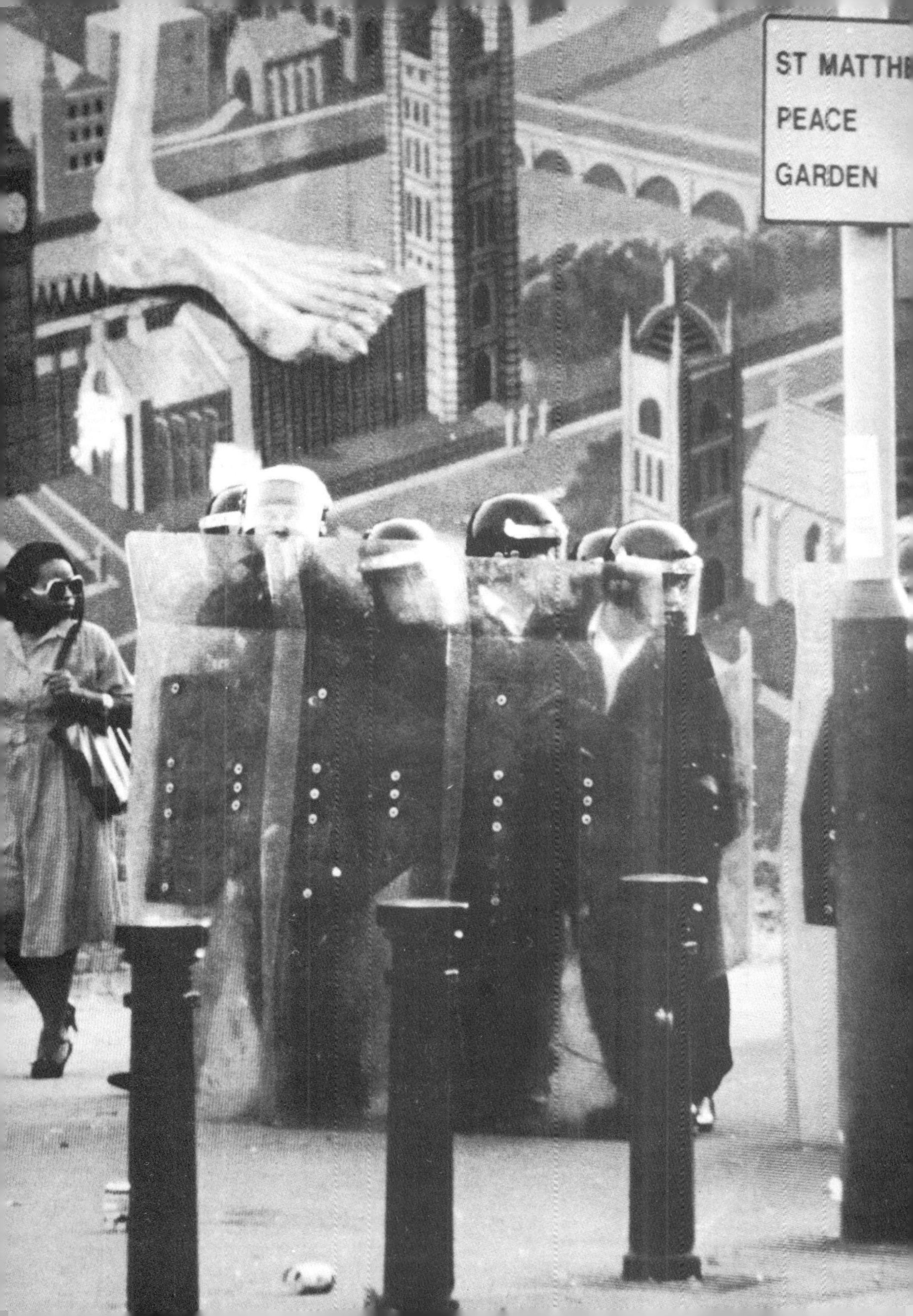
ST MATTH
PEACE
GARDEN

Massiter says that a typical way in which the government and MI5 operate in obtaining information on potential *political* adversaries is the way in which MI5 provided information on individual CND members to a propaganda unit – DS19 – which had been created by Michael Heseltine when he was Minister of Defence. It is not surprising to find out that this operation was set up just before the 1983 General Election, when nuclear disarmament was a key issue in the Labour Party manifesto.

So Tory politicians use the British Secret Service not only to combat terrorists and spies, but also to obtain information on their innocent political adversaries in the hope of discrediting them before the electorate and pre-empting their political plans.

Again, the comparisons between Thatcher's smug claims of 'freedom' in Britain and the reality of life in the USA are embarrassing. Watergate brought down an entire government. Massiter's well documented claims here have hardly made a ripple. Indeed, few people would even know who Massiter is.

Even when faced with such indictable evidence, however, public hysteria and prejudices can be whipped up so that any infringements of people's right to privacy are acceptable. Speaking in the House of Commons in March '85, after the Post Office-CND revelations, Conservative MP Robert Audley said that as people involved with CND must share a worldview "indistinguishable" from that held in the Kremlin, "they should expect such treatment". His statement was greeted with approval from the Government benches.

In many other countries, such an attitude is not tolerated. It is indicative of the British situation to note how our government is treated in Europe. In May 1984, for example, when the Government was questioned by the opposition on the subject, Lord Elton was forced to say that – at that moment alone – the European Court of Human Rights had before it 30 applications relating to the interference of correspondence within the U.K. against the British Government. By far the highest number of complaints against any EEC member, even though very few cases are ever taken out against the government by individuals having their mail tampered with, meaning that even this figure represents only a fraction of the mail involved.

Personal information of all kinds can be pried into by the Government – even the most confidential medical information. Mere patients are actually prevented from gaining full access to their own medical records. These records are not the property of the patient, nor even the property of the patient's doctor. They belong to the local Health Authority. Without the knowledge of the patient, or his doctor, the police have access to the personal data recorded on the patient's file via the Health Authority.

In a situation such as this, it is perhaps not surprising that many people fear consulting fully with their GP, and may suffer physically and mentally as a result. A person may be worried about having VD for example, but not go for testing or treatment because he is afraid that his confidentiality may be breached.

In these days when the question of compulsory AIDS screening is a subject of serious debate, as too is the incarceration of AIDS victims and carriers (HIV positive prostitutes are already being held against their will by the Social Services in some hospitals), it is perhaps worrying – when police can refer to patients' records at will – when powerful policemen display their true attitudes towards people who don't conform to their own narrow personal set of beliefs.

In December 1986, James Anderton, Chief Constable of Greater Manchester, said, *"People with AIDS are swirling around in a cesspool of their own making"*. Anderton, a devout Christian and lay preacher, is the same policeman who set up armed police patrols in Manchester city centre, and was also accused by other police officers of bugging their phones. This writer can find no quotes from Anderton on the subject of Human Rights. Perhaps he should study the works of J. Christ more carefully – or at least listen harder when he speaks to him on his intercom. *"Judge not and you shall not be judged; condemn not and you shall not be condemned; forgive and you shall be forgiven."*

Anyone who raises their eyes above street level in London will find police video surveillance cameras in numerous positions above the capital – there are six in Trafalgar Square alone. Police helicopters and 'hoolivans' are now a common sight in most large cities. Any patrolling officer can radio base and find the identity and records of any member of the public within seconds. Official phone taps are increasing, as is the use of all manner of computerised information-gathering technology. Individual officers add to police data by getting information from the Inland Revenue, Social Security offices, Customs & Excise, Education and Health Authorities, even banks and other private institutions.

With a few real safeguards, this information can be passed on to private security firms, employment officers, foreign governments and police forces – even though much of the information cannot be checked and may be incorrect, and a lot of it is based on unsubstantiated hearsay from informants and officers. In the estimation of one former Chief Constable – John Alderson (not to be confused with James Anderton) over a third of the information held by the police alone is totally useless in the pursuit of law breakers. In a variety of ways, police build up information on members of the public who have no convictions.

Since May 1984, beat policemen have been encouraged to add to this mass of information on non-convicted members of the public by completing very brief green 'Intelligence Debriefing Reports', listing car and telephone numbers, names and addresses of suspects and potential trouble makers, etc. etc. and filing these at their station for other officers to refer to. Police patrols regularly note the registration numbers of cars seen parked outside such innocuous events as charity village fetes in aid of CND, or in the car parks of certain pubs used by known criminals and nightclubs frequented by gays. Serious allegations have been made, aired on Channel 4 TV, saying that some police officers have actually staged burglaries into new offices and the homes of newcomers to an area, as a cover for a clandestine search of the property to see what business is done there. The reported 'burglaries' are then investigated in the normal way, involving an official police visit with questions being asked and fingerprints being taken. Even in legitimate enquiries, such as murder investigations, thousands of innocent people may be interviewed and information stored on them relating to their work, their lifestyles, their friends etc. Even when the specific inquiry is resolved, this information can be kept by the police in perpetuity.

The enormous amount of trivial information, held in the form of brief notes on computer and likely to be ambiguous, though often inferring that individuals are in some way criminally minded or subversive, can then be passed on through the information system. Years later, a foreign police force, for example, could request information on a citizen, leading to a false impression being created based on the ambiguous info received.

If you happen to be stopped by the police three times within a month – even if you are guilty of no crime – some constabularies automatically put you on file as being a 'suspected person'. Meaning you are "someone who is actively engaged in crime but who has not been convicted of any offence". No matter how innocent or law-abiding you are, this information will no doubt affect the way you are treated by the police in future.

Driving away from Plymouth in May 1983, Mrs B. – who was eight months pregnant – was stopped by the police because her car registration number was routinely checked through the computer which revealed that the car was connected with an address at which there had been a drugs raid in 1981. Taken to the police station, she was stripped, searched, and held for four hours on 'suspicion'. True, police *had* raided her home two years before – but only because they went to the wrong address. In other words, incorrect and misleading information had been held on computer for 2 years.

In September 1984 Dr Brian Richards was arrested by police in Los Angeles on the basis of information which they had been sent by Scotland Yard (information which had been stored on the 'C' Computer at Hendon, which alone holds information on over two million people). The information supplied to the L.A.P.D. was misleading and later proved to be incorrect. When asked about this particular incident, the under-Secretary of State admitted that the information was wrong and that the Met. were wrong to have supplied it. However, he added, the problem was that the information was *"now in the possession of the U.S. authorities, and, regretfully, cannot be withdrawn"*. Tough luck, Doctor.

The cogent fact is that data, however irresponsibly gathered, can be held against an individual for life if stringent rules are not applied. Even in a 'free' society such as ours, citizens have little control over the information held on them, how it is used, or to whom it is disseminated.

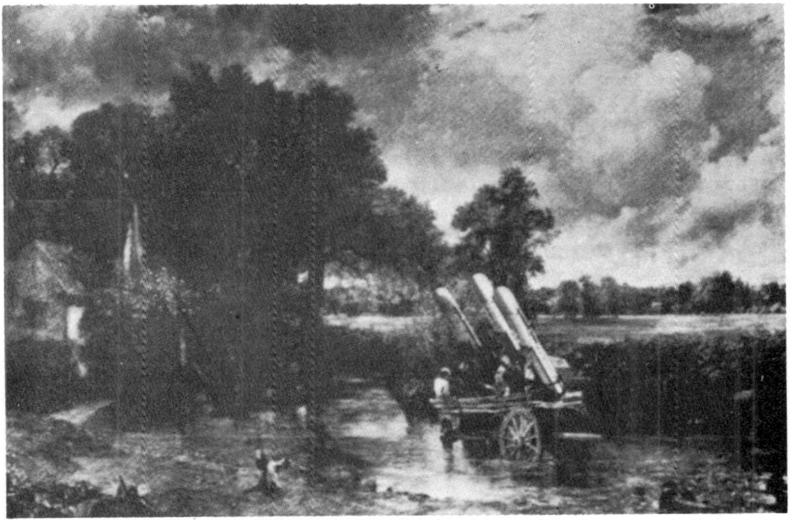

Jerusalem? (Photomontage by Pete Kennard)

The case of Dr Richards and the case of 'Mrs B.' (when the National Council for Civil Liberties reported her case she asked for her name to be kept secret) are not isolated ones. It recently came to light that MI5 vetted all the journalists applying for jobs at the BBC, and have done so secretly for years. The only reason this fact came out was because of the case of Isabel Hilton. In 1976, Ms Hilton applied for a television job with the Corporation. The BBC Board unanimously chose her from the many candidates for the post, but they were informed by MI5 that she was a "security risk", as she was Secretary of an academic cultural group called the Scotland/China Association, which the 'Intelligence' Services wrongly thought was a 'subversive' organisation. So she couldn't have the job.

The position went to someone else, despite the wishes of Ms Hilton and the BBC Under British law, Ms Hilton has *no right* to challenge the accuracy of the information passed on to prospective employers about her. Determined to clear her name and highlight the unjust system that operates in Britain, with great determination she took the case to the European Court. (It was one of three cases regarding British Intelligence services heard by the court in February 1987 alone.) Though hundreds of similar cases here have come to light, one can only speculate on how many thousands of other cases have not.

Public accountability is not a high priority in Britain, whether it be about the use of personal information regarding a private citizen, or the release of information that is in the public interest.

Under the Public Records Act, records of the Cabinet and central government departments are placed in the PR office where they must be made available to the public...but only after a period of *thirty years* has elapsed, and even then only at the discretion of the Lord Chancellor of the time. Even this necessity can be avoided if "sensitive" information is involved. In all government departments, a constant process of sieving is going on so as to reduce the enormous amount of paper stored. During this process, the vast bulk of governmental records are destroyed. Of course, most of these records are of no interest to anyone, but historians and journalists have made accusations of government departments conveniently destroying records that may be embarrassing to them in later years. (Incidentally, records of criminal proceedings brought by the government are made available to the public not after 30, but only after 100 years.)

Such injustices flourish almost unnoticed because this government is a master in the art of public relations, and a genius at wrapping restrictive new laws and practices in an appealing package. For example, the public is told that the system of collecting local council rates is "unfair", so the government, deeply concerned with fairness and justice, will help everybody by radically changing the system. The Poll Tax is introduced. No longer are rates to be paid by the householder and determined purely by the size and value of the building and the wealth of the person. Now everybody is to pay. Conveniently, this means that every person in the land must declare where they are living, who they are living with, how much time they spend at an address etc. etc. An ongoing census is introduced, albeit by the back door.

The information on the new tax register is collected by thousands of Registration Officers, who have the power to investigate any household in the country. The information which they seek must be given by every citizen (if you refuse to co-operate you can be sent to prison). The extensive personal data collected will *not* be safeguarded by the law. More worryingly, behind the Register itself is what is called a Second File, recording the notes, anecdotes and suspicions of the local authority officers about individuals made in order to assist them in catching evaders. A citizen is not allowed to see his or her entry on the Second File, as the Local Authority can deny access on the grounds that the file is related to the collection of a tax. Any information collected by the local council can be passed on to other governmental departments on request. The government have said that to build up information on individuals living in a house, it may be possible to cross reference Tax Register files with records kept by estate agents, insurance companies, local libraries, housing departments, bus companies (season ticket lists), landlords, trade associations, British Telecom, the local Electricity and British Gas Boards, the local press, education bodies, health authorities etc. etc. The new Tax Register will also include an individual's National Insurance Number – which is interesting when one considers what is happening to people's National Insurance Cards.

The old cards (which every person over 16 has) are suddenly no longer any good, so a new type of card is introduced. Gone is the scruffy, ordinary looking piece of cardboard (which can be read by the card holder), to be replaced by a shiny new plastic card, which just happens to have a mysterious magnetic strip on the back of it (which cannot be read by the card holder).

In June 1988, Metropolitan Police Commissioner Sir Peter Imbert forecast that Identity Cards would be carried by all British adults by the mid 1990s – embarrassed Government Ministers denied all knowledge of the plan.

By November of '88, however, Douglas Hurd announced the introduction of a 'voluntary' national ID Card scheme to be phased in over the next few years. One wonders what the police would say to people they stop who have not chosen to co-operate with this scheme (got something to hide 'ave we?) Of course, after the voluntary 'run-in' period an excuse will be found to make the cards compulsory. This happened when Sports Minister Colin Monyhan announced that due to the success of a voluntary card scheme at Luton Town Football Club (the scheme was not voluntary with fans nor was it successful) all seven million people who attended football matches would be required by law to register for, buy and carry such a card to all matches – regardless of their previous behaviour. Something which the clubs, the fans, the Police Federation and many local Councils opposed. Despite this, and the public safety problems that will arise when 50,000 people turn up at a stadium ten minutes before kick-off, Thatcher liked the idea. So, the idea was that unless you have a card you cannot watch our national sport. Freedom – loving England was the only country in the world to consider adopting such a scheme.

In response to growing public concern over the gathering, storage and use of personal information, the Government – as keen as ever to win votes – passed the Data Protection Act in 1984 amid a blaze of positive publicity. (In fact the law had been forced on the British Government by the European Government.) Everybody is happy as superficially, the Act, which came into force in November 1987, purports to give private citizens sweeping new rights of access to all material held on them. On closer inspection, one finds that any information held on computer which is deemed to relate in any way to the safeguard of "national security" (as defined by officials at the time) is exempted. So too is any information held on manual (paper) systems of storage. Also, although the publicity surrounding the Act claimed that it outlawed the secret transfer of information from one agency to another, there are in fact several exemptions in the small print. For example, any government department, local authority, bank, employer or any other body can release any information in secret to the Police, Customs, and Tax officials in the interests of "preventing crime". (Note the word "prevention", which means the Police and others can still gain secret access to any records even if no crime has been committed.) In everyday reality, the Act only means that citizens can pay to see what information is held on them in the computers of mailorder and credit card companies and their ilk. The law does *not* mean that individuals can see, and perhaps challenge, files held on them by several government departments, which are still withheld, regardless of how inaccurate or misleading they may be.

Besides the shortage of rights a British subject has relating to personal information, Britain also gives few opportunities for the electorate to find out exactly what is being done in the name of the country by the

Government in control. The much-abused '30 Year Rule' is just one example of how this situation is tolerated with little or no criticism.

The outmoded and unfair Official Secrets Act (particularly Section 2), has, however, been criticised by many politicians, judges and private individuals over the last few years, though it remains defiantly on the statute book and has been used by successive governments. It is not only seen as being morally correct for a government to have secrets from the citizens who elect it into power to serve them, but it is also apparently acceptable for this wide-ranging Act to be used to cover up a variety of truths that cannot conceivably affect the nation's security.

In 1979 an attempt was made to reform the Act by introducing a fairer 'Protection of Information Bill', but this failed to get through Parliament. In 1988, backbencher Richard Shepherd introduced a 'Protection of Official Information Bill', which proposed to effectively replace Section 2 with a better code. The Government used their majority to defeat the Bill.

The ubiquitous Official Secrets Act gags over 2,500,000 British citizens, forbidding them from talking in any way about any aspect of their work. It also makes it an offence to *receive* any such information. So, for example, if you read the first copy of the now-defunct left wing tabloid the *'News on Sunday'* in July '87 which contained a list of innocuous 'official secrets', *you* broke the law.

So did a postman who wrote to his local paper saying that the post office was undermanned. He was threatened with prosecution under the Act. So was a journalist who published nothing more important than the dress regulations of the Police Force. Although such examples did not make it to court, the *threat* of imprisonment remains hanging over almost all of us, whether we have signed the Act or not.

In a blatant P.R. move in November '88 the Government published its own proposed changes to the Act. Despite some good publicity, the small print of the 'reformed' law shows it to be every bit as unjust and open to abuse as the previous Act.

Regardless of one's opinion about war, few people would expect any government to divulge such things as troop movements to the press during hostilities, as this would inevitably cost lives. It is generally believed that it is clear-cut cases such as this which make the Act necessary. However, not many people outside of the government would agree that it would be justifiable for that government to invoke the Act in order to cover up military movements retrospectively, particularly when several years had passed since conflict ceased. To reveal the whereabouts of military units after the event could have no effect on the outcome of the war.

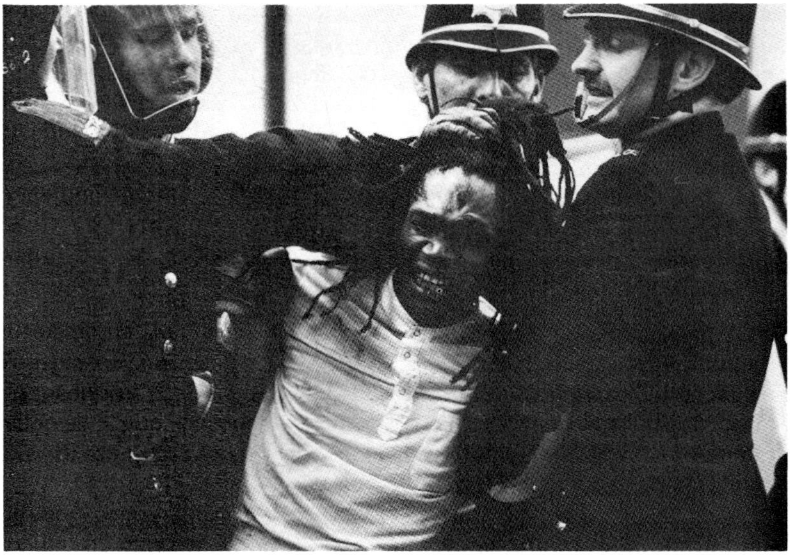

Community policing in Birmingham.

Yet governments ignore the concept of accountability and invoke the spectre of 'National Security' whenever it suits them to do so. And in Britain, there is *nothing* anybody can do to stop them.

Ignoring the political fact that, as Head of National Security, the Prime Minister of the day is accountable for getting us into any war, and that as Head of the Intelligence Services, she was also responsible for ignoring information received two months ahead of the Argentine invasion of the Falklands in 1982 – for which she has not been brought to account – as leader of the War Cabinet at the time, she has also never explained several military decisions which were taken during the course of the conflict. Everyone knows about the repugnant Belgrano and Clive Ponting affairs, and the way in which Sarah Tisdall was imprisoned for six months for leaking politically embarrassing information to the *Guardian* but other, perhaps more important matters just do not seem to have been spotlighted by the press and remain unanswered by the government.

It has long been the boast of the British Foreign Office that we, the third country to develop and arm ourselves with nuclear weapons, were the first country to promise never to threaten a non-nuclear power. It is in this context that we should look at the mystery of the Falklands submarines.

Why were three nuclear-powered Fleet submarines (HMS Conqueror, HMS Spartan and HMS Splendid) kept in the Falklands war zone for so long that they came close to running out of food? Why were they not relieved by other nuclear-powered submarines in their class which were not otherwise engaged in their normal NATO duties at the time? At the time, the Royal Navy had 32 submarines, twelve of which were of this nuclear-powered 'Fleet' type. According to a variety of reputable sources, six of these Fleet Submarines were free at the time of the Falklands crisis (those 3 already mentioned, plus HMS Warspite, HMS Superb and HMS Courageous), but these three 'spare' subs did not relieve their starving sister ships in the war zone because they were in fact being used secretly to escort one of Britain's four SSBNs (otherwise known as Polaris submarines) in the South Atlantic between the military base at Ascension Island and the Falklands.

Given Britain's long standing promise to the world about the limited use of its nuclear weapons, what was such a powerful unit of Britain's 'nuclear deterrent' doing *sailing out of range of the Soviet Union,* but within range of the non-nuclear capable Argentine mainland? Who was it 'deterring'? Labour MP Tam Dalyell has been asking such questions for several years, but not only has he never received any satisfactory answers from the Government, he has been pictured as something of a crank by the media for being interested in the answers.

It has also been reported that several frigates and two carriers leaving the largest naval base in Europe, Devonport Dockyard in Plymouth, and others sailing from the naval bases at Portsmouth, Rosyth and Chatham, were armed with fully charged nuclear weapons on board. Asked about these reports in the House of Commons after the war, Margaret Thatcher refused to answer any such questions "in the interests of national security".

The same excuse was rolled out for the actions that sprang from the Zircon affair in early 1987.

In 1983, the government was approached by the signals intelligence branch – GCHQ at Cheltenham – with technical plans for the Zircon spy satellite. Only the USA and USSR have spy satellites. Their development and deployment is costly and technically difficult and, like nuclear weapons systems, they are a defence acquirement that gives a nation a childish prestige in a field not shared by anyone else. Not surprisingly in Thatcher's Britain, the plans were approved in June '83 and, unbeknown to the taxpayer and despite a climate of cut-backs in the social services and even in conventional defence, a budget of £700,000,000 was earmarked for the project.

At this point it should be remembered that even if the Soviet Union did not know of the plans (which is doubtful given the history of MI5 and GCHQ) it would have been able to detect the new satellite from the moment it was launched.

Duncan Campbell, a freelance investigative journalist working on a BBC TV series, discovered details of the project and started filming a documentary about it in 1986, for transmission in November of that year. The government stepped in, however, and had secret talks with BBC governors instructing them not to air the programme, which was obligingly shelved. In January '87 Campbell, somewhat disappointed, wrote an article in the *New Statesman* magazine which talked in general terms about the satellite and concerned itself primarily with the way in which Parliament had supposedly been duped by the government over the £700m Zircon budget.

The magazine's offices were promptly raided by the police. Special Branch officers also raided Campbell's home (twice) in January and seized documents. A few days later, detectives raided the BBC's Broadcasting House in Glasgow at night, and confiscated the master tapes of the Zircon programme and those of all the other programmes in the projected series. In a supposedly unconnected incident a few days later, Sir Alistair Milne, Director General of the BBC, resigned. He had already been under pressure to do so from Norman Tebbit, then Chairman of the Conservative Party, for supposed political bias against the Tories.

In free Britain, then, police swept into the private home of a well known journalist, the offices of a widely-read magazine and, under cover of darkness, the studios of our country's National TV station, broke down doors (Campbell's), and took away material that was destined for public consumption. Labour MP Gerald Kaufman compared the actions with those being carried out in South Africa and East Germany. The government denied all responsibility for the raids, saying that the police had "acted without instructions from Whitehall"!

Some found it hard to believe that the chain of command, from Chief Constable, to Home Secretary to Prime Minister, was broken in a case of such national importance.

Of the 15 member nations of N.A.T.O., only two governments refuse to publicise or debate their emergency civil defence plans for times of war. It will be no surprise to learn that one of these two countries is Britain.

Since 1979, Home Defence arrangements in Britain have been

completely revised, and government powers over the internment of citizens, setting up of new courts, conscription of civilians to work parties, reinstatement of the death penalty, commandeerment of private transport and buildings, plans to block road and rail routes out of major cities and so on have been extended far beyond the emergency powers which operated in Britain during World War II.

Secret Bills are now known to have been drawn up since the Thatcher government signed the 1983 Joint Logistics Plan, an unpublicised agreement with the Americans which led to these secret Bills being devised. The elected government of this country have denied even the existence of these mysterious Bills and refuse to debate their contents openly in Parliament, but it is now accepted that they do exist.

It may perhaps be necessary for governments to have emergency powers in case of the outbreak of war, and also to keep certain military plans secret from potential enemies, but why is Britain almost unique in making these plans for the *civilian* population totally secret and undebatable by MPs and the British people? The answer seems obvious. If real information about government plans in the event of war were known, serious, *informed* debate would take place resulting in public pressure on the government to change these plans and, probably, added pressure would also be brought to close down British and American nuclear bases throughout Airstrip One.

Unlike the Germans, Dutch, Italians and almost everyone else, the British people and their elected representatives are flatly *refused the right* to find out what they may be letting themselves in for.

Nobody can change this situation. Politicians learn from the experience of Tam Dayell that their questions are either not answered truthfully – or not answered at all. Civil Servants have seen Clive Ponting charged for speaking the truth, and journalists must heed the message sent out by the Zircon affair. Don't investigate the government, don't listen to the truth, don't publicise the facts.

So the censorship of reality goes on and on. It is a way of life. There are, of course, numerous examples of censorship of material which cannot remotely affect National Security.

In November '87 the American Alza Corporation, marketing a new IUD contraceptive, wished to supply patients with an 8 page booklet explaining the possible longterm effects of using IUDs and giving women instructions on their correct use. The British Health Department banned the booklet (which was distributed freely in all the other countries taking the contraceptive) saying it was *"inappropriate for use in the U.K."* Social Audit, a consumer research group on pharmaceuticals, said that the British decision *"reflected the British Government's tight-fistedness with information"*. The DHSS said that it would not comment on this, or any other of its decisions, which are confidential. The leaflet, and the product, were withdrawn by Alza, who refused to supply women with IUDs without informing them of the possible health risks involved. This is by no means an isolated example of the peculiar secrecy adopted by the British Government in order to maximise its power and limit public awareness.

The government gets detailed reports on defects of all models of car, but will not reveal the findings to the general public; the government's Department of Health tests the relative toxicity of all brands of cigarettes, but won't tell of the results; the government has lists of areas in Britain that are hazard sites, liable to be unfit for human habitation due to "fall out" of dangerous chemicals if accidents occur at local factories and stores – the information is classified. And so on. In 1984 a Social Security ruling which allows young people studying part time to claim benefits during their first three months of study was not publicised, nor even did the DHSS inform any Social Security office of the ruling, until news of the situation was leaked to *The Guardian* newspaper: a report commissioned by the DHSS on healthier eating was suppressed by the government as the Ministry of Agriculture predicted that its recommendations to reduce the consumption of red meat would affect farmers' sales...

The Government not only conceal the truth, they distort it. Since 1979, the methods of calculating and publishing the unemployment figures have been 'altered' more than 27 times. Each 'alteration' has caused an apparent drop in the numbers of unemployed, trying to conceal the true rise from 1 million to nearly 4 million.

ENFORCERS (GUNS, COMPUTERS, ARMOURED CARS – BUT NO BLUE LAMP)

The UK has 125,000 police officers. (The police recently asked for 15,000 more.) There are also a variety of specialist internal security branches, such as MI6, the UDF, Int.Corps, C13, and the Special Branch.

At any time, these civil forces can be supported by the military, who number around 250,000. The army were last called onto the streets of U.K. cities to support the police in 1969. They have also been used in England to break strikes which affect the "national interest", such as the Dockers' Dispute in the 1970s.

The vast majority of law enforcement, of course, is carried out by the police alone. Contrary to a totally hollow piece of rhetoric which people like to repeat, they are an armed force. (If they were not, 5 year old John

Shorthouse, who was shot accidentally by police in 1985, would still be alive today. Londoner Steven Waldorf would not have been crippled by a hail of police bullets as he sat innocently in his car at some traffic lights. Fourteen people would not have been killed by police plastic bullets alone since Thatcher took over in 1979.) Of course the police are armed; they probably need to be – but let's not pretend they are not.

The police arsenal *in England and Wales alone* includes more than 30,000 plastic bullets, 2,000 rounds of CS gas, stun grenades, 9mm Heckler & Koch MP5K sub machine guns (which are of German design but clandestinely manufactured in the U.K.), Parker Hale rifles, Smith & Wesson handguns, armoured personnel carriers and assorted other weaponry.

The police make no secret of the fact that they are, primarily, the heavies of the State machinery by requiring recruits to be of a certain physical, rather than intellectual stature. The police are employed to enforce laws created by the government. Laws defined by judges – individuals who have been selected by the Lord Chancellor – in the courts. These are the nuts and bolts of the legal system. The *manner* in which this system operates is dictated by the attitudes of those at the top, in the cabinet. These attitudes are illustrated not only by looking at the spate of new laws which the British people have been subjected to, but also by the priority given to the Police and other law enforcement agencies in terms of spending.

Although NHS waiting lists have increased by 70% since Thatcher assumed power, and there are some 500,000 more homeless people now than there were in 1979 when the Tories were elected, this government has seen fit to increase Law & Order spending by more than 35% in real terms over the last ten years (costing us now around £6,500,000,000 per year). Spending on the police alone has – even after allowing for inflation – increased by more than 50% since 1977. One would assume that such a vast increase would have halted the steady growth in real crime, but nothing could be further from the truth. For example, in this time burglary has increased by 61% and theft has increased by nearly 40%. And since 1979, under the Tory 'Law & Order' Government, notifiable offences increased from 2.3 million annually to 5.5 million, while police clear-up rates fell from 42% to under 35%.

Perhaps the police themselves are not to blame. They didn't use to have to spend their time raiding so many bookshops, cinemas, or TV stations.

The Tory Government has certainly increased the police workload, by inventing new offences through new laws and adjustments to existing ones. Everything seems geared towards giving the law enforcement agencies and the State prosecutors more and more power. More reasons for arrest. More chances of conviction.

The 1986 Public Order Act is one such example. Among other things, it created a whole new offence called "disorderly conduct" (which covered just about anything) and also gave the police powers to ban peaceful, formerly legal marches and protests, infringing the British public's age-old right to assemble peacefully and hold a march or public demonstration.

The local police can even ban a demonstration if they believe it may simply cause some disruption to the "life of the community" (traffic and shoppers). Unlike in Moscow, where it is now common in the Glasnost era to see demos that have not received the necessary police clearance, if you try to organise a demonstration of any kind in Britain despite police instructions, you can now be imprisoned for three months and fined – regardless of how peaceful the demonstration is. (Even before the new Act came into force the Home Secretary has been able to ban marches, and this potentially undemocratic habit has become more common under this Government than ever before, as State interference in all areas of life has become more acceptable. Between 1970 and 1980, 11 demonstrations were banned, most of them in N. Ireland. In the years 1981 to 1984, 75 demos were banned, all over the country.)

A father in the North of England was arrested under this new Public Order 'offence' when his son's birthday party was thought "too noisy". A street theatre group in Hereford were threatened with arrest under this new law for singing songs about our beloved Prime Minister. Four people were arrested and charged with the offence in London for putting up a satirical poster of Margaret Thatcher in December '87.

The new law also gives police more powers to ban any other type of gathering of 20 people or more. They have already recently banned some pop festivals and football matches. Now, the Public Order Act, in conjunction with the Sporting Events Act 1985, can be used with equally new Trade Union laws to stop almost anyone going anywhere if the police don't like the look of them. For instance, if you are on your way to a sporting event in a private mini bus with two or three friends you can be stopped and searched by police. If you have a can of alcohol with you in the van, you can be arrested. This quite ridiculous law is a typically inept response to the isolated tragedy of the Heysel Stadium disaster and the disproportionate reporting of football-related violence in the gutter press. As usual, the Government disregard personal freedoms and pass a law that will have no effect whatsoever on fighting at football matches.

Both the Alliance and Labour parties vowed to repeal the Public Order Act if they came to power in the '87 election, but so little publicity had been given to the Act anyway that nobody bothered to make it an election issue.

It's undoubtedly true that many ordinary police officers are becoming increasingly resentful of the way in which they are being used by the present government to prop up an ever more totalitarian regime. Unfortunately, in the present climate, precious few such officers get promoted to the top jobs in the force. Such jobs are reserved for the likes of James Anderton, or less well known officers such as Mike Dixon, President of the Police Superintendents Association. In September 1987, the Association pressed for jurors to be informed of a defendant's previous police record *before* a trial – the implications of which are obvious to all. In defending their position, Superintendent Dixon said that it was "time civil liberty took a step backwards." Perhaps Mr Dixon should have said "another step backwards", as there are numerous examples of this steady backward shuffle which are already enshrined in Law, or soon to be added to the statute book.

The Criminal Justice Bill is yet another such example. Traditionally, the defence council has been able to challenge and remove up to three jurors prior to the case being heard, without having to give any reason. This is to try and give the defence the benefit of rejecting anyone who they think may not be an unbiased judge of the evidence at hand (for a hypothetical example, if a black person saw some white skinheads take seats on a jury about to try him, he could reject them). The government's new bill proposes to deny people this tried and trusted right of peremptory challenge completely. Meanwhile, in other countries such as the USA, the opposite is the case, as the rights of the defence to reject jurors is increased. Once more, age-old rights of the individual citizen are being reduced, and the chances of the State to convict people of crime are increased, against the worldwide trend.

During the 'Persons Unknown' trial it was revealed that in some cases potential jurors are vetted and – contrary to the British principle that juries should be randomly selected – excluded if they were considered by the Prosecution to be 'unsuitable'. The Secretary General's guidelines on jury rigging say that potential jurors should be checked against local police, Special Branch, and other records (the Special Branch computer alone has more than 1,000,000 people's details stored on it). People can be barred from jury service if the State feels they may have 'extreme political beliefs' and the Special Branch do not consider them 'loyal' citizens. These guidelines have never been approved by Parliament.

Parliament was neatly bypassed (again) when obscure local bylaws were introduced for Molesworth and Greenham Common (coincidentally, both places where a foreign government has dumped its weapons) in 1985. Suddenly, trespass on MoD land in these specific areas became a criminal (rather than a civil) offence. It also became an offence for anyone to attach anything to the perimeter fences of Air Force bases. This includes, of course, the priests and nuns who have regularly attached crosses and crucifixes to the fences over the years. In July '87, the common moorland near RAF Fylingdales became out of bounds to ordinary British people. Now, MoD police can tell any person to leave the moors without giving any reason, and direct them not to return within 12 months. If one protests at this, one can be charged with a criminal offence. The new 'Controlled Area' is 50% Common Land.

Apart from such changes in the law, the legal system itself is changing its practices within the existing legal framework in order to fit in with the current almost totalitarian atmosphere.

There is, for example, a growing trend for trials to be held behind closed doors. In one sample week in 1987, a published survey of London courts showed that more than 366 hearings were held with both the Press and the Public excluded. In several cases, Contempt orders were also placed on trials so that certain pieces of evidence could not be reported. This secretive style of justice is common practice in the country's major courts today. Decisions which effect the freedom of thousands of people are made behind closed doors, or with reporting restrictions which stop newspapers and TV from releasing pertinent facts. Even more insidious is the fact that more general, far-reaching judgements – which alter and re-interpret areas of the law and therefore affect all of us – are being made without public scrutiny or discussion.

Lord Scarman said a few years ago that *"Justice is done in public so that it can be discussed and criticised in public"*. Now, in this era of almost imperceptible clampdown, the rights of discussion and serious criticism are effectively being denied. All too often, justice is not being seen to be done.

Even in normal 'open' court there is a widespread practice of preventing members of the public from taking notes during a trial. Some instances have been reported of police moving into the public gallery and removing notebooks from onlookers in the court. There is no legal authority for police to restrict people's freedom to take notes in this way, other than on the orders of the judge.

Even journalists reporting on open trials are not always allowed a copy of the transcript of the court proceedings. The procedure is that the journalist must apply to the Attorney General for permission to purchase a copy of the transcript (the fee itself is substantial), and this permission may be refused without reason. Journalists who have been refused trial records include such potential subversives as Ludovic Kennedy.

The courts are given special protection against criticism by the doctrine of contempt of court. Unlike in some other countries, judges are not elected, and cannot be voted out. They cannot, in effect, be controlled or disciplined. Complaints against them are heard by their colleagues and, in practice, usually come to nothing.

What is not generally known about judges is that, when an accused person is brought to trial, his or her past record of convictions is given to the judge. (This explains why the Statue of Justice on top of the Old Bailey is not blindfolded, as she is in other countries.) Some people think that, as the attitude and stature of the judge influences often nervous and easily-led jurors, the accused person's past record should not be made available to judges in this way before the evidence is even heard.

Although journalists have many complaints about the judicial decisions which deny them reporting rights, they find their rights to appeal blocked by The Supreme Court Act, which prevents reviews of actions of Crown Court judges. This law came into force in 1981. Thanks to this, the only way people have of obtaining a proper legal review of a dubious reporting ban is to break it, and risk prosecution and a prison sentence for contempt of court.

In State-inspired mythology, every person accused of a crime must be convicted on the grounds of hard evidence – not hearsay or accusation – by twelve of his fellow citizens who sit as a jury. Quite right too. A shame that this is just not true.

There are numerous types of case where *no hard evidence, no defence witnesses,* and *no jury* are needed. For instance, if Customs Officers enter and search your premises (they do not need a warrant and are free to take anything they wish) they can forfeit any item unless, within a month, you decide to take them to court to argue your case. No jury can be present at such hearings and the only evidence acceptable is for you to convince the judge that you are not breaking any subjectively interpreted law by having the articles in your house.

There are far more sinister possible injustices than this, however. The law relating to the evidence of informers is exactly the same all over the United Kingdom of England, Wales, Scotland and N. Ireland, or so the Home Secretary once assured Enoch Powell, and offers one such possibility. In all these parts of the country, it is possible for an individual to be accused by the police of a crime and tried without the right to have a jury, solely on the evidence of a police informer. The informer, in most circumstances, is in turn granted immunity from prosecution, or leniency himself if his evidence is sufficient to ensure the desired results. He is thus put in the position in which his 'evidence' must have the maximum effect on the judge. This method of justice has frequently been used, often with startling results.

A judge in Belfast, trying ten men without a jury in May '84, sentenced the ten to a total of 1,001 years imprisonment on the basis of the accusations made by a police informant.

Although there is little public concern over the fate of people who may be guilty of crimes of brutal, bigoted violence, many people have expressed reservations about this dubious practice and its future implications. How is it, they ask, that the country which most prides itself on its fair legal system, can imprison people for over 100 years each without a jury being present, and purely on the basis of hearsay evidence given by a confessed criminal out to save his own neck?

The law of the UK, as administered in the microcosm of Ulster, is an example of the State's powers over its citizenry when protest and revolt are in the air, even when this protest is only manifested in the hands of a tiny minority. It is important to realise that it is in no way inconceivable that the heavy-handed practices of State interference operating in the province be put to use in any other part of the country. The law already allows for this and, after all, special measures adopted to handle the specific case of N. Ireland have been imported into Britain before. The Special Branch, for example, was formed in 1883 as a secret police unit purely to combat the bombings of Fenian extremists. It is now used to infiltrate and keep watch on the National Front, Communist Party, CND, Scottish Nationalist Party, Trades Union officials, journalists, and a host of others throughout Britain. The legal system already exists to allow the government to pass powers such as internment without trial all over the UK mainland if it so wished, because we have no written constitution forbidding it.

The Prevention of Terrorism Act was an 'emergency' Bill passed through Parliament in 1974. This very stringent Act was only passed because, at the time, the Government said that it would only exist for a maximum of six months, and would help the security forces net dozens of active I.R.A. members operating in Britain. *Nearly twenty years later, it remains on the statute book.* Despite the fact that the then Home Secretary admitted that the Act was "wholly unacceptable and inimical to our tradition of civil liberties". The powers of the Act were extended in 1984.

The unfortunate individual detained under the Act can be detained for 7 days without any charge and is effectively put in the position of having to prove his innocence of a crime of which he may not even have been told.

Perhaps Governments need extra powers with which to combat violent terrorists, but the Act has proved to be neither necessary nor effective in this fight. Available figures show that between 25th November 1974 and 30th September 1983, 5,683 people were detained under this Act. Of these, only 21 (twenty-one) were found to be involved in anything resembling terroristic activity. The overwhelming majority of those arrested and detained under this sweeping law were guilty of no offence of *any* kind. Most detentions occurred in Liverpool, and included innocent people attending Trades Union meetings, weddings, and even the funerals of relatives.

The Act also allows the State to place an 'Exclusion Order' on any individual, stopping their movement from one part of the country to the next (usually from N.Ireland to England or vice versa). No one who has their freedom of movement restricted in this way has a right to be told why, nor to appeal. Sean Stitt, a student from Belfast, had no idea why he was placed under an Exclusion Order for over a decade. Despite being a UK passport holder, and never having been a member or supporter of any illegal or terrorist organisation, he found himself 'exiled' to N. Ireland and unable to visit Britain to see his sister or attend National Union of Students functions to which he was invited. Despite appeals, the Government refuse to discuss his case.

In the early '70s, the Labour Government reintroduced the practice of internment without trial and – as in the South Africa the Labour Party criticises today – hundreds of people were dragged from their beds and arrested within days of the decision being taken. As revealed in the Compton Report, many were hooded and forced to spend long periods spreadeagled against walls. As reported by the Parker Commission, many people were also beaten, kicked, and deprived of sleep. Many detainees claimed that police had put plastic bags over people's heads, not allowing them to breathe for long periods during interrogation, and others spoke of electric shock treatment as favoured in some South American countries (countries which, like South Africa, are rightly heavily criticised in the UK media, who largely ignore such accusations when they are levelled against our own security forces). Lord Gardiner, of the Parker Commission, found that the procedures adopted by the police were "secret, illegal, not morally justifiable and alien to the traditions of the greatest democracy in the world". Yet another investigation, The Bennett Report, said in 1979 that prisoners had "sustained injuries which were not self-inflicted". The Secretary of State at the time accepted the inquiries' broad conclusions, though now, over a decade after the British Government was hauled before the European Commission of Human Rights and found guilty of the use of torture, numerous comparable accusations are still being made.

Torture has, of course, been used by almost every country in the world to extract information and admissions from suspects. The Catholic inquisitions and Protestant witch hunters of previous centuries had demonstrated that physical pain is a good key with which to open up the mind. Torture victims are not usually imprisoned because of what they have done, but because of what they know and because of what they might do. Because of what they *think*.

THOUGHT CRIME

We all know that to attempt a crime is in itself an offence, and to conspire with others to commit a crime is also an offence. Did you know, though, that under the Police & Criminal Evidence Act of 1984, it is now tantamount to an offence *for you to have in your mind the intention to commit a crime,* even if you keep silent about it. To have criminal thoughts – even if they are not acted upon in any way – in the privacy of one's own mind is now itself good reason for the police to act against you. *"For the police to now have powers to do things such as set up roadblocks in order to find people who they merely believe may be intending to commit an offence takes us dangerously near to the Thought-Crime of George Orwell,"* commented Lord Gifford.

He was not alone in his condemnation of the Tories' new law. The Law Society said that it was 'absolutely against' parts of the Act. Also, in a *Sunday Times*/MORI poll, more than 65% of the public opposed the Act. Nowadays, in our free country, one cannot move around freely if the authorities perceive that you may be thinking of committing an offence, regardless of your behaviour. Miners, during the Coal Strike of 1985, were the first large group to fall victim of the Thought Police, as they were intercepted on roads and turned back at county borders in case they were planning to join a picket.

If you listen to Government Ministers and their cronies in the right wing press, the police only used this tactic occasionally, when imminent violence was obvious in the vicinity. The Chief Constable of Nottinghamshire admitted, however, that 164,508 people who were guilty of no crime, were prevented from entering the county of Nottinghamshire in one 27-week period during the strike. The police roadblocks effectively cut off the counties of Nottinghamshire, Derbyshire, Yorkshire and many other mining areas, turning them into 'no-go' areas for hundreds of thousands of ordinary people. Any individual who was told to turn back but who insisted on exercising his right as a British citizen to freedom of movement was promptly arrested.

When the generally peaceful Stonehenge Festival was outlawed in 1985, 1,363 policemen massed around the nearby site on which the convoy camped, harassing and abusing the six or seven hundred picnicking hippies who had gathered. The report investigating the incident was highly critical of police tactics and behaviour, and also of the manner in which hippies were detained after arrest – in overcrowded cells without proper toilet facilities. When the report was published in April 1987, the toothless nature of such inquiries was revealed when the Chief Constable of Somerset said that he "would do the same again" if the hippies ever returned. Not *one* of the tabloid newspapers covered the findings of the report, which found that "some officers used excessive force". It also concluded that the 537 arrests which took place "were largely wrong", and that "a number of incidents took place in which members of the public were hit by police with truncheons...the police accept the truth of these incidents [but] it has not been possible to identify *any* of the officers concerned" (my emphasis).

Surely, in this free country, one asks, the armed thugs guilty of beating up innocent men, women and children have been arrested, imprisoned, or at least drummed out of the Force?

The answer is all too predictable. Not one policeman was charged with any offence after the Stonehenge debacle. Shame on them.

Kate Adie is a well known TV Reporter who has worked in Libya and Lebanon, among other places. In none of these 'oppressive' nations has she been attacked by the police. However, in common with other journalists and TV camera crews, the British police refused her entry to certain areas of Wapping when she was covering the print workers dispute. A good old British Bobby also hit her with a truncheon in the course of his duty.

Adie is far from being alone in her experience with the police. Cameras covering protests at Greenham Common, Toxteth, Aldgrave, Stonehenge and numerous other places have been covered up by the ubiquitous police glove, and the National Union of Journalists has had many complaints about the police from their members. Journalists covering police actions are now fair game, it seems; as is anyone who may be vaguely identified with a group that has been socially stigmatised, such as hippies, football fans, punks, pickets etc. All are legitimate targets as the new rules give police greater powers and allow far more scope for any personal bigotry which they may have to be vented. An individual's behaviour and intent may be peaceful and law-abiding. But it doesn't matter anymore. The police, it seems, can now read minds.

If you are a male and police see you talking to someone who they know to be a prostitute, you can both be arrested under The Sexual Offences Act 1985. This typically Victorian piece of legislation was supposed to make the streets safer for women. In fact, it merely gave police more powers to intervene in the voluntary sexual transactions of consenting adults, and diverted the police from their real task – to arrest and convict rapists. According to the organisation Women Against Rape, the Act "makes women more, not less, vulnerable to rape and other sexual assault." It does, however, appeal to the moralists of the Tory party and to the type of policemen who are obviously keen to exercise their new-found mind-reading powers.

All of this may be alright if you're white, middle class, middle aged and female (in fact, just like Margaret Thatcher). But don't be young, don't look different, don't be male and, above all, don't be black...

"There was a time, in Nazi Germany, when police were instructed in a similar way to look at the features of a person. If he had Semitic features he could be arrested."

(Lord Molloy speaking on the Government's new laws.)

Mark Bravo is not a criminal, but he is black. On his 16th birthday he got a Suzuki motorbike, and started riding it near his home in North London. In the first *week* he was stopped by police seven times. This was only the beginning, as over the next few months, he was stopped dozens of times. It got so bad, his mother started keeping a diary of the general police harassment of the boy. It revealed that, for example, in the period between March 31st and April 14th, he was stopped 24 times (nearly twice every day). By the end of the year, fed up with dozens of more incidents, Mark sold his bike.

In December '84, Derek Donaldson, a musician with the group Sons of Jah, was injured while being "searched" by police in the street. He was charged with assault, but Judge Suckling QC dismissed the charges against him, noting that the arresting officers had given evidence saying that "anyone in the Notting Hill area is suspected of being in possession of a controlled drug."

On May 6th, 1982, Matthew Paul, a 19 year-old "black youth" was found dead in his cell at Leman Street Police Station. He had been detained, without charge, for 36 hours without access to his family, friends or a solicitor – this is perfectly legal (in fact new laws allow police to keep you without charge for up to 96 hours). Paul had hanged himself (after being questioned by police) from a flap on his cell door which had been left open by police officers despite regulations to the contrary and regardless of a recommendation made by a West London coroner after a similar death had occurred in another station. What's unusual about Matthew's case is that the inquest jury returned a verdict of "suicide due to lack of care". In this case, though, it's strange to note that in the official Home Office records *the jury's verdict is not recorded.* Also, in new coroners rules which came into force shortly after the Paul case, the list of available verdicts open to a jury was altered so as to exclude the use of the words "lack of care" where death resulted from violence, accident or suicide in police cells.

It is common practice for people to be held, incommunicado and without charges being made, for long periods of time in police cells. It is also quite common for people to die while being held in custody for one reason or another. In 1983, the most recent year's figures which are available, 106 people died while in cells. Although perhaps not too much importance should be attached to statistics, it is strange to note that between 1970 and 1983, the number of annual deaths while in police custody has increased by 300%.

When a death occurs in a police cell, a public inquiry is held. There are literally dozens of cases which record such deaths as being caused by violence, though they are usually very briefly reported. Unfortunately, one has to die while in custody in order to get a public inquiry. If you are merely beaten, you apparently have little cause for concern.

It seems that the general attitude is that anyone who finds himself in a police station deserves to be there and can therefore expect such treatment. The system is geared towards acceptance of the fact that as any such complaints are so difficult to prove, they should remain unanswered. So *no* independent jurors sit in on complaints made against the police. Most complainants therefore do not bother to go through official channels. This is hardly good for public confidence in the police.

Someone who had his confidence in the police severely impaired was reggae singer Junior Service. He was arrested in February 1984 and charged with handling a stolen cheque. Later the same day he was stretchered out of Brixton Police Station to Kings College Hospital. An emergency operation was performed after doctors at the hospital found that he had "severe injuries" to his penis resulting in an inability to pass water.

At 10.40 pm on the 1st January, 1987, Police arrested 19-year-old Trevor Monerville for breaking the window of a parked car. His family were not informed of the arrest, and Monerville's worried father visited Stoke Newington Police Station on several occasions during the following few days, asking the police if they knew what had happened to his son. On one occasion, he even brought in a photo of Trevor to show the desk sergeant while asking for him to be put on the Missing Persons list. On each occasion, the police claimed to have no knowledge of Trevor's whereabouts, even though, in fact, he was in cells at Stoke Newington Police Station itself. The following Sunday, Mr Monerville was shocked to learn that his son was in Brixton Prison Hospital. When he had last seen him, on the evening of the 31st December, he had appeared perfectly normal and well. A few days later, after being held secretly in police cells, he needed a brain operation. Anthony Strong, the consultant neurosurgeon at Maudsey Hospital where Trevor was taken to be treated, indicated that Trevor's head injuries which made the operation necessary were likely to have been caused by a blow with an instrument. The police custody records, later obtained by Monerville's solicitor, show that six officers were involved in taking Trevor's fingerprints "by force". It also shows that Trevor's clothes were somehow destroyed. Police did not make any charge against Trevor, who is now partially paralysed.

In December 1982, police shot dead Rod Carroll and another man. Constable John Robertson was subsequently charged with murder. During his trial, Robertson gave evidence saying that the police had lied at the time of the shootings when they claimed that the two men had crashed through a police roadblock. The police did not challenge this evidence at the trial. P.C. Robertson was acquitted. The local coroner was later asked to investigate the double killing. A few days later, he resigned.

The British Crime Survey of 1984 revealed that fewer than one person in ten who had a complaint against the police took it to the authorities. If you do make such a complaint about the behaviour of a policeman, it will, on average, take 216 days for your complaint to be processed. All complaints made against police officers are carried out by their colleagues on the force. Of those complaints which are received, only 10% lead to a police officer being disciplined or 'advised'. So, the statistics suggest that if a policeman were to hit you for no reason, he has less than a 1 in a 100 chance of being reprimanded by his superiors – let alone being convicted of assault.

Often, however, it seems that when a general complaint about police behaviour is made, the force suffers lapses of memory, loses documentation, and the culprits cannot be identified. In 1986 it was revealed by former officers that detectives in Kent, keen to increase their crime clear-up rate, bribed criminals with promises of bail if they would admit to crimes other than those for which they had been arrested. More than 150 officers were investigated, but it was reported that, as many crucial files had mysteriously "gone missing", not one prosecution was made.

When Liverpool football fans contributed to the Heysel Stadium disaster at the 1985 European Cup Final at which 38 Juventus fans died, police, under pressure from Downing Street, spent months studying TV and video footage of the event, along with hundreds of blown-up newspaper stills, so that they could identify trouble makers in the crowd and track them down. They did very well, too, arresting fans months after the event and deporting them to Belgium for trial. It seems then that they can manage to make identifications of nameless faces in the melee of a fighting football crowd, but when presented with clear, close-up TV film of their own officers, identification is impossible. As happened at Stonehenge, for example.

Such was also the case at the Orgrave Coking Plant in 1985, when opposition MPs wanted some officers disciplined or charged with criminal offences after watching the violent scenes on TV. The force didn't take such action due to "the problems of identifying officers in the crowd." Weird.

ONE MAN'S RIOT

A riot was started by the police when, in a raid on her home, Mrs Cynthia Jarret – an innocent woman accused of no crime – died after being flung to the ground by police. (The start of this riot was similar to the beginning of the Handsworth riot, when Cheryl Groce was attacked by police.) In the Broadwater Farm riot which followed a few hours after the Jarret incident, a policeman was brutally killed.

Many feel that this incident led the police, and the courts, into actions that Lord Gifford QC said exceeded zealousness and clearly broke the law. In the days following the riot, hundreds of police in full riot gear occupied the flats of the Estate and – in the words of the Queen's Council's report – "terrorised" innocent residents, smashed down dozens of doors unnecessarily, and arrested hundreds of young men. The official inquiry found that when the arrested people's parents and legal advisers inquired at police stations as to the whereabouts of the young men, they were deliberately lied to and misled.

"Those being questioned were being hidden away in police stations" said Gifford. The inquiry found that in very many cases, the police held people far longer without charge than the law allowed (36 hours), and denied them any right to legal advice or contact with the outside world until a confession was signed. As a result of the many 'confessions' which somehow appeared, the courts were faced with a procession of cases involving juveniles and people of 17 and 18 who apparently had admitted to a variety of serious allegations entirely of their own free will. Not surprisingly, jurors did not know that many such confessions had come

from terrified young people who had been isolated and questioned for days without any legal counselling. So, when presented with such confessions, many jurors – who had themselves recently been horrified to read of the barbaric killing of the young PC – went unquestioningly with the police view and took such confessions at face value. Once defendants were convicted, the judges were severe.

In January '88, Government Minister David Mellor visited the Gaza Strip. In a well-publicised incident which outraged the Israelis, he criticised the housing conditions of the Palestinians and carpeted an accompanying Israeli official for the arrest of a youth, near his entourage, who was throwing stones. The British Foreign Office spokesman told the Israeli hosts that *"in Britain we don't arrest young men for throwing stones"*.

Tell that to the judge. One young (black) man arrested in Tottenham for throwing stones during the riot was sentenced to eight (8) years' imprisonment.

One 13 year old 'confessed' after being held incommunicado for three days in a police cell, after being interrogated regularly and only allowed to wear his underpants during his confinement.

The comparisons with the type of charges brought by the police and the punishments meted out by the courts between the Tottenham cases and those arising from the earlier Handsworth riot add fuel to the belief that zealousness against specific murderers had given way to a police policy of outright discrimination against a whole community.

After the far longer, bigger and more violent Handsworth riot, in which petrol bombs caused more damage, and during which two (Asian) men were killed, the type of charges brought were far less serious. At Tottenham, 71 were charged with affray, 13 with riot and 6 with murder (though charges were dropped against 2 as the judge found discrepancies in the police evidence). At Birmingham, only 16 people were charged with serious offences such as affray, and nobody with murder (even the manslaughter charges were reduced). Sentences were also strangely different. Arsonists convicted in Birmingham were given shorter sentences than those convicted of less serious offences in Tottenham.

The Report into the causes of the Tottenham riot found that the local community had "justified anger" stemming from the long term history of policing of the area, sparked by the death of Mrs Jarret on that October night.

Since the days of the Peterloo Massacre, the U.K. has, of course, been a nation of rioters and of swift action against those involved in any such violent protest. A classic modern example was Bloody Sunday, when the army shot dead 13 of the United Kingdom's residents.

Although there have been scores of riots in Belfast and Londonderry regardless of the political climate in London, and although there are intermittent shudders on the UK 'mainland' such as at Red Lion Square, Grunwick and Lewisham (where Blair Peach was killed with a police truncheon and no-one was charged with his death), we have not had such troubled streets since the social unrest of the Industrial Revolution. Thatcher's extremist policies have, perhaps, truly taken us back to 'Victorian values'.

History clearly shows that in any country where freedom of expression is denied, where the concepts of equality and education are openly abused, and where people are patronised, oppressed and dissatisfied, there will be riots. St. Pauls, Toxteth, Brixton, Tottenham, Nothing Hill, Wapping – we are informed about riots which occur at the focal points of media attention, but what of the incidents in cities such as Southampton, Leeds, Wolverhampton and Plymouth, or those at new towns such as Skelmersdale, which have only been reported locally?

In the case of Skelmersdale, reporters from Radio Piccadilly in Manchester telephoned the local police for news of what was happening during the riot, but were told that "nothing unusual" was, in fact, going on. Is it true that such "riots" are now fairly commonplace, and that police chiefs are simply denying that they have occurred? The evidence from around the country suggests that this is so. (500 people turning over cars and looting shops would have been national news in 1970, one thinks.) Perhaps the reason for such a cover-up is that police fear creating a knock-on effect of 'copycat' riots nationwide, which Tory MPs accused the Media of doing after the first Brixton riots. Perhaps the policy expressed by Mary Whitehouse at the time, to censor the news, was, in fact, adopted.

Perhaps the answer to the paranoid idea of a mass cover-up is far more simple. Nationally, such events are just not reported. The Media is not interested any more, because the nation is bored with watching images of blazing cars, baton charges and rubber bullets being fired. (When was the last time you saw a Belfast riot reported? Have they stopped?) Protest and oppression are now so tolerable, they're no longer news; and if they're no longer news, they might as well not be real.

PRISON

All countries have prisons; few have as high a percentage of their people inside them as we do. Britain has far more people in prison than any other European country. As you read this, nearly one person in every thousand is in jail.

In some countries, prisons are seen as places of rehabilitation rather than punishment. The impression Britain gives to the outside world is that we, too, look upon prisons largely as places of reform. Incarceration is merely a last resort, used to protect the general public from its most violent and habitually criminal members. A prison sentence is more of an inconvenience to the prisoner, not a denial of all rights spent in a place of misery and despair etc. We are, after all, a modern, liberal and just society.

Barry Foster was kept imprisoned for more than two years before his case came to trial. He had admitted while under police questioning to a crime which it was proved that he did not commit. Despite this, he was kept in prison. The Home Office gave his MP, Robert MacLennan, no explanation for keeping Foster imprisoned for so long without him being found guilty of any crime.

The Secretary of State for the Home Office (the person appointed by the Prime Minister to be in charge of prison affairs and know what he's talking about) claims to have "no record" of the number of people held in jail in England and Wales without trial. The official government estimate (likely to be conservative) is that, at any one time, there are about 1,500 people in prison who have been held there for *over three months without being found guilty of any crime.* (This figure does not include those in prison in Scotland and N. Ireland.) What the Government does not publicise is that, in some parts of the U.K., it will on *average* take you 178 days in prison before your case even comes to trial.

There was a time, not so long ago, when such remand prisoners were allowed a few privileges not shared by convicted prisoners. Relatives were able to visit more often, and food, toothpaste and other items were allowed to be sent in to these inmates who had not been convicted of any crime. No more. In December 1987 the Government announced that drugs were being smuggled into prisons in food parcels, so all privileges enjoyed by previous generations of remand prisoners were immediately curtailed. The Prison Officers' unions said it would be easy for their members to search parcels to prevent this happening, if they had enough staff. Cutting citizens' rights was cheaper than employing an adequate number of prison officers.

In January 1988, the main Prison Officers' Union balloted its members on the question of industrial action in protest at low manning levels throughout Britain's jails. The overwhelming majority of members – over 90% – voted for such action. The Government, however, said that the vote for action only amounted to just over 45% of the *total* workforce, so "we do not consider that 45% gives them a mandate" (said the Home Office).

Strange, that. The same Government, after all, was voted in by only 19% of the total U.K. population. No more prison officers were employed. Unemployment carried on rising. Prisoners' rights continued to erode due to "lack of staff".

As anyone who has spent time in prison will tell you, British prisons are often dangerous, old fashioned and overcrowded (official reports show that we have 9,000 more prisoners than we have authorised prison places). Violence among inmates and between inmates and warders is said to be common. Once inside, justice is rare.

In a test case, a former prisoner claimed damages against the Home Office for assault and battery, and the administration of drugs against his will while in custody. (Unusually, the prisoner concerned also continued to protest his innocence of the crime for which he was imprisoned, long after he was sent down. As such protests can lengthen one's stay in jail, this is something few convicts do). In the case, the Home Office denied that the prisoner was forced to take drugs or that he was assaulted, saying that he expressly consented to the administration of the drugs. However, the man claimed that five prison officers had entered his cell, held him down, wrenched off his trousers and pushed a needle into his buttocks – injecting Stelesine. He claimed that these forced injections happened on several occasions. The judge accepted the evidence of the prison officers, however, who claimed to be "totally unaware of the absence of any consent to the injections", and the case was dismissed. The ex-prisoner appealed, but the case was dismissed again.

Legal expert Sir John Donaldson says that a prisoner cannot, as a matter of law, give an effective consent to treatment under any circumstances. Lord Avebury claims that even if a prisoner agrees to medication, it is often due to the fact that any refusal can be interpreted as a refusal to co-operate with the prison authorities, thus lengthening the stay in prison.

The practice of injecting prisoners with drugs is not uncommon. In 1984, the Home Office admitted that in 1983 alone, 8,220 doses of psychotropic drugs were injected into prisoners. These *mind-related* drugs were, we should stress, not injected into people incarcerated in mental institutions, but into inmates of normal prisons. No figures for orally-administered drugs in prisons are available for publication.

Although the particular test case mentioned may or may not have had a basis in fact, such accusations of forced drugging and other forms of mistreatment are very common indeed. It has even been pointed out in Parliament that "there is a pattern and consistency about ex-prisoners' allegations of brutality which lends substance to such claims."

Such accusations are almost impossible to prove. Even when presented with a corpse, it seems that the legal establishment is unable to come up with many cases in which either police or prison officers have been jailed for acts of violence, let alone murder. Often, it seems, when someone is badly injured or dies while in prison the motions of a concerned society are gone through, inquests are held...and nothing happens.

Let us take the example of just one of the prisons in England and Wales, the example of Wandsworth Prison in South London.

At Wandsworth, Terry Smerdon was recently found dead in his cell with bruises to his body. The inquest returned an "open" verdict.

Ian Methven was another prisoner to meet his end in a Wandsworth cell. The inquest verdict this time was "death due to lack of care".

Lennie Turner alleges that while in Wandsworth, he was assaulted and denied food and drink for five days.

Jimmy Anderson, who actually went as far as asking a court's permission to take legal proceedings against some prison officers at Wandsworth, said in court that other prison officers had threatened him with death unless he dropped his charges. He applied to the High Court to allow him to take the legal action necessary to try the prison officers who had assaulted him, but Lord Justice Tasker Williams ruled against him, stopping him from taking legal action on the grounds that there was "adequate protection against abuse within the prison system". No prison officers were even brought to trial.

Although *thousands* of similar complaints have been made about the illegal actions of prison officers, many totally legal punishments pass without comment. At the discretion of Prison Officers alone, a variety of extreme punishments and restraints can be imposed on a prisoner. Under Rule 43, prisoners can be segregated and put into solitary confinement; they can be strapped into the notorious Body Belt (a sort of leather straight-jacket); or they can be incarcerated in 'Strong Box' cells (otherwise known as 'Strip Cells').

Strip-searching is common. In 1982, some prisons introduced the practice of strip searching women prisoners. In *one* prison, 97 prisoners were strip searched a total of 772 times in a period of 4 months – almost eight strip searches per prisoner. In June 1983 records show that one woman at the same prison was strip searched 28 times. This practice continues, and is quite legal.

Contrary to popular opinion, most criminals who are sent to prison have been convicted of crimes not against people, but against the property of people – victimless crimes. Of all crimes reported in England and Wales in 1986, *96% were committed against property.* Despite the headlines and the propaganda put about by the Home Office and the Police, the vast majority of people now in prison are *not* violent, are *not* sexually motivated, and do *not* represent a physical danger to other members of society. They are far more likely to have stolen a car, evaded tax, sold a pornographic video, or taken marijuana than they are of raping or killing anyone. But in a society obsessed with materialism, censorship and restriction, they are dumped into a prison system that does not properly differentiate between the violent and the unlucky. Although some prisons are better than others, if you are put in prison in this country, even for a victimless crime, it is not only possible that you may be injected with drugs, stripped and caged in a bare cell and – if certain members of the House of Lords are to be believed – beaten up by guards and other inmates; it is also possible that if you have a mental or physical problem, you will not be given the medical attention expected by any civilised society.

Take the example of Alan Tschelbinski. When he arrived at the aptly-named Strangeways prison, he was suffering from fits. Instead of being hospitalised, he was transferred to a cell with bare brick walls, a concrete floor, and no furniture except for a bare mattress which lay on the floor. He was stripped naked and left alone in this cell for several days. Most of the time he spent lying on the cell floor, the last couple of days in his own excrement. When the fits took hold of him, he would run against the cell walls. He was not treated for any of the bruising and other injuries that occurred. Despite his appalling condition, the prison authorities refused to allow his parents admission when they came to visit him, even though they knew that his mother had dealt with him successfully on many occasions in the past when he had been suffering from fits. Alan died within a week of being imprisoned. At his inquest, which uncovered the details of his death listed here, the prison authorities still maintained that the cell was "the proper place" for Alan.

Although our prisons and detention centres are hopelessly overcrowded, there is a remedy that would not involve a great deal of public expenditure. That would be to de-criminalise several offences, such as the possession of certain drugs, instruct magistrates to sentence people to shorter terms for minor crimes which are not carried out against the person, and, instead of punishing offenders by simply sending them to prison, make them do community service work and pay compensation to the owners of the property which they have stolen or damaged. Despite the common sense of these suggestions, which have been made in a number of reports, courts seem reluctant to change, as every year the prison population increases and the penal system sags under the pressure. One other alternative answer to the problem of prison overcrowding is to let prisoners die, particularly if they are as troublesome as Tschelbinski. Alan was not unique. Someone dies in a cell in this country every two days.

The National Council for Civil Liberties (now called 'Liberty') receives, on average, 2,000 letters a year concerning the abuse of prisoners. A typical case they have highlighted was that of 18 year old Jim Heather-Hayes. He committed suicide while at Ashford Remand Centre, just after being examined by the Prison Doctor. At the inquest into his death the doctor gave evidence which revealed what Ashford's medical care really entailed. *"I go into a cell with a warder and I say 'Are you alright?'. Heather-Hayes did not reply, so I left the cell."*

Risley Remand Centre is another prison which holds people who have been found guilty of no crime. In a report on the Centre, published in June '88, it was found that the centre was "infested with cockroaches and other pests, toilet facilities were practically non-existent and overall conditions ranged from bad to disgusting". In Risley's twenty odd years of existence, there have been 25 suicides.

Of course, not all prisons are hell-holes. The Government would point to some that are very good, and indeed they are. But surely, we do not need to be concerned about what goes on in good prisons, but as a caring society we *must* be concerned with the many bad ones.

The message is, perhaps we British should not be as complacent about our own prison system, nor as quick to condemn the prisons in other countries (such as those in Turkey or the USSR, for instance) until we have made reforms here.

The problem is that MPs, newspapers and the general public are not very concerned about what goes on inside the prison walls, and of those few campaigners that are concerned, many find it impossible to judge the situation themselves as their sources, the former prisoners themselves, are automatically discredited as witnesses due to their previous law breaking, and officialdom blocks any inquiries with a wall of silence and suspicion. We are back to the question of Information. Information about what goes on inside prisons is considered to be extraordinarily sensitive in free Britain.

Home office rules relating to prisoners writing books while serving their sentences say that inmates wishing to write a book while in custody may do so, and the book may be published after release, *"provided there is no reference to prison conditions, or members of the staff or fellow prisoners"*. On top of this, no manuscript can be sent out of prison, even after vetting, during the writer's sentence.

Books, letters, notes and even personal diaries written by prisoners while in custody are prison property, and may be censored or confiscated at any time, for any reason, and kept – even after the prisoner's release from gaol.

Compare this with unfree Russia. When convicted spy Peter Kroger was exchanged for British spy Gerald Brooke, all of his notebooks were taken from him by the prison authorities and he was not allowed to leave prison with them. Brooke, coming back to England from the USSR brought back all his 30-odd prison notebooks to the U.K.

HEALTH, SEX AND MORALITY (THE CONDOMS GO ON AND THE GLOVES COME OFF)

The many areas that we have already covered seem to give the impression that there is a great deal of repression in the land of the free. Anyone who endeavours to bring information to the public which highlights this fact is open to persecution, regardless of their motives. The right wing monopoly that controls the news media and the extremist, censorious, amateurish attempts of the political left to counter-balance this on 'alternative' TV shows and in magazines means that 'political' avenues of expression are also, in practice, limited and compartmentalised.

Having said that, however, there is a great deal more tolerance shown to political dissenters (who retain a small degree of power due to their voting capacity), than there is to people who publish information relating to Religion and Sex. Even the lethargic British would, one thinks, protest if anything like the same degree of open interference and censorship were shown in public political matters as in private sexual ones. Our freedom to complain about the government, sometimes even to criticise the government (though not the State) is considered fundamental, and infinitely more important than our freedom to do with our own bodies what we wish.

As the only alternative to the government is another government, which acts in much the same way as the one that went before it, the State System can afford to encourage superficial criticism of Downing Street and accept government personnel changes if the system is to survive without serious questions being asked of the very structure of British society.

A real necessity of Control is to control each individual as a single entity, thereby controlling the masses. This control over the individual is no more apparent, and at the same time no more apparently unnecessary, as it is in the area of sex.

The social pressures put on an individual so that he or she conforms to 'normality' are so enormous and widely experienced that we need not even cite examples of this here. The British seem totally obsessed with sex, and the law is full of the results of this unhealthy obsession. Here are a few examples.

The Post Office Acts make it an offence for anyone to send "indecent" material through the post, even if it is packaged in such a way as to cause no possible offence to prudish postmen...

Anal intercourse between men and women is illegal – even if the participants are married...

In 1985, a Midland based contact magazine called *'Rendezvous'* was prosecuted, and production of the magazine stopped. The magazine published no erotic stories or letters, no photographs of models or genitalia. What it did do was feature lists of personal adverts placed voluntarily by adult members of the public wishing to meet others, primarily for sex. The magazine accepted no adverts from minors or prostitutes or pornographers, and was only on sale to people over the age of 18. This did not stop it being fined...

Nightshift was a nightclub operating in central London that was frequented primarily by suburban married couples interested in the "swinging" scene. Although no on-premises sex was permitted by the management and the club was only used as a meeting point for likeminded adults, the police raided the club in November '87, saying that they were "investigating possible licensing infringements and (unspecified) indecent behaviour." The club was forced to close...

Homosexuality is still forbidden in the armed forces. It is thought that nearly 100 men a year are locked up in Colchester Military Training Centre, guilty of nothing more than being gay. In a flagrant breach of an individual's right to privacy, the military question candidates about their personal sexual habits prior to admission. It also goes to great lengths to root-out individuals who it suspects of being gay, and court marshals them, kicking them out. This means, in effect, that thousands of pounds of taxpayer's money is wasted on their training, and the military lose hundreds of competent, professional individuals.

After a series of police raids on private homes in 1990, codenamed Operation Spanner, sixteen men were convicted of assaults causing actual bodily harm and wounding at the Old Bailey, under sections 47 and 20 of the Offences Against the Person Act, 1861. Their crime had been to indulge in heavy homosexual S/M activities with each other, and commit some of these scenes to video. The video was not sold or distributed, but was discovered by police in one of the initial raids. All the defendants were over the age of twenty one. Sentences varied, but some of the convicted men were given up to four and a half years in prison. The Court of Appeal cut some of the sentences, but upheld the convictions. Lawyers for the convicted men took the case on through to the House of Lords, where, on 11th March 1993, the original judgement was upheld by the Law Lords by a small majority. One of the judges, Lord Lowry, said: *"Homosexual activity cannot be regarded as conducive to the welfare of society or the enhancement of family life."* Another, Lord Templeman, said: *"Society is entitled to protect itself against a cult of violence. Pleasure derived from the infliction of pain is an evil thing."* So, regardless of the fact that the men involved were all above the legal age of consent, acted in private and through their own volition, and, prior to the new interpretation of this ancient law, had no reason to believe that they were acting illegally, they still went to Brixton prison. At the time of writing, several of the defendants are thus languishing in jail for inflicting minor, short term injuries on each other, while successful boxers are lauded and respected members of society for doing the same thing. Britain, as a member of the EC, is a signatory to the European Convention on Human Rights, Article 8 of which guarantees respect for the private life of each European citizen. The case is being taken to the European Commission of Human Rights. Co-incidentally, on the day the Law Lord's ruling was reported, some newspapers carried a small item on the case of doctors who had acquiesced with the Jehovah's Witness parents of a 13-day-old baby by refusing to give medical attention that, in the words of the doctors, would have saved the mother's life. Some gay men, who, by their sexual orientation, do not contribute in the normal way to the "enhancement of family life" were given prison sentences for consentual activities that caused no permanent injury or damage, let alone death. On the same day, a Christian sect is, on the other hand, allowed to let people die, thus depriving their children of the "enhancement of family life". Extremists with "Christian" motives are apparently alright, even if their activities lead to the death of others. Extremists who have personal, sexual motives, are punished by the law, even if their activities harm no-one.

New York has Times Square, Paris has The Pigalle, Hamburg has The Reeperbahn – London had Soho. Due to the connivance of the Metropolitan Police, Westminster Council and the Government, there are no longer any shops in Soho selling only sexually-related literature. There are no filmclubs screening explicit adult movies.

This may be no great loss, but it is indicative of the current puritanical crackdown that's taking place in this country. It has also caused problems. When the Recreational Sex industry is driven underground, rather than regulated by public scrutiny, a situation is created where gangsters, rip-off merchants and black marketeers of all kinds move in. This is bad for the police, bad for the hapless customers, and bad for those involved – who are far more likely to be treated badly and exploited and less likely to be given regular health checks. Thatcher's Britain prefers to sweep Sex under the carpet. If one compares the situation in Copenhagen, which has council-run brothels, legal gay clubs etc., with that in Bangkok, which outlaws prostitution and therefore has a terrible record of child exploitation and disease, one wonders why the British authorities adopt such an unrealistic and restrictive policy.

Politicians can say what they like, but the bottom line in all political debate is the allocation of resources. The splitting up of the cake. And the State, in this allocation of resources and set of priorities, reveals in this way its true attitude towards certain sections of society, and the way in which they behave. The most obvious and topical case in question at present is how the British government, NHS, DHSS, scientific establishment and the media have reacted to the HIV virus and its spread of AIDS.

The Syndrome was first identified by doctors in America at the turn of the decade, and by 1983 the sexually transmitted nature of the virus' spread was well known. In the first few years the problem confined itself almost entirely to gay men, mainline drug users and a relatively minuscule number of haemophiliacs. Information about the disease was, however, left largely to the gay press, the Terence Higgins Trust charity and a handful of aware doctors in STD clinics. Despite warnings from the USA, which were heeded in countries such as Holland and Sweden, the British government left it more than three years, until the end of 1986, to take serious action. Was it coincidental that this happened just as health experts warned that the disease had started to spread into the heterosexual community? At the time, it was estimated that over 50,000 British people had already been infected with the virus. Besides a few thousand haemophiliacs, a few hundred junkies and only six heterosexual women, all these 50,000 were thought to be gay men.

When the evidence showed that heterosexuals were becoming at risk, the government allocated £4 million to fund 21 AIDS related projects (only four of which were engaged in looking for a cure for the disease.) To put this into perspective, this sum represents the equivalent of one third of the cost of one Tornado fighter, of which the RAF have 220. At the beginning of 1987, £20 million was spent on an advertising campaign warning about the disease (compared to the £40 million spent on advertising shares in British Gas a few months earlier). One survey showed that the public thought the government had reacted well to the threat, though the gay press wondered publicly why the government had waited so many years to take action. And why was its research budget one of the lowest per capita of any Western country? Why hadn't the government acted three years earlier, when the problem was perceived as being almost solely one for homosexuals? At least, at last, 'ordinary' people were being made aware of the problem, even though the battle against 'ignorance' was fought not with Durex – who the IBA initially refused permission to advertise on TV – but with volcanoes and icebergs.

In February '87 Junior Health Minister Edwina Curry spoke her Government's mind at a speech in Liverpool. *"Good, Christian people don't get AIDS,"* she assured the nation, and went on to say that *"only people who misbehave are at risk"*. It seems, then, that as the virus only affects what one must logically assume from her speech are bad, godless people who obviously disagree with the perverse pseudo-Victorian values of the Government, there is no reason for their health to be any concern.

Meanwhile, that other pillar of the establishment, the Christian Church, set about offering constructive advice on the problem. *"The AIDS TV adverts encourage sex amongst the young,"* boomed one helpful Catholic Bishop, adding that the tombstone shape used in the ads was *"too phallic"*. (Quite how the threat of death and the allure of a gravestone encouraged sex was not made clear.) A vicar in Kent refused to allow the burial of a young gay victim of the disease in his graveyard, saying *"We don't want people like that buried here."* True compassion.

There are many pleasant, well-meaning people involved with the Christian Church, and the faith and rhetoric it generates may be very helpful to many people. But the hard fact, like it or not, is that the Church is the enemy of Freedom of Choice. When faced with difficult, real issues, the Church always agrees with the concept of interference, rather than persuasion by example. As it is a supposedly Christian set of morals which are the foundation of the State's attitudes to sex and sexuality, it is always the followers of the Church in this country who persecute any sexually (or otherwise) identified minority. So, "good" reasons are always drummed up to support such persecution. British Communists are bugged as they are assumed to be in league with the Anti-Christ in Moscow; gays are victimised and denied entry to the Church as Ministers as they pervert youngsters and spread disease; antisemitism is still rife as the Jewish faith opposes the validity and power of Christ; videos are censored to protect children from being led astray. And so it goes on (and on).

Although we do not want to dwell on the question of AIDS, or the persecution of male homosexuals, in recent years it is this group of individuals who have suffered most obviously as the State looks for 'deviants' and minorities to make scapegoats of – and it is their experience that provides a classic example of how 'free' we really are in the last decade of the millenium.

In December '87, under pressure from Tory backbenchers, the Government sneaked a new clause into the Local Government Bill – a bill which, in itself, went further in taking power from democratically elected local councils and transferring it to Whitehall than anything that had gone before. Clause 28 said that local councils would now be "prohibited from the teaching in any maintained school of the acceptability of homosexuality..." and barred from "intentionally promoting homosexuality" in any way.

Incredibly (or not), the Parliamentary Labour Party supported the Clause, though their spokesman Jack Cunningham expressed reservations, asking if the public realised that the new legislation might prevent school and public libraries from stocking books by such eminent authors as Truman Capote, Oscar Wilde and Gore Vidal – all of whom described and 'promoted' homosexual lifestyles. Only *one* Tory MP – Michael Brown – opposed the Clause.

On the 9th January 1988, 12,000 people took part in an OLGA march demonstrating against Clause 28 in London. During the peaceful demo 20 people were arrested – two men for kissing in public, and others for carrying offensive weapons, the "weapons" being flag poles used to carry banners. The *Sunday Mirror*, Britain's only supposedly 'left wing' tabloid paper, devoted one column inch on an inside page to the march. When 40,000 demonstrated against the Clause in Manchester, most national papers ignored the event completely.

In March '87 Barrister Adrian Fulford reported that *"since the advent of AIDS, it seems that the number of arrests of gay men has gone up. And, whereas before most people arrested for importuning were normally cautioned or bound over without the case coming to trial, now it is more the case that the prosecutors insist that cases go to court."* The self-righteous, religious right wing have manipulated public opinion so brazenly since the appearance of AIDS that homosexuals in some areas are being treated in the same bigoted and often violent fashion as were Jews in Germany in the years preceding WWII. Rugby Council in Warwickshire refuse to employ homosexual men; an HIV carrier in Southampton has been banned from using his local council swimming pool; hundreds of gays have lost their jobs, and, since 1985, polls show that in the 1985/87 period, reported attacks on gay men increased by 1,000 percent.

The lesson to learn is that, whenever an excuse crops up which allows society to vent its true, barely-concealed hatred of any individual who seeks to live in a slightly different fashion, all civilised concepts of compassion, respect and tolerance go out the window. The gloves come off...

Or, in the case of the police, the gloves go on. Many gay men have reported that in recent raids on gay clubs, police have worn surgical gloves and joked about not wanting to touch any 'queers' when arresting them in case they catch the disease. (Our police are wonderful.)

Pressure is mounting from reactionary groups on all sides, particularly within the government. The Conservative Family Campaign, supported by a number of Tory MPs, is calling for a repeal of the 1967 Act which legalised homosexual acts between consenting adult men in the privacy of their own home. Though not, incidentally, in the privacy of their hotel room or any other 'public' place. (Homosexuality was still illegal in N. Ireland until 1982. It is also still illegal on the Isle of Man).

Geoffrey Dickens MP – a Tory backbencher – is not a member of the campaign, but he nevertheless has a lot to say about the subject. *"The family life of this country is eroding,"* due, he says, to liberal sexual attitudes. *"Homosexuals entice and corrupt others into their unnatural net. The 1967 Act should be repealed."* When asked about the question of Civil Rights, the exceptionally well-proportioned person says *"We have to interfere with civil liberties to do what's right,"* (don't they always) *"...normal people are appalled about the way homosexuality is spreading in this country."* But how would such a change in the law be enforced? *"Policing such a change in the law would include closing down all gay and lesbian clubs and pubs and limiting certain publications."*

Would this enforcement include police raids on the private bedrooms of adults living together who were *suspected* by the police of being homosexual, one wonders. *"Oh yes,"* he replies. *"Absolutely."* (Incidentally, Dickens has also been calling on the Government to introduce laws which will effectively ban any 'occult' practice in Britain. Something that would be constitutionally impossible for the Federal government to do in America, but is easy to do in free-thinking Britain.)

Such a change in the law would inevitably mean fewer gay men attending clinics for check-ups, for fear of a visit from policemen like the aforementioned James Anderton. This would no doubt facilitate the spread of diseases like AIDS. So, although Public Health is the excuse, it seems that a bigoted idea of 'Public Decency' is the real question behind such a change.

The Conservative Party is said to be seriously considering making such a change during their next period in office. Should the law be altered, police would be given even more discretionary powers to stop and question individuals, read minds, confiscate books, and raid private property. At the same time diverting manpower from the fight against rape, murder, mugging and other violent crimes that we are told are the threats that they are there to protect us from. The protection of the individual from physical attack, and the protection of his or her civil rights, are obviously not as important as implementing laws that are considered 'right' by a few hundred absolutist MPs and the Government's ventriloquist dummies in the Tory-owned right-wing press.

As a society, the British seem far less worried about the threat of violence than the perceived threat posed by people who *think differently*. Whether they be gay, communist, vegan, pagan, or 'mad'.

The threat that worries us as a Society is not that these or any other factions may somehow violently overthrow the systems to which we adhere, but that they may actually convince us that they are right. There may be ways of living which may be more practical and enjoyable. Why else would we harass peaceful organisations like CND, or make illegal certain sexual acts between adults? This is why alternative lifestyles and literature are treated with contempt and derision in the popular press. This is why we are encouraged not to think or act differently. This is why there is hardly ever any talk about what happens to people when they have mental problems.

Incredible as it may seem, there is now a growing body of opinion within the psychiatric profession that holds the previously unthinkable view that there is no such thing as mental illness unless the brain is injured or diseased, just variety and deviation in numerous – sometimes extreme – forms. Although this revolutionary opinion may be erroneous, and does sound something to be debated by eager 6th Form sociology students, the point is that over the years anti-social behaviour of all kinds in an individual has been seen as being the result of some vague mental "derangement". (Up until the 1920s, we still used to lock up epileptics, people who were catatonic, homosexual men and even unmarried mothers – who were thought to have a mental illness which explained their lack of morals.) Oddly enough, the behaviour of an individual is often the only 'proof' of any cerebral disorder we have, while at the same time the disorder itself is sometimes explained as originating from such behavioral experience. Although diagnosis and treatment of mental illness is undoubtedly well-intentioned, a Free Society must be very careful when it diagnoses people as being sick without their having any physical damage. Often, it seems that the basic criterion we have for judging mental disorder seems to be how inconvenient the person has become to their family, friends and doctors. No clear or consistent distinction has ever been made between criminals and mentally sick offenders, but a mental patient is robbed of even more rights – we even assume the right to tamper with the workings of their mind without their informed consent.

Of course, even in a free society, some such decisions have to be made. However, in a truly free and caring society, adequate safeguards which make incarceration of sane, anti-social people impossible should be in place. The files of the Mental Health charity MIND would suggest that in Britain, they are not.

It's generally believed that nobody here can be committed to a mental institution against their will unless several psychiatrists commit a patient referred to them for the protection of society as a whole. Not so. Under Section 4 of the Mental Health Act 1983, a Social Worker can apply for someone to be admitted and detained against their will if they think it necessary. Only one Doctor, a G.P. who may never before have met the 'patient' or have had any specialist training, is all that is now required to have a person forcibly admitted. Once the G.P. has given the go-ahead, the (usually old) person concerned can be forcibly taken from their home (usually by police and social workers), detained in a secure hospital, and forcibly drugged.

The 'patient' is left totally at the mercy of the doctor concerned, who can administer drugs such as neuroleptics which may be detrimental to his longterm general health. (Although any patient is to some degree at the mercy of his doctor, people with physical illness and injury have the right to refuse treatment, discharge themselves from hospital, or ask for a second opinion. Mental patients do not.) When they are diagnosed, often inaccurately, all their usual rights are taken away. Doctors, obsessed with the idea of 'psychosis', are often keen to treat behavioral difficulties with a flood of chemicals and little else.

The Mental Health Act does not forbid people other than doctors from administering drugs. Prison officers, nurses and health workers at mental hospitals forcibly administer drugs to inmates daily. The only legal right they have to do this is in cases of "urgent necessity" when the patient (or, it seems, prisoner) is unable to give his informed consent. (If, for example, he had been injured and was unconscious and therefore unable to agree to the administration of life-saving drugs.)

In reality, even when patients and prisoners are quite conscious, and involved in no urgent life or death situation they have no right to refuse injections of drugs. Such anti-social people, whether they can be called insane or criminal, are easier to handle when they are drugged up to the eyeballs, so the practice is widespread and officially condoned, though not publicised.

Despite persistent calls for reform, the government has not altered the law, and in passing the 1983 Act, threw away an opportunity to make the medical establishment and DHSS more accountable for its treatments and give more recognition to the question of individual patients' rights. In typical fashion, the British Government has, at the same time, been highly critical of the forcible drugging and incarceration of subversive and difficult individuals in other countries.

GOD'S POLITICS

The present Conservative Government is the most marvellous political animal to emerge in this country in the last 40 years because it has learnt first to influence public opinion, then reflect it. At least, reflect the parts of it which it finds useful.

There has been a media-manufactured change in attitudes towards Public Morality in the last few years, and in any country, such shifts in Public Opinion have a nasty habit of showing up as changes in the law. (Clause 28 is a classic example, in that it reflects rampant homophobia induced by AIDS.) Such changes also show-up in the way in which the State spends the tax payers' money.

For example. The government feels it wants to spend more money on the Police Force, so as to combat social unrest caused primarily by its uncaring economic programme and enforce its plethora of restrictive new laws. It cannot justify this vast increase in spending to the electorate in the light of the huge cutbacks in Health and Education, so it must carry support for such spending. The Police Force, happy to oblige as it always wants more muscle, concocts crime figures which show a crime wave of tidal proportions. So, in the 1986 statistics for example, there are hundreds more rapes than in 1985. In fact, as the Police later admitted, there were probably not, but methods of cataloguing reported rapes had changed, giving a misleadingly large apparent increase.

Of course, even in a democracy, the private attitudes and morals of an individual have nothing to do with changes in the law at all. What matters is Public Opinion. Public Opinion and Individual Morality are often confused. Public Opinion can be changed by whipping up hysteria in the news media, and by releasing distorted statistics. The private morals of each individual cannot be changed quite so easily. We live through our media, and in the media world, Public Opinion is formed not through a collection of independent thought or informed debate, but by the media's image of Public Opinion. The opinion represented in the views of a thin stratum of society – the 'personalities' who feature on TV, on radio, and in newspapers.

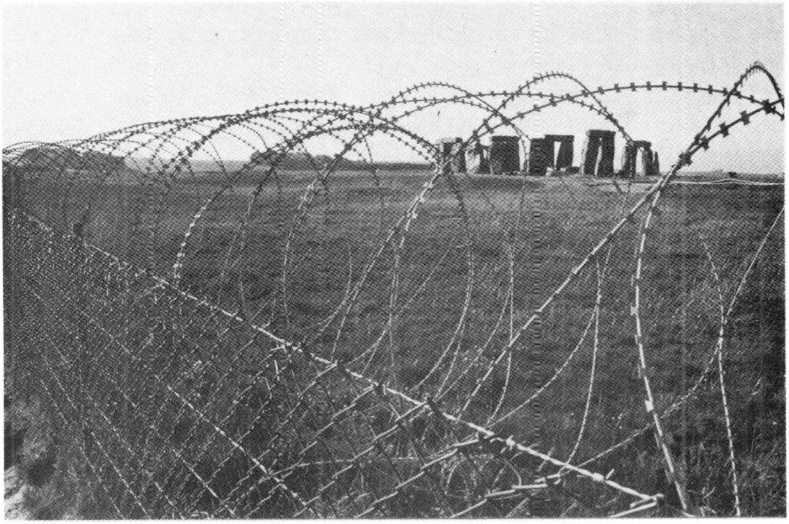

"...how shall we extol thee, who are born of thee?"

For the majority of people it's probably fair to say that their image of Public Opinion is drawn solely from the reporting of Public Opinion – usually by people with political axes to grind. Most 'news' is in fact taken up with the opinions of publicity-seeking individuals. (For example, in the report 'Mass Media & N.Ireland' it was found that the largest category of 'news' coverage of the province was devoted to the speeches and interviews of politicians.

So in Britain today there exists a genuine silent majority of people who, for instance, don't really mind about people cavorting around Stonehenge or watching sexually explicit films or having their genitals pierced or setting up pirate radio stations or picketing at closed factory gates. These people are told that they are in a minority. They do not get on TV shows. Their privately held opinions are not held by those in power. They cannot argue against all the evidence, and anyway, a public silence breeds a private fear of speaking up in public against the government and what must be the majority. So, although the majority really don't want to see our traditional rights eroded, the minority that sees itself as the guardian of Public Morality manipulates and amplifies publicly voiced opinion as loudly as possible, so as to excuse its excesses.

In areas of finite fact, such as the physical sciences, successful deviations from the accepted norm are called 'inspiration'. Deviants who challenge what is accepted, and prove it to be wrong, are given Nobel Prizes. Their research is encouraged and their findings are supported with tangible physical evidence.

In areas of Art, Morality, Philosophy, Theology and so on, practically no opinion, vision or revelation can be supported by physical evidence of any kind. The only chance one has of encouraging evolution is to convince the majority of people that what one thinks and does may be interesting and beneficial. That changes can be made for the better. The only way one can do this is through the imaginative use of the communications media. Through cinema, novels, magazines, paintings, newspapers, music etc. When such free forms of expression are denied and censored, progress is made impossible. Everything is geared towards support for the present system, however limited and unsatisfactory that system may be. Everyone must pay lip service to it. To the idea of retrogression rather than advancement. To static, septic status quo rather than illumination and change.

In the current climate, where morality is seen in the monochrome, it is Human Evolution itself which suffers. When you distort reality and censor the media, changes in people's perceptions become impossible. In scientific terms, radical changes in what is accepted as being fact is called a paradigm shift. A paradigm is, quite literally, a frame of thought (from the Greek word 'paradigma' – pattern). So a paradigm shift is a new way of thinking about our old problems. The interesting thing about paradigm shifts is, of course, that with the passage of time, each 'shift' eventually becomes the established mode of thought and naturally becomes redundant itself whenever a new shift occurs. A shift is evoked by someone. At first (perhaps for decades) it is scorned by adherents to the old paradigm, but it is eventually accepted as being a reasonable framework within which to operate. So in evolutionary terms the concept of such shifting of the 'truth' provides the perfect argument against blind faith, dogmatism and censorship, as each paradigm seems to have an in-built self destruct mechanism. That is, each framework, each idea, each answer, throws up another idea, another question. New pieces of data turn up that don't fit into the old frame of reference, so eventually you are left with a mountain of questions that cannot be held within the structure of the old paradigm and – pricked by a Cezanne or an Einstein – it bursts open. The unsolved questions flood into a new frame of reference to be answered, and so it goes on until the next shift. Sadly, in social terms, this evolutionary experience can no longer happen in Britain.

The truth is that we live in a society that cannot accommodate progressive change. This country had started to make some real advances in the years between the end of the war and the introduction of Thatcherism. The invention of the NHS, the improvement of the educational system, the relaxation of many unjust laws and so on. It still had a long way to go, but it might have got there. The reason this slow progress was stopped was because it was decided that we could not pay for our advancement. As usual, the World Banks saw to that. Now the Conservatives have rolled things back nearly a century, to make the country backward, isolated, but safe in its ignorance. The Capitalist State has recuperated any longterm changes quite successfully. The present Government have proved that we are a society that will not look at the present and into the future, but cling to an image of the past. Politicians on both the left and right preach censorship, ignorance, and the need for adherence to outmoded values and ways of thinking. The church, meanwhile, believe that the ancient principles and methods of living are sacrosanct, and can be applied to the problems of today. The legal system and social climate reflect all this in an icy permafrost, where the only movements made are small and always backward. All ignore the theory of evolution. The theory that makes credible and necessary the need for individuals to be able to express themselves, research life for themselves, vent their views and experience new sensations so as to allow for, encourage, and inspire change. Growth. Progress.

We live in a country run through fear by yesterday's men. Men who control through a myriad of mummified, unfathomable laws underlined by the threat of real physical violence and deprivation. Men who do this not necessarily because they are evil or stupid, but because they are so conceited as to be convinced that they are right, and that the ends justify the means.

The reason for the State's absolute belief in itself is deeply rooted, and stems from its symbolic relationship with Religion.

From Egypt, Babylon and Greece – the areas from which Christianity most heavily borrowed – come the schematic idea of humanised gods. Gods who made laws and ruled the Earth. These deities had to be pleased, so that crops would grow. Clever leaders of dominant groups seized on the idea well, and claimed divine and mysterious links with the gods. So, it's not surprising to find that the first legal system ever recorded – in Babylon – was said not to have been drawn up by a man, but by a God. King Hanmurali (2067 – 2025 BC) said that the law had been given to him by

Merduk (not just any god, but the Babylonian version of the later, all-powerful Greek god Zeus.) And so, although throughout history the names of the gods and the details of the laws have changed, the concept remains the same.

The Head of State in Britain is the Monarch, who is also head of the Church of England. Bishops are given automatic seats in Parliament (in the House of Lords) and any laws passed by MPs cannot become law until they are rubber-stamped by the Monarch (given 'Royal Assent'). Implied associations with God, and with what is Good, are everywhere. So, by inference, that State is given the right to rule.

From clever King Hanmurali onwards, God has become inexorably connected with the State. God has become politicised, and the appeal of God has been utilised by all those who seek to exercise control over others. 'His' laws have been propagated and freely adapted by people who claim, perhaps not to have spoken to him, but through a study of his laws (an association with the Church) have therefore assumed not only their right to control others, but a monopoly on morality. So all wars are holy wars and all laws are good laws. The more laws we have, the better we must be. It's lovely.

Regrettably, this unspoken association with All Things Bright and Beautiful has led us into a situation in which those who are convinced they are right, must believe to some degree that everyone else is wrong. In the ultimate Nanny State, their poor souls must be saved and they must be made to behave. Naughty children.

As Britain's position in the world has slumped, the temptation has been for governments not to look forward and tackle today's problems in a realistic manner, but to look back, to a golden vision of the country when everyone knew their place and when it ruled a quarter of the planet. In a simpleton's equation, the current government have sought to encourage and enforce a return to old values of the Victorian era, as if social retardation to a blatantly unjust and uncaring time would by some weird science restore Britain's world status.

This notion is not only a fallacy, it is indicative of the survival instinct of the State Machine. To this enormous, almost abstract entity, individual people do not matter. So if, for the system to run smoothly, individuals have to submit to injustice, unnecessary hardship and lack of liberty, it doesn't matter. So long as the image of a squeaky-clean, new British Motherland emerges. Not strong in itself, but appearing strong and wholesome to the outside world again. A strength measured not in individual liberty and contentment, but in share prices and nuclear warheads.

Our civilisation is locked into the dialectic of Conflict and Competition on an international stage, and the preservation of its control in the domestic area at all costs. In this nuclear age, where co-operation and compromise are the real keys to survival, our system is clearly as dangerous as it is outmoded.

As research and reform are relegated, civilisation itself suffers, Education, Art, Literature all take a back seat, as individuals who seek to express new ideas are gagged. People who do not conform are made to look foolish, and even criminal, so the new criminal class is not composed of violent gangsters or rapists, but people who sell books and make films. Of old ladies who protest at Greenham and Civil Servants who reveal the truth about the workings of our Government.

Our story is truly a chilling one. A sad and depressing one. Think about it. The country that was once the Cradle of Democracy and the birthplace of the fairest legal system in the world has been damaged, perhaps beyond repair. The long term consequences, not only of the Government's new laws but of its disregard for the truth are genuinely crippling to both Individual Liberties and to the social health of the nation. We are left with only a false external appearance of democracy, manifested in long queues to the ballot box every five years, giving our support to one idiotic set of values against another. Our choice is totally controlled and predicted by the system to which we have submitted. A system which elevates megalomaniacs and liars to superstardom.

In systematically lying more so than any government in modern times, in editing and covering-up the truth, Thatcher, and to a lesser extent, John Major and their cronies have created what communication scientists call a 'disinformation situation'. In America, Paul Watzlonick and others conducted experiments during which totally sane people were lied to in a systematic and calculating manner. The results were that the subjects started to behave with all the irrationality of schizophrenics and paranoid patients. I would suggest that this is starting to happen now, as people abandon all hope, and all interests in politics and the structures of this society. This has the effect of leaving more space for the insidious and unchecked growth of centralised power, more distant and less accountable than ever. The rise in narcotic and alcohol abuse, suicide and violent crime is a product not of TV, but of alienation and mistrust of a system that denies people any hope.

Few realists would argue the need for some reasonable and generally agreed laws and levels of policing those laws. We all want protection from violence and intimidation, warnings about exposure to dangerous drugs and so on. This is not the issue here. What we are discussing is a heavily disguised undemocratic use of power. Of blind assumptions that the preservation of the present social system is a paramount importance, and the belief that the elected government's own narrow set of values are so perfect that any serious dissent must be silenced.

Have we not illustrated that we condone an educational system that openly indoctrinates children? That our belief in 'good' and 'evil' has been so perverted that adherents to the State's dictums actually believe that they have the monopoly on godliness, justice, good taste and common sense? That we have created a bureaucracy that assumes the right to interfere in people's private lives and sit in judgement on even the most noble acts of any individual? Are we not saddled with a blatantly undemocratic electoral system which will not be overturned by those who ride this same system to total power, and an all too often corrupt, stupid, violent police force and a demonstrably biased, unjust and senile legal structure? On top of this, history shows us to be stuck with a governmental monolith that exists supposedly to serve the people and administer to their well being, but which has grown into a latterday Godking. To be served (particularly during times of war) and serviced. Our sense of freedom is abstract, our feelings of oppression are all too real.

The system is not perfect, and all governments have their faults, but this present government has changed all the rules, and is getting away with it. As Stuart Bell pointed out, John Donne may have had a lot to say on the matter.

The government tolls the bell for egalitarianism in a society that we once believed was opposed to authoritarianism. It tolls the bell for liberties that are known, understood, and were once enjoyed by all of us. It tolls for our children. They will be brought up in a society that takes as a matter of course arbitrary searches of people's homes without warrant, the interception of private mail, seven days' detention without charge, 3 months' imprisonment without trial, regular deaths in custody, systematic roadblocks, plastic bullets fired on children, the outlawing of peaceful demonstrations, trial without jury and enforced drugging of prisoners, the effective removal of the right to strike or picket, the abolition of local democracy, the banning of books...

Perhaps the last words should go to an outsider, who can provide a more objective view. In this case, American Professor Ronald Dworkin, an international commentator on politics, philosopher and a lecturer based in Oxford: *"A truly civilised society is vigilant about the question of civil rights. The number of minorities which are hated in this country is indefinite. Each person who is in some way or another a member of a minority – not only black people, not only homosexuals – but people who hold unpopular convictions of all sorts, have got to band together. They've got to say that they're not going to allow it when on every possible occasion people use some trumped-up excuse as justification for tearing the veneer of civilisation away."*

But the words of the Tory ad man repeat on the video machine, cold and hollow... **"Man is born free...his natural state...his god-given right. Nowhere is this tradition more deeply rooted than in Britain...we are a proud nation of individuals...Freedom has been both our strength and our battle cry..."** The television beams lies to a nation that doesn't believe anything anymore.

Our claims to be the most free country in the world have no validity any longer. We hold these truths to be self-evident. This is the last of England.

SEX, CRIME, AND THE 'OCCULT'

COLIN WILSON

I was recently re-reading my *Origins of the Sexual Impulse*, written more than twenty-five years ago, to see whether it is worth republishing. Within twenty pages, I had become convinced that the problems I discuss there are more relevant than ever. In 1981, a 22-year-old sex killer called Steven Judy was executed in Indianapolis for the murder of a mother and her two children; before his execution, he admitted that he had killed more women than he could remember, leaving a trail of bodies across the United States. In recent years, the American police have become aware that killers like Steven Judy are an increasing problem. They are known as 'serial killers', and they travel around the country committing murder as casually as a different type of criminal might rob gas stations. They may not travel around; California's 'freeway killers', who murdered and raped more than forty young men, stuck roughly to the same area. In nearly all cases, the basic motivation of serial killers is sexual.

But why is it happening? Why are such crimes – rare when I wrote the book in 1963 – becoming increasingly frequent? We even have a recent example in England, in Dennis Nielsen, who killed fifteen youths.

Origins of the Sexual Impulse raises the basic question: what is sexual perversion, and how and why does it develop? The name of the Marquis de Sade appears again and again. And two years after it came out, the Moors murderer Ian Brady revealed in court how deeply he had been influenced by de Sade. In fact, de Sade might almost be regarded as the patron saint of serial killers.

De Sade's basic argument is that sex is one of the greatest pleasures in life, and that every man and woman has a right to as much of it as they can get. To de Sade's contemporaries, that proposition meant a great deal more than it does to us, because most of us take it for granted that sex is pleasant and harmless. Sade's contemporaries were still dominated by the Catholic Church. They felt that, strictly speaking, sex is *'forbidden'* – except in the marriage bed – and that adultery and fornication are a kind of delightful poison that should be taken only in very small doses. De Sade shocked everybody by arguing that if sex is a delicious poison, that is only another reason for taking it in very large doses. What made it worse was that de Sade claimed to be a philosopher, and argued his case with great intellectual seriousness. It was rather as if a modern dietary expert should write a book urging that we should all eat exactly what we want, especially cream cakes, saturated fats and sticky sweets.

There is, as de Sade recognised, a basic problem here. For human beings, sex tends to be enjoyable because it involves surmounting certain *social* barriers. For a male, all the pretty girls he went to school with, all the girls he passes in the street, are forbidden fruit. If he was Haroun Al Raschid, he would order his Grand Vizier to escort most of them to his bedroom. But he isn't, so he has to get used to the idea that he is allowed to look, but not touch... But if, as de Sade suggests, we break down all the social barriers and make sex more easily accessible, it becomes less fun. De Sade agrees. His answer is: seek out new barriers to surmount. Find ever more 'forbidden' kinds of sex. He himself seduced his wife's sister, and hired prostitutes to allow him to flog them and inflict other indignities. To the objection that this will also become boring eventually, de Sade replies chortling: *"No, there are always plenty of forbidden things to do."*

De Sade symbolises the central question of sexual perversion. And my own analysis of perversion – from harmless forms of fantasy to sexual murder – led me to a conclusion which I will try to summarise as follows. When we ask the question: What *is* sexual perversion? we are envisaging sex as a kind of continuous scale, like a thermometer. At Zero lies sexual 'normality', the kind of sex that the Archbishop of Canterbury would approve of. Between Zero and '10', there are various mild deviations from the norm, beginning with masturbation, harmless forms of fetishism, and so on. Masochism comes next; then the milder forms of sadism, then more violently aggressive behaviour in which the sexual partner becomes a 'victim'. De Sade did his best to get higher still, with perversions like shooting pregnant women out of canons.

It struck me that this narrowly sexual view of the problem is a mistake. At its best, the sexual orgasm is a kind of explosion of light – a combination of energy and insight. Yet the same is true of what the philosopher is trying to achieve. And the scientist. And the artist. And the saint. De Sade's great mistake was in failing to see that the 'Zero' point on the thermometer is *not* 'normality'. A man who had devoted his life to trying to achieve that explosion of energy and insight might pass *through* point Zero, seeking entirely different methods of achieving his aim. Most saints and mystics, for example, begin by renouncing sex, or at least abstaining for a certain period. For de Sade, that was an incomprehensible absurdity.

However, a mystic who has achieved his *'explosion of light'* would assure de Sade that it really works. Sex in itself is a ball and chain in the search for the *'explosion of light...'*

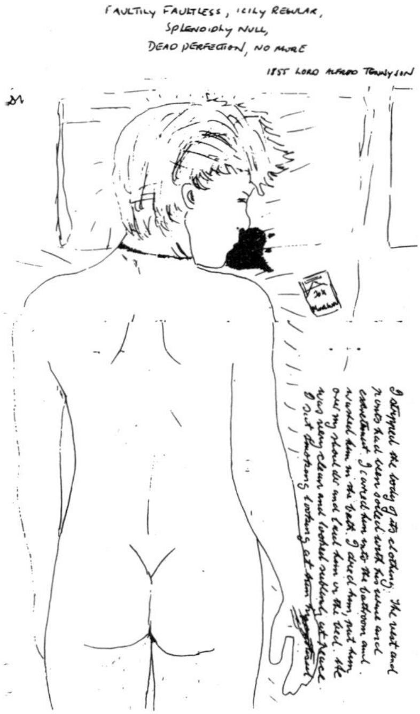

One of the grisly collection of drawings produced by Dennis Nilsen.

The truth is that long before I wrote my first book *The Outsider* in 1955, I had already arrived at my own conclusion about the purpose of life. It was the highly unfashionable view known as 'Vitalism', and it had been expounded by Henri Bergson, Bernard Shaw and Hans Driesch. T. E. Hulme expressed it clearly in an essay on Bergson. The force we call 'life' is attempting to 'insert' itself into matter, and so to achieve more freedom. The amoeba could be regarded as a small leak through which freedom could be inserted into the world. Fishes are bigger 'leaks', animals bigger leaks still, and (on Earth at least) Man is the largest leak so far. The philosopher is a man who is deliberately setting out to enlarge the leak.

De Sade found sex one of the best ways of enlarging the leak. When he had experienced a violent orgasm, it made him feel more free. But the intensity of the orgasm depended on the sense of 'forbiddenness'. He had better orgasms with his sister-in-law than with his wife because she was supposed to be taboo... He reasoned that if he could find some ultimately forbidden sexual act, he would have an orgasm to end all orgasms, and turn into a kind of god...

It was, in a way, quite sound reasoning. But de Sade was leaving one important factor out of account. The man who makes a habit of doing 'forbidden' things will begin to *see* himself as a criminal. And a criminal is, by definition, someone who does 'wrong'. He sees himself as an outcast from society. He may shake his fist and shout defiance, but in doing so he is acknowledging that society has the right to treat him as a pariah. A man in this state of mind cannot experience any true sense of freedom. He is trapped in a thoroughly *limited view of himself*. No sooner is the orgasm over than he ceases to feel like a god and feels like a naughty schoolboy.

And this is precisely why Steven Judy stood up in court and demanded to be executed. He was, apparently, a fairly intelligent individual. Yet he had committed acts that made him an outcast, and which he knew he would go on committing as long as he was alive. His personal evolution had reached a dead end. The same applies to many other habitual criminals – as I have pointed out in my *Criminal History of Mankind*.

We can see that the increasing problem of criminal violence – particularly the problem of 'serial killers' – is the de Sade problem blown up to horrifying proportions. Most serial killers are vagrants, without a home or a regular job. Life offers no exciting challenges, no interesting obstacles to overcome. The daily pattern of experiences is a dreary, predictable round. But the sexual itch remains as persistent as ever. The act of sexual violence offers a momentary 'high'. Then the greyness closes in again, like a fog... The basic problem here, of course, is lack of direction. But then, this a problem that faces us all. Compared to many animals on the surface of this Earth, man is a fairly young creature – no more than a few million years old. Most of that time he has spent fighting grimly to stay alive. And then, quite suddenly, he created civilisation. His intelligence had constructed a form of security such as no other animal had ever achieved – even the great dinosaurs lounging on their tropical beaches. It makes him lose his sense of direction. I remember talking to a man who had worked on the Burma railroad as a prisoner of war; his picture of their sufferings was graphic, and he made it clear that every one of them dreamed of freedom. Yet now he had his freedom, he was wasting it – drifting from pub to pub and drinking far too much. He had already lost his sense of direction...

From *The Outsider* onward, I had been obsessed by this problem. Why do we lose sense of direction so easily? Why can we not cling on to it? This problem of maintaining a sense of direction is the greatest of all challenges to our intelligence. Why can we not solve it as we have solved so many other problems? Why can we not *seize* that vision of the *'explosion of light',* the sudden moment of insight, and use it as a compass that would prevent us ever becoming bored or depressed or discouraged?

Because an American publisher asked me to write a book on the 'occult', I began to study the evidence for the paranormal. I began by assuming that most of it was self delusion or wishful thinking, but it didn't take long to realise that the evidence for telepathy, clairvoyance, precognition, ghosts and poltergeists is as strong as the evidence for the existence of atoms. And suddenly I realised that fate had given me a nudge in the right direction. My study of the paranormal proved one thing beyond all doubt: that the powers of the human mind are far greater – and far stranger – than we generally think. I have written very widely about these powers, as well as more 'specialist' books about witchcraft, poltergeists and psychometry.

But there was one subject I have always been inclined to avoid: the problem of life after death. A few years ago I was asked to write a book on reincarnation. I was tempted for a while, but when the publisher took an unconscionably long time producing a contract, I was glad to make it an excuse to drop the idea; I felt I couldn't apply to it the high standards of investigation and analysis I had set myself in *The Occult.*

Two years ago, another publisher asked me if I would be willing to write a book investigating the evidence for life after death; after some initial reluctance, I agreed. I should explain that this was not entirely a matter of scepticism about the evidence. I knew that some of it was very convincing indeed. Yet the same applies to Flying Saucers, and I am not particularly interested in Flying Saucers. My own feeling is that it would certainly be a very pleasant bonus if 'survival' proved to be a reality. But it doesn't have much to do with the 'existential' problems we face when we open our eyes every morning. For Human Beings, the basic problem is: what are we doing here, and what are we supposed to do now we're here? To reply: *'You will continue to live in another world after your death'* seems totally irrelevant.

I must also admit that I expected to find much of the evidence too silly for words: 'spirit' messages from Aunt Edna saying *'Don't forget to wear your woolly underwear dear',* and that kind of thing. There was, indeed, a certain amount of *'that kind of thing'.* But it was unimportant in comparison to the more interesting evidence. Briefly, this falls into two categories: evidence of so-called 'near-death experiences', in which people believe they have, in some sense, died and then 'returned', and evidence through 'mediums' that certain people have survived death. The evidence for 'near death experiences' is dubious because it obviously is possible that it was all some kind of dream or illusion, perhaps some psychological defence mechanism against death. But when taken together with the second kind of evidence, the case for 'survival' began to look very convincing indeed.

The 'near death experience' (usually abbreviated to NDE) has become the subject of a great deal of study in recent years. An American doctor, Raymond Moody, collected the accounts of 150 people who believed they had died and then 'returned', and was astonished by the similarity of the accounts. Pain or discomfort suddenly changed to a sense of blissful relaxation, immense peace and serenity. Many patients felt they were drawn into a long tunnel with a light at the end. Many found themselves looking down on their own bodies. A large number thought they were met by dead relatives. Many felt they were offered the choice of 'going on' or returning to their physical bodies; most felt reluctant to come back to life.

Other doctors had collected similar observations, and Moody's book *Life After Life* caused many more to question patients who had been close to death (in some cases, they had been pronounced dead). There could be no doubt about it: an enormous number had been through the identical experience.

The investigators are all in agreement that NDEs prove nothing whatsoever about 'life after death'. Yet most of them gradually found themselves developing the conviction that human beings somehow survive bodily death. And one of the leading investigators, Kenneth Ring, speaks for many of them when he says: *"My own understanding of these near death experiences leads me to regard them as 'teaching'. They are, it seems to me, REVELATORY EXPERIENCES."* Their real importance is what they teach the person who has been through them. In most cases, they remove all fear of death.

But, more important, they seem to produce a sense of meaning and purpose that was not present before. Life no longer seems (as Yeats once put it) *"a long preparation for something that never happens"*, but a meaningful and purposeful exercise.

This is what interests me so much. From *The Outsider* onward, I have always been fascinated by such moments – such as when Hermann Hesse's *Steppenwolf* tastes a glass of wine and is suddenly reminded of *'Mozart and the stars'*, or his feeling, in bed with a girl: *'The kernel of this life of mine was noble, and turned, not on trifles, but on the stars'.* Such moments of *'affirmation'* have been experienced again and again by the great mystics. The psychologist Abraham Maslow called them *'peak experiences'*. And it has always been obvious to me that if we could 'switch on' the peak experiences at will, we would have solved that basic problem of lack of direction...

For me, this insight was, in a sense, far more important than my conviction that humans probably survive death. For it led me back to that problem about Vitalism that had always been my central preoccupation. It is significant that the two major philosophers of the 20th Century, Hans Driesch and Henri Bergson, were both presidents of the Society for Psychical Research. Why should Vitalists find it easy to accept the evidence for the paranormal? Because Vitalism is the belief that life is a force quite separate from matter, and is engaged in a struggle to 'conquer' the material universe. Shaw believed that life is a more or less blind, instinctive force, struggling to achieve self-awareness. But if we can accept the evidence for the 'paranormal' (and my experience is that everyone who is willing to study it impartially ends up by accepting it), then it strongly suggests that there are intelligences that are not attached to physical bodies like ours. The evidence seems to point to the existence of other realms of reality existing, so to speak, in another dimension, or perhaps just at a higher rate of 'vibration' than our physical world. And this raises the interesting possibility that the force of life may have already 'conquered' these levels, to some extent, but that our own densely physical universe is a harder nut to crack. This is roughly the view held by Bergson and Driesch.

Where the conquest of matter is concerned, the problem seems to be that when 'life' descends into matter, it *loses its memory* (Wordsworth was making the same point in the *'Immortality Ode'*.) It could be compared to a child who has been sent out on an errand, but who has forgotten his instructions. For human beings, this 'forgetfulness' leads to the feeling of being trapped in a meaningless world of matter, and to Sartre's conviction that *'it is meaningless that we live and meaningless that we die'*.

So we could say that the basic problem for the 'life force' is how to prevent us forgetting our instructions – the purpose with which we set out.

Let us consider this problem as if we were angels sitting up in heaven, looking down on human beings and wondering how we could prevent them from forgetting their instructions and wandering back home with nothing accomplished.

The purpose of life is to increase its power over matter, to enlarge the 'leak'. So the last thing we want is a race of creatures who feel that life is pointless and futile, and that the sooner they can escape from *'this dim vale of tears'* the better. Ideally, we want creatures who feel that life is immensely interesting and exciting, and that no problem remains permanently unsolvable. We want creatures with an enormous *'appetite for reality'*. And the trouble with these human beings is that they all start out full of the feeling that life is going to be marvellous, and that the world is *'apparelled in celestial light'* and end up bored, disillusioned and defeated. And what makes it more annoying is that they are now so close to achieving their objective. For hundreds of thousands of years they have fought grimly against cold and starvation and predators, frequently on the point of extinction. Then they began to use their intelligence to make weapons, and to build weather-proof shelters, and life began to improve steadily. They created civilisation, and suddenly man's chief enemy became other men. Still, they laboured on and gradually learned to make life more and more worth living. They created art and literature and learned to live in the realms of the mind. At last it began to look as if they had achieved their basic purpose – to make an impregnable bridgehead in the world of matter. But then, unfortunately, a new problem arose. They had become so accustomed to struggling and fighting that they began to grow bored with the civilisation their ancestors had built with so much labour. Instead of struggling for more consciousness, they began to choose the road of least resistance. Most of them seem to feel that life would be perfect if they had a car and colour television and a video...

We could say that, in the remote past, the 'higher intelligences' kept in touch with the human race through certain individuals who were highly sensitive 'receiving sets'. These people – called prophets and messiahs – could be shown the purpose of life through mystical revelations, and they then used their enormous powers of persuasion to induce everyone to live as if the purpose was to achieve a passport to heaven. For thousands of years, this method of preventing human beings from 'forgetting their instructions' was immensely successful, and the great religions kept man working at the central aim of increasing human optimism and intelligence. But the development of his intelligence caused him to outgrow these religions. And the increasing complexity of his civilisation created more and more 'drop outs', people who felt life was totally meaningless. (Many of these have been awarded the Nobel Prize for literature...)

So what could be done? One committee of angels was allowed to try out the idea of a more direct form of communication, to convince men that there was life after death. The experiment started about 1850, and in the form of religious movement known as Spiritualism, spread across the world. Unfortunately, it tended to attract the wrong type of person – feeble minded sentimentalists. The scientists and philosophers were inclined to remain aloof. Another committee of angels suggested the near death experience as a 'teaching method', and this also achieved some success. But on far too small a scale to do much good...

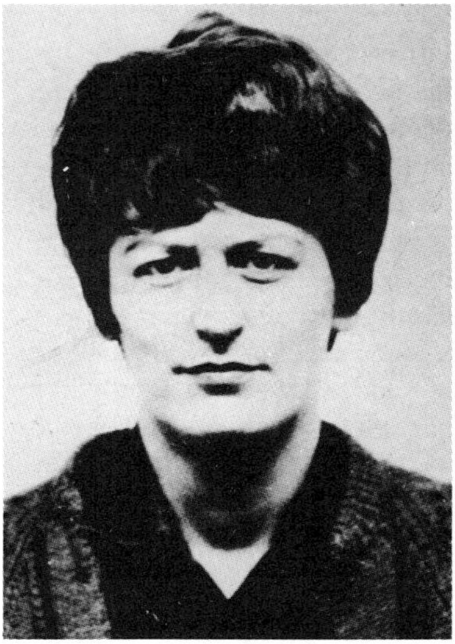

Fleet Street's Heart of Darkness.
Myra Hindley, prisoner 964005.

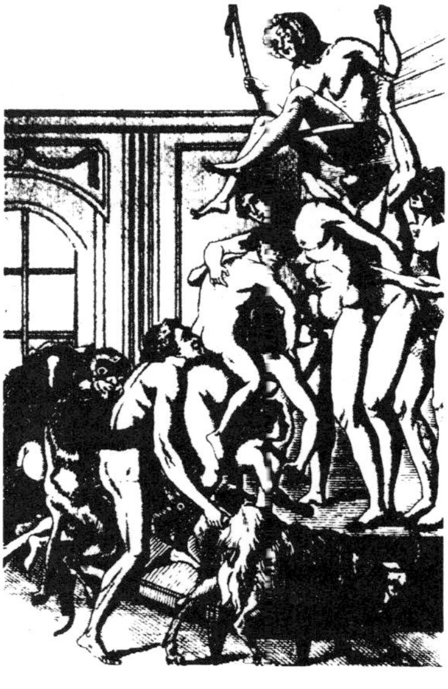

Illustration from De Sade's 'Justine & Juliette'

And there, I suggest, we have the problem in a nutshell. It makes no difference if you regard life after death as a lamentable superstition, and the near death experience as a psychological defence mechanism against the fear of death – such scepticism is healthy. But anyone who spends half an hour brooding on the problem of evil and our human tendency to be defeated by it will agree that our real task is to cling to the insight of the 'moments of affirmation', and to refuse to allow ourselves to be persuaded that life is futile. And we are living in a world in which increasing numbers of people are losing all sense of direction, and turning to all kinds of dubious methods of inducing 'highs', from heroin to casual sex murder.

There is, at least, one good reason for optimism. Anyone who surveys the cultural history of the past two and a half centuries will see that man has changed a great deal for the better. Compared to the average Elizabethan, modern man has learned to make far more use of his intelligence and imagination. There is many a down-and-out living in Salvation Army hostels who would have struck the Elizabethans as a man of formidable intelligence and imagination. The invention of the novel, then of cinema and television, has raised human intelligence to a remarkable degree. Millions of children have experienced that feeling of becoming totally absorbed in a story. This increased capacity to be carried away into a world of imagination – so we are responding often physically to an imaginary world as if it were real – is our most encouraging prospect for the future. For the chief problem of human existence is that feeling of being 'negated' by physical reality, as if the world of brute force and brute matter always had the last word. Every time we read a book or see a film and find ourselves carried away into the world of imagination, we know that this is not true. It is the power of the mind that has the last word. I am inclined to believe that man is on the brink of a new evolutionary 'leap', and that it will come about through the *deliberate investigation and control of the power of imagination.* This may not seem to offer much comfort in our crime-ridden world, but nevertheless suspect that it will prove to be the answer.

HELTER SKELTER

Much has been written concerning the so-called 'Manson Family' and the involvement of its various members in the Hinman and Tate-La Bianca murders in Los Angeles in July/August 1969; but seldom have the accused parties themselves been allowed to tell their own side of the story in public.

This situation has led to misunderstanding and inaccuracy. Some people, for example, believe that the Family was an organised devil-worshipping cult, and many incorrectly think that Manson himself was charged with the murder of Roman Polanski's wife, Sharon Tate. Others worship Manson as a Sixties anti-hero who attacked the hypocrisy of America at its core.

RAPID EYE now attempts to put the record straight by presenting verbal testimony from the main protagonist in those legendary events: Charles Manson himself.

The Charles Manson Trial Testimony
(November 19, 1970)

On Sunday, October 12, 1969, Charles Manson and nine members of his "family" were arrested at the Barker Ranch near Death Valley, California, in connection with the murders of Sharon Tate, Voityck Frykowski, Abigail Folger, Jay Sebring, Leon and Rosemary La Bianca, and Steve Parent.

Later charged with conspiracy to murder in the case, Charles Manson was consistently denied the opportunity to plead for his own defence, or call his own witnesses, during his lengthy front-page trial. Only at the very end was he allowed to make a concluding statement, an attempt to vindicate himself. Yet even then, prosecutor Vincent T. Bugliosi, apparently fearful of Manson's mesmeric rhetorical abilities, successfully applied to have the jury prevented from hearing the speech – rendering it impotent.

The resulting testimony, a transcript of which follows, lasted over an hour and was an often incoherent, repetitive, rambling, borderline-psychotic declamation of the Manson philosophy offered knowingly in the face of hostile judicial censorship. With hindsight, Bugliosi needn't have worried – such words would possibly have only served to doubly assure the court of the defendant's guilt.

JUDGE OLDER: Do you have anything to say?

CHARLES MANSON: Yes, I do. There has been a lot of charges and a lot of things said about me and brought against me and brought against the co-defendants in this case, of which a lot could be cleared up and clarified to where everyone could understand exactly what the family was supposed to have been, what the philosophies in regards to the family were, and whether or not there was any conspiracy to commit murder, to commit crimes, and to explain to you who think with your minds. It is hard for you to conceive of a philosophy of someone that may not think.

I have spent my life in jail, and without parents. I have looked up to the strongest father-figure, and I have always looked to the people in the free world as being the good people, and the people in the inside of jail as being the bad people. I never went to school, so I never growed up in the respect to learn to read and write so good, so I have stayed in jail and I have stayed stupid, I have stayed a child while I have watched your world grow up, and then I look at the things that you do and I don't understand. I don't understand the courts, and I don't understand a lot of things that are brought against me.

You write things about my mother in the newspaper that hasn't got anything to do with anything in particular. You invent stories, and everybody thinks what they do, and then they project it from the witness stand on the defendant as if that is what he did. For example, Danny DeCarlo's testimony. He said that I hate black men, and he said that we thought alike, that him and I was a lot alike in our thinking. But actually all I ever did with DeCarlo or any other human being was reflect himself back at himself. If he said he did not like the black man, I would say: "Okay." I had better sense than tell him I did not dislike the black man. I just listened to him and I would react to his statement. So consequently he would drink another beer and walk off and pat me on the back and he would say to himself: "Charlie thinks like I do." But actually he does not know how Charlie thinks because Charlie has never projected himself.

But maybe the girls and women in your world outside... Being by yourself for such a long time when you do get out you appreciate things that people don't even see, you walk over them every day. Like in jail you have a whole new attitude or a whole different way of thinking. I don't think like you people. You people put importance on your lives. Well, my life has never been important to anyone, not even in the understanding of the way you fear the things that you fear, and the things you do.

I know that the only person I can judge is me. I judge what I have done and I judge what I do and I look and I live with myself every day. I am content with myself. If you put me in the penitentiary, that means nothing because you kicked me out of the last one. I didn't ask to get released. I liked it in there because I like myself. But in your world it's hard because your understanding and your values are different.

These children that come at you with knives, they are your children. You taught them. I didn't teach them. I just tried to help them stand up. Most of the people at the ranch that you call The Family were just people that you did not want, people that were alongside the road, people that their parents had kicked them out or they did not want to go to Juvenile Hall, so I did the best I could and I took them up on my garbage dump and I told them this: that in love there is no wrong.

I don't care. I have one law and I learned it while I was a kid in reform school. It's: don't snitch. And I have never snitched. And I told them that anything they do for their brothers and sisters is good, if they do it with a good thought. It is not my responsibility. It is your responsibility. It is the responsibility you have towards your own children who you are neglecting, and then you want to put the blame on me again and again and again. Over and over you put me in your penitentiary. I did not build the penitentiary. I would not lock one of you up. I could not see locking another human being up.

You eat meat with your teeth and you kill things that are better than you are, and in the same respect you say how bad, and even killers, that your children are. You make your children what they are. I am just a reflection of every one of you. I have never learned anything wrong. In the penitentiary, I have never found a bad man. Every man in the penitentiary has always showed me his good side, and circumstances put him where he was. He would not be there, he is good, human, just like the policeman that arrested him is a good human.

I have nothing against none of you. I can't judge any of you. But I think it is high time that you all started looking at yourselves, and judging the lie that you live in. I sit and watch you from nowhere, and I have nothing in my mind, no malice against you and no ribbons for you. But you stand and you play the game of money. As long as you can sell a newspaper, some sensationalism, and you can laugh at someone and look down at someone, you know. You just sell those newspapers for public opinion, just like you are all hung on public opinion, and none of you have any idea what you are doing. You are just doing what you are doing for the money, for a little bit of attention from somebody.

I can't dislike you, but I will say this to you: You haven't got long before you are all going to kill yourselves because you are all crazy. And you can project it back onto me, and you can say that it's me that cannot communicate, and you can say that it's me that don't have any understanding, and you can say that when I am dead your world will be better, and you can lock me up in your penitentiary and you can forget about me. But I'm only what lives inside you, each and every one of you.

These children, they take a lot of narcotics because you tell them not to. Any child you put in a room and you tell them: 'Don't go through that door," he never thought of going through that door until you told him to go through the door. You go to the high schools and you show them pills and you show them not what to take, how else would they know what it was unless you tell them? And then you tell them what you don't want them to do in the hopes they will go out and do it and then you can play your game with them and then you can give attention to them, because you don't give them any of your love. You only give them frustration, you only give them your anger, you only give them the bad part of you rather than give them the good part of you. You should all turn around and face your children and start following them and listening to them.

The music speaks to you every day but you are too deaf, dumb and blind to stop what you are doing. You point and you ridicule. But it's okay, it's all okay. It doesn't really make any difference because we are all going to the same place anyway. It's all perfect. There is a God. He sits right over here beside me. That is your God. This is your God. But let me tell you something: There is another Father and he has much more might than you imagine.

If I could get angry at you I would try to kill every one of you. If that's guilt, I accept it. These children, everything they have done, they have done for love of their brother. Had you not arrested Robert Beausoleil for something he did not do...

[Interruption]

I have killed no one and I have ordered no one to be killed. I may have implied on several occasions to several different people that I may have been Jesus Christ, but I haven't decided yet what I am or who I am. I was given a name and a number and I was put in a cell, and I have lived in a cell with a name and a number. I don't know who I am. I am whoever you make me, but what you want is a fiend; you want a sadistic fiend because that is what you are. You only reflect on me what you are inside of yourselves, because I don't care anything about any of you and I don't care what you do.

I can stand here in front of this court and smile at you, and you can do anything you want to do with me, but you cannot touch me because I am only my love, and it is all for me, and I give it to myself for me, because I look out for me first and I like me, and you can live with yourselves and your opinion of yourselves. I know what I have done.

If I showed someone that I would do anything for my brother, include giving my life for my brother in the battlefield, or give where else that I may want to do that, then he picks his banner up and he goes off and does what he does. That is not my responsibility. I don't tell people what to do. If we enter into an agreement to build a house, I will help you build the house and I will offer suggestions for that house, but I won't put myself on you because that is what made you weak, because your parents have offered themselves to you. You are not you, you are just reflections, you are reflections of everything that you think that you know, everything that you have been taught. Your parents have told you what you are. They made you before you were six years old, and when you stood in school and you crossed your heart and pledged allegiance to the flag, they trapped you in truth because at that age you didn't know any lie until that lie was reflected on you.

No, I am not responsible for you. Your karma is not mine. My father is the jail house. My father is your system, and each one of you, each one of you are just a reflection of each one of you, and you all live by yourselves, no matter how crowded you may think that you are in a room full of people, you are still by yourself, and you have to live with that self forever and ever and ever and ever. To some people this would be hell, to some people it would be heaven.

I have mine, and each one of you will have to work out yours, and you cannot work it out by pointing your fingers at people. I have ate out of your garbage cans to stay out of jail. I have wore your second-hand clothes. I have accepted things and given them away the next second. I have done my best to get along in your world and now you want to kill me, and I look at you and I see how incompetent you all are, and then I say to myself: "You want to kill me, ha! I'm already dead, have been all my life – I've lived in your tomb that you built."

I did seven years for a thirty-seven dollar check. I did twelve years because I didn't have any parents, and how many other sons do you think you have in there? You have many sons in there, many, many sons in there; most of them are black and they are angry. They are mad, and they are mad at me. I look and I say: "Why are you mad at me?" He said: "I am mad at you because of what your father did." And I look at him and I say; "Well," and I look at my fathers and I say: "If there was ever a devil on the face of this earth I am him." And he's got my head anytime he wants it, as all of you do too, anytime you want it. Sometimes I think about giving it to you. Sometimes I think about just jumping on you and let you shoot me. Sometimes I think it would be easier than sitting here and facing you in the contempt that you have for yourself, the hate that you have for yourself. It's only the anger you reflect at me, the anger that you have got for you.

I do not dislike you. I cannot dislike you, I am you. You are blood. You are my brother. That is why I can't fight you. If I could I would jerk this microphone out and beat your brains out with it because that is what you deserve, that is what you deserve. Every morning you eat that meat with your teeth. You're all killers, you kill things better than you. And what can I say to you that you don't already know? And I have known that there is nothing I can say to you. There is nothing I can say to any of you. It is you that has to say it to you, and that is my whole philosophy: you say it to you and I will say it to me.

I live in my world, and I am my own king in my world, whether it be a garbage dump or if it be in the desert or wherever it be. I am my own human being. You may restrain my body and you may tear my guts out, do anything you wish, but I am still me and you can't take that. You can kill the ego, you can kill the pride, you can kill the want, the desire of a human being. You can lock him in a cell and you can knock his teeth out and smash his brain, but you cannot kill the soul. You could never kill the soul. It's always there, the beginning and the end. You cannot stop it, it's bigger than me. I'm just looking into it and it frightens me sometimes.

The truth is now, the truth is right here, the truth is this minute, and this minute we exist. Yesterday – you cannot prove yesterday happened today, it would take you all day and then it would be tomorrow, and you can't prove last week happened. You can't prove anything except to yourself.

My reality is my reality, and I stand within myself on my reality. Yours is yours, and I don't care what it is. Whatever you do is up to you and it's the same with anyone in my family, and anybody in my family is a white human being, because my family is of the white family. There is the black family, a yellow family, the red family, a cow family and a mule family. There is all kind of different families. We have to find ourselves first, God second, and kind, k-i-n-d, come next. And that is all I was doing. I was working on cleaning up my house, something Nixon should have been doing. He should have been on the side of the road picking up his children. But he wasn't. He was in the White House sending them off to war.

I don't know the different people that have got on the stand; one friend said I put a knife to his throat. I did. I put a knife to his throat. And he said I was responsible for all these killings.

I have done the best I know how, and I have given all I can give and I haven't got any guilt about anything because I have never been able to say any wrong. I never found any wrong. I looked at wrong, and it is all relative. Wrong is if you haven't got any money. Wrong is if your car payment is overdue. Wrong is if the TV breaks. Wrong is if President Kennedy gets killed. Wrong is, wrong is – you keep on, you pile it in your mind. You become belaboured with it, and in your confusion...

I make up my own mind. I think for myself. I look at you and I say: "Okay, you make up your own mind, you think for yourself, then you see your mothers and fathers and your teachers and your preachers and your politicians and your presidents, and you lay in your brain with your opinions, considerations, conclusions..." And I look at you and I say: "Okay, if you are real to you it's okay with me but you don't look real to me. You only look like a composite of what someone told you you are. You live for each others' opinion and you have pain on your face and you are not sure what you like, and you wonder if you look okay." And I look at you and I say: "Well, you look alright to me," you know, and then you look at me and you say: "Well, you don't look alright to me."

Well I don't care what I look like to you. I don't care what you think about me and I don't care what you do with me. I have always been yours anyway. I have always been in your cell. When you were out riding your bicycles I was sitting in your cell looking out the window and looking in pictures in magazines and wishing I could go to high school and go to the proms, wishing I could go to the things you could do, but oh so glad, oh so glad, brothers and sisters, that I am what I am. Because when it comes down around your ears and none of you know what you are doing, you better believe I will be on top of my thought. I will know what I am doing. I will know exactly what I am doing. If you ever let me go before you kill me. And then I don't really particularly care anyway, because I still will be there and I will still know what I am doing.

In my mind I live forever. In my mind I live forever, and in my mind I have always lived forever. I am only what you made me, I am only a reflection of you.

I have done everything I have always been told. I have mopped the floor when I was supposed to mop the floor. And I have swept when I was supposed to sweep. I was smart enough to stay out of jail and too dumb to learn anything. I was too little to get a job there, and too big to do something over here. I have just been sitting in jail thinking nothing. Nothing to think about. Everybody used to come in and tell me about their past and their lives and what they did. But I could never tell anybody about my past or what my life was or what I did because I have always been sitting in that room with a bed, a locker, and a table.

So, then it moves on to awareness: how many cracks can you count in the wall? It moves to where the mice live and what the mice are thinking, and see how clever mice are. And then, when you get on the outside, you look into people's heads. You take Linda Kasabian and you put her on the witness stand and she testifies against her father. She never has liked her father, and she has always projected her wrong off to the man-figure. So, consequently, it is the man's fault again, and the woman turns around and she blames it on the man. The man made her do it. The man put her up to it. The man works for her, the man slaves for her, the man does everything for her, and she lays around the house and she tells him what he should do, because, generally, she is an extension of his mother. His mother told him what to do and she trained him for twenty years and passed him on to the wife. Then the woman takes him and tells him what to wear, when to get up, when to go to work. Then when she gets on the stand and she says when she looked in that man's eyes that was dying, she knew it was my fault.

She knew that it was my fault because she couldn't face death. And if she cannot face death, that is not my fault. Why should she blame it on me? I can face death. I have all the time. In the penitentiary you live with it, with constant fear of death, because it is a violent world in there, and you have to be on your toes constantly. So, it is not without violence that I live. It is not without pain that I live.

I look at the projection that comes from this witness stand often to the defendants. It isn't what we said, it is what someone thought we said. A word is changed: "in there" to "up there", "off of that" to "on top". The semantics get into a word game in the courtroom to prove something that is gone in the past. It is gone in the past, and when it is gone, it is gone, sisters. It is gone, brother. You can't bring the past back up and postulate or mock up a picture of something that happened a hundred years ago, or nineteen-seventy years ago, as far as that goes. You can only live in the now, for what is real is now.

The words go in circles. You can say everything is the same, but it is always different. It is the same, but it is always different. You can "but" it to death. You can say: "You are right, but, but, but..."

You sat here for nineteen days questioning that girl. She got immunity on seven counts of murder. She got. I don't know how much money she is going to make in magazines and things. You set her up to be a hero, and that is your woman. That is the thing that you worship. You have lost sight of God. You sing your songs to woman. You put woman in front of man. Woman is not God. Woman is but a reflection of her man, supposedly. But a lot of times, man is a reflection of his woman. And if a man can't rise above a woman's thought, then that is his problem, it is not my problem. But you give me this problem when you set this woman against me.

You set this woman here to testify against me. And she tells you a sad story. How she has only taken every narcotic that is possible to take. How she has only stolen, lied, cheated and done everything that you have got there in that book. But it's okay, she is telling the truth now. She wouldn't have any ulterior motive like immunity for seven counts of murder.

And then comical as it may seem, you look at me and you say: "You threatened to kill a person if they snitched." Well, that is the law where I am from. Where I am from, if you snitch, you leave yourself open to be killed. I could never snitch because I wouldn't want someone to kill me. So, I have always abided by that law. It is the only law that I know of, and it is the law that I have always abided by. But she will come up here and you enshrine her, you put her above you, and you strive to be as good as something below you.

It is circles that just don't make any sense in my reality. But of course again that is my reality and it has nothing to do with you, because you have got your reality and you have to live with what you believe in. But this woman has got here and she has testified. She said she wasn't sure, but maybe.

Then the magical mystery tour wouldn't be able to be explained to you. A magical mystery tour is when you pick up somebody else and play a part. You may pick up a cowboy today, and you go around all day and play like a cowboy. You put on a hat and you ride a horse.

This is all we have done. We have played like mom and dad. We have loved each other. We have done everything we could to stay outside the frame of the law, the shakedowns. Nothing has been stolen. I have got better sense than to break the law. I give to the law what it has coming. It is his law. If I break his law, he puts me back in the grave again.

I haven't broken his law yet but it seems as if somebody lays around and somebody needs to fulfil a spot, they snatch it up and say: "This will do. We will put this over here. We can hang this on him, or we can do this to that."

Then the words go onto another meaning and another level of understanding. Why a woman would stand up and project herself into a man and say: "Actually he never told me anything, but I knew it all came from him." Her assumption. Am I to be found guilty on her assumption?

You assume what you would do in my position, but that doesn't mean that is what I did in my position. It doesn't mean that my philosophy is valid. It's only valid to me. Your philosophies – they are whatever you think you are, and I don't particularly care what you think they are. But I know this: that in your hearts and in your souls, you are as much responsible for the Vietnam war as I am for killing these people.

I knew a guy that used to work in the stockyards and he used to kill cows all day long with a big sledgehammer and then go home at night and eat dinner with his children and eat the meat that he slaughtered. Then he would go to church and read the bible, and he would say: "That is not killing." And I look at him and say: "That doesn't make any sense, what are you talking about?" Then I look at the beast, and I say: "Who is the beast?" I am the beast. I am the beast. I am the biggest beast walking the face of the earth. I kill everything that moves. As a man, as a human, I take responsibility for that. As a human, it won't be long, and God will ask you to take responsibility for it. It is your creation. You live in your creation. I never created your world, you created it. You create it when you pay taxes, you create it when you go to work, then you create it when you foster a thing like this trial.

Only for vicarious thrills do you sell a newspaper and do you kow-tow to public opinion. Just to sell your newspapers. You don't care about the truth. You take another Alka-Seltzer and another aspirin and hope that you don't have to think of the truth and you hope that you don't have to look at yourself with a hangover as you go to a Helter Skelter party and make fun of something that you don't understand.

JO: Please confine your remarks to the issues in this case, Mr. Manson.

CM: The issues in this case? The issues in this case? The issues in this case are that Mr. Younger is Attorney General, and I imagine he is a good man and does a good job. I don't know him. I can't judge him. But I know he has got me here. He set me in this seat. Mr. Bugliosi is doing his job for a paycheck. That is an issue. He is doing whatever he is doing. Whether he thinks it is right or not, I couldn't say. That is up to him.

The only way that I have been able to live on that side of the road was outside the law. I have always lived outside the law. When you live outside the law it is pretty hard, you can't call the man for protection. You have got to pretty much protect your own. You can't live within the law and protect yourself. You can't knock the guy down when he comes over and starts to rape one of the girls, or starts to bring some speed or dope up there. You can't enforce your will over someone inside the law.

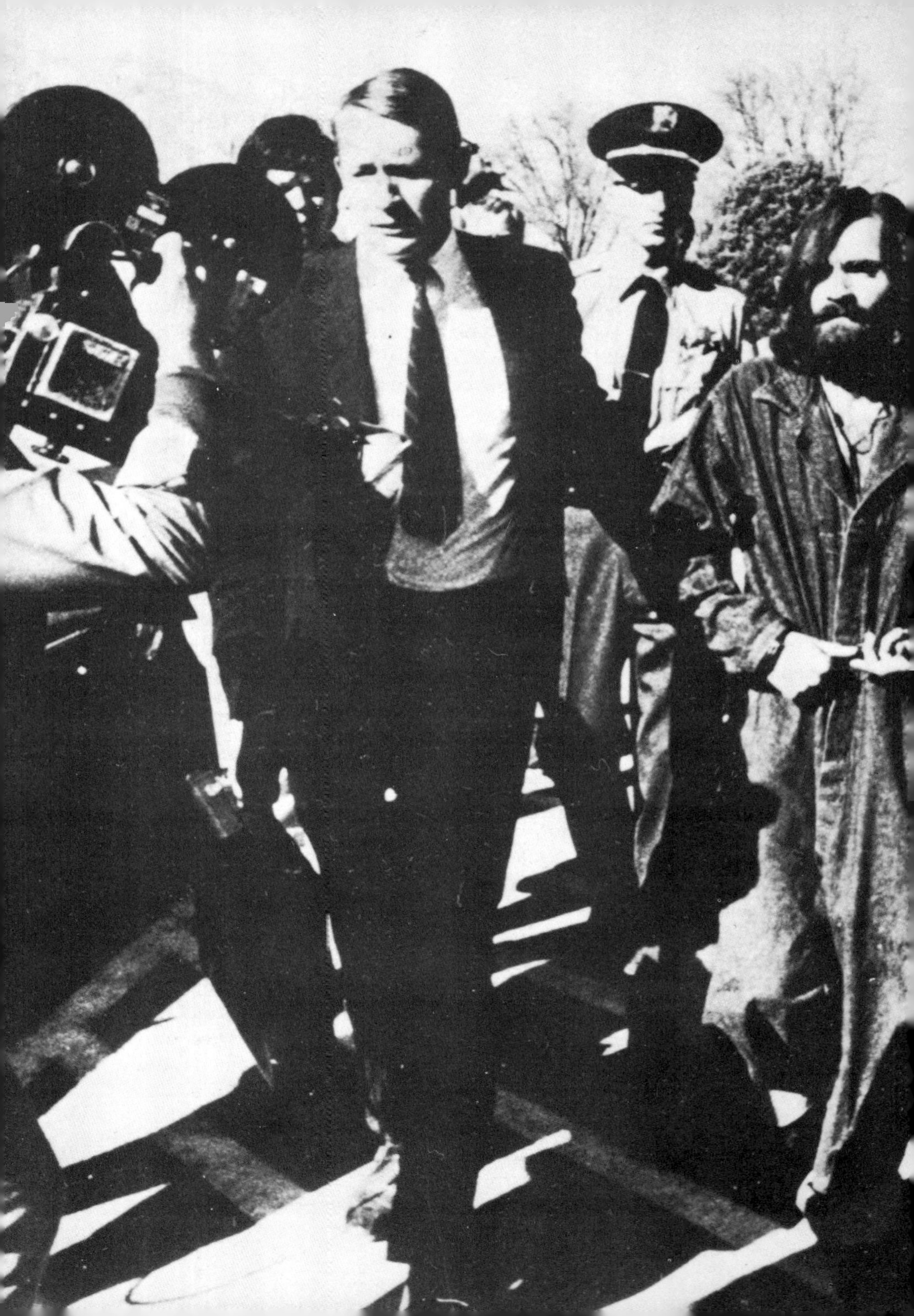

Facing Page: December 1969, Manson is taken under arrest to Independence Court House as a suspect in the Tate/LaBianca murders. (Photo: Michael Haering/L.A. Herald Examiner.)

I gave everything I could think of to that old man and that ranch for permission to stay there, and I have given the people that stayed on that ranch my all. When no one wanted to clean the toilets, I would go and clean them. People would see me and they would see what I do and see the example that I set. They see, when I am cleaning out a cesspool, that I am happy and smiling and making a game of it. Like I was on a chain gang somewhere once upon a time and they come and pass the water. I make a game out of it, or I make a pleasure out of a job. We turn it into a magical mystery tour.

We speed down the highway in a 1958 automobile that won't go but fifty, and an SKE Jaguar goes by, and I state to Clem: "Catch him, Clem, and we'll rob him or steal all of his money," you know. And he says: "What shall we do?" And I say: "Hit him on the head with a hammer." And we magical mystery tour it.

Then Linda Kasabian gets on the stand and says: "They were going to kill a man, they were going to kill a man in an automobile." To you, it seems serious. But like Larry Kramer and I would get on a horse and we would ride over to Wichita, Kansas, and act like cowboys. We make it a game on the ranch.

Like, Helter Skelter is a nightclub. Helter Skelter means confusion, literally. It doesn't mean any war with anyone. It doesn't mean that those people are going to kill other people. It only means what it means. Helter Skelter is confusion. Confusion is coming down fast. If you don't see the confusion coming down fast around you, you can call it what you wish.

It is not my conspiracy. It is not my music. I hear what it relates. It says: "Rise!" It says: "Kill!" Why blame it on me? I didn't write the music. I am not the person who projected it into your social consciousness, that sanity that you projected into your social consciousness, today. You put so much into the newspaper, and then you expect people to believe what is going on. I say: back to the facts again.

How many witnesses have you got up here and projected only what they believe in. What I believe in is right now. I don't believe in anything past now. I speak to you from now. Because there is nothing here to worry about, nothing here to think about, nothing here to be confused over. My house is not divided. My house is one with me, myself.

Then I look at the facts that you have brought in front of this court, and I look at the twelve facts that are looking at me and judging me. If I were to judge them, what scale would that balance? Would the scale balance if I was to turn and judge you? How would you feel if I were to judge you? Could I judge you? I can only judge you if you try to judge me. That is the fact.

Mr. Bugliosi is a hard-driving prosecutor, with a polished education. Semantics, words. He is a genius. He has got everything that every lawyer would want to have – except one thing: a case. He doesn't have a case. Were I allowed to defend myself, I could have proven this to you. I could have called witnesses and showed you how these things lay, and I could have presented my picture.

You are dealing with facts and positive evidence. If you are dealing with things that are relative to the issues at hand, then you look at the facts. What else do you look at? Oh, the thong. How many people have ever worn moccasins with a leather thong in it? So you have placed me in the desert with leather clothes on and you took a leather thong from my shoe. How many people could we take leather thongs from? That is an issue. Then you move on and you say I had one around my neck. I always tie one around my head when my hair is long, it keeps it out of my eyes. And you pull it down on your neck. And I imagine a lot of long-haired people do.

There are so many aspects to this case that could be dug into and a lot of truth could be brought up, a lot of understanding could be reached. It is a pretty hideous thing to look at seven bodies, one hundred and two stab wounds. The prosecutor, or the doctor, gets up and he shows how all the different stab wounds are one way, and then how all the different stab wounds are another way; but they are the same stab wounds in another direction. They put the hideous bodies on display and they say: "If he gets out see what will happen to you." Implying it. I am not saying he did this. This is implied. A lot of diagrams are actually, in my opinion, senseless to the case.

Then there is Paul Watkins' testimony. Paul Watkins was a young man who ran away from his parents and wouldn't go home. You could ask him to go home and he would say no. He would say: "I don't got no place to live. Can I live here?" And I'd say: "Sure." So, he looks for a father image. I offer no father image. I say: "To be a man, boy, you have got to stand up and be your own father." And he still hungers for a father image. So he goes off to the desert and finds a father image. When he gets on the stand, I forget what he said, whether it had any relative value; oh, I was supposed to have said to go get a knife and kill the Sheriff of Shoshone. Go get a knife and kill the Sheriff of Shoshone? I don't know the Sheriff of Shoshone. I don't think I have been there but once. I am not saying that

I didn't say it, but if I said it, at that time I may have thought it was a good idea. Whether I said it in jest and whether I said it in joking, I can't recall and reach back into my memory. I could say either way. I could say: "Oh, I was just joking." Or I could say I was curious. But to be honest with you I don't ever recall saying: "Get a knife and change of clothes and go do what Tex said." Or I don't recall saying: "Get a knife and go kill the Sheriff."

I don't recall saying to anyone: "Go get a knife and kill anyone or anything." In fact it makes me mad when someone kills snakes or dogs or cats or horses. I don't even like to eat meat because that is how much I am against killing. So you have got the guy who is against killing on the witness stand, and you are all asking him to kill you. You are asking him to judge you. Because with my words, each of your opinions or diagrams, your thoughts, are dying. What you thought was true is dying. What you thought was real is dying. Because you all know, and I know you know, and you know that I know you know. So, let's make that circle.

You say: "Where do we start from there?" Back to the facts again. You say that the facts are elusive in my mind. Actually, they just don't mean anything. The District Attorney can call them facts. They are facts. You are facts. But the facts of the case aren't even relative, in my mind. They are relative to the Thirteenth Century. They are relative to the Eighth Century. They are relative to how old you are or what kind of watch you wear on your arm. I have never lived in time. A bell rings, I get up. A bell rings and I go out. A bell rings, and I live my life with bells. I get up when a bell rings and I do what a bell says. I have never lived in time. When your mind is not made in time, the whole thought is different. You look at time as being man-made. And you say time is only relative to what you think it is. If you want to think me guilty then you can think me guilty and it is okay with me. I don't dislike any of you for it. If you want to think me guilty it is okay with me. I know what I know and nothing and no one can take that from me.

You can jump up and scream: "Guilty!" and you can say what a no-good guy I am, and what a devil, fiend, eeky-sneaky slimy devil I am. It is your reflection and you're right, because that is what I am. I am whatever you make me. You see, it is what happens inside the now that ... the words just lose meaning. A motion is more real than a word. The Indians spoke with it. They could explain to you with motions what they felt. This is what I intended to do if I could represent myself. Explain to you what is inside of me, how I feel about things. Because words are your words. You invented the words, and you made a dictionary and you gave me the dictionary and you said: "This is what the words mean." Well, this is what they mean to you, but to someone else, they've got a different dictionary. And things mean different things to different people, and to match the symbols up as you talk back and forward. Then you put a witness up here to say what you said. I could never say what someone else said. I could only say what I said.

You tell me something and, tomorrow, I try to repeat it; if I didn't write it down, I couldn't tell you what you said. Let alone a year ago, let alone eight months ago. let alone a week ago. I am forgetful. I forget one day to the next. I forget what day it is or what month it is or what year it is. I don't particularly care because all that real to me is right now. But then, the case is real to me, and I say: "What do I have to do to make you people let me go back to the desert with my children?"

You have your world. You are going to do whatever you do with it. I don't have the schooling in it. I don't believe in your church. I don't believe in anything you do. I am not saying you are wrong, and I hope that you say I am not wrong for believing what I believe in.

Murder? Murder is another question. It is a move, it is a motion. You take another's life. Boom! and they're gone. You say: "Where did they go?" They are dead. You say: "Well, that person could have made the motion. He could have taken my life just as well as I took his." If a soldier goes off to the battlefield, he goes off with his life in front. He is giving his life. Does that not give him permission to take one? No. Because then we bring our soldiers back and try them in court for doing the same thing we sent them to do. We train them to kill, and they go over and kill, and we prosecute them and put them in jail because they kill. If you can understand it, then I bow to your understanding. But in my understanding I wouldn't get involved with it.

My peace is in the desert or in the jail cell, and had I not seen the sunshine in the desert I would be satisfied with the jail cell much more over your society, much more over your reality, and much more over your confusion, and much more over your world, and your word games that you play.

And each witness got up here and only testified for what was best for them, they did not testify for what was best for me. They testified for what was best for them, their own benefit. So you say: "Okay, and then what else did she say?" She said: "You only see in me what you want to see in me." You only see in her what you put in her, because when you take LSD enough times you reach a stage of nothing. You reach a stage of no thought. An example of this: if you were to be standing in a room with someone and you were loaded on LSD and the guy says: "Do you like my sports coat?" And you would probably not pay any attention to him.

About two or three minutes later the guy loaded on LSD will turn around and say: "My, you have a beautiful sports coat," because he is only reacting. He is only reacting to the individual terminology, the person that he has in the room. As you would put two people in a cell, so would they reflect and flow on each other like as if water would seek a level.

I have been in a cell with a guy eighty years old and I listened to everything he said. "What did you do then?" And he explains to me his whole life and I sat there and listened, and I experienced vicariously his whole being, his whole life, and I look at him and he is one of my fathers. But he is also another one of your society's rejects. Where does the garbage go? As we have tin cans and garbage alongside the road, and oil slicks in your water, so you have people, and I am one of your garbage people. I am one of your motorcycle people. I am one of what you want to call hippies. I never thought about being a hippie. I don't know what a hippie is. A hippie is generally a guy that's pretty nice. He will give you a shirt and a flower, and he will give you a smile, and he walks down the road. But don't try to tell him nothing. He ain't listening to nobody. He got his own thoughts. You try to tell him something and he will say: "Well, if that's your bag." He is finding himself. You, those children there were finding themselves. Whatever they did, if they did whatever they did, is up to them. They will have to explain to you that. I'm just explaining to you what I am explaining to you. Everything is simple to me. It is what it is because that is what it is. It doesn't go any farther. What? That is all there is. Why?

Why? Why comes from your mother. Your mother teaches you why, why, why. You go around asking your mother why and she keeps telling you: "Because, because," and she laces your little brain with because and because. "Why?" "Because." "Why?" And you don't know any different. If you had two mothers, one to tell you one thing and one to tell you another, then your mind might be left where mine was. If you had a dozen parents that you went around with and couldn't believe anything you were told and then you couldn't disbelieve anything you were told. And it's the same thing with this court. I don't believe what these witnesses get up here and say but I don't disbelieve them either. I won't challenge them. If the guy says: "You're no good," I say: "Okay. If that's what you want me to believe it's okay with me."

I don't care what you believe. I know what I am. You care what I think of you? Do you care what I think of you? No, I hardly think so. I don't think that any of you care about anything other than yourselves because when you find yourself, you find that everyone is out for themselves anyway. It looks that way to me here, the money that has been made, the things that I cannot talk about, and I know I can't talk about, I won't talk about and I will keep quiet about these things. How much money has passed over this case? How sensational do you think that you have made this case? I never made it sensational. I was hiding in the desert. You come and got me, remember? Or could you prove that? What could you prove? The only thing you can prove is what you can prove to yourselves, and you can sit here and build a lot in that jury's mind, and they are still going to interject their personalities on you. They are going to interject their inadequate feelings; they are going to interject what they think. I look at the jury and they won't look at me. So I wonder why they won't look at me. They are afraid of me. And do you know why they are afraid of me? Because of the newspapers.

You projected fear. You projected fear. You made me a monster and I have to live with that the rest of my life because I cannot fight this case. If I could fight this case and I could present this case, I would take that monster back and I would take that fear back. Then you could find something else to put your fear on, because it's all your fear. You look for something to project it on and you pick a little old scroungy nobody who eats out of a garbage can, that nobody wants, that was kicked out of the penitentiary, that has been dragged through every hellhole you can think of, and you drag him up and put him in a courtroom.

You expect to break me? Impossible – you broke me years ago. You killed me years ago. I sat in a cell and the guy opened the door and he said: "You want out?" I looked at him and I said: "Do you want out?" You are the jail, all of you, and your whole procedure. The procedure that is on you is worse than the procedure that is on me. I like it in there. I like it in there – it's peaceful. I just don't like coming to the courtroom. I would like to get this over with as soon as possible. And I'm sure everyone else would like to get it over with too.

Without being able to prepare a case, without being able to confront the witnesses and to bring out the emotions, and to bring out the reasons why witnesses say what they say, and why this hideous thing has developed into the drama that it's moved into, would take a bigger courtroom, and it would take a bigger public, a bigger press, because you all, as big as you are, know what you are as I know what you are, and I like you anyway. I don't want to keep rehashing the same things over. There are so many things that you can get into, Your Honour, that I have no thoughts on. It is hard to think when you really don't care too much one way or the other.

[Interruption]

I was released from the penitentiary and I learned one lesson in the penitentiary: you don't tell nobody nothing. You listen. When you are little you keep your mouth shut, and when someone says: "Sit down," you sit down unless you know you can whip him, and if you know you can whip him you stand up and whip him and you tell him to sit down. Well, I pretty much sit down. I have learned to sit down because I have been whipped plenty of times for not sitting down and I have learned not to tell people something they don't agree with. If a guy comes up to me and he says: "The Yankees are the best ball team," I am not going to argue with that man. If he wants the Yankees to be the best ball team, it's okay with me, so I look at him and I say: "Yeah, the Yankees are a good ball club." And somebody else says: "The Dodgers are good," I will agree with that; I will agree with anything they tell me. That is all I have done since I have been out of the penitentiary. I agreed with every one of you. I did the best I could to get along with you, and I have not directed one of you to do anything other than what you wanted to do.

I have always said this: You do what your love tells you and I do what my love tells me. Now if my love tells me to stand up there and fight I will stand up there and fight if I have to. But if there is any way that my personality can get round it, I try my best to get around any kind of thing that is going to disturb my peace, because all I want is to be just at peace, whatever that takes. Now in death you might find peace, and soon I may start looking in death to find my peace.

I have reflected your society in yourselves, right back at yourselves, and each one of these young girls was without a home. Each one of these young boys was without a home. I showed them the best I could what I would do as a father, as a human being, so they would be responsible to themselves and not to be weak and not to lean on me. And I have told them many times, I don't want no weak people around me. If you are not strong enough to stand on your own, don't come and ask me what to do. You know what to do. This is one of the philosophies that everyone is mad at me for, because of the children, I always let the children go. "You can't let the children go down there by themselves." I said: "Let the children go down. If he falls, that is how he learns, you become strong by falling." They said: "You are not supposed to let the children do that. You are supposed to guide them." I said: "Guide them into what? Guide them into what you have got them guided into? Guide them into dope? Guide them into armies?" I said: "No, let the children loose and follow them." That is what I did in the desert. That is what I was doing, following your children, the ones you didn't want, each and every one of them. I never asked them to come with me – they asked me.

[Recess]

There's been a lot of talk about a bottomless pit. I found a hole in the desert that goes down to a river that runs North underground, and I call it a bottomless pit, because where could a river be going North underground? You could even put a boat on it. So I covered it up and I hid it and I called it "The Devil's Hole" and we all laugh and we joke about it. You could call it a Family joke about the bottomless pit. How many people could you hide down in this hole?

Again you have a magical mystery tour that most of the time there's forty or fifty people at the ranch playing magical mystery tour. Randy Starr thought he was a Hollywood stunt man. He had a car all painted up and like never done any stunts. Another guy was a movie star, but he had never been in any movies, and everybody was just playing a part, you know; like most people get stuck in one part, but we were like playing different parts every day. One day you put on a cowboy hat and say: "Shoot somebody," or the next you might have a knife fighter, or go off in the woods for a month or two to be an Indian, or just like a bunch of little kids playing. Then you establish reality within that reality of play-acting.

And then you get to conspiracy. The power of suggestion is stronger than any conspiracy that you could ever enter into. The powers of the brain are so vast, it's beyond understanding. It's beyond thinking. It's beyond comprehension. So to offer a conspiracy might be to sit in your car and think bad thoughts about someone and watch them have an accident in front of you. Or would it be a conspiracy for your wife to mention to you twenty times a day: "You know, you're going blind, George, you know how your eyes are, you're just going blind; we pray to God and you're going blind, and you're going blind."? And she keeps telling the old man he's going blind until he goes blind. Is that a conspiracy? Is it a conspiracy that the music is telling youth to rise against the establishment because the establishment is rapidly destroying things? Is that a conspiracy? Where does conspiracy come in? Does it come in that?

I have showed people how I think by what I do. It is not as much as what I say as what I do that counts, and they look at what I do and they try to do it also, and sometimes they are made weak by their parents and cannot stand up. But is that my fault? Is it my fault that your children do what they do?

Now the girls were talking about testifying. If the girls come up here to testify and they say anything good about me, you would have to reverse it and say that it was bad. You would have to say: "Well, he put the girls up to saying that. He put the girls up to not telling the truth." Then you say the truth is as I am saying, but then when it's gone, tomorrow it is gone, it changes, it's another day and it's another truth, as it constantly moves thousands of miles an hour through space.

Hippie cult leader; actually, "hippie cult leader", that is your words. I am a dumb country boy who never grew up. I went to jail when I was eight years old and I got out when I was thirty-two. I have never adjusted to your free world. I am still that stupid, corn-picking country boy that I have always been.

If you tend to compliment a contradiction about yourself, you can live in that confusion. To me it's all simple, right here, right now; and each of us knew what we did and I know what I did, and I know what I'm going to do and what you do is up to you. I don't recognize the courtroom, I recognize the press and I recognize the people.

JO: Have you completed your statement, Mr. Manson?

CM: You could go on forever. You can just talk endless words. It don't mean anything. I don't know that it means anything. I can talk to the witnesses and ask them what they think about things, and I can bring the truth out of other people because I know what the truth is, but I cannot sit here and tell you anything because like basically all I want to do is try to explain to you what you are doing to your children.

You see, you can send me to the penitentiary, it's not a big thing. I've been there all my life anyway. What about your children? These are just a few, there is many, many more coming right at you.

JO: Anything further?

CM: No. We're all in our own prisons, we are each all our own wardens and we do our own time. I can't judge anyone else. What other people do is not really my affair unless they approach me with it.

Prison's in your mind... Can't you see I'm free?

TWO DRAGONS PLAYING WITH A PEARL

NANCY MACKENZIE

"The moon shines through a window; it is in the depths of the night. Waiting for his return, she has fallen asleep from fatigue, and the red tips of tiny shoes emerge slightly from the corner of the bedcovers. He returns and is delighted by the sight. Drawing down the curtains, he eagerly grasps and plays with the phoenix tips. He is still not satisfied, so she removes embroidered shoes and bindings. Her white lotuses are pointed and fine, beautiful as polished jade or a mound of powder. She lifts twin hooks and caresses his sex by rubbing them up and down against it, and they bull it about like two dragons playing with a pearl. It finally becomes as soft as if a mere breeze could blow it down; the intense delight is such as he has never before enjoyed. This marvel is still another special benefit accruing from the lotus."

Foot-binding probably started in China, towards the end of the 10th Century, innovated by palace dancers of the time. The dancers' feet were probably only slightly compressed, and not severely enough to seriously hamper movement, but the image of the small and delicate foot was to start a fashion that, by the 12th Century, had become widely accepted and even customary.

The actual process of binding the feet was to wind thin cloths of between two and three inches wide and five to twelve feet long tightly around and under the foot, binding until all cloth was used. The big toe was left unfettered as this was essential for any balance, but the remaining toes were forced underneath and pushed as close to the heel as was physically possible. Many rituals were performed during the binding process; one was to soak the feet in urine as this was believed to soften the bones. Festival or auspicious days in the lunar calendar were co-ordinated with certain beliefs; an auspicious day was one in which female and male elements in the universe were harmonious. While the binding was taking place the young victim might hold or bite a slim, pointed object believing that this would be a symbol encouraging her foot to become slim and pointed.

The binding process started at the ages of between three and twelve years while the feet were small and the bones relatively soft and pliable. The young girls were forced to walk on their bound feet every day so that they would be able to stand without fainting. Every few weeks the bindings would be tightened, and a new pair of shoes one tenth smaller would be worn after each tightening. The aim was to achieve the three inch 'Golden Lotus'. This was, in fact, very difficult; only about one in a hundred were successful.

The three main reasons for foot-binding were:

1) Vanity. Small meant beautiful and, anyway, large feet on either sex were associated with the lower classes.

2) Sexual. The fleshy, deep crevice formed by the tight binding was seen and used as an alternative vagina.

3) Status. A man who married a woman with bound feet showed he was wealthy enough to keep his wife and to afford many servants to perform her chores for her. Her bound feet also had the effect of preventing his wife from ever being able to leave the home.

The mystery of the bound foot could only enhance its appeal. Men craved the opportunity to see and touch the foot, and for a man to be allowed this privilege always meant the woman was his exclusive possession.

Licking the foot while it was being cleansed was termed 'Eating steamed dumplings in pure water'! The southern Fukienese woman would prepare a special treat for her husband on the night before their wedding: she would put two cooked eggs in a basin of hot water, in which she would bathe her unbound feet. After cleansing she removed the eggs from the water and took them to the home of her husband-to-be, where she boiled them in sugar and made an offering of them to him! Some men would willingly drink the water which had just been used to cleanse and pedicure the feet, and then complete the ritual by eating small delicacies from between their loved ones' toes.

A woman's feet were the possession of her husband and were used for his pleasure only. The woman would go to great lengths to make them desirable; special shoes were worn for different occasions. For sleeping the shoes were of scarlet silk or satin, adorned with rich embroidery and tiny gems, often with soft satin socks worn inside. A woman would reach the heights of ecstasy through having her feet rubbed, although upper class women kept their socks on during this prelude to sexual intercourse!

It was necessary for a woman to have bound feet if she wished to marry, as a man would rarely propose to a woman with large feet, let alone consider sexual relations with her. Men, too, were often subjected to the painful process of binding; especially the young adopted boys of homosexuals.

Male prostitutes also had bound feet, and transvestites and drag artists simply squeezed their feet into lotus-like shoes and mimicked the walk of the bound-footed woman; a walk about which one doctor wrote: "Footbinding had a physical influence on a woman's body. When the bound-footed women went walking, the lower part of her body was in a state of tension. This caused the skin and flesh of her legs and also the skin and flesh of her vagina to become tighter. The woman's buttocks, as a result of walking, became larger and more attractive sexually to the male. We can thus see that these are definite reasons why men formerly liked to marry women with bound feet." It was thought that binding the feet tightly forced the blood upwards, tightening the vagina and buttocks, thus giving the sensation of having sexual intercourse with a virgin. In one sense this was correct, as the pain suffered by the binding would often cause the vagina and buttocks to tense and therefore tighten up, but any claim of influence on the actual sex organs of the woman was proved scientifically invalid.

Many rituals were performed with the feet either in or out of shoes and bindings. There were women who liked to fondle the male member with their tiny feet. "When intoxicated, they would remove the bindings, place the organ between their feet, and rub it back and forth until the aroused male scattered his sperm about in profusion. This delighted the woman. Touching of the genital organs by the tiny feet provokes the male thrill of an indescribable voluptuousness. And great lovers know that in order to awaken the ardour, far too cold, of their old clients, to take the rod between their two feet is worth more than all the aphrodisiacs of the Chinese pharmacopoeia and kitchen."

For many years the pain would be so excruciating that walking or standing, no matter how slight the pressure, would prove unbearable, and releasing the bindings in hope of relief would only add to the discomfort.

Bound feet forced women into the confines of the boudoir, rendering them fettered young playthings for the sole desire and amusement of men. The naked foot was, however, rarely seen by anyone other than the husband, and even relatives and close friends avoided contact with the naked flesh.

Over a period of centuries, almost every woman in China had her feet bound. It was customary for the aristocracy and essential for prostitutes and concubines. One man of wealth never had relations with a prostitute, but insisted on smelling the foot and removing dirt between the toes and in the plantar with his finger nails. He was careful to remove every speck, made a tablet out of it with his hands, and swallowed it as if it were a delicious tid-bit.

Many men would lose interest if the feet were washed or perfumed. They were washed as little as possible, as it was feared that removing the bindings too often would allow the feet to spread and grow. The rarity of the feet being washed had greater consequences as the odourous flesh began to putrefy, and the skin slough off from the sole. Sometimes the rot would eat so deeply into the flesh that one or more toes would actually drop off. Many males found the smell of the feet sexually arousing – so much so that they would willingly smell, lick and chew the naked, unbathed flesh. A small proportion of lotus admirers were, however, offended by the stench of the decaying deformed object of their lust.

The list of sexual activities that involved the lotus foot was endless. Apart from smelling and licking etc., it was also used as a pseudo-vagina with which the women whose feet, released from the bindings, could successfully use for podocoitus. The two feet, crescent shaped, could be placed sole to sole, forming an orifice for the male member to enter. The women would also give pleasure by inserting the tiny bare foot into the man's mouth until he could take no more, and he would suck and nibble it with great joy.

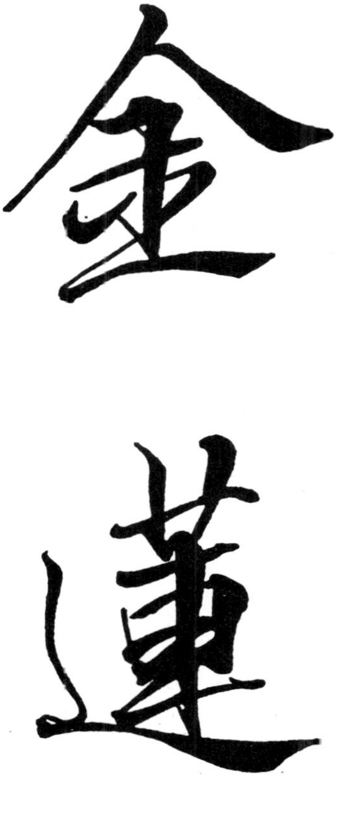

TORTURE

As well as the pleasure a man could give a bound-footed women, he could also administer great pain. Husbands of bound women often punished their wives by squeezing the foot hard. This alone would cause great pain.

The harshest treatment was always taken out on prostitutes, by bandits. Nails were driven through the hands and feet, crucifixion style, and the women were left for several days until they died. Another form of torture was to tie up the women so that their legs dangled down in mid-air, and then to attach small but heavy rocks to each toe, increasing the weight until the toes straightened out and eventually dropped off. The toes were often so rotten anyway that they didn't need too much weight to pull them off. One writer stated that in a bandit area in east Kiangsi around 1931, where bound-footed women were unable to flee from the bandits by whom they had been taken captive, the bandits, angered by their captives' inability to walk and keep file, forced the women to remove their shoes and bindings and to run about barefoot in a large field covered with sharp stones and rocks. This caused immense pain and discomfort in addition to the suffering caused by the continuous whipping they were receiving simultaneously. The bandits then played a dancing game; they would take a woman each and force her to dance barefoot on the sharp ground. This ripped the flesh and soaked the area with blood.

In the Sino-Russian War, Russian troops were accused of committing atrocities against women in some areas of China. They sexually abused the women, then strung the tiny shoes around their own necks as mementos of their 'conquests'.

ABOLITION

As the 19th Century closed, Chinese leaders began to fight for women's rights, and this naturally included moves against foot-binding. These led to the first step towards abolishing foot-binding, with an imperial decree in 1902. The Manchus were opposed to the practice from the start, but during their centuries of rule, attempts at eradication were sporadic and unsuccessful, and the custom continued to grow in popularity.

The abolition of foot-binding by imperial decree did finally have some effect, but it was not until the 15th April 1915, when an official order of prohibition was issued, that foot-binding legislation really had the desired effect. By August of the same year more than 763,000 women had removed their bindings and the custom virtually disappeared. Only in remote villages might you see very old women with bound feet today.

BODYSHOCKS

The Mr Sebastian Interview

SIMON DWYER

"The human body is always treated as an image of society and there can be no natural way of considering the body that does not involve at the same time a social dimension."

Mary Douglas, *Natural Symbols*

"One must be a work of art, or wear a work of art."

Oscar Wilde

A small, clean room in London, Radio 4 drifts out of the open window over the rows of sun-baked rooftops. A semi naked man lies on a medical couch. He notices a crack in the ceiling. An anglepoise lamp creaks into position and hangs above him, like a praying mantis. A honeyed voice, deep and hypnotic, soothes away the last minute beads of anxiety, "you may just feel a slight tingling sensation". Odour of surgical alcohol bends images the way heat does. The peace is broken by the nauseating buzz of the tiny metal needle, glinting blue ink. Fleeting thoughts of dental torture, Klaus Barbie or Laurence Olivier, gently subside, taut muscles relax as the body realises that it really doesn't hurt at all. It's all very peaceful.

The last time I'd ventured into a tattooist's grandly titled 'studio' had been when I was sixteen. I'd sat, squashed into a queue of sailors' and skinheads' spotty white flesh, watching with a mixture of fascination and barely concealed horror at the Mickey Moused beer bellies, 'Love' engraved fists and skull infested backsides. All were being produced indelibly in a matter of minutes by an artiste of Hulk Hoganesque proportions, a bad case of Delirium Tremens and the personal hygiene of a hippo. Gritted teeth grinned inanely as the painted punters bared various hairy white hams and accepted their doses of hepatitis like men. Suddenly, I remembered a previous engagement.

It took me nearly a decade before I was inexorably drawn back. This time, though, things could hardly have been more different. Now I was in the capable hands of Mr Sebastian, a legendary figure among tattoo aficionados who enjoys the reputation as one of the the best tattooists and piercers on this side of the Atlantic.

If you want a job done by Sebastian you don't join a queue for an hour, you join a waiting list for four or five months. Like any good surgeon or lawyer, this man exudes an air of elitism and appointment-only authority, and in his presence it's easy to elevate the craft of the body artist to the vocation of the professional. It's quite simple, if you want your body adorned and you're fashionable, professional, or just plain sensible, you go to Mr Sebastian. Your body is worth it.

But how does such a man become involved in a world that, even now, implies associations with subterranean machismo? His introduction was traditional enough. His first tattoo – a small star on his hand – was a DIY job done in the army during his National Service, but that, for the time being, was that. Unusually, Sebastian (real name Alan Oversby) became interested in piercing before tattoos.

Unemployed and unwilling to follow his father's footsteps into an Insurance firm in Liverpool, 22-year-old Alan caught a steamer to South America to become an Overseer on a sugar plantation in British Ghiana. It was while he was there that he first came into contact with piercing.

"I saw two fieldhands with pierced nipples, with little gold rings through them. As soon as I saw them I knew that's what I wanted. So I got to know them and then one evening they took me to this strange little man who was a Portuguese West Indian, who lived in one of those houses on stilts in the jungle. He was the man who had done their piercing. I remember we sat around drinking rum and his pet monkey kept running around the room pissing everywhere. We got a little drunk, but that didn't really help with the pain. He knew what he was doing, but he used an old fashioned syringe type piercer."

On his return to Britain, Sebastian decided that his gold rings were positioned a little too near the front of his nipples, so he decided to move them back, making new piercings himself with the aid of some disinfectant, whisky, and an embroidery needle. "Bloody painful", but it worked.

Reactions to his piercings were surprisingly good, and in response to the demand, Sebastian invested in a piercing syringe and gave nipple piercings to a few friends.

A piercing has the effect of baring nerve endings and, as a result, increasing sensitivity in the area of the piercing when the ring is touched. Generally, men's nipples are far less sensitive than those of a woman, but after piercing the man discovers two new, highly sensitive erogenous zones. Piercing is partly aesthetic, primarily sexual. This is part of the underlying reason why body adornment is generally frowned upon in polite society, though it is by no means the only reason. The whole culture of Body Art is still tinged with the lustre of rebelliousness and riddled with unspecific underworld associations for simple historical reasons.

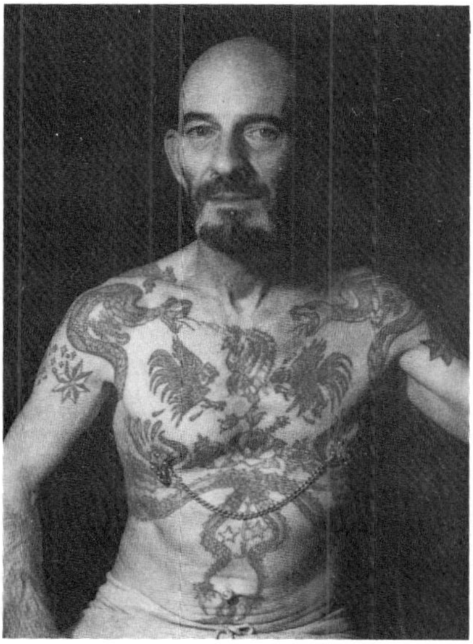

The Illustrated Man – Mr Sebastian.

Tattooing, piercing and scarification of the body existed in dozens of quite separate tribal and national cultures all over the world before the global domination of the white man, and his religion. As the European empires spread around the planet like a plague, the accompanying shadow of Christianity spread with them. In its wake, all forms of body-marking were crushed. The logic was typically crass: The bible said that God had made Man in his own image, so, any attempt to alter that image was seen as being a departure from God – the work of the Devil. Tattooing and piercing were seen as satanic, or at best, godless traditions.

Sebastian was having none of that. He realised then what we should all know now: our bodies are our own, to do with as we please, regardless of the opinions and interfering laws of our society. Often, our bodies are all that we have left.

Impressed with what he called his two new "jolly buttons", he decided it only natural to extend his attentions to his genitals. *"I used to practice on myself with needles"* he grins, as this interviewer crosses his legs involuntarily. *"I was working as an Art Teacher by this time and had a few more tattoos done. Becoming more and more adventurous as I went along. Then a few years later I went to the States and stayed with four or five tattooists, learning as I went along. Then I met Doug Malloy who'd been interested in tattooing for years and was really quite knowledgable. So with advice from him and a doctor friend of his, I also learnt about piercing. About what you could do and what you couldn't do."*

RE: So there was really nobody who could actually train you.

"No. Even Doug Malloy had only done a few piercings at that time and Jim Ward who runs ***P.F.I.Q.*** *(Piercing Fans International Quarterly), didn't have any piercings. So between us talking about it and pooling what experience we had we worked out the best way of doing it."*

Twenty years on, Sebastian has perfected the delicate art like few others. The photos in his studio are his testament, and a wonder to behold. Roses etched around arseholes; snakes extended up cocks, rings through labia. Men with 3, 4, and even 5 gold rings or steel 'bolts' through the shaft of their cock. Other photos show smiling couples joined together (temporarily!) with thin steel chains extending from one foreskin or helmet ring to the other. (Quite properly, Sebastian declined us permission to re-print these pictures so as to preserve his clients anonymity).

Besides the amusing, the novel, and the bizarre, there are of course a few horrors. Some customers come to Sebastian having divided their own penis completely from tip to base.

Many people may find it hard to believe, but there are quite a few obsessives who do sit at home with a carving knife and a bottle of painkillers and hack pieces from their own glands. Psychiatrists and Sociologists would probably have a field day with these characters, but the reasons they do this are – in their minds – aesthetic, and also to increase the novel sexual kicks one apparently gets from having intercourse with a dick that has thousand of nerve-endings exposed beneath only a thin layer of scar tissue. There's also a certain degree of one-upmanship involved. People enjoy the kudos of being the only man at a party who owns a penis that is, in itself, a work of art. And just as it's often the case that one tattoo leads to another and leaves the entire body ending up looking like a patchwork quilt, piercers often come back for more and more extreme and novel additions.

One regular visitor is a respectable middleaged businessman who – in effect – now has two cocks. His penis having been completely bificated along its entire length. He claims to get two (thin) erections (and no doubt a few curious double-takes in the urinals). The urethra, through which the urine and semenal fluid passes, is preserved down one side of the 'tube', though apparently some people do experience a lot of 'leaking' and 'dribbling' during both urination and ejaculation. (Even with a straightforward cock piercing, one has to learn to 'adjust your aim'.)

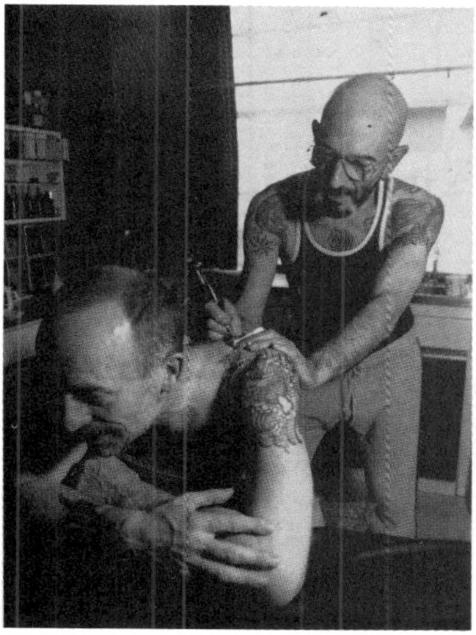

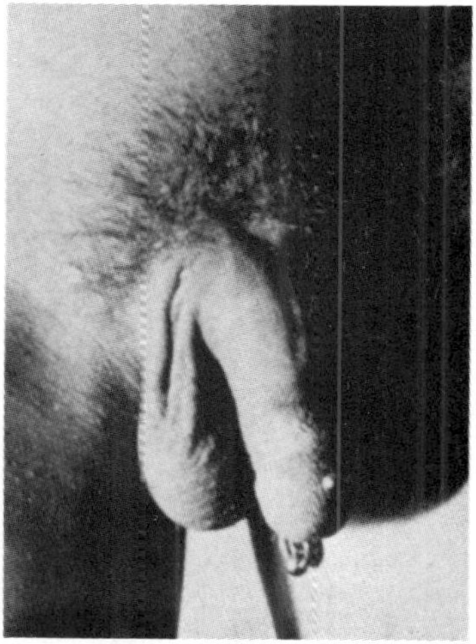

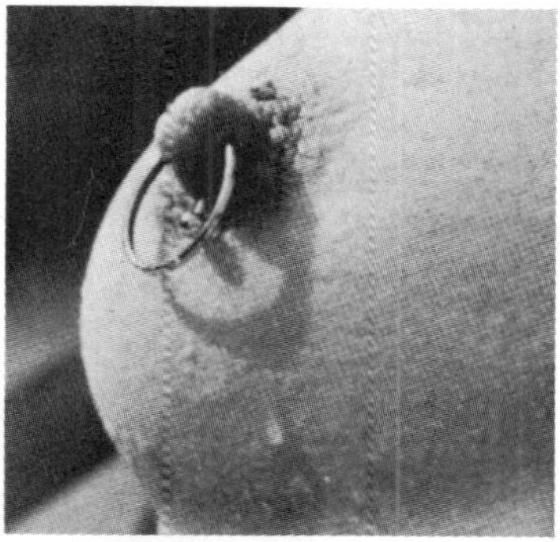

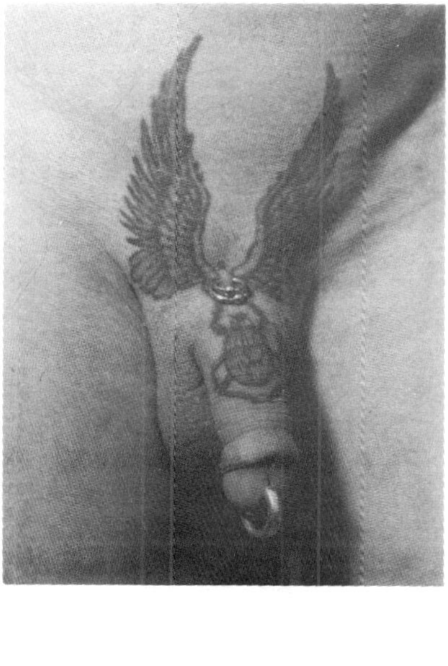

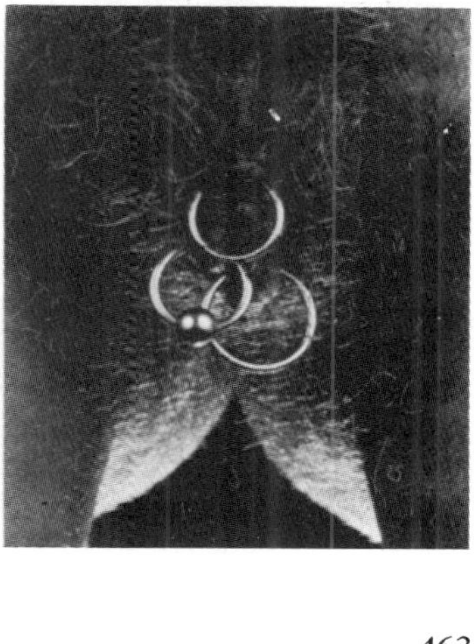

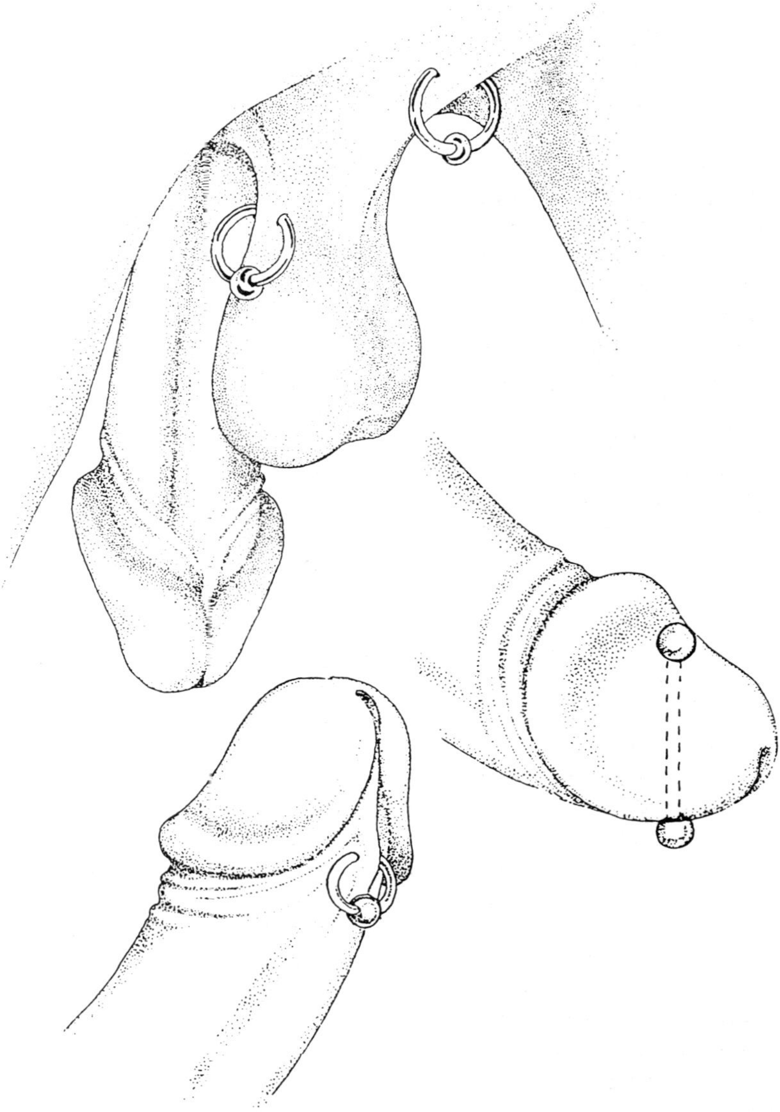

TOP: 'GUICHE' – Through the ridge of the skin between scrotum and anus. 'HAFADA'- Piercing through side of scrotum.
LEFT: 'FRENUM' – Through web of flesh beneath glands.
RIGHT: 'APADRAVYA' – Pierced vertically up through glands.

This particular customer's wife is pleased with her husband's unusual genitalia. *"He brings her along with him, she's most keen!"* In fact, Sebastian had one wife telephone to thank him for her husband's nipple piercings, saying they were "Magic. Things have started happening now he's got nipples that work."

Mainly, though, Sebastian's clientele is gay, middleaged, respectable. *"I don't get a lot of skinheads, but I'm sure I would if I had an open shop. Lal Hardy, who does some excellent work, gets a lot but I wouldn't really care for a lot of skinheads myself. Not being snotty, but I wouldn't really want to do bulldogs and Union Jacks or whatever. I realised when I started that there was a need for somebody to do work by appointment. There are an awful lot of businessmen – for want of a better word – who want to have tattoos but wouldn't be happy walking into an open shop...that type of person usually wants something small and discreet, mostly something on their arse or cock."*

The most 'respectable' cock piercing of all is that of the 'Prince Albert', a metal ring which is inserted through the urethra and through the underneath of the (punctured) glands. It's so named because there were strong rumours in Victorian times that the Prince himself sported such a device. Of course, the only person who could confirm or deny this was Queen Victoria – and she wasn't saying.

Small tattoos and a fair deal of piercing was in fact said to be quite common among Society men in the late 19th Century, and, unlike tattooing and most types of piercings, nipple piercing was a purely English invention.

RE: What's the most difficult place to tattoo?

"The inside of the foreskin, which some secretive people want. That's very difficult. There's one fellow who comes in who's cut his foreskin completely in two and I'm in the process of tattooing the inside of that now, a little at a time. It's very hard, as it's mostly scar tissue, and the ink tends to seep along the tissue beneath the skin if you're not very careful. For a tattoo to be done properly the skin really needs to be stretched tight, so it's difficult. I don't think it looks nice either."

Despite what one may at first think, there are instances when he will not work on a client. Nobody under the age of 18 (that's the law anyway). Also, any young men who come in asking for tattoos on their heads are turned away, as are people who want tattoos on their hands and other permanently visible areas. The same rule applies to piercings. If the customer looks young or undecided, Sebastian asks them to go away and think about it.

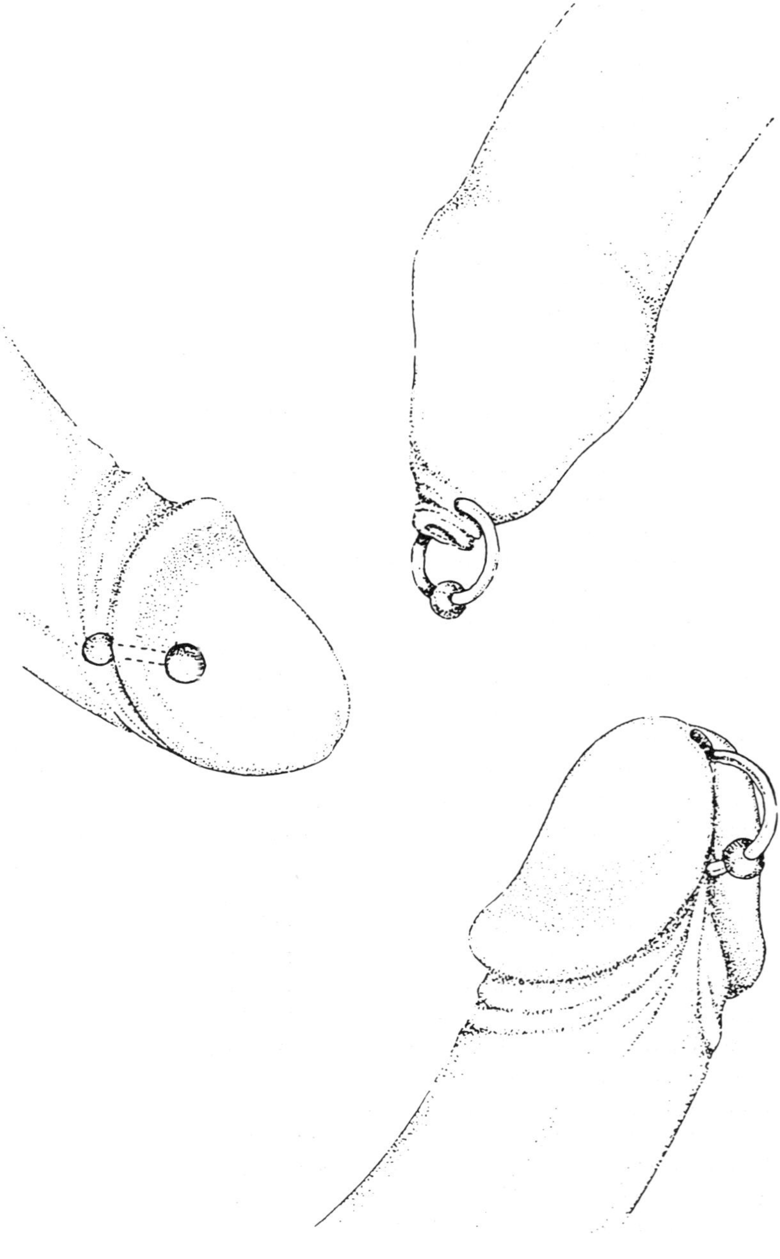

One can easily become very anthropological about man's innate desire to make marks when considering the subject of Body Art, but the real reasons people have tattoos and so on are quite simple.

We live in a Society that is synthetic and automatic. Never before has mankind been so distanced from his body, so the sensual, physical and mental kick of bodymarking – which heightens one's feeling of being physical – has perhaps never before been so necessary. And anyway, the body – the point at which our mind meets the outside universe – is also a good advertising hoarding.

Besides the straightforward decorative and physical effects, having a tattoo or series of piercings is a sign of some sort of self-realisation. Of arrival. Of commitment to a certain kind of attitude and life. Hence the high number of homosexual men who visit Sebastian for tattoos. This also explains, to a degree, why so many members of gangs and cults, from Hells Angels to punks to Triad members, go in for permanent body marks. An indelible sign not only to your peer group, but to yourself.

In Arab countries the tattoo was used both decoratively and as a protection against evil spirits and physical harm by way of sympathetic magic and, not surprisingly, many people in Britain connected with formal 'occult' groups come to Sebastian for a variety of secretive images that mean little to the tattooist (Ray Sherwin & co. may be interested to know that I saw several Chaos insignia in Seb's photo album). Of course, such activities are nowadays more acceptable than they were in the past, but the interest in tattooing does seem to vary at geographical borders.

Relatively few people have tattoos in Holland, but there are now three full time piercers in Amsterdam (one bad, two good). The Dutch do, however, have more tattoos than the Spanish, who have practically none. One survey showed that some 50% of the male prison population in both Britain and America have tattoos before they go inside (largely a remnant of the fact that both countries have been the world's major naval powers). In Germany the figure's down to about 20%, in France less than 10%, and in Italy and most other countries it's next to nothing. Tattoos are still illegal in Japan, having as they do unpleasant connections to outlawed gangs and also serving to remind the Japanese of the occupying American soldiers and sailors shortly after the bombs on Hiroshima and Nagasaki.

In Britain, tattoos and piercings have never been more popular. Now, with years of experience and state-of-the-art equipment at his disposal, more and more people are hearing of, and trusting themselves to Mr Sebastian. His repertoire is imaginative. Both men and women can have several nipple piercings, through which studs, rings and chains can be worn. Most people who have this type of piercing find that not only is the sensitivity of the area pleasurably heightened, but the actual size of the nipple is increased. A ring or stud can also be worn on or near the navel, and a small piercing in the skin beneath the lower lip can provide a perfect resting place for the occasionally worn piece of jewellery (Sebastian himself wears a tiny diamond in his). Apart from the ears, of course, other head piercings include the nose – either outside or inside, (through the tissue between the nostrils). Besides the Prince Albert, many men also go in for short bolts – ampallangs – through the head of the penis, and smaller rings through the foreskin and down at the base of the shaft. All of which have the effect of increasing the intensity, and duration, of the orgasm. Women, too, occasionally come into the studio. Besides the normal small tattoos and head and nipple piercings, many have rings put through both the outer and inner labia. And although Sebastian advises customers against it, many also have their clitoris pierced. Men's scrotums are pierced, and for the more masochistically inclined, Sebastian also supplies and can advise on the use of stainless steel weights which can be worn round the balls to stretch the scrotum to quite remarkable lengths.

Indeed, the word 'tattoo' still implies a sense of pain. It was, in fact, introduced to the language by Captain Cook (who else) on his return from the South Seas and comes from the Tahitian 'taku' – meaning 'to strike' - referring to the painful technique of holding a sharp-pointed instrument, usually made of human bone, against the skin and tapping it with a small hammer.

The ritual, painful 'initiation' aspect of tattooing is still evident and will be known to all small boys who own a blood and ink stained compass, and even though in Sebastians hands the operation is practically painless, I wonder aloud if masochism does play its part.

"I don't think so. I know a few people have got erections when I've tattooed or pierced them, but it's very very rare. One tattooist told me of an old customer who asked him to make it hurt more once, and actually wanted him to dress up as a doctor and bend the needle so it caused him more pain! But he was the only one I've heard of."

The writer knows six or seven people who have 'erotic' piercings, and every single one of them have said that they were glad they took the plunge.

One of these is John Norton. John used to be an Advertising Executive, but he became bored and decided to drop out. Now he lives on the 17th floor of a block of council flats in South London, behind a mass of security cameras and broken lifts, with his wife and baby. A normal couple, under the skin. If one wants to pontificate, one could say that John's new 'birth' into a more free lifestyle was ritually marked by him undergoing a process of being tattooed and pierced, and talk about his innate need for a lasting initiation into this different world. An initiation that's left his body so marked with dancing dragons and serpents that it would be socially impossible for him to return to his old job in the city. But, really, that's all obvious. To John, tattoos are sexy and fun and, rather like motorbikes or stamp collections, provide the holder with a passport to a sub-culture that, in this case, is obsessed with body decoration.

The cult is served by magazines such as the aforementioned **P.F.I.Q.** and Britain's own **Body Art**, run by old **Maitresse** regular Henry Fergusson. John also contributes to this relatively new mailorder industry by producing the **Body Shock** videos and distributing them through his own company, Dragon Video. The tapes include interviews with a variety of tattooists and their subjects and a section showing Sebastian performing a piercing operation.

John Lomax of Brighton's Wildcat Productions also says that he's never had it so good. Wildcat have a thriving mailorder business specialising in body modification videos, books, and an amazing array of Ball weights, Bar Closure rings, Barbells with Stirrups, Ball Closure rings, Chunk rings, Tusks, Labret studs, Flesh Tunnels, Nipple clamps, Nipple discs and Cock rings. Wildcat also run party nights called **The Steel Ball** at a variety of venues that are a truly eye-popping experience. One party John threw recently had a guest who, as his party piece, could pass a large dead fish through a hole in his penis! What once may have been the domain of men in dirty raincoats is now a realm of fantasy, fashionable fetishism and, above all, SAFE FUN. You cannot take yourself too seriously if you have a dead fish hanging out of your willy.

The burgeoning interest in relatively safe sexual practices that do not require the exchange of bodily fluids has led to an enormous interest in the bondage and S/M scene. Now, it is quite de rigor for trendy couples to attend clubs like **The Torture Garden** in leathers, rubbers and plastics, and the demand for piercing and tattooing has never been greater.

Unlike tattoos, which require painful surgery to remove and leave an often horrendous looking scar, one can change heart over a piercing by removing the inserted rings. This will either have the effect of making the piercing all but invisible, or, in some cases, allow the hole to seal up for good.

Interestingly, no one I know has allowed this to happen. It also says something for the allure of piercing when one realises that after the 'operation', men cannot have any kind of sex (including masturbation) until the piercing is completely healed; sometimes taking up to 10 weeks. From all accounts the frustrating wait is worth it (even though – and don't

tell Sebastian – nobody I've met has lasted the full 10 weeks before indulging). But is it legal?
Sebastian rolls his eyes. *"Well, it's not actually illegal. I just don't think the powers that be really know much about it, unless they read books like this. I do have a licence to pierce ears and I'm also officially allowed to tattoo people. The health inspector has been around here and checked the place and my equipment so...it's legal!"*
Perhaps Her Majesty knows something that we don't?

Wildcat International, 16 Preston Street, Brighton BN1 2HN, England. (Send A5 SAE for free brochure).

Body Art Magazine, Blake House Studios, Blake House, Rayne, Braintree, Essex CM7 8SH.

Skin Two Magazine, BCM Box 2071, London WC1N 3XX

Tattoo International, 389 Cowley Road, Oxford OX4 2BS.

HIS NAME WAS MASTER

(Brion Gysin – In Memory)

GENESIS P-ORRIDGE

In 1916 Brion arrived screaming and kicking, suffering, (forever) he said, from thee adverse effects of constricted vaginal muscle. Projected through a world that was like Disneyland into a world that became Disneyland via a port of entry charged by light. Brion travelled in Time and Light and made us all cry easier than lose out in our own Earthbound domesticity. E am coumvinced, always will be, that Brion is, was and will be a Master Cultural Alchemist. He could be so negative, stubborn and cantankerous that screaming suicide off high buildings became more enlightening than his clammed up viscosity of no-speak. Frustrating all attempts to get a direct answer to a direct question he would benignly draw on his kif and, eyes twinkling, play magickal cat and mouse for literally hours on end. E have never met a more knowledgeable, more capable teacher anywhere, either as myth or saint, or, as in Brion's case, as human. At thee end of the day he was thee only Man E ever wrote love letters to. To Master, a long Goodnight...

And now, in present Time. He's not here. And it hurts. It hurts coumpletely. In thee way that sneaks into us unannounced, cutting nerves and emotions, crippling our coumplacent daily stance and opening up our pain synapses to snapping point.

In 1975 E wrote to Brion. E was co-editor of a reference book of mammoth proportions called *Contemporary Artists* and E was determined that Brion should be rightfully represented in that tome as a radical visual artist and painter. Not dismissed as an eccentric dilettante as appeared to have happened so far in thee deceptual artworld. For ten yera's E had, like so many, been tracking down these renegades via deleted Beach Books, often found in Soho porn shops. Exploding with multiple recognitions of a contemporary arcane knowledge that appeared to coumfirm youthful instincts and institutions, Brion was always thee hardest to find. He remained that way forever. He had becoum light. There was no focus, only reverberating frequencies and pulses, crystals at his centre. He had become, quite literally and physically, a Dreamachine that had assumed human form for thee reassurance of us mere observers. We stare still with closed eyes. He flickers bright on our retina and generates vivid signals. E see all about Brion as Magick and Light. E re-discover perception through him.

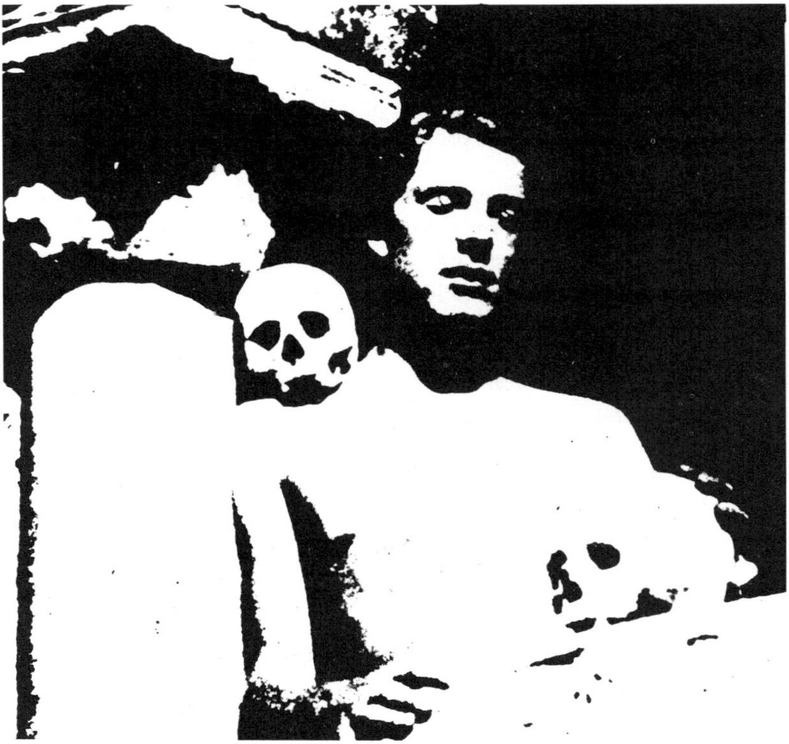

Brion Gysin, Greece, 1935

Out to Brion went a list of questions about his life so far. Back came a cultured exclamation of surprise coupled with a note: *"Even the CIA don't know THIS much about me"*.

Through correspondence we met in Paris. He would make tea in his tiny kitchen, Moroccan style. Naming thee different bubbles as thee water heated. As thee fish eyes appeared he poured thee water onto thee tea. Exploding its flavour. Thee alchemists believe water boils at 101 degrees he explained. We soon developed a tradition, chocolate biscuits and tea in thee afternoons. A small pasta meal in thee evening, with spirits to accompany it. Coffee later on. E would sit. Thee sound of drumming outside thee Pompidou Centre. Flashes of Marakesh. Sunlight catching thee flowers on his white table, smell of hash smoke. Swiss dreamachine in thee corner. Calligraphic paintings on thee easel. Notebooks in rows. Moroccan trinkets reminding me of his influence over Brian Jones. And he would talk. It was like a children's fairytale. Thee child looking up spellbound and thee grandfather enrapturing with his amazing tales and anecdotes. Never enough time. Yellow light cutting across thee later shadows and dreams. There is no way to describe how proud E was to know this man.

> *"The hallucinated have come to tell you that your utilities are being shut off, dreams monitored, thought directed, sex is shutting down everywhere you are being sent.*
> *all words are taped.*
> *agents everywhere. marking down the live ones to exterminate.*
> *they are turning out the lights.*
> *no they are not evil, nor*
> *the devil, but men on a mission with a spot of work to do.*
> *this,*
> *dear friends, they intend to do on you.*
> *you have been offered a*
> *choice between liberty and freedom and NO! you can not have both."*

B.G. *Minutes To Go* (1986)

Thee way to write is to simply tell thee truth. Thee way to right is to simply, tell thee truth.

> *"Dearest Gen,*
> *There is not much point in telling you just how negative I am feeling these days...daze. I have not much recovered from my fall in the stairs. After all is said and done, I felt only one thing...finished. I don't feel any necessity to do all these things but I guess I'll do them if I am still stuck here and have to do them. I'll do them as best I can and that may not be much. Don't worry. Nothing much more to be said but dumb numb no-news.*
> *Love, Brion"* 17 March 1982

And within everything else there is coumthing else. It's a spark. E live forever surrounded by Brion. His paintings on thee walls, his face in snapshots on thee mantelpiece. Thee glow of Paris light. Caresse calls him *"Grandad, my grandad"*, and she is right. Thee wise old man of thee lowlands. When E took Paula to meet Brion for thee first time E was nervous. He's a bit of a misogynist, E warned. Well, he tries to be, butter E have always found him charming to women nevertheless.

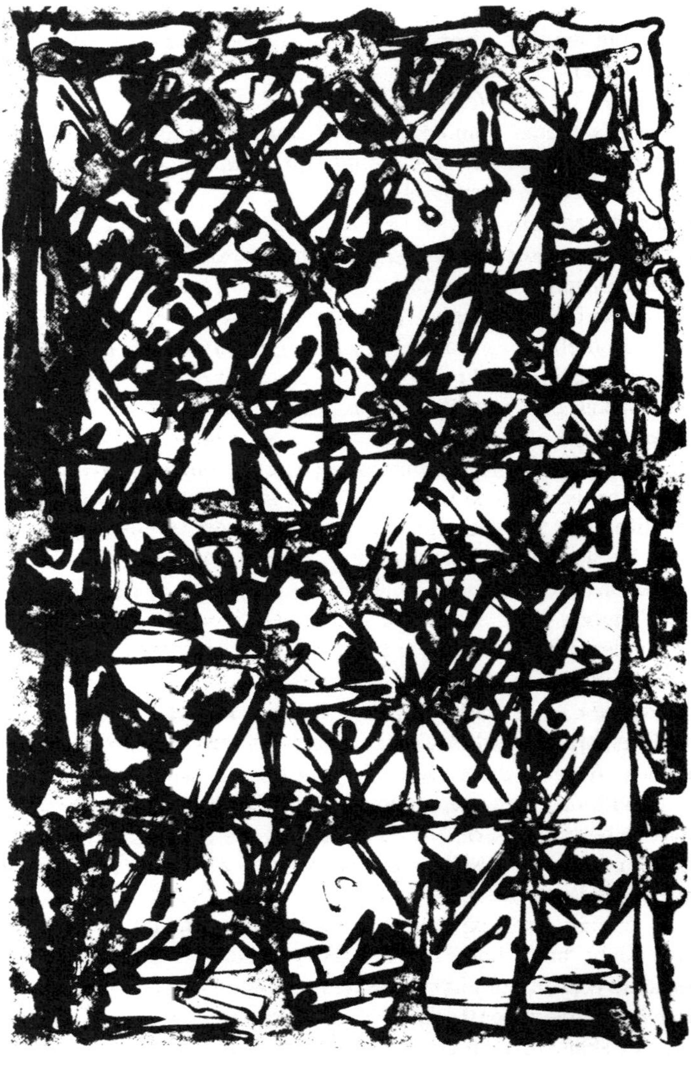

'Peggy Guggenheim's Window on The Grand Canal, Venezia, Italy'
– Brion Gysin, 1962

Paula knew nothing about Brion except my love for him. Her love for him was instant and pure. He coumgratulated us on our impulsive marriage in Tijuana in 1981. Chance had it, that two boys from Joujouka were staying with him in Paris that week. Brion made us relaxed. Paula used thee dreamachine. Unprompted by any prior information about what it was. Thee TG LP *Heathen Earth* played as she and thee Arab boys stared, eyes closed. E filmed on video. Soon Paula was swirling through psychedelic patterns and vivid colours. Then desert scapes, eyes of Horus, so many archetypal symbols and places. Proof positive that the dreamachine actually works, is not triggered by preconceptions. And afterwards thee most beautiful, priceless and special meal of my whole life. Cooked and served by thee musicians of Joujouka. As we ate and talked, Brion full of energies; thee boys played sacred musick of Pan on pipes in candlelight. E was once more in a fairytale, thee old magician conjuring sensations and rewards. E have never lost my joy and thanks for such a special gift from Brion. Nothing could have been more literally priceless than that dark, orange, flamelit evening. At thee end of thee evening he gave us a painting. Our pagan wedding present, which he inscribed for us. All thee fears and illnesses, all thee betrayals and losses of his life, his bitternesses and flirtations with socialites became as nothing. He was thee wisest, kindest man in our world and we loved him totally for it.

Brion's work and friendship is a reminder. A notice of work to be done and a challenge to thee stagnant coumplacency of thee dreamless minds that would drown us. Magick begins in dreams, dreaming what we would like to happen, programming our subconscious. If you take those dreams seriously enough they do happen. Dreams are descriptions of how things really are. A product of thee Third Mind, of perceptual editing and focused will. Dreams are accurate transmissions. There should be no separation between work, life, dreams. We must all aim for coumplete integration of every possible and impossible facet of our minds, emotions, responses and relationships and then express that integration through popular culture and expressive arts, through friendships and events, through light and time. Brion was a philosophical and alchemical transmitter/receiver. His ideas are frequencies that travel and confront as intimately as television butter with thee content of full knowledge and potency of shamanic, ritual magick. No wonder he fell in love with thee pipes of Pan and thee sunlight of thee desert. There should be no separation. Separation would be dishonest, would go against a dream of evolution through knowledge and psychic development, would go against our potential. A book, a film, music, paintings, love, are all thee person who makes and feels them. This is a Magickal process and it makes things happen. It reveals even more. Thee first time E looked at Brion's drawings they appeared abstract calligraphics. Then he told me they were portrayals of Arab market places. E could suddenly see they were indeed photographically accurate pictures of everyday scenes. They simply included thee nature of reality and time that engages our receptors in a manner we are unused to. Now E always introduce his paintings as figurative works to make this point. Man dreams before he talks, and since our first dreams we have felt that therein are messages. Prophecies, descriptions and events that cannot be ignored. Arcane societies and civilisations in their wisdom, and to their credit, employed people to interpret and record these dreams. Priests would stand on towers and pass their hands before their eyes rapidly creating a flicker effect against thee sun, eventually 'tripping out' and speaking of visions that were coumsidered holy and powerful. Today, a society and culture with a vested interest in thee suppression of imagination, self assurance, creativity, questioning and aspiration discards dreams and esoteric techniques as trivia. Dreams are merely disturbed nights, or entertainment. Brion saw dreams as a parallel and interconnected universe. A commentary upon Man's potential and hopes. He was in many ways a traditional artist yet by thee nature of his personality he was simultaneously and without self-contradiction thee most radical thinker of our age in thee area of magickal creativity and cross-discipline possibilities. No surprise then that his greatest political and behavioral achievement was dubbed the *Dreamachine*. A simple machine able to decondition and reactivate our perceptions. Society's controllers try to ensure that dreams are represented as vestigial trappings of intuition and are kept in their place. For Brion and for those who revere his work, that way lies death. When you cease to dream you cease to exist. Shut your eyes. Thee world doesn't die, open them and in a sense, half of it does. Dreams generate ideas, liberate behaviour, enhance sexuality, empower magick and most of all create possibilities. Dangerous stuff. No wonder Brion was frozen out into thee sideshows of painting and writing. Too real. Too close to functional and practical techniques. Now through Brion we have thee Dreamachine. Perhaps a crucial tool for thee arousal of vision, perception and inner space that has becoum our heritage. Make no mistake, its suppression in subtle ways was no accident. A machine that for the price of a lightbulb leads you drugless into thee core of your being, taps you into thee mass subconscious, stimulates thee mind and bridges thee abyss between sleep and wakefulness, conscious and unconscious life. Brion recognised that we are at war. Thee fight is between expression and suppression, suppression and perception, sexuality and guilt; and between all those things that bolster and assist control, manipulation and darkness and those that encourage freedom, evolution, hope and light.

In thee eleven years we were friends thee question E most asked was *"Tell me about Magick"*. Thee question he most studiously avoided answering was thee same. Yet once he graciously gave me a clue. *"Do you know your real name?"* he said. E did. And then he told me his. It was as E expected.

There was never a superiority, or generation gap with Brion. He was always living in now and thee future. In present time. Thinking of new projects, working with young people, making music, records, paintings. Holding soirées for young fans and seekers. Always outgoing and moving, always absorbing and thinking. Thee last time we saw him was in Paris in 1986, ten days before he died. Paula and E sat and held his hand. Being physically alive had becoum a struggle. *"I just never guessed it would hurt so much"*, he said. And really there was nothing more to say. It was over.

Brion was sure he was here to go. We are left here to do. And what we do is described by, defined by, and contained within our dreams.

During that last afternoon thee undertaker came to discuss death arrangements with Brion. Paula and E went walking round Rue St Martin. We couldn't articulate thee craziness of life and death. There was nothing to say. Two boys from behind thee Iron Curtain stopped us and told us of their work in electrical sculpture and words. They said they were influenced by thee ideas of Brion Gysin who they'd heard lived in Paris. We drank coffee and took their address. Exiles in America. *"He doesn't live in Paris anymore,"* E said. We felt euphorically disconnected, yet cold. Suppressing our emotions and terrors because they meant nothing. Had no value measured against losing Brion. So many people who love him so much. All knowing they will lose him soon. Frail images of his room. Now a hospice. Thee air itself thee colour of thee plastic tubes and bags of liquid. Casting a cold bluish tinge through everything. As thee light was going from him his space was becoming transparent.

Ten days later Paula came rushing into thee room crying, sobbing uncontrollably. *"Brion's dead..."* she said.

THE GARDEN

DEREK JARMAN

I walk in this garden
Holding the hands of dead friends
Old age came quickly for my frosted generation
Cold, cold, cold, they died so silently
Did the forgotten generations scream?
Or go full of resignation
Quietly protesting their innocence
Cold, cold, cold, they died so silently

Linked hands at four AM
Deep under the city you slept on
Never heard the sweet flesh song
Cold, cold, cold, they died so silently

I have no words
My shaking hand
Cannot express my fury
Sadness is all I have
Cold, cold, cold, they died so silently

Matthew fucked Mark fucked Luke fucked John
Who lay in the bed that I lie on
Touch fingers again as you sing this song
Cold, cold, cold, they died so silently

My gilly flowers, roses, violets blue
Sweet garden of vanished pleasures
Please come back next year
Cold, cold, cold, I die so silently

Goodnight boys,
Goodnight Johnny,
Goodnight,
Goodnight.

A THANKSGIVING PRAYER

WILLIAM BURROUGHS

(For John Dillinger, in the hope that he is still alive.
Thanksgiving Day November 28th 1986.)

Thanks for the wild turkey and the passenger pigeons, destined to be shit-out through wholesome American guts.
Thanks for a continent to despoil and poison.
Thanks for Indians to provide a modicum of challenge and danger.
Thanks for vast herds of Bison to kill and skin, leaving the carcasses to rot.
Thanks for bounties on wolves and coyotes.
Thanks for the American Dream – to vulgarise and falsify until the bear lies shine through.
Thanks for the K.K.K.
For nigger-killing lawmen feeling their notches.
For decent, church-going women with their mean, pinched, bitter evil faces.
Thanks for 'Kill A Queer For Christ' stickers.
Thanks for laboratory AIDS.
Thanks for prohibition, and the war against drugs.
Thanks for a country where nobody is allowed to mind his own business.
Thanks for a nation of finks.
Yes, thanks for all the memories – 'Alright, let's see your arms.'
You always were a headache and you always were a bore.
Thanks, for the last and greatest betrayal, of the last and greatest of human dreams...

Appendix

This book is not for sale to minors. Readers are reminded that it is an offence to tattoo any individual under the age of 18. Do not attempt any of the piercings or body modifications described herein. If you must, the publishers strongly suggest that you seek out the help of a professional. Neither the contributors, publishers nor distributors will assume any responsibility for the use or misuse of any information contained in this book.

Photographs. Some additional unaccredited photographs have been used in this book. Although efforts have been made to trace the copyright owners concerned, this has not been possible in every case. Should copyright holders wish to contact Rapid Eye, the publishers will be pleased to re-imburse them at our standard rates and credit them in future editions.

The Tantra article was sent to us by C R Morgan of Mandrake Publishing, Oxford. Mandrake produce their own magazines, exhibitions and seminars and can put serious enquirers in touch with pagan/thelemic groups. (PO Box 250, Oxford OX1 1AP, England).

Nick Toczek is a published poet and writer – he is currently writing a book, 'The Gemstone File Investigation', which questions some of Bruce Robert's assertions and backs up others. It also goes into a detailed exploration of the key events and personalities that crop up in the File. Nick also hopes to extend this project into a film on the subject. If anyone has further information about The Gemstone File, please get in touch with him by writing to him care of 5 Beech Terrace, Undercliffe, Bradford, BD3 OPY, W.Yorkshire, England.

'The Fall of Art' and 'Johnson Family' are extracts from 'The Adding Machine', published by John Calder Ltd. Thanks to WSB, James Grauerholz, Susan Herbert at John Calder and also A D Peters and Co. for their co-operation. 'Rover' has never before been published. 'A Thanksgiving Prayer' was originally published in 'Tornado Alley', Cherry Vale Editions, USA, 1989. Dedicated to Keith Haring at the Apocalypse, with whom Burroughs worked on a series of visual and sound works in New York. Also available on the CD 'Dead City Radio', a recording of WSB reading works with backing music supplied by Sonic Youth, John Cale, Chris Stein, the NBC Symphony Orchestra and others, produced by Hal Willner and Nelson Lyon (Island Records, 1991).

Thanks also to Vale for contributing the Burroughs Interview. Vale edits ReSearch magazine - essential reading. Send $50 for three large issues, ReSearch, 20 Rombolo B, San Francisco, CA 94133, USA. Of particular interest; Issue 4/5, on TG., Burroughs, Gysin etc. with contributions from Simon Dwyer and Jon Savage. Also Issue 12, Modern Primitives, on body modification in America, and Issue 8/9, on and by J.G.Ballard.

'Mescalin and Mysticism' is an extract from Christopher Mayhew's autobiography 'Time to Explain' (Century Hutchinson). Thanks to Baron Mayhew for his permission and help, and also to The Observer.

Pat Hollis is co-editor of 'Pandemonium' magazine in America. Pandemonium covers several topics similar to those featured in Rapid Eye, especially interested in strange films and criminals. Pandemonium, 171 Auburn Street, Apt #11, Cambridge, MA 02139, USA.

The 'Brazil' article was inspired by Dr.Terence DuQuesne. Terence DuQuesne is a former contributor to Rapid Eye, and writes widely on many subjects. His books include 'Catalogi Librorum Eroticorum', 'A Handbook of Psychoactive Medicines', and volumes of poetry. He is a clinical pharmacologist and writes extensively on human rights, oriental studies, the classics, poetry and art criticism. Simon Dwyer would like also to thank Liberty for their co-operation in his researching of this piece.

'The Garden' by Derek Jarman is from his film of the same name. The poem also appears in his book 'Modern Nature' (Century).

The Black Box appears courtesy of OMNI magazine.

A more complete transcript of the Jonestown tape is now available from Temple Press, PO Box 227, Brighton BN2 3GL. A free catalogue is available from them on request.

Readers should not try to order PTV/TOPY merchandise from this publication. Rapid Eye is, and always has been, an independent publication and is not any part of the Temple organisation, nor are individuals 'members' of same. Unsolicited loony letters, collages, photos etc. thrown in the bin. Grow up.

Having said that, we welcome serious contributions to Rapid Eye, be they written or visual. Also, if you have any comments, suggestions etc., please feel free to write to **The Editor, Rapid Eye, c/o Annihilation Press, 83 Clerkenwell Road, London EC1, England.** Although every reasonable care is taken, neither the Editor nor the publisher can accept responsibility for manuscripts and artwork that are lost or damaged. Make copies.

Any contributors or interview subjects featured in Rapid Eye can be contacted via the publishers. All letters will be forwarded, but please enclose a forwarding stamp.

Annihilation Press is a division of Creation Press, specialising in non-fiction books of a transgressive nature.

Rapid Eye was founded in Poplar, east London, on 23rd January 1979. It does not strive to be academic or definitive, but to provide readers with entertainment and avenues for possible further exploration. It has taken several different forms, as magazine, mailart campaign, series of booklets and audio tapes etc. This version of Rapid Eye brings new readers up to date, and is the first in a projected series of deluxe editions that will span the final decade of the 20th Century. The last supper. In widening our readership we intend to fulfil the project's original aim: To put Art and Magick onto the street, where they belong, in order to facilitate the process of understanding and civilisation in a wilfully ignorant and manifestly uncivilised society.

In a world that experiences life only through its media, to re-invent and contribute to a popular medium is to question reality itself, and, in the '90s, when all solely 'moral' arguments become redundant, to be civilised will mean having the power and conviction to take your dreams seriously. 'Truth' never sets you free. It is only your questions which will bring you emancipation. Suffer little children!

In the media culture of the post-industrial, postmodernist mess, influence over the deepest areas of social consciousness is the only issue. There is no conclusion. 24 hours a day. Nothing short of total war. Nothing short of total love. Do not be afraid. It's not to be feared, it's not to be feared, it's a friend. Be realistic, demand the impossible. And please, come back next year.

All facts and opinions expressed in Rapid Eye are liable to change without notice.

ECSTATIC INCISIONS

The Collages of Freddie Baer

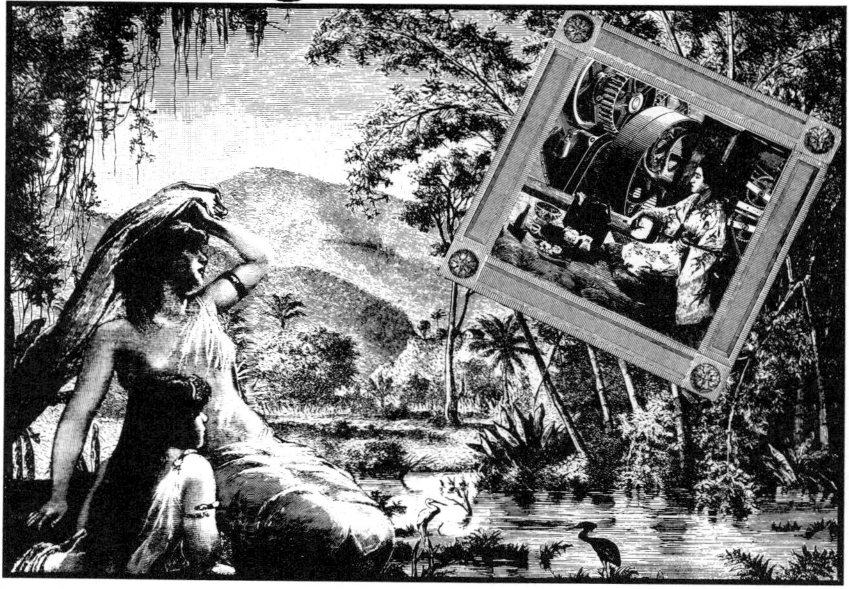

Ecstatic Incisions: The Collages of Freddie Baer with a preface by Peter Lamborn Wilson. ISBN# 1 873176 60 0; 8 1/2 x 11, 80 pages; a perfect bound paperback with a three color cover; 71 illustrations, 44 full page; £7.95.

Ecstatic Incisions is Freddie Baer's first collection of collage work. Over the last decade her illustrations, ranging from the bitingly political to the sublimely surreal, have appeared on numerous magazine covers, t-shirts, posters, and album sleeves. This anthology draws from all her previously published pieces, new material, and her collaborations with Hakim Bey, T. Fulano, Jim Gilman, Jason Keehn, and David Watson. Freddie Baer is a graphic artist and illustrator who currently resides in San Francisco. Her collage work has been featured in *Semiotext(e). SF, Science Fiction Eye, Interzone, Fifth Estate, Factsheet Five, Xerox Pirates,* and *Anarchy: A Journal of Desire Armed,* amongst others.

Available from AK Press, 3 Balmoral Place, Stirling, Scotland FK8 2RD.

"RED HEDZ" Michael Paul Peter

The hardcore horror classic; an extreme onslaught of shape-shifting, psycho-sexual tyranny and mutation.

"Horror fiction on the edge." – **RAMSEY CAMPBELL**

"Would make a perfect David Cronenberg film if translated to the screen." **– JÖRG BUTTGEREIT**

"...takes writers like William Burroughs and Clive Barker as merely the starting-point for a mixture of poetry, cut-up fiction, hallucinatory rantings and keenly-observed characterisation." – **SKELETON CREW**

£5.95

"THE BLACK BOOK" Tony Reed (Ed.)

The sex and death show.

A disturbing collection of urban horror and psycho-sexual derangement by new writers and illustrators presenting their own personal vision of Hell.

"Genuinely painful, and worth investigating" – **i-D**

£4.95

"RED STAINS" Jack Hunter (Ed.)

A lexicon of lesions, bible of blood.

New stories of extreme biological fantasy and the psycho-sexual imagination. A successor to the **"Black Book"**. Authors include: **Ramsey Campbell, Jeremy Reed, Tony Reed, Terence Sellers, James Havoc, Paul Buck, DF Lewis, Michael Paul Peter Philbin, Adèle Olivia Gladwell.**

"The most unrelenting collection of sexual horror fiction that I've ever read." **– DIVINITY**

£5.95

"INTERREGNUM" Geraldine Monk

In 1612, ten people from the Pendle area of East Lancashire were hanged as witches in the city of Lancaster. Unquestionably, they fell victim to a *language-magic* far more powerful and effective than their own: the language-magic possessed by, and misused by, the governing authorities, rendering the witches' magic meaningless. A state of interregnum was created, whereby accepted codings no longer applied and the relationship between words and actions became completely arbitrary. Contemporary and historical abuse and misuse of language-magic, which determines degrees of freedom, is the recurring theme in the text of **Interregnum**, and culminates in the nemesis of the witches' monologues.

"Parallel texts, image chains, ikon-like symmetrical designs are all animated by Monk's special willingness to submerge herself completely into her experience." **– THE GUARDIAN**

£7.95

"A HOLYTHROAT SYMPOSIUM" Aaron Williamson

The assembled 'acts of writing' orbit the poet's deafness with a static insistency; an explosive poetry surfaces, squalling, devouring the pages. Williamson has burdened his work with the weight of the physical world; at the heart of the book is an unspeakable surdity, a silent flickering language ravenous for release, possessing any and every faculty: a primal world of violence and estrangement of one who is 'anatomically exiled' from the language he uses. **A Holythroat Symposium** is vertiginously layered, accumulating a physical impact; an irritant compulsion contorting its anatomical intelligence.

"A merciless winnowing to gist. Savage in rhetoric. Farctate. Exploring all the dark resources of fault." – **IAIN SINCLAIR**

£7.95

"BRIDAL GOWN SHROUD" Adèle Olivia Gladwell

Short fiction, prose-poems and illuminating essays dealing with sexual/textual politics. Using a subversive motif of menstruation, the writer explores the gulf between the symbolic and the imaginary to comment upon the abjection and fragmentation of the misplaced woman. Includes essays on Nick Cave, Religious Ecstasy, Pornography etc.

"The missing link between Lydia Lunch and Julia Kristeva." – **LOADED**

"Compelling, strangely addictive...violent images of sex and blood."

– **OUTLOOK**

£6.95

"THE RISEN" Peter Whitehead

Sexual magick, Shamanism, crystallography, Egyptology, Virtual Reality, psychopharmacology, Grail mythology – author Peter Whitehead has taken themes and images from all of these and more, to produce an authentic picture of the transformed consciousness mankind will need to adopt in the not too distant future. Two truth-seekers conduct seemingly unconnected, simultaneous experiments – one splitting a pyramid-shaped diamond with X-ray lasers, the other splitting his mind by ingesting a crystalline psychedelic drug. Their parallel researches are destined to lead them to the only conceivable meeting-point – infinity. **The Risen** charts their collision course through a labyrinth of disturbing eroticism, dismemberment and reincarnation, drawing the reader through the half-silvered mirror of reason into its own time-space, a virtual inscape fusing magical imagery from holography and morphic resonance, fetishistic sex and pagan initiation rites: an occult *tour-de-force* which may well alter our perception of reality – forever.

PETER WHITEHEAD is the former 60's *avant-garde* film-maker and Rolling Stones documentarist.

"This highly original work may well be the future of the novel"

– **ANDREW SINCLAIR**

£8.95

"THE HAUNTED PALACE" **Edgar Allan Poe** *Creation Classics I*
Death Poems & Vampire Tales
The quintessence of Poe's artistic vision: a body of obsessive work which stands as one of the great testaments to the inseparable passions of love and death. As well as his darkest poetry, this new, revised edition contains the "vampire" cycle of 5 stories which in many ways forms the nucleus of his prose work. In these stories Poe investigates the vampiric nature of human relationships, including love and lust both "normal" and incestuous, and develops his theme to observe the vampiric qualities inherent in the creative or artistic process.
The texts are accompanied by lithographs by the 19th century Symbolist **Odilon Redon**, taken from his series dedicated to Poe in 1882.
£7.95

"PHILOSOPHY IN THE BOUDOIR" **De Sade** *Creation Classics II*
Probably the single most representative (and concise) text out of all the Marquis de Sade's works, containing all his libertine doctrines expounded in full, as well as liberal doses of the unbridled eroticism for which he is (unfairly) more renowned. The renegade philosophies put forward here are amongst the main cornerstones of the Surrealist manifesto.
This seminal text is here presented in a *brand new*, modern and authentic translation by Meredith Bodroghy, herself a former dominatrix descended of Hungarian aristocracy. Second, revised edition.
£7.95

"BLOOD AND ROSES" *Creation Classics III*
Edited by James Havoc and Adèle Olivia Gladwell
An anthology of 19th century literature in which the vampire appears as a metaphor for erotic delirium, menstruation etc. Translators new and old include Lafcadio Hearn, Alexis Lykiard and Jeremy Reed.
Authors include: **Poe, Lautréamont, Gautier, Oscar Wilde, Huysmans, Baudelaire, Bram Stoker, Sheridan le Fanu** and many others. Possibly the definitive book on its subject. Illustrated throughout with the Satanic/Erotic works of **Felicien Rops**.
"As near to definitive as anyone's ever got" – **MELODY MAKER**
£7.95

"CRAWLING CHAOS" **H. P. Lovecraft** *Creation Classics IV*
At last, a quality single edition of the best works of Lovecraft. Contains 23 stories, prose-poems and collaborative pieces from 1920 to 1935, including several unusual items. With a brand new introduction by Colin Wilson.
"Step forward for a round of applause Creation Press, for this thoughtful collection" –**DARKSIDE**
368 pages, large de-luxe format.
£9.95

"THE GREAT GOD PAN" **Arthur Machen** *Creation Classics V*

First published in 1894, *THE GREAT GOD PAN* is Arthur Machen's first, and greatest, opus of Decadence and Horror. With his singular eye for the bizarre and macabre, Machen unfurls this tale of a young girl cursed by her supernatural parentage. This new, exclusive edition from Creation Press includes a set of complementary "automatic" drawings by Machen's contemporary and fellow mystic, **Austin Osman Spare**, and a brand new introductory essay on Machen and his works by Iain Smith of the Arthur Machen Society, as well as Machen's own illuminating introduction from the 1916 edition.

"What can I say about a writer whose influence has been acknowledged by H.P. Lovecraft, Peter Straub, and Clive Barker? Perhaps that he managed to communicate a sense of the inexpressibly and awesomely supernatural with more power than he ever knew." – **RAMSEY CAMPBELL**

"Of creators of cosmic fear raised to its most artistic pitch, few can hope to equal Arthur Machen" – **H. P. LOVECRAFT**

£7.95

"SALOME" **Oscar Wilde** *Creation Classics VI*

Written – and banned – in 1892, **Salome** is Oscar Wilde's ultimate, most *outré* statement of Decadence. Composed in French, this bizarre Biblical psychodrama was eventually translated from the original French by his friend Lord Alfred Douglas.

Blasphemous, erotic-charged, masturbatory, oneiric, hypnotic: this concentric tale of lust, sexual jealousy and violent murder is above all a savage attack on the hypocritical misogyny of Christianity.

This brand new edition from Creation Press includes original illustrations drafted by **Aubrey Beardsley** for the English translation, and also features an archaic translation of The Book of Revelation (whence Wilde drew much of the apocalytic imagery in **Salome**): the book of Armagideon and the Beast 666.

£7.95

BAD BLOOD

Transgressive Art & Literature

"THE SLAUGHTER KING" Simon Whitechapel *Bad Blood 1*

A sadistic serial killer is leaving a seemingly random trail of butchered corpses, both male and female, across Europe. He kills and mutilates with the skill and anatomical precision of a surgeon, the flair of a surrealist painter, the insatiable ferocity of a beast. *El Rey.* The Slaughter King.

With only the help of the dying girl who alone holds the key to the slaughter, policewoman Alanna Kirk trails this psychopathic destroyer from Northern Spain through a dark underworld of S&M sex, organized suicide and police corruption, to the industrial North of England – only to find that there are those who want the Slaughter King very much alive and on the streets...

"Whitechapel is one of the new breed of crime writers, ready to slice through narrative as easily as slicing through flesh. It's about time that the crime genre was infected by the blood of these people, intent on dragging its razored corpse into the age of AIDS, the Serial Killer and end-of-millennium sexual psychosis."

– **PAUL BUCK** (Author, "The Honeymoon Killers")

£7.95

"SEX MURDER ART" – The Films of Jörg Buttgereit *Bad Blood 2*

HEADPRESS co-editor David Kerekes has produced the definitive book on the controversial young German director whose films, such as **NEKROMANTIK, NEKROMANTIK 2,** and **DER TODESKING** have already earned him a reputation as one of the most original, innovative and *dangerous* of all modern film-makers. Buttgereit's films deal explicitly with death, and feature graphic images of necrophilia, grave-robbing, murder and suicide.

The author uses detailed analysis of all the films, dozens of rare and often disturbing photographs, plus extensive personal interviews with not only Buttgereit but also his principal players, to create a comprehensive and illuminating study: possibly the ultimate testament to the obsession, paranoia and politics of modern underground film-making.

"SEX MURDER ART" is published to coincide with the British premiere of Buttgereit's new film **SCHRAMM.**

*"**DER TODESKING** is the first truly post-modern horror film."*

– **RAMSEY CAMPBELL**

£9.95

"HEADPRESS ONE" – The Best of Headpress Magazine *Bad Blood 3*

The very best articles, interviews and photographs from HEADPRESS – the magazine of Sex, Religion & Death – whose early issues are already notorious, long-deleted collectors' items.

HEADPRESS ONE will feature a wide range of subjects, including bizarre sexual activities, weird crime cases, underground performance artists, writers and film-makers, religious manias and fanaticism, and many other little-covered or misrepresented facets of "apocalypse culture". Interviewees range from porno queen Annie Sprinkle, through body-piercer Patrick to film director Alejandro Jodorowski, plus dozens of other unrepentant characters.

The book will be illustrated throughout with rare photographs and artworks.

"Particularly bizarre ... disturbing and sometimes delightful." – **TIME OUT**

"Remarkable ... one of the most most turbo-charged publications to appear in mnan a month." – **DARK SIDE**

"An entirely healthy interest in violent death and deviant sex." - **i-D**

£9.95

ANNIHILATION PRESS

Cinema, Art, Music, True Crime, Occult

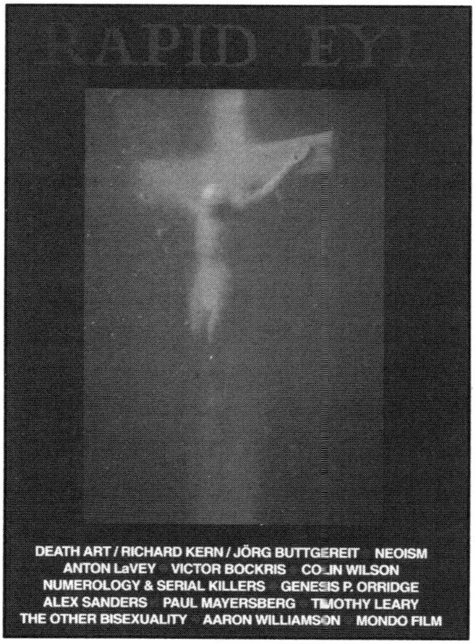

RAPID EYE 2

Simon Dwyer (Editor)
ISBN 1 871592 23 2
400 pages A5 Illustrated £9.95
Available now.

**JÖRG BUTTGEREIT * RICHARD KERN
GENESIS P-ORRIDGE * ANTON LAVEY
PAUL MAYERSBERG * ALEX SANDERS
THE OTHER BISEXUALITY * CIA
MONDO MOVIES * TIMOTHY LEARY
TWILIGHT LANGUAGE * VICTOR
COLIN WILSON * VICTOR BOCKRIS
KENNETH ANGER * SAVOY BOOKS
H.P. LOVECRAFT * LOBSANG RAMPA
AARON WILLIAMSON * JEFF KOONS**
and much more...

"The second volume of this essential counter culture journal...seek out Richard Dyer's audibly clear introduction to the arresting work of deaf poet Aaron Williamson; cult author Paul Buck's journey into the psyche of screen writer and Nic Roeg collaborator Paul Mayersberg, and editor Simon Dwyer's disturbing, fragmentary 'The Plague Yard', a 'Fear and Loathing' for the post beat generation. Examining and affirming an array of differences, Rapid Eye 2 attempts to contextualise an increasingly disparate culture of resistance. Recommended."

THE PINK PAPER

"Second issue of the heavyweight Brit periodical devoted to documenting apocalypse culture... with good pieces on Death Art and a great extended travelogue through the United States of Sleaze from Simon Dwyer. Recommended reading."

i-D MAGAZINE

"To read Rapid Eye 2 is to descend into chaos... This is the first and final battle."

MELODY MAKER

"Rapid Eye 2 is a slick, streetwise affair. Editor Simon Dwyer once again manages to tap into some of the more necessary themes in the medium of Transgression, and comes up with an original, valid, and highly entertaining work that isn't bound to the usual motifs. The book includes an excellent glimpse into the life of Alex Sanders, murder, Fortean and conspiracy theories, film extremes, sex, and David Flint rollercoaster-riding through that white knuckled genre, Mondo Movies. Simon Dwyer's travelogue encompasses delirium with every footfall in a land that somehow successfully manages to market everything from Aids Christ to Vampira. Dwyer's journey tells us more about the media than it does about plasticland itself, because THIS is the reality. A most excellent read."

HEADPRESS